"This new book is a thoughtful and useful addition to the field. It addresses many important, common scenarios typically encountered in eating disorders work, yet rarely discussed. A variety of unique situations are examined in detail. The adaptation of evidence-based approaches to novel settings and delivery methods will be highly valuable to practicing clinicians. I recommend the book highly!"

Scott Crow, Ph.D., Professor of psychiatry, University of Minnesota

"This book, edited and written by eating disorder experts from across the globe, attempts to bridge the gap between research and clinical practice: as ED treatments evolve, clinicians need to know how to effectively administer treatments with populations and in environments that were not part of the original clinical trials. This work will be a great resource for those practitioners looking for guidance in working with patients from diverse backgrounds and presentations."

Lucene Wisniewski, Ph.D., FAED, Clinical Director, Center for Evidence Based Treatment Ohio and Case Western Reserve University

"This is a very welcome book that takes the reader beyond the usual account of evidence-based treatments. It is a good reminder that a large number of patients do not fit the stereotype of the 'typical' patient, indeed novel populations and settings are very much what every clinician encounters in their practice all the time. A key aspect of evidence-based practice is respecting the needs and preferences of clients and their families and this book provides an excellent guide how to achieve this."

Ivan Eisler, OBE, Ph.D., FAED, joint head of the Maudsley Centre for Child and Adolescent Eating Disorders at the South London and Maudsley NHS Foundation Trust and Emeritus Professor, Kings College, London

Adapting Evidence-Based Eating Disorder Treatments for Novel Populations and Settings

This comprehensive text provides practical approaches to adapting empirically supported treatments for eating disorders for clinicians working with patients of diverse backgrounds and presentations, or within non-traditional treatment settings across levels of care.

The book describes empirically- and clinically-informed treatment adaptations that impact delivery of real-world services for eating disorder patients and generate interest in testing adapted treatments in randomized controlled trials. Featuring contributions from researchers and clinicians with expertise in developing, delivering, and testing interventions for eating disorders, each chapter focuses on a specific population, setting, or training approach. Practical applications are then illustrated through case examples and wisdom gleaned through the contributors' own clinical studies and experiences.

Readers working with a diverse population of eating disorder patients will gain the necessary skills to support their patients on the journey to recovery and self-acceptance.

Christina C. Tortolani, Ph.D., is an Associate Professor at Rhode Island College, adjunct faculty at Brown Medical School, and a licensed psychologist specializing in eating disorders.

Andrea B. Goldschmidt, Ph.D., is an Associate Professor (Research) at Brown Medical School who conducts research on maladaptive eating and overweight/obesity across the lifespan.

Daniel Le Grange, Ph.D., holds a distinguished professorship at the University of California, San Francisco, and is Director of the Eating Disorders Program in the Department of Psychiatry and Behavioral Sciences. He is also Emeritus Professor of Psychiatry and Behavioral Neuroscience at the University of Chicago.

Adapting Evidence-Based Eating Disorder Treatments for Novel Populations and Settings

A Practical Guide

Edited by
Christina C. Tortolani,
Andrea B. Goldschmidt,
and Daniel Le Grange

NEW YORK AND LONDON

First published 2021
by Routledge
52 Vanderbilt Avenue, New York, NY 10017

and by Routledge
2 Park Square, Milton Park, Abingdon, Oxon, OX14 4RN

Routledge is an imprint of the Taylor & Francis Group, an informa business

© 2021 Taylor & Francis

The right of Christina C. Tortolani, Andrea B. Goldschmidt, and Daniel Le Grange to be identified as the authors of the editorial material, and of the authors for their individual chapters, has been asserted in accordance with sections 77 and 78 of the Copyright, Designs and Patents Act 1988.

All rights reserved. No part of this book may be reprinted or reproduced or utilised in any form or by any electronic, mechanical, or other means, now known or hereafter invented, including photocopying and recording, or in any information storage or retrieval system, without permission in writing from the publishers.

Trademark notice: Product or corporate names may be trademarks or registered trademarks, and are used only for identification and explanation without intent to infringe.

Library of Congress Cataloging-in-Publication Data
Names: Tortolani, Christina C., editor. | Goldschmidt, Andrea B., editor. | Le Grange, Daniel, editor.
Title: Adapting evidence-based eating disorder treatments for novel populations and settings : a practical guide/edited by Christina C. Tortolani, Andrea B. Goldschmidt, Daniel Le Grange.
Description: New York, NY : Routledge, 2021. | Includes bibliographical references and index. |
Identifiers: LCCN 2020021230 (print) | LCCN 2020021231 (ebook) | ISBN 9780367142728 (hardback) | ISBN 9780367142742 (paperback) | ISBN 9780429031106 (ebook).
Subjects: LCSH: Eating disorders–Treatment. | Evidence-based medicine.
Classification: LCC RC552.E18 A33 2021 (print) | LCC RC552.E18 (ebook). |
DDC 616.85/26–dc23
LC record available at https://lccn.loc.gov/2020021230
LC ebook record available at https://lccn.loc.gov/2020021231

ISBN: 978-0-367-14272-8 (hbk)
ISBN: 978-0-367-14274-2 (pbk)
ISBN: 978-0-429-03110-6 (ebk)

Typeset in Baskerville
by MPS Limited, Dehradun

Printed in the United Kingdom
by Henry Ling Limited

Contents

List of Figures, Tables, and Boxes	x
About the Editors	xii
List of Contributors	xiii
Acknowledgments	xxiv
Preface	xxv

PART I
Adapting Evidence-Based Treatments
for Novel Populations — 1

1 Cultural Adaptations of Evidence-Based
Treatments for Eating Disorders — 3
MAE LYNN REYES-RODRÍGUEZ and DEBRA FRANKO

2 Modifying Treatments to Recognize the
Pursuit of Muscularity, and Related Eating
Psychopathology, Among Men — 31
MITCHELL L. CUNNINGHAM, JASON M. NAGATA, and STUART B. MURRAY

3 Where is the Evidence of Evidence-Based Treatment
for LGBTQIA+ Individuals Experiencing
Eating Disorders? — 50
JEREL P. CALZO, ETHAN E. LOPEZ, SCOUT SILVERSTEIN,
TIFFANY A. BROWN, and AARON J. BLASHILL

4 Utilizing Alternate Caregivers and Support Persons
in Eating Disorder Treatment — 74
CRISTIN D. RUNFOLA and LINSEY UTZINGER

viii *Contents*

5 Implementing Eating Disorder Treatment
Before and After Bariatric Surgery   103
KASEY P.S. GOODPASTER, ALLYSON DIGGINS, and LESLIE J. HEINBERG

6 Evidence-Based Treatments for Youth with
Overweight/Obesity   128
ASHLEY F. JENNINGS, ABIGAIL R. COOPER, SARA FRUCHTER,
GINA DIMITROPOULOS, and KATHARINE L. LOEB

7 Adapting Evidenced-Based Therapies for
Avoidant/Restrictive Food Intake Disorder   146
KENDRA R. BECKER, LAUREN BREITHAUPT, JENNY H. JO,
KAMRYN T. EDDY, and JENNIFER J. THOMAS

8 Treating Eating-Related Problems in Non-Eating
Disordered Populations   169
REBECCA BERNARD, JESSIE MENZEL, and KERRI BOUTELLE

9 Eating Disorders and Disordered Eating
in the Military Family   194
ALEXANDRIA MORETTINI, NATASHA A. SCHVEY,
DAKOTA GILLMORE, and MARIAN TANOFSKY-KRAFF

10 Integrating Evidence-Based Treatments for
Eating Disorder Patients with Comorbid PTSD
and Trauma-Related Disorders   216
TIMOTHY D. BREWERTON, KATHRYN TROTTIER, JULIE TRIM,
TRICIA MEYERS, and STEPHEN WONDERLICH

11 Treating Eating Disorders in Pregnancy
and the Postpartum Period   238
BRONWYN RAYKOS and HUNNA WATSON

12 Tailoring Treatments to Middle-Aged
and Older Adults   268
LISA SMITH KILPELA, FRANCESCA GOMEZ, and CAROLYN BECKER

Contents ix

PART II
Applying Evidence-Based Treatments
in Nontraditional Treatment Settings 291

13 Delivering Evidence-Based Treatments for
Eating Disorders in the Home-Based Setting 293
EVA-MOLLY PETITTO DUNBAR, CHRISTINA C. TORTOLANI,
SANDRA M. ESTRADA, and ANDREA GOLDSCHMIDT

14 Using Remote Methods to Deliver Evidence-Based
Treatment for Eating Disorders 313
CLAIRE TRAINOR, SASHA GORRELL, KRISTEN ANDERSON, and
DANIEL LE GRANGE

15 Using FBT and Adjunctive Family Interventions
in a Partial Hospitalization Program for Adolescents
with Eating Disorders 335
TERRA L. TOWNE, STEPHANIE K. PECK, and ROXANNE E. ROCKWELL

16 Ensuring Continuity of Family-Based Care across
Levels of Treatment 352
RENEE D. RIENECKE and ELIZABETH WALLIS

17 Primary Care-Based Treatment for Eating Disorders 367
RICHARD CHUNG and DEVDUTTA SANGVAI

18 eHealth Interventions for Eating Disorders 376
JOHANNA SANDER, SALLY BILIĆ, and STEFFI BAUER

Afterword: Novel Research, Training, and Supervision
Opportunities for Evidence-Based Treatment Adaptations 397
CAROL B. PETERSON, EMILY M. PISETSKY, and LISA M. ANDERSON

Index 409

List of Figures, Tables, and Boxes

Figures

1.1	Summary of Cultural Adaptation Process	8
1.2	Comprehensive Intervention Approach for Latinas in the United States	21
3.1	Recommendations for Advancing Research and Evidence-Based Treatment for Eating Disorders among LGBTQIA+ Populations	67
6.1	A Summary Diagram of Hypothesized Links Between Risk Factors for Children with Overweight/Obesity Status and Corresponding Treatment Modalities	133
11.1	Sally's Clinical Formulation	249
11.2	Self-Evaluation Pie Chart	255
13.1	Natalie's Weight Gain Trajectory Throughout Home-Based FBT	304
15.1	UCSD Adolescent Partial Hospitalization Program Schedule	337
15.2	Meal-Coaching Consultation Example During Multifamily Meal	342

Tables

1.1	Frameworks, Models, and Guidelines for Cultural Adaptation of Evidence-Based Treatments	6
1.2	Publications on Culturally Sensitive Treatment and Randomized Clinical Studies on Eating Disorders Targeting Diverse Populations	10
4.1	How Significant Others Might Aid in Recovery within CBT-E	90
5.1	Common Session Topics in Presurgical Eating Disorder Treatment	110

List of Figures, Tables, and Boxes xi

5.2	Common Session Topics in Postsurgical Eating Disorder Treatment	117
5.3	Bariatric Lifestyle Recommendations	118
6.1	Hypothesized Weight Range Target at Which Health/Remission is likely to be Achieved	131

Boxes

4.1	Couple-Based Approaches	87
7.1	Our Team's Operational Definitions for Criterion A of the ARFID Diagnosis in *DSM-5*	147
7.2	Three Tips in Deciding Which Maintaining Mechanism to Target First	157
7.3	Five "Tips from the Trenches" in Treating Individuals with ARFID	164
11.1	Evidence-Based Guidelines	240
11.2	Assessment	242
11.3	Establishing a Treating Team	245
11.4	Recommended Caloric Intake in Pregnancy and for Breastfeeding Women	246
11.5	Recommended Weight Gain During Pregnancy	247
11.6	Psychoeducation	248
11.7	Formulation	248
11.8	Weekly Weighing	251
11.9	Self-Monitoring and Addressing Dietary Restriction and Dietary Restraint	252
11.10	Mood Intolerance and Emotional Triggers	253
11.11	Overevaluation of Eating, Weight, and Shape	254
11.12	Negative Body Image	257
11.13	Maintenance and Relapse Prevention	258
12.1	Case Illustration: Charlene	275
12.2	Case Illustration: Dorothy	276
12.3	Case Illustration: Sue	278
18.1	Summary	379
18.2	Summary	382
18.3	Summary	386
A.1	Research Considerations for Adaptations of Evidence-Based Treatment Investigations	399

About the Editors

Christina C. Tortolani, Ph.D., is an Associate Professor and Clinical Director at Rhode Island College's Graduate program in Mental Health Counseling. She also serves as an adjunct Associate Professor of Psychiatry and Human Behavior at Brown Medical School. As a licensed psychologist, she has worked with children, adolescents, and adults with eating disorders within various settings and levels of treatment, utilizing a number of evidence-based treatment models. Her research interests focus on the adaptation and dissemination of evidence-based treatments. She is currently an investigator on several grant-funded research projects.

Andrea Goldschmidt, Ph.D., FAED, is an Associate Professor (Research) at Brown Medical School who conducts research on maladaptive eating and obesity across the lifespan. Her specific areas of interest include the etiology and course of binge eating in children and adolescents, and dissemination and implementation of evidence-based treatments for adolescent eating disorders. She is currently a PI on several federally funded grants, and has authored or co-authored over 100 peer-reviewed publications, book chapters, and edited books.

Daniel Le Grange, Ph.D., FAED, is a Benioff UCSF Professor in Children's Health, and Director of the Eating Disorders Program in the Department of Psychiatry and Behavioral Sciences UCSF Weill Institute for Neurosciences at the University of California, San Francisco. He is also Emeritus Professor of Psychiatry and Behavioral Neuroscience at The University of Chicago. He is a past recipient of the Leadership Award in Research from the Academy of Eating Disorders and his work has been supported by the National Institute of Mental Health for two decades now. He is the author of over 500 articles, books, book chapters, and published abstracts.

List of Contributors

Kristen Anderson, M.A., L.C.S.W., is an eating disorder therapist practicing in Chicago, Illinois. She specializes in the treatment of adolescent restrictive eating disorders.

Lisa M. Anderson, Ph.D., is an Assistant Professor in the National Institute of Mental Health postdoctoral fellowship in eating disorders research within the Department of Psychiatry and Behavioral Sciences at the University of Minnesota. Dr. Anderson's research seeks to elucidate biological and behavioral mechanisms underlying anxiety-related psychopathology and eating disorders, with the goal of translating these findings to inform the development and optimization of treatments for eating disorders.

Steffi Bauer, Ph.D., is the Director of the Center for Psychotherapy Research at the University Hospital Heidelberg. Her work focuses on psychotherapy research and service research with a focus on e-mental health. Over the past two decades, her team has developed and evaluated a number of technology-enhanced interventions for the prevention, treatment, and relapse prevention of various mental illnesses.

Carolyn Becker, Ph.D., is a Professor of Psychology and a board-certified, licensed clinical psychologist who specializes in eating disorders, anxiety disorders, and PTSD. Her work primarily focuses on the implementation of scientifically supported interventions in "real world" settings. Dr. Becker is past president of both the Academy for Eating Disorders (AED) and the Society for a Science of Clinical Psychology, and she has received numerous awards including the Lori Irving Award for Excellence in Eating Disorders Prevention and Awareness granted by the National Eating Disorders Association and the Research Practice Partnership Award from the AED.

Kendra R. Becker, Ph.D., is a Clinical Staff Psychologist at the Eating Disorder Clinical and Research Program (EDCRP) at the Massachusetts General Hospital and an Instructor in Psychology at Harvard Medical School. She has expertise in delivering evidenced-based treatments for feeding and eating disorders including family-based treatment, cognitive

xiv   *List of Contributors*

behavior therapy, and dialectical behavioral therapy for children, adolescents, and adults with eating disorders. She is a co-author of more than 35 scientific publications and has received federal and foundation funding for her research on the neurobiology of restrictive eating disorders.

Rebecca Bernard, Ph.D., is an (Health Sciences) Associate Clinical Professor in the Department of Pediatrics at the University of California, San Diego, and the Clinical Director of the UC San Diego Center for Healthy Eating and Activity Research (CHEAR). Dr. Bernard is a licensed clinical psychologist with expertise in the evaluation and treatment of overeating, obesity, eating disorders, disruptive behavior disorders, and comorbid medical and psychiatric conditions. Her research interests include treatment development and outcome research and she currently is involved in treatment outcome studies at CHEAR.

Sally Bilić (née Kindermann), Ph.D., is a graduated psychologist. At the Center for Psychotherapy Research at the University Hospital, Heidelberg, she has been involved in several research projects on e-mental health, for example, projects related to eating disorder prevention, chat-based counseling, and clinical aftercare.

Aaron J. Blashill, Ph.D., is an Associate Professor in the Department of Psychology at San Diego State University, and the SDSU/UC San Diego Joint Doctoral Program in Clinical Psychology. His research focuses on sexual and gender minority health disparities, including body image disturbance and eating pathology.

Kerri Boutelle, Ph.D., is a Professor in the Departments of Pediatrics, Family Medicine and Public Health, and Psychiatry at the University of California, San Diego, and the director of the UC San Diego Center for Healthy Eating and Activity Research. Dr. Boutelle is a licensed clinical psychologist and has specialized in studying and treating obesity, overeating, binge eating, and eating disorders since 1992. Dr. Boutelle has pioneered treatments based on extinction theory for overeating in children and adults, including the development of a novel clinical treatment program, named Regulation of Cues (ROC), that shows promise in preliminary clinical trials with children and adults.

Lauren Breithaupt, Ph.D., is a clinical psychologist at Massachusetts General Hospital/Harvard Medical School specializing in evidenced-based treatment of eating disorders. Her research focuses on identifying a biomarker for eating disorder risk and recovery.

Timothy D. Brewerton, M.D., is Affiliate Professor of Psychiatry and Behavioral Sciences at the Medical University of South Carolina in Charleston, South Carolina, where he is in private practice, and he also currently serves as the Director of Clinical Outcomes and Research for Monte Nido and Affiliates. He is: Distinguished Life Fellow of the American

Psychiatric Association; Distinguished Fellow of the American Academy of Child and Adolescent Psychiatry; Founding Fellow of the Academy of Eating Disorders; and former president of the Eating Disorders Research Society and the South Carolina Psychiatric Association. Dr. Brewerton has been instrumental in exploring the overlaps between trauma, PTSD, and eating disorders, as well as promoting integrated treatment approaches for eating and related comorbid disorders.

Tiffany A. Brown, Ph.D., is an Assistant Project Scientist in the Department of Psychiatry at the University of California, San Diego, and a Research Scientist at the San Diego State University Research Foundation. Her research focuses on developing and evaluating eating disorder prevention and treatment programs for male and LGBTQIA+ populations. Her research also focuses on identifying novel biobehavioral targets for the treatment of restrictive eating disorders, with a particular focus on interoception and gastric specific anxiety.

Jerel P. Calzo, Ph.D., M.P.H., is Associate Professor in the Division of Health Promotion and Behavioral Science at San Diego State University School of Public Health. His research examines the development of gender and sexual orientation health disparities in adolescence and young adulthood, with a particular focus on eating disorders and substance use. In addition, he utilizes survey, mixed-method, and community-based participatory research approaches to examine and evaluate school- and community-based programs to promote the health and positive youth development of gender and sexual minority adolescents and young adults.

Richard Chung, M.D., is the Director of Adolescent Medicine at Duke University Medical Center, Medical Director of the Duke Center for Eating Disorders, and an Associate Professor of internal medicine and pediatrics at Duke. Dr. Chung's clinical and research interests include chronic illness in adolescence and the role of positive developmental trajectories in driving successful transitions to independent adulthood. As Medical Director of the Duke Center for Eating Disorders, he oversees medical services in an active interdisciplinary program caring for the full spectrum eating disorders across the lifespan.

Abigail R. Cooper is a graduate of Colby College and is currently a third-year Ph.D. student in clinical psychology at Fairleigh Dickinson University. Her research interests include sleep disorders and anorexia nervosa as bidirectionally driven comorbidities in the context of treatment trajectory and outcomes.

Mitchell L. Cunningham is a third-year doctoral student in the School of Psychology at the University of Sydney, Australia. His research revolves around the drive for muscularity among men and women, as well as its

List of Contributors

antecedents (e.g., social media use) and negative consequences (e.g., maladaptive eating and exercise behaviors).

Allyson Diggins, Ph.D., is an Associate Staff Psychologist at the Cleveland Clinic Bariatric & Metabolic Institute. She is an associate member of the American Society for Metabolic and Bariatric Surgery, a member of The Obesity Society, and member of the Society of Behavioral Medicine. Her research and clinical interests include the interaction between culture and health, behavioral interventions for obesity, and predictors of postoperative outcomes following bariatric surgery.

Gina Dimitropoulos, Ph.D., is an Associate Professor with the Faculty of Social Work at the University of Calgary. She is cross-appointed with the Department of Psychiatry and Pediatrics at UofC. She is the research leader for the Calgary Eating Disorder Program at the Alberta Children's Hospital whose work focuses on family-based treatments for adolescents and young adults with anorexia nervosa and avoidant/restrictive food intake disorder (ARFID).

Eva-Molly Petitto Dunbar, M.A., is a Clinical Psychology doctoral candidate at the University of Rhode Island (URI) with a focus on Health Psychology. Ms. Dunbar has experience providing evidence-based eating disorder treatment across the lifespan and levels of care. She conducts research in the areas of health behavior change and eating disorder treatment and prevention. She co-founded URI's Eating Concerns Advisors (UReca!) program and was the Project Coordinator on a state-funded grant, where she worked with the project PIs and team to disseminate eating disorder training, education, and treatment approaches to the Rhode Island healthcare workforce.

Kamryn T. Eddy, Ph.D., is a clinical psychologist, an Associate Professor of Psychology at Harvard Medical School, and the Co-Director of the Massachusetts General Hospital Eating Disorders Clinical and Research Program. She is a fellow of the Academy for Eating Disorders and president-elect of the Eating Disorders Research Society and her research, supported through the National Institutes of Health and private foundations, focuses on understanding the neurobiological bases of eating disorders to inform treatment. Along with her colleague, Dr. Jennifer Thomas, Dr. Eddy developed a novel manualized cognitive-behavioral therapy for ARFID (CBT-AR).

Sandra M. Estrada, M.A., is a licensed clinical social worker (LCSW) in the state of Rhode Island. She has 15 years of experience working with children, families, and victims of domestic violence. Sandra graduated from Boston College with her master's degree in social work. In the last 5 years, Ms. Estrada has been working with clients with eating disorders providing FBT treatment in home settings.

List of Contributors   xvii

Debra Franko, Ph.D., is Senior Vice-Provost for Academic Affairs at Northeastern University and a Professor in the Department of Applied Psychology. Her clinical interests in eating disorders span depression, suicide, and substance abuse and she has particular expertise in issues related to pregnancy and eating disorders. She has published extensively, including over 150 journal articles and book chapters on eating disorders, body image, and obesity. Dr. Franko was elected secretary of the Board of Directors of the Academy of Eating Disorders in 2011, where she served for 5 years, and was the recipient of the 2015 National Eating Disorders Association Award for Excellence in Prevention and Advocacy.

Sara Fruchter is a graduate of Barnard College and is currently a second-year Ph.D. student in Clinical Psychology at Fairleigh Dickinson University. Her current research interests involve mixed methods designs to study the effects of social media on body image and anxiety in young women.

Dakota Gillmore is a graduate student in the Department of Medical and Clinical Psychology at the Uniformed Services University in Bethesda, Maryland. He is a member of the Developmental Research Laboratory on Eating and Weight Behaviors and is involved in research examining barriers to mental health care utilization among military personnel. He completed an M.A. in Sport and Exercise Psychology from Minnesota State University, Mankato, in 2016.

Francesca Gomez completed her undergraduate degree at Trinity University and is currently a post-baccalaureate research assistant in Dr. Carolyn Becker's lab at Trinity. She has contributed to ongoing research projects in the field of eating disorders concerning food insecurity and Latinx populations. She will begin graduate training in clinical psychology at Arizona State University in the fall of 2020.

Kasey P.S. Goodpaster, Ph.D., received her doctorate in Counseling Psychology from Purdue University. Currently, she is the Director of Behavioral Services at the Cleveland Clinic Bariatric & Metabolic Institute and an Assistant Professor of Medicine at the Cleveland Clinic Lerner College of Medicine of Case Western Reserve University. She also serves as the co-chair of the ASMBS Integrated Health Clinical Issues and Guidelines Committee. Her clinical and research interests include bariatric surgery evaluation, eating disorders, cognitive behavioral treatment, and infusing body positivity into weight loss treatment.

Sasha Gorrell, Ph.D., is a NIMH-funded T32 Postdoctoral Research Fellow in the Eating Disorders Program, at University of California, San Francisco. Dr. Gorrell earned her Ph.D. in Clinical Psychology from the University at Albany in 2018. The overarching goal of her research is to identify translational mechanisms that contribute to unhealthy eating and exercise behavior, in efforts to inform treatment development for adolescents with eating disorders.

xviii *List of Contributors*

Scott Griffiths, Ph.D., is a Lecturer in Psychology at the University of Canberra, a visiting fellow at the Australian National University and an executive board member of the National Association for Males with Eating Disorders.

Leslie J. Heinberg, Ph.D., is Director of Enterprise Weight Management at the Cleveland Clinic and Vice-Chair for Psychology in the Center for Behavioral Health Department of Psychiatry and Psychology, and the Director of Behavioral Services for the Bariatric and Metabolic Institute at the Cleveland Clinic. She is a Professor of Medicine in the Cleveland Clinic Lerner College of Medicine of Case Western Reserve University and is a staff member of the Digestive Diseases Institute and the Neurological Institute. Her clinical and research interests include obesity, bariatric surgery, eating disorders, and disorders of body image.

Ashley F. Jennings is a graduate of Drake University and is currently a third-year Ph.D. student in Clinical Psychology at Fairleigh Dickinson University. Her research interests include emotional overcontrol as a common substrate between anorexia nervosa and OCD.

Jenny H. Jo, M.A., is a senior clinical research coordinator at the Neuroendocrine Unit and Eating Disorder Clinical and Research Program (EDCRP) at the Massachusetts General Hospital. She is pursuing her doctorate in Clinical Psychology at Ohio University under Dr. Jean Forney's mentorship. She is passionate about investigating the biological and psychological underpinnings of eating disorders in hopes of improving treatment adherence and outcome.

Lisa Smith Kilpela, Ph.D., is an Assistant Professor at the University of Texas Health Science Center at San Antonio Long School of Medicine, in the Department of Psychiatry and Behavioral Sciences and in the Barshop Institute for Longevity and Aging Studies. She is a licensed clinical psychologist specializing in the clinical characterization of eating disorders in older adults, specifically focusing on aging-related factors that impact the experience of older women with disordered eating and have implications for treatment. Dr. Smith Kilpela is a 2019 recipient of the Paul B. Beeson Emerging Leaders in Aging Career Development Award, funded by the National Institute on Aging (NIA) and the American Federation for Aging Research (AFAR).

Katharine L. Loeb, Ph.D., is Professor of Psychology in the Ph.D. Program in Clinical Psychology at Fairleigh Dickinson University (FDU). She has been inducted as a fellow in the Academy for Eating Disorders and in the Association for Psychological Science and is a recipient of the FDU Distinguished Faculty Award for Research and Scholarship. Dr. Loeb's research involves improving case identification of and parenting capacities in managing child and adolescent eating disorders, and systems-level strategies, including applied behavioral economics, for pediatric overweight and obesity.

Ethan E. Lopez (He/They) is a queer and transgender community activist with a bachelor's degree in Lesbian Gay Bisexual Transgender and Queer (LGBTQ+) Studies awarded from San Diego State University. He is a team member of Trans Folx Fighting Eating Disorders (T-FFED) and a passionate advocate for the trans community's representation in research.

Jessie Menzel, Ph.D., is an (Health Sciences) Assistant Clinical Professor in the Department of Psychiatry at the University of California, San Diego, and the founder of the Pediatric Program at the UCSD Eating Disorder Center for Treatment and Research. Dr. Menzel has extensive treatment experience working with children, adolescents, and adults with eating disorders at all levels of care. Dr. Menzel has published research in the fields of eating and anxiety disorders and her current research interests are in the development and evaluation of treatments for ARFID.

Tricia Meyers, Ph.D., is the Chair of Eating Disorders for Sanford Health in Fargo, North Dakota. She is also the director of Training for the Treatment Collaborative for Traumatized Youth (TCTY) in Sanford Research. She has extensive experience in delivering family-based treatment for eating disorders and also trauma-focused cognitive behavior therapy for trauma-related disorders in children and adolescents.

Alexandria Morettini, Ph.D., is a Lieutenant in the U.S. Navy and has served on active duty since 2006. LT Morettini is a member of the Developmental Research Laboratory on Eating and Weight Behaviors. Her research focuses on the disparities in access to and delivery of mental health care for military children.

Stuart B. Murray, Ph.D., is Associate Professor, and the Director of the Eating Disorders Program, and the Translational Research in Eating Disorders lab, at the University of Southern California. His NIMH-funded program of research is oriented toward the identification of mechanisms underpinning eating disorder psychopathology.

Jason M. Nagata, M.D., M.Sc., is an Assistant Professor of Pediatrics in the Division of Adolescent and Young Adult Medicine at the University of California, San Francisco. He is an expert in the medical management of eating disorders and researches body image in understudied populations including males, sexual minorities, and gender minorities. In 2019, he was the recipient of the American Academy of Pediatrics Emerging Leader in Adolescent Health Award, the Society for Pediatric Research Fellow's Clinical Research Award, and the Grumbach Award for Excellence in Research at UCSF.

xx *List of Contributors*

Stephanie K. Peck, Ph.D., is a clinical psychologist and Director of the Intensive Family Treatment Programs at UCSD. In addition to her clinical work, she has also co-developed Temperament-Based Treatment with Supports (TBT-S), a treatment approach for individuals and their family members that addresses core temperament and neurobiology of eating disorders.

Carol B. Peterson, Ph.D., is an Associate Professor in the Department of Psychiatry and Behavioral Sciences at the University of Minnesota and the chief training officer of The Emily Program. The recipient of federal and foundation grants, Dr. Peterson has published widely on the topics of eating disorders treatment, assessment, and maintenance mechanisms. She is a fellow of the Academy for Eating Disorders and a member of the Editorial Board of the *International Journal of Eating Disorders* as well as a practicing clinician.

Emily M. Pisetsky, Ph.D., is an Assistant Professor in the Department of Psychiatry and Behavioral Sciences at the University of Minnesota. She received her undergraduate degree from Wesleyan University and her Ph.D. in clinical psychology from the University of North Carolina at Chapel Hill. Dr. Pisetsky conducts research, provides direct patient care, and trains psychology graduate students and psychiatry residents.

Bronwyn Raykos, Ph.D., is head of the Eating Disorders Program at the Centre for Clinical Interventions (CCI) in Western Australia. She is passionate about delivering, evaluating, disseminating, and improving evidence-based treatments for individuals with eating disorders. Bronwyn is a member of the Australian and New Zealand Academy of Eating Disorders (ANZAED) and is currently on the editorial board of the *International Journal of Eating Disorders*.

Mae Lynn Reyes-Rodríguez, Ph.D., is Clinical Associate Professor at Center of Excellence for Eating Disorders (CEED), Psychiatry Department of the University of North Carolina at Chapel Hill. As a researcher and clinical psychologist, she has devoted her career to adapting eating disorders treatments for the Latino population in Puerto Rico during her early career years and later with Latinos in the mainland, particularly in Central North Carolina. She is the expert of content for Latinos and underrepresented populations for the National Center of Excellence for Eating Disorders (NCEED) funded by Substance Abuse and Mental Health Services Administration (SAMHSA).

Renee D. Rienecke, Ph.D., FAED, is Director of Research for Eating Recovery Center/Insight Behavioral Health Centers and Associate Professor in the Department of Psychiatry and Behavioral Sciences at Northwestern University. She has over 20 years of experience in the treatment of eating disorders, particularly in family-based treatment, and

List of Contributors xxi

has built and developed two eating disorder programs, at the University of Michigan and at the Medical University of South Carolina. Her research interests include the role of expressed emotion in treatment outcome for adolescent anorexia nervosa and bulimia nervosa.

Roxanne E. Rockwell, Ph.D., is a clinical psychologist and Associate Clinical Professor in the Department of Psychiatry at UC San Diego. She was a founding member of the UC San Diego Eating Disorders Center for Treatment.

Cristin D. Runfola, Ph.D., is a licensed clinical psychologist specializing in the treatment and research of eating disorders, and a Clinical Assistant Professor in the Department of Psychiatry and Behavioral Sciences. She has worked across all levels of care, including outpatient, partial hospitalization, and inpatient settings, while also developing and studying protocols for delivering therapy in individual, group, and couple-based formats delivered in person, online, or via video conferencing. She supervises clinical trainees, is on the editorial board of *Eating Disorders: The Journal of Treatment and Prevention*, and has held leadership positions in the Academy for Eating Disorders.

Johanna Sander, M.Sc. Psych., studied psychology with a focus on developmental and clinical psychology at Heidelberg University. She currently works as a Research Fellow at the Center for Psychotherapy Research at the University Hospital Heidelberg. Her research focuses on the link between e-mental health and the prevention and early intervention in eating disorders.

Devdutta Sangvai, M.D., is Vice President for Population Health Management and Executive Director of the Population Health Management Office at Duke University Health System. He is Associate Professor of Family Medicine, Pediatrics, & Psychiatry at the Duke University School of Medicine. Dr. Sangvai has over 15 years of experience in working with patients with eating disorders.

Natasha A. Schvey, Ph.D., is an Assistant Professor in the Department of Medical and Clinical Psychology at the Uniformed Services University in Bethesda, Maryland. Dr. Schvey's research focuses on the intersection of stigma and health among vulnerable populations including youth and adults with overweight and obesity, military service members and dependents, and sexual and gender minorities. She has published over 50 scientific papers and chapters, and has presented to academic, professional, and community organizations throughout the country.

Scout Silverstein focuses on cultural competence among health care professionals, harm reduction, healing justice, and accessibility. They have degrees in human development as well as health policy & advocacy. They

xxii *List of Contributors*

are a team member of Trans Folx Fighting Eating Disorders and aim to close the gaps of health disparities in transgender and intersex populations.

Marian Tanofsky-Kraff, Ph.D., is Professor in the Departments of Medical and Clinical Psychology and Medicine at the Uniformed Services University of the Health Sciences and researcher in the Section on Growth and Obesity at the Eunice Kennedy Shriver National Institute of Child Health and Human Development at the NIH. She is also Director of the Developmental Research Laboratory on Eating and Weight Behaviors and Research Director for the Military Cardiovascular Outcomes Research Program (MiCOR). Dr. Tanofsky-Kraff's research program involves the intersection of obesity and eating disorders and emphasizes endophenotyping eating patterns that promote excess weight gain. She has carried out intervention trials aimed at preventing adult obesity and eating disorders in targeted and special populations.

Jennifer J. Thomas, Ph.D., is the Co-Director of the Eating Disorders Clinical and Research Program at Massachusetts General Hospital, and an Associate Professor of Psychology in the Department of Psychiatry at Harvard Medical School. She is currently a principal investigator on several studies investigating the neurobiology and treatment of ARFID, funded by the U.S. National Institute of Mental Health and private foundations. She is the author or co-author of more than 125 scientific publications and three books, serves as secretary for the Academy for Eating Disorders, and is Associate Editor for the *International Journal of Eating Disorders*.

Terra L. Towne, Ph.D., is a clinical psychologist and Global Foundation for Eating Disorders Scholar at the UC San Diego Eating Disorders Center. She is involved in both treatment development research and the Intensive Family Treatment (IFT) programs for adolescents and young adults.

Claire Trainor currently works as a clinical research coordinator in the Eating Disorders Program at the University of California, San Francisco. Her research interests are focused on understanding personality risk factors in eating disorders, how individual traits impact treatment outcomes, and treatment development for eating disorders in both children and adults. Claire will be starting the Doctoral Program in Clinical Psychology at Drexel University in the Fall of 2020.

Julie Trim, Ph.D., is an Assistant Professor of Psychiatry at UC San Diego (UCSD). She served as Director of the UCSD Adult Eating Disorder IOP and PHP programs for 11+ years, and is now in private practice. Her primary clinical and research interests include eating disorders and trauma or PTSD, emotion regulation, and dialectical behavior therapy (DBT).

Kathryn Trottier, Ph.D., is a psychologist in the Eating Disorder Program at University Health Network, and Assistant Professor in the Department of Psychiatry at the University of Toronto. Through her clinical work in the Toronto General Hospital's Eating Disorders Program, Kathryn became interested in the role of trauma-related symptoms in maintaining eating disorder symptoms and psychopathology. Her recent research has focused on developing and evaluating empirically-based integrated treatment protocols for co-occurring eating disorders and posttraumatic stress disorder.

Linsey Utzinger, Psy.D., is a clinical psychologist at Park Nicollet's Melrose Center in Minneapolis, Minnesota, where she specializes in evidence-based treatments for eating disorders across the lifespan. She completed her doctoral training in the PGSP-Stanford Consortium, predoctoral internship at Children's Hospital Colorado, and a T32 postdoctoral fellowship with the Midwest Regional Postdoctoral Training Grant in Eating Disorders Research. She was most recently a Clinical Assistant Professor in the Department of Psychiatry and Behavioral Sciences at Stanford University.

Elizabeth Wallis, M.D., M.S., is an Assistant Professor in the Departments of Pediatrics and Psychiatry and Behavioral Sciences, and the Director of Division of Adolescent Medicine and the Friedman Center for Eating Disorders at the Medical University of South Carolina in Charleston, South Carolina. She has research and clinical expertise in eating disorders and primary care behavioral health. She and Dr. Renee Rienecke opened the first family-based treatment program for eating disorders in South Carolina in June 2016.

Hunna Watson, Ph.D., is a clinical psychologist and Assistant Professor in the Department of Psychiatry and Center of Excellence for Eating Disorders at the University of North Carolina at Chapel Hill. She also holds the positions of adjunct research fellow at The University of Western Australia and adjunct lecturer at Curtin University in Australia. She is on the editorial board of the *International Journal of Eating Disorders* and the *Journal of Eating Disorders*, is a steering committee member of the National Eating Disorders Collaboration, and is a member of the Academy for Eating Disorders.

Stephen Wonderlich, Ph.D., is the Chester Fritz Distinguished Professor, University of North Dakota School of Medicine & Health Services and serves as Vice President for research at Sanford Health. He currently sits on the editorial board for several professional journals, is a past-president of the Academy for Eating Disorders, and was a member of the Eating Disorder Workgroup for *DSM-5*.

Acknowledgments

This book was a collective effort, with more than 60 authors contributing their wisdom and expertise. Our multidisciplinary researchers and clinicians share a commitment to adapting empirically-supported treatments for eating disorders and grounding them in real-world, clinical experience. These researchers and clinicians have helped to make our vision a reality, and we thank them for helping to improve treatments for eating disorder patients and also heighten interest in the testing of these treatments. We would also like to thank Routledge/Taylor & Francis for supporting our ideas and guiding us through the publication process. Finally, and most importantly, we thank the patients and families who collectively entrusted us to guide them through treatment and recovery using the adaptations described in this volume.

Christina Tortolani, Ph.D.
My collaborators, Andrea and Daniel, have made the process of writing this book both fun and enriching – thank you both! I also wish to express my profound gratitude to my professional mentors for their guidance and wisdom, and to my family and friends for their unfailing love and support. To my parents, Alan and Gail, you have always been my champions. To my partner, Seth Schulman, you have been and continue to be my rock. My children, Michaela, Stella, and Marco, you make my world go round!

Andrea Goldschmidt, Ph.D.
I would like to thank my family, particularly my husband, for their love, support, and unwavering belief that the work I do matters.

Daniel Le Grange, Ph.D., FAED
This one is for little Zoë who has put a smile on my face from the day she was born.

Preface

Like many ideas in science, the idea for this book emerged from a casual conversation. For several years, the first two authors of this text (CT and ABG) had been providing group supervision in eating disorders treatment to clinicians at a community-based mental health agency. These clinicians lacked experience with the eating disorders population, and we were tasked with helping them to implement an evidence-based treatment approach for adolescents with anorexia nervosa within their child and family intensive outreach services home-based team. One day, after reviewing the clinicians' progress, we remarked on the massive divide that exists between researchers, who typically evaluate treatment efficacy in "ivory tower" academic settings with what often amounts to a highly selective group of patients, and clinicians, who encounter in their practice settings individuals who represent the spectrum of gender identity, sexual orientation, sociocultural background, and comorbid presenting concerns. Many clinicians at this agency and elsewhere seemed to lack information about the state-of-the-science with respect to eating disorder treatment, and particularly how they might effectively adapt existing treatments for diverse populations and settings. Surely there had to be other researchers and practitioners who struggled with the quandary of how to apply existing manualized treatments to best fit the enormous heterogeneity and complexity of patients who exist in the real world. Wouldn't it be great if clinicians everywhere had access to resources instructing them how to finely tailor the most efficacious treatments for eating disorders to accommodate the unique presentations of their clientele?

After reviewing the literature, it was clear that a book like this was sorely needed. Eating disorders are devastating psychiatric illnesses with potentially fatal medical consequences. These disorders affect at least 5% of the population,[1] impede quality of life,[2] and lead to increased mortality due to high rates of suicidality, self-injurious behaviors, and physical health complications.[3] Although lay people often assume that eating disorders primarily impact white adolescent females of a higher socioeconomic class, studies suggest that these disorders actually cut across all demographics, including older adults, males, gender non-conforming individuals, ethnic or racial and sexual minorities, those for whom English is not a first language, xxvi *Preface*

and those of a lower socioeconomic strata.[4-6] These individuals often fail to seek treatment due to stigma, lack of access to quality treatment providers, and financial or transportation-related barriers. Meanwhile, providers often fail to recognize early signs of eating disorders in patients with diverse backgrounds and complex symptom profiles because of biases in expected eating disorder presentation. Even when eating disorders are appropriately recognized and referred for treatment, clinicians may experience challenges delivering evidence-based care that meets the unique needs of their patients' specific identity- and culture-related issues. As a consequence, patients may become frustrated and abandon treatment, while clinicians themselves may experience higher rates of burnout due to lack of confidence in their ability to tailor interventions to patient nuances, as well as subsequent feelings of ineffectiveness in helping their patients get well.

Although there are several manualized treatments for eating disorders that have a strong evidence base, these treatments, in their original conceptualizations, may not be appropriate for all populations and treatment settings. Because treatment manuals were written to apply to a broad spectrum of eating disorder patients, they often fail to address patient- and setting-related features that are critical to their effective implementation. At the time the idea for this text was conceived, there was not a single book that described how to adapt evidence-based eating disorder treatments for specific populations and clinical settings.

Adapting Evidence-Based Treatments for Eating Disorders for Novel Populations and Settings fills this gap. Intended for both novice and experienced clinicians and drawing on real-world clinical experience, the book illuminates how to adapt empirically supported treatments for eating disorders for patients of diverse backgrounds and presentations, and within non-traditional treatment settings across levels of care. Each chapter focuses on a specific population, setting, or training approach and is written by researchers and/or clinicians with expertise in developing, delivering, and/or testing interventions for eating disorders. Collectively, the chapters offer practical applications as well as illustrative case examples and clinical "pearls of wisdom." The primary goal of this volume is to bring the latest research about eating disorders and their treatment out of the ivory tower and into the clinic, where it can do the greatest good for patients with specific needs receiving care in specific treatment contexts. A secondary, aspirational goal is for this text to drive more research on adapted treatments to confirm their efficacy and effectiveness in unique populations and settings.

This volume is organized into two parts, the first of which explores application of evidence-based treatments in populations beyond those typically studied. In Chapter 1, Mae-Lynn Reyes Rodriquez, Ph.D., and Debra Franko, Ph.D., explore how cultural issues related to race, ethnicity, religion, and socioeconomic status might help or hinder the treatment process, and how therapists might adapt evidence-based treatments for patients from diverse cultural backgrounds. In Chapter 2, Mitchell L. Cunningham, Jason M. Nagata, M.D., M.Sc., Scott Griffiths, Ph.D., and Stuart B. Murray, Ph.D.,

Preface xxvii

describe the unique appearance-related concerns experienced by males that are often unaddressed by manualized treatments, and how evidence-based interventions can be modified to incorporate these distinct concerns. Chapter 3, by Jerel Calzo Ph.D., M.P.H., Ethan E. Lopez, Scout Silverstein, Tiffany A. Brown, Ph.D., and Aaron J. Blashill, Ph.D., describes adaptations for eating disorder patients who identify as transgender, gender non-conforming, intersex, or a sexual minority and who might have unique body image issues to consider in treatment.

In Chapter 4, Cristin Runfola, Ph.D., and Linsey Utzinger, Psy.D., discuss how clinicians can incorporate alternate caregivers or support persons – including partners or spouses, roommates, and guardians appointed by the legal system – to improve outcomes of evidence-based treatments. Chapter 5, by Kasey Goodpaster, Ph.D., Allyson Diggins, Ph.D., and Leslie Heinberg, Ph.D., examines how to adapt evidence-based treatments for patients who have undergone bariatric surgery, who may be at elevated risk for problematic eating behaviors in the post-surgical period that can impact their health and surgical outcomes. Ashley Jennings, Abigail R. Cooper, Sara Fruchter, Gina Dimitropoulos, Ph.D., and Katharine Loeb, Ph.D., lead us in Chapter 6 through the intricacies of adapting evidence-based treatments for youth struggling with overweight or obesity. Chapter 7, by Kendra R. Becker, Ph.D., Lauren Breithaupt, Ph.D., Jenny H. Jo, M.A., Kamryn T. Eddy, Ph.D., and Jenny Thomas, Ph.D., discusses the unique clinical features of avoidant/restrictive food intake disorder (ARFID) that require a new treatment approach. In some patients, eating-related problems are secondary to other illnesses or comorbid conditions such as autism spectrum disorders, obsessive-compulsive disorder, and Celiac disease. Rebecca Bernard, Ph.D., Jessie Menzel, Ph.D., and Kerri Boutelle, Ph.D., describe how to adapt treatments for these patients in Chapter 8.

Active and inactive members of the armed forces and their families have unique needs when it comes to treating eating disorders – a topic covered by Alexandria Morettini, Natasha Schvey, Ph.D., Dakota Gillmore, and Marian Tanofsky-Kraff, Ph.D., in Chapter 9. Chapter 10, co-authored by Timothy Brewerton, M.D., Kathryn Trottier, Ph.D., Julie Trim, Ph.D., Tricia Meyers, Ph.D., and Stephen Wonderlich, Ph.D., considers how to use evidence-based treatments to treat patients struggling with comorbid eating disorders and post-traumatic stress disorder. In Chapter 11, Bronwyn Raykos, Ph.D., and Hunna Watson, Ph.D., examine how to adapt evidence-based treatments to help patients who are pregnant or who have recently given birth. Concluding Part I, Chapter 12, by Lisa Smith Kilpela, Ph.D., Francesca Gomez, and Carolyn Becker, Ph.D., examines the treatment adaptations that clinicians might find necessary when treating middle-aged and older adults, who often struggle with feelings of isolation and other aging-related stressors that contribute to the onset and/or maintenance of their eating disorder symptoms.

Part II of the volume shifts away from population-related adaptations and considers how practitioners might best apply evidence-based treatments in

xxviii *Preface*

non-traditional treatment settings. Chapter 13, by Eva-Molly Petitto Dunbar, M.A., Christina Tortolani, Ph.D., Sandra Estrada, M.A., and Andrea Goldschmidt, Ph.D., focuses on how to address the unique challenges and opportunities presented by offering eating disorders treatment in the home as opposed to the clinic. As many patients lack access to treatment in their local areas and require delivery of evidence-based treatments by phone, video-conferencing, or other remote methods, Claire Trainor, Sasha Gorrell, Ph.D., Kristen Anderson, M.S.W., and Daniel Le Grange, Ph.D., describe how best to modify treatments for telehealth settings in Chapter 14.

Family-based treatment was designed for delivery in the outpatient setting. As Terra Towne, Ph.D., Stephanie Peck, Ph.D., and Roxanne Rockwell, Ph.D., reveal in Chapter 15, family-based treatment concepts and strategies and adjunctive family interventions can be utilized in partial hospitalization settings, where higher levels of care might make it challenging for parents to take charge of an adolescent's eating. Renee Rienecke, Ph.D., and Elizabeth Wallis, M.D., M.S., examine the challenges of transitioning between outpatient care and inpatient or partial hospitalization in Chapter 16, suggesting how we might facilitate the transition by embedding evidence-based practice into these higher levels of care.

In Chapter 17, Richard Chung, M.D., and Devdutta Sangvai, M.D., M.B.A., discuss primary care as a viable setting for providing evidence-based assessment and treatment of eating disorders. This chapter also considers how primary care providers can serve as critical members of the treatment team when psychotherapy is being implemented elsewhere. Chapter 18, by Johanna Sander, M.Sc., Sally Bilić, Ph.D, and Steffi Bauer, Ph.D., considers the unique technical, ethical, and legal challenges that arise during online e-health and m-health interventions, suggesting how clinicians might best meet these challenges to improve patient access and treatment outcomes. The book concludes with an Afterword by Carol Peterson, Ph.D., Emily M. Pisetsky, Ph.D., and Lisa Anderson, Ph.D., which considers the novel research, training, and supervision opportunities presented by evidence-based treatment adaptations.

Evidence-based treatments for eating disorders offer great potential for patients suffering from these devastating illnesses. But that potential can only be realized if treatments are perceived as relevant and appropriate for the patients whom they are intended to reach. We hope that this book will provide clinicians with the knowledge and confidence to apply principles and interventions of evidence-based treatments to their patients, in all their complexity and individuality, in the unique settings in which they present. We further hope that researchers will feel inspired to test novel cultural and setting-related adaptations of evidence-based treatments for eating disorders in scientifically rigorous efficacy and effectiveness studies. Everyone in the eating disorders community benefits when we bridge the gap between science and practice – clinicians, researchers, carers, and most importantly, patients.

Part I

Adapting Evidence-Based Treatments for Novel Populations

1 Cultural Adaptations of Evidence-Based Treatments for Eating Disorders

Mae Lynn Reyes-Rodríguez and Debra Franko

Introduction

The tremendous growth of populations from diverse cultural backgrounds across the United States poses unique challenges for providing culturally competent care, particularly for mental health. According to the U.S. Census projections, it is expected that the U.S. population will become a majority–minority nation for the first time in 2043 (Colby & Ortman, 2014). Due to the new geographic composition, the use of the term *"culturally sensitive"* or *"cultural competence"* has increased in relevance in the mental health literature with the aim to address and reduce ethnic disparities in mental health care access and outcomes (Alarcon et al., 2009). Culture, context, and language are essential considerations for culturally competent care. The American Psychological Association provides guidelines as a way to educate psychologists about issues of diversity (APA, 2003). The importance of providing culturally sensitive practices and being well informed about culture, race, ethnicity, national origin, and language is not only an ethical issue, but also essential for the effective implementation of services or research (APA, 2017).

The literature on culturally sensitive treatments for eating disorders in the United States within diverse populations is limited. This is due, in part, to the misconception that eating disorders primarily affect White females from a specific socioeconomic background, and do not occur in other ethnic/racial groups; as a result, most treatment and assessment protocols have been developed primarily for Whites and may not be valid for use with other ethnic groups (Smolak & Striegel-Moore, 2001). Contrary to this misconception, it is well documented that eating disorders affect people from diverse ethnic and racial backgrounds (Franko, Becker, Thomas, & Herzog, 2007; Rodgers, Berry, & Franko, 2018; Udo & Grilo, 2018). Furthermore, functional impairment associated with a lifetime history of eating disorders is comparable or higher in diverse populations (i.e., Latinos, Asian Americans, and African Americans) as compared with non-Latino Whites (Marques et al., 2011). There is considerable need for understanding the complex interactions between race/ethnicity and the psychological factors that contribute to the development of eating disorders (Rodgers et al., 2018).

The research on ethnicity-based disparities in psychiatric diagnosis and access to care reflects three main issues that can lead to lack of appropriate treatment and impede access to care: (1) the poor fit of psychiatric diagnostic categories with ethnically diverse explanatory models and presentations of illness that could potentially lead to improper diagnosis (Alegria et al., 2008); (2) the differential help-seeking patterns for illness across racial/ethnic groups which requires different approaches to enhance engagement into treatment (Alegria et al., 2006); and (3) clinician error or bias due to the misperception that eating disorders are not prevalent in members of diverse populations. Culturally sensitive guidelines and protocols are suggested for potential modifications in the treatment content and delivery process that could affect outcomes by enhancing treatment effects, engagement, or retention and therefore reduce mental health disparities.

The purpose of this chapter is to provide the most updated information about culturally sensitive treatments for eating disorders for diverse populations. The first part of the chapter is devoted to defining what entails a cultural adaptation, discussing cultural adaptation frameworks, and determining when it is appropriate and necessary to integrate a culturally sensitive approach. The second part includes a review of research of culturally sensitive evidence-based treatments (EBTs) conducted with diverse populations in the United States. Finally, other relevant factors to take into consideration when working with diverse populations are discussed.

What is a Cultural Adaptation?

Cultural adaptation of treatments is one means for ensuring that EBTs that have been primarily developed and evaluated with study population representative of the majority culture are feasible, acceptable, and effective across diverse ethnic and social groups (Bernal, Jiménez-Chafey, & Domenech-Rodríguez, 2009; Domenech Rodríguez & Bernal, 2012). Dissonance can emerge when EBTs are applied untested in ethnic minority groups (Barrera & Gonzalez Castro, 2006). According to Bernal et al. (2009), cultural adaptation involves a systematic modification of an intervention to integrate clients' relevant cultural factors (e.g., language and values). Whaley and Davis (2007) emphasized that the modification could be either in the content or in the delivery of an EBT or both, in order to accommodate values, attitudes, and practices of the target population.

Guidelines or systematic approaches for treatment adaptation in clinical trials and for the implementation of treatment in practice have been developed (APA, 2003). The DSM-5 Cross-Cultural Issues Subgroup developed a cultural formulation interview for implementation in diagnostic assessment to ensure that clinicians tap relevant domains of social, cultural, and ethnic identities (Alarcon et al., 2009). Furthermore, Griner and Smith (2006) made specific recommendations for the cultural modification of mental health interventions which emphasize the integration of the cultural values of the client in the therapy process (i.e., language, extended family, and spiritual traditions) and matching clients with therapists of the same race/ethnicity when possible. Bernal, Bonilla, and Bellido (1995) and Gonzalez Castro, Barrera, and Holleran-Steiker (2010) emphasized the importance of combining culturally adapted EBTs with culturally competent trained clinicians in the delivery of the intervention. Culturally adapted treatments appear to be especially valuable and acceptable to Latino individuals in the United States with low levels of acculturation (Griner & Smith, 2006).

Domenech Rodríguez and Bernal (2012) discussed ten models/frameworks and one guideline that have been published to address cultural adaptation of EBTs. Although there are some nuances among these models/frameworks, they concur that an initial exploratory phase, including gathering feedback from the target population and a literature review, should be the first step taken to inform the need for the cultural adaptation for the target population. Each model/framework emphasizes some specific steps of the cultural adaptation process with diverse levels of involvement of the target population but with the goal of providing a culturally sensitive approach congruent with the original EBT (Table 1.1).

Although the need for culturally sensitive treatments is clear (Bernal & Domenech Rodríguez, 2009; Falicov, 2009), specific guidelines about when and how to conduct a cultural adaptation are not explicit in the literature (Domenech Rodríguez, Baumann, & Schwartz, 2011) and the implementation of standards is limited (Smith, Domenech Rodríguez, & Bernal, 2011). Gonzalez Castro et al. (2010) summarized four basic conditions to justify a cultural adaptation: ineffective patient engagement; unique risk or resilience factors in a subcultural group; unique symptoms of a common disorder that the original EBT was not designed to influence; and poor intervention effectiveness with a particular subcultural group. Figure 1.1 summarizes the basic steps for a cultural adaptation process.

Brief Review of Existing Literature

Prevalence Studies

Eating disorders, disordered eating, unhealthy weight control behaviors, and body image concerns are well documented among racially and ethnically diverse individuals across the United States and around the world (Reyes-Rodríguez et al., 2010; Rodgers et al., 2018; Sinha & Warfa, 2013). While current stereotypes that eating disorders only affect affluent White females remain (Sonneville & Lipson, 2018), the scientific literature is replete with empirical data and epidemiological studies providing ample evidence to support dismissing this common stereotype (Blostein, Assari, & Caldwell, 2017; Perez, Ohrt, & Hoek, 2016; Rodgers et al., 2018; Swanson, Crow,

Table 1.1 Frameworks, Models, and Guidelines for Cultural Adaptation of Evidence-Based Treatments

Name	Year	Authors	Key Elements
The Multidimensional Model for Understating Culturally Responsive Psychotherapies (Framework)	1992	Koss-Chioino and Vargas	Two dimensions: (1) culture (context and context); and (2) structure (process and form)
Ecological Validity Framework	1995	Bernal, Bonilla, and Bellido	Eight elements: (1) language; (2) persons; (3) metaphors; (4) content; (5) concepts; (6) goals; (7) methods; and (8) context
Cultural Accommodation Model	1996	Leong	Three steps: (1) cultural gaps are identified; (2) literature review to inform the content that will fill the gap; and (3) testing the intervention to improve validity
Cultural Sensitivity Framework	2002	Resnicow, Soler, Braith-waite, Ahluwalia, and Butler	Two dimensions: (1) surface (appearance); and (2) deep (contextual influences on behaviors)
Cultural Adaptation Process Model	2004	Domenech-Rodríguez and Wieling	Three phases: (1) setting the stage; (2) initial adaptations; and (3) adaptation iterations
Hybrid Prevention Program Model	2004	González Castro, Barrera, and Martinez	Three dimensions: (1) cognitive information processing; (2) affective motivational characteristics; and (3) environmental characteristics
Selective and Directed Treatment Adaptation Framework	2006	Lau	Adaptation would target: (1) engagement or (2) treatment outcomes, or both.

Heuristic Framework	2006	Barrera and González-Castro	Four steps: (1) gather information; (2) make preliminary adaptations to the intervention; (3) test the preliminary adaptations; and (4) refine adaptations
Culturally Specific Prevention (Framework)	2006	Whitbeck	Five stages: (1) search for existing research models; (2) existing research of ethnic minorities is reviewed; (3) engaging in cultural translation of key risk and protective factors; (4) unique cultural risk and protective factors are identified and measured; and (5) undertake culturally specific interventions trials and assessments
Integrated Top-Down and Bottom-Up Approach to Adapting Psychotherapy (Model)	2006 and 2009	Hwang	Six domains: (1) dynamic issues and cultural complexities; (2) orientation; (3) cultural belief; (4) client-therapist relationship; (5) cultural differences in expression and communication; and (6) cultural issues of salience
Adaptation for International Transport (Guidelines)	2008	Kumpfer, Pinyuchon, Teixiera de Melo, and Whiteside	Implemented in 17 countries focused on cultural adaptation but keeping treatment fidelity

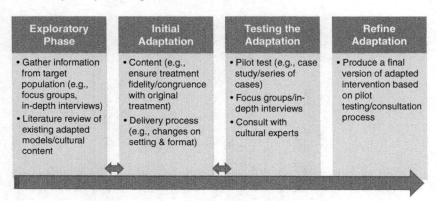

Figure 1.1 Summary of Cultural Adaptation Process.

Le Grange, Swendsen, & Merikangas, 2011). We begin this section with a very brief review of robust epidemiologic studies.

In a large nationally representative comparative study in the United States, Marques et al. (2011) found that in a sample of Latino/as, African Americans, Asian Americans, and Whites, the prevalence of anorexia nervosa (AN) and binge eating disorder (BED) was similar across all four of these groups. However, both lifetime and 12-month prevalence of bulimia nervosa (BN) was higher in Latino/as and African Americans relative to Asian Americans and Whites. In contrast to Whites, lifetime prevalence of "any binge eating" was higher and mental health service utilization was lower in all the three minority groups. Using a subset of the same nationally representative sample, Taylor et al. (2013) studied 5,191 adults and 1,170 adolescents who were either African American or Caribbean Black and found that while the lifetime prevalence of AN and BN was low (0–1.98%, depending on diagnosis and group), the prevalence of BED was 5.02% for African Americans and 5.78% for Caribbean Blacks. Nicdao, Hong, and Takeuchi (2007) found in a study of 2,095 Asian Americans that few were diagnosed with AN or BN and that women were more likely to have been diagnosed with BED than men. In one of the only studies to include Native Americans, Neumark-Sztainer et al. (2002) reported that African American adolescents had lower weight concerns and engaged in fewer weight loss behaviors than White adolescents. Notably, however, Hispanic, Asian American, and Native American adolescents were similar on these variables to White adolescents. Finally, in a study examining both eating disorder symptoms and body image concerns, Smith et al. (2018) found that body dissatisfaction was similar across three racial/ethnic groups ($n = 473$ Hispanic; $n = 341$ White; $n = 83$ Native American females university students); however, White women indicated more eating disorder symptoms than the other two groups.

To briefly summarize, our review of the literature finds that individuals from diverse racial and ethnic groups, particularly women and adolescent girls, present with eating disorders, eating disorder behaviors, body dissatisfaction, and problematic weight control behaviors. However, the literature is mixed as to whether prevalence rates are similar to, greater than, or less than Whites. We would argue that relative comparisons do not actually matter that much and what is important is that we recognize that these problems exist across the racial/ethnic spectrum in the United States. It is of note though that while the prevalence of frank eating-related issues in Native Americans is likely low, this group has rarely been studied in the eating disorders field (Striegel-Moore et al., 2011).

For our purposes, we assume that eating disorders and related behaviors occur across racial and ethnic minority groups in the United States. Before we begin our discussion of culturally tailored treatment for eating disorders, we consider two studies that have actually examined the question of whether there are differential intervention effects on those from minority backgrounds relative to Whites. Rodríguez, Marchand, Ng, and Stice (2008) and Stice, Marti, and Cheng (2014) found that outcomes did not differ significantly between White participants and African American/Asian/Hispanic participants in a four-session clinician-led prevention program titled the Body Project, and further, that a clinician match to participant race/ethnicity did not affect the results. This led the authors to conclude, *"The Body Project eating disorder prevention program produces similar reductions in eating disorder risk factors and symptoms for African Americans, Asian Americans, European Americans, and Hispanic young women who voluntarily enroll in trials of body acceptance interventions."* (Stice et al., 2014, p. 63). Of note, the authors further stated that *"It would be interesting to test whether this prevention program could produce even larger effects (emphasis ours) for ethnic minority groups if the intervention were specifically tailored for specific ethnic groups."* (Stice et al., 2014, p. 63).

This issue is the focus of this chapter. While differential outcomes were not found in these two studies, the more interesting and yet-to-be answered question is whether intervention outcomes would be enhanced for diverse groups if culturally sensitive and tailored programs were utilized, particularly with the less acculturated members.

Treatment Studies

Table 1.2 provides a comprehensive list of all studies published between 2010 and 2018 on topics relevant to the subject of this chapter (e.g., culturally sensitive treatments and treatment studies with diverse populations). Not surprisingly, these studies are very few in number. In fact, the only culturally adapted treatments published to date come from two research groups: one headed by Reyes-Rodríguez and the other by Cachelin, both working with Latino samples. While some interesting work has been published using Appetite Awareness Training (AAT) with African Americans (Goode et al., 2018), the authors note that because this type of treatment had not been tested previously with this

Table 1.2 Publications on Culturally Sensitive Treatment and Randomized Clinical Studies on Eating Disorders Targeting Diverse Populations

Authors	Year	Sample	Methods
Cultural adaptation studies **Asian Americans**			
Cheng and Merrick	2016	Case study, Chinese woman	Singe case, 24-year-old student, culturally adapted DBT treatment for AN-binge/purge type. (English language)
Smart	2010	No sample used	Qualitative study exploring cultural competency in therapy. Illustrated scenario of E-CBT for eating disorders
Latino/Hispanic population			
Binkley and Koslofsky	2016	Case study, Mexican American	Single case, adolescent, brief modified FBT-BN (five FBT sessions) combined with narrative humility approach. (Spanish/English language)
Cachelin et al.	2014	31 Mexican Americans women	Culturally adapted version of a CBT-based self-help program with eight guidance sessions for binge type eating disorders. (English language)
Reyes-Rodriguez, Baucom, and Bulik	2014	Case study, adult Latina	Single-case culturally adapted CBT-BN with six family sessions as an adjunct of individual CBT. (Spanish language)
Randomized clinical trials			
Reyes-Rodriguez, Watson, Woods-Smith, Baucom, and Bulik	Submitted	25 Latina women	Proof-of-principle study, culturally adapted CBT for binge eating type disorders, randomized to individual CBT ($n = 13$) versus individual CBT plus six family sessions ($n = 12$). (Spanish/English language)
Cachelin et al.	2018	40 Latina women	

			Small RCT culturally adapted GSH ($n = 21$) for BED versus waitlist ($n = 19$). (English language)
Goode et al.	2018	31 non-Latino black women	Small RCT Appetite Awareness training via eight, 60-minute sessions for binge or LOC eating ($n = 16$) versus waitlist ($n = 15$)
Mazzeo et al.	2016	45 adolescents (44.4% Whites and 42.2% Blacks)	Randomized to DBT-based intervention-LIBER8 for loss of control eating disorder or BED versus weight management group (2Bfit)
Mama et al.	2015	180 women (86.6% African Americans and 15.4% Hispanic)	Randomized to physical activity versus dietary intervention group, with six intervention sessions over 24 weeks
Stice, Marti, and Cheng	2015	Study 1: 426 female undergraduates (72 Asian Americans, 27 African Americans, 52 Hispanics, and 275 European Americans). Study 2: 189 female undergraduates (56 Asian Americans, 13 African Americans, 40 Hispanics, and 80 European Americans)	Study 1: randomized to clinician-led *Body Project* groups or an educational control group. Study 2: randomized to peer-led *Body Project* groups or a waitlist control condition
Grilo et al.	2014	104 obese patients (45.2% Caucasian, 34.6% African Americans, and 13.5% Hispanic)	Randomized to four conditions: medication, placebo, medication/CBTsh, placebo/CBTsh for BED
Grilo and White	2013	79 obese Latino adults (65 women and 14 men)	BED patients ($n = 40$) versus without BED randomized to orlistat-plus-BWL versus placebo-plus-BWL

Abbreviations: AN, anorexia nervosa; BED, binge eating disorder; BN, bulimia nervosa; BWL, behavioral weight loss; CBT, cognitive behavioral therapy; CBTsh, cognitive behavioral therapy self-help; DBT, dialectical behavior therapy; E-CBT, enhanced cognitive behavioral therapy; FBT-BN, family-based therapy for bulimia nervosa; GHS, guided self-help; LIBER-8, linking individuals being emotionally real; LOC, loss of control; RCT, randomized controlled/clinical trial.

population, they believed "*it was important to determine the feasibility of the original intervention (e.g., no cultural tailoring).*" (Goode et al., 2018, p. 84).

It is of note that no culturally relevant or adapted treatment studies for either Asian Americans or Native Americans have been published to date. While there are several relevant literature reviews and case reports with these groups (see Smart, 2010, for review of Asian Americans and Native Americans for obesity prevention program considerations), we could find no systematic trials with treatments tailored to these two groups. This is an area in need of research. Further, while some eating disorder treatment studies have included large diverse samples (Lydecker, Gueorguieva, Masheb, White, & Grilo, 2019), none utilized culturally adapted treatments. Finally, there are multiple studies that have examined the topics of help-seeking patterns, symptom presentation, dropout, and differential treatment response in diverse samples (Becker, Franko, Speck, & Herzog, 2003; Franko, Jenkins, & Rodgers, 2012; Sinha & Warfa, 2013; Thompson-Brenner et al., 2013). Although a review of these studies is beyond the scope of this chapter, briefly, the studies exploring race as a predictor and moderator of treatment outcomes for BED found no significant differences (Lydecker et al., 2019; Thompson-Brenner et al., 2013). Thompson-Brenner et al. (2013) found that Blacks were more likely to drop out from treatment compared with Whites; however, Blacks appear to have similar or better outcomes in BED treatment than Whites (Lydecker et al., 2019; Thompson-Brenner et al., 2013).

Culturally Tailored Treatment Studies

Studies conducted with Latinas have documented personal factors (i.e., motivation, knowledge, and stigma; Cachelin & Striegel-Moore, 2006) and system factors (i.e., clinician bias, lack of bilingual services; Becker et al., 2003; Cachelin & Striegel-Moore, 2006; Franko et al., 2007) as barriers for eating disorder treatment. In early work, Reyes-Rodríguez, Ramírez, Davis, Patrice, and Bulik (2013) identified several such barriers in this population, including clinician bias, providers' lack of knowledge of and skills with eating disorders, and lack of bilingual services. One of the main findings was that providing practical facilitators such as bilingual treatment and affordable care was not sufficient to encourage Latinas with eating disorders to seek help (Reyes-Rodríguez et al., 2013). Among the key elements that prevented Latinas with eating disorders from seeking treatment were stigma, fear of not being understood, not being ready to change, and privacy issues. Having the support of a family member or friend was found to be a facilitator of treatment retention. Other studies have also highlighted the influence of family in treatment engagement in Latinas with eating disorders (Cachelin & Striegel-Moore, 2006; Reyes-Rodríguez et al., 2019; Shea et al., 2012).

A comprehensive approach addressing the different components and barriers that contribute to health disparities in Latinos with eating disorders is necessary. Considering the low levels of service utilization and the dearth of culturally appropriate EBTs for Latinos (Miranda et al., 2005), a study of treatment effectiveness and acceptability of culturally adapted interventions that consider the context combined with evidence-based care is likely to facilitate treatment engagement and successful outcomes (Domenech Rodríguez et al., 2011; Miranda et al., 2005; Shea et al., 2012). Cognitive behavioral therapy (CBT) was found to be a feasible approach for Latina women in a study conducted in Puerto Rico (Reyes, Roselló, & Calaf, 2005). Further, the feasibility of CBT has been documented with Latinas with eating disorders in the United States (Cachelin, Shea, et al., 2014; Reyes-Rodríguez, Baucom, & Bulik, 2014; Shea, 2012). However, Reyes-Rodríguez et al. (2013) found that the community-based approach appears to be the most appropriate way to incorporate EBTs in the Latino community living in the United States. This work demonstrated the importance of using a community-based approach to tackle the distrust that Latinos often have in the system due to their immigration status. In a proof-of-principle study (Reyes-Rodríguez, Watson, Woods Smith, Baucom, & Bulik, submitted), 25 Latina adults with binge-type eating disorders ($M \pm SD$: 37 $\pm$ 9 years, range = 18–75 years) were recruited and randomized to two conditions: 25 individual CBT sessions ($n = 13$) versus 19 individual CBT + 6 family sessions ($n = 12$). Community therapists were trained and treatment was delivered at local community mental health facilities. The results of this study in terms of retention rate are impressive (completion of $\geq 75\%$ of sessions); 72% of patients remained in treatment, which is substantially higher than typical dropout rates in CBT trials for BN which can be near 40% (Schnicker, Hiller, & Legenbauer, 2013).

Using this community-based approach, multiple system and patient barriers were addressed. First, the knowledge and skills needed to recognize eating disorders in Latinos by community clinicians increased. Second, community therapists were receptive to training on evidence-based care. Third, patients were able to receive all services in their language of preference. Fourth, services were delivered at community clinics close to their residence in order to reduce transportation issues. Finally, using the community-based clinic facilitated the referral process for those who needed additional treatment. However, other barriers were identified.

The lack of health insurance or bilingual services in the area prevented Latino patients who were referred to outside specialist services to get the treatment (Reyes-Rodríguez, 2014; submitted). Although some community therapists were receptive to being trained in EBTs, at first, some community therapists were reluctant to use a different treatment approach than that in which they had been trained. Also, some of them shared concerns about the potential medical complications of eating disorders, which could indicate some reluctance to treat eating disorders and concerns about how to integrate medical care for this population. Establishing a trusting relationship with community clinics by the research team was important to engaging therapists and other administrative staff in the community clinics. However, this effort was not sufficient to prevent turnover of therapists, which is a common issue in community clinics.

Despite the critical importance that family plays in Latino culture, the literature about how best to incorporate family into treatment for eating disorders for Latinos is sparse. Reyes-Rodríguez et al. (submitted) found that treatment retention was higher in those randomized to the family condition (83%) compared with those randomized to the individual condition (69%). Results revealed small effect size differences in favor of the family condition on treatment acceptability, adherence, caregiver burden, family conflict from the patient's perspective, and follow-up eating disorder symptoms. Patients in the family condition attended more sessions compared with those in the individual CBT and reported greater treatment satisfaction. This proof-of-principle study shows that family enhancement, as an adjunct to individual CBT, is effective in the reduction of eating disorder symptoms in Latinas and could improve treatment acceptability, adherence, and treatment outcomes (Reyes-Rodríguez et al., submitted). In both groups, we observed reductions in eating disorder symptoms from baseline to the end of treatment and those changes were sustained into the 3-month follow-up. Similar to the finding in a case study (Reyes-Rodríguez et al., 2014), changes in eating disorder symptoms were observed after Week 6. This result is not consistent with the observations in Caucasian populations, where early change predicts good treatment outcome (Fernandez-Aranda et al., 2009; Le Grange, Peter, Ross, & Eunice, 2008), raising questions whether the course of treatment in Latina women differs from Caucasians (Reyes-Rodríguez et al., 2014).

The second research group working with Latino samples (primarily Mexican-American) is Cachelin et al. In a study by Shea, Cachelin, Gutierrez, Wang, and Phimphasone (2016) treated 12 Mexican-American women with BN or BED who were provided the CBT-Guided Self-Help (GSH) manual *Overcoming Binge Eating* and then participated in posttreatment focus groups. Themes that emerged included ideas about the social/cultural construction of both eating behaviors and body image ideals; the need for a "multifaceted support system" for effective treatment; and the conclusion that while the CBT-GSH treatment was feasible and relevant, the program would be improved with greater support from both friends and family.

Cachelin et al. (2018) provided results of a randomized controlled (RCT) trial with 40 overweight and obese Latinas with BED using a culturally adapted CBT-GSH program. Reductions in binge eating, depression, and psychological distress were reported by intervention group relative to controls. Nearly half (47.6%) of the intervention group reported no binge eating at 12 weeks after CBT-GSH. This RCT, using a culturally adapted treatment with Latina women with an eating disorder, provides an excellent model for such work in other populations.

Scott, Gil-Rivas, and Cachelin (2018) worked with 16 African American women with BED to explore their ideas about adaptations needed to make the treatment more effective; they found that participants had minimal

Cultural Adaptations of Evidence-Based Treatments 15

awareness about the diagnosis, identified cultural issues related to the thin ideal, and recognized that the connections between eating behaviors and interpersonal relationships, religion, coping with adversity, and motivation were all important treatment considerations.

Goode et al. (2018) recently tested an existing intervention for binge eating with a group of African American women. AAT is designed to train individuals to recognize hunger and satiety and use physiological signals to guide eating decisions. AAT has been found to be effective in prior studies of White adult women (Blumenthal et al., 2010; Hill, Craighead, & Safer, 2011), but was only recently tested with an African American sample. Goode et al. (2018) utilized AAT in the original format (not culturally tailored), and found decreases in binge eating and improvements in eating self-efficacy at the end of this 8-week treatment. However, the treatment was not culturally adapted, as noted earlier.

To conclude, very few studies of culturally adapted treatment with Latino/Hispanic participants have been published to date and no studies with Asian, Native American, or African American participants are available. Only two research groups, one spearheaded by Reyes-Rodríguez and the other by Cachelin, have actually implemented and measured the effect of culturally adapted interventions, both with Latino/Hispanic populations. There is much work to be done.

Working with Racially and Ethnically Diverse Individuals with Eating Disorders

In the meantime, while we wait (and encourage readers to engage in this work), many clinicians will find themselves treating racially and ethnically diverse individuals with eating disorders. In the next section, we highlight specific elements to consider.

The issue of therapist–client matching in relation to race and ethnicity has been a matter of some debate over the years; however, a meta-analysis concluded that patient–therapist match does not affect treatment outcome (Cabral & Smith, 2011). Even so, many suggest that becoming comfortable discussing race and ethnicity with clients may promote better treatment outcome (Cardemil & Battle, 2003). Cardemil and Battle (2003) provided a roadmap for ways to discuss this topic with clients, which included suspending one's own preconceptions about race/ethnicity, recognizing individual differences, considering potential effects on the therapy, acknowledging the ways that power, privilege, and racism might affect therapist–client work, being willing to take risks with clients, and staying open to learning.

We echo a number of points raised by these authors and highlight that acknowledging important differences both in dialogues with the client and within clinical supervision are critical to treatment success. We also encourage clinicians to admit their lack of knowledge, experiences, and ability to understand what it is like to be in the shoes of a client whose race or ethnicity

16   *Mae Lynn Reyes-Rodríguez and Debra Franko*

differs from their own. As noted by Cardemil and Battle (2003), engaging in these conversations with clients, while potentially uncomfortable, provides rich opportunities to put issues on the table and is likely to be of great value in the therapeutic process. It is fine for the therapist to note the sensitivity of this discussion both in terms of his/her own discomfort and/or in the context of the current political climate, where race and ethnicity are particularly charged topics. Finally, therapists need to educate themselves as they prepare for and engage in the work with clients who look different from themselves. We provide suggestions in the next section.

There is a vast literature describing the cultural values, customs, and ethnic identities of the four main racial/ethnic groups in the United States (Lum, 1995; Vargas & Kemmelmeier, 2013) and this is likely much too large a body of work for a clinician to become familiar with while working in a busy practice. We suggest that the papers by Hansen, Pepitone-Arreola-Rockwell, and Greene (2000) and Andrés-Hyman, Ortiz, Añez, Paris, and Davidson (2006) provide a blueprint for this work. The first provides criteria and case examples related to multicultural competence (Hansen et al., 2000) and the second offers extremely detailed recommendations related to culture and clinical practice when working with Puerto Ricans and other Latina/os in the United States (Andrés-Hyman et al., 2006). Readers are encouraged to use these papers as excellent guideposts for working with culturally diverse groups. In addition, the work of Sue and Sue provides specific guidelines on treating patients from diverse cultural backgrounds and how to navigate through our own cultural assumptions, values, and biases in order to develop appropriate strategies to work with diverse populations (Sue & Sue, 2003).

There are several specific elements to be considered when working with individuals with eating disorders of varied racial and ethnic backgrounds. Please note that these are *general* areas to explore; the perspectives of an individual client may well vary from the overarching cultural mores. That said, the first area to learn about, both in the culture at-large and with the individual client during the treatment, is the values placed on eating-related issues (food, customs and rituals, preference for body size and type, and the importance of appearance) as well as values of the culture, the society, and the role of the family in that particular cultural group. Ethnic identity is another area that should be explored in the therapeutic setting (Rakhkovskaya & Warren, 2014; Rhea & Thatcher, 2013).

To provide a very specific example, the work of Reyes-Rodríguez and colleagues is illuminating (Bernal & Scharrón-del-Río, 2001; Reyes-Rodríguez et al., 2014). The integration of cultural values in the treatment of Latinos with eating disorders is essential (Kempa & Thomas, 2000). Particularly, the family dynamic around food and body image (Altabe & O' Gara, 2002; Reyes-Rodríguez et al., 2016; Shea et al., 2012) and the profound interdependence between parents and their offspring (La Roche, 2002), also known as *familismo*, are some of the traditional values that should be considered into treatment. In Latino culture, food is associated with cultural values such as *familismo*,

Cultural Adaptations of Evidence-Based Treatments 17

hospitality, and prosperity (Altabe & O' Gara, 2002; Shea et al., 2012), and provides a sense of identity and "belonging" (Cachelin, Gil-Rivas, & Vela, 2014). The centrality and emotional valence of food in Latino culture could pose a challenge to those who are struggling with eating disorders fostering family conflicts around eating behaviors (Cachelin, Shea, et al., 2014; Shea et al., 2012). Addressing those family conflicts around eating behaviors could help to reduce the tension during family meals. Providing psychoeducation to the family about how eating disorders change the dynamic around food has found to be helpful to decrease the tension and increasing the support from the family to the patient.

Other particular issue that has been found in the Latino population is food insecurity and it relation to eating disorder symptoms. In the work conducted by Reyes-Rodríguez et al. (2016), patients who experienced starvation during the border crossing also experienced emotional distress and loss of control over eating due to the uncertainty of when food would be available. Food insecurity is not only associated with the border crossing but also with socioeconomic status as minority, with less access to variety of foods due to cost or due to double working shifts making very difficult to follow the treatment recommendations of having a regular eating pattern. The contributing effect of food insecurity and eating disorders is a recent topic that has been explored and should be object of clinical attention, particularly when working with vulnerable populations (Becker, Middlemass, Taylor, Johnson, & Gomez, 2017; Becker et al., 2018; Lydecker & Grilo, 2019; West, Goldschmidt, Mason, & Neumark-Sztainer, 2019).

In the study by Reyes et al. (2005), six sessions were dedicated to working with family members of patients with BN. Although 95% of the patients were adults, in this study both primary and extended family members (e.g., grandmother, aunt, and boyfriends/partners) were closely involved with the patient. Content analysis revealed two key factors for treatment success: (1) family incorporation early in treatment was a necessary cultural adaptation to treatment for Latinos; and (2) successfully incorporating family members into treatment requires more than one session. This finding was confirmed more recently in a qualitative study where Latina patients and family discussed their experiences of having a family member involved in the treatment (Reyes-Rodríguez et al., 2019). For Latinos living in the United States, the role of family, migration, language, and specific cultural values (e.g., *familismo*, ethnic identity, dependence, and independence) differs depending on the length of time an individual has spent in the United States, as well as on the experience of migration and relationship to the dominant majority culture (Bernal & Reyes, 2008; Shea et al., 2012). A study conducted with 12 Mexican Americans with eating disorders found that the role of family, the meaning of food, cultural expectations, and acculturation differences were key elements that should be integrated in a culturally competent intervention (Shea et al., 2012). The experience of tensions and family conflicts due to eating problems is the result of different cultural beliefs, values, and acculturation levels that Latino families face in their transition to a new culture (Shea et al., 2012). The need for support from family members has been recognized an important factor for treatment outcome in Latinas with eating disorders (Cachelin, Shea, et al., 2014).

In addition to clinicians educating themselves toward a better understanding of cultural values, norms, and customs within a given racial or ethnic group, we describe later a number of systemic issues that may come into play in the therapy room that clinicians need to consider. When working with clients from diverse racial and ethnic backgrounds, a number of variables are relevant in the therapeutic context: language, access to services (both financially and logistically), immigration status and the extent to which fears related to this issue loom large, acculturation, discrimination, and racism. Obviously, any one of these issues can (and likely does) play a major role in an individual's life and potentially in the development and maintenance of an eating disorder or body image concerns. The key for the therapist is to be aware of the potential for these issues to be "in the room," and to be ready and open to discussing these topics in the therapeutic setting. For further information as related to eating disorders, see Assari (2018) and Cheng, Tran, Miyake, and Kim (2017).

Finally, we note several challenges as we work toward the goal of developing and implementing culturally sensitive treatments for eating disorders. (1) There are few studies on this topic to guide the work. (2) Most clinicians are not from minority backgrounds, and so they have not lived many of the issues that their diverse clientele will experience over the course of their lives. (3) Empirically supported treatments for eating disorders are actually quite few in number, and even those that are deemed successful (CBT or family-based treatment) are only helpful to a relatively small portion of patients over the long term. (4) Few patients receive empirically supported treatment (von Ranson, Wallace, & Stevenson, 2013). (5) Working with patients with eating disorders is difficult by virtue of the multifaceted and complex nature of the disorder itself; learning another's culture and incorporating culturally relevant interventions add nuanced elements to an already difficult enterprise. To expand, keeping in mind the cultural and systemic factors that might affect an individual, while at the same time working on the eating disorder, can be daunting for a clinician. Actively participating in supervision and being willing to discuss the difficulties are key to a successful outcome.

Other Cultural Factors: What Therapists Need to Know for Clinical Practice

Level of Acculturation and Acculturative Stress

Acculturation is a dynamic process of changes that every migrant faces when moving from his or her native country to contact with a new culture (Schwartz, Unger, Zamboanga, & Szapocznik, 2010). Acculturative stress is defined as the stress experienced by individuals during the cultural adaptation process (Berry, 2006). In the eating disorder field, acculturation and acculturative stress have been identified as potential moderators of the association between body dissatisfaction and eating disorder symptoms in the Latino population (Gordon, Castro, Sitnikov, & Holm-Denoma, 2010; Perez, Voelz, Pettit, & Joiner, 2002), and as risk factors for mood disturbance and anxiety (Revollo, Qureshi, Collazos, Valero, & Casas, 2011). Particularly, body dissatisfaction and acculturative stress appear to interact as cross-sectional predictors of bulimic behaviors (Perez et al., 2002). Assessing the level of acculturation of the patient would inform therapists about which approach or techniques should be integrated into treatment. A multi-dimensional integrative acculturation assessment includes language use and preference, ethnic identity and classification, cultural heritage and behaviors, and ethnic interaction. In order to determine with whom the acculturation assessment should be conducted, questions about race, ethnicity, and cultural background are recommended as part of the standard intake procedure with all patients. It is important to highlight that a patient could self-identify as White, but come from a different country (e.g., Poland) and struggle with acculturation and acculturative stress; therefore, we should not underestimate this process with patients who come to the United States from a different country, even when they are not members of a minority group. Exploring these dimensions prior to treatment is essential for a culturally sensitive approach. Patients with low levels of acculturation might require more assistance with the healthcare system due to both the language barrier and mistrust in the system (see case study by Reyes-Rodríguez et al., 2014). In contrast, when working with minors, differing levels of acculturation between minors and parents could increase stress and tension in relation to family dynamics. Mediating and addressing the conflicts in session by improving communication skills could increase the collaboration of patient and family in the treatment process. Special attention is needed when working with undocumented patients or parents. The fear of being deported could prevent patients and/or parents from following through on some of the recommendations. Having open communication and developing a trusting relationship with both patients and parents would be essential for a competent care and better treatment outcomes.

Use of Interpreters

Acknowledging that the population in the United States is becoming more diverse, the possibility of encountering clients/patients from a different ethnic/racial background has increased. As mentioned beforehand, although matching client/patient in relation to race/ethnicity does not affect treatment outcome, patient satisfaction is greater when treated by a provider with the same cultural and language background (Cabral & Smith, 2011). The first choice, if the resource is available, is to match the patient with a culturally sensitive therapist and with fluency in the patient's primary language. However, finding bilingual therapists who speak the variety of languages (i.e., Spanish, Chinese, Arabic,

20 Mae Lynn Reyes-Rodríguez and Debra Franko

Burmese, among others) that we can encounter in the United States is almost impossible. Physicians have reported over 20 languages in their practice (Karliner, Perez-Stable, & Gildengorin, 2004). The use of professional interpreters for health care has been associated with improved clinical care, communication, service utilization, and satisfaction (Karliner, Jacobs, Chen, & Mutha, 2007). However, for psychiatric care, the limited data to inform evidence-based guidelines for improving quality of care (Bauer & Alegria, 2010) and the complexity of conducting psychotherapy with interpreters (Kuay, Chopra, Kaplan, & Szwarc, 2015) raise multiple challenges. For example, the presence of a third party in session could affect the therapeutic alliance, treatment fidelity, and communication errors due to language nuances. In a specific example, Spanish language varies across Hispanic countries. Spanish from Spain differs from Spanish from Mexico, Central America, and Puerto Rico, so communication among Latinos/Hispanics from different countries of origin could increase errors and misunderstandings. Based on the first author's clinical experience (M.L.R.R.), sometimes professional interpreters add their own recommendations outside of the provider's office. This dynamic could add another layer of complexity for treatment compliance and therapeutic alliance, if the interpreter' suggestions are not in line with the provider's recommendations. The use of minors, such as siblings, for interpretation purposes is not recommended. Having a minor patient serving as an interpreter could diminish the authority role of parents, therefore affecting the hierarchy and power in the family dynamic. The use of a professional interpreter should be the option if no other resource is available (i.e., bilingual therapist, community clinic with culturally competent services for the target population).

Final Remarks

As documented in this chapter, culturally sensitive EBTs for eating disorders for diverse populations are scarce. The few culturally adapted EBT studies available in the literature have been conducted primarily with the Latino population and only one study has been published with African Americans. The small sample size of those studies brings into question the generalizability of those findings; therefore, larger clinical trials are essential. The lack of inclusion of diverse populations in eating disorders clinical trials contributes to the vacuum in the field. With the exception of some studies (Grilo, Milsom, Morgan, & White, 2012; Grilo & White, 2013), most of the clinical trials include the most acculturated minorities. Although the domain of English language is only one dimension of the acculturation process, certainly members of diverse populations with no language barrier have different access to services than those less acculturated. Approximately 46 million people in the United States do not speak English as their primary language, affecting their access to primary and preventive health care (Jacobs, Shepard, Suaya, & Stone, 2004). There is a call for researchers to include participants from diverse populations and with different levels of acculturation in clinical trials in order to have a better understanding of the generalizability of EBTs among diverse populations and the potential culturally sensitive modifications to enhance engagement, retention, and treatment outcomes. Case studies and case series documenting the use of EBTs with diverse populations could be the first steps toward understanding the feasibility and potential cultural adaptations that are needed. Although the existence of EBTs for binge-type eating disorders has been found to be feasible and adequate for Latinas, cultural adaptation seems to enhance retention, patient satisfaction, and family dynamic. Engagement and retention of Latino patients in mental health treatment are two of the main barriers for access to specialized treatment and therefore contribute to health disparities (Alegria et al., 2002). A comprehensive intervention approach for Latinas in the United States is proposed in Figure 1.2. Assessing and addressing the interconnection between family, culture (patient's own cultural values and dominant culture, acculturation,

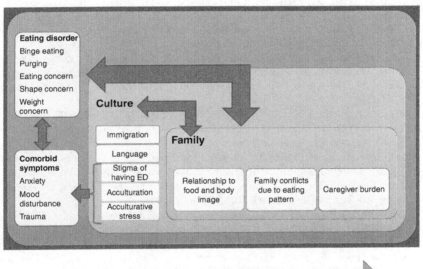

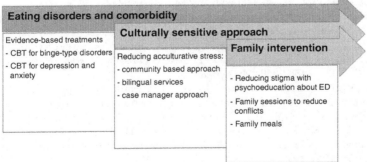

Figure 1.2 Comprehensive Intervention Approach for Latinas in the United States.

22　*Mae Lynn Reyes-Rodríguez and Debra Franko*

acculturative stress), and eating disorder symptoms are fundamental in a culturally sensitive approach. For patients from other racial and ethnic backgrounds, it would be essential to assess how family and cultural values interconnect with eating disorder symptoms in order to be sensitive and modify the EBT to the patient's own cultural reality.

References

Alarcon, R. D., Becker, A. E., Lewis-Fernandez, R., Like, R. C., Desai, P., Foulks, E., Gonzales, J., Hansen, H., Kopelowicz, A., Lu, F. G., Oquendo, M. A., & Primm, A. (2009). Issues for DSM-V: The role of culture in psychiatric diagnosis. *The Journal of Nervous and Mental Disease, 197*(8), 559–660. doi:10.1097/NMD.0b013e3181b0cbff.

Alegria, M., Canino, G., Rios, R., Vera, M., Calderon, J., Rusch, D., & Ortega, A. N. (2002). Inequalities in use of specialty mental health services among Latinos, African Americans, and non Latino whites. *Psychiatric Services, 53*(12), 1547–1555. doi:10.1176/appi.ps.53.12.1547.

Alegria, M., Cao, Z., McGuire, T. G., Ojeda, V. D., Sribney, B., Woo, M., & Takeuchi, D. (2006). Health insurance coverage for vulnerable populations: Contrasting Asian Americans and Latinos in the United States. *Inquiry, 43*(3), 231–254. doi:10.5034/inquiryjrnl_43.3.231.

Alegria, M., Chatterji, P., Wells, K., Cao, Z., Chen, C. N., Takeuchi, D., & Meng, X. L. (2008). Disparity in depression treatment among racial and ethnic minority populations in the United States. *Psychiatric Services, 59*(11), 1264–1272. doi:10.1176/ps.2008. 59.11.1264.

Altabe M., & O' Gara, K. (2002). Hispanic body images. In T. Cash & T. Pruzinsky (Eds.), *Body image: A handbook of theory, research, and clinical practice* (pp. 251–477). New York, NY: The Guilford Press.

Andrés-Hyman, R. C., Ortiz, J., Añez, L. M., Paris, M., & Davidson, L. (2006). Culture and clinical practice: Recommendations for working with Puerto Ricans and other Latinas(os) in the United States. *Professional Psychology: Research and Practice, 37*(6), 694–701. doi.org/10.1037/0735-7028.37.6.694.

Assari, S. (2018). Perceived discrimination and binge eating disorder; Gender difference in African Americans. *Journal of Clinical Medicine, 7*(5), 89. doi:10.3390/jcm7050089.

American Psychological Association. (2003). Guidelines on multicultural education, training, research, practice and organizational change for psychologists. *American Psychologist, 58*(5), 377–402. doi:doi.org/10.1037/000-066X.58.5.377.

American Psychological Association. (2017). *Ethical principles of psychologists and code of conduct.* Washington, DC.

Barrera, M. Jr., & González Castro, F. (2006). A heuristic framework for the cultural adaptation of interventions. *Clinical Psychology—Science and Practice, 13*(4), 311–316. doi:10.1111/j.1468-2850.2006.00043.x.

Bauer, A. M., & Alegria, M. (2010). Impact of patient language proficiency and interpreter service use on the quality of psychiatric care: A systematic review. *Psychiatric Services, 61*(8), 765–773. doi:10.1176/ps.2010.61.8.765.

Becker, A. E., Franko, D. L., Speck, A., & Herzog, D. B. (2003). Ethnicity and differential access to care for eating disorder symptoms. *International Journal of Eating Disorders, 33*(2), 205–212. doi:10.1002/eat.10129.

Cultural Adaptations of Evidence-Based Treatments 23

Becker, C. B., Middlemass, K., Johnson, C., Taylor, B., Gomez, F., & Sutherland, A. (2018). Traumatic event exposure associated with increased food insecurity and eating disorder pathology. *Public Health Nutrition, 21*(16), 3058–3066. doi:10.1017/S1368980018001738.

Becker, C. B., Middlemass, K., Taylor, B., Johnson, C., & Gomez, F. (2017). Food insecurity and eating disorder pathology. *International Journal of Eating Disorders, 50*(9), 1031–1040. doi:10.1002/eat.22735.

Bernal, G., Bonilla, J., & Bellido, C. (1995). Ecological validity and cultural sensitivity for outcome research: Issues for the cultural adaptation and development of psychosocial treatments with Hispanics. *Journal of Abnormal Child Psychology, 23*(1), 67–82. doi:10.1007/BF01447045.

Bernal, G., & Domenech Rodríguez, M. M. (2009). Advances in Latino family research: Cultural adaptations of evidence-based interventions. *Family Process, 48*(2), 169–178. doi:10.1111/j.1545-5300.2009.01275.x.

Bernal, G., Jiménez-Chafey, M. I., & Domenech-Rodríguez, M. M. (2009). Cultural adaptation of treatments: A resource for considering culture in evidence-based practice. *Professional Psychology: Research and Practice, 40*(4), 361–8. doi:10.1037/a0016401.

Bernal, G., & Reyes, M. L. (2008). Psychosocial treatments for depression with adult Latinos. In S. A. Aguilar-Guaxiola & T. P. Gullotta (Eds.), *Depression in Latinos: Assessment, treatment and prevention* (pp. 189–204). New York: Springer-Verlag.

Bernal, G., & Scharrón-del-Río, M. R. (2001). Are empirically supported treatments valid for ethnic minorities? Toward an alternative approach for treatment research? *Cultural Diversity & Ethnic Minority Psychology, 7*(4), 328–342. doi:10.1037/1099-9809.7.4.328.

Berry, J. W. (2006). Acculturative stress. In P. T. P. Wong, & L. C. J. Wong (Eds.), *Handbook of multicultural perspectives on stress and coping* (pp. 287–298). New York, NY: Springer.

Binkley, J., & Koslofsky, S. (2016). Una familia unida: Cultural adaptation of family-based therapy for bulimia with a depressed Latina adolescent. *Clinical Case Studies, 16*(1), 25–41. doi:10.1177/1534650116668268.

Blostein, F., Assari, S., & Caldwell, C. H. (2017). Gender and ethnic differences in the association between body image dissatisfaction and binge eating disorder among Blacks. *Journal of Racial and Ethnic Health Disparities, 4*(4), 529–538. doi:10.1007/s40615-016-0255-7.

Blumenthal, J. A., Babyak, M. A., Hinderliter, A., Watkins, L. L., Craighead, L., Lin, P. H., & Sherwood, A. (2010). Effects of the DASH diet alone and in combination with exercise and weight loss on blood pressure and cardiovascular biomarkers in men and women with high blood pressure: The ENCORE study. *Archives of Internal Medicine, 170*(2), 126–135. doi:10.1001/archinternmed.2009.470.

Cabral, R. R., & Smith, T. B. (2011). Racial/ethnic matching of clients and therapists in mental health services: A meta-analytic review of preferences, perceptions, and outcomes. *Journal of Counseling Psychology, 58*(4), 537–554. doi:10.1037/a0025266.

Cachelin, F. M., Gil-Rivas, V., Palmer, B., Vela, A., Phimphasone, P., de Hernandez, B. U., & Tapp, H. (2018). Randomized controlled trial of a culturally-adapted program for Latinas with binge eating. *Psychological Services, 16*, 504–512. Advance online publication. doi:10.1037/ser0000182.

24 Mae Lynn Reyes-Rodríguez and Debra Franko

Cachelin, F. M., Gil-Rivas, V., & Vela, A. (2014). Understanding eating disorders among Latinas. *Advances in Eating Disorders*, *2*(2), 204–208. doi:10.1080/21662630.2013.869391.

Cachelin, F. M., Shea, M., Phimphasone, P., Wilson, G. T., Thompson, D. R., & Striegel, R. H. (2014). Culturally adapted cognitive behavioral guided self-help for binge eating: A feasibility study with Mexican Americans. *Cultural Diversity and Ethnic Minority Psychology*, *20*(3), 449–457. doi:10.1037/a00353452014-29268-013 [pii].

Cachelin, F. M., & Striegel-Moore, R. H. (2006). Help seeking and barriers to treatment in a community sample of Mexican American and European American women with eating disorders. *International Journal of Eating Disorders*, *39*(2), 154–161. doi:10.1002/eat.20213.

Cardemil, E. V., & Battle, C. L. (2003). Guess who's coming to therapy? Getting comfortable with conversations about race and ethnicity in psychotherapy. *Professional Psychology: Research and Practice*, *34*(3), 278–286. doi:10.1037/0735-7028.34.3.278.

Cheng, H. L., Tran, A., Miyake, E. R., & Kim, H. Y. (2017). Disordered eating among Asian American college women: A racially expanded model of objectification theory. *Journal of Counseling Psychology*, *64*(2), 179–191. doi:10.1037/cou0000195.

Cheng, P., & Merrick E. (2016). Cultural adaptation of dialectical behavior therapy for a Chinese international student with eating disorder and depression. *Clinical Case Studies*, *16*(1), 42–57. doi:10.1177/1534650116668269.

Colby, S. L., & Ortman, J. M. (2014). *Projections of the size and composition of the U.S. population: 2014 to 2060, current population reports, P25-1143*. Washington, DC: U.S. Census Bureau.

Domenech Rodríguez, M. M., Baumann, A. A., & Schwartz, A. L. (2011). Cultural adaptation of an evidence based intervention: From theory to practice in a Latino/a community context. *American Journal of Community Psychology*, *47*(1–2), 170–186. doi:10.1007/s10464-010-9371-4.

Domenech Rodríguez, M. M. & Bernal, G. (2012). Frameworks, models, and guidelines for cultural adaptation. In G. Bernal & M. M. Domenech Rodríguez (Eds.), *Cultural adaptations: Tools for evidence based practice with diverse populations* (pp. 23–44). Washington, DC: American Psychologist Association. doi:10.1037/13752-000.

Domenech-Rodríguez, M., & Wieling, E. (2004). Developing culturally appropriate, evidence-based treatments for interventions with ethnic minority populations. In M. Rastogi & E. Wieling (Eds.), *Voices of color: First-person accounts of ethnic minority therapists* (pp. 313–333). Thousand Oaks, CA: Sage.

Falicov, C. J. (2009). Commentary: On the wisdom and challenges of culturally attuned treatments for Latinos. *Family Process*, *48*(2), 292–309. doi.org/10.1111/j.1545-5300.2009.01282.x.

Fernandez-Aranda, F., Alvarez-Moya, E. M., Martinez-Viana, C., Sanchez, I., Granero, R., Penelo, E., & Penas-Lledo, E. (2009). Predictors of early change in bulimia nervosa after a brief psychoeducational therapy. *Appetite*, *52*(3), 805–808. doi:10.1016/j.appet.2009.03.013.

Franko, D. L., Becker, A. E., Thomas, J. J., & Herzog, D. B. (2007). Cross-ethnic differences in eating disorder symptoms and related distress. *International Journal of Eating Disorders*, *40*(2), 156–164. doi:10.1002/eat.20341.

Franko, D. L., Jenkins, A., & Rodgers, R. F. (2012). Toward reducing risk for eating disorders and obesity in Latina college women. *Journal of Counseling and Developmental*, *90*(3), 298–307. doi:10.1002/j.1556-6676.2012.00038.x.

Gonzalez Castro, F., Barrera, M. J., & Holleran-Steiker, L. K. (2010). Issues and challenges in the design of culturally adapted evidence-based interventions. *Annual Review of Clinical Psychology, 6*, 213–239. doi:10.1146/annurev-clinpsy-033109-132032.

Gonzalez Castro, F., Barrera, M. Jr., & Martinez, C. R., Jr. (2004). The cultural adaptation of prevention interventions: Resolving tensions between fidelity and fit. *Prevention Science, 5*(1), 41–45. doi.org/10.1023/B:PREV.0000013980.12412.cd.

Goode, R. W., Kalarchian, M. A., Craighead, L., Conroy, M. B., Wallace, J., Jr., Eack, S. M., & Burke, L. E. (2018). The feasibility of a binge eating intervention in Black women with obesity. *Eating Behaviors, 29*, 83–90. doi:10.1016/j.eatbeh.2018.03.005.

Gordon, K. H., Castro, Y., Sitnikov, L., & Holm-Denoma, J. M. (2010). Cultural body shape ideals and eating disorder symptoms among White, Latina, and Black college women. *Cultural Diversity and Ethnic Minority Psychology, 16*(2), 135–143. doi:10.1037/a0018671.

Grilo, C. M., Masheb, R. M., White, M. A., Gueorguieva, R., Barnes, R. D., Walsh, B. T., & Garcia, R. (2014). Treatment of binge eating disorder in racially and ethnically diverse obese patients in primary care: Randomized placebo-controlled clinical trial of self-help and medication. *Behaviour Research and Therapy, 58*, 1–9. doi:10.1016/j.brat.2014.04.002S0005-7967(14)00056-4 [pii].

Grilo, C. M., Milsom, V. A., Morgan, P. T., & White, M. A. (2012). Night eating in obese treatment-seeking Hispanic patients with and without binge eating disorder. *International Journal of Eating Disorders, 45*(6), 787–791. doi:10.1002/eat.22011.

Grilo, C. M., & White, M. A. (2013). Orlistat with behavioral weight loss for obesity with versus without binge eating disorder: Randomized placebo-controlled trial at a community mental health center serving educationally and economically disadvantaged Latino/as. *Behaviour Research and Therapy, 51*(3), 167–175. doi:10.1016/j.brat.2013.01.002S0005-7967(13)00013-2.

Griner, D., & Smith, T. B. (2006). Culturally adapted mental health interventions: A meta-analytic review. *Psychotherapy: Theory, Research, Practice, Training, 43*(4), 531–548. doi:10.1037/0033-3204.43.4.531.

Hansen, N. D., Pepitone-Arreola-Rockwell, F., & Greene, A. F. (2000). Multicultural competence: Criteria and case examples. *Professional Psychology: Research and Practice, 31*(6), 652–660. doi:10.1037/0735-7028.31.6.652.

Hill, D. M., Craighead, L. W., & Safer, D. L. (2011). Appetite-focused dialectical behavior therapy for the treatment of binge eating with purging: A preliminary trial. *International Journal of Eating Disorders, 44*(3), 249–261. doi:10.1002/eat.20812.

Hwang, W. (2006). The psychotherapy adaptation and modification framework: Application to Asian Americans. *American Psychologist, 61*(7), 702–715. doi:10.1037/0003-066X.61.7.702.

Hwang, W. (2009). The Formative Methods for Adapting Psychotherapy (FMAP): A community-based developmental approach to culturally adapting therapy. *Professional Psychology: Research and Practice, 40*, 369–377. doi:10.1037/a0016240.

Jacobs, E. A., Shepard, D. S., Suaya, J. A., & Stone, E. L. (2004). Overcoming language barriers in health care: Costs and benefits of interpreter services. *American Journal of Public Health, 94*(5), 866–869. doi:10.2105/ajph.94.5.866.

Karliner, L. S., Jacobs, E. A., Chen, A. H., & Mutha, S. (2007). Do professional interpreters improve clinical care for patients with limited English proficiency? A systematic review of the literature. *Health Services Research, 42*(2), 727–754. doi:10.1111/j.1475-6773.2006.00629.x.

Karliner, L. S., Perez-Stable, E. J., & Gildengorin, G. (2004). The language divide. The importance of training in the use of interpreters for outpatient practice. *Journal of General Internal Medicine, 19*(2), 175–183. doi:10.1111/j.1525-1497.2004.30268.x.

Kempa, M. L., & Thomas, A. J. (2000). Culturally sensitive assessment and treatment of eating disorders. *Eating Disorders, 8*(17–30). doi:10.1080/10640260008251209.

Koss-Chioino, J. D., & Vargas, L. A. (1992). Through the cultural looking glass: A model for understanding culturally responsive psychotherapies. In L. A. Vargas & J. D. Koss-Chioino (Eds.), *Working with culture: Psychotherapeutic interventions with ethnic minority children and adolescents* (pp. 1–22). San Francisco, CA: Jossey-Bass.

Kuay, J., Chopra, P., Kaplan, I., & Szwarc, J. (2015). Conducting psychotherapy with an interpreter. *Australasian Psychiatry: Bulletin of Royal Australian and New Zealand College of Psychiatrists, 23*(3), 282–286. doi:10.1177/1039856215581294.

Kumpfer, K. L., Pinyuchon, M., Teixeira de Melo, A., & Whiteside, H. O. (2008). Cultural adaptation process for international dissemination of the Strengthening Families Program. *Evaluation & The Health Professions, 31*(2), 226–239. doi:10.1177/0163278708315926.

La Roche, M. J. (2002). Psychotherapeutic considerations in treating Latinos. *Harvard Review of Psychiatry, 10*(2), 115–122. doi:10.1093/hrp/10.2.115.

Lau, A. S. (2006). Making the case for selective and directed cultural adaptations of evidence-based treatments: Examples from parenting training. *Clinical Psychology: Science and Practice, 13*(4), 295–310. doi:10.1111/j.1468-2850.2006.00042.x.

Le Grange, D., Peter, D., Ross, D. C., & Eunice, C. (2008). Early response to treatment in adolescent bulimia nervosa. *International Journal of Eating Disorders, 41*(8), 755–757. doi:10.1002/eat.20566.

Leong, F. T. L. (1996). Toward an integrative model for cross-cultural counseling and psychotherapy. *Applied and Preventive Psychology, 5*(4), 189–209. doi:10.1016/S0962-1849(96)80012-6.

Lum, D. (1995). Cultural values and minority people of color. *Journal of Sociology and Social Welfare, 22*(1), 59–74.

Lydecker, J. A., & Grilo, C. M. (2019). Food insecurity and bulimia nervosa in the United States. *International Journal of Eating Disorders, 52*(6), 735–739. doi:10.1002/eat.23074.

Lydecker, J. A., Gueorguieva, R., Masheb, R., White, M. A., & Grilo, C. M. (2019). Examining race as a predictor and moderator of treatment outcomes for binge-eating disorder: Analysis of aggregated randomized controlled trials. *Journal of Consulting and Clinical Psychology, 87*(6), 530–540. doi:10.1037/ccp0000404.

Mama, S. K., Schembre, S. M., O'Connor, D. P., Kaplan, C. D., Bode, S., & Lee, R. E. (2015). Effectiveness of lifestyle interventions to reduce binge eating symptoms in African American and Hispanic women. *Appetite, 95*, 269–274. doi:10.1016/j.appet.2015.07.015.

Marques, L., Alegria, M., Becker, A. E., Chen, C. N., Fang, A., Chosak, A., & Diniz, J. B. (2011). Comparative prevalence, correlates of impairment, and service utilization for eating disorders across US ethnic groups: Implications for reducing ethnic disparities in health care access for eating disorders. *International Journal of Eating Disorders, 44*(5), 412–420. doi:10.1002/eat.20787.

Mazzeo, S. E., Lydecker, J., Harney, M., Palmberg, A. A., Kelly, N. R., Gow, R. W., & Stern, M. (2016). Development and preliminary effectiveness of an innovative treatment for binge eating in racially diverse adolescent girls. *Eating Behaviors, 22*, 199–205. doi:10.1016/j.eatbeh.2016.06.014.

Miranda, J., Bernal, G., Lau, A., Kohn, L., Hwang, W. C., & La Framboise, T. (2005). State of the science on psychosocial interventions for ethnic minorities. *Annual Review of Clinical Psychology, 1,* 113–142. doi:10.1146/annurev.clinpsy.1. 102803.143822.

Neumark-Sztainer, D., Croll, J., Story, M., Hannan, P. J., French, S. A., & Perry, C. (2002). Ethnic/racial differences in weight-related concerns and behaviors among adolescent girls and boys: Findings from Project EAT. *Journal of Psychosomatic Research, 53*(5), 963–974. doi:10.1016/S0022-3999(02)00486-5.

Nicdao, E. G., Hong, S., & Takeuchi, D. T. (2007). Prevalence and correlates of eating disorders among Asian Americans: Results from the National Latino and Asian American Study. *International Journal of Eating Disorders, 40* Suppl, S22–S26. doi:10.1002/eat.20450.

Perez, M., Ohrt, T. K., & Hoek, H. W. (2016). Prevalence and treatment of eating disorders among Hispanics/Latino Americans in the United States. *Current Opinion in Psychiatry, 29*(6), 378–382. doi:10.1097/YCO.0000000000000277.

Perez, M., Voelz, Z. R., Pettit, J. W., & Joiner, T. E., Jr. (2002). The role of acculturative stress and body dissatisfaction in predicting bulimic symptomatology across ethnic groups. *International Journal of Eating Disorders, 31*(4), 442–454. doi:10. 1002/eat.10006.

Rakhkovskaya, L. M., & Warren, C. S. (2014). Ethnic identity, thin-ideal internalization, and eating pathology in ethnically diverse college women. *Body Image, 11*(4), 438–445. doi:10.1016/j.bodyim.2014.07.003.

Resnicow, K., Soler, R., Braithwaite, R. L., Ahluwalia, J. S., & Butler, J. (2002). Cultural sensitivity in substance use prevention: Bridging the gap between research and practice in community-based substance abuse prevention. *Journal of Community Psychology, 28*(3), 271–290. doi.org/10.1002/(SICI)1520-6629(200005) 28:3<271::AID-JCOP4>3.0.CO;2-I.

Revollo, H. W., Qureshi, A., Collazos, F., Valero, S., & Casas, M. (2011). Acculturative stress as a risk factor of depression and anxiety in the Latin American immigrant population. *International Review of Psychiatry, 23*(1), 84–92. doi:10.3109/ 09540261.2010.545988.

Reyes, M. L., Rosselló, J., & Calaf, M. (2005). Cognitive Behavioral Therapy for Bulimia Nervosa in Latinos: Preliminary findings of case studies. Poster presented at the Eating Disorders Research Society, Annual Meeting, Toronto, Ontario, Canada, September 2005.

Reyes-Rodríguez, M. L., Ramírez, J., Davis, K., Patrice, K., & Bulik, C. M. (2013). Exploring barriers and facilitators in the eating disorders treatment in Latinas in the United States. *Journal of Latina/o Psychology, 1*(2), 112–131. doi:10.1037/a0032318.

Reyes-Rodríguez, M. L., Baucom, D. H., & Bulik, C. M. (2014). Culturally sensitive intervention for Latina women with eating disorders: A case report. *Revista Mexicana de Trastornos Alimentarios, 5*(2), 135–146. doi.org/10.1016/S2007-1523(14) 72009-9.

Reyes-Rodríguez, M. L., Franko, D. L., Matos-Lamourt, A., Bulik, C. M., Von Holle, A., Camara-Fuentes, L. R., & Suarez-Torres, A. (2010). Eating disorder symptomatology: Prevalence among Latino college freshmen students. *Journal of Clinical Psychology, 66*(6), 666–679. doi:10.1002/jclp.20684.

Reyes-Rodríguez, M. L., Gulisano, M., Silva, Y., Pivarunas, B., Luna-Reyes, K. L., & Bulik, C. M. (2016). "Las penas con pan duelen menos": The role of food and

28 *Mae Lynn Reyes-Rodríguez and Debra Franko*

culture in Latinas with disordered eating behaviors. *Appetite, 100*, 102–109. doi:10. 1016/j.appet.2016.02.029S0195-6663(16)30064-2 [pii].

Reyes-Rodríguez, M. L., Watson, H. J., Barrio, C., Baucom, D. H., Silva, Y., Luna-Reyes, K. L., & Bulik, C. M. (2019). Family involvement in eating disorder treatment among Latinas. *Eating Disorders: The Journal of Treatment & Prevention, 27*(2), 205–229. doi:10.1080/10640266.2019.1586219.

Reyes-Rodríguez, M. L., Watson, H., Woods Smith T., Baucom, D. H., & Bulik, C. M. Promoviendo una Alimentación Saludable (PAS) results: Engaging Latino families in eating disorder treatment (submitted).

Rhea, D. J., & Thatcher, W. G. (2013). Ethnicity, ethnic identity, self-esteem, and at-risk eating disordered behavior differences of urban adolescent females. *Eating Disorders, 21*(3), 223–237. doi:10.1080/10640266.2013.779177.

Rodgers, R. F., Berry, R., & Franko, D. L. (2018). Eating disorders in ethnic minorities: An update. *Current Psychiatry Reports, 20*(10), 90. doi:10.1007/s11920-018-0938-3.

Rodríguez, R., Marchand, E., Ng, J., & Stice, E. (2008). Effects of a cognitive dissonance-based eating disorder prevention program are similar for Asian American, Hispanic, and White participants. *International Journal of Eating Disorders, 41*(7), 618–625. doi:10.1002/eat.20532.

Schnicker, K., Hiller, W., & Legenbauer, T. (2013). Drop-out and treatment outcome of outpatient cognitive-behavioral therapy for anorexia nervosa and bulimia nervosa. *Comprehensive Psychiatry, 54*(7), 812–823. doi:10.1016/j.comppsych.2013.02.007.

Schwartz, S. J., Unger, J. B., Zamboanga, B. L., & Szapocznik, J. (2010). Rethinking the concept of acculturation: Implications for theory and research. *American Psychologist, 65*(4), 237–251. doi:10.1037/a0019330.

Scott, T. N., Gil-Rivas, V., & Cachelin, F. M. (2018). The need for cultural adaptations to health interventions for African American women: A qualitative analysis. *Cultural Diversity and Ethnic Minority Psychology, 25*, 335–341. doi:10.1037/cdp0000228.

Shea, M., Cachelin, F., Uribe, L., Striegel, R. H., Thompson, D., & Wilson, G. T. (2012). Cultural adaptation of a cognitive behavior therapy guided self-help program for Mexican American women with binge eating disorders. *Journal of Counseling Development, 90*(3), 308–318. doi:10.1002/j.1556-6676.2012.00039.x.

Shea, M., Cachelin, F. M., Gutierrez, G., Wang, S., & Phimphasone, P. (2016). Mexican American women's perspectives on a culturally adapted cognitive-behavioral therapy guided self-help program for binge eating. *Psychological Services, 13*(1), 31–41. doi:10.1037/ser0000055.

Sinha, S., & Warfa, N. (2013). Treatment of eating disorders among ethnic minorities in western settings: A systematic review. *Psychiatria Danubina, 25* (Suppl 2), S295–S299.

Smart, R. (2010). Treating Asian American women with eating disorders: Multicultural competency and empirically supported treatment. *Eating Disorders, 18*(1), 58–73. doi:10.1080/10640260903439540.

Smith, J. M., Smith, J. E., McLaughlin, E. A., Belon, K. E., Serier, K. N., Simmons, J. D., & Delaney, H. D. (2018). Body dissatisfaction and disordered eating in Native American, Hispanic, and White college women. *Eating and Weight Disorders, 25*, 347–355. doi:10.1007/s40519-018-0597-8.

Smith, T. B., Domenech Rodríguez, M., & Bernal, G. (2011). Culture. *Journal of Clinical Psychology, 67*(2), 166–175. doi.org/10.1002/jclp.20757.

Cultural Adaptations of Evidence-Based Treatments 29

Smolak, L., & Striegel-Moore, R. H. (2001). Challenging the myth of the golden girl. In Striegel-Moore, R. H. & Smolak, L. (Eds.), *Eating disorders: Innovative directions in research and practice* (pp. 111–132). Washington, DC: American Psychological Association.

Sonneville, K. R., & Lipson, S. K. (2018). Disparities in eating disorder diagnosis and treatment according to weight status, race/ethnicity, socioeconomic background, and sex among college students. *International Journal of Eating Disorders, 51*(6), 518–526. doi:10.1002/eat.22846.

Stice, E., Marti, C. N., & Cheng, Z. H. (2014). Effectiveness of a dissonance-based eating disorder prevention program for ethnic groups in two randomized controlled trials. *Behaviour Research and Therapy, 55,* 54–64. doi:10.1016/j.brat.2014.02.002.

Striegel-Moore, R. H., Rosselli, F., Holtzman, N., Dierker, L., Becker, A. E., & Swaney, G. (2011). Behavioral symptoms of eating disorders in Native Americans: Results from the ADD Health Survey Wave III. *International Journal of Eating Disorders, 44*(6), 561–566. doi:10.1002/eat.20894.

Sue, D. W., & Sue, D. (2003). *Counseling the culturally diverse: Theory and practice.* Hoboken, NJ: John Wiley & Sons, Inc.

Swanson, S. A., Crow, S. J., Le Grange, D., Swendsen, J., & Merikangas, K. R. (2011). Prevalence and correlates of eating disorders in adolescents. Results from the national comorbidity survey replication adolescent supplement. *Archives of General Psychiatry, 68*(7), 714–723. doi:10.1001/archgenpsychiatry.2011.22archgenpsychiatry.2011.22 [pii].

Taylor, J. Y., Caldwell, C. H., Baser, R. E., Matusko, N., Faison, N., & Jackson, J. S. (2013). Classification and correlates of eating disorders among Blacks: Findings from the National Survey of American Life. *Journal of Health Care for the Poor and Underserved, 24*(1), 289–310. doi:10.1353/hpu.2013.0027.

Thompson-Brenner, H., Franko, D. L., Thompson, D. R., Grilo, C. M., Boisseau, C. L., Roehrig, J. P., & Wilson, G. T. (2013). Race/ethnicity, education and treatment parameters as moderators and predictors of outcome in binge eating disorder. *Journal of Consulting and Clinical Psychology, 81*(4), 710–721. doi:10.1037/a0032946.

Udo, T., & Grilo, C. M. (2018). Prevalence and correlates of DSM-5-defined eating disorders in a nationally representative sample of U.S. adults. *Biological Psychiatry, 84*(5), 345–354. doi:10.1016/j.biopsych.2018.03.014.

Vargas, J. H., & Kemmelmeier, M. (2013). Ethnicity and contemporary American culture: A meta-analytic investigation of horizontal-vertical individualism-collectivism. *Journal of Cross-Cultural Psychology, 44*(2), 195–222. http://dx.doi.org/10.1177/0022022112443733.

von Ranson, K. M., Wallace, L. M., & Stevenson, A. (2013). Psychotherapies provided for eating disorders by community clinicians: Infrequent use of evidence-based treatment. *Psychotherapy Research, 23*(3), 333–343. doi:10.1080/10503307.2012.735377.

West, C. E., Goldschmidt, A. B., Mason, S. M., & Neumark-Sztainer, D. (2019). Differences in risk factors for binge eating by socioeconomic status in a community-based sample of adolescents: Findings from Project EAT. *International Journal of Eating Disorders, 52*(6), 659–668. doi:10.1002/eat.23079.

Whaley, A. L., & Davis, K. E. (2007). Cultural competence and evidence-based practice in mental health services: A complementary perspective. *American Psychologist, 62*(6), 563–574. doi:10.1037/0003-066X.62.6.563.

Whitbeck, L. B. (2006). Some guiding assumptions and a theoretical model for developing culturally specific preventions with Native American people. *Journal of Community Psychology, 34*(2), 183–192. doi:10.1002/jcop.20094.

2 Modifying Treatments to Recognize the Pursuit of Muscularity, and Related Eating Psychopathology, Among Men

Mitchell L. Cunningham, Jason M. Nagata, and Stuart B. Murray

Introduction

Historically, eating disorders (EDs) are considered some of the most pernicious and gendered psychiatric conditions. However, there is a need to address the pervasive misconception that EDs are sparse across male populations. In fact, men have been estimated to represent up to 25% of ED diagnoses, yet regrettably have only been the focus of less than 1% of published empirical research related to EDs (namely, anorexia nervosa) (Murray, Griffiths, & Mond, 2016a; Murray et al., 2017a). This underrepresentation has meant that the conceptualization of EDs and their presentations among men have been largely extrapolated from findings using female samples (Lavender, Brown, & Murray, 2017). The inference one could draw from this is that ED-related cognitions and behaviors, as well as influencing factors, manifest similarly across the sexes, despite growing evidence of noteworthy differences, particularly around the pursuit of the muscular appearance ideal (Pope, Phillips, & Olivardia, 2000) and associated eating pathology, both of which are more common among men than women. These sex differences are likely to have important implications for cognitive-behavioral models underpinning ED symptomatology, and in turn, the prevention and treatment efforts based on such models.

This chapter describes how treatment approaches may need to be modified to better address ED experiences specifically among men. First, to provide the reader with an appreciation of the specific challenges facing males with EDs, we highlight medical complications and presentations of EDs as they pertain to males specifically. Second, this chapter will illustrate the importance of the unique muscular body ideal commonly pursued by males, the muscular-oriented eating pathology that is likely to accompany this pursuit, and the possibility that established psychological treatment protocols (namely cognitive behavioral therapy [CBT]) may need to be tailored to better address these issues. Third, we underscore the need for ED treatment protocols to screen for and potentially address muscle dysmorphia (MD), a psychiatric condition marked by an extreme preoccupation with muscularity, and for which men

32 Cunningham, Nagata, and Murray

may be particularly vulnerable. Lastly, we discuss the directions for future research that will be critical in helping conceptualize, better understand, and treat muscularity-oriented concerns and related eating pathology among men.

Medical Complications of EDs in Males

Before highlighting male-specific prevalence rates and presentations of EDs, it is important to acknowledge the growing literature on the medical consequences of EDs in males (Nagata & Golden, 2018). Current evidence in males has demonstrated that EDs can affect the cardiovascular, hematological, gastrointestinal, liver, endocrine, skeletal, and neurological systems as well as electrolyte balance (Nagata & Golden, 2018). Over *half* of adolescent boys, upon first presentation to ED specialty services, urgently required hospitalization due to physiological instability (Vo, Lau, & Rubinstein, 2016).

The most common cardiovascular complications of EDs in males include sinus bradycardia and orthostatic hypotension. One study of adolescent boys with ED found that bradycardia was present in 39.4%, with a mean heart rate of 58.7 beats per minute (Vo et al., 2016). The average orthostatic heart rate change was 22.0 beats per minute when changing from the lying to standing position. Other cardiovascular complications reported in anorexia nervosa (AN) include poor myocardial contractility, mitral valve prolapse, and reduced thickness and mass of the left ventricular wall (Sachs, Harnke, Mehler, & Krantz, 2016).

Hematological complications in all blood cell lines have been documented in males with EDs; one study found abnormalities in hematocrit (33%), platelets (19%), white blood cells (24%), and absolute neutrophil counts (10%) (Vo et al., 2016). Male sex is associated with higher risk for having elevated liver enzymes (alanine aminotransferase [ALT] $\geq$ 40) in AN (Nagata, Park, Colditz, & Golden, 2015). Approximately 40% of men with an ED diagnosis report previously having a body mass index in the overweight or obese range (Vo et al., 2016) and may have greater ultimate nutritional needs during nutritional rehabilitation (Silber et al., 2004). Other gastrointestinal complications of EDs can include constipation, pancreatitis, and delayed gastric motility (Norris et al., 2016).

In terms of endocrine complications in males, malnutrition suppresses the hypothalamic-pituitary-gonadal axis, which in males may lead to low testosterone and decreased libido (Misra et al., 2008). Of note, amenorrhea was previously a criterion for the diagnosis of AN in the Diagnostic and Statistical Manual of Mental Disorders, Fourth Edition (DSM-IV), which precluded males from receiving this diagnosis; however, this is no longer a diagnostic criteria for the DSM-5 (American Psychiatric Association, 2013). Skeletal complications of AN in males include low bone mineral density (Misra et al., 2008; Nagata, Golden, Peebles, Long, Leonard, et al., 2017) and a greater risk for fractures (Nagata, Golden, Leonard, Copelovitch, & Denburg, 2017). Males with AN have also been shown to have significant deficits in fat mass and lean body mass (Nagata, Golden, Peebles, Long, Murray, et al., 2017), as well as having a linear growth interruption (Modan-Moses et al., 2003).

Modifying Treatments among Men 33

Neurological complications of EDs and malnutrition include structural brain changes as evidenced in brain imaging studies. One study of adolescent males with EDs found evidence of cortical atrophy on brain computerized tomography (CT) scans in seven of nine patients (Siegel, Hardoff, Golden, & Shenker, 1995). Finally, EDs can lead to electrolyte abnormalities, with one study demonstrating low potassium (25%) and low phosphorous levels (5%) among adolescent males with EDs (Vo, Lau, & Rubenstein, 2016). In sum, there is limited but growing evidence in male populations that EDs can cause substantial medical issues affecting all organ systems within the body.

Sex Differences in Prevalence Rates and Presentations of EDs[1]

Anorexia Nervosa

In the community, the lifetime prevalence of AN among men is estimated to be 0.2% (ranging 0–0.3%); this is in comparison to an analogous estimate of 1.4% (ranging 0.1–3.6%) among women (Galmiche, Dechelotte, Lambert, & Tavolacci, 2018). Based on these statistics, the sex ratio for AN appears to be approximately 7 : 1. Across psychiatric settings, males are believed to comprise 5–11% of adult patients treated for EDs (including AN) (Sweeting et al., 2015). Researchers argue that the marked disparity in prevalence estimates of EDs among men may in part be attributed to issues around seeking help and stigmatization faced particularly by male populations (e.g., associated with the misnomer that EDs are exclusively a 'feminine' problem) (Griffiths et al., 2015; Murray et al., 2017a).

Presentations of AN across sex are also subtly distinct in a number of ways. For example, instead of the pursuit of an extremely thin figure, engagement in caloric restriction or fasting (i.e., core AN symptoms) among males with AN may be undertaken to attain muscular leanness and minimize body fat so muscles are increasingly visible (Murray et al., 2017a; Pope et al., 2000). This aligns with the common desire among males to have a "six-pack" of abdominal muscles, which can typically only be achieved with very low body fat, as opposed to the flat stomach often desired by women and reflective of the excessively thin ideal (Darcy et al., 2012). Moreover, regular episodes of extreme dietary restriction (defined as 3 or more episodes per week during past month) are estimated to be around five times as prevalent among females than males (11.5% of females engaged in this behavior versus 2.3% of males) (Mond et al., 2014). It is plausible that some boys and men may be deterred from extreme caloric restriction out of fear of impeding muscle gains, which require the consumption of special macronutrients (namely protein). Notwithstanding this clear difference in dietary restriction, the study found comparable levels of excessive exercise as a way of influencing weight and shape across the sexes (Mond et al., 2014). Although idealized body types may be different between the sexes (which will be described in detail later in

34   *Cunningham, Nagata, and Murray*

this chapter), these findings suggest that both men and women are vulnerable to unhealthy thinness-oriented eating and exercise behaviors where a reduction of body adiposity might be a key goal (Murray et al., 2017a).

Bulimia Nervosa

The lifetime prevalence of bulimia nervosa (BN) among men in the community is estimated to be 0.6% (ranging 0.1–1.3%) (Galmiche et al., 2018). This is compared to a corresponding estimate of 1.9% (ranging 0.3–4.6%) in women, suggesting a prevalence rate sex ratio of around 3 : 1. Similar to AN, research and clinical reports suggest a number of sex differences in symptom presentation.

Adolescent males report less concern around eating and are less likely to report feelings of loss of control compared to females of the same age (8.3% of boys reported regular loss of control versus 24.7% of girls; Mond et al., 2014). However, significant proportions of adolescent males still report regular episodes of objective binge eating and perceptions of loss of control associated with eating (6.0% and 8.3%, respectively) (Mond et al., 2014). Moreover, boys appear to be less likely to purge as evidenced through lower prevalences of regular self-induced vomiting (0.8%) and laxative misuse (0.2%) than girls (3.3% and 1.1%, respectively).

A dietary practice which has only garnered recent empirical attention, and which may be particularly important to acknowledge in the context of muscularity concerns, is "cheat meal" engagement. A cheat meal is often portrayed as the consumption of a excessively large amount of calorie-dense food in a sitting, typically comprising of a high caloric intake similar to traditional objective binge episodes (e.g., 1,000–9,000+ calories) (Pila, Mond, Griffiths, Mitchison, & Murray, 2017). Due to these meals largely consisting of assorted high fat food items with limited nutritional value, they tend to represent a brief reprieve from one's otherwise regimented and "healthy" diet (Lavender et al., 2017; Murray et al., 2016b; Pila et al., 2017). Men wishing to improve their muscularity may be particularly drawn to this eating practice, which purportedly confers a temporary boost in metabolic function to accelerate muscle gains (Lavender et al., 2017; Murray et al., 2016b). Speaking to this point, Murray and colleagues (2016b) in their analysis of pro-muscularity websites gleaned the following 'advice' – "One day a week of HIGH calories is all that you need to shift your body out of a metabolic slur and keep fat burning as your main source of energy. What can you eat? ANYTHING! Eat KFC or my favourite, Popeye's. Remember, however, ONE meal. This is NOT a cheat day" (p. 18). While only a minority of social media images related to cheat meals depicted people, the preponderance of these individuals (60.7%) showed off a body that was highly and visibly muscular, likely further perpetuating the association between cheat meals and the attainment of a muscular appearance (Pila et al., 2017). Further qualitative analysis of content related to cheat meals exposes other resemblances to hallmark components of BN such as feelings of loss of control over eating (e.g., [social media content notes] "Snaccident: eating an entire pizza/box of

Modifying Treatments among Men 35

chocolates/family size bag of chips by mistake", p. 701) as well as subsequent compensatory behaviors (e.g., reinforced adherence to restricted diet) (Pila et al., 2017). However, unlike objective binge episodes in BN, we currently do not have empirical support that engaging in cheat meals is associated with significant distress and/or psychosocial impairment (Lavender et al., 2017). Yet, we have evidence that content related to cheat meals may strive to minimize the potential health risks associated with the eating practice such as through idealization of overconsumption and overindulgence (e.g., [social media content notes] "I don't want to look back one day and think 'I could have eaten that'", Pila et al., 2017, p. 703), and anecdotally, could be associated with negative affect (e.g. "When you just ate an entire pizza and you can't decide if you're disgusted with yourself or you want to finish strong with a cake", Pila et al., 2017, p. 703).

Binge Eating Disorder

The lifetime prevalence of binge eating disorder (BED) of men in the community is estimated to be 1.0% (ranging 0.3–2.0%) (Galmiche et al., 2018). This is compared to a corresponding estimate of 2.8% (ranging 0.6–5.8%) in women, suggesting a prevalence rate sex ratio of approximately 3 : 1. However, Gornell and Murray (2019) expect that such estimates could be an underestimation given the relaxation of diagnostic criteria from requiring at least two binge eating episodes per week (in DSM-IV) to only one per week in the previous three months (DSM-5) (American Psychiatric Association, 2013). However, despite these prevalence figures, estimates of BED-related symptomatology across sex appears somewhat inconsistent in the community. For example, there is research suggesting that adult males are approximately three times as likely as females to report subthreshold BED symptoms (1.9% versus 0.6%, respectively) (Hudson 2007), whereas another study has found that significantly smaller proportions of adolescent males report objective and subjective binge episodes (as noted previously) than adolescent females (Mond et al., 2014). These latter findings are supported by recent research among 5191 Australian adolescents, finding that males were less likely to exhibit subthreshold BED symptoms (0.0% versus 0.5%) and probable BED (0.2% versus 1.8%) than females (Mitchison et al., 2020).

The Muscular Male Body Ideal and Muscular-Oriented Disordered Eating

It is crucial that researchers and clinicians continue to pinpoint factors that may be driving these important differences in the prevalence and presentations of EDs across sex. A comprehensive understanding of such factors will undoubtedly inform the modification of ED screening and treatment efforts to better address the experience of EDs in males. In this section, we first highlight the critical difference in the overvalued idealized appearance across the sexes, with men endorsing more muscular ideals and women endorsing a drive for thinness. With these distinct appearance-related pursuits in mind, we must consider the different types of eating pathology that may appear as a result. In particular, muscularity-oriented disordered eating may be the result of a pursuit toward hypermuscularity. Second, we discuss the lack of specificity and sensitivity of existing assessment instruments in indexing ED symptoms among men, particularly those related to the drive for muscularity. It is imperative that both researchers and clinicians have a grasp of these issues to ensure male EDs are not overlooked or described solely in terms of thinness-oriented pathology which may not adequately capture the spectrum of ED symptoms experienced in this population.

The Muscular Body Ideal

Given that most ED research to date has involved females (and rarely males), it is not surprising that the manner in which EDs are conceptualized and treated predominantly derives from a female-centric diagnostic framework (Murray et al., 2017a). Cognitive-behavioral models for EDs tend to conceptualize the development and maintenance (and therefore treatment) of symptomatology around a drive for thinness, allowing for cardinal symptoms such as an un-abating desire to lose weight and fear of weight gain, extreme caloric restriction, fasting, binge-purging behaviors, and other forms of thinness-oriented eating pathology (Fairburn, Cooper, & Shafran, 2003; Murray, Griffiths, & Mond, 2016a). However, the underlying assumption of theoretical models often borne out of research in exclusively female samples is that the overvalued ideal appearance is one characterized primarily by thinness (Murray et al., 2017a). Whether these same models and related treatment efforts adequately capture ED pathology in men, for whom the overvalued appearance may not be one primarily of thinness, but of overt muscularity, remains questioned in the literature (Mitchison & Mond, 2015; Murray et al., 2017a).

Juxtaposing the slim and slender body ideal often endorsed by women in Westernized nations, many men instead strive to attain an increasingly muscular physique (Cafri et al., 2005; Leit, Gray, & Pope, 2002; Pope, Phillips, Olivardia, 2000). Specifically, this muscular appearance is typically described as comprising prominent upper-body muscularity with minimal body adiposity so one's muscles appear defined (Murray et al., 2017a; Ridgeway & Tylka, 2005). A more nuanced assessment indicates that men place particular value on the attainment of a developed abdominal region (i.e., 'six-pack' abdominal muscles and visible obliques), large and defined arms (i.e., biceps and triceps), as well as toned and strong pectoral muscles (Ridgeway & Tylka, 2005). And akin to the excessively thin ideal for women, this overtly lean and muscular body ideal represents an unattainable goal for most men, and one likely to elicit body dissatisfaction when efforts to acquire it fall short. Indeed, we see that muscularity dissatisfaction is relatively common across various male populations. Research suggests that over 90% of U.S. university men desire greater muscularity (Frederick et al., 2007), findings which are not confined to U.S. men, with large proportions of Ukranian (69%) and Ghanaian (49%) men also expressing this desire. These results also appear to extend to East Asian men, with one study showing that 75–77% of their male university sample in Hong Kong were dissatisfied with their current muscularity, slightly less than analogous figures from the U.S. men sampled as part of the same study (81–84%; Jung, Forbes, & Chan, 2010). Younger male populations do not appear to be immune from the desire for greater muscularity either. For instance, a recent analysis of a large nationally (U.S.) representative sample of adolescent boys note that 39.6% reported attempts to gain weight despite being of a normal BMI (Nagata et al., 2019a). Within this same normal BMI stratum, 24.3% of boys still perceived themselves to be underweight. A study of more than 5,700 children aged 8–12 years across Guangzhou, China, found that, of those classified as having a healthy weight, 49.5% still believed they were too thin (and ostensibly wanting to be bigger; Liu et al., 2019). Even among boys as young as 6 years of age, almost one third displayed preferences for higher levels of muscularity and expect greater positive rewards from this facet of appearance compared to thinness (McLean, Wertheim, & Paxton, 2018). Together, these findings converge to clearly demonstrate the value that a preponderance of boys and men place on the attainment of an increasingly muscular physique. And just as an overvaluation of the thin body ideal can precipitate thinness-oriented eating pathology, the endorsement and pursuit of the muscular body ideal common in men are likely to engender a distinct array of eating patterns and behaviors aimed at moving one closer to reaching it (i.e., muscularity-oriented disordered eating patterns; Lavender et al., 2017; Murray et al., 2017a).

Muscularity-Oriented Disordered Eating and Associated Behaviors

Established treatments for EDs must recognize the constellation of unique muscular-oriented disordered eating patterns that may accompany an overvaluation of, and drive for, muscularity common among men. However, to better understand the array of such ED behaviors, it is crucial that researchers and clinicians understand precisely the components of the drive for muscularity.

As alluded earlier, a drive for muscularity is believed to have two primary and somewhat mutually exclusive constituents: (1) muscular growth/size, and (2) muscular leanness (Lavender et al., 2017; Murray et al., 2017a; Tylka, 2011). The former pertains to the building of muscle volume or density, while the latter is characterized through the reduction of body fat to ensure one's muscles are not obscured and look 'cut' (Lavender et al., 2017; Murray et al., 2017a; Tylka, 2011). With these two components in mind, efforts to improve muscularity (i.e., through eating and exercise practices) may be elicited via two different pathways (Murray et al., 2017a; Tylka, 2011). For instance, *muscle growth* typically requires a consumption of surplus calories including a large intake of protein (Griffiths, Murray, & Touyz, 2013; Murray et al., 2017a). Interestingly, protein consumption may strictly abide by arbitrary rules regarding both amount (e.g., [stated on pro-muscularity website] "Total protein should be your goal bodyweight in pounds X 1.5"; Murray et al., 2016b, p. 19) and a fixed frequent schedule (e.g., every few hours) (Mosley, 2009). Adherence to such a rigid dietary regime can mean one feels compelled to eat even after satiety to meet one's macronutrient quota (e.g., [case study writes] "... I don't feel like eating at all, but I force it down knowing that it is helping me get bigger", p. 165), or wake up multiple times during the night solely to consume protein to ensure one's body does not slip into a catabolic state from insufficient intake (Murray et al., 2011). There may also be a proclivity to bulk prepare meals in advance (i.e., 'meal prep'). These meals would often be scrupulously prepared, involving the precise calculation of macronutrients to ensure they align with one's body change goals (e.g., high protein with low carbohydrates), and facilitate compliance to one's restrictive diet by providing continual access to 'acceptable' foods (Lavender et al., 2017; Mosley, 2009; Murray et al., 2012a). In cases where muscularity is of extreme concern, there may even be an outright refusal to consume any foods that have not been personally prepared (Murray et al., 2011).

In contrast, the pursuit of *muscular leanness* may precipitate a distinct array of ED behaviors, typically centered around the consumption of a caloric deficit to expedite fat loss. In particular, this could (and often does) entail a radical restriction of dietary carbohydrates, whilst maintaining a sufficient intake of lean protein to preserve muscle mass (Griffiths, Murray, & Touyz, 2013; Murray et al., 2017a). Mosley's (2009) case study with MD captures this point, stating, "When I'm in a cutting phase I'll restrict my carb intake to almost nothing so as to lean up and make my muscles stand out" (p. 4). Considering their attendant eating behaviors, the concurrent focus on both maximizing muscle growth and minimizing body adiposity may be conflicting (e.g., calorie surplus for the former versus calorie deficit for the latter). These individuals may therefore engage in rigid and prolonged 'bulk-cut' dieting, an oscillating cycle of eating and training regimes dedicated to the expedition of muscle growth (i.e., 'bulk' up), followed by a period dedicated to enhancing leanness (i.e., 'cut' body fat) (Lavender et al., 2017).

Research suggest that special muscularity-oriented eating and exercising behaviors appear to be relatively common among men. For instance, earlier research found that over 90% and around 68% of adolescent males reported exercising more and amending eating habits, respectively, in order to improve muscularity within the previous year (Eisenberg, Wall, & Neumark-Sztainer, 2012). Further, almost 35% of boys had used protein powders/shakes, with 6.3% reporting having used such supplements often. Among 14–16 year old Australian adolescent boys, Yager and McLean (2020) found that 49.8% reported having used protein powder and 8.4% having used creatine monohydrate. When asked about their intention to use such supplements in the future, these figures inflated to 62.0% and 25.7%, respectively. In an analysis of earlier data from adolescent

Modifying Treatments among Men 39

boys across the U.S. (n = 4,710), Nagata and colleagues (2020) found close to 30% attempted to gain weight, with 22.7% engaging in concerted efforts to increase weight or muscle (e.g., eating greater volumes, using supplements) – figures which remained relatively stable (within ~5%) at a 7-year follow up. To put these findings in perspective, less than 5% of boys reported engaging in weight loss behaviors (16% at follow up). We also see a similar trend in men, where recent findings among a nationally representative sample of 7,018 young men across the U.S. showed that around 22.4% perceived themselves to be underweight, and 21.9% having engaged in muscularity-oriented eating behaviors to increase muscle mass (e.g., eating more or different foods, taking food supplements) (Nagata et al., 2019b). Considering this body of emerging research illustrating the nature and prevalence of muscularity-oriented concerns and concomitant engagement in special eating behaviors, it is vital that existing screening and treatment protocols for EDs recognize this unique constellation of muscularity-oriented ED pathology (Murray et al., 2017a).

Although not eating per se, men who are preoccupied about being insufficiently muscular may also be drawn to using illicit substances to expedite the growth of lean muscle mass. These substances contrast those which have been historically linked to EDs and the facilitation of weight loss, such as laxatives or diuretics. Arguably the most infamous and researched class of muscularity-enhancing substances is androgenic-anabolic steroids (AAS), pharmacological substances which include testosterone and its chemical derivatives that are typically administered via intramuscular injection (Goldman, Pope, & Bhasin, 2019; Pope et al., 2014b). In the U.S., among those aged 13 to 50 years, it was estimated that up to 4 million people had used AASs in their lifetime, and around 98% of whom are predicted to be male (Pope et al., 2014a). In their study of adolescents across the U.S., Eisenberg et al. (2012) found that almost 6% of boys reported AAS use over the past year, which is comparable to figures found among Australian adolescents (4.2%; Yager & Mclean, 2020). A preoccupation with the idea of not being muscular enough is believed to be an important risk factor for AAS use (Kanayama, Hudson, & Pope, 2020; Pope, Kanayama, & Hudson, 2012), and understandably so, given their ability to cultivate lean muscle mass at a rate exceeding that typically possible through conventional exercise and diet alone (Bhasin et al., 1996). And while AAS use may have a marked effect on one's muscularity in the short term, it could inadvertently place one at a high risk of longer term physical and psychological harm (see for review Pope et al., 2014b).

Gold Standard Assessments of EDs and Muscularity Concerns

Given that prominent cognitive-behavioral models of EDs are geared toward an overvaluation of a thin ideal appearance, many ED assessment tools may be limited in capturing muscularity concerns and related ED pathology among males. For instance, the widely used self-report Eating Disorder

Examination Questionnaire (EDE-Q; Fairburn & Beglin, 1994), which has been validated to index core tenets of ED pathology (e.g., overvaluation of body weight or shape, binge and purging behaviors), contains certain items which may lack sensitivity among men (Griffiths et al., 2013). For instance, the items "*Have you have a definite desire to have a totally flat stomach?*" may not adequately gauge the motivation for many men to acquire the "six-pack" abdominal muscles. Items relating to weight (e.g., "*Have you had a definite fear that you might gain weight?*") may not capture fears that men may hold about being too small or thin, and actually wanting to gain weight in the form of lean muscle mass. Items pertaining to the misuse of laxatives (or diuretics) to control weight and shape would not capture the ideation or actual use of substances (e.g., AAS) that men might use to instead increase weight and muscle size as opposed to weight loss. The profound implication of this could be that some of our most widely utilized measures of ED psychopathology are limited in their sensitivity and specificity to adequately index muscularity-oriented ED psychopathology (Murray et al., 2017a). Compounding this issue further is the lack of items specifically directed towards gauging the unique ED cognitions and behaviors that are concomitant with the drive for greater muscularity (Murray et al., 2017a; 2019). This could help account for why men have been found to exhibit significantly lower scores on standard ED assessments than females (Mond et al., 2014; Murray et al., 2017a; Smith, Mason, & Murray, 2017), despite having comparable clinical presentations (Darcy et al., 2012), suggesting that current tools may be failing to capture an important component of ED pathology in men. Given that screening and treatment protocols often employ such "gold standard" self-report and interview-based assessments to track symptom changes over time, this lack of specificity to muscularity-oriented ED pathology is concerning.

The recent development of the Muscularity Oriented Eating Test (MOET) addresses this important gap (Murray et al., 2019). This 15-item self-report questionnaire is the first standalone measure to specifically index the attitudinal and behavioral components of disordered eating behaviors that occur in the context of the drive for muscularity. Items assess a broad range of affective (e.g., "I have felt anxious when I run out of protein-based supplements"), attitudinal (e.g., "What I ate has influenced how I think about myself as a person"), and behavioral (e.g., "I have used meal replacement supplements when I felt full") aspects of muscularity-oriented eating pathology. The MOET demonstrates excellent psychometric properties evaluated through sound internal consistency and test-retest reliability, and convergent validity indicated through correlations with other muscularity-related constructs (Murray et al., 2019). The measures shows a one-factor structure among U.S. college men, providing a global measure of muscularity-oriented eating pathology (Murray et al., 2019); however, it is crucial these psychometric properties are replicated (or examined) across more diverse samples. Nonetheless, the measure is an important advancement in helping us index and understand the nature and extent of muscularity-oriented eating pathology. However, given its novelty and recent development, further research is necessary to extend our understanding of how

Modifying Treatments among Men   41

this ED pathology manifests in relevant at-risk clinical populations and give careful consideration for how we might adapt existing ED treatments to incorporate such measurements (discussed further) (Murray et al., 2019).

Muscle Dysmorphia

With increasing recognition of appearance concerns focused on muscularity in men, we must adapt ED treatment efforts to recognize the potential for, and possibly address, comorbid MD among men presenting with ED pathology. MD is a psychiatric condition hallmarked by a pathological drive for muscularity and a preoccupation with the perception that one is insufficiently muscular (Choi, Pope, & Olivardia, 2002; Pope et al., 1997). Once conceptualized as a type of ED and coined the colourful name "reverse anorexia nervosa" (Pope, Katz, & Hudson, 1993), MD was later categorized as a specifier of body dysmorphic disorder (BDD) in DSM-V (APA, 2013) as eating pathology was purported to be only an auxiliary component of the disorder (Murray et al., 2017a; Pope et al., 1997).

Despite its diagnostic classification, research continues to highlight the significant ED pathology exhibited by men with MD. For instance, case studies of men with MD demonstrate the primacy of maladaptive eating practices in their clinical presentation (Mosley, 2009; Murray et al., 2011, 2012a). These case reports describe many of the muscularity-oriented eating practices alluded to earlier, including excessively rigid diets centred around protein intake, eating in fixed intervals even if not hungry, the strict cutting of carbohydrates during periods in which leanness is the key goal, and the meticulous preparation of meals in advance to ensure dietary compliance. And from these case studies, it is clear these behaviors can be associated with distress and functional impairment. One case notes, "I have to eat every 3 hours, even if I'm not hungry, to make sure that my body has enough protein to get bigger. Sometimes it is actually hard to eat that much ... but I force it down knowing it is helping me get bigger" (Murray et al., 2011, p. 165). Another case notes in relation to their excessively calculated dietary regime, "it is really hard to keep this kind of diet up and maintain any kind of normal life" (Mosley, 2009, p. 4). Research even suggests that men with MD exhibit comparable dietary restraint and concerns about body shape and weight to men with AN (Murray et al., 2012b). The centrality of unhealthy eating practices among those with severe preoccupations with muscularity is further demonstrated by research highlighting that disordered eating beliefs and attitudes could help differentiate those who may be more likely to have MD from body building controls (i.e., pathological vs. non-pathological drives for muscularity), whereas exercise could not (Mitchell et al., 2017; Murray et al., 2017a). Consequently, the appropriate nosology of MD and its categorization as a form of BDD, rather than a type of ED, remains debated in the literature today (Murray et al., 2010; 2017a).

Together, despite its nosological classification, these findings underscore the susceptibility of those with extreme drives for muscularity (i.e., MD) to engage in both maladaptive thinness- and muscularity-oriented eating practices.

42 Cunningham, Nagata, and Murray

Consequently, it would be prudent for assessment tools and efforts to not screen for MD related symptomatology, and consider negative appraisals of muscularity more generally, which may be driving ED pathology in presenting men.

Directions for Future Research

There are several important directions for future research to help us understand the experience of EDs among men and inform their treatment. Perhaps the most fruitful direction involves the continual improvement of tools to be used by both researchers and clinicians to accurately gauge muscularity-oriented eating pathology. It is vital that future studies examine the sensitivity of the MOET, and other emerging instruments designed to tap into muscularity-oriented eating, in clinical populations and throughout interventions intended to alter muscularity-oriented psychopathology (Murray et al., 2019). This research will assist with determining appropriate 'cut-off' MOET scores that can be used to help screen for individuals engaging in, or at high risk of engaging in, muscular-oriented disordered eating and related pathologies (e.g., MD) (Murray et al., 2019). A related issue requiring further careful consideration would then be how to best incorporate such questionnaire items into existing ED assessment and treatment protocols to ensure that muscularity-oriented pathology does not go undetected or inaccurately indexed.

Future research should also endeavour to further characterize muscularity-oriented disordered eating and qualify precisely when an eating-related attitude or behavior may be considered "disordered". Murray et al. (2017a) note that any muscularity-oriented eating attitudes or behaviors to be considered disordered must produce clinically significant distress and/or impaired psychosocial functioning. One may argue that some muscle change behaviors should be considered categorically disordered and maladaptive (e.g., illicit AAS use), however, others are not so clearly delineated. For example, consuming extra protein, muscle-building dietary supplements, and/or frequent exercise should not be considered intrinsically disordered or dangerous (Murray et al., 2017a). However, these behaviors may be considered facets of disordered eating and related pathological behaviors if an individual becomes significantly distressed if they cannot engage in them (e.g., becoming markedly anxious about insufficient daily protein intake) or if they interfere with one's day-to-day functioning (e.g., neglecting important events and duties to workout at the gym) (Murray et al., 2017a). As discussed earlier, further studies of men with MD could provide a vital platform for expanding our understanding of what clinically relevant muscularity-oriented disordered eating may entail (Murray et al., 2017a). Addressing this knowledge gap will inform the judgements of researchers and clinicians as to what specific attitudes and behaviors, and under what circumstances, may be particularly useful to gauge in their assessments of ED pathology.

We are also not currently aware of any purposive treatments to address muscularity-oriented disordered eating in males. This is perhaps unsurprising given that we have only recently begun to index the pathology empirically. Nonetheless, a handful of relevant treatment studies might help us to grasp what these may encompass and understand other important considerations in the context of muscularity issues in men. In treating an adolescent male with MD, Murray and Griffiths (2015) adapted a form of family-based treatment with positive outcomes. The patient presented with significant muscularity-oriented disordered eating, restricting intake to very select food items that were high in protein and low in fat, as well as presenting other excessive behaviors (e.g., adding protein powder to meals). Parental intervention was mobilized to curtail such behaviors and diversify the repertoire of foods the boy consumed (Murray & Griffiths, 2015). Concurrently, the parents of the patient were required to closely monitor his excessive exercise behaviors both in the morning and at night, with a temporary ban put in place until he no longer feared certain foods and was not driven to exercise (as a compensatory behavior) after consuming them. Over the seven month treatment, the patient's MD-related symptoms were significantly attenuated (Murray & Griffiths, 2015). Although promising, particularly for younger boys with a preoccupation with muscularity, the findings are likely to have limited generalizability to men outside of the family/home context.

A more recent case report even highlights that thinness-oriented eating pathology may even evolve into muscularity-oriented pathology throughout conventional treatment (Murray et al., 2017b). Here, an individual presented with AN, was treated successfully using FBT, and was discharged after he had restored sufficient weight and exhibited a marked decline in his motivation to be thin and lose weight (Murray et al., 2017b). During this time, however, the patient developed a drive to be increasingly muscular, a clear change in motivation that was undetected. Regrettably, this drive transitioned into a severe preoccupation with muscularity and concomitant maladaptive muscularity-oriented eating, thus necessitating further treatment (Murray et al., 2017b). It is unclear how such a drastic transition could occur covertly; it may be the case that the move away from a severely low body weight was viewed as positive progress and therefore misconstrued as innocuous (Murray et al., 2017b). Nonetheless, these findings further emphasize the importance of modifying existing ED treatment protocols to include additional measures for screening muscularity-related concerns in males at the outset and throughout treatment for thinness-oriented ED pathologies such as AN (Murray et al., 2017b).

Finally, future research is required to expose the physical health complications linked to an excessive drive for muscularity and attendant maladaptive eating practices. Indeed, we have preliminary evidence of associated medical concerns. Murray and colleagues (2018) describe the case study of a 16-year old male who presented to a clinic with muscularity-oriented psychopathology. The patient was a wrestler who engaged in restrictive eating practices in a bid to become leaner to meet certain weight limits for competitive wrestling. In achieving this, he over-regulated his protein intake (e.g., drinking up to 8 cups of milk daily), obsessively kept track of weight fluctuations and counted calories and macronutrients of food, as well as refusing to eat in contexts where the precise nutritional contents of his food could not be ascertained (e.g., at a restaurant). He also reportedly made efforts to stand instead of sit while at home, fearing the latter would attenuate muscularity in his legs. The patient was referred for a psychiatric evaluation where he did not exhibit scores considered to be of clinical severity on formal ED measures. However, the patient required urgent hospitalization due to medical instability. He exhibited bradycardia (displaying a slowed heart rate of 45 beats per minute), which was particularly prominent overnight (reducing to 38 beats per minute), and other medical complications including normocytic anemia. Due to the patient's relentless drive for muscular leanness, his weight dropped from being at the 75th percentile to the 30th percentile for BMI in approximately 1 year. Although it is unclear exactly what factors engendered such complications, Murray and colleagues (2018) call for future research on the medical dangers associated with muscularity-oriented disordered eating and extremely high protein diets. This information will likely serve as a crucial resource for physicians to help identify and manage this ED pathology in clinical practice, especially given this pathology may not be fully captured by conventional ED assessment tools as exemplified in this case.

Summary and Conclusion

Because men have been systematically overlooked in ED research, our 'understanding' of EDs among males has largely been informed by empirical and clinical studies on the disorders among females. And yet, sex differences exist in the idealized appearance that may give rise to distinct constellations of ED-related behaviors and cognitions. Research has consistently demonstrated that men have a preference for an increasingly muscular physique as opposed to one primarily characterized by thinness. At the same time, many well-known cognitive behavioral ED models, and treatment protocols, are geared toward addressing the latter. This chapter sought to create awareness about and provide readers with an appreciation of the pursuit of muscularity and attendant eating psychopathology among men, and in doing so, stimulate thought regarding how existing ED assessment and treatment protocols may need to be modified to better address these phenomena. Treatment protocols need to recognize that the over-valued muscular appearance common among men is distinct from that often found among women, and that it might precipitate a unique array of ED pathologies. Relatedly, existing and widely used ED assessment and treatment tools may be insensitive to, and inadequately index, muscularity-oriented ED pathology. It would be beneficial for ED treatment protocols to screen for, and potentially address concurrently, MD, because individuals with muscularity concerns may be particularly vulnerable to experiencing muscularity-oriented eating pathologies. Although the recent recognition of muscularity-oriented eating pathology as a phenomenon of clinical relevance, as well as recent advances in quantitatively indexing this pathology, represent advances in the field, future research will be critical in furthering our understanding of the nature of this pathology in populations of clinical relevance to aid in their treatment. Furthermore, emerging knowledge of muscularity-oriented disordered eating necessitates careful thought about how to optimally incorporate its measurement into existing and widely used ED assessment and treatment tools and how best to manage the pathology.

Note

1 For a detailed review relevant to sections of this chapter, we refer the reader to Murray et al. (2017a).

References

American Psychiatric Association. (2013). *Diagnostic and statistical manual of mental disorders (5th ed.)*. Arlington, VA: American Psychiatric Publishing.

Bhasin, S., Storer, T. W., Berman, N., Callegari, C., Clevenger, B., Phillips, J., Bunnell, T. J., Tricker, R., Shirazi, A., & Casaburi, R. (1996). The effects of supraphysiologic doses of testosterone on muscle size and strength in normal men. *New England Journal of Medicine, 335*, 1–7. 10.1056/nejm199607043350101.

Cafri, G., Thompson, J. K., Ricciardelli, L., McCabe, M., Smolak, L., & Yesalis, C. (2005). Pursuit of the muscular ideal: Physical and psychological consequences and putative risk factors. *Clinical Psychology Review, 25*, 215–239.

Choi, P. Y. L., Pope, H. G., Jr., & Olivardia, R. (2002). Muscle dysmorphia: A new syndrome in weightlifters. *British Journal of Sports Medicine, 36*, 375–377.

Eisenberg, M. A., Wall, M., & Neumark-Sztainer, D. (2012). Muscle-enhancing behaviors among adolescent girls and boys. *Pediatrics, 130*, 1019–1026.

Darcy, A. M., Doyle, A. C., Lock. J., Peebles, R., Doyle, P., & Le Grange, D. (2012). The eating disorders examination in adolescent males with anorexia nervosa: How does it compare to adolescent females? *International Journal of Eating Disorders, 45*, 110–114.

Fairburn, C. G., Cooper, Z., & Shafran, R. (2003). Cognitive behaviour therapy for eating disorders: A "transdiagnostic" theory and treatment. *Behaviour Research and Therapy, 41*, 509–528.

Fairburn, C. G., & Beglin, S. J. (1994). Assessment of eating disorders: Interviews or self-report questionnaire? *International Journal of Eating Disorders, 16*, 363–370.

Frederick, D. A., Buchanan, G. M., Sadehgi-Azar, L., Peplau, L. A., Haselton, M. G., Berezovskaya, A., & Lipinski, R. E. (2007). Desiring the muscular ideal: Men's body satisfaction in the United States, Ukraine, and Ghana. *Psychology of Men & Masculinity, 8*(2), 103–117.

Galmiche, M., Déchelotte, P., Lambert, G., & Tavolacci, M. P. (2019). Prevalence of eating disorders over the 2000–2018 period: A systematic literature review. *The American Journal of Clinical Nutrition, 109*, 1402–1413.

Goldman, A. L, Pope, H. G., & Bhasin, S. (2019). The health threat posed by the hidden epidemic of anabolic steroid use and body image disorders among young men. *The Journal of Clinical Endocrinology & Metabolism, 104*, 1069–1074.

Gorrell, S., & Murray, S. B. (2019). Eating disorders in males. *Child and Adolescent Psychiatric Clinics of North America, 28*, 641–651.

46 Cunningham, Nagata, and Murray

Griffiths, S., Murray, S. B., & Touyz, S. W. (2013). Disordered eating and the muscular ideal. *Journal of Eating Disorders*, *1*, 15.

Griffiths, S., Mond, J. M., Li, Z., Gunatilake, S., Murray, S. B., Sheffield, J., & Touyz, S. (2015). Self-stigma of seeking help and being male predicts an increased likelihood of having an undiagnosed eating disorder. *International Journal of Eating Disorders*, *48*(6), 775–778.

Hudson, J. I., Hiripi, E., Pope, H. G., & Kessler, R. C. (2007). The prevalence and correlates of eating disorders in the National Comorbidity Survey replication. *Biological Psychiatry*, *61*, 349–358.

Jung, J., Forbes, G. B., & Chan, P. (2010). Global body and muscle satisfaction among college men in the United States and Hong Kong-China. *Sex Roles*, *63*, 104–117.

Kanayama, G., Hudson, J. I., & Pope, Jr., H. G. (2020). Anabolic-androgenic steroid use and body image in men: A growing concern for clinicians. *Psychotherapy and Psychosomatics*, *89*, 65–73.

Lavender, J. M., Brown, T. A., & Murray, S. B. (2017). Men, muscles, and eating disorders: An overview of traditional and muscularity-oriented disordered eating. *Current Psychiatry Reports*, *19*(6), 32.

Leit, R. A., Gray, J. J., & Pope, H. G. (2002). The media's representation of the ideal male body: A cause for muscle dysmorphia? *International Journal of Eating Disorders*, *31*(3), 334–338.

Liu, W., Lin, R., Guo, C., Xiong, L., Chen, S., & Liu, W. (2019). Prevalence of body dissatisfaction and its effects on health-related quality of life among primary school students in Guangzhou, China. *BMC Public Health*, *19*, 213.

McLean, S. A., Wertheim, E. H., & Paxton, S. J. (2018). Preferences for being muscular and thin in 6-year-old boys. *Body Image*, *26*, 98–102.

Misra, M., Katzman, D. K., Cord, J., Manning, S. J., Mendes, N., Herzog, D. B., et al. (2008). Bone metabolism in adolescent boys with anorexia nervosa. *The Journal of Clinical Endocrinology and Metabolism*, *93*(8), 3029–3036.

Mitchell, L., Murray, S. B., Hoon, M., Hackett, D., Prvan, T., & O'Connor, H. (2017). Correlates of muscle dysmorphia symptomatology in natural bodybuilders: Distinguishing factors in the pursuit of hyper-muscularity. *Body Image*, *22*, 1–5.

Mitchison, D., & Mond, J. M. (2015). Epidemiology of eating disorders, eating disordered behaviour, and body image disturbance in males: A narrative review. *Journal of Eating Disorders*, *3*, 20.

Mitchison, D., Mond, J., Bussey, K., Griffiths, S., Trompeter, N., Lonergan, A., Pike, K. M., Murray, S. B., & Hay, P. (2020). DSM-5 full syndrome, other specified, and unspecified eating disorders in Australian adolescents: Prevalence and clinical significance. *Psychological Medicine*, *50*, 981–990.

Modan-Moses, D., Yaroslavsky, A., Novikov, I., Segev, S., Toledano, A., Miterany, E., & Stein, D. (2003). Stunting of growth as a major feature of anorexia nervosa in male adolescents. *Pediatrics*, *111*(2), 270–276.

Mond, J., Hall, A., Bentley, C., Harrison, C., Gratwick-Sarll, K., & Lewis, V. (2014) Eating-disordered behavior in adolescent boys: Eating disorder examination questionnaire norms. *International Journal of Eating Disorders*, *47*(4), 335–341.

Mosley, P. E. (2009). Bigorexia: Bodybuilding and muscle dysmorphia. *European Eating Disorders Review*, *17*(3), 191–198.

Murray, S. B., Accurso, E. C., Griffiths, S., & Nagata, J. M. (2018). Boys, biceps, and bradycardia: The hidden dangers of muscularity-oriented disordered eating. *Journal of Adolescent Health*, *62*, 352–355. 10.1016/j.jadohealth.2017.09.025.

Murray, S. B, Brown, T. A., Blashill, A. J., Compte, E. J., Lavender, J. M., Mitchison, D., Mond, J. M., Keel, P. K., & Nagata, J. M. (2019). The development and validation of the Muscularity-Oriented Eating Test (MOET): A novel measure of muscularity-oriented disordered eating. *The International Journal of Eating Disorders, 52*, 1389–1398.

Murray, S. B., & Griffiths, S. (2015). Adolescent muscle dysmorphia and family-based treatment: A case report. *Clinical Child Psychology And Psychiatry, 20*(2), 324–330.

Murray, S. B., Griffiths, S., Hazery, L., Shen, T., Wooldridge, T., & Mond, J. M. (2016b). Go big or go home: A thematic content analysis of pro-muscularity websites. *Body Image, 16*, 17–20.

Murray, S. B., Griffiths, S., & Mond, J. M. (2016a). Evolving eating disorder psychopathology: Conceptualizing muscularity-oriented disordered eating. *British Journal of Psychiatry, 208*, 414–415.

Murray, S. B., Griffiths, S., Mitchison, D., & Mond, J. M. (2017b). The transition from thinness-oriented to muscularity-oriented disordered eating in adolescent males: A clinical observation. *The Journal of Adolescent Health, 60*(3), 353–355.

Murray, S. B., Maguire, S., Russell, J., & Touyz, S. W. (2012a). The emotional regulatory features of bulimic episodes and compulsive exercise in muscle dysmorphia: A case report. *European Eating Disorders Review, 20*(1), 68–73.

Murray S. B., Nagata, J. M., Griffiths S., Calzo, J. P., Brown, T. A., Mitchison, D., Blashill, A. J., & Mond, J. M. (2017a). The enigma of male eating disorders: A critical review and synthesis. *Clinical Psychology Review, 57*, 1–11.

Murray, S. B., Rieger, E., Hildebrandt, T., Karlov, L., Russell, J., Boon, E., Dawson, R. T., & Touyz, S. W. et al. (2012b). A comparison of eating, exercise, shape, and weight related symptomatology in males with muscle dysmorphia and anorexia nervosa. *Body Image, 9*, 193–200.

Murray, S. B., Rieger, E., Touyz, S. W., & De la Garza García, Y. (2010). Muscle dysmorphia and the DSM-V conundrum: Where does it belong? A review paper. *International Journal of Eating Disorders, 43*, 483–491.

Murray, S. B., Rieger, E., & Touyz, S. W. (2011). Muscle dysmorphia symptomatology during a period of religious fasting: A case report. *European Eating Disorders Review, 19*, 162–168.

Nagata, J. M., Bibbins-Domingo, K., Garber, A. K., Griffiths, S., Vittinghoff, E., & Murray, S. B. (2019a). Boys, bulk, and body ideals: Sex differences in weight-gain attempts among adolescents in the United States. *Journal of Adolescent Health, 64*, 450–453.

Nagata, J. M., Domingue, B. W., Darmstadt, G. L., Weber, A. M., Meausoone, V., Cislaghi, B., & Shakya, H. B. (2020). Gender norms and weight control behaviors in U.S. adolescents: A prospective cohort study (1994–2002). *Journal of Adolescent Health, 66*, S34–S41.

Nagata, J. M., & Golden, N. H. (2018). Sex differences in eating disorders. *Adolescent Medicine: State of the Art Reviews, 29*, 245259.

Nagata, J. M., Golden, N. H., Leonard, M. B., Copelovitch, L., & Denburg, M. R. (2017). Assessment of sex differences in fracture risk among patients with anorexia nervosa: A population-based cohort study using the health improvement network. *Journal of Bone and Mineral Research: The Official Journal of the American Society for Bone and Mineral Research, 32*(5), 1082–1089.

Nagata, J. M., Golden, N. H., Peebles, R., Long, J., Leonard, M. B., & Carlson, J. L. (2017). Assessment of sex differences in bone deficits among adolescents with anorexia nervosa. *International Journal of Eating Disorders, 50*(4), 352–358.

Nagata, J. M., Golden, N. H., Peebles, R., Long, J., Murray, S. B., Leonard, M. B., & Carlson, J. L. (2017). Assessment of sex differences in body composition among adolescents with anorexia nervosa. *The Journal of Adolescent Health: Official Publication of the Society for Adolescent Medicine, 60*(4), 455–459.

Nagata, J. M., Park, K. T., Colditz, K., & Golden, N. H. (2015). Associations of elevated liver enzymes among hospitalized adolescents with anorexia nervosa. *The Journal of Pediatrics, 166*(2), 43.e1.

Nagata, J. M., Murray, S. B., Bibbins-Domingo, K., Garber, A. K., Mitchison, D., & Griffiths, S. (2019b). Predictors of muscularity-oriented disordered eating behaviors in U.S. young adults: A prospective cohort study. *International Journal of Eating Disorders, 52*, 1380–1388.

Norris, M. L., Harrison, M. E., Isserlin, L., Robinson, A., Feder, S., & Sampson, M. (2016). Gastrointestinal complications associated with anorexia nervosa: A systematic review. *The International Journal of Eating Disorders, 49*(3), 216–237.

Pila, E., Mond, J. M., Griffiths, S., Mitchison, D., & Murray, S. B. (2017). A thematic content analysis of #cheatmeal images on social media: Characterizing an emerging trend. *International Journal of Eating Disorders, 50*(6), 698–706.

Pope, H. G., Jr., Gruber, A., Choi, P., Olivardia, R., & Phillips, K. (1997). Muscle dysmorphia: An underrecognized form of body dysmorphic disorder. *Psychosomatics, 38*(6), 548–557.

Pope, H. G., Jr., Kanayama, G., Athey, A., Ryan, E., Hudson, J. I., & Baggish, A. (2014a). The lifetime prevalence of anabolic-androgenic steroid use and dependence in Americans: Current best estimates. *The American Journal on Addictions, 23*, 371–377.

Pope, H. G., Jr., Kanayama, G., & Hudson, J. I. (2012). Risk factors for illicit anabolic-androgenic steroid use in male weightlifters: A cross-sectional cohort study. *Biological Psychiatry, 71*, 254–261. 10.1016/j.biopsych.2011.06.024.

Pope, H. G., Jr., Katz, D. L., & Hudson, J. I. (1993). Anorexia nervosa and "reverse anorexia" among 108 male bodybuilders. *Comprehensive Psychiatry, 34*(6), 406–409.

Pope, H. G., Jr., Phillips, K. A., & Olivardia, R. (2000). *The Adonis complex: The secret crisis of male body obsession.* New York: The Free Press.

Pope, H. G., Jr., Wood, R. I., Rogol, A., Nyberg, F., Bowers, L., & Bhasin, S. (2014b). Adverse health consequences of performance-enhancing drugs: An endocrine society scientific statement. *Endocrine Reviews, 35*, 341–375.

Ridgeway, R. T., & Tylka, T. L. (2005). College men's perceptions of ideal body composition and shape. *Psychology of Men and Masculinity, 6*, 209–220.

Sachs, K. V., Harnke, B., Mehler, P. S., & Krantz, M. J. (2016). Cardiovascular complications of anorexia nervosa: A systematic review. *The International Journal of Eating Disorders, 49*(3), 238–248.

Siegel, J. H., Hardoff, D., Golden, N. H., & Shenker, I. R. (1995). Medical complications in male adolescents with anorexia nervosa. *The Journal of Adolescent Health: Official Publication of the Society for Adolescent Medicine, 16*(6), 448–453.

Silber, T. J., Robb, A. S., Orrell-Valente, J. K., Ellis, N., Valadez-Meltzer, A., & Dadson, M. J. (2004). Nocturnal nasogastric refeeding for hospitalized adolescent boys with anorexia nervosa. *Journal of Developmental & Behavioral Pediatrics, 25*, 415–418.

Smith, K. E., Mason, T. B., Murray, S. B., Griffiths, S., Leonard, R. C., Wetterneck, C. T., Smith, B. E. R., Farrell, N. R., Riemann, B. C. & Lavender, J. M. (2017). Clinical norms and sex differences on the Eating Disorder Inventory (EDI) and the Eating Disorder Examination Questionnaire (EDE-Q). *International Journal of Eating Disorders, 50*, 769–775.

Sweeting, H., Walker, L., MacLean, A., Patterson, C., Räisänen, U., & Hunt, K. (2015). Prevalence of eating disorders in males: A review of rates reported in academic re-search and UK mass media. *International Journal of Men's Health, 14*, 2.

Tylka, T. L. (2011). Refinement of the tripartite influence model for men: Dual body image pathways to body change behaviors. *Body Image, 8*, 199–207.

Vo, M., Lau, J., & Rubinstein, M. (2016). Eating disorders in adolescent and young adult males: Presenting characteristics. *Journal of Adolescent Health, 59*, 397–400.

Yager, Z., & McLean, S. (2020). Muscle building supplement use in Australian adolescent boys: relationships with body image, weight lifting, and sports engagement. *BMC Pediatrics, 20*, 89.

3 Where is the Evidence of Evidence-Based Treatment for LGBTQIA+ Individuals Experiencing Eating Disorders?

Jerel P. Calzo, Ethan E. Lopez, Scout Silverstein, Tiffany A. Brown, and Aaron J. Blashill

Introduction

Eating disorders (e.g., anorexia nervosa and binge eating disorder) and disordered weight and shape control behaviors (e.g., overeating and purging) affect individuals across all demographic strata and indicators of social location, including sex, age, weight, ability, socioeconomic position, race, and ethnicity. Two diverse subpopulations that have been identified as exhibiting elevated prevalence of eating disorders and disordered weight and shape concerns are sexual minorities (i.e., individuals who are not exclusively heterosexual in their attractions, sexual behaviors, or identities) and gender minorities (i.e., individuals whose gender identity or expression do not align with the sex they were assigned at birth; Calzo, Blashill, Brown, & Argenal, 2017; Diemer, Grant, Munn-Chernoff, Patterson, & Duncan, 2015; Duffy, Henkel, & Joiner, 2019). The goals of this chapter are threefold: (1) to review the state of the research on eating disorders and eating disorders treatment and prevention among sexual and gender minorities, including relevant theory and epidemiology on health inequities; (2) to discuss the state of evidence-based treatment and critical gaps in research and clinical practice that have impeded the development of tailored and targeted eating disorders treatment and prevention for sexual and gender minority populations; and (3) to describe recommendations for future research and clinical practice, as informed by the literature and original data collected from providers, advocates, and individuals with lived experience.

Writing this chapter was challenging. Despite overall growth in sexual orientation and gender health equity research, there continues to be a dearth of published research on evidence regarding the effectiveness of treatments to address the disparate burden of body image concerns and disordered eating behaviors among sexual and gender minority populations. Too often, researchers and treatment providers do not assess sexual orientation or gender in a way that enables attention to sexual orientation and gender diversity. The lack of systematic assessment precludes the ability to report whether sexual and/or gender minority individuals were included in research or clinic-based samples, or whether there may be differential prevention or treatment effects based on aspects of sexual orientation and/or gender. Thus, we (the authors) identified that an immediate recommendation to the eating disorders field (as proposed in the foundational Institute of Medicine report on lesbian, gay, bisexual, and transgender people [Institute of Medicine, 2011]), is for **research studies and clinic-based records to collect and report data on indicators of sexual orientation and gender in a systematic fashion to build an evidence base of the effectiveness of all current and newly developed treatments as they relate to sexual orientation and gender diversity (Recommendation 1)**. In the absence of information on evidence-based treatment considerations for sexual and gender minorities, we infer recommendations from epidemiologic research and perspectives from providers and individuals with lived experience with eating disorders to provide insights for how existing evidence-based treatments might be adapted for enhanced treatment of eating disorders among sexual and gender minorities. In particular, we noted a paucity of research on the diverse experiences of transgender and gender nonconforming individuals, with limited research focused on their lived experiences with eating disorders, or experiences as health providers and advocates. In order to prevent additional harms to gender minority communities, we deemed it vital for transgender and gender nonconforming people living with eating disorders to be included as direct voices and advocates in shaping future recommendations. Accordingly, throughout the chapter we made concerted efforts to center on the voices of transgender and gender nonconforming individuals with lived experiences with eating disorders, drawing from an original, brief online open-response survey we (coauthors EL and SS) collected via a community listserv that provides support and resources to sexual and gender minority individuals with eating disorders and to sexual and gender minority-serving health providers. The survey methods and procedures were reviewed and approved by the Institutional Review Board of San Diego State University.

Epidemiology and Engagement

How to Gather Information on Sexual Orientation and Gender, and the Need for Institutional Commitment to Change

Although we use the terms "sexual minority" and "gender minority" throughout the chapter, we acknowledge that these terms are largely demographic and public health terms, and may differ from the actual labels and identifiers that individuals who are categorized as belonging to sexual and gender minority populations may use to describe themselves. For example, a gay or lesbian patient may not self-identify as a "sexual minority," even if that is the term ascribed to gay men and lesbian women in scientific literature. "Sexual minorities" – a term often used in demographic and health research

52 *Jerel P. Calzo et al.*

to describe individuals who do not identify as heterosexual (e.g., those who identify as lesbian, gay, bisexual, and pansexual) – also include individuals who report attractions to people of same or multiple genders, and/or individuals who report engaging in sexual contact with people of the same or multiple genders (Institute of Medicine, 2011; Sexual Minority Assessment Research Team (SMART), 2009). Not all dimensions of sexual orientation are necessarily aligned. For example, a person who self-identifies as a lesbian (identity dimension) may have sex with both women and men (behavioral dimension); a man may identify as straight (identity dimension) and be attracted to individuals of all genders (sexual attractions dimension). "Gender minority" is a term used in demographic and health research to describe individuals whose current gender identity differs from the sex they were assigned at birth (e.g., an individual who was assigned female at birth and currently identifies as a man; individuals who identify as transgender or genderqueer; and individuals who do not identify as cisgender), and/or who express gender nonconformity (Institute of Medicine, 2011; The GenIUSS Group, 2014). Examples of gender minority identities include transgender man, trans woman, and non-binary people.

Becoming familiar with terminology for sexual orientation and gender, and the variable use of such important terms by sexual and gender minority individuals, researchers, and clinicians, are critical first steps in conducting research and implementing clinical practices to promote health equity. It may seem unorthodox to discuss language and terminology at length in the context of epidemiology, yet in our experience as researchers and health advocates, we believe that the overwhelming lack of basic training around concepts of sexual orientation and gender diversity – as fundamental aspects of human identity, culture, and health – are at the very root of the perpetuation of many health inequities faced by sexual and gender minority individuals. For instance, in the U.S.A. and Canada, the median time spent on LGBT content in medical schools is 5 hours (Obedin-Maliver et al., 2011). As two participants in the listserv survey stated:

> *I was an inpatient for about a year and never really felt comfortable talking about my identity (nonbinary transgender, asexual, panromantic) because it would inevitably end with me having to explain what it meant to my treatment team. I didn't feel like my treatment team could competently discuss the intersection between my eating disorder and my gender and sexuality, even when it might be relevant, because their knowledge and understanding was too limited and simplified.*

> *At the very baseline, not having to do "Gender 101" with every provider I see would be nice.*

Language, particularly the language ascribed to identity, is a working and living concept that transforms throughout time. Unfortunately, as has become apparent in research on sexual and gender minority health policy (e.g., health intake forms and electronic health records; Cahill et al., 2014), and survey research conducted for this chapter, institutional language is not always up to date. Problematic or outdated language can take the form of offering solely binary sex and gender fields on patient intake forms and surveys, "using potentially outdated" because many older transgender individuals may still use the terms "transsexual" or "gender reassignment surgery," whereas contemporary transgender youth may consider these terms to be outdated. **When interacting directly with patients and research participants, we recommend utilizing the terminology and identifiers that they themselves utilize (Recommendation 2).** For example, it is vital for providers to ask a patient what language they prefer to use in relation to their body or identity. A patient may feel uncomfortable being referred to as "male to female" and prefer to be called a trans woman. An intersex patient may not necessarily identify as transgender. As described by participants in the listserv survey, including and acknowledging an individual's sexual orientation and gender identity is critical to providing high-quality eating disorders care:

> *During my most recent experience with PHP treatment, I encountered intake forms that were heavily dependent on the gender binary, which made it difficult to disclose how my gender identity was impacting my eating behavior, as I didn't expect the staff to be competent at addressing that part of my presentation.*

> *People won't seek resources if they're non-binary for fear of being misgendered or misunderstood and doctors not knowing how to talk to trans people.*

Furthermore, sexual orientation and gender identity should not be confused or conflated with one another. Although sexual and gender minorities may be aggregated together under a community acronym, such as "LGBTQIA+" (lesbian, gay, bisexual, transgender, queer, intersex, asexual, aromantic, two spirit, and other identities and expressions), **all individuals have a sexual orientation and a gender identity** (e.g., straight/heterosexual transgender woman and pansexual cisgender man). As not all aspects of sexual orientation necessarily align, and not all aspects of gender necessarily align, **one cannot necessarily make overall assumptions about an individual's sexual orientation and gender based on limited information from singular aspects of identity.** For example, one cannot infer that a man who self-identifies as heterosexual or straight only has sex with women; it is possible for a transgender woman to identify as heterosexual and to be attracted to and have sex with people of all genders. **Taken together, the complexity of sexual orientation and gender indicate that gaining a comprehensive understanding of someone's sexual orientation and gender requires asking for information on multiple facets of sexual orientation and gender (Recommendation 3).**

54 *Jerel P. Calzo et al.*

Resources continue to grow on how to gather sexual orientation and gender data, as well as best practices for establishing environments that foster disclosure and discussion of sexual orientation and gender. In research, a compendium of tools to measure sexual orientation and gender is available via the National Institutes of Health Sexual & Gender Minority Research Office (https://dpcpsi.nih.gov/sgmro/measurement). In clinical and health practice settings, individuals may consult resources such as the National LGBT Health Education Center (https://www.lgbthealtheducation.org/), which contains training resources and modules, including a brief report on addressing eating disorders, body dissatisfaction, and obesity among sexual and gender minority youth (https://www.lgbthealtheducation.org/wp-content/uploads/2018/04/EatingDisordersBodyImageBrief.pdf). **At minimum, we recommend creating a research and clinical space that makes one comfortable to disclose sexual orientation and gender information. Establish norms that create a context of respect and inclusion of sexual orientation and gender diversity. Rather than assuming sexual orientation and gender identity, actively ask patients and participants about their identities and experiences (Recommendation 4).** For example, focusing on gender identity and expression, one practice to implement is to include the sharing of pronouns in all standard verbal introductions and intake forms to help make an environment comfortable and safe for everyone (e.g., verbal: "Hi, my name is Sam, I use they/them. What's your name?" written form: "Which pronouns do you use? She/her, He/him, They/them, Different pronouns than what are listed here _____ ").

However, given that training in LGBTQIA+ health in preparatory programs for health professions is generally insufficient (Obedin-Maliver et al., 2011; White et al., 2015), an ongoing institutional commitment to lifelong learning around LGBTQIA+ topics in health is imperative. As one listserv participant described:

> *Treatment providers need to be well educated on LGBTQ+ healthcare and need to show obvious signs that they are inclusive, including but not limited to appropriate terminology on forms, proper education of front-desk staff (if present), clinical and informational materials that illustrate a wide variety of people using services.*

Due to the shifting landscape of language and terminology used to describe the experiences of LGBTQIA+ populations, and the growing body of research on LGBTQIA+ populations, it is unlikely that the static content of standalone, competency-based education materials are sufficient to meet the training needs of a research and clinical workforce that will interact with diverse and dynamic LGBTQIA+ populations. Institutions that support researchers and health providers must commit to evaluating their practices to ensure they are respecting the populations they are engaging with, that they are learning from past mistakes and imbalances of power, and that they are continually focusing on new ways to foster connection. **Thus, beyond the**

need to develop more comprehensive substantive educational content on LGBTQIA+ populations for health researchers and professionals, we also recommend that institutions incorporate cultural humility approaches to pedagogy and practice that encourage self-evaluation and critique, acknowledgement of power imbalances, and a commitment to lifelong learning (Calzo et al., 2017; Grubb, Hutcherson, Amiel, Bogart, & Laird, 2013; Tervalon & Murray-García, 1998; **Recommendation 5)**.

Listserv participants described one concrete method by which institutions can foster connection to LGBTQIA+ communities – through networking with local community-based organizations. Such connections can be useful for developing additional supports and referrals for patients with eating disorders, and developing guidance for particular LGBTQIA+ subpopulations with eating disorders, such as LGBTQIA+ youth:

> *Create a network with other Queer and Trans organizations. Work collaboratively with local LGBTQIA+ organizations such as Gay Straight Alliances or Gender and Sexuality Alliances (GSAs) in schools in order to create support groups or workshops.*

Theoretical Frameworks for Understanding Disparities in Eating Disorder Risk

Theoretical models to account for sexual orientation and gender disparities in eating disorder risk generally center on minority stress and stigma and differential sociocultural exposures as underlying greater risk. In support of these theoretical models, data from clinical surveillance and case reports, community survey, and large-scale epidemiologic surveillance indicate that sexual and gender minority individuals overall report and experience a greater burden of disordered eating symptoms and clinical diagnoses of a range of eating disorders relative to their heterosexual and cisgender peers (Calzo et al., 2017; Diemer et al., 2015; Diemer, White Hughto, Gordon, Guss, Austin, & Reisner, 2018; McClain & Peebles, 2016). Although it is important for researchers, clinicians, and advocates to acknowledge the greater population-level risk for disordered eating among LGBTQIA+ populations, it is also important to avoid treating sexual minority and gender minority populations as monoliths, and assume that all sexual minority and gender minority individuals have eating disorders (i.e., that sexual orientation or gender identity *cause* eating disorders). **Researchers and clinicians should recognize that categorical representations of sexual orientation and gender are actually representing any number of processes that could be connected to eating disorder risk, including biological processes, discrimination, trauma, culture, and socialization (Krieger, 2003; Piran, 2017). Focus on the processes and determinants underlying eating disorders, which may or may not have a direct connection to sexual orientation and**

gender (Recommendation 6). This recommendation was illustrated by a listserv participant who, when asked, "What information would you want providers to know in serving LGBTQIA+ populations," wrote:

> *What microaggressions are, what heteronormativity is, that gender is performative, that there can be a link between mental illness and LGBTQIA+ identity without one causing the other, that eating disorders don't happen because "girls are afraid of becoming women."*

Growing research indicates that LGBTQIA+ individuals share in common the threat of facing elevated risk for victimization, discrimination, and harassment based on having socially stigmatized identities that are deemed a violation of society's cisnormative (i.e., binary gender as the norm) and heteronormative hegemonies (Institute of Medicine, 2011). With regard to eating disorder risk, such minority stress can directly and indirectly increase risk for disordered eating by increasing negative mental health states and use of disordered eating behaviors as a form of coping (Gordon, Austin, Krieger, White Hughto, & Reisner, 2016; Gordon, Austin, Pantalone, Baker, & Eiduson, 2019; Katz-Wise et al., 2015; Sevelius, 2013). Accordingly, researchers have found that shame, concealing one's sexual orientation, and experiencing discrimination can elevate eating disorder risk among sexual minorities (Bayer, Robert-McComb, Clopton, & Reich, 2017; Wang & Borders, 2017; Watson, Velez, Brownfield, & Flores, 2016). Furthermore, systemic stigma and discrimination against sexual and gender minority individuals in health care settings may mean that LGBTQIA+ individuals are less likely to seek healthcare when experiencing disordered eating symptoms or behaviors, to be screened for eating disorders, or to have access to eating disorders treatment that is affirming of their sexual orientation and/or gender-related experiences (Hatzenbuehler, Phelan, & Link, 2013; Jones et al., 2018). Inability to access treatment that is accepting of one's sexual orientation or gender identity can lead to elevation of eating disorder symptom severity and prevalence of untreated eating disorders among sexual and gender minority populations.

Regarding socialization factors, LGBTQIA+ individuals may be at risk for disordered eating due to differential sociocultural norms (e.g., community norms about attractiveness and ideal body types) that lead to the internalization of appearance ideals promoting disordered eating behaviors (e.g., drive for thinness and drive for muscularity; Feldman & Meyer, 2007; Gordon et al., 2016; McClain & Peebles, 2016; Tylka & Andorka, 2012). For example, norms regarding the centrality of physical attractiveness and appearance in sexual and dating partners among sexual minority men may contribute to elevated body dissatisfaction and disordered eating behaviors, including use of supplements and drugs in the pursuit of muscularity (Blashill, 2010; Brennan, Craig, & Thompson, 2012; Tiggemann, Martins, & Kirkbride, 2007; Tylka, 2012). **Stress and socialization factors underlying elevated risk for eating disorders are often interrelated**, as research on transgender and gender nonconforming populations highlights (Bockting et al., 2016; Bockting, Miner, Swinburne Romine, Hamilton, & Coleman, 2013; Gordon et al., 2016; Sevelius, 2013). One explanatory framework for heightened eating disorder risk among gender minorities is focused on body dissatisfaction connected to **gender dysphoria**. Gender dysphoria can be described as feelings of disconnectedness to and discomfort with one's birth-assigned gender and body. Dysphoria can be experienced around certain parts of the body (bottom dysphoria), gender presentation, or embodiment in general. Dysphoria in transgender men may present as wanting to "spot reduce" in certain areas of the body such as the chest or hips in order to gain a more Western-ideal "masculine" appearance. Dysphoria in transgender women may present as wanting to gain hips and a chest for a more Western-ideal "feminine" appearance. Nonbinary individuals may also experience dysphoria, which may elevate eating disorder risk. In a recent study, gender nonbinary individuals were found to be 3.16 times more likely to be diagnosed with an eating disorder than individuals with a binary gender identity (Diemer et al., 2018). Intersex individuals who have been subjected to nonconsensual surgery as children to conform to binary sex norms may experience dysphoria in a more complicated way. Intersex individuals are often assigned a sex at birth that they may not later identify with, a rate that studies estimate to be between 5% and 60% (Dutchen, 2020). Additionally, intersex individuals who have hormonal imbalances that manifest in hirsutism, gender-typical stature differences, and height differences also may experience an increased level of dysphoria. Lack of control over one's body, such as by means of forced intersex surgery or biological hormonal processes, can be sources of trauma and take agency away from a person's bodily autonomy. As one listserv participant described:

> Intersex has affected my eating disorder because for a long time I saw myself as different and have struggled with low-self esteem for a long time. I didn't have control over my body when I was young so the eating disorder helped me control my body and it also made me like myself better when I was thin.

However, while intersex and transgender identities can have overlap, they are distinctly different. It cannot be assumed that intersex individuals self-identify as members of transgender and gender nonconforming communities.

Gender dysphoria can manifest in myriad of ways, yet it is also important to remember that some transgender and gender nonconforming individuals do not experience gender dysphoria. Body dissatisfaction and disordered eating behaviors may disappear or lessen when transgender and gender non-conforming individuals experience gender affirmation or have access to gender affirming procedures (social [e.g., correct name used], legal [e.g., correct gender markers on identification cards], and medical [e.g., hormone therapy]; Sevelius, 2013; Testa, Rider, Haug, & Balsam, 2017).

58   Jerel P. Calzo et al.

Although not all gender minority individuals seek or obtain medicalized gender affirmation, the pursuit of gender affirmation is *paramount to survival* for many gender minorities, as experiencing gender affirmation can mitigate exposure to transphobia and violence (Bockting et al., 2016; Bockting et al., 2013; Sevelius, 2013). Seeking gender affirmation can either motivate adaptive behaviors (e.g., seeking social support, legal services, and medical services), or maladaptive behaviors (e.g., disordered eating behaviors and medically unsupervised hormone and silicone injections; Sevelius, 2013). For gender minorities, the binary gendered appearance ideal not only impacts body dissatisfaction, as it does for cisgender individuals, but is also a primary source of stress as it creates the standard by which gender nonconformity is defined and transphobia emerges (Gordon et al., 2016). Highlighting the complex interplay of gender dysphoria, gender identity, and eating disorder risk, one participant from the listserv shared:

> *My eating disorder was so completely tied up with my gender identity that the only way I have been able to recover has been to come out completely and transition. Treatment providers need to know that if they're not asking about gender and sexuality they may be missing the key pieces that will allow someone to recover.*

However, although gender affirmation may alleviate body dissatisfaction, it is not always a cure for eating disorders. That is, the "transition as cure" narrative (Algars, Alanko, Santtila, & Sandnabba, 2012; Jones et al., 2018; Testa et al., 2017) may not apply to all transgender and gender nonconforming individuals. Testimonials highlighted diversity of experiences, indicating that, for some people, gender affirmation procedures (e.g., hormones) can help, but that such procedures can also introduce a host of new stressors and unpredicted complications (e.g., sexual objectification and appearance ideals). Listserv participants also noted that intersex individuals may have no single way to "transition," and may opt out of altering their bodies.

Prevalence of Eating Disorders among Sexual Minority and Gender Minority Populations

A comprehensive review of the magnitude and direction of specific eating disorders and disordered eating behaviors is beyond the scope of this chapter; examples of recent systematic and scoping reviews on eating disorders and disordered eating behaviors among sexual minority populations include Calzo et al. (2017) and Meneguzzo et al. (2018), and Jones et al. (2016) for gender minority populations. Overall, relative to heterosexual peers, sexual minorities are at higher risk for presenting disordered eating symptoms (Laska et al., 2015; Shearer et al., 2015; Smith, Hawkeswood, Bodell, & Joiner, 2011; Yean et al., 2013) and specific disordered eating behaviors. Sexual minority females have a greater risk than heterosexual females of reporting overeating and binge eating (Laska et al., 2015; Mason & Lewis, 2015; Mason, 2016), purging (Austin,

Nelson, Birkett, Calzo, & Everett, 2013; Calzo, Sonneville, Scherer, Jackson, & Austin, 2016), fasting (Watson, Adjei, Saewyc, Homma, & Goodenow, 2017), and using diet pills (Austin et al., 2013; Watson et al., 2017). Similarly, sexual minority males have a greater risk than heterosexual males of purging (Austin et al., 2013; Matthews-Ewald, Zullig, & Ward, 2014; Watson et al., 2017), fasting (Watson et al., 2017), restrictive dieting (Matthews-Ewald et al., 2014), diet pill use (Austin et al., 2013; Matthews-Ewald et al., 2014; Watson et al., 2017), and using drugs and supplements to increase muscle mass (Blashill & Safren, 2014; Blashill, Calzo, Griffiths, & Murray, 2017). In their review of recent sexual orientation eating disorder disparities research, Calzo et al. (2017) found that studies with adequate power to examine differences in sexual orientation by subgroups or dimensions of sexual orientation (i.e., behavior, identity, and attractions) indicate that not all sexual minority subgroups are at significantly greater risk for disordered eating behaviors compared to heterosexuals. In addition, sexual orientation disparities appear to be more pronounced among cisgender men than among cisgender women (Calzo et al., 2017).

Scant research on gender minorities indicates elevated risk for disordered eating behaviors (Guss, Williams, Reisner, Austin, & Katz-Wise, 2017) and eating disorder diagnoses (Avila, Golden, & Aye, 2019; Diemer et al., 2018; Donaldson et al., 2018) relative to cisgender individuals, with potentially elevated risk among transgender individuals who are also sexual minorities (Diemer et al., 2015). Consistent with the gender affirmation framework for understanding elevated risk for health inequities among gender minorities, there is evidence that transgender men and women exhibit elevated body dissatisfaction for gender-identifying body parts (Witcomb et al., 2015), that transgender individuals may engage in disordered eating behaviors, particularly dietary restriction, as a means of suppressing the expression of biological sex characteristics (Algars et al., 2012; Strandjord, Ng, & Rome, 2015), and that experiencing gender affirmation and access to gender affirmation procedures can mitigate risk for body dissatisfaction and disordered eating behaviors (Testa et al., 2017). However, other research indicates that body dissatisfaction and disordered eating behaviors can persist even after experiencing gender affirmation procedures (Gordon et al., 2016; Gordon et al., 2019).

A limited number of studies have investigated intersectionality by race/ethnicity, with studies noting elevated prevalence of overall symptoms (De Santis et al., 2012), diet pills and purging (Austin et al., 2013), and steroid use (Blashill et al., 2017) among racial/ethnic sexual minorities and among racial/ethnic gender minorities (Gordon et al., 2016; Gordon et al., 2019). The small, but growing literature on intersectional influence of sexual orientation, gender identity, and race/ethnicity in eating disorder risk indicates that the concepts of sexual minority identity and gender minority identity cannot be treated as monoliths. Additionally, much of the epidemiologic surveillance studies of disordered eating behaviors is derived from large national surveys and cohorts, such as National College Health Assessment, Youth Risk Behavior

60 *Jerel P. Calzo et al.*

Surveillance Survey, and the Growing Up Today Study. Although a benefit of using such data is providing adequate power for health disparities analyses, limitations include the predominant focus on the experiences of adolescents and young adults, inadequate assessment of body image and disordered eating behaviors that encapsulate the diverse range of experiences of sexual and gender minority individuals, and inadequate assessment of risk and protective factors that are unique to sexual and gender minority populations. Large-scale epidemiologic studies may enable analysis of the magnitude of health disparities; yet, they may mask (due to lack of assessment of relevant constructs) the processes contributing to the health disparities. **More research is needed on examining intersectionality and diverse identities among sexual and gender minority populations, and the specific processes (stress, socialization, or otherwise) contributing to health disparities (Recommendation 7).** Sexual and gender minority populations are themselves diverse populations, whose variegated health experiences are likely shaped by diversity related to age, weight, socioeconomic position, race, ethnicity, and other factors (Brennan et al., 2013; Gordon et al., 2016; Moore, 2012).

The relative absence of research on diverse sexual and gender minority populations echoed the sentiments of listserv participants. For example, participants indicated the lack of representation of LGBTQIA+ people of color, and lack of portrayals of fat people in positive ways in outreach materials in research and clinical treatment settings:

> *Take a look at your marketing strategies, do your posters, pamphlets, social media, and website include images of trans and gender nonconforming folx? Do they portray QTPOC (Queer trans people of color) positively?*

Participants indicated the need to shift the stereotype of eating disorders (i.e., that they only affect thin, cisgender, white, and upper-class adolescent girls) to be broader and more inclusive. In addition, the participants noted that the lack of diverse representation was not only apparent in outreach materials, but also among those represented in the academic and clinical spaces.

> *[I recommend] increased racial diversity in treatment settings—both patients and clinicians.*

> *Having different kinds of people giving treatment that aren't white doctors would be a big help. It's important to see yourself.*

> *For me, personally, and others I know who are people of color, the biggest barrier is honestly just that when you go on the website or ask others about their experiences with treatment programs around here, every single person that is on their staff page is what appears to be a skinny cis white woman. And their websites often feature yoga and*

meditation in ways that feel culturally appropriative. I guess my feeling is that if they don't even have any people of color on staff, they don't really seem to value diversity and it makes me feel like they probably won't be competent around gender stuff either. So much of what I am able to eat is centered around my ethnic culture, and I don't trust that white women using culturally appropriative yoga will be able to understand and respect that.

The lack of diversity described by listserv participants highlights perceptions of systemic issues of racism, homophobia, transphobia, and weightism that foster academic and medical mistrust among LGBTQIA+ individuals. As potential systemic issues, insufficient diversity among researchers and treatment staff may also constrain epidemiologic research on diverse experiences and the development of evidence-based treatment for diverse sexual and gender minority populations. Building upon the previous recommendation for fostering an institutional commitment to critical self-evaluation and connection, an additional institutional commitment toward diversity and inclusion of diverse research and clinical staff may enhance progress toward development of eating disorders research and treatment programming for diverse LGBTQIA+ populations.

Treatment

We begin this section by reviewing the state of the evidence on evidence-based treatment for sexual and gender minority individuals with eating disorders. We then provide our recommendations for how to advance to field, drawing from our review of theory, epidemiology, and original data collection from individuals with lived experience and health providers. Overall, the lack of evidence for evidence-based treatment is generally due to the systematic exclusion of LGBTQIA+ individuals from research evaluating evidence-based treatment and intervention techniques, either through lack of measurement of sexual orientation and gender at intake, and/or inadequate inclusion and recruitment. In addition, as we note in the recommendations, systemic challenges and barriers in academic research and clinical practice with sexual and gender minority populations must be addressed in order to advance LGBTQIA+ health equity overall, particularly around eating disorders.

The Current State of Evidence-Based Treatment for LGBTQIA+ Individuals with Eating Disorders

Despite overwhelming evidence of sexual orientation and gender disparities in disordered eating behaviors, there is very limited data on whether existing treatments are as effective for sexual and gender minorities. Indeed, few eating disorder treatment outcome studies have explicitly assessed sexual orientation or gender identity and we are unaware of any published studies evaluating the efficacy of eating disorder treatment among sexual or gender minority patients. In the absence of these data, empirically supported treatments within the broader eating disorder literature may be helpful for sexual and gender minority patients, including enhanced cognitive behavioral therapy for eating disorders (CBT-E; Fairburn, 2008), family-based treatment (FBT; Courturier, Kimber, & Szatmari, 2013), and dialectical behavior therapy (DBT; Safer, Telch, & Agras, 2001). These treatments and potential areas for expansion to sexual and gender minority patients are briefly described below.

CBT-E was developed based on the transdiagnostic cognitive behavioral theory of eating disorders, which suggests that the core psychopathology of eating disorders involves overevaluation of shape and weight, and, as a result, individuals engage in maladaptive behaviors to achieve body change (Fairburn, 2008). CBT-E is delivered across approximately 20 sessions and is highly individualized, which allows for flexibility when working with sexual and gender minorities. CBT-E focuses on regularizing food intake (Stage 1), reviewing progress (Stage 2), targeting individualized maintenance factors for eating pathology including weight and shape concerns, daily stressors, and extreme dietary restraint (Stage 3), and relapse prevention (Stage 4). A promising future direction for research in this area may be adapting current evidence-based treatments, such as CBT-E, to incorporate more directly minority stressors, as has been done in the broader mental health field (Pachankis, Hatzenbuehler, Rendina, Safren, & Parsons, 2015).

FBT has demonstrated efficacy for adolescents with eating disorders, particularly those with anorexia nervosa, and consists of approximately 20 sessions delivered in three phases (Loeb & Le Grange, 2009). Phase I focuses on weight restoration (for anorexia nervosa only) and normalization of eating behaviors. During this phase, parents are given control over their child's eating. In Phase II, control over eating is gradually returned to the adolescent. Phase III consists of focusing on interpersonal difficulties and other developmental issues that may play a role in the child's eating pathology. Phase III provides opportunities to incorporate issues relevant to sexual and gender minorities, including family's and others' support of the child's identity and the role of sociocultural influences or stressors (e.g., bullying and discrimination) in influencing eating disorder symptoms. Given that family acceptance is key for sexual and gender minorities, particularly among youth, family-based therapy may be particularly relevant (McClain & Peebles, 2016). However, special considerations may need to be made when using FBT with families that may be rejecting, as may be the case for some LGBTQIA+ individuals. Indeed, preliminary research supports that a separated family therapy may be more efficacious for families with high levels of parental criticism (Eisler et al., 2000), and this may extend to non-affirming families as well. Many transgender people may have complex relationships with their families of origin. Providers must also recognize that there may be a lack of spousal/partner acceptance. Treatment providers should take greater care from first point of contact (screening) in understanding that chosen family, case managers, or if vocalized – nobody – may be involved during treatment and that the treatment team may have to work with the client to build a support network or care web. This is especially important in treatment centers which have scheduled times for family therapy, inpatient centers which have visiting hours, or treatment centers which use the Maudsley Method approach.

DBT is a cognitive behavioral treatment originally developed for borderline personality disorder and incorporates both behavioral and acceptance-based interventions across 20 individual and group therapy sessions. The theoretical model underlying DBT suggests that maladaptive eating behaviors function as a misguided attempt to regulate unwanted emotions (Wiser & Telch, 1999). As such, DBT focuses on the acquisition of effective emotion regulation strategies. DBT skills training groups focus on mindfulness, emotion regulation, distress tolerance, and interpersonal effectiveness skills modules. Individual sessions focus on three primary targets: life-threatening behaviors (e.g., suicidality), therapy-interfering behaviors (e.g., homework noncompletion and therapy nonattendance), and quality-of-life interfering behaviors (e.g., body checking, restriction, and eating disorder behaviors). DBT's individualized focus may allow for flexibility in incorporating factors related to minority stress and interpersonal victimization and many of the distress tolerance and mindfulness skills may help buffer against more general minority stressors.

Limited research has focused on developing or adapting novel prevention or treatment protocols. Indeed, the only such programs we are aware of within the eating disorder field are eating disorder prevention programs focused on sexual minority men (Brown & Keel, 2015; Feldman, Torino, & Swift, 2011). Both programs focused on adapting the Body Project (Becker, Smith, & Ciao, 2005) a dissonance-based, peer-led intervention designed to reduce eating disorder risk, previously developed for college women. Feldman et al. (2011) adapted aspects of the Body Project to improve body satisfaction and eating behaviors among gay and bisexual men living with HIV/AIDS; however, the published work in this area focused predominately on acceptability of the intervention and did not provide data on efficacy (Feldman et al., 2011). Brown & Keel (2015) successfully adapted the Body Project into the PRIDE Body Project for use with 18–30 years old, sexual minority men, and demonstrated reductions in eating pathology, body dissatisfaction, body-ideal internalization, and self- and potential partner-objectification at postintervention though a 4-week follow-up (Brown & Keel, 2015). Results supported that the impact of the treatment was primarily through reductions in body-ideal internalization, which supports prior studies emphasizing the role of sociocultural influences on eating disorder risk. Although these results are promising, **more work is needed to develop evidence-based practices to prevent eating disorders and disordered eating behaviors in sexual minority individuals of all genders (Recommendations 8)**.

Similar to treatment research in sexual minorities, minimal research on specific treatments for gender minorities has been conducted. However, initial

64 *Jerel P. Calzo et al.*

qualitative work on treatment experiences and recommendations for providers has yielded critical information for future research in this area. A qualitative survey of treatment experiences for transgender and gender-diverse individuals with an eating disorder identified multiple themes regarding unique factors affecting treatment and barriers to treatment (Duffy, Henkel, & Earnshaw, 2016). These included the unique role of body dysphoria and relationship with the physical body as an underlying factor contributing to the eating disorder (e.g., restriction of food intake to minimize of breast tissue), negative experiences with clinicians, and fear of disclosure of identity with therapists or treatment centers due to stigma and discrimination. Participants also noted the need for greater facilitation of access to care within the transgender community. Consistent with this, qualitative research and results from case series highlight the importance of interdisciplinary care with gender management and mental health specialists (Donaldson et al., 2018) to ensure affirmative treatment. In terms of specific treatment strategies, research on gender confirming medical interventions and cross-sex hormones treatment support that these intervention may help alleviate body image concerns and eating disorder symptoms in transgender populations, potentially via gender affirmation (Jones et al., 2018; Testa et al., 2017). Critically, future research is needed to help better understand whether specific eating disorder prevention programs and treatments are effective with gender minority populations and how specific risk factors for this group may be incorporated more directly into intervention efforts.

Enhancing Evidence-Based Treatments for Eating Disorders among LGBTQIA+ Individuals

Come from a Position of Humility, Sensitivity, and Respect (Recommendation 9)

In the absence of evidence evaluating the formal efficacy of various treatments for sexual and gender minority patients, practices rooted in cultural humility, sensitivity, and respect for persons are fundamental to building trust and preventing additional harm when providing care and treatment. For example, providers with inadequate training around transgender identity can create an ineffective or harmful treatment environment (Duffy et al., 2016). Participants in the listserv who provided testimonials described situations in which access to gender affirmation was limited, or even actively withheld (potentially as a means of enforcing compliance with eating disorders treatment):

> *Ensure that your center or practice allows trans patients to have access to hormone therapy. Train your staff in being considerate to trans patients needs. Hormones should be treated like any other medication prescribed to a patient and they should be delivered on time and not withheld as punishment.*

> *Withholding gender-affirming treatment is harmful. Best practice is to treat both the*

eating disorder and support folks in gender affirming care (hormones, using the patient's pronouns, using the patient's chosen name if applicable, allowing gender affirming clothing, etc.).

Furthermore, lack of sensitivity to the needs and experiences of transgender individuals can lead to harmful assumptions about the applicability of messaging and techniques derived from other (likely cisgender female) populations. For example, promoting messages about body positivity and body acceptance without consideration of gender identity or gender affirmation can be disrespectful or potentially harmful to transgender and gender non-conforming individuals:

I was not out to everyone when I started treatment and I did not feel comfortable coming out in that setting I am a trans man and I found the emphasis on "loving my body" and "embracing my curves" to be counterproductive.

"Love your body" is not a useful message. Transition-related care is essential to the well-being of a person, and therefore much more likely to help than hurt in ED treatment.

Acknowledge and Address LGBTQIA+ Oppression-Related Trauma (Recommendation 10)

Although it is understood that trauma is connected to the development of eating disorders, and that sexual and gender minority populations experience elevated discrimination and trauma due to social stigma (Hatzenbuehler et al., 2013; Hendricks & Testa, 2012; Testa et al., 2017), there is a gap in translational research in applying the understanding of LGBTQIA+ trauma to eating disorders treatment. Treatment providers should always be aware of the possibility that LGBTQIA+ patients have experienced trauma due to social stigma. For example, gender minorities are more likely than cisgender individuals to experience family rejection, homelessness, and bullying, and to participate in sex work (Fitzgerald, Patterson, Hickey, Biko, & Tobin, 2015; Mizock & Lewis, 2008). These traumatic experiences can alter the ways in which an eating disorder may develop and how a treatment team may approach treating a client. As one listserv participant described:

Trans people are often very scared of institutions and hospitals, for very good reason. Validate those fears, find ways to address needs without them needing to interact with those systems, and do everything you can to make sure they are safe within those systems. Trans people are often used to lying in order to get the care they need. Don't be surprised. Don't judge or label that. It comes from what we need to survive. If a patient needs to be sent to a medical hospital from a clinic or eating disorder unit, always send them with a staff member that they trust.

66   Jerel P. Calzo et al.

Increase Accessibility of Eating Disorders Treatment (Recommendation 11)

Sexual and gender minorities face multiple forms of oppression that may affect their access to eating disorders treatment. Based on testimonials gathered, "accessibility" included not only financial accessibility (i.e., fiscal and health insurance), but also physical accessibility to individuals of diverse genders, bodies, and abilities:

> *A significant barrier is financial access to appropriate providers. Most providers do not accept insurance and very few accept state funded insurance. Organizations that fund services are helpful.*

> *Understand the reality that poverty and food insecurity are often contributors to our eating disorders. It is difficult to face that reality as a provider but a successful treatment plan depends on it.*

> *Increased accessibility of treatment (on bus lines, cheaper, covered by Medicaid, wheelchair accessible, blind/Deaf/HoH accessible, etc.).*

> *Gender neutral bathrooms, not being gender separated for groups or meals.*

> *Making sure your centers are ramp accessible, providing captions on all videos shown in treatment, ASL interpreters available, sensory (not using perfumes or fragrances in centers).*

Increase the Diversity of Treatment Center Staff, and Support Diversity, Equity, and Inclusion Practices (Recommendation 12)

As described previously, issues of diversity, equity, and inclusion are of critical importance for advancing health equity research and evidence-based treatment for sexual and gender minority populations. The review of the epidemiologic research and data collected for this chapter reveal the dearth of studies focused on diverse LGBTQIA+ populations (i.e., by race and ethnicity, weight, socioeconomic status, etc.) and the perception that eating disorders research and treatment teams are not inclusive of diverse LGBTQIA+ individuals. In the words of listserv participants, recommendations include:

> *Hire openly queer and trans staff. It is important for your patients to have someone they connect to and see themselves represented even before entering any kind of treatment.*

> *Fat dietitians or researchers in the nutrition fields [who] promote Health at Every Size (HAES). It can be life saving in LGBTQIA+ folks to learn to love their bodies.*

Recommendation 1	Collect and report data on indicators of sexual orientation and gender in a systematic fashion to build an evidence base of the effectiveness of treatments as they relate to sexual orientation and gender diversity
Recommendation 2	When interacting with patients and research participants, use the sexual orientation and gender terms and identifiers that they use
Recommendation 3	Gaining a comprehensive understanding of someone's sexual orientation and gender requires asking for information on multiple facets of sexual orientation and gender
Recommendation 4	Create a research and clinical space that makes one comfortable to disclose sexual orientation and gender information. Establish norms that create a context of respect and inclusion of sexual orientation and gender diversity. Rather than assuming sexual orientation and gender identity, actively ask patients and participants about their identities and experiences.
Recommendation 5	Incorporate cultural humility approaches to pedagogy and practice that encourage self-evaluation and critique, acknowledgement of power imbalances, and a commitment to lifelong learning
Recommendation 6	Sexual orientation and gender are not the only relevant aspects of an individual's identity or experience. Furthermore, sexual orientation and gender do not cause eating disorders. Focus on the processes and determinants underlying eating disorders, which may or may not have a direct connection to sexual orientation and gender.
Recommendation 7	More research is needed on examining intersectionality and diverse identities among sexual and gender minority populations, and the specific processes (stress, socialization, or otherwise) contributing to health disparities.
Recommendation 8	More work is needed to develop evidence-based practices to *prevent* eating disorders and disordered eating behaviors in sexual and gender minorities.
Recommendation 9	Come from a position of humility, sensitivity, and respect
Recommendation 10	Acknowledge and address LGBTQIA+ oppression-related trauma
Recommendation 11	Increase accessibility of eating disorders treatment
Recommendation 12	Increase the diversity of treatment center staff, and support diversity, equity, and inclusion practices

Figure 3.1 Recommendations for Advancing Research and Evidence-Based Treatment for Eating Disorders among LGBTQIA+ Populations.

However, as one listserv participant noted, it is also important to acknowledge that LGBTQIA+ staff have more to contribute than just their experiences as being members of a specific community, "Be careful not to tokenize trans staff either trans folks are NOT just their identity!" Other methods to create a welcoming clinical space include visible allyship:

68 *Jerel P. Calzo et al.*

Be a visible ally. This means hanging up rainbow and trans flags or posters on the wall in your centers.

Make sure your staff are enforcing other patients to use the correct names and pronouns for your trans patients. If someone is bullying a trans patient, make sure there is a safety plan or regulation policy at your workplace for zero tolerance.

Atmospheres of inclusivity at all treatment locations, with a willingness to back that up (i.e., if a cis-person is uncomfortable with the trans person there, the facility will back up the trans person's right to be there).

Conclusion

We offer a brief review of the state of the research on eating disorders and eating disorders treatment among sexual and gender minorities, discussed the state of evidence-based treatment, and provide 12 recommendations to advance research and the development of evidence-based practices for eating disorders treatment among sexual and gender minority populations (summarized in Figure 3.1). We hope that the evidence reviewed and critical limitations highlighted in this chapter, and particularly the original and powerful insights presented by the LGBTQIA+ community members and health providers who shared their experiences with eating disorders treatment, spark conversations about how the eating disorders field can make essential advances to address the gaps in evidence-based treatment for underserved LGBTQIA+ populations with eating disorders.

References

Algars, M., Alanko, K., Santtila, P., & Sandnabba, N. K. (2012). Disordered eating and gender identity disorder: A qualitative study. *Eating Disorders*, *20*(4), 300–311. https://doi.org/10.1080/10640266.2012.668482.

Austin, S. B., Nelson, L. A., Birkett, M. A., Calzo, J. P., & Everett, B. (2013). Eating disorder symptoms and obesity at the intersections of gender, ethnicity, and sexual orientation in US high school students. *American Journal of Public Health*, *103*(2), e16–e22. https://doi.org/10.2105/ajph.2012.301150.

Avila, J. T., Golden, N. H., & Aye, T. (2019). Eating disorder screening in transgender youth. *The Journal of Adolescent Health: Official Publication of the Society for Adolescent Medicine*. https://doi.org/10.1016/j.jadohealth.2019.06.011.

Bayer, V., Robert-McComb, J. J., Clopton, J. R., & Reich, D. A. (2017). Investigating the influence of shame, depression, and distress tolerance on the relationship between internalized homophobia and binge eating in lesbian and bisexual women. *Eating Behaviors*, *24*, 39–44. https://doi.org/10.1016/j.eatbeh.2016.12.001.

Becker, C. B., Smith, L. M., & Ciao, A. C. (2005). Reducing eating disorder risk factors in sorority members: A randomized trial. *Behavior Therapy*, *36*, 245–253. Retrieved from http://ac.els-cdn.com/S0005789405800735/1-s2.0-S0005789405800735-main.pdf?_tid=0a57709a-0db1-11e7-9752-00000aacb362&acdnat=1490044149_48dea0ab83bb5b2d491d627506a31b79.

Treatment for LGBTQIA+ Individuals 69

Blashill, A. J. (2010). Elements of male body image: Prediction of depression, eating pathology and social sensitivity among gay men. *Body Image, 7*(4), 310–316. https://doi.org/10.1016/j.bodyim.2010.07.006.

Blashill, A. J., Calzo, J. P., Griffiths, S., & Murray, S. B. (2017). Anabolic steroid misuse among US adolescent boys: Disparities by sexual orientation and race/ethnicity. *American Journal of Public Health, 107*(2), 319–322. https://doi.org/10.2105/AJPH.2016.303566.

Blashill, A. J., & Safren, S. A. (2014). Sexual orientation and anabolic-androgenic steroids in US adolescent boys. *Pediatrics, 133*(3), 469–475. https://doi.org/10.1542/peds.2013-2768.

Bockting, W. O., Coleman, E., Deutsch, M. B., Guillamon, A., Meyer, I., Meyer, W., ... Ettner, R. (2016). Adult development and quality of life of transgender and gender nonconforming people. *Current Opinion in Endocrinology & Diabetes and Obesity, 23*(2), 188–197. https://doi.org/10.1097/MED.0000000000000232.

Bockting, W. O., Miner, M. H., Swinburne Romine, R. E., Hamilton, A., & Coleman, E. (2013). Stigma, mental health, and resilience in an online sample of the US transgender population. *American Journal of Public Health, 103*(5), 943–951. https://doi.org/10.2105/AJPH.2013.301241.

Brennan, D. J., Asakura, K., George, C., Newman, P. A., Giwa, S., Hart, T. A., ... Betancourt, G. (2013). "Never reflected anywhere": Body image among ethnoracialized gay and bisexual men. *Body Image, 10*(3), 389–398. https://doi.org/10.1016/j.bodyim.2013.03.006.

Brennan, D. J., Craig, S. L., & Thompson, D. E. A. (2012). Factors associated with a drive for muscularity among gay and bisexual men. *Culture, Health & Sexuality, 14*(1), 1–15. https://doi.org/10.1080/13691058.2011.619578.

Brown, T. A., & Keel, P. K. (2015). A randomized controlled trial of a peer co-led dissonance-based eating disorder prevention program for gay men. *Behaviour Research and Therapy, 74*, 1–10. https://doi.org/10.1016/j.brat.2015.08.008.

Cahill, S., Singal, R., Grasso, C., King, D., Mayer, K., Baker, K., & Makadon, H. (2014). Do ask, do tell: High levels of acceptability by patients of routine collection of sexual orientation and gender identity data in four diverse American Community Health Centers. *PLoS One, 9*(9), e107104. https://doi.org/10.1371/journal.pone.0107104.

Calzo, J. P., Blashill, A. J., Brown, T. A., & Argenal, R. L. (2017). Eating disorders and disordered weight and shape control behaviors in sexual minority populations. *Current Psychiatry Reports, 19*(8), 49. https://doi.org/10.1007/s11920-017-0801-y.

Calzo, J. P., Melchiono, M., Richmond, T., Leibowitz, S., Argenal, R., Goncalves, A., ... Burke, P. (2017). Lesbian, gay, bisexual, and transgender adolescent health: An interprofessional case discussion. *MedEdPORTAL Publications, 13*(13). https://doi.org/10.15766/mep_2374-8265.10615.

Calzo, J. P., Sonneville, K. R., Scherer, E. A., Jackson, B., & Austin, S. B. (2016). Gender conformity and use of laxatives and muscle-building products in adolescents and young adults. *Pediatrics, 138*(2). Retrieved from http://pediatrics.aappublications.org/content/138/2/e20154073.abstract.

Courturier, J., Kimber, M., & Szatmari, P. (2013). Efficacy of family-based treatment for adolescents with eating disorders: A systematic review and meta-analysis. *International Journal of Eating Disorders, 46*, 3–11.

De Santis, J. P., Layerla, D. M., Barroso, S., Gattamorta, K. A., Sanchez, M., & Prado, G. J. (2012). Predictors of eating attitudes and behaviors among gay hispanic

70 *Jerel P. Calzo et al.*

men. *Archives of Psychiatric Nursing, 26*(2), 111–26. https://doi.org/10.1016/j.apnu. 2011.06.003.

Diemer, E. W., Grant, J. D., Munn-Chernoff, M. A., Patterson, D. A., & Duncan, A. E. (2015). Gender identity, sexual orientation, and eating-related pathology in a National Sample of College Students. *The Journal of Adolescent Health: Official Publication of the Society for Adolescent Medicine, 57*(2), 144–149. https://doi.org/10.1016/j.jadohealth. 2015.03.003.

Diemer, E. W., White Hughto, J. M., Gordon, A. R., Guss, C., Austin, S. B., & Reisner, S. L. (2018). Beyond the binary: Differences in eating disorder prevalence by gender identity in a transgender sample. *Transgender Health, 3*(1), 17–23. https:// doi.org/10.1089/trgh.2017.0043.

Donaldson, A. A., Hall, A., Neukirch, J., Kasper, V., Simones, S., Gagnon, S., ... Forcier, M. (2018). Multidisciplinary care considerations for gender nonconforming adolescents with eating disorders: A case series. *International Journal of Eating Disorders, 51*(5), 475–479. https://doi.org/10.1002/eat.22868.

Duffy, M. E., Henkel, K. E., & Earnshaw, V. A. (2016). Transgender clients' experiences of eating disorder treatment. *Journal of LGBT Issues in Counseling, 10*(3), 136–149. https://doi.org/10.1080/15538605.2016.1177806.

Duffy, M. E., Henkel, K. E., & Joiner, T. E. (2019). Prevalence of self-injurious thoughts and behaviors in transgender individuals with eating disorders: A national study. *The Journal of Adolescent Health: Official Publication of the Society for Adolescent Medicine, 64*(4), 461–466. https://doi.org/10.1016/j.jadohealth.2018.07.016.

Dutchen, S. (2020, January). The body, the self: The care of people with intersex traits evolves as clinicians and researchers learn more – and listen more. *Harvard Medicine Magazine.* Retrieved from https://hms.harvard.edu/magazine/lgbtq-health/body-self.

Eisler, I., Dare, C., Hodes, M., Russell, G., Dodge, E., & Le Grange, D. (2000). Family therapy for adolescent anorexia nervosa: The results of a controlled comparison of two family interventions. *Journal of Child Psychology and Psychiatry, and Allied Disciplines, 41*(6), 727–736. Retrieved from http://www.ncbi.nlm.nih.gov/pubmed/11039685.

Fairburn, C. G. (2008). *Cognitive behavior therapy and eating disorders.* New York, NY: Guildford Press.

Feldman, M. B., & Meyer, I. H. (2007). Eating disorders in diverse lesbian, gay, and bisexual populations. *The International Journal of Eating Disorders, 40*(3), 218–226.

Feldman, M. B., Torino, J. A., & Swift, M. (2011). A group intervention to improve body image satisfaction and dietary habits in gay and bisexual men living with HIV/AIDS. *Eating Disorders, 19*(5), 377–391. https://doi.org/10.1080/10640266.2011.609084.

Fitzgerald, E., Patterson, S., Hickey, D., Biko, C., & Tobin, H. (2015). *Meaningful work: transgender experiences in the sex trade.* Retrieved from https://www.transequality.org/ sites/default/files/Meaningful Work-Full Report_FINAL_3.pdf.

Gordon, A. R., Austin, S. B., Krieger, N., White Hughto, J. M., & Reisner, S. L. (2016). "I have to constantly prove to myself, to people, that I fit the bill": Perspectives on weight and shape control behaviors among low-income, ethnically diverse young transgender women. *Social Science & Medicine (1982), 165*, 141–149. https://doi.org/10.1016/j.socscimed.2016.07.038.

Gordon, A. R., Austin, S. B., Pantalone, D. W., Baker, A. M., & Eiduson, R. (2019). Appearance ideals and eating disorders risk among LGBTQ college students: The Being Ourselves Living in Diverse Bodies (BOLD) study. *Journal of Adolescent Health, 64*(2), S43–S44.

Grubb, H., Hutcherson, H., Amiel, J., Bogart, J., & Laird, J. (2013). Cultural humility with lesbian, gay, bisexual, and transgender populations: A novel curriculum in LGBT health for clinical medical students. *MedEdPORTAL Publications, 9.* https:// doi.org/doi.org/10.15766/mep_2374-8265.9542.

Guss, C. E., Williams, D. N., Reisner, S. L., Austin, S. B., & Katz-Wise, S. L. (2017). Disordered weight management behaviors, nonprescription steroid use, and weight perception in transgender youth. *The Journal of Adolescent Health: Official Publication of the Society for Adolescent Medicine, 60*(1), 17–22. https://doi.org/10.1016/j.jadohealth. 2016.08.027.

Hatzenbuehler, M. L., Phelan, J. C., & Link, B. G. (2013). Stigma as a fundamental cause of population health inequalities. *American Journal of Public Health, 103*(5), 813–821. https://doi.org/10.2105/ajph.2012.301069.

Hendricks, M., & Testa, R. (2012). A conceptual framework for clinical work with transgender and gender nonconforming clients: An adaptation of the Minority Stress Model. *Professional Psychology, Research and Practice, 43,* 460–7.

Institute of Medicine. (2011). *The health of lesbian, gay, bisexual, and transgender people: Building a foundation for better understanding.* Washington, DC: The National Academies Press. https://doi.org/10.17226/13128.

Jones, B. A., Haycraft, E., Bouman, W. P., Brewin, N., Claes, L., & Arcelus, J. (2018). Risk factors for eating disorder psychopathology within the treatment seeking transgender population: The role of cross-sex hormone treatment. *European Eating Disorders Review, 26*(2), 120–128. https://doi.org/10.1002/erv.2576.

Jones, B. A., Haycraft, E., Murjan, S., & Arcelus, J. (2016). Body dissatisfaction and disordered eating in trans people: A systematic review of the literature. *International Review of Psychiatry (Abingdon, England), 28*(1), 81–94. https://doi.org/10.3109/09540261. 2015.1089217.

Katz-Wise, S. L., Scherer, E. A., Calzo, J. P., Sarda, V., Jackson, B., Haines, J., & Austin, S. B. (2015). Sexual minority stressors, internalizing symptoms, and unhealthy eating behaviors in sexual minority youth. *Annals of Behavioral Medicine: A Publication of the Society of Behavioral Medicine.* https://doi.org/10.1007/s12160-015-9718-z.

Krieger, N. (2003). Genders, sexes, and health: What are the connections–and why does it matter? *International Journal of Epidemiology, 32*(4), 652–657. Retrieved from http://www.ncbi.nlm.nih.gov/pubmed/12913047.

Laska, M. N., Van Kim, N. A., Erickson, D. J., Lust, K., Eisenberg, M. E., & Rosser, B. R. S. (2015). Disparities in weight and weight behaviors by sexual orientation in college students. *American Journal of Public Health, 105,* 111–121.

Loeb, K. L., & Le Grange, D. (2009). Family-based treatment for adolescent eating disorders: Current status, new applications and future directions. *International Journal of Child and Adolescent Health, 2*(2), 243–254.

Mason, T. B. (2016). Binge eating and overweight and obesity among young adult Lesbians. *LGBT Health, 3*(6), 472–476. https://doi.org/10.1089/lgbt.2015.0119.

Mason, T. B., & Lewis, R. J. (2015). Minority stress and binge eating among lesbian and bisexual women. *Journal of Homosexuality, 62*(7), 971–992. https://doi.org/10. 1080/00918369.2015.1008285.

Matthews-Ewald, M. R., Zullig, K. J., & Ward, R. M. (2014). Sexual orientation and disordered eating behaviors among self-identified male and female college students. *Eating Behaviors, 15*(3), 441–444. https://doi.org/10.1016/j.eatbeh.2014. 05.002.

72 *Jerel P. Calzo et al.*

McClain, Z., & Peebles, R. (2016). Body image and eating disorders among Lesbian, Gay, Bisexual, and Transgender youth. *Pediatric Clinics of North America, 63*(6), 1079–1090. https://doi.org/10.1016/j.pcl.2016.07.008.

Meneguzzo, P., Collantoni, E., Gallicchio, D., Busetto, P., Solmi, M., Santonastaso, P., & Favaro, A. (2018). Eating disorders symptoms in sexual minority women: A systematic review. *European Eating Disorders Review: The Journal of the Eating Disorders Association, 26*(4), 275–292. https://doi.org/10.1002/erv.2601.

Mizock, L., & Lewis, T. K. (2008). Trauma in transgender populations: Risk, resilience, and clinical care. *Journal of Emotional Abuse, 8*, 335–354. https://doi.org/10.1080/10926790802262523.

Moore, M. R. (2012). Intersectionality and the study of black, sexual minority women. *Gender & Society, 26*(1), 33–39. https://doi.org/10.1177/0891243211427031.

Obedin-Maliver, J., Goldsmith, E. S., Stewart, L., White, W., Tran, E., Brenman, S., ... Lunn, M. R. (2011). Lesbian, Gay, Bisexual, and Transgender–related content in undergraduate medical education. *Journal of the American Medical Association, 306*(9), 971–977. https://doi.org/10.1001/jama.2011.1255.

Pachankis, J. E., Hatzenbuehler, M. L., Rendina, H. J., Safren, S. A., & Parsons, J. T. (2015). LGB-affirmative cognitive-behavioral therapy for young adult gay and bisexual men: A randomized controlled trial of a transdiagnostic minority stress approach. *Journal of Consulting and Clinical Psychology, 83*(5), 875–889. https://doi.org/10.1037/ccp0000037.

Piran, N. (2017). *Journeys of embodiment at the intersection of body and culture.* Cambridge, MA: Elsevier.

Safer, D. L., Telch, C., & Agras, W. S. (2001). Dialectical behavior therapy for bulimia nervosa. *American Journal of Psychiatry, 158*, 632–634.

Sevelius, J. M. (2013). Gender affirmation: A framework for conceptualizing risk behavior among transgender women of color. *Sex Roles, 68*(11–12), 675–689. https://doi.org/10.1007/s11199-012-0216-5.

Sexual Minority Assessment Research Team (SMART). (2009). *Best practices for asking questions about sexual orientation on surveys.* Retrieved from http://www.palmcenter.org/files/active/0/SMART_FINAL_Nov09.pdf.

Shearer, A., Russon, J., Herres, J., Atte, T., Kodish, T., & Diamond, G. (2015). The relationship between disordered eating and sexuality amongst adolescents and young adults. *Eating Behaviors, 19*, 115–119. Retrieved from http://www.sciencedirect.com/science/article/pii/S147101531500104X.

Smith, A. R., Hawkeswood, S. E., Bodell, L. P., & Joiner, T. E. (2011). Muscularity versus leanness: An examination of body ideals and predictors of disordered eating in heterosexual and gay college students. *Body Image, 8*(3), 232–236. https://doi.org/10.1016/j.bodyim.2011.03.005.

Strandjord, S. E., Ng, H., & Rome, E. S. (2015). Effects of treating gender dysphoria and anorexia nervosa in a transgender adolescent: Lessons learned. *International Journal of Eating Disorders, 48*(7), 942–945. https://doi.org/10.1002/eat.22438.

Tervalon, M., & Murray-García, J. (1998). Cultural humility versus cultural competence: A critical distinction in defining physician training outcomes in multicultural education. *Journal of Health Care for the Poor and Underserved, 9*(2), 117–125. Retrieved from http://www.ncbi.nlm.nih.gov/pubmed/10073197.

Testa, R. J., Rider, G. N., Haug, N. A., & Balsam, K. F. (2017). Gender confirming medical interventions and eating disorder symptoms among transgender individuals. *Health Psychology, 36*(10), 927–936. https://doi.org/10.1037/hea0000497Eating disorders.

The GenIUSS Group. (2014). *Best practices for asking questions to identify transgender and other gender minority respondents on population-based surveys.* Herman J. L. (Ed.). Los Angeles, CA: The Williams Institute.

Tiggemann, M., Martins, Y., & Kirkbride, A. (2007). Oh to be lean and muscular: Body image ideals in gay and heterosexual men. *Psychology of Men & Masculinity, 8*(1), 15–24. https://doi.org/10.1037/1524-9220.8.1.15.

Tylka, T. L., & Andorka, M. J. (2012). Support for an expanded tripartite influence model with gay men. *Body Image, 9*(1), 57–67. https://doi.org/10.1016/j.bodyim.2011.09.006.

Wang, S. B., & Borders, A. (2017). Rumination mediates the associations between sexual minority stressors and disordered eating, particularly for men. *Eating and Weight Disorders: EWD, 22*(4), 699–706. https://doi.org/10.1007/s40519-016-0350-0.

Watson, L. B., Velez, B. L., Brownfield, J., & Flores, M. J. (2016). Minority stress and bisexual women's disordered eating. *The Counseling Psychologist, 44*(8), 1158–1186. https://doi.org/10.1177/0011000016669233.

Watson, R. J., Adjei, J., Saewyc, E., Homma, Y., & Goodenow, C. (2017). Trends and disparities in disordered eating among heterosexual and sexual minority adolescents. *The International Journal of Eating Disorders, 50*(1), 22–31. Retrieved from http://www.ncbi.nlm.nih.gov/pubmed/27425253.

White, W., Brenman, S., Paradis, E., Goldsmith, E. S., Lunn, M. R., Obedin-Maliver, J., ... Garcia, G. (2015). Lesbian, Gay, Bisexual, and Transgender patient care: Medical students' preparedness and comfort. *Teaching and Learning in Medicine, 27*(3), 254–263. https://doi.org/10.1080/10401334.2015.1044656.

Wiser, S., & Telch, C.F. (1999). Dialectical behavior therapy for Binge-Eating Disorder. *Journal of Clinical Psychology, 55*(6), 755–768. https://doi.org/10.1002/(sici)1097-4679(199906)55:6<755::aid-jclp8>3.0.co;2-r.

Witcomb, G. L., Bouman, W. P., Brewin, N., Richards, C., Fernandez-Aranda, F., & Arcelus, J. (2015). Body image dissatisfaction and eating-related psychopathology in trans individuals: A matched control study. *European Eating Disorders Review, 23*(4), 287–293. https://doi.org/10.1002/erv.2362.

Yean, C., Benau, E. M., Dakanalis, A., Hormes, J. M., Perone, J., & Timko, C. A. (2013). The relationship of sex and sexual orientation to self-esteem, body shape satisfaction, and eating disorder symptomatology. *Frontiers in Psychology, 4*, 1–11. https://doi.org/10.3389/fpsyg.2013.00887.

4 Utilizing Alternate Caregivers and Support Persons in Eating Disorder Treatment

Cristin D. Runfola and Linsey Utzinger

Introduction

Eating disorders are maintained by intra and interpersonal processes (Arcelus, Haslam, Farrow, & Meyer, 2013; Blomquist, Ansell, White, Masheb, & Grilo, 2012; Schmidt & Treasure, 2006) and, thus, typically require pooled resources in the medical, psychiatric, and social realms if they are to be overcome. Importantly, individuals recovered from eating disorders report that supportive relationships are the most important factor in their recovery (Tozzi, Sullivan, Fear, McKenzie, & Bulik, 2003). Yet, individuals with eating disorders are often socially isolated and have poor interpersonal relationships (Arcelus et al., 2013; Arkell & Robinson, 2008; Tiller et al., 1997). As caregivers' responses can either facilitate or hinder motivation for recovery in the individual affected (Jones, Lindekilde, Lübeck, & Clausen, 2015; Steiger et al., 2017), including close others in treatment may be essential.

Caregivers of individuals with eating disorders may benefit from support as well. Caregivers often believe they are to blame for the development of the eating disorder or feel guilty for not recognizing it sooner, and subsequently feel responsible for caring for the affected individual (Fox, Dean, & Whittlesea, 2017). Indeed, caregivers experience high caregiver burden (Fischer, Baucom, Kirby, & Bulik, 2015; Graap et al., 2008; Perkins, Winn, Murray, Murphy, & Schmidt, 2004; Treasure et al., 2001; Zabala, Macdonald, & Treasure, 2009), negative emotional health effects, including stress, high expressed emotion, depression, and anxiety (Agh et al., 2016; Anastasiadou, Medina-Pradas, Sepulveda, & Treasure, 2014; Romero-Martínez & Moya-Albiol, 2017; Treasure et al., 2001), as well as a lack of self-efficacy in their role as carers (Sadeh-Sharvit et al., 2018). Factors influencing caregiving experiences include their knowledge of the illness, level of expressed emotion, the individual's illness duration, stigma, and the level of contact with the individual affected by the eating disorder (Anastasiadou et al., 2014). Family members typically express a desire to help their loved one, but often report not knowing how (Branch & Eurman, 1980; Haigh & Treasure, 2003). They report wanting more eating disorder education and practical guidance (Haigh & Treasure, 2003; Winn, Perkins, Murray, Murphy, & Schmidt, 2004). Consequently, existing evidence-based treatments (EBTs) for eating disorders recommend embedding significant others who are in the patient's immediate social network into the therapeutic setting (Pisetsky, Utzinger, & Peterson, 2016).

Whereas early approaches to working with families are derived from an explanatory model of family functioning, current treatment approaches, including manualized treatments, emphasize the family as a key resource. Although treatment manuals can be extremely valuable, they do not always respond to every context or situation clinicians face when treating patients with eating disorders. Furthermore, research evaluating the efficacy of existing manuals is insufficient (Fisher, Skocic, Rutherford, & Hetrick, 2019). First, for children and adolescents, the term "family" has been generally conceptualized as parents or primary caregivers, and, thus, most research has investigated the efficacy of family therapies with this family configuration. For some patients, particularly young adults and adults with eating disorders, there can be challenges or contraindications to including parents or primary caregivers in treatment. Second, for adults, few studies exist that have studied family-based interventions for eating disorders. Relatedly, although many individually based EBTs (e.g., cognitive-behavioral therapy [CBT]) recommend involving support persons in treatment, there is little guidance and a dearth of research into how exactly to include them. Finally, not all patients respond to existing treatments or live within family contexts or settings that are well-suited to these treatments.

In everyday clinical practice, clinicians must balance the need for implementing EBTs with the complexities of settings and patients seen outside of research trials. Indeed, this is what the term "evidence-based practice" implies. Thus, when current EBTs do not seem to apply to a given patient or setting, or when attempts to use them have failed, a clinician must combine the best available evidence with clinical expertise. However, without clear research-informed blueprints for addressing these challenges, clinicians may be understandably hesitant about including alternate support persons in treatment, even when it might be in the best interest of the patient.

This chapter is intended to draw from the best available evidence and clinical experience to help guide clinicians in making decisions about who in the individual's social network to involve in treatment and how. We provide an overview of current EBTs for individuals with eating disorders that may have potential for including alternate caregivers and support persons, and discuss considerations related to their inclusion. Insights are offered into how one may adapt interventions to include other support individuals. However, it must be noted that there is no systematic research to date supporting these adaptations. These possible adaptations may be future directions for eating disorder treatment research. It is recommended that first-line treatments be utilized when possible and that adaptations are considered with caution and consultation only as secondary treatment options.

Involving Support Persons in the Treatment of Adolescents

A growing body of research on family therapy, including a limited number of randomized controlled trials (RCTs), has shown that families are an integral resource in the treatment of adolescents with eating disorders (Lock, 2015). Family therapies have evolved over time, integrating principles and approaches from several different schools of family therapy. Although the existing evidence base is insufficient for determining whether one type of family therapy is significantly better than another (Fisher et al., 2019), current guidelines recommend that interventions for adolescents with anorexia nervosa (AN) or bulimia nervosa (BN) should be family-based and include parents, family members, or carers (Hilbert, Hoek, & Schmidt, 2017; National Institute for Health Care Excellence [NICE], 2017). In contrast, individual or group formats are currently recommended for adolescents with binge-eating disorder (BED; Hilbert et al., 2017; NICE, 2017). Although research on treatments for BED in youth is lacking, individual interventions often have a parental component (Boutelle et al., 2011; Hilbert, 2013). From both theoretical and practical standpoints, parents or primary caregivers are necessarily involved in the treatment of adolescents with eating disorders. However, in rare or extraordinary circumstances, involving parents or primary caregivers may not be possible and considerations may need to be made for involving alternate caregivers in treatment.

Family-Based Treatment

One specific form of family therapy for adolescents with AN, family-based treatment for AN (FBT-AN), is particularly effective and widely disseminated (Agras et al., 2014; Lock, 2015). In FBT, the entire family is asked to attend treatment (Lock & Le Grange, 2013). The term "family" includes anyone living in the home with the patient and anyone (e.g., grandparents and secondary household members) with whom the patient spends significant amounts of time and might be involved in any aspect of refeeding (Lock, Le Grange, Agras, & Dare, 2001). Having the entire household present for treatment allows the clinician to begin enhancing parental authority, specifically, over the process of refeeding. Indeed, parental involvement is viewed as being crucial to the recovery process in family therapy for eating disorders (Whitney & Eisler, 2005). However, many obstacles exist in the implementation of FBT, including that clinicians may be uncomfortable with whole family sessions or have difficulty impressing upon families the importance of attendance, or families may have difficulty prioritizing treatment, may lack resources, or may be experiencing caregiver burnout. Another reason manualized FBT may be difficult to implement is because the adolescent's family or living situation is atypical, such as the patient having court-appointed guardians, or living in foster care, a group home, with other relatives, or at home with parent(s) suffering from acute mental or medical health issues. In such circumstances, implementing FBT with alternate caregivers might be considered. However, almost no data exists examining or supporting the implementation of FBT without the inclusion of parents.

Alternate caregivers in FBT could include grandparents, relatives (e.g., aunts, uncles), adult siblings, or court-appointed person(s). Clinicians and families need to consider the living arrangement, availability, relationship, and motivation of the alternate support person(s). First, will the alternate carer be present in the patient's life on a daily basis for the duration of treatment? The carer would need to live in the same home as the patient, even if only temporarily, to take charge of the refeeding process. The carer must also be available to attend all treatment sessions. Second, is the alternate carer a relative or loved one or in a paid position (e.g., staff member at a group home)? Notably, individuals in paid positions are subject to voluntary or involuntary changes in employment, as well as potentially having other work demands, that may impact consistency of care. Finally, what is the level of motivation the alternate carer has for the patient to get well? FBT places significant demands on the person(s) in the parental role. As such, they need to be invested and have the fortitude to continue helping the patient in a recovery process that is difficult and not always linear. In addition to the above considerations, parents or legal guardians would need to consent to any alternative arrangements.

Drawing from research on FBT in adolescents involving parents, a variety of factors would need to be addressed in therapy with alternate caregivers. First, anyone involved in the patient's care should be present for the assessment process, which would allow the clinician to observe interactions, coalitions, and to engage everyone in treatment. Second, clinicians must emphasize effective communication strategies and clarify roles and boundaries between participating caregivers. Relatedly, all involved must understand the alternate caregiver's chief role with responsibility for refeeding. As such, therapists would need to build alternate caregiver authority. Like parents, alternate carers may benefit from hearing that they are not to blame for the child's illness. As parental self-efficacy may be a mechanism that helps achieve good outcomes in FBT (Byrne, Accurso, Arnow, Lock, & Le Grange, 2015), the self-efficacy of the alternate caregiver may need to be a focus as well. Third, as research shows that a longer course of treatment may be needed for adolescents from non-intact (i.e., separated, divorced, single-parent, or reconstituted) families to achieve better outcomes (Lock, Agras, Bryson, & Kraemer, 2005), it is possible that an expanded version of FBT may be needed with alternate caregivers. Fourth, attention to expressed emotion may be important. In families where increased expressed emotion (i.e., parental criticism or overinvolvement) is present at the start of FBT, outcomes have been negatively impacted (Allan, Le Grange, Sawyer, McLean, & Hughes, 2018; Eisler et al., 2000; Le Grange, Eisler, Dare, & Hodes, 1992; Le Grange, Eisler, Dare, & Russell, 1992; Szmukler, Eisler, Russell, & Dare, 1985). Thus, if warranted when working with alternate caregivers, clinicians may consider utilizing adaptations and alternatives to

78   *Cristin D. Runfola and Linsey Utzinger*

conjoint FBT aimed at enhancing outcomes specifically relevant to family communication styles, including intensive parental coaching (Lock et al., 2015) and parent-focused therapy (PFT; Le Grange et al., 2016).

In one case example of FBT-AN delivered without the involvement of parents, two staff members at a group home for foster children were enlisted to participate in a shared "parent" role to help a 16-year old male diagnosed with AN (Aspen & Boutelle, 2014). In this case, because parents were unavailable and the adolescent needed treatment, and because two staff members initially agreed to participate in treatment to help the patient, providers felt this was the best approach. At first, the two alternate carers both attended treatment sessions and took shifts at the group home to ensure meals were monitored and supported. The carers solved problems in sessions and implemented strategies outside of session, resulting in early weight gain. However, by the fourth session, one carer left her position and, shortly after, the other carer reduced his hours. As a result, meals were inconsistently monitored, and the patient's weight gain faltered. The "family" also prematurely moved to Phase II of treatment and decreased sessions to monthly due to the availability of the remaining carer. Despite these particular obstacles, the patient's ideal body weight (IBW) increased from 76% at the start of treatment to 87% at the end of treatment, dropping to 81.5% IBW at follow-up. Several significant challenges were encountered utilizing this approach, most importantly the inconsistent caregiving that occurred as a result of staff turnover and employment changes. It also highlights a problematic division of responsibility, as other group home staff were not involved in treatment, yet were asked to provide meal and other support to the patient. Nevertheless, there were also clear benefits to the approach taken in this case. Most notably, the patient received a modified version of an evidence-based, first-line treatment for adolescents with AN and achieved and maintained some weight gain and significant symptom reduction in outpatient care, where he was able to remain living in his group home.

Although it may be possible to include alternate caregivers in the "parent" role in FBT, the theoretical rationale behind this approach necessitates family involvement. Moreover, completed RCTs examining FBT have included parents/families (Lock, 2015). Thus, the first-line treatment recommendation when implementing FBT for adolescents is to involve parents. In extraordinary circumstances where parents are unavailable or their involvement is contraindicated, the pros and cons of adapting FBT to include alternate caregivers must be thoughtfully considered.

Other Family-Based Options

There are several other family-based therapy approaches for adolescents that may be promising for the treatment of eating disorders, though the effectiveness of these is yet to be fully established. These approaches include family therapy for AN (Eisler et al., 2016), systemic family therapy (Agras et al.,

Utilizing Alternate Caregivers/Support Persons   79

2014), PFT (Le Grange et al., 2016), separated family therapy (Eisler et al., 2000), intensive family therapy (Rockwell, Boutelle, Trunko, Jacobs, & Kaye, 2011), and multifamily group therapy (Eisler et al., 2016). As is true for FBT, it is strongly recommended that parents or primary caregivers be included in treatment as the first-line approach. If this is contraindicated or not possible, the same considerations should be weighed as for FBT, including the living arrangement, availability, relationship, and motivation and commitment of the potential support person(s).

Involving Support Persons in the Treatment of Transitional-Age Youth

During typical development, the transition between adolescence and adulthood is a time when greater autonomy is sought out and achieved in various domains of life and individuals become less dependent on their parents (Arnett, 2015). Transitions that commonly occur during this life stage include moving out of or away from home, as well as acquiring post-secondary education, increased fiscal responsibility, and increased personal responsibility (Arnett, 2015). However, this period of growth is often disrupted if the older adolescent or young adult develops or has a chronic history of an eating disorder. Transition age youth ([TAY] approximately 16–25 years of age) with eating disorders are thought to be distinct from adolescent and adult populations in that these individuals often continue to live with their family of origin and require familial support, yet simultaneously desire independence (Dimitropoulos & Freeman, 2016; Dimitropoulos et al., 2015). This is also a period of higher rates of comorbid psychiatric illness (Fischer & Le Grange, 2007; Le Grange, Swanson, Crow, & Merikangas, 2012; Swanson, Crow, Le Grange, Swendsen, & Merikangas, 2011) and increased risk of mortality (Crow et al., 2009; Fischer & Grange, 2007). Unfortunately, the ego-syntonic nature of the illness often hinders engagement in treatment (Bulik, Berkman, Brownley, Sedway, & Lohr, 2007; Roncero, Belloch, Perpiñá, & Treasure, 2013). Furthermore, despite the importance of family support, there may be significant resistance to parental involvement in treatment, particularly for those with a later onset of illness who have already achieved a certain level of independence from their parents. Early intervention is known to positively impact outcome, and recognizing and treating AN in its early stages is imperative (Campbell & Peebles, 2014). Unfortunately, though, as adolescents transition to adulthood, treatment options for AN become more limited and are characterized by poor treatment outcomes and high rates of relapse (Berkman, Lohr, & Bulik, 2007; Bulik et al., 2007; Hay, 2013; Hay, Touyz, & Sud, 2012). Accounting for these factors, together with the importance of familial support in eating disorder treatment, emerging research is examining an adapted version of manualized FBT (Le Grange & Lock, 2007; Lock & Le Grange, 2013) for TAY with restrictive-type eating disorders.

Family-Based Therapy for Transition Age Youth (FBT-TAY)

FBT-TAY is tailored to respond to the unique developmental needs of older adolescents and young adults. Compared with the adolescent manuals, FBT-TAY is longer, sessions offer more individual time prior to family meetings, and the approach endeavors to build a more collaborative relationship between the young adult and caregivers (Dimitropoulos, Lock, Le Grange, & Anderson, 2015). FBT-TAY is divided into three phases (Dimitropoulos et al., 2015). As with traditional FBT, the first phase relentlessly targets weight restoration. The support adult(s) is charged with the task of refeeding and the young adult is asked to accept this support. The second phase is focused on returning control over eating, with an emphasis on helping the young adult to acquire and master the necessary skills to manage eating and weight-related concerns independently. The third phase explores issues related to autonomy and independence, relapse prevention, and developing an identity that is separate from the eating disorder.

Two preliminary studies, one using the FBT-TAY manual (Dimitropoulos et al., 2018) and another using a separate, but similar, adaptation to FBT for young adults (FBTY; Chen et al., 2016), have demonstrated acceptability and feasibility for TAY. In an open trial of 26 participants (aged 16–25), eating disorder symptomatology was significantly improved and weight restoration achieved and maintained at end of treatment and 3-month follow-up (Dimitropoulos et al., 2018). In a pilot study of 22 participants (aged 18–26), weight restoration was achieved and there were improvements in eating disorder symptomatology, both of which were maintained at a 12-month follow-up (Chen et al., 2016). Notably, though, and similar to findings from adult AN treatment trials (Watson & Bulik, 2013), dropout rates in both studies were high (Chen et al., 2016; Dimitropoulos et al., 2018), suggesting concerns with the acceptability of this approach.

In both FBT-TAY and FBTY, family is defined broadly and young adults are allowed greater input into how "family" is conceptualized and which support person(s) are included in treatment (Dimitropoulos et al., 2015). Individuals could elect to include a support adult who is not a parent. This particular approach is meant to appeal to the burgeoning independence of the young adult by enhancing engagement and accounting for any obstacles or contraindications, such as the patient no longer living in the home; the patient living at a significant physical distance from parents (e.g., the patient may be away at college); the parents being acutely impaired by mental or medical illness; or the existence of a history of abuse within the family (Dimitropoulos et al., 2015). In addition, sibling involvement is encouraged but not required, depending on the patient's perspective on the advantages or disadvantages of including siblings (Dimitropoulos et al., 2015).

Nevertheless, preliminary evidence suggests that patients choose to involve their parents in treatment (Chen et al., 2016; Dimitropoulos et al., 2018). In an open trial of FBT-TAY, the majority of participants already lived with or

Utilizing Alternate Caregivers / Support Persons 81

elected to live with their families during the first phase of treatment (Dimitropoulos et al., 2018). Greater than 95% of participants included their families in treatment despite having the option to include alternate support persons. This is consistent with the FBTY study, in which 64% of participants elected to include their parents in treatment; the others nominated a friend, sibling, partner and parent dyad, and sibling and parent dyad (Chen et al., 2016). One could postulate that young adults with AN, although potentially resistant to parental involvement in treatment, remain embedded within their families and recognize that their families are the most invested in their recovery and are best equipped to help them. Individuals with AN, particularly those with a more chronic course, also tend to experience significant social isolation (Arkell & Robinson, 2008; Ratnasuriya, Eisler, Szmukler, & Russell, 1991; Robinson, Kukucska, Guidetti, & Leavey, 2015; Treasure, Crane, McKnight, Buchanan, & Wolfe, 2011), further limiting the availability of alternate support persons. Nevertheless, considering the desire of TAY for autonomy and control, allowing the young adult to select whom to include may be a valuable intervention in and of itself.

Clinicians should work together with patients to determine who is the most appropriate and willing support person(s) to include in treatment (Pisetsky et al., 2016). Treatment for those over the age of 18 is voluntary and the patient must provide consent for the participation of a parent or alternate support person, requiring discussion of confidentiality and communication from the outset of treatment. Although FBT-TAY is intended to be more collaborative and attentive to issues of autonomy and independence, it is important to note that the first phase of treatment, similar to FBT-AN, targets weight restoration and normalization of eating and tasks the supportive adult with great responsibility for these goals. This should be made very clear at the outset of treatment. Although FBT-TAY is a promising treatment for TAY with restrictive-type eating disorders, effectiveness studies are needed. Moreover, further research is needed to determine whether outcome-related differences exist when including alternate support persons in lieu of parents.

Involving Support Persons in the Treatment of Adults

Similar to adolescents, practice guidelines recommend involving family members or significant others in the assessment and treatment of adults with eating disorders (NICE, 2017). It is recommended that carers of adults with eating disorders take a collaborative support stance, defined as respecting the individual's autonomy while offering unconditional support or encouraging change (Geller et al., 2017). In addition, carers of adults report benefit from learning motivational interviewing skills as a means for communicating with their loved one (Macdonald, Murray, Goddard, & Treasure, 2011). Improving communication may be essential given that the eating disorder can be a way individuals communicate their distress or meet essential needs (Serpell, Teasdale, Troop, & Treasure, 2004). Additionally, accommodation and enabling behaviors need to be considered. Accommodation and enabling occurs when, in an attempt to minimize an individual's distress in the short term, the caregiver engages in behavior that inadvertently reinforces eating disorder behaviors in the long term (Treasure & Todd, 2016). Across psychiatric disorders, accommodation and enabling behaviors in partners have been associated with more severe symptoms (Boeding et al., 2013; Caporino et al., 2012; Salerno et al., 2016), worsened treatment response (Boeding et al., 2013; Salerno et al., 2016), and lower relationship satisfaction (Boeding et al., 2013; Fredman, Vorstenbosch, Wagner, Macdonald, & Monson, 2014). Notably, the more time caregivers spend with patients, the more frequent accommodation and enabling behaviors become (Anastasiadou et al., 2014). It is important to note that caregivers might have difficulty tolerating their loved one's distress (Boeding et al., 2013; Fischer et al., 2015) and engage in these behaviors to regulate their own emotions. Given that the onset of eating disorders typically occurs in adolescence or young adulthood, adults with eating disorders may have a longer duration of illness, which is associated with higher caregiver burden (Anastasiadou et al., 2014). Thus, caregivers often need strategies for managing their own distress. Adult interventions including caregivers must appropriately account for these developmental differences and caregiving experiences.

There are a number of interventions for adults with eating disorders that engage significant others in a developmentally appropriate way. These interventions vary based on the frequency and nature of sessions, as well as in their focus in treatment. All interventions including significant others have demonstrated at least preliminary efficacy, positively influencing the eating disorder, comorbid psychopathology, and/or family-related outcomes. However, it remains unclear whether any one intervention is superior to another. Thus, whether and how to involve a significant other in treatment should be decided collaboratively with the patient (NICE, 2017).

As part of the decision process on whether to include a significant other in treatment, clinicians should discuss the potential pros and cons. A thorough family history and relationship assessment exploring the individual's interactions and experiences with close others over time will help aid in the decision. Discussing the ways in which others have benefitted from additional support in treatment may also expand this list and address any irrational help-seeking concerns. Notably, contrary to data (Haigh & Treasure, 2003; Winn et al., 2004), individuals with eating disorders often feel that their loved ones do not want to help or that they would be a burden to others. Clinicians should discuss the various options for including close others in treatment, including the rationale for doing so and the existing evidence base, based on their case conceptualization. For example, if there is a clear reciprocal relationship between the eating disorder and interpersonal interactions, the patient may benefit from identifying this relationship and the ways in which the treatment could help break the negative cycle. Another concern patients may have is disclosure of information. Patients may prefer to keep some information private and fear that personal information will be disclosed to others without their consent. As with young adults, a thorough discussion of confidentiality and explicit guidelines on what will be disclosed and when needs to be agreed upon in advance.

Significant others can play a crucial role in helping their loved one get into treatment. Clinicians are frequently contacted by significant others for guidance on how to express their concerns to their loved one and to access appropriate treatment. Normalizing the challenges of communicating with an individual with an eating disorder and reinforcing the significant other's ability to reach out for support from a specialist can validate their experiences and promote their effective help-seeking behavior. Brief education about eating disorders and their treatment may improve this process as well. To prevent a defensive response and enhance one's willingness to listen, clinicians can provide guidance to significant others on how to express their observations and feelings compassionately and tactfully while maintaining appropriate boundaries. For example, discussing strategies for rolling with resistance to prevent conflict in the relationship may help if the patient is struggling to see they have a safe, trusted loved one to turn to for support. In addition, sharing eating disorder resources and providing contacts to providers with eating disorder specialization will enable the loved one to share appropriate resources with the prospective patient. Finally, significant others can help contact professionals, set up initial assessments, and, at a minimum, provide instrumental support by transporting patients to and from their appointment or providing childcare, as appropriate.

Significant others can be involved in treatment in various ways. Below, we briefly review the existing interventions involving significant others in treatment for adults with eating disorders, beginning with those that are family-based, followed by those that are couple-based, and then individually based.

Family-Based Interventions

In general, data suggest that including family members in treatment is acceptable and feasible, and can reduce eating disorder symptoms for patients with AN, as well as those with an early onset and shorter duration of illness. One RCT comparing a family therapy with individual-only specialist treatments for adult AN found equivalence in outcomes (Dare, Eisler, Russell, Treasure, & Dodge, 2001). Another RCT comparing family therapy with individual therapy in adolescents and adults with either AN or BN found differences in efficacy between the two interventions based on the individual's pretreatment diagnosis, age, and illness factors both at 1-year and 5-year follow-up (Eisler et al., 1997; Russell, Szmukler, Dare, & Eisler, 1987). The family therapies studied lasted 6 months–1 year and were similar to FBT-AN for adolescents. In this treatment model, families are seen as the solution, not the problem, and the eating disorder is viewed as affecting all family members. However, in contrast to FBT-AN, in Phase I, adult patients and their families decided whether the patient or family member(s) would have control over the patient's eating. Phase II, like FBT-AN, continues to focus on eliminating the eating disorder and achieving weight gain.

84   Cristin D. Runfola and Linsey Utzinger

In Phase III, more normal family concerns were similarly addressed, but the central theme was on establishing healthy adult relationships between the individual affected by the eating disorder and their included family member(s), without the eating disorder symptoms being used as a medium for communication. Anyone living in the same household as the patient is invited to participate, as are children of the family who left the home. However, studies suggest that most adults participating in this treatment lived with either parents or partners and, thus, included these members in treatment (Dare et al., 2001; Eisler et al., 1997). Of concern, dropout from treatment remained high (Dare et al., 2001; Eisler et al., 1997). Data are inconclusive on whether there are differences in dropout between family and individual therapies (Dare et al., 2001; Eisler et al., 1997).

In another family-based intervention, The Maudsley Model of Treatment for Adults with Anorexia Nervosa (MANTRA, Treasure, Schmidt, & Macdonald, 2009), family member involvement is flexible with significant others included as necessary, as determined by the clinician and adult patient with AN. One study of this treatment found lower drop out (25% versus 41%) and better acceptability and credibility ratings than a specialist supportive clinical management individual therapy (Schmidt et al., 2015). Both interventions were associated with increased body mass index and reduced eating disorder and comorbid symptoms at 1- and 2-year follow-up, with no differences between groups (Schmidt et al., 2015; Schmidt et al., 2016). MANTRA targets the intra and interpersonal maintaining factors of AN from a cognitive-behavioral model and evolutionary approach to psychopathology while drawing from neuropsychological, social cognitive, and personality trait AN research (Schmidt & Treasure, 2006; Schmidt, Wade, & Treasure, 2014). The interpersonal maintenance factor targeted is the response of close others, including anxiety, worry, blame, criticism, or hostility (i.e., high expressed emotion), as well as enabling or accommodation behaviors (Target 4). Although these studies typically include parents as caregivers, MANTRA was developed for partner or other caregiver (e.g., sibling) involvement as well.

Pilot studies of other family therapies exist. For example, preliminary data suggest an intervention similar to MANTRA, ECHOMANTRA, which is a transition support intervention for patients and carers, can augment the acceptability and efficiency of inpatient care by preparing them better for the transition from inpatient to community care (Adamson et al., 2019). In addition, both outpatient (Tantillo, 2006) and intensive outpatient multifamily therapies (Dimitropoulos et al., 2015; Wierenga et al., 2018) for adult AN have demonstrated feasibility and high acceptability with adults, and were suggestive of benefiting both the patient and their support. Parents and partners are most often involved in these treatments.

Little research has examined the impact of specific caregivers on outcome in these family therapies. However, research suggests that fathers, in particular, can have powerful and positive impacts on eating disorder symptomatology (Agras, Bryson, Hammer, & Kraemer, 2007; Hibbs, Rhind,

Leppanen, & Treasure, 2015; Johnson, Cohen, Kasen, & Brook, 2002; Keery, Boutelle, van den Berg, & Thompson, 2005; Kyriacou, Treasure, & Schmidt, 2008) and can improve treatment outcomes (Bulik, Sullivan, Fear, & Pickering, 2000; Castro, Toro, & Cruz, 2000). Yet, fathers are often less involved in treatment (Hughes, Burton, Le Grange, & Sawyer, 2018). One case illustration of an adult female with AN specifically examined the role of fathers in the implementation of MANTRA (Treasure, Schmidt, & Kan, 2019). The formulation in this case was that the patient's father was avoiding dealing with the eating disorder, whereas much of its management was left to the patient's mother, and the nature of this division of responsibility was allowing the patient's AN to be accommodated and persist (Treasure et al., 2019). Parental counseling and a skills-based workshop were utilized to support and engage the patient's father, ultimately helping both parents to work together to help their daughter (Treasure et al., 2019).

It is recommended that providers initially consider including parents or partners in treatment given most of the above research has included these significant others. As with adolescents, extraordinary circumstances may call for the involvement of alternate caregivers or support persons. Alternate caregivers willing to help may include an adult sibling or child, close friend/roommate, or court-appointed person(s). When including caregivers in treatment, it is important to consider their level of contact with the individual affected, the patient's duration of illness, and the degree of emotional effects. These factors will help the patient and clinician determine which of the above treatments might be most feasible, and the family factors (such as expressed emotion and accommodating and enabling behaviors) that might need to be addressed to achieve good results.

Couple-Based Interventions

For individuals in committed relationships, a cognitive-behavioral couple-based intervention appears more promising than the above family-based therapy for keeping adults with eating disorders in treatment. Data from an open pilot trial of Uniting Couples in the Treatment of Anorexia Nervosa (UCAN) suggests that working with partners in committed relationships (defined as being together for at least 6 months) for the 22-week duration of treatment, as an adjunctive treatment to individual therapy, reduced dropout by 15% (from the 25% figure reported in the MANTRA trial and the average 25% figure reported in a systematic review of psychotherapy trials for adult AN; Baucom et al., 2017; Berkman et al., 2007). At both post-treatment and 3-month follow-up, this study showed that patients improved on various AN-related measures, anxiety and depression, and relationship adjustment. Partners benefitted as well as they had reduced anxiety and depression and improved relationship adjustment. Benchmarking analyses comparing the multicomponent couple intervention to RCTs of individual therapy for AN revealed that the couple intervention compared favorably on AN-related outcomes. Furthermore, a pilot study of an adaptation of this couple-based approach for binge-eating type disorders (Uniting couples In the Treatment of Eating disorders [UNITE]) found high acceptability (with low drop out at 10%), feasibility, and preliminary efficacy (Runfola et al., 2018; Weber et al., 2018). These data are consistent with a review on the efficacy of cognitive-behavioral couple-based interventions across psychiatric disorders, which found that they are at least as effective as individual CBT but had the unique added benefit of improving relationship functioning (Fischer, Baucom, & Cohen, 2016).

Most adults affected by eating disorders report relying on their partners for support in their recovery (Linville, Cobb, Shen, & Stadelman, 2016; Tozzi et al., 2003). However, receiving support from partners can be difficult. Studies show women with eating disorders report lower marital satisfaction, less frequent positive interaction, sexual concerns, and increased negative interaction in their relationships than women without eating disorders (Pinheiro et al., 2010; Whisman, Dementyeva, Baucom, & Bulik, 2012). Partners also report experiencing challenges, indicating that they find it difficult to understand eating disorders, struggle with eating disorder-related secrecy and issues of trust, and express powerlessness and ineffectiveness in their attempts to help (Huke & Slade, 2006; Linville et al., 2016). Notably, when caregivers experience self-blame and fear, they are more likely to lack self-efficacy (Stillar et al., 2016). In this context, partners may become avoidant (due to fear of saying or doing something counterproductive), overtly critical or blaming, or passive aggressive in their remarks (Huke & Slade, 2006; Linville et al., 2016). These communication patterns can inadvertently reinforce or exacerbate the eating disorder symptoms as well as its shame, secrecy, and self-critical nature (Arcelus et al., 2013; Linville et al., 2016).

UCAN and UNITE address the above concerns as well as negative interaction cycles while using the power of the relationship to overcome the eating disorder. As such, incorporating romantic partners into the treatment setting following the UCAN or UNITE approach warrants significant consideration as an approach for couples in which one partner has an eating disorder.

UCAN and UNITE

UCAN/UNITE integrates enhanced cognitive-behavioral couple-based therapy (Epstein & Baucom, 2002) with CBT for eating disorders (Fairburn, 2008) to help couples navigate recovery together. They target the eating disorder and reduce stress by improving communication around its symptoms (Target 1), enhancing interpersonal problem-solving/behavioral change skills (Target 2), and improving emotion regulation skills (Target 3). In doing so, couples make joint decisions as to how to address mealtimes, manage triggers (e.g., stress, holidays, and body comments), and effectively respond to eating disorder urges and behaviors (e.g., restriction, binge eating, and purging) while meeting both partners' needs as well as building support, trust, and open

Utilizing Alternate Caregivers/Support Persons 87

communication within the relationship. Partners can also improve the therapeutic process when more intensive treatment for the individual with the eating disorder is being discussed (Kirby, Baucom, La Via, & Bulik, 2016). Similar to FBT, partners are taught they are not to blame for the eating disorder, but that they can instead be the patient's best resource in recovery. Unlike FBT for adolescent eating disorders, though, which provides parents or caregivers with initial control over the recovery process, UCAN/UNITE works with loved ones to reach mutual decisions regarding treatment and recovery. As such, the partner is incorporated into treatment in a developmentally appropriate way, as a partner of equal status, and a team-like approach to recovery is emphasized. UCAN/UNITE targets similar interpersonal issues presumed to maintain eating disorders as MANTRA. Although the interventions were originally tested as a multidisciplinary treatment including individual therapy, whether the intervention can be a stand-alone treatment is being investigated.

There are three phases of UCAN/UNITE covered over 22 sessions. Phase I focuses on creating a shared understanding of the eating disorder via psychoeducation and assessment of severity and functionality. A thorough relationship assessment and evaluation of the couple's communication, presence of enabling and accommodating behaviors, expressed emotion, and strengths is conducted. The latter end of this phase focuses on building communication skills, namely by reviewing guidelines for emotional expression (i.e., sharing thoughts and feelings) and decision-making, and practicing these two types of conversations in the sessions. Phase II helps couples, using these communication skills, to make decisions around addressing the eating disorder and to target emotion regulation difficulties and related eating disorder challenges, such as body image, physical affection, and sexuality. For example, partners might accompany the patient on an exposure outing, such as to a restaurant to confront feared foods. Within sessions, the patient and partner make concrete decisions on how they will work together during these experiences and troubleshoot potential barriers to their completion. This degree of collaboration is crucial to preventing conflict. Phase III focuses on relapse prevention, both for the eating disorder and couple relationship. Throughout these phases, three couple-based approaches are used to target eating disorder maintenance factors: partner-assisted interventions, disorder-specific interventions, and couple therapy (see Box 4.1 for definitions).

Box 4.1 Couple-Based Approaches

Partner-assisted interventions employ the partner as a surrogate therapist or coach in addressing the eating disorder, including providing structure to the environment conducive to treatment change, helping the patient complete behavioral experiments (or homework) outside of session, and reinforcing positive changes.

Disorder-specific interventions target the couple's interaction patterns or roles as they relate to the eating disorder. Thus, these interventions target

> maladaptive symptom accommodation and enabling behaviors, by helping the couple redefine roles and responsibilities in an adaptive way.
>
> *General couple therapy* is used when relationship distress or interpersonal challenges appear to contribute to the eating disorder development or maintenance. This is often the case when there is an excess of negative interactions, built up resentment, and lack of support, which may contribute to the relationship becoming a global, recurrent stressor for the individual. [Note: Creating a more positive environment for the couple, by disrupting hostility and lack of cooperation between partners, would be necessary to facilitate the partner-assisted and disorder-specific interventions. As mentioned previously, interpersonal stressors frequently occur in women with eating disorders (Whisman et al., 2012). Because pre-treatment interpersonal problems predict poorer treatment response and higher dropout (Jones et al., 2015), it is not uncommon that general couple therapy occurs in the treatment of eating disorders.]

UCAN/UNITE was developed and tested for adults in committed relationships. Most individuals in the studies mentioned above lived together with their partner, with few living in separate homes; thus, the efficacy of UCAN/UNITE for couples living apart is not yet known. It is possible that even long-distance relationship couples could benefit from treatment. Technology, such as video conferencing, can be leveraged to enable couple interactions during or after meals. Clinicians could also video conference a partner into a session with the patient or vice versa, depending on the state's ethical guidelines. As UCAN/UNITE were recently developed, research on their efficacy is in its infancy and no studies to date have examined mediators or moderators or predictors of outcome.

UCAN/UNITE would not be feasible with adults whose partners are unable to attend sessions (either due to work travel, childcare challenges, lack of interest, etc.). Whether these interventions can be adapted to include other individuals in the patient's life has not been tested. For example, it is possible that the intervention could work with a relative, roommate, close friend, or a court-appointed person. Clinicians could also alter the frequency of partner involvement or evidence-based individual therapy delivered. These adaptations have not yet been tested. However, it is important to note that, in general, couple-based interventions often appear more effective than individual-based ones when partners are substantially involved in treatment (Fischer et al., 2016); this may be true of other carers as well.

Individually Based Treatments

Conceptually, at times, it makes the most sense to include significant others in an individual EBT for eating disorders. Enhanced cognitive behavior therapy

Utilizing Alternate Caregivers / Support Persons 89

(CBT-E) has the strongest evidence base and is often recommended as the first line individually-based treatment for eating disorders (NICE, 2017). CBT-E was developed based on the transdiagnostic view of eating disorder psychopathology and targets cognitive and behavioral maintenance mechanisms thought to be common across eating disorder diagnoses (Fairburn, 2008). The CBT-E manual suggests that adult patients can invite others to the initial assessment appointment to provide emotional support and information and to their therapy sessions for support. For underweight adults, it is recommended that clinicians discuss the possible inclusion of support persons in treatment, particularly if the patient lives with family or a partner who the patient believes might be helpful in the process of weight regain. It is recommended that psychoeducation be provided and that the patient and support person(s) work out their roles, which may include ensuring that adequate food supplies are available, providing emotional support at meals, or assisting with urge surfing (Fairburn, 2008). See Table 4.1 for more guidance on how significant others might aid in recovery.

The manual recommends that support person(s) join sessions at regular intervals during the weight regain phase of treatment, but discontinue attendance later so that mastery of normalized eating and relapse prevention can be achieved by the patient independently. However, there is no research to support what level of involvement of support persons or caregivers is helpful in CBT-E for adults. Thus, it would behoove clinicians to work with patients in determining the amount and nature of involvement of others in treatment. Depending on the severity or duration of illness, caregivers may be more or less involved in treatment sessions and the work between sessions.

A case study of a 31-year-old, undocumented Latina woman with BN-purging type treated with CBT illustrates the feasibility of including a partner based on clinical needs of the patient (Reyes-Rodriguez, Baucom, & Bulik, 2014). For this case, the clinician collaboratively worked with the patient and partner to plan the frequency and timing of couple sessions, resulting in six total sessions planned every 2 weeks interspersed with individual sessions for a total of 26 sessions. Based on the conceptualization of couple-specific stressors playing a key role in maintaining the patient's symptoms, couple sessions initially addressed the following issues: a domestic violence episode, parenting skills, the disciplinary process with children, expression of affection and love, and intimacy issues. The remaining couple sessions were devoted to psychoeducation about the eating disorder and teaching and practicing communication skills to help the couple address the eating disorder symptoms directly. By the end of treatment, the patient was free from symptoms. The authors concluded that, consistent with Latinos/as' value of family, including her partner and incorporating parenting goals was important and contributed to the patient's adherence to treatment. This observation was supported by a subsequent qualitative investigation of ten Latina women and their relatives (Reyes-Rodríguez et al., 2019). Furthermore, this case study reveals that when

90 *Cristin D. Runfola and Linsey Utzinger*

Table 4.1 How Significant Others Might Aid in Recovery within CBT-E

Intervention Target	Significant Other's Role[1]
Strict dieting; noncompensatory weight-control behavior	Aid in grocery shopping and/or meal preparation
	Eat meals or snacks with patient
	Send texts prompting patient to eat/have patient share pictures of meals and reinforce adaptive eating behavior
	Create a positive experience around eating, e.g., lighting a candle, playing calming music, engaging in light conversation about non-food related topics, and discussing food in non-judgmental way using mindfulness skills
	Engage in activities with patient during high risk times for eating disorder behavior
	Provide emotional support when needed
Binge eating	Schedule activities after meals, or during high risk times for binge eating, as a distraction
	Keep certain foods out of the house
	Aid in grocery shopping and/or meal preparation
	Provide emotional support when needed
Compensatory vomiting/ laxative misuse	Schedule activities after meals or eating exposures for distraction
	Lock laxatives in secure place or get rid of them
	Provide emotional support when needed
Overevaluation of control over eating, shape or weight	Engage in nonfood related activities together
	Support patient's involvement in non-food related values-based behaviors, e.g., volunteering on weekends
	Eliminate body talk or comments about appearance/focus on body functionality
	Change the channel if dieting ads present on TV and throw away any magazines reinforcing the diet mentality or showing unrealistic body ideals
	Get rid of the scale
	Help eliminate maladaptive food- or body-related use of social media (e.g., close or sign out of accounts, particularly those reinforcing negative messages)
Events and associated mood change	Help patient problem solve to reduce exposure to stressors
	Support patient in following schedule or plan for normalized eating in the face of current stressors

Note
1 The significant other and patient both agree on the role of the significant other in treatment including when and what type of support is provided.

Utilizing Alternate Caregivers/Support Persons 91

including significant others in CBT, important interpersonal challenges and stressors may need to be addressed, which may lengthen treatment.

Carer Skills Workshops and Self-Help

There may be times when it is not feasible, appropriate, or clinically indicated for a caregiver to attend therapy sessions with patients. Skill-based workshops for carers may be more appropriate.

"The Maudsley eating disorder collaborative care skills workshops" (AKA "New Maudsley Method") is an intervention for carers of children or adults with eating disorders consisting of one full day (Jenkins et al., 2018) or six 2-hour workshops (Álvarez, Sepúlveda, Anastasiadou, & Parks, 2013; Pépin & King, 2016; Sepulveda, Lopez, Todd, Whitaker, & Treasure, 2008). Carers can be parents/step-parents, partners, siblings, grandparents, or others. Notably, the carer most commonly involved in studies of these programs was a parent. The workshops are based on psychological theories of caregiver coping, which highlight issues such as denial of symptoms, the stigma of eating disorders, and behaviors that can reinforce symptoms (Treasure, Whitaker, Whitney, & Schmidt, 2005). As such, the workshop assists carers in developing an understanding of the disease, effective communication strategies, and problem-solving skills. The workshop also assists caregivers in reflecting on their loved one's readiness to change and encourages them to engage in self-care.

In general, studies evaluating the efficacy of these carer skill workshops show significant reductions in carer distress, burden, and behaviors (e.g., expressed emotion) thought to maintain eating disorders (Hibbs et al., 2015), as well as improvements in carer self-efficacy (Jenkins et al., 2018). These changes are sustained over time (Hibbs et al., 2015). Whether the individual with an eating disorder was an adult or youth did not appear to affect results; however, carers of older individuals endorsed feeling less confident in managing eating pathology than carers of younger individuals (Jenkins et al., 2018). This could be due to differences in duration of illness, with adult patients more likely to have been affected by the eating disorder for a longer time and, thus, have a more entrenched disorder that is resistant to change (Linacre, Green, & Sharma, 2016; Treasure et al., 2005; Treasure, Stein, & Maguire, 2015). Different responsibilities of carers between age groups could also explain this finding.

Another option for supporting carers is a 2-day, group-based, emotion-focused family therapy transdiagnostic intervention for parents of children and adults with eating disorders. This group intervention appeared more effective than the above workshops at enhancing parental self-efficacy in its participants (Lafrance Robinson, Dolhanty, Stillar, Henderson, & Mayman, 2016). Program goals were to educate and support parents in mastering skills involved in recovery coaching, emotion coaching, and processing emotional blocks to effective caregiving using the New Maudsley's animal models (Treasure, Smith, & Crane, 2007). The nature and intensity of involvement in

92 Cristin D. Runfola and Linsey Utzinger

the program could vary slightly according to the child's developmental age, motivation, and symptom pattern.

A meta-analysis of studies on carer interventions found that the addition of these interventions to patient treatment improves patient outcome as well as reduces service use and burden on carer (Hibbs et al., 2015). In addition, qualitative studies of patients and partners who participated in skills groups revealed positive changes, including increased understanding and enhanced communication, as well as decreased critical remarks and emotional over-involvement (Goddard et al., 2011; Macdonald et al., 2011; Toubøl, Koch-Christensen, Bruun, & Nielsen, 2019). Participants found the following program components most helpful for increasing self-efficacy: psychoeducation, role play, practicing new skills, and exchange of ideas with other carers (Jenkins et al., 2018).

Self-help and guided self-help programs (via workbooks, DVDs, and web) for carers based on the interpersonal maintenance model of eating disorders also have been successful in reducing carers' distress and perceived reductions in accommodating and enabling behaviors (Albano, Hodsoll, Kan, Lo Coco, & Cardi, 2019; Dimitropoulos et al., 2019; Goddard et al., 2011). Caregivers report the interventions as essential for helping manage the illness and improve self-care (Zucker, Marcus, & Bulik, 2006).

Additional Considerations on Alternate Caregivers in the Treatment of Adults

The interventions mentioned in this chapter have been mostly studied in heteronormative couples and mothers. Therefore, scant research exists on whether many of the reported observations apply to fathers and to other couple and parenting configurations such as adoptive, LGTBQ, and single parents. In addition, there is little research on the experiences of alternate caregivers, such as siblings and friends. These individuals may be an untapped resource that could present a crucial link in the effort to connect individuals with eating disorders to treatment resources, as well as to provide support during recovery.

Notably, siblings report being willing to take on a primary caretaking role when parents are unable to do so (Dimitropoulos, Klopfer, Lazar, & Schacter, 2009). According to a qualitative study, when including siblings in treatment, there are important factors to consider (Dimitropoulos et al., 2009). First, siblings often strongly identify with the role of "mediator and protector" within the family; thus, clinicians may need to work with siblings to reestablish roles and responsibilities. As familial conflict has contributed to the role of mediator, clinicians may need to provide a forum for siblings to express their thoughts and feelings about the ways in which the family communicates about the eating disorder. Teaching siblings to problem-solve and communicate more effectively may help reduce conflict in the family. Second, siblings prefer to have in-formation about eating disorders and the ways in which that information applies to their situation. Thus, like parents and partners, siblings need psychoeducation and skills. Third, it may be important to address sibling's thoughts and feelings about how they are involved in helping their sibling, and to ensure that, in collaboration with their sibling, they agree on their roles. This collaboration is crucial to prevent feelings of resentment, guilt, anger, or burden. Previous research shows siblings typically have been agreeable to helping parents with tasks such as housekeeping and meal preparation but have been more conflicted about supervising meals and disclosing confidential information. Fourth, as siblings have reported coping better when externalizing the illness, using narrative therapy techniques is important. Finally, reinforcing the positive aspects the eating disorder has had on the sibling relationship may further strengthen the bond between the affected and non-affected sibling. Similar to work with other caregivers, siblings prefer working with clinicians who are non-blaming, empathic, and supportive. All interventions for adults described in this chapter address these concerns or provide room for doing so.

Friends may be incorporated into treatment as well. College students report being more willing to seek help for a friend's eating disorder than their own (Tillman & Sell, 2013). If help is sought, students report being more likely to turn to peers over parents and formal sources for guidance and support (Prouty, Protinsky, & Canady, 2002). Friends, like others, often do not know how to help their peer with an eating disorder. Only 20% of campuses offer education and training about eating disorders (National Eating Disorders Association, 2013). With less than 20% of the college students screening positive for an eating disorder receiving treatment (Dooley-Hash, Lipson, Walton, & Cunningham, 2013; Eisenberg, Nicklett, Roeder, & Kirz, 2011), such educational experiences may help funnel more students to appropriate treatment. Once in treatment, peers may be willing to help in an ongoing way. Anecdotal data suggest friends are willing to cook meals at home, eat out, and spend time with patients who reach out for support. Thus, including friends in the above treatments or workshops may be effective.

Although most interventions involving support persons are delivered in person, a range of methods of delivery (such as online delivery and bibliotherapy) is likely to fit the broad needs of carers (Haigh & Treasure, 2003; Harding & Higginson, 2003). Additionally, online blogs, telephone hotlines, and support groups may provide adjunct support for family and friends (LaMarre, Robson, & Dawczyk, 2015; Prior et al., 2018).

Conclusions and Implications

For adolescents, TAY, and adults with eating disorders, it is important to include family members in treatment. At the very least, other adults whom the patient finds emotionally supportive and invested in his or her recovery may also be included. Across age groups and EBTs, key interventions that may be useful when working with significant others and caregivers include psychoeducation, externalization of the eating disorder, improving communication, teaching skills for targeting eating disorder behaviors, managing emotions, and relapse prevention. Most research, particularly studies of family-based therapies for adolescents, have involved parents and, thus, it is strongly recommended that parents be included in treatment. For TAY and adults, there is preliminary evidence to suggest that including alternate support persons or caregivers, or at least providing the option to include such others, may be helpful. Even if carers are not included in treatment, they may benefit from separate psychoeducational interventions aimed at improving their coping skills and efficacy. Although this chapter presented options for including alternate caregivers and support persons in evidence-based eating disorder treatments across the age spectrum, further research is needed to examine the effectiveness of these alternative applications.

References

Adamson, J., Cardi, V., Kan, C., Harrison, A., Macdonald, P., & Treasure, J. (2019). Evaluation of a novel transition support intervention in an adult eating disorders service: ECHOMANTRA. *International Review of Psychiatry. 31*(4), 382.

Agh, T., Kovács, G., Supina, D., Pawaskar, M., Herman, B. K., Vokó, Z., & Sheehan, D. V. (2016). A systematic review of the health-related quality of life and economic burdens of anorexia nervosa, bulimia nervosa, and binge eating disorder. *Eating and Weight Disorders-Studies on Anorexia, Bulimia and Obesity, 21*(3), 353–364.

Agras, W. S., Bryson, S., Hammer, L. D., & Kraemer, H. C. (2007). Childhood risk factors for thin body preoccupation and social pressure to be thin. *Journal of the American Academy of Child & Adolescent Psychiatry, 46*(2), 171–178.

Agras, W. S., Lock, J., Brandt, H., Bryson, S. W., Dodge, E., Halmi, K. A., ... Wilfley, D. (2014). Comparison of 2 family therapies for adolescent anorexia nervosa: A randomized parallel trial. *JAMA Psychiatry, 71*(11), 1279–1286.

Albano, G., Hodsoll, J., Kan, C., Lo Coco, G., & Cardi, V. (2019). Task-sharing interventions for patients with anorexia nervosa or their carers: A systematic evaluation of the literature and meta-analysis of outcomes. *International Review of Psychiatry, 31*(4).

Allan, E., Le Grange, D., Sawyer, S. M., McLean, L. A., & Hughes, E. K. (2018). Parental expressed emotion during two forms of family-based treatment for adolescent anorexia nervosa. *European Eating Disorders Review, 26*(1), 46–52.

Álvarez, E. G., Sepúlveda, A. R., Anastasiadou, D., & Parks, M. (2013). Familia y Trastornos del Comportamiento Alimentario: Avances en Evaluación y Diseño e Intervención Psicoeducativa Family and Eating Disorders: Advances in Evaluation, Design and Psychoeducational. *Clínica, 4*(2), 107–117.

Anastasiadou, D., Medina-Pradas, C., Sepulveda, A. R., & Treasure, J. (2014). A systematic review of family caregiving in eating disorders. *Eating Behaviors, 15*(3), 464–477.

Arcelus, J., Haslam, M., Farrow, C., & Meyer, C. (2013). The role of interpersonal functioning in the maintenance of eating psychopathology: A systematic review and testable model. *Clinical Psychology Review, 33*(1), 156–167.

Arkell, J., & Robinson, P. (2008). A pilot case series using qualitative and quantitative methods: Biological, psychological and social outcome in severe and enduring eating disorder (anorexia nervosa). *International Journal of Eating Disorders, 41*(7), 650–656.

Arnett, J. J. (2015). *The Oxford Handbook of Emerging Adulthood.* Oxford, UK: Oxford University Press.

Utilizing Alternate Caregivers/Support Persons 95

Aspen, V., & Boutelle, K. (2014). Family-based treatment without a family: Case report of an adolescent with anorexia nervosa. *Eating and Weight Disorders-Studies on Anorexia, Bulimia and Obesity*, *19*(1), 119–123.

Baucom, D. H., Kirby, J. S., Fischer, M. S., Baucom, B. R., Hamer, R., & Bulik, C. M. (2017). Findings from a couple-based open trial for adult anorexia nervosa. *Journal of Family Psychology*, *31*(5), 584.

Berkman, N. D., Lohr, K. N., & Bulik, C. M. (2007). Outcomes of eating disorders: A systematic review of the literature. *International Journal of Eating Disorders*, *40*(4), 293–309.

Blomquist, K. K., Ansell, E. B., White, M. A., Masheb, R. M., & Grilo, C. M. (2012). Interpersonal problems and developmental trajectories of binge eating disorder. *Comprehensive Psychiatry*, *53*(8), 1088–1095.

Boeding, S. E., Paprocki, C. M., Baucom, D. H., Abramowitz, J. S., Wheaton, M. G., Fabricant, L. E., & Fischer, M. S. (2013). Let me check that for you: Symptom accommodation in romantic partners of adults with Obsessive–Compulsive Disorder. *Behaviour Research and Therapy*, *51*(6), 316–322.

Boutelle, K. N., Zucker, N. L., Peterson, C. B., Rydell, S. A., Cafri, G., & Harnack, L. (2011). Two novel treatments to reduce overeating in overweight children: A randomized controlled trial. *Journal of Consulting and Clinical Psychology*, *79*(6), 759.

Branch, H., & Eurman, L. J. (1980). Social attitudes toward patients with anorexia nervosa. *The American Journal of Psychiatry*, *137*(5), 631–632.

Bulik, C. M., Berkman, N. D., Brownley, K. A., Sedway, J. A., & Lohr, K. N. (2007). Anorexia nervosa treatment: A systematic review of randomized controlled trials. *International Journal of Eating Disorders*, *40*(4), 310–320. doi:10.1002/eat.20367.

Bulik, C. M., Sullivan, P. F., Fear, J. L., & Pickering, A. (2000). Outcome of anorexia nervosa: Eating attitudes, personality, and parental bonding. *International Journal of Eating Disorders*, *28*(2), 139–147.

Byrne, C. E., Accurso, E. C., Arnow, K. D., Lock, J., & Le Grange, D. (2015). An exploratory examination of patient and parental self-efficacy as predictors of weight gain in adolescents with anorexia nervosa. *International Journal of Eating Disorders*, *48*(7), 883–888.

Campbell, K., & Peebles, R. (2014). Eating disorders in children and adolescents: State of the art review. *Pediatrics*, *134*(3), 582–592.

Caporino, N. E., Morgan, J., Beckstead, J., Phares, V., Murphy, T. K., & Storch, E. A. (2012). A structural equation analysis of family accommodation in pediatric obsessive-compulsive disorder. *Journal of Abnormal Child Psychology*, *40*(1), 133–143.

Castro, J., Toro, J., & Cruz, M. (2000). Quality of rearing practices as predictor of short-term outcome in adolescent anorexia nervosa. *Psychological Medicine*, *30*(1), 61–67.

Chen, E. Y., Weissman, J. A., Zeffiro, T. A., Yiu, A., Eneva, K. T., Arlt, J. M., & Swantek, M. J. (2016). Family-based therapy for young adults with anorexia nervosa restores weight. *International Journal of Eating Disorders*, *49*(7), 701–707.

Crow, S. J., Peterson, C. B., Swanson, S. A., Raymond, N. C., Specker, S., Eckert, E. D., & Mitchell, J. E. (2009). Increased mortality in bulimia nervosa and other eating disorders. *American Journal of Psychiatry*, *166*(12), 1342–1346.

Dare, C., Eisler, I., Russell, G., Treasure, J., & Dodge, L. (2001). Psychological therapies for adults with anorexia nervosa: Randomised controlled trial of outpatient treatments. *The British Journal of Psychiatry*, *178*(3), 216–221.

Dimitropoulos, G., Farquhar, J. C., Freeman, V. E., Colton, P. A., & Olmsted, M. P. (2015). Pilot study comparing multi-family therapy to single family therapy for

96   Cristin D. Runfola and Linsey Utzinger

adults with anorexia nervosa in an intensive eating disorder program. *European Eating Disorders Review*, *23*(4), 294–303.

Dimitropoulos, G., & Freeman, V. E. (2016). The perceptions of individuals with anorexia nervosa regarding their family's understanding of their illness, treatment, and recovery. *Eating Disorders*, *24*(4), 375–382.

Dimitropoulos, G., Freeman, V. E., Allemang, B., Couturier, J., McVey, G., Lock, J., & Le Grange, D. (2015). Family-based treatment with transition age youth with anorexia nervosa: A qualitative summary of application in clinical practice. *Journal of Eating Disorders*, *3*(1), 1.

Dimitropoulos, G., Klopfer, K., Lazar, L., & Schacter, R. (2009). Caring for a sibling with anorexia nervosa: A qualitative study. *European Eating Disorders Review: The Professional Journal of the Eating Disorders Association*, *17*(5), 350–365.

Dimitropoulos, G., Landers, A. L., Freeman, V., Novick, J., Garber, A., & Le Grange, D. (2018). Open trial of family-based treatment of anorexia nervosa for transition age youth. *Journal of the Canadian Academy of Child and Adolescent Psychiatry*, *27*(1), 50.

Dimitropoulos, G., Landers, A., Freeman, V., Novick, J., Schmidt, U., & Olmsted, M. (2019). A feasibility study comparing a web-based intervention to a workshop intervention for caregivers of adults with eating disorders. *European Eating Disorders Review*, *27*(6), 641–654.

Dimitropoulos, G., Lock, J., Le Grange, D., & Anderson, K. (2015). Family therapy for transition youth. In *family therapy for adolescent eating and weight disorders: New applications*, (pp. 230–255).

Dooley-Hash, S., Lipson, S. K., Walton, M. A., & Cunningham, R. M. (2013). Increased emergency department use by adolescents and young adults with eating disorders. *International Journal of Eating Disorders*, *46*(4), 308–315.

Eisenberg, D., Nicklett, E. J., Roeder, K., & Kirz, N. E. (2011). Eating disorder symptoms among college students: Prevalence, persistence, correlates, and treatment-seeking. *Journal of American College Health*, *59*(8), 700–707.

Eisler, I., Dare, C., Hodes, M., Russell, G., Dodge, E., & Le Grange, D. (2000). Family therapy for adolescent anorexia nervosa: The results of a controlled comparison of two family interventions. *Journal of Child Psychology and Psychiatry*, *41*(6), 727–736.

Eisler, I., Dare, C., Russell, G. F., Szmukler, G., Le Grange, D., & Dodge, E. (1997). Family and individual therapy in anorexia nervosa: A 5-year follow-up. *Archives of General Psychiatry*, *54*(11), 1025–1030.

Eisler, I., Simic, M., Hodsoll, J., Asen, E., Berelowitz, M., Connan, F., … Treasure, J. (2016). A pragmatic randomised multi-centre trial of multifamily and single family therapy for adolescent anorexia nervosa. *BMC Psychiatry*, *16*(1), 422.

Epstein, N. B., & Baucom, D. H. (2002). *Enhanced cognitive-behavioral therapy for couples: A contextual approach*. Washington, D.C.: American Psychological Association.

Fairburn, C. G. (2008). *Cognitive behavior therapy and eating disorders*. New York, NY: Guilford Press.

Fischer, M. S., Baucom, D. H., & Cohen, M. J. (2016). Cognitive-behavioral couple therapies: Review of the evidence for the treatment of relationship distress, psychopathology, and chronic health conditions. *Family Process*, *55*(3), 423–442.

Fischer, M. S., Baucom, D. H., Kirby, J. S., & Bulik, C. M. (2015). Partner distress in the context of adult anorexia nervosa: The role of patients' perceived negative consequences of AN and partner behaviors. *International Journal of Eating Disorders*, *48*(1), 67–71.

Fischer, S., & Le Grange, D. (2007). Comorbidity and high-risk behaviors in treatment-seeking adolescents with bulimia nervosa. *International Journal of Eating Disorders, 40*(8), 751–753.

Fisher, C. A., Skocic, S., Rutherford, K. A., & Hetrick, S. E. (2019). Family therapy approaches for anorexia nervosa. *Cochrane Database of Systematic Reviews* (5). https://www.ncbi.nlm.nih.gov/pmc/articles/PMC6497182/.

Fox, J. R., Dean, M., & Whittlesea, A. (2017). The experience of caring for or living with an individual with an eating disorder: A meta-synthesis of qualitative studies. *Clinical Psychology & Psychotherapy, 24*(1), 103–125.

Fredman, S. J., Vorstenbosch, V., Wagner, A. C., Macdonald, A., & Monson, C. M. (2014). Partner accommodation in posttraumatic stress disorder: Initial testing of the Significant Others' Responses to Trauma Scale (SORTS). *Journal of Anxiety Disorders, 28*(4), 372–381.

Geller, J., Srikameswaran, S., Iyar, M., Zelichowska, J., Thibodeau, M., Brown, K. E., & Dunn, E. C. (2017). Support stance in carers of adults with eating disorders: Factors associated with collaborative versus directive approaches. *International Journal of Eating Disorders, 50*(5), 498–505.

Goddard, E., Macdonald, P., Sepulveda, A. R., Naumann, U., Landau, S., Schmidt, U., & Treasure, J. (2011). Cognitive interpersonal maintenance model of eating disorders: Intervention for carers. *The British Journal of Psychiatry, 199*(3), 225–231.

Graap, H., Bleich, S., Herbst, F., Trostmann, Y., Wancata, J., & de Zwaan, M. (2008). The needs of carers of patients with anorexia and bulimia nervosa. *European Eating Disorders Review: The Professional Journal of the Eating Disorders Association, 16*(1), 21–29.

Haigh, R., & Treasure, J. (2003). Investigating the needs of carers in the area of eating disorders: Development of the Carer's Needs Assessment Measure (CaNAM). *European Eating Disorders Review: The Professional Journal of the Eating Disorders Association, 11*(2), 125–141.

Harding, R., & Higginson, I. J. (2003). What is the best way to help caregivers in cancer and palliative care? A systematic literature review of interventions and their effectiveness. *Palliative Medicine, 17*(1), 63–74.

Hay, P. (2013). A systematic review of evidence for psychological treatments in eating disorders: 2005–2012. *International Journal of Eating Disorders, 46*(5), 462–469.

Hay, P. J., Touyz, S., & Sud, R. (2012). Treatment for severe and enduring anorexia nervosa: A review. *Australian & New Zealand Journal of Psychiatry, 46*(12), 1136–1144.

Hibbs, R., Rhind, C., Leppanen, J., & Treasure, J. (2015). Interventions for caregivers of someone with an eating disorder: A meta-analysis. *International Journal of Eating Disorders, 48*(4), 349–361.

Hilbert, A. (2013). Cognitive-behavioral therapy for binge eating disorder in adolescents: Study protocol for a randomized controlled trial. *Trials, 14*(1), 312.

Hilbert, A., Hoek, H. W., & Schmidt, R. (2017). Evidence-based clinical guidelines for eating disorders: International comparison. *Current Opinion in Psychiatry, 30*(6), 423.

Hughes, E. K., Burton, C., Le Grange, D., & Sawyer, S. M. (2018). The participation of mothers, fathers, and siblings in family-based treatment for adolescent anorexia nervosa. *Journal of Clinical Child & Adolescent Psychology, 47*(sup1), S456–S466.

Huke, K., & Slade, P. (2006). An exploratory investigation of the experiences of partners living with people who have bulimia nervosa. *European Eating Disorders Review: The Professional Journal of the Eating Disorders Association, 14*(6), 436–447.

Jenkins, P. E., Bues, S., Cottrell, J., Hawkins, J., Pinder, L., Price, S., & Stewart, A. (2018). A collaborative care skills workshop for carers: Can it be delivered in 1 day? *Clinical Psychology & Psychotherapy, 25*(1), 130–137.

Johnson, J. G., Cohen, P., Kasen, S., & Brook, J. S. (2002). Childhood adversities associated with risk for eating disorders or weight problems during adolescence or early adulthood. *American Journal of Psychiatry, 159*(3), 394–400.

Jones, A., Lindekilde, N., Lübeck, M., & Clausen, L. (2015). The association between interpersonal problems and treatment outcome in the eating disorders: A systematic review. *Nordic Journal of Psychiatry, 69*(8), 563–573.

Keery, H., Boutelle, K., van den Berg, P., & Thompson, J. K. (2005). The impact of appearance-related teasing by family members. *Journal of Adolescent Health, 37*(2), 120–127.

Kirby, J. S., Baucom, D. H., La Via, M. C., & Bulik, C. M. (2016). Helping couples address higher level of care treatment for anorexia nervosa. In Murray, S., Anderson, L., & Cohn, L. (Eds.), *Innovations in Family Therapy for Eating Disorders: Novel Treatment Developments, Patient Insights, and the Role of Carers.* (pp. 144–151). Abingdon: Routledge.

Kyriacou, O., Treasure, J., & Schmidt, U. (2008). Understanding how parents cope with living with someone with anorexia nervosa: Modelling the factors that are associated with carer distress. *International Journal of Eating Disorders, 41*(3), 233–242.

Lafrance Robinson, A., Dolhanty, J., Stillar, A., Henderson, K., & Mayman, S. (2016). Emotion-focused family therapy for eating disorders across the lifespan: A pilot study of a 2-day transdiagnostic intervention for parents. *Clinical Psychology & Psychotherapy, 23*(1), 14–23.

LaMarre, A., Robson, J., & Dawczyk, A. (2015). Mothers' use of blogs while engaged in family-based treatment for a child's eating disorder. *Families, Systems & Health, 33*(4), 390.

Le Grange, D., Eisler, I., Dare, C., & Hodes, M. (1992). Family criticism and self-starvation: A study of expressed emotion. *Journal of Family Therapy, 14*(2), 177–192.

Le Grange, D., Eisler, I., Dare, C., & Russell, G. F. (1992). Evaluation of family treatments in adolescent anorexia nervosa: A pilot study. *International Journal of Eating Disorders, 12*(4), 347–357.

Le Grange, D., Hughes, E. K., Court, A., Yeo, M., Crosby, R. D., & Sawyer, S. M. (2016). Randomized clinical trial of parent-focused treatment and family-based treatment for adolescent anorexia nervosa. *Journal of the American Academy of Child & Adolescent Psychiatry, 55*(8), 683–692.

Le Grange, D., & Lock, J. (2007). *Treatment manual for bulimia nervosa: A family-based approach.* New York, NY: Guilford.

Le Grange, D., Swanson, S. A., Crow, S. J., & Merikangas, K. R. (2012). Eating disorder not otherwise specified presentation in the US population. *International Journal of Eating Disorders, 45*(5), 711–718.

Linacre, S., Green, J., & Sharma, V. (2016). A pilot study with adaptations to the Maudsley Method approach on workshops for carers of people with eating disorders. *Mental Health Review Journal, 21*(4), 295–307.

Linville, D., Cobb, E., Shen, F., & Stadelman, S. (2016). Reciprocal influence of couple dynamics and eating disorders. *Journal of Marital and Family Therapy, 42*(2), 326–340.

Lock, J. (2015). An update on evidence-based psychosocial treatments for eating disorders in children and adolescents. *Journal of Clinical Child & Adolescent Psychology, 44*(5), 707–721.

Lock, J., Agras, W. S., Bryson, S., & Kraemer, H. C. (2005). A comparison of short- and long-term family therapy for adolescent anorexia nervosa. *Journal of the American Academy of Child & Adolescent Psychiatry, 44*(7), 632–639.

Utilizing Alternate Caregivers/Support Persons 99

Lock, J., & Le Grange, D. (2013). *Treatment manual for anorexia nervosa: A family-based approach (2nd ed.).* New York, NY: Guilford Press.

Lock, J., Le Grange, D., Agras, W., & Dare, C. (2001). *Treatment manual for anorexia nervosa: A family-based approach.* New York, NY: Guilford Publications, Inc.

Lock, J., Le Grange, D., Agras, W. S., Fitzpatrick, K. K., Jo, B., Accurso, E., ... Stainer, M. (2015). Can adaptive treatment improve outcomes in family-based therapy for adolescents with anorexia nervosa? Feasibility and treatment effects of a multi-site treatment study. *Behaviour Research and Therapy, 73*, 90–95.

Macdonald, P., Murray, J., Goddard, E., & Treasure, J. (2011). Carer's experience and perceived effects of a skills based training programme for families of people with eating disorders: A qualitative study. *European Eating Disorders Review, 19*(6), 475–486.

National Eating Disorders Association (2013). *Collegiate survey project.* Retrieved from https://www.nationaleatingdisorders.org/CollegiateSurveyProject.

National Institute for Health and Care Excellence (2017). *Eating Disorders: Recognition and Treatment.* (NICE guideline NG69). Retrieved from https://www.nice.org.uk/guidance/NG69.

Perkins, S., Winn, S., Murray, J., Murphy, R., & Schmidt, U. (2004). A qualitative study of the experience of caring for a person with bulimia nervosa. Part 1: The emotional impact of caring. *International Journal of Eating Disorders, 36*(3), 256–268.

Pinheiro, A. P., Raney, T., Thornton, L. M., Fichter, M. M., Berrettini, W. H., Goldman, D., ... Treasure, J. (2010). Sexual functioning in women with eating disorders. *International Journal of Eating Disorders, 43*(2), 123–129.

Pisetsky, E. M., Utzinger, L. M., & Peterson, C. B. (2016). Incorporating social support in the treatment of anorexia nervosa: Special considerations for older adolescents and young adults. *Cognitive and Behavioral Practice, 23*(3), 316–328.

Prior, A.-L., Woodward, D., Hoefkens, T., Clayton, D., Thirlaway, K., & Limbert, C. (2018). Telephone helplines as a source of support for eating disorders: Service user, carer, and health professional perspectives. *Eating Disorders, 26*(2), 164–184.

Prouty, A. M., Protinsky, H. O., & Canady, D. (2002). College women: Eating behaviors and help-seeking preferences. *Adolescence-San Diego, 37*, 353–364.

Pépin, G., & King, R. (2016). Collaborative care skill training workshop: How Australian carers support a loved one with an eating disorder. *Advances in Eating Disorders, 4*(1), 47–58.

Ratnasuriya, R. H., Eisler, I., Szmukler, G. I., & Russell, G. (1991). Anorexia nervosa: Outcome and prognostic factors after 20 years. *The British Journal of Psychiatry, 158*(4), 495–502.

Reyes-Rodríguez, M. L., Baucom, D. H., & Bulik, C. M. (2014). Culturally sensitive intervention for Latina women with eating disorders: A case study. *Revista Mexicana de Trastornos Alimentarios, 5*(2), 136–146.

Reyes-Rodríguez, M., Watson, H., Barrio, C., Baucom, D., Silva, Y., Luna-Reyes, K., & Bulik, C. (2019). Family involvement in eating disorder treatment among Latinas. *Eating disorders, 27*(2), 205–229.

Robinson, P. H., Kukucska, R., Guidetti, G., & Leavey, G. (2015). Severe and enduring anorexia nervosa (SEED-AN): A qualitative study of patients with 20+ years of anorexia nervosa. *European Eating Disorders Review, 23*(4), 318–326.

Rockwell, R. E., Boutelle, K., Trunko, M. E., Jacobs, M. J., & Kaye, W. H. (2011). An innovative short-term, intensive, family-based treatment for adolescent anorexia nervosa: Case series. *European Eating Disorders Review, 19*(4), 362–367.

Romero-Martínez, Á., & Moya-Albiol, L. (2017). Stress-induced endocrine and immune dysfunctions in caregivers of people with eating disorders. *International Journal of Environmental Research and Public Health, 14*(12), 1560.

Roncero, M., Belloch, A., Perpiñá, C., & Treasure, J. (2013). Ego-syntonicity and ego-dystonicity of eating-related intrusive thoughts in patients with eating disorders. *Psychiatry Research, 208*(1), 67–73.

Runfola, C. D., Kirby, J. S., Baucom, D. H., Fischer, M. S., Baucom, B. R., Matherne, C. E., ... Bulik, C. M. (2018). A pilot open trial of UNITE-BED: A couple-based intervention for binge-eating disorder. *International Journal of Eating Disorders, 51*(9), 1107–1012.

Russell, G. F., Szmukler, G. I., Dare, C., & Eisler, I. (1987). An evaluation of family therapy in anorexia nervosa and bulimia nervosa. *Archives of General Psychiatry, 44*(12), 1047–1056.

Sadeh-Sharvit, S., Arnow, K. D., Osipov, L., Lock, J. D., Jo, B., Pajarito, S., ... Johnson, C. (2018). Are parental self-efficacy and family flexibility mediators of treatment for anorexia nervosa? *International Journal of Eating Disorders, 51*(3), 275–280.

Salerno, L., Rhind, C., Hibbs, R., Micali, N., Schmidt, U., Gowers, S., ... Coco, G. L. (2016). An examination of the impact of care giving styles (accommodation and skilful communication and support) on the one year outcome of adolescent anorexia nervosa: Testing the assumptions of the cognitive interpersonal model in anorexia nervosa. *Journal of Affective Disorders, 191*, 230–236.

Schmidt, U., Magill, N., Renwick, B., Keyes, A., Kenyon, M., Dejong, H., ... Yasin, H. (2015). The Maudsley Outpatient Study of Treatments for Anorexia Nervosa and Related Conditions (MOSAIC): Comparison of the Maudsley Model of Anorexia Nervosa Treatment for Adults (MANTRA) with specialist supportive clinical management (SSCM) in outpatients with broadly defined anorexia nervosa: A randomized controlled trial. *Journal of Consulting and Clinical Psychology, 83*(4), 796.

Schmidt, U., Ryan, E. G., Bartholdy, S., Renwick, B., Keyes, A., O'Hara, C., ... Dejong, H. (2016). Two-year follow-up of the MOSAIC trial: A multicenter randomized controlled trial comparing two psychological treatments in adult outpatients with broadly defined anorexia nervosa. *International Journal of Eating Disorders, 49*(8), 793–800.

Schmidt, U., & Treasure, J. (2006). Anorexia nervosa: Valued and visible. A cognitive-interpersonal maintenance model and its implications for research and practice. *British Journal of Clinical Psychology, 45*(3), 343–366.

Schmidt, U., Wade, T. D., & Treasure, J. (2014). The Maudsley Model of Anorexia Nervosa Treatment for Adults (MANTRA): Development, key features, and preliminary evidence. *Journal of Cognitive Psychotherapy, 28*(1), 48–71.

Sepulveda, A. R., Lopez, C., Todd, G., Whitaker, W., & Treasure, J. (2008). An examination of the impact of "the Maudsley eating disorder collaborative care skills workshops" on the well being of carers. *Social Psychiatry and Psychiatric Epidemiology, 43*(7), 584–591.

Serpell, L., Teasdale, J. D., Troop, N. A., & Treasure, J. (2004). The development of the P-CAN, a measure to operationalize the pros and cons of anorexia nervosa. *International Journal of Eating Disorders, 36*(4), 416–433.

Steiger, H., Sansfaçon, J., Thaler, L., Leonard, N., Cottier, D., Kahan, E., ... Gauvin, L. (2017). Autonomy support and autonomous motivation in the outpatient treatment of adults with an eating disorder. *International Journal of Eating Disorders, 50*(9), 1058–1066.

Stillar, A., Strahan, E., Nash, P., Files, N., Scarborough, J., Mayman, S., ... Orr, E. S. (2016). The influence of carer fear and self-blame when supporting a loved one with an eating disorder. *Eating Disorders, 24*(2), 173–185.

Utilizing Alternate Caregivers/Support Persons 101

Swanson, S. A., Crow, S. J., Le Grange, D., Swendsen, J., & Merikangas, K. R. (2011). Prevalence and correlates of eating disorders in adolescents: Results from the national comorbidity survey replication adolescent supplement. *Archives of General Psychiatry*, *68*(7), 714–723.

Szmukler, G. I., Eisler, I., Russell, G., & Dare, C. (1985). Anorexia nervosa, parental 'expressed emotion' and dropping out of treatment. *The British Journal of Psychiatry*, *147*(3), 265–271.

Tantillo, M. (2006). A relational approach to eating disorders multifamily therapy group: Moving from difference and disconnection to mutual connection. *Families, Systems & Health*, *24*(1), 82.

Tiller, J. M., Sloane, G., Schmidt, U., Troop, N., Power, M., & Treasure, J. L. (1997). Social support in patients with anorexia nervosa and bulimia nervosa. *International Journal of Eating Disorders*, *21*(1), 31–38.

Tillman, K. S., & Sell, D. M. (2013). Help-seeking intentions in college students: An exploration of eating disorder specific help-seeking and general psychological help-seeking. *Eating Behaviors*, *14*(2), 184–186.

Toubøl, A., Koch-Christensen, H., Bruun, P., & Nielsen, D. S. (2019). Parenting skills after participation in skills-based training inspired by the New Maudsley Method: A qualitative study in an outpatient eating disorder setting, *Scandinavian Journal of Caring Sciences*, *33*(4), 959–968.

Tozzi, F., Sullivan, P. F., Fear, J. L., McKenzie, J., & Bulik, C. M. (2003). Causes and recovery in anorexia nervosa: The patient's perspective. *International Journal of Eating Disorders*, *33*(2), 143–154.

Treasure, J., Crane, A., McKnight, R., Buchanan, E., & Wolfe, M. (2011). First do no harm: Iatrogenic maintaining factors in anorexia nervosa. *European Eating Disorders Review*, *19*(4), 296–302.

Treasure, J., Murphy, T., Szmukler, T., Todd, G., Gavan, K., & Joyce, J. (2001). The experience of caregiving for severe mental illness: A comparison between anorexia nervosa and psychosis. *Social Psychiatry and Psychiatric Epidemiology*, *36*(7), 343–347.

Treasure, J., Schmidt, U., & Kan, C. (2019). An illustration of collaborative care with a focus on the role of fathers in Maudsley Anorexia Nervosa Treatment for Adults (MANTRA). *Journal of Clinical Psychology*, *75*(8), 1403–1414.

Treasure, J., Schmidt, U., & Macdonald, P. (2009). *The clinician's guide to collaborative caring in eating disorders: The New Maudsley Method*. Abingdon, UK: Routledge.

Treasure, J., Smith, G., & Crane, A. (2007). *The Maudsley model of collaborative caring: Skills based learning in caring for a loved one with an eating disorder*. London, UK: Routledge.

Treasure, J., Stein, D., & Maguire, S. (2015). Has the time come for a staging model to map the course of eating disorders from high risk to severe enduring illness? An examination of the evidence. *Early Intervention in Psychiatry*, *9*(3), 173–184.

Treasure, J., & Todd, G. (2016). Interpersonal maintaining factors in eating disorder: Skill sharing interventions for carers. In *Bio-psycho-social contributions to understanding eating disorders* (pp. 125–37). New York, NY: Springer.

Treasure, J., Whitaker, W., Whitney, J., & Schmidt, U. (2005). Working with families of adults with anorexia nervosa. *Journal of Family Therapy*, *27*(2), 158–170.

Watson, H., & Bulik, C. (2013). Update on the treatment of anorexia nervosa: Review of clinical trials, practice guidelines and emerging interventions. *Psychological Medicine*, *43*(12), 2477–2500.

102 *Cristin D. Runfola and Linsey Utzinger*

Weber, D. M., Fischer, M. S., Baucom, D. H., Baucom, B. R., Kirby, J. S., Runfola, C. D., ... Bulik, C. M. (2018). The association between symptom accommodation and emotional coregulation in couples with binge eating disorder. *Family Process, 58*(4), 920–935.

Whisman, M. A., Dementyeva, A., Baucom, D. H., & Bulik, C. M. (2012). Marital functioning and binge eating disorder in married women. *International Journal of Eating Disorders, 45*(3), 385–389.

Whitney, J., & Eisler, I. (2005). Theoretical and empirical models around caring for someone with an eating disorder: The reorganization of family life and interpersonal maintenance factors. *Journal of Mental Health, 14*(6), 575–585.

Wierenga, C. E., Hill, L., Peck, S. K., McCray, J., Greathouse, L., Peterson, D., ... Kaye, W. H. (2018). The acceptability, feasibility, and possible benefits of a neurobiologically-informed 5-day multifamily treatment for adults with anorexia nervosa. *International Journal of Eating Disorders, 51*(8), 863–869.

Winn, S., Perkins, S., Murray, J., Murphy, R., & Schmidt, U. (2004). A qualitative study of the experience of caring for a person with bulimia nervosa. Part 2: Carers' needs and experiences of services and other support. *International Journal of Eating Disorders, 36*(3), 269–279.

Zabala, M. J., Macdonald, P., & Treasure, J. (2009). Appraisal of caregiving burden, expressed emotion and psychological distress in families of people with eating disorders: A systematic review. *European Eating Disorders Review: The Professional Journal of the Eating Disorders Association, 17*(5), 338–349.

Zucker, N., Marcus, M., & Bulik, C. (2006). A group parent-training program: A novel approach for eating disorder management. *Eating and Weight Disorders-Studies on Anorexia, Bulimia and Obesity, 11*(2), 78–82.

5 Implementing Eating Disorder Treatment Before and After Bariatric Surgery

Kasey P.S. Goodpaster, Allyson Diggins, and Leslie J. Heinberg

Introduction

Obesity is increasingly prevalent in both developed and developing countries (Kang & Le, 2017; Wang & Beydoun, 2007). In fact, according to the National Health and Nutrition Examination Surveys, more than one out of three adults in the United States meet the criteria for obesity (Hales, Carroll, Fryar, & Ogden, 2017). Obesity is characterized by an excessive accumulation of body fat and is clinically defined by measures that estimate adiposity from body weight, body build, and height (ASMBS, 2017). Body mass index (BMI) is most commonly used to define overweight and obesity and is determined by dividing weight in kilograms by height in meters squared (BMI = kg/m^2). A BMI of ≥ 30 is defined as obesity.

Obesity is associated with conditions such as cardiovascular disease, dyslipidemia, hypertension, cerebrovascular disease, type 2 diabetes, certain types of cancer, and all-cause mortality (Engin, 2017). Recent research suggests that bariatric surgery is the most effective and durable treatment for severe obesity (Kang & Quang, 2017). To qualify for bariatric surgical procedures, patients must have a BMI ≥ 40 or BMI ≥ 35 with at least one obesity-related comorbidity (e.g., type 2 diabetes, hypertension, and sleep apnea), and an inability to achieve healthy weight loss for a sustained period of time with prior weight loss efforts (ASMBS, 2017).

According to the American Society for Metabolic and Bariatric Surgery, 228,000 bariatric surgeries were performed in the United States in 2017, a 44.31% increase since 2011 (ASMBS, 2017). Of bariatric procedures performed, sleeve gastrectomy (59.39% of bariatric cases), and Roux-en-Y gastric bypass (RYGB; 17.80%) are the most common. Sleeve gastrectomy involves removing approximately 80% of the stomach, whereas RYGB involves creating a small stomach pouch and bypassing a segment of the small intestine. Compared to lifestyle interventions and pharmacotherapy, these surgical procedures are more effective in achieving significant weight loss, long-term weight maintenance, improvements in medical comorbidities, and reductions in mortality (Buchwald et al., 2004; Colquitt, Pickett, Loveman, & Frampton, 2014; Jumbe, Hamlet, & Meyrick, 2017). For instance, both the Longitudinal

104 *Goodpaster, Diggins, and Heinberg*

Assessment of Bariatric Surgery-2 (LABS-2) and Swedish Obese Subjects (SOS) studies provide evidence for significant and sustained benefits of bariatric surgery including reductions in obesity-related illnesses (Sjöström et al., 2009; Sjöström et al., 2012), and improvements in health-related quality of life (Karlsson, Taft, Rydén, Sjöström, & Sullivan, 2007) between 7 years (LABS-2 study) and 15 years (SOS study) postoperatively (Devlin et al., 2018). Nevertheless, longitudinal studies have found that different weight loss patterns and associated benefits are observed postoperatively for patients who have undergone the same surgical procedure. Thus, increased attention has been given to the identification of factors that promote optimal responses postsurgically including eating behaviors (Devlin et al., 2018).

Eating disorders (EDs) are common among preoperative bariatric surgery populations (Mitchell et al., 2015), and may persist or emerge postoperatively (Conceição et al., 2014). In fact, active EDs are one of the most commonly cited contraindications for bariatric surgery (Walfish, Vance, & Fabricatore, 2007). To date, research on the prognostic significance of preoperative disordered eating (e.g., graze eating, binge eating, night eating, and loss of control [LOC] over eating) on postsurgical outcomes has been mixed, in part as a result of variable operationalizations and measurements across studies (Courcoulas et al., 2013; Konttinen, Peltonen, Sjöström, Carlsson, & Karlsson, 2014). However, accumulating evidence highlights the connection between disordered eating behaviors before and after bariatric surgery and poor surgical outcomes. For instance, a recent review conducted by Meany, Conceição, and Mitchelll (2014) concluded that 14 of the 15 studies examined provided support for the association between binge/LOC eating and poorer weight loss and greater weight regain postoperatively. In addition, disordered eating behaviors before surgery have been shown to increase the risk for medical complications, and return to LOC eating postoperatively (Meany et al., 2014; Niego et al., 2007; Chao et al., 2016).

As research begins to focus on presurgical eating behaviors on postsurgical outcomes, there has also been increased attention paid to eating behaviors postsurgically. Relatedly, King et al. (2019) found that binge eating accounted for an additional weight regain of 8% of maximum weight lost, whereas more common eating behaviors such as disinhibited eating, graze eating, and eating past fullness were also independently related. Colles, Dixon and O'Brien (2008) found that 94% of individuals who engaged in graze eating presurgery continued this eating pattern after surgery, and both preoperative and postoperative graze eating independently predicted poorer postsurgical weight loss. Additionally, postsurgical LOC eating was associated with regaining 20% of maximum weight lost at Year 7 (Devlin et al., 2018).

Of importance, disorders involving LOC and overeating are not the only maladaptive eating patterns that may be present after bariatric surgery. In fact, case reports have suggested that some individuals may be susceptible to a pattern of extreme control and rigid dietary rules postoperatively (Meany et al., 2014). Thus, targeting all manifestations of maladaptive eating patterns at all-time points throughout the surgical process appears to be of clinical importance.

In this chapter, we will review the prevalence of EDs before and after surgery, pre and postoperative treatment of EDs in this population, and special considerations when adapting ED treatment to bariatric patients. Illustrative case examples will be used throughout.

Prevalence of EDs Before and After Bariatric Surgery

Patients presenting for bariatric surgery have high rates of problematic eating behaviors and EDs compared to patients without severe obesity and compared to patients with severe obesity who do not present for treatment (Engel, Mitchell, de Zwaan, & Steffen, 2012; Kalarchian et al., 2007). As noted above, a subset of patients will continue to exhibit these problems after surgery, and new disordered eating can emerge following bariatric procedures. In this section, we will describe EDs and problematic eating behaviors most frequently seen prior to surgery, prevalence of EDs and disordered behavior following surgery, and impact of pre and postsurgical eating difficulties on outcomes.

Presurgical Disordered Eating

Binge Eating Disorder/LOC Eating

Binge eating disorder (BED) is the most common ED among individuals presenting for bariatric surgery (Brode & Mitchell, 2019). BED is defined as eating an unusually large amount of food in a short period of time (approximately 2 hours) with perceived LOC and other associated symptoms. Bariatric surgery candidates presenting with BED are more likely to have other disordered eating behaviors (Mitchell et al., 2015). LOC appears to be a particularly important factor, as greater reported LOC is linked to higher rates of psychopathology (Colles et al., 2008b). Prevalence rates are quite variable across studies due to methodological differences and use of self-report instruments versus structured interviews. However, using structured clinical interviews, a multisite study of five bariatric programs found that 10% of participants met full Diagnostic and Statistical Manual of Mental Disorders (DSM-5) diagnostic criteria for BED (Mitchell et al., 2012), whereas population base rates are approximately 1.2% (Brode & Mitchell, 2019). These rates may be an underestimate as patients presenting for bariatric surgery may be motivated to underreport any problematic eating behavior for fear of not being approved for surgery.

Graze Eating

Graze eating (also referred to as picking and nibbling) is not a recognized DSM-5 ED but has been frequently described in the bariatric and ED research literature. Conceição et al. (2014) proposed a clinical definition which included unplanned, repetitive eating of small/modest amounts between meals and snacks in which the patient does not know how much will be consumed at the onset of eating, and not in response to hunger/satiety signals. The graze eating behavior can be accompanied with LOC or can be more consistent with eating in a distracted/mindless manner. Graze eating has been previously reported to be quite common (44%) among patients with BED but is also very common in patients with bulimia nervosa (57.6%) and anorexia nervosa (34.3%). Because of differing criteria, prevalence rates in bariatric surgery populations are quite variable (19.5–59.8%) across studies (Conceição et al., 2014). However, in a bariatric surgery sample in which 33% reported graze eating behavior, 32% of those had LOC during episodes of graze eating (Goodpaster et al., 2016).

Night Eating Syndrome (NES) and Sleep-Related Eating Disorder (SRED)

NES is characterized by a delay in the circadian pattern of dietary intake. It includes evening hyperphagia and awakening from sleep to eat. Although not recognized as a DSM-5 ED (generally coded as an "Other Specified Feeding or Eating Disorder"), proposed research criteria include excessive food consumption (>25% of daily calories) after the evening meal and/or nocturnal ingestions either of which occur at least twice per week for 3 months (Allison et al., 2010). Beyond its associated features, it also includes an awareness of eating (to distinguish from other parasomnias) and significant emotional distress and/or impairment in functioning. Although there is overlap with BED, NES may be differentiated by the cognition that one needs to eat in order to sleep at night (de Zwaan, Marschollek, & Allison, 2015). Prevalence of NES in patients presenting for bariatric surgery range from 1.9% to 20%, and NES is associated with higher prevalence of other types of psychopathology (Allison et al., 2006; de Zwaan et al., 2015).

SRED is a parasomnia characterized as a form of sleepwalking. In SRED, there is a lack of conscious awareness of food intake, the food consumed may be unusual or even inedible, and dangerous behavior can occur in the quest for food (e.g., using knife, stove, etc.; Vinai et al., 2012). Research has not examined prevalence rates of SRED in bariatric surgery populations.

Postsurgical Disordered Eating

Binge Eating Disorder/LOC eating

The objective binge eating (OBE) component of BED (eating a large amount of food in a short period of time) often resolves early after surgery due to physiologic changes from the restrictive aspects of the surgical procedures (Opozda, Chur-Hansen, & Wittert, 2016). However, OBE can persist over time (Colles et al., 2008; Engel et al., 2012; Opozda et al., 2016). More commonly, patients may continue to experience LOC and describe subjective episodes of binge eating (Conceição et al., 2017). Prevalence estimates indicate that between 10% and 39% of postoperative patients report LOC within 24 months of surgery (Conceição et al., 2017). This problematic eating behavior can present shortly after surgery or may occur over time as more food is tolerated and/or when cravings return (Conceição et al., 2017; Colles et al., 2008b; White, Kalarchian, & Masheb, 2010).

Numerous studies have examined whether a presurgical diagnosis of BED is a contraindication for surgery or if it results in poorer weight loss outcomes. The majority of the findings do not support a link between BED and suboptimal outcomes (Opozda et al., 2016). Not surprisingly, however, postsurgical LOC eating is linked to suboptimal weight loss and weight regain (Meany et al., 2014; White et al., 2010). Most recently, 7-year prospective data from the LABS study have shown LOC to be a risk factor for poorer weight loss outcomes and weight regain (Devlin et al., 2018). Additionally, LOC has been shown to be linked to increased postsurgical problems (Meany et al., 2014; Müller, Mitchell, Sondag, & de Zwaan, 2013), depression, and poorer health related quality of life (de Zwaan et al., 2010; White et al., 2010). As a history of BED is linked to postsurgical LOC, it has been suggested that patients with BED be closely monitored (Brode & Mitchell, 2019) and/or undergo brief BED treatment (Ashton, Drerup, Windover, & Heinberg, 2009; Ashton, Heinberg, Windover, & Merrell, 2011).

Graze Eating

Graze eating is the most common postsurgical problematic eating behavior with studies reporting prevalence rates ranging from 20% to 38% of postsurgical patients (Colles et al., 2008; Conceição et al., 2013; Conceição et al., 2014). Although patients are not able to consume large volumes of food in one sitting, some patients develop new onset graze eating postsurgery without a history of BED or OBE due to their altered physiology and ease with which small amounts can be consumed over longer periods of time.

One difficulty with differentiating graze eating from normative eating behavior is that postsurgical patients are often instructed to eat multiple small meals throughout the day. However, graze eating can be distinguished by its occurrence without planning and that it may be accompanied by LOC. It has also been hypothesized that patients with BED presurgically may evolve into graze eating postsurgically and thus may be at a greater risk for this problematic eating behavior (de Zwaan et al., 2010). Graze eating has also been linked to poorer weight loss outcomes and weight regain (Conceição et al., 2014; Conceição et al., 2017). Both patients with BED and presurgical graze eating patterns should be monitored postsurgically and may benefit from treatment at either time-point (Goodpaster et al., 2016).

108   *Goodpaster, Diggins, and Heinberg*

NES and SRED

Unlike BED, LOC, and graze eating behaviors, little research has focused on NES following bariatric surgery (Conceição, Utzinger, & Pistsky, 2015). A recent study found that NES symptoms improved in patients with depression following surgery versus those without depression in spite of similar post-surgical weight loss (Pinto et al., 2017). However, the impact of depression on sleep and other vegetative symptoms may be at least partially explanatory as well as the improvement in depression and sleep that is often found within the first year after surgery (Brode & Mitchell, 2019).

Other Problematic Eating Behaviors / Subthreshold Disorders

A number of less common problematic eating behaviors have been described in the literature including chewing and spitting, intentional vomiting, and purposefully eating foods known to induce dumping syndrome (de Zwaan et al., 2010). Dumping syndrome occurs after the consumption of high sugar, high carbohydrate, or high fat foods, characterized by dizziness, diaphoresis, flushing, palpitations, and diarrhea, and can occur frequently after bariatric surgery (Ahmad et al., 2019; Berg & McCallum, 2016). A smaller percentage of patients may also develop postsurgical EDs resembling traditional EDs such as anorexia nervosa (Conceição et al., 2013).

Presurgical Treatment

Research suggests that longstanding disordered eating patterns may be resistant to surgical intervention and that presurgical patients engaging in maladaptive eating behaviors may benefit from intervention prior to the surgical procedure (Leahey, Bond, Irwin, Crowther, & Wing, 2009). Although psychological interventions that address maladaptive eating patterns are not routinely offered within bariatric programs, programs that include ED treatments show the initial utility of incorporating these multimodal treatments into the presurgical process (Brandenburg & Kotlowski, 2005; Cassin et al., 2013; Liu, 2016; Paul et al., 2015). Generally, presurgical interventions have been found to positively influence disordered eating behaviors along with mood and anxiety symptoms (Gade, Friborg, Rosenvinge, Småstuen, & Hjelmesæth, 2015).

Treatment Outcomes

As bariatric surgery grows in use and acceptance, there have been an increasing number of intervention studies focusing on providing lifestyle interventions to presurgical patients. Of these studies, a limited number have examined the effectiveness of preoperative ED treatment.

Gade et al. (2015) assessed the effects of a 10-week cognitive behavioral therapy (CBT) intervention aimed at reducing disordered eating behaviors (i.e., exerting rigid control, LOC eating, or eating for emotional reasons rather than hunger or appetite) among individuals presenting for bariatric surgery. The researchers presumed that disordered eating behaviors occur in relation to negative mood states or a tendency to experience LOC over eating, and, thus, involve cognitive, emotional, and behavioral components that are positively influenced by CBT. Results demonstrated that patients in the CBT intervention group evidenced a decrease in maladaptive eating patterns, moderate alleviation of depression and anxiety, and weight loss following treatment. Results are consistent with previous studies that have examined the effects of CBT on eating behaviors.

Ashton et al. (2009) conducted a brief four-session CBT intervention for binge eating among 243 bariatric surgery patients. Session topics included eating as a habit, self-monitoring, stimulus control, stress management, mindful eating, body image, postoperative expectations, and cognitive restructuring. Patients experienced statistically significant improvements in binge eating episodes, cognitions, and behaviors. Additionally, patients were categorized as responders or nonresponders based on their eating disordered behaviors postintervention. Across bariatric surgical procedures, patients who were categorized as responders lost significantly more weight at 6 and 12 months postsurgically.

Adding to the evidence base, Kalarchian and Marcus and colleagues (2013) conducted a randomized prospective study of a presurgical lifestyle intervention based on a standard behavioral weight management program and adapted for bariatric surgery candidates. Patients ($N = 240$) were assigned to the 6-month lifestyle intervention or to usual care. Initial results indicated that patients who participated in the intervention experienced greater weight loss, had a greater probability of achieving $\geq$ 5% weight loss, reported improvements in maladaptive eating patterns, and were more likely to remain surgical candidates after the intervention. Of note, 53% of patients in the intervention group achieved at least 5% weight loss, which has been associated with shorter operating room times (Alami et al., 2007) and greater weight loss 1 year following RYGB (Solomon, Liu, Alami, Morton, & Curet, 2009).

In addition, patients in Spain participated in a 3-month presurgical CBT intervention (Abilés et al., 2013). Prior to the intervention, patients with BED were more likely to have anxiety, depression, low self-esteem, fear, and guilt; have a lower quality of life; be more concerned with food, weight, and figure; have greater hunger; and be more influenced by contextual factors. Following the intervention, many of these domains improved. Specifically, patients experienced improvements in self-esteem, depression, and EDs.

Finally, a study conducted in Germany involved an outpatient group intervention offered to patients with mood, anxiety, and/or EDs. The authors concluded that the program resulted in clinically relevant reductions in depression, improvement in quality of life, and transition in ED behaviors (i.e., decoupled association between eating behavior and depression; Wild et al., 2011).

110   *Goodpaster, Diggins, and Heinberg*

Taken together, current evidence from multiple countries suggests pre-surgical treatment may have a favorable impact on EDs as well as depression, anxiety, and health-related quality of life; however, further studies are warranted to ascertain longitudinal benefits (Kalarchian & Marcus, 2015).

Common Elements in Presurgical ED Treatment

Studies assessing presurgical interventions have primarily been based on CBT, acceptance and commitment therapy (ACT), and mindfulness based approaches (see Table 5.1). Theoretical principles from CBT that have been commonly incorporated into presurgical ED treatments include learning to recognize triggers to disordered eating behaviors, identifying associated cognitions and emotions, introducing plans for change, goal setting, self-monitoring, implementing stimulus control procedures, establishing a regular eating pattern, engaging in self-reinforcement, and use of cognitive and behavioral assignments outside of session (Gade et al., 2015; Leahey, Crowther, & Irwin, 2008).

In addition, treatment focuses on cognitive restructuring and problem-solving. In particular, patients are instructed to identify and challenge cognitive patterns that sustain problematic eating behaviors (e.g., all-or-nothing thinking and minimization) and learn problem-solving skills to manage stressors that are connected to eating behaviors (Leahey et al., 2008). Furthermore, interventions commonly include strategies to enhance intrinsic motivation and use motivational interviewing techniques to address resistance to change. Finally, treatment addresses maintaining change and relapse prevention with an emphasis on reviewing high-risk situations and developing adaptive coping strategies to reduce the likelihood of relapse.

In addition to traditional CBT approaches, ACT has also been used as a basis for presurgical interventions for bariatric surgery patients. ACT targets changes in avoidance behaviors such as eating to avoid experiencing unpleasant emotions (Weineland, Arvidsson, Kakoulidis, & Dahl, 2012). These interventions focus less on reducing problematic eating behaviors, and focus

Table 5.1 Common Session Topics in Presurgical Eating Disorder Treatment

Characteristics of eating disordered behaviors	Overview of CBT model
Regulating eating pattern	Stress management
Goal-setting and self-monitoring	Body image
Problem-solving	Preparing for surgery (and life after surgery)
Nonfood rewards	Changes in relationships/ social situations
Managing cravings	Mindful eating
Stimulus control	

more on increasing valued actions. Within bariatric surgery populations, ACT strategies have been used to increase activity in areas which were previously avoided due to weight gain including intimate relationships and exercising.

In mindfulness-based approaches, presurgical patients are encouraged to focus on emotions and physical sensations with nonjudgmental awareness and self-acceptance (Kabat-Zinn, 1982). Supporting emotional acceptance, reducing reactive behavioral responses, incorporating mindfulness strategies, and increasing use of adaptive coping practices may lead to decreased use of food as an emotional escape mechanism (Heatherton & Baumeister, 1991). For bariatric candidates, mindfulness interventions may address unique needs as these patients must adhere to strict dietary guidelines postsurgically and may have experienced significant difficulty altering their eating patterns prior to the surgical procedure (Stunkard, Stinnett, & Smoller, 1986; Wadden, Sarwer, & Berkowitz, 1999).

Format

Presurgical ED treatments vary in intervention length, treatment modality, and background of intervention facilitators. With regard to intervention length, presurgical interventions are generally brief, ranging from 4 weeks to 6 months. Intervention brevity has been supported by research suggesting the efficacy of short-term treatment (Grilo, Masheb, & Wilson, 2006). In addition, brief treatment offers the benefit of allowing for optimizing outcomes without causing undue delay for bariatric surgeries, which, though elective, are often considered medically necessary (Creel, 2009).

Treatment modalities include group versus individual treatment and in-person versus telephone. Of the studies reviewed previously, there was a relatively equal number of interventions delivered in group (Abilés et al., 2013; Ashton et al., 2009; Wild et al., 2011) and individual formats (Cassin et al., 2013; Gade et al., 2015; Kalarchian & Marcus, 2015). The majority of the studies included combined face-to-face sessions and e-health approaches. For instance, the lifestyle intervention delivered by Kalarchian & Marcus (2015) included 8 weekly face-to-face sessions lasting an hour followed by 16 weeks of alternating face-to-face sessions and telephone coaching lasting 15–20 minutes. Finally, the study conducted by Gade et al. (2015) included five intervention sessions that were delivered to patients at the treatment study center, whereas the remaining six sessions were delivered through scheduled telephone calls. Across studies, treatment facilitators included psychiatrists, psychologists, physiotherapists, clinical psychology doctoral candidates, and interventionists who had received training in behavioral and surgical management of obesity (Abilés et al., 2013; Ashton et al., 2009; Cassin et al., 2013; Gade et al., 2015; Kalarchian & Marcus, 2015; Wild et al., 2011).

112   *Goodpaster, Diggins, and Heinberg*

Special Considerations for Presurgical Patients

Presurgical ED treatment for bariatric surgery patients includes a number of unique components, such as increasing education on disordered eating behaviors and risks of postsurgical challenges, identifying alternative coping strategies, mindfulness, becoming mentally prepared for surgery, and developing realistic expectations for life after surgery. A case study is provided to illustrate the application of ED interventions to a presurgical patient.

Case Study – Samantha

"Samantha" is a 22-year-old Caucasian female who presented for presurgical psychological evaluation seeking RYGB. Her goals postsurgery were increased energy, increased self-worth, and increased social life. Samantha described childhood onset obesity with gradual weight gain despite several weight loss attempts. She attributed weight gain to genetic predisposition, "feeling overwhelmed," childhood influences (e.g., mother emphasized weight and dieting), irregular eating patterns, suboptimal physical activity, and consumption of processed foods. Her weight at initial psychological evaluation was 280 lbs. (BMI = 45). During the course of the evaluation, she reported recent binge eating, graze eating, and limited social support. As part of preparation for the surgical procedure, Samantha participated in the four-session CBT group initially created by Ashton et al. (2009) and summarized below.

SESSION 1

During the first session, individuals complete a pregroup assessment and are provided with an overview of treatment. Group members are given the opportunity to discuss motivators for the surgical procedure, pros/cons of program participation, and barriers to weight management. The goal of session one is to provide patients with greater education on how disordered presurgical eating behaviors may compromise postsurgical outcomes, as well as emphasize the value of modifying eating behaviors prior to surgery (Ashton et al., 2009; Leahey et al., 2008). Patients are also introduced to the importance of self-monitoring and setting behavioral goals.

Samantha was open about her difficulty with managing her eating behaviors. She acknowledged that her main motivators for undergoing the surgical procedure included "needing to learn how to eat again." She described how binge eating and graze eating behaviors have served as a barrier to weight management. She was an active participant in the group and set a goal to separate eating and drinking, and increase daily water intake over the next week.

Treatment Before and After Bariatric Surgery   113

SESSION 2

During the second session, patients review food diaries with an emphasis on triggers to maladaptive eating patterns, discuss antecedents for eating disordered behaviors including emotions (e.g., stress, depression, and anger) and thoughts, identify alternative stress management and cognitive strategies, and review body image expectations postsurgery. The psychologist facilitates a relaxed breathing exercise in this session.

Samantha expressed challenges with compliance with food diaries noting that she filled them out at the end of the week, which may have compromised accuracy. Despite challenges with completing food diaries, she reported increased awareness of her eating patterns and her vulnerabilities for making unhealthy food choices. She was unable to achieve her goal from Session 1; however, she set a new goal to eat breakfast every morning and exercise twice per week.

SESSION 3

In the third session, food diaries are reviewed with an emphasis on behavioral techniques for weight management (e.g., stimulus control), strategies for managing cravings, behavior chaining, and developing an exercise plan. In addition, time is spent learning mindfulness-based practices that encourage greater awareness of the environment, reducing distractions, engaging the five senses in the process of eating, and physical sensations that ultimately promote patients' adherence to postsurgical dietary and behavioral recommendations (Leahey et al., 2008). The psychologist facilitates a mindful eating exercise in this session.

During this session, Samantha reported she partially completed food diaries. In addition, she was able to partially achieve her goal of eating breakfast and going to the gym. She reported reduced evening cravings attributed to eating more regularly throughout the day. To build upon this progress, Samantha set a new goal of eating breakfast daily, exercising 4 days per week, and establishing regular mealtimes (eating 3 meals and 2 snacks).

SESSION 4

During the last session, emphasis is placed on preparing for surgery and life after surgery. Session topics include eating in social situations, assertiveness training, mental preparation for surgery, and preparing the support system. In addition, food diaries are reviewed with a focus on eating in social situations. The session concludes with a guest speaker 1 year postsurgery to answer participants' questions about life after surgery. Finally, patients complete postgroup assessments. Throughout the session, patients are encouraged to develop realistic expectations for life postoperatively as unmet postsurgical expectations can contribute to distress and frustration among patients and may influence postoperative eating behaviors (Leahey et al., 2008). As such, discussion centers on nonscale victories and nonjudgmental acceptance.

Samantha acknowledged limited adherence with food diaries and discussed barriers to achieving goals including busyness. She problem-solved strategies for establishing regular mealtimes such as setting a timer on her phone as a reminder to eat. Samantha shared her pleasure with her reduced preoccupation with food and choosing and enjoying healthier food options. She was engaged in the discussion and asked thoughtful questions. On postgroup assessments, Samantha evidenced improved eating behaviors (i.e., denied engagement in binge, night, or graze eating) and improved motivation and confidence in her ability to manage her weight and be physically active long term.

OUTCOMES

Overall, throughout the course of treatment, Samantha struggled with keeping food diaries and meeting stated goals. Despite challenges, her self-report suggested improvements in mindset, motivation, and eating habits. She acknowledged hesitancy about participating in the group initially; however, she ultimately cited benefits including accountability, goal setting, group interaction, and learning how to better manage cravings. Samantha felt mentally prepared for surgery and underwent RYGB with minimal medical or psychological complications. She followed up after surgery in shared psychology appointments at 1 and 3 months postoperatively. By her 6 month appointment with the bariatric team, Samantha had lost 100 lbs. (73% of excess body weight) and denied return to disordered eating behaviors. Although long-term benefit of preoperative ED treatment cannot be established, Samantha was able to reduce disordered eating behaviors in the short term and displayed increased ability to problem-solve strategies for adjusting to life postsurgically through participation in the presurgical intervention. She was educated about early warning signs of ED relapse and given resources for treatment if problematic eating behaviors reemerged.

Postsurgical Treatment

Although the hope is that presurgical ED treatment can provide patients with coping skills needed to avoid ED relapse postsurgery, patients may not receive such treatment. Some barriers to consider here include unavailable treatments, underreporting of ED symptoms for fear of not being "cleared" for surgery, and patients not seeing the value in behavioral treatment. Indeed, some patients view surgery alone as a cure for overweight and disordered eating, which reduces motivation for participating in behavioral intervention prior to surgery. One study comparing patients' willingness to participate in pre and postsurgical ED interventions demonstrated that patients referred after surgery are more likely to follow up on the referral, attend more sessions,

Treatment Before and After Bariatric Surgery   115

and complete the intervention, than those referred before surgery (Leahey et al., 2009). The authors suggested that before surgery, patients may overestimate the power of surgery in preventing maladaptive eating; yet, after surgery, they realize that behaviors continue to drive outcomes, thus enhancing motivation for treatment. Evidence-based ED treatment is needed to address lingering or new onset ED symptoms.

Treatment Outcomes

Outcome research regarding postsurgical ED treatment is limited, and typically consists of small pilot studies. Nevertheless, results have been encouraging, and many of these interventions share common elements (i.e., CBT and mindfulness) that clinicians may incorporate into their evidence-based practice. However, note that dismantling studies have not been conducted, thus it is unknown which elements of treatment are essential in contributing to outcomes.

One of the earliest studies examining an intervention for bariatric patients experiencing subjective binge eating showed good promise. Over the course of a 10-week group intervention, which combined traditional CBT with mindfulness elements, patients reduced LOC/binge eating, reduced urges to eat in response to emotions, decreased depression, decreased emotional regulation difficulties, and increased self-efficacy with eating (Leahey et al., 2008).

Another small, randomized controlled trial compared ACT to treatment as usual (TAU) for postsurgical patients (Weineland, Arvidsson, Kakoulidis, & Dauhl, 2012). Although patients with ED were not specifically recruited for the study, ED symptoms were measured before and after the randomly assigned intervention. ACT treatment involved two face-to-face sessions and a six-week Internet course. Compared to the TAU condition, those participating in the ACT condition evidenced more improvement in ED behaviors, body dissatisfaction, quality of life, and acceptance of weight-related thoughts and feelings.

In an intervention designed by Cassin et al. (2013), the authors suggested that pre and postsurgical patients can be combined to receive one intervention to address binge eating symptoms. In this small pilot study, consisting of a mix of presurgical ($n = 2$) and postsurgical patients ($n = 6$), a six-session course of CBT was delivered either in person or telephonically. The majority of patients (four of six) evidenced improvements in binge eating frequency, associated binge eating symptoms, depression, and urges to eat to soothe negative emotions.

Another small, but randomly controlled pilot study of postsurgical patients suggested that a 10-week group mindfulness-based intervention reduced emotional eating, although binge eating was not present among participants neither before nor after the intervention (Chacko, Yeh, & Davis, 2016). Given the authors' mixed findings regarding perceived stress and associated binge eating behaviors (i.e., discrepancies between qualitative and quantitative results in these domains), they concluded that "explicit instruction in complementary coping skills" (p. 18) paired with mindfulness may improve treatment outcomes.

Finally, Robinson, Adler, Darcy, Osipov, and Safers (2016) shedded light on the length of treatment needed to achieve successful outcomes. They examined early intervention for patients who were beginning to engage in maladaptive eating behaviors (e.g., graze eating and mindless eating) in the first 6 months postsurgery. A total of 13 patients participated in targeted sessions delivered mostly by phone. The number of sessions recommended were determined by participants' responses on a dietary adherence questionnaire. Thus, only session topics relevant to patients' distinct challenges were covered. Findings suggested that most patients were able to improve adherence and reduce engagement in maladaptive eating behaviors with only a few sessions (average of 4.5 out of 12 possible sessions). Thus, a brief course of targeted sessions may help address barriers to regular follow-up after surgery.

Common Elements in Postsurgical ED Treatment

Clearly, interventions supported by research have differed in their focus, format, length, and theoretical approach. However, multiple studies share common elements, which include group support, CBT, and mindfulness. Cognitive-behavioral elements (i.e., self-monitoring, goal-setting, psychoeduction, cognitive restructuring, problem-solving, behavioral activation, stimulus control, and relapse prevention), which were reviewed earlier in this chapter, also apply to postsurgical treatment (Cassin et al., 2013, Leahey et al., 2008).

In particular, mindfulness techniques may supplement traditional CBT interventions and help address postsurgical patents' grieving process as they let go of the role food played in their lives. In this context, mindfulness involves realistic goal-setting, self-compassion, mindful awareness and acceptance of emotions, mindful eating, and meditation. Patients are helped to practice nonjudgmental acceptance of current weight, lifestyle changes needed, and unmet expectations for surgery and weight loss (Weineland, Arvidsson, Kakoulidis, & Dahl, 2012). In-vivo mindfulness practice coupled with didactic content may include mindful eating strategies to help patients better discern hunger and fullness given their new anatomy, as well as accept negative emotions that tend to prompt maladaptive eating. Additional guided meditations may be used for "homework" between sessions to improve self-care (Chacko et al., 2016; Leahey et al., 2008).

Format

Research supports that individual or group formats can be effective in reducing ED symptoms. However, the group format offers benefits of time- and cost-effectiveness, and ability for patients to receive and provide support to others with similar challenges. Given that ED symptoms can feel isolating, the group format provides a sense of validation. Indeed, in Chacko et al.'s (2016, p. 18) postintervention interview, participants universally cited the group format as beneficial, "specifically the benefit of hearing others' experiences, trust and safety, and cohesion and friendship."

Previously studied group interventions have ranged from 4 to 12 weeks of 30–90 minute sessions. Sessions begin with a "check in" in which food diaries are reviewed and patients share successes and challenges since the last session. Didactic content focused on the session topic is then reviewed in a semi-structured manner, with patient examples and experiences elicited during the session. Sessions end with a "check out" in which patients set goals on which to focus their efforts until the next session. Table 5.2 includes common session topics in postsurgical ED treatment.

Special Considerations for Postsurgical Patients

Although many CBT and mindfulness interventions are used in other populations with EDs, postsurgical bariatric patients have unique needs to be addressed in treatment, including dietary restrictions, fear of failure/weight regain, grieving the loss of food, social/relationship changes, and body image concerns. A case study is provided to illustrate the application of ED interventions to a postsurgical patient.

Case Study – Ruby

"Ruby" is a 65-year-old African American woman who underwent the RYGB in 2010. Prior to surgery, she was noted to have binge eating and depression, and was required to participate in the four-session CBT group described earlier in this chapter for binge eating. In addition, she was required to establish therapy to address depression. She made good progress through presurgical treatment, and with surgery, lost from her highest weight of 269 lbs. to a nadir of 164 lbs. Ruby returned to the bariatric program in 2017 after a 2-year gap in follow-up, at which point she had regained to 232 lbs. She was motivated to reestablish treatment to address weight regain after learning that her diabetes was returning.

Table 5.2 Common Session Topics in Postsurgical Eating Disorder Treatment

Overview of CBT Model	Cognitive reframing
Goal-setting and self-monitoring	Behavioral activation
Problem-solving	Stress management techniques
Nonfood rewards	Mindful eating
Developing a regular eating pattern	Social aspects of eating
Managing cravings	Assertive communication training
Stimulus control	Relapse prevention

118   *Goodpaster, Diggins, and Heinberg*

During her reevaluation with the psychologist, Ruby evidenced daily graze eating and NES, frequent dumping syndrome, and poor adherence to nutritional recommendations. She reported moderately severe depression and anxiety as well as a stressful living environment in a high crime neighborhood, and these contributed to low motivation. She had discontinued mental health treatment shortly after surgery, thinking she no longer needed therapy. She had questions about whether her anatomy could be contributing to weight regain and whether she would qualify for a revision surgery. Rather than being referred back to the surgeon, Ruby was referred to the dietitian and to a therapy group designed for postsurgical patients experiencing weight regain.

BARIATRIC LIFESTYLE RECOMMENDATIONS

Bariatric patients such as Ruby have unique dietary needs that should be addressed in treatment. In a multidisciplinary settings, dietitians are able to provide guidance for specific dietary recommendations, but these lifestyle changes should also be integrated into ED programming. Table 5.3 lists typical lifestyle recommendations, which may vary slightly by bariatric program.

Behavioral health providers who are accustomed to emphasizing mindfulness and a "non-dieting" approach may be challenged by what appear to be additional "food rules." Indeed, some patients' attempt to adhere to postsurgical dietary recommendations can take on an obsessive quality and, in extreme cases, contribute to the onset of EDs such as anorexia nervosa (Conceição et al, 2013). Thus, behavioral health providers generally strive to assist patients in following the bariatric lifestyle while acknowledging the need for balance, sustainable lifestyle change, and self-compassion.

RUBY'S BARIATRIC LIFESTYLE ADHERENCE

During Ruby's psychological evaluation, she evidenced poor adherence to the bariatric lifestyle. She was typically eating only one to two meals per day, and these meals tended to be high in carbohydrates and low in protein. In addition, she was no longer separating eating and drinking, and was consuming

Table 5.3 Bariatric Lifestyle Recommendations

1 Consume five to six small, planned meals per day
2 Slow the pace of eating to 20–30 minutes
3 Chew food thoroughly; approximately 30 chews per bite of food
4 Separate eating and drinking by 30 minutes
5 Eliminate alcohol, caffeine, and carbonated beverages
6 Reduce portions to saucer-sized plates
7 Prioritize protein and reduce sweets/carbohydrates
8 Increase water

Treatment Before and After Bariatric Surgery   119

three cups of coffee per day. Her diet quality contributed to a sense of sluggishness, frequent dumping syndrome, and overeating at night. Specifically, skipped meals earlier in the day led to high levels of physical hunger later on, and this sense of urgency led her to resort to snack foods, consumed at a rapid pace. Evening snacking, in turn, contributed to reduced appetite the next day, and thus reinforced the cycle of skipped meals and overeating. The psychologist worked together with the dietitian to reinforce education about bariatric lifestyle recommendations and problem-solve how to improve the timing and quality of her food intake.

FEAR OF WEIGHT REGAIN

Fear of weight regain is rather common and tends to increase over time (14.3% at 1 month and 20.7% at 3 months postoperatively; Heinberg, Mohun, Goodpaster, Peterson, & Lavery, 2017). Bariatric surgery can seem like a "last resort" when all previous diets have resulted in only short-term weight loss and, ultimately, weight regain. A sense of failure may be internalized, and many bariatric patients report an overwhelming pressure for bariatric surgery to be effective when nothing else was. Given the more rapid and visible weight loss associated with surgical treatment, patients may also face greater scrutiny and questions about weight loss, eating habits, and regain. Additionally, weight loss plateaus, which are normal in the weight loss progression, can compound fears of failure and lead patients to assume they are doing something wrong.

Incidentally, although some mild anxiety may increase motivation for continued healthy eating habits, more severe symptoms may prove to be counterproductive and lead to increased emotional eating. Thus, behavioral health providers are tasked with helping patients break down negative thought patterns to prevent fear of weight regain from becoming a self-fulfilling prophecy. Cognitive restructuring may be a helpful intervention to address these fears.

RUBY'S FEAR OF WEIGHT REGAIN

Fear of weight regain was not one of Ruby's primary challenges. In fact, her mild fear of weight regain was, in some ways, helpful in providing the impetus to return to the bariatric program. She was aware if she continued to gain weight, her diabetes would return. However, concern regarding weight regain turned to demoralization or a sense of resignation that weight regain was occurring. She lacked an internal locus of control, and was instead focused on a surgical or medical solution to her weight management difficulties. Food diaries were the most important tool in increasing her awareness about disordered eating patterns (e.g., skipped meals contributing to night eating), and the connection between her food choices (e.g., sweets) and physical symptoms (i.e., dumping syndrome). When she started changing her behaviors and noticed the resultant weight loss, she began to feel more in control and confident in her ability to manage her health. Mild fear of weight regain motivated her to return for follow-up appointments more regularly than she had initially postsurgery.

GRIEVING THE LOSS OF FOOD

Before surgery, food can serve many needs: to reduce physical hunger, connect socially, celebrate, and soothe emotions. When food takes on a different role after surgery, patients sometimes describe a grieving process similar to losing a loved one. In a recent study of psychological complications between 1 and 3 months after surgery, approximately 5% of patients endorsed this grieving process (Heinberg et al., 2017). Those who felt out of control of their eating prior to surgery may feel disappointed if they continue to feel out of control after surgery, but perhaps with graze eating rather than binge eating. Grieving the loss of food may involve moving through stages of denial, anger, depression, bargaining, and acceptance, not always in a cyclical manner (Kübler-Ross, 1969). Behavioral health providers assist patients in moving through this grieving process using supportive, grief counseling techniques. They may also help patients explore underlying feelings (e.g., boredom and stress), needs (e.g., stimulation and relaxation), and nonfood strategies for meeting these needs (e.g., taking a quick walk and practicing meditation).

RUBY'S EXPERIENCE OF GRIEVING THE LOSS OF FOOD

Ruby shared that initially after surgery, she was relieved that food was not appealing and she had decreased physical hunger. However, as time passed, she began to experience what she perceived to be "excessive hunger." As she had expected that hunger would be diminished indefinitely, her increased urges to eat were alarming. Treatment involved helping Ruby discern physical hunger from mental cravings. One of her biggest clues that she was having a craving was her sudden, strong desire for specific foods (i.e., sweets) during those times. As she began to reduce sweets again, she initially reported increased emotional distress which seemed related to her no longer using sweets to numb her emotions. The psychologist used mindful eating strategies to help her derive enjoyment from food, including sweets, in smaller amounts. Ruby also explored nonfood strategies for addressing underlying emotional needs for comfort. Having adaptive coping strategies in place helped to alleviate grief, and she began to feel empowered about her control over eating.

BODY IMAGE CHANGES

Many patients expect that weight loss associated with bariatric surgery will improve body image. In fact, Libeton and colleagues (2004) found that approximately one-third of bariatric candidates rated "distress about physical appearance" or "embarrassment socially about weight" as the primary motivators for surgery. However, reduced weight does not guarantee concomitant improvements in perceptions of one's body. A systematic literature review revealed that although several studies found general improvements in body image following surgery, others found that some body image domains improve, but others do not, and that body image does not necessarily improve "enough" to match norms in the general population (Ivezaj & Grilo, 2018). Indeed, dissatisfaction with excess skin is common, and is related to body image problems, physical irritation, impaired movement, and intimacy concerns (Ivezaj & Grilo, 2018). Poor body image has the potential to negatively affect eating behavior by either leading to (1) obsessiveness about weight loss and fears of weight regain, which could, in turn, trigger compensatory behaviors or restriction, and/or (2) increased LOC eating and avoidance of exercise (due to impaired motivation or fear of judgment). Thus, body image is an important issue to address in postsurgical treatment.

RUBY'S BODY IMAGE CHANGES

Ruby's body image improved soon after surgery, particularly as her diabetes became better controlled and she felt less pain. She was weighing herself daily and was excited by her weight loss. However, as weight loss began to slow and she reached plateaus, her frequent weighing began to take a toll on motivation. The scale became a trigger for shame, depression, and thoughts that she was "failing" the surgery. Eventually, she stopped weighing altogether because she did not want to face how much she had gained. Poor body image reached an all-time high when she learned that her diabetes was returning. Poor body image only served to increase emotional eating. The psychologist worked with Ruby to create a "bariatric bucket list" of nonscale goals she had wanted to achieve before surgery. She then checked off several items that were accomplished despite weight regain, and was encouraged to practice gratitude for these improvements. As she began to improve her diet, she was cautioned not to weigh too frequently, knowing that slow but sustainable weight loss might deter motivation. Ruby decided to weigh only at doctor's appointments and instead focus on behavioral goals and quality of life indictors. Meanwhile, cognitive restructuring, acceptance, and exposure techniques were used to help her reprocess her body image.

SOCIAL/RELATIONSHIP ASPECTS

Bariatric patients often report a mix of positive and negative changes in relationships, some of which may affect eating behaviors. Patients may need to field many questions about weight loss, which can increase feelings of vulnerability, exacerbate the pressure for weight loss, and affect body image. Some friends and family may "food police" (e.g., make critical comments about food choices such as, "Should you be eating that?") generally out of concern or desire to support patients. However, these comments can feel stigmatizing or shaming. Other social supports may "food push" (i.e., encourage patients to eat larger portions or consume certain foods that may not align with bariatric lifestyle recommendations, e.g., "Is that all you're going to eat?"). Food pushing can be unintentional, as social supports may be accustomed to showing their love and appreciation through food, or intentional and sabotaging. Thus, patients need support increasing assertive communication skills to help navigate social dynamics.

RUBY'S EXPERIENCE OF SOCIAL ASPECTS OF EATING

Ruby was challenged by social eating, specifically at community potlucks in which members urged her to consume the special "comfort foods" they prepared and she had historically enjoyed. Ruby was afraid of appearing rude by turning down their offers for these foods. At first, she suggested she should avoid church potlucks. However, church was one of the few places she found joy and socialization. Instead, the psychologist helped her to brainstorm specific strategies she could use during potlucks. For example, she ate regular meals beforehand to avoid high levels of hunger during the potluck, brought bariatric-friendly recipes to share, scanned all options before selecting those she most wanted to eat, consumed protein before vegetables and carbohydrates, and used rehearsed responses when others offered her more food (e.g., "No thank you, I ate before I came" or "That looks really good, I might get some later"). She found she received much less "pushback" than she had expected.

Overall, multidisciplinary postsurgical treatment proved effective in reducing disordered eating and, in turn, facilitated additional weight loss. A year after her reentry into the bariatric program, Ruby had lost to 178 lbs. (BMI = 30), blood glucose levels were in the normal range, and she no longer saw the need for a revision surgery. She continues to maintain regular follow-up appointments, having learned that long-term support is a key component in her long-term success.

Conclusion

Bariatric surgery is a powerful weight loss tool, yet EDs before and after surgery are not uncommon and can compromise outcomes. Although patients may expect that surgery itself will help them feel in control of eating, these procedures do not preclude graze eating, LOC eating, restriction, or other maladaptive behaviors. Presurgical ED treatment thus plays a valuable role in aligning patients' expectations about what the surgical procedures will and will not solve; practicing adaptive coping skills to manage emotions, thoughts, and activities related to eating that will likely remain with altered anatomy; and identifying early warning signs of ED relapse postsurgery.

Though research suggests promising short-term outcomes of presurgical ED treatment, many patients do not access this treatment before surgery due to not disclosing their eating pathology or such treatment being unavailable. Postsurgical patients experiencing reemergence of eating pathology and/or weight regain may have more intrinsic motivation to participate in ED interventions. CBT, mindfulness, and other brief evidence-based interventions are helpful in preventing and treating EDs when they emerge throughout the pre- and postsurgical process.

References

Abilés, V., Rodríguez-Ruiz, S., Abilés, J., Obispo, A., Gandara, N., Luna, V., & Fernández-Santaella, M. C. (2013). Effectiveness of cognitive-behavioral therapy in morbidity obese candidates for bariatric surgery with and without binge eating disorder. *Nutricion Hospitalaria, 28*(5), 1523–1529.

Ahmad, A., Kornrich, D. B., Krasner, H., Eckardt, S., Ahmad, Z., Braslow, A., & Brogglewirth, B. (2019). Prevalence of dumping syndrome after laparoscopic sleeve gastrectomy and comparison with laparoscopic Roux-en-Y gastric bypass. *Obesity Surgery, 29*, 1506–1513.

Alami, R. S., Morton, J. M., Schuster, R., Lie, J., Sanchez, B. R., Peters, A., & Curet, M. J. (2007). Is there a benefit to preoperative weight loss in gastric bypass patients? A prospective randomized trial. *Surgery for Obesity and Related Diseases, 3*(2), 141–145.

Allison, K. C., Lundgren, J. D., O'Reardon, J. P., Geliebter, A., Gluck, M. E., Vinai, P., ... Stunkard, A. J. (2010). Proposed diagnostic criteria for night eating syndrome. *International Journal of Eating Disorders, 43*, 241–247.

Allison, K. C., Wadden, T. A., Sarwer, D. B., Fabricatore, A. N., Crerand, C. E., Gibbons, L. M., ..., Williams, N. N. (2006). Night eating syndrome and binge eating disorder among persons seeking bariatric surgery: Prevalence and related features. *Obesity, 14*, 77S–82S.

American Society for Bariatric and Metabolic Surgery (2017). Retrieved from https://asmbs.org/.

Ashton, K., Drerup, M., Windover, A., & Heinberg, L. J. (2009). Efficacy of a four-session cognitive behavioral group intervention for binge eating among bariatric surgery candidates. *Surgery for Obesity and Related Diseases, 5*, 262–276.

Ashton, K., Heinberg, L. J., Windover, A., & Merrell, J. (2011). Positive response to binge eating intervention enhances postsurgical weight loss and adherence. *Surgery for Obesity and Related Diseases, 7*, 315–320.

Berg, P. & McCallum, R. (2016). Dumping syndrome: A review of the current concepts of pathophysiology, diagnosis, and treatment. *Digestive Diseases and Sciences, 61*, 11–18.

Brandenburg, D., & Kotlowski, R. (2005). Practice makes perfect? Patient response to a prebariatric surgery behavior modification program. *Obesity Surgery, 15*(1), 125–132.

Brode, C. S. & Mitchell, J. E. (2019). Problematic eating behaviors and eating disorders associated with bariatric surgery. *Psychiatric Clinics of North America, 42*, 287–297.

Buchwald, H., Avidor, Y., Braunwald, E., Jensen, M. D., Pories, W., Fahrbach, K., & Schoelles, K. (2004). Bariatric surgery: A systematic review and meta-analysis. *Journal of the American Medical Association, 292*(14), 1724–1737.

Cassin, S. E., Sockalingham, S., Wnuk, S., Strimas, R., Royal, S., Hawa, R., & Parikh, S. V. (2013). Cognitive behavioral therapy for bariatric surgery patients: Preliminary evidence for feasibility, acceptability, and effectiveness. *Cognitive and Behavioral Practice, 20*, 529–543.

124   Goodpaster, Diggins, and Heinberg

Chacko, S. A., Yeh, G. Y., & Davis, R. B. (2016). A mindfulness-based intervention to control weight after bariatric surgery: Preliminary results from a randomized controlled pilot trial. *Complementary Therapies in Medicine, 28*, 13–21.

Chao, A. M., Wadden, T. A., Faulconbridge, L. F., Sarwer, D. B., Webb, V. L., Shaw, J. A., ... Williams, N. N. (2016). Binge-eating disorder and the outcome of bariatric surgery in a prospective, observational study: Two-year results. *Obesity, 24*(11), 2327–2333.

Colquitt, J. L., Pickett, K., Loveman, E., & Frampton, G. K. (2014). Surgery for weight loss in adults. *Cochrane Database of Systematic Reviews,* (8), 1–184.

Colles, S. L., Dixon, J. B., & O'Brien, P. E. (2008a). Loss of control is central to psychological disturbance associated with binge eating disorder. *Obesity, 16*, 608–614.

Colles, S. L., Dixon, J. B., & O'Brien, P. E. (2008b). Grazing and loss of control related to eating: Two high-risk factors following bariatric surgery. *Obesity, 16*, 615–622.

Conceição, E. M., Crosby, R., Mitchell, J. E., Engel, S. G., Wonderlich, S. A., Simonich, H. K., ... Le Grange, D. (2013). Picking or nibbling: Frequency and associated clinical features in bulimia nervosa, anorexia nervosa, and binge eating disorder. *International Journal of Eating Disorders, 46*, 815–818.

Conceição, E. M., Mitchell, J. E., Engel, S. G., Machado, P. P., Lancaster, K., & Wonderlich, S. A. (2014). What is grazing? Reviewing its definition, frequency, clinical characteristics, and impact on bariatric surgery outcomes, and proposing a standard definition. *Surgery for Obesity and Related Diseases, 10*, 973–982.

Conceição, E. M., Mitchell, J. E., & Pinto-Bastos, A. (2017). Stability of problematic eating behaviors and weight loss trajectories after bariatric surgery: A longitudinal observational study. *Surgery for Obesity and Related Diseases, 13*, 1063–1070.

Conceição, E. M., Mitchell, J. E., Vaz, A. R., Bastos, A. P., Ramalho, S., Silva, C., ... Machado, P. P. (2017). The presence of maladaptive eating behaviors and weight loss trajectories after bariatric surgery: A longitudinal observational study. *Surgery for Obesity and Related Diseases, 13*, 1063–1070.

Conceição, E. M., Orcutt, M., Mitchell, J. E., Engel, S., Lahaise, K., Jorgensen, M., ... Wonderlich, S. (2013). Eating Disorders after bariatric surgery: A case series. *International Journal of Eating Disorders, 46*, 274–279.

Conceição, E. M., Utzinger, L. M., & Pistsky, E. M. (2015). Eating disorders and problematic eating behaviours before and after bariatric surgery: Characterization, assessment and association with treatment outcomes. *European Eating Disorders Review, 23*, 417–425.

Courcoulas, A. P., Christian, N. J., Belle, S. H., Berk, P. D., Flum, D. R., Garcia, L., ... Wolfe, B. M. (2013). Weight change and health outcomes at 3 years after bariatric surgery among individuals with severe obesity. *Journal of the American Medical Association, 310*(22), 2416–2425.

Creel, D. B. (2009). Comment on: When is the best time to deliver behavioral intervention to bariatric surgery patients: Before or after surgery?. *Surgery for Obesity and Related Diseases, 5*(1), 102–103.

Devlin, M. J., King, W. C., Kalarchian, M. A., Hineman, A., Marcus, M. D., Yanovski, S. Z., & Mitchell, J. E. (2018). Eating pathology and associations with long-term changes in weight and quality of life in the longitudinal assessment of bariatric surgery study. *International Journal of Eating Disorders, 51*, 1322–1330.

de Zwaan, M., Hilbert, A., Swan-Kremeier, L., Simonich, H., Lancaster, K., Howell, L. M., ... Mitchell, J. E. (2010). Comprehensive interview assessment of

Treatment Before and After Bariatric Surgery 125

eating behavior 18–35 months after gastric bypass surgery for morbid obesity. *Surgery for Obesity and Related Diseases, 6*, 79–85.

de Zwaan, M., Marschollek. M., & Allison, K. C. (2015). The night eating syndrome (NES) in bariatric surgery patients. *European Eating Disorders Review, 23*, 426–434.

Engel, S. G., Mitchell, J. E., de Zwaan, M. & Steffen. K. J. (2012). Eating disorders and eating problems pre-and postbariatric surgery. In *Psychosocial assessment and treatment of bariatric surgery patients* (pp. 87–98). New York, NY: Routledge.

Engin, A. (2017). The definition and prevalence of obesity and metabolic syndrome. In *Obesity and lipotoxicity* (pp. 1–17). Cham, Switzerland: Springer.

Gade, H., Friborg, O., Rosenvinge, J. H., Småstuen, M. C., & Hjelmesæth, J. (2015). The impact of a preoperative cognitive behavioural therapy (CBT) on dysfunctional eating behaviours, affective symptoms and body weight 1 year after bariatric surgery: A randomised controlled trial. *Obesity Surgery, 25*(11), 2112–2119.

Goodpaster, K. P. S., Marek, R. J., Lavery, M., Ashton, K., Rish, J. & Heinberg, L. J. (2016). Graze eating among bariatric surgery candidates: Prevalence and psychosocial correlates. *Surgery for Obesity and Related Diseases, 12*, 1091–1097.

Grilo, C. M., Masheb, R. M., & Wilson, G. T. (2006). Rapid response to treatment for binge eating disorder. *Journal of Consulting and Clinical Psychology, 74*(3), 602.

Hales, C. M., Carroll, M. D., Fryar, C. D., & Ogden, C. L. (2017). *Prevalence of obesity among adults and youth: United States, 2015–2016. NCHS Data Brief* (288), 1–7. https:// stacks.cdc.gov/view/cdc/49223.

Heatherton, T. F., & Baumeister, R. F. (1991). Binge eating as escape from self-awareness. *Psychological Bulletin, 110*(1), 86.

Heinberg, L., Mohun, S., Goodpaster, K., Peterson, N., & Lavery, M. (2017). Early psychological complications: Pre-operative psychological factors predict post-operative regret, fear of failure, and grieving the loss of food. *Surgery for Obesity and Related Diseases, 13*, S42–S43.

Ivezaj, V. & Grilo, C. M. (2018). The complexity of body image following bariatric surgery: A systematic review of the literature. *Obesity Reviews, 19*, 1116–1140.

Jumbe, S., Hamlet, C., & Meyrick, J. (2017). Psychological aspects of bariatric surgery as a treatment for obesity. *Current Obesity Reports, 6*(1), 71–78.

Kabat-Zinn, J. (1982). An outpatient program in behavioral medicine for chronic pain patients based on the practice of mindfulness meditation: Theoretical considerations and preliminary results. *General Hospital Psychiatry, 4*, 33–47.

Kalarchian, M. A., & Marcus, M. D. (2015). Psychosocial interventions pre and post bariatric surgery. *European Eating Disorders Review, 23*(6), 457–462.

Kalarchian, M. A., Marcus, M. D., Courcoulas, A. P., Cheng, Y., & Levin, M. D. (2013). Preoperative lifestyle intervention in bariatric surgery: Initial results from a randomized, controlled trial. *Obesity, 21*(2), 254–260.

Kalarchian, M. A., Marcus, M. D., Levine, M. D., Courcoulas, A. P., Pilkonis, P. A., Rinham, R. M., ... Rofey, D. L. (2007). Psychiatric disorders among bariatric surgery candidates: Relationship to obesity and functional health status. *American Journal of Psychiatry, 164*, 328–334.

Kang, J. H., & Le, Q. A. (2017). Effectiveness of bariatric surgical procedures: A systematic review and network meta-analysis of randomized controlled trials. *Medicine, 96*(46), e8632.

Karlsson, J., Taft, C., Ryden, A., Sjöström, L., & Sullivan, M. (2007). Ten-year trends in health-related quality of life after surgical and conventional treatment for severe obesity: The SOS intervention study. *International Journal of Obesity, 31*(8), 1248.

126 *Goodpaster, Diggins, and Heinberg*

King, W. C., Belle, S. H., Hinerman, A. S., Mitchell, J. E., Steffen, K. J., & Courcoulas, A. P. (2019). Patient behaviors and characteristics related to weight regain after Roux-en-Y gastric bypass: A multicenter prospective cohort study. *Annals of Surgery* (e-pub ahead of print). https://pubmed.ncbi.nlm.nih.gov/30950861/.

Konttinen, H., Peltonen, M., Sjöström, L., Carlsson, L., & Karlsson, J. (2014). Psychological aspects of eating behavior as predictors of 10-y weight changes after surgical and conventional treatment of severe obesity: Results from the Swedish Obese Subjects intervention study. *The American Journal of Clinical Nutrition, 101*(1), 16–24.

Kübler-Ross, E. (1969). *On death and dying.* New York, NY: The Macmillan Company.

Leahey, T. M., Bond, D. S., Irwin, S. R., Crowther, J. H., & Wing, R. R. (2009). When is the best time to deliver behavioral intervention to bariatric surgery patients: Before or after surgery?. *Surgery for Obesity and Related Diseases, 5*(1), 99–102.

Leahey, T. M., Crowther, J. H., & Irwin, S. R. (2008). A cognitive-behavioral mindfulness group therapy intervention for the treatment of binge eating in bariatric surgery patients. *Cognitive and Behavioral Practice, 15*, 364–375.

Libteton, M., Dixon, J. B., Laurie, C., & O'Brien, P. E. (2014). Patient motivation for bariatric surgery: Characteristics and impact on outcomes. *Obesity Surgery, 14*, 392–398.

Liu, R. H. (2016). Do behavioral interventions delivered before bariatric surgery impact weight loss in adults? A systematic scoping review. *Bariatric Surgical Practice and Patient Care, 11*(2), 39–48.

Niego, S. H., Pratt, E. M., & Agras, W. S. (1997). Subjective or objective binge: Is the distinction valid? *International Journal of Eating Disorders, 22*, 291–298.

Meany, G., Conceição, E., & Mitchell, J. E. (2014). Binge eating, binge eating disorder and loss of control eating: Effects on weight outcomes after bariatric surgery. *European Eating Disorders Review, 22*, 87–91.

Mitchell, J. E., King, W. C., Courcoulas, A., Dakin, G., Elder, K., Engel, S., … Wolfe, B. (2015). Eating behavior and eating disorders in adults before bariatric surgery. *International Journal of Eating Disorders, 48*, 215–222.

Mitchell, J. E., Selzer, F., Kalarchian, M. A., Devlin, M. J., Strain, G. W., Elder, K. A., Marcus, M. D., Wonderlich, S., Christian, N. J., & Yanovski, S. Z. (2012). Psychopathology before surgery in the Longitudinal Assessment of Bariatric Surgery-3 (LABS-3) Psychosocial Study. *Surgery for Obesity and Related Diseases, 8*, 533–541.

Müller, A., Mitchell, J. E., Sondag, C., & de Zwaan, M. (2013). Psychiatric aspects of bariatric surgery. *Current Psychiatry Reports, 15*, 397.

Opozda, M., Chur-Hansen, A., & Wittert, G. (2016). Changes in problematic and disordered eating after gastric bypass, adjustable gastric banding and vertical sleeve gastrectomy: A systematic review of pre-post studies. *Obesity Reviews, 17*, 770–792.

Paul, L., van Rongen, S., van Hoeken, D., Deen, M., Klaassen, R., Biter, L. U., & … van der Heiden, C. (2015). Does cognitive behavioral therapy strengthen the effect of bariatric surgery for obesity? Design and methods of a randomized and controlled study. *Contemporary Clinical Trials, 42*, 252–256.

Pinto, T. F., de Bruin, P. F. C., de Bruin, V. M. S., Lemos, F. N., Lopes, F. H. A., & Lopes, P. M. (2017). Effects of bariatric surgery on night eating and depressive symptoms: A prospective study. *Surgery for Obesity and Related Diseases, 13*, 1057–1062.

Robinson, A. H., Adler, S., Darcy, A. M., Osipov, L., & Safer, D. L. (2016). Early adherence targeted therapy (EATT) for postbariatric maladaptive eating behaviors. *Cognitive and Behavioral Practice, 23*, 548–560.

Sjöström, L., Peltonen, M., Jacobson, P., Sjöström, C. D., Karason, K., Wedel, H., & ... Bouchard, C. (2012). Bariatric surgery and long-term cardiovascular events. *Journal of the American Medical Association, 307*(1), 56–65.

Sjöström, L., Gummesson, A., Sjöström, C. D., Narbro, K., Peltonen, M., Wedel, H., & ... Jacobson, P. (2009). Effects of bariatric surgery on cancer incidence in obese patients in Sweden (Swedish Obese Subjects Study): A prospective, controlled intervention trial. *The Lancet Oncology, 10*(7), 653–662.

Solomon, H., Liu, G. Y., Alami, R., Morton, J., & Curet, M. J. (2009). Benefits to patients choosing preoperative weight loss in gastric bypass surgery: New results of a randomized trial. *Journal of the American College of Surgeons, 208*(2), 241–245.

Stunkard, A. J., Stinnett, J. L., & Smoller, J. W. (1986). Psychological and social aspects of the surgical treatment of obesity. *The American Journal of Psychiatry, 143*(4), 417–429.

Vinai, P., Ferri, R., Ferini-Strambi, L., Cardetti, S., Anelli, M., Vallauri, P., ... Manconi, M. (2012). Defining the borders between sleep-related eating disorder and night eating syndrome. *Sleep Medicine, 13*, 686–690.

Wadden, T. A., Sarwer, D. B., & Berkowitz, R. I. (1999). Behavioural treatment of the overweight patient. *Best Practice & Research Clinical Endocrinology & Metabolism, 13*(1), 93–107.

Walfish, S., Vance, D., & Fabricatore, A. N. (2007). Psychological evaluation of bariatric surgery applicants: Procedures and reasons for delay or denial of surgery. *Obesity Surgery, 17*(12), 1578–1583.

Wang, Y., & Beydoun, M. A. (2007). The obesity epidemic in the United States—gender, age, socioeconomic, racial/ethnic, and geographic characteristics: A systematic review and meta-regression analysis. *Epidemiologic Reviews, 29*(1), 6–28.

Weinland, S., Arvidsson, D., Kakoulidis, T. P., & Dahl, J. (2012). Acceptance and commitment therapy for bariatric surgery patients, a pilot RCT. *Obesity Research & Clinical Practice, 6*, e21–e30.

White, M. A., Kalarchian, M. A., & Masheb, R. M. (2010). Loss of control over eating predicts outcomes in bariatric surgery: A prospective 24-month follow-up study. *Journal of Clinical Psychiatry, 71*, 175–181.

Wild, B., Herzog, W., Wesche, D., Niehoff, D., Müller, B., & Hain, B. (2011). Development of a group therapy to enhance treatment motivation and decision making in severely obese patients with a comorbid mental disorder. *Obesity Surgery, 21*, 588–594.

6 Evidence-Based Treatments for Youth with Overweight/ Obesity

Ashley F. Jennings, Abigail R. Cooper, Sara Fruchter, Gina Dimitropoulos, and Katharine L. Loeb

Introduction

Rising rates of childhood obesity (Ogden, Carroll, Fryar, & Flegal, 2015; Ogden, Carroll, Kit, & Flegal, 2014; Ogden et al., 2016) have prompted a range of efforts directed at prevention and intervention, including the adaptation and application of core eating disorder (ED) treatments for youth with overweight or obesity (OW/OB) given that these conditions frequently overlap. Childhood overweight status is defined as a body mass index (BMI) range from the 85th up to the 95th percentile for age and sex, and obesity is characterized by a BMI percentile at or above 95 (Barlow & Expert Committee, 2007), although increased attention to variables beyond BMI-based measures has been advocated in the literature (Cambuli et al., 2008; Speiser et al., 2005). EDs are marked by pathological eating behaviors and psychological experience of food and/or body, leading to functional impairment and distress (Diagnostic and Statistical Manual of Mental Disorders, Fifth Edition [DSM-5]; American Psychiatric Association, 2013). This chapter will review OW/OB considerations in ED presentations, with a particular emphasis on binge ED (BED) and atypical anorexia nervosa (AAN). The following will also discuss the rationale for and data on adapting specific ED interventions for the distinct and overlapping presentations of OW/OB in youth.

Weight and EDs

OW/OB can be comorbid with ED, by history or concurrently, and within ED; weight status can differentiate diagnosis. For example, binge eating and purging in the context of underweight and other symptoms of anorexia nervosa (AN) would be classified as AN, binge eating/purging type rather than as bulimia nervosa (BN). In addition, although AN is partially diagnosed by an underweight status, individuals with AAN, BN, and BED fall within the normal-to-obese weight range according to diagnostic criteria (American Psychiatric Association, 2013). Moreover, historical and current growth curve data carry implications for treatment goals and planning,

Youth with Overweight/Obesity   129

particularly in pediatric populations. For instance, expected weight is informed by growth history and is also conceptualized as a moving target for youth, which necessitates ongoing adjustment in intervention targets (Flegal, Tabak, & Ogden, 2006).

BED in Youth with OW/OB

There is a general positive correlation between binge eating and weight status (Kessler et al., 2013), and BED is associated with increased risk for weight gain and obesity among children and adolescents (Stice et al., 1999; Stice, Presnell, & Spangler, 2002; Tanofsky-Kraff et al., 2006). In addition, risk factors for both BED and BN include childhood obesity (Gonçalves, Machado, Martins, Hoek, & Machado, 2016; Striegel-Moore et al., 2005). Research has signified differences between ED and non-ED OW/OB presentations in youth. For example, overweight adolescents with BED are distinguishable from their non-BED counterparts by elevated ED (e.g., shape and weight concerns) and mood symptoms (Eddy et al., 2007; Glasofer, 2006; Goldschmidt, Wall, Loth, & Neumark-Sztainer, 2015; Kass et al., 2017). Even infrequent binge eating among overweight adolescents is associated with significantly greater eating-related and general psychopathology (Eddy et al., 2007).

Loss-of-control (LOC) eating (Tanofsky-Kraff, Marcus, Yanovski, & Yanovski, 2008), which reflects only a component criterion for binge eating, operates as a key indicator of eating and weight problems in youth. LOC eating is highly comorbid with obesity and metabolic dysfunction in youth and carries negative prognostic significance with regard to onset of EDs, anxiety disorders, and depression (Byrne, LeMay-Russell, & Tanofsky-Kraff, 2019; He, Cai, & Fan, 2017). In fact, it has been argued that the size of an overeating episode matters less than the experience of LOC eating and other behavioral and psychological symptoms in predicting disordered eating and OW/OB (Shomaker et al., 2009), in part because the context of child development can render the size criterion for binge eating ambiguous. LOC eating in childhood and adolescence has therefore been conceptualized in multiple ways, including as a developmentally specific manifestation of BED (He et al., 2017), as an other specified feeding or ED (Tanofsky-Kraff et al., 2008), or as a correlate or early risk signal for future BED and increase in BMI (Hilbert & Brauhardt, 2014; Sonneville et al., 2013; Tanofsky-Kraff et al., 2011).

The overlap between BED and OW/OB, in combination with the negative prognostic significance of lower frequency binge eating and LOC eating, renders the distinction in the treatment literature between OW/OB in isolation, and OW/OB with ED behaviors among youth, as rather diffuse. The research reflects this continuum of OW/OB presentation in its characterization of symptomology and in the corresponding selection of relevant ED prevention and intervention approaches for OW/OB adaptation. Thus, treatments for, and in association with, LOC eating will be reviewed in this chapter, highlighting that LOC eating, independently of BED, confers psychiatric and medical implications for youth.

In the adult BED treatment literature, although binge eating is the primary target, weight is often considered an important secondary outcome variable under the assumption that facilitating remission from BED should arrest a prior weight gain trajectory, optimally, and yield weight reduction. The weight loss effect in this population has been minimal at best (Wilson, 2011). In examining the inverse relationship, the presence of binge eating attenuates weight outcomes among adults involved in weight loss interventions (Chao et al., 2017) as well as adolescents undergoing bariatric surgery (Goldschmidt, Lavender, Hipwell, Stepp, & Keenan, 2018) or receiving family-based behavioral treatment (Wildes et al., 2010).

AAN in Youth with OW/OB

The term "atypical AN" has been used historically in the ED literature to represent subthreshold AN and other variants of AN spectrum presentations. More recently, DSM-5 categorized AAN as an other specified eating and feeding disorder, and defined it specifically as meeting all criteria for AN except that despite significant weight disruption, current weight falls within or above the normal range (American Psychiatric Association, 2013). Among children and adolescents, normal range can span 80 percentile points at the population level (Kuczmarksi et al., 2002); it is therefore critical to use individualized growth curves to determine benchmarks for expected weight (Golden et al., 2015). One complicating factor in doing so is that a history of OW/OB is common in AAN (Sawyer, Whitelaw, Le Grange, Yeu, & Hughes, 2016) and, according to the diagnostic criteria, can also be present at treatment initiation or case identification. (Indeed, weight loss in AAN might be reinforced, and further weight loss even encouraged by health professionals, peers, parents, and others in the patient's environment.) This raises key questions about clinically indicated growth curve targets during a course of treatment for AAN, a disorder with a severity of physical and psychological morbidity on par with AN (Sawyer et al., 2016), and thus a similar urgency for full and sustained remission. Although some clinicians may be tempted to set goal weights in accordance with population-based normal range (Dimitropoulos et al., 2019), research on degree of weight suppression, disentangled from absolute weight status in AN (e.g., Berner, Shaw, Witt, & Lowe, 2013), suggests that an idiographic, iterative decision-making process may yield superior outcomes.

Beyond prospective markers of improvement in AAN such as medical stability, background variables that could have influenced premorbid weight status must also be considered in hypothesizing weight targets, i.e., future growth percentiles that will likely correspond to return of health. Relevant factors include prior weight/growth trajectory (stable or unstable), history of health behaviors (presence or absence of binge eating, LOC eating, other

Youth with Overweight/Obesity 131

problematic eating patterns, and sedentary behavior), and affective state (presence or absence of affect dysregulation, depression, and mood lability). The degree to which concerns in these domains are applicable can inform the necessity of full versus partial weight percentile restoration in the context of increasing variety and quantity of food to facilitate renourishment. For example, an adolescent with AAN who maintained a stable 85th BMI-for-age percentile for most of her development, ate nutritiously and flexibly, participated in team sports, and experienced minimal mood fluctuations before her ED would likely need to return to her premorbid growth percentile; there were no obvious modifiable variables premorbidly to suggest that her weight status could be adjusted further through reasonable, sustainable measures. Conversely, an adolescent with AAN whose historical BMI-for-age percentile had deviated significantly upward following a significant interpersonal loss and period of depression, during which she started binge eating and spending her free time in her room on screens, should not be expected to return to her immediately premorbid weight status; rather, the comorbidities should also be treated and more distal growth curves examined for indicators of her personalized "normal."

Although these two starkly contrasting scenarios illustrate the principle at its extreme, more typically, adolescents with AAN and prior or current OW/OB will present with a mixed profile, requiring thoughtful case conceptualization and multidisciplinary treatment planning with regard to weight goals. Table 6.1 presents relevant decision-making factors for youth with AAN and other presentations involving past or present OW/OB. Importantly, clinicians must be prepared to help patients with AAN work toward acceptance of the limitations of a human body's mutability when a healthy, durable approach to eating and exercise is implemented. Data on the degree to which weight stigma and bias are internalized even by ED professionals (Puhl, Latner, King, & Luedicke, 2014) suggest that this is an important area for future research and training.

Table 6.1 Hypothesized Weight Range Target at Which Health/Remission is likely to be Achieved

Maladaptive Eating or Activity Behavior and/or Relevant Psychiatric Comorbidity, Prior to Onset of Eating/Weight Disorder	*Weight History*	
	Unstable[1]	*Stable*[2]
Present	Prior healthy range	(Prior) normal to overweight range
Absent	Prior healthy range	(Prior) normal to overweight range

Notes

1 Unstable weight history: History indicates that weight was stable and healthy for child/adolescent, then increased significantly prior to onset of eating/weight disorder.

2 Stable weight history: History indicates that weight was stable at any range (normal, overweight, and obese), and remained so, prior to onset of ED.

132   Ashley F. Jennings et al.

Adapting ED Interventions to Prevent or Treat OW/OB in Youth

Rationale

The justification for utilizing ED treatments for a population without diagnostic-level eating pathology has both overarching and treatment-specific rationales. First, treatment approaches that have proven useful for regulating dietary behavior in the service of facilitating recovery from an ED may also have face-valid or mechanism-level applications to an overlapping set of maladaptive eating behaviors that may appear in non-ED OW/OB presentations. Second, capitalizing on parenting capacities to improve eating- and weight-related health behaviors among children and adolescents has been shown to be effective in both the ED and weight disorder literatures (Couturier, Kimber, & Szatmari, 2013; Jamilian, Malekirad, Farhadi, Habibi, & Zamani, 2014; Niemeier, Hektner, & Enger, 2012; Sung-Chan, Sung, Zhao, & Brownson, 2013). Third, mood and interpersonal pathways can lead to dysregulated behavior, including emotional eating, in youth (Kelly et al., 2016). Certain evidence-based treatments for EDs target improvement of mood dimensions like depression by working on relational functioning (i.e., interpersonal psychotherapy [IPT] or IPT techniques included in cognitive behavior therapy [CBT] for EDs). Other interventions (e.g., dialectical behavior therapy [DBT]) more directly focus on mood regulation and distress tolerance in an effort to reign in impulsivity, which is intrinsic to the developmental stage of adolescence (Pehlivanova et al., 2018). Given these hypothesized links between risk factors for OW/OB in youth and corresponding treatment modalities (see Figure 6.1), early identification, prevention, and intervention are all critical.

IPT

IPT, a therapy with a focus on the interpersonal context, was originally developed for adults with major depressive disorder (Klerman, Weissman, Rounsaville, & Chevron, 1984), and was later modified for adults with EDs (Agras, Walsh, Fairburn, Wilson, & Kraemer, 2000; Fairburn, 1991; McIntosh, Bulik, McKenzie, Luty, & Jordan, 2000; Wilfley et al., 2002). More recently, IPT has been adapted as an early intervention program for adolescents who are at risk for excessive weight gain due to overweight status and engagement in LOC eating (Tanofsky-Kraff et al., 2007). Some research has substantiated the interpersonal model for LOC eating which posits that interpersonal distress causes negative affect, resulting in the engagement of LOC eating (Ansell, Grilo, & White, 2011; Elliott et al., 2010; Goldschmidt et al., 2018). However, other studies have found that only the experience of interpersonal distress, not negative affect, was related to LOC eating (Ranzenhofer et al., 2014). For example, in a sample of adolescent girls ranging from a healthy to obese BMI, recent social stress, regardless of premeal affect, was

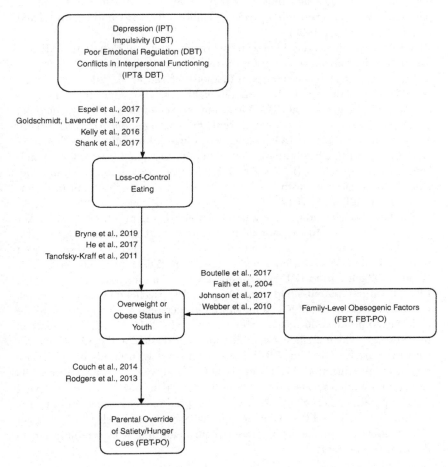

Figure 6.1 A Summary Diagram of Hypothesized Links Between Risk Factors for Children with Overweight/Obesity Status and Corresponding Treatment Modalities (DBT, Dialectical Behavior Therapy; FBT, Family-Based Treatment for Weight Loss; FBT-PO, Family-Based Treatment for Pediatric Obesity [Adapted from Eating Disorder Treatment]; IPT, Interpersonal Therapy)

related to increased consumption of dessert and snack foods (Shank et al., 2017).

IPT as prevention of excessive weight gain (IPT-WG) is based on former adaptations of IPT including IPT Adolescent Skills Training (AST; Young, Mufson, & Davies, 2006) and IPT for BED (Wilfley, Frank, Welch, Spurrell, & Rounsaville, 1998). IPT-AST is a prevention program for adolescents who are at risk of developing major depressive disorder (Young et al., 2006; 2012). IPT for BED aims to reduce binge eating through improving interpersonal

134 *Ashley F. Jennings et al.*

functioning deficits which may precipitate maladaptive behavior via mood pathways, while also providing psychoeducation on obesity and health-related issues (Wilfley et al., 1998).

IPT-WG, which targets adolescents who fall within the 75th–97th BMI-for-age percentile and engage in LOC eating, aims to reduce LOC eating to, in turn, prevent excess weight gain (Tanofsky-Kraff et al., 2007). Recently, IPT-WG was compared with a general health education control condition in a randomized control trial (RCT) focusing on weight as a primary outcome. Participants experienced significant reductions in age-adjusted BMI z-score and percentile, adiposity, LOC eating, and binge eating behaviors (Tanofsky-Kraff et al., 2014). These outcomes were maintained at a 3-year follow-up and lend further support to IPT as a successful early intervention program, specifically for adolescents with baseline anxiety and social adjustment problems (Tanofsky-Kraff et al., 2017).

IPT has also been adapted as a family-based treatment (FB-IPT; Shomaker et al., 2015) to prevent weight gain in overweight preadolescents (aged 8–13) with LOC eating. The intervention techniques in FB-IPT were derived from IPT for preadolescents with depression (Dietz, Mufson, Irvine, & Brent, 2008), and from IPT-WG for adolescents (Tanofsky-Kraff et al., 2007). FB-IPT targets parent–child conflict, provides psychoeducation about the relationship between LOC eating and interpersonal conflict, and teaches children communication skills (Shomaker et al., 2015). FB-IPT consists of three phases, which include a combination of individual and conjoint sessions with the parent and child. FB-IPT was compared with family-based weight management education (Wilfley et al., 2007), and was found to reduce LOC eating in preadolescents and prevent increases in BMI z-score at 1-year follow-up (Shomaker et al., 2015). These preliminary results indicate the potential efficacy of FB-IPT in preventing obesity in at-risk youth. Longer term follow-up assessments are required to determine if the stabilization in BMI z-score persists.

Family-Based Treatment for Adolescent EDs

Family-based behavioral treatment developed and implemented without selection for, or attention to, ED concerns has a robust established efficacy base in the literature and is discussed extensively in Chapter 8 (Boutelle et al., 2017; Epstein, Roemmich, & Raynor, 2001). In addition, another form of family-based treatment, an established intervention for adolescents with AN (Lock & Le Grange, 2013) and BN (Le Grange & Lock, 2007), has been adapted to address OW/OB in adolescents, in the absence of an ED diagnosis. The three-phased intervention for ED initially enlists parents as the primary agents of symptom management, and reduces their involvement over time, allowing the adolescent to regain autonomy in treatment as symptoms cease (Couturier et al. 2013; Le Grange & Lock, 2007; Lock & Le Grange, 2013; Stiles-Shields, Hoste, Doyle, & Le Grange, 2012). Loeb et al. (2015)

developed the adaptation of this ED-informed intervention, family-based treatment for pediatric obesity (FBT-PO), retaining the underlying principles of the original ED protocol, and tested the efficacy of the adolescent module in a pilot RCT (Loeb et al., 2019; Stiles-Shields, Doyle, Le Grange, & Loeb, 2018). This study compared FBT-PO (consisting of conjoint family sessions) to nutrition education counseling (NEC; delivered to patient and parents in divided sessions), and found that FBT-PO, while not yielding a marked decrease in BMI z-score, appeared to arrest an otherwise-occurring weight-gain trajectory as seen in the NEC control condition.

Key elements of FBT-PO include the following: (1) empowering parents to manifest a health-promoting home environment; (2) adjusting environmental modifications to be applicable to all family members; and (3) transitioning the child to a developmentally appropriate level of autonomy around positive health choices related to energy intake and expenditure. The extent of parental involvement is based on developmental stage, with the tested adolescent module allowing for parent–child collaboration early on in treatment. Unlike the classic family-based behavioral treatment (Boutelle et al., 2017; Epstein et al., 2001), FBT-PO does not directly aim for weight loss, and instead focuses on parents' capacity to combat components of their environment that may contribute to pediatric OW/OB. Some of these "obesogenic" environmental risk factors (Townshend & Lake, 2017) can be addressed through parent-related variables including parental modeling (Ong et al., 2017; Rodgers et al., 2013), parenting style (Kakinami, Barnett, Séguin, & Paradis, 2015), parental response to children's hunger/satiety cues (Couch, Glanz, Zhou, Sallis, & Saelens, 2014; Johnson et al., 2017; Rodgers et al., 2013), and the parent–child relationship (Blewitt, Bergmeier, Macdonald, Olsson, & Skouteris, 2016). Studies have shown parental feeding practices to be influenced by a child's OW/OB rather than feeding practices leading to weight gain (Faith et al., 2004; Webber, Cooke, Hill, & Wardle, 2010). Furthermore, there have been two RCTs showing that parent-only interventions are non-inferior to parent and child family-based treatment (Boutelle, Cafri, & Crow, 2011; Boutelle et al., 2017); as such, it is important to focus on parent-related variables directly. FBT-PO, while not specifically adapted for BED, does address antecedents to and correlates of LOC eating, including negative affect and behaviors such as eating in secret and the consumption of "forbidden" foods (Loeb et al., 2015).

DBT

DBT is a treatment that combines mindfulness and acceptance principles with CBT techniques, and was originally developed for individuals with borderline personality disorder (Linehan, 1993). DBT focuses on four key skill domains: emotion regulation, distress tolerance, mindfulness, and interpersonal effectiveness. In the context of EDs, DBT has been successfully adapted for BN (Safer, Telch, & Chen, 2009), BED (Safer, Robinson, & Jo, 2010), and more recently, emotional eating in OW/OB adults (Roosen, Safer, Adler, Cebolla, & van Strien, 2012). Poor emotion regulation (Goldschmidt, Lavender, Hipwell, Stepp, & Keenan, 2017), and impulsivity in the context of negative affect (Espel, Muratore, & Lowe, 2017), may play a significant role in the development and maintenance of LOC eating. Moreover, extensive research has shown that emotion dysregulation in youth predicts excess weight gain and onset of OW/OB status (Graziano, Calkins, & Keane, 2010), particularly among those with LOC eating (Kelly et al., 2016).

Boutelle, Braden, Knatz-Peck, Anderson, and Rhee (2018) developed the Preventing Emotional Eating Routines (PEER) intervention program, which integrates DBT emotion regulation skills with parenting techniques and behavioral weight loss, for OW/OB adolescents and their parents. Results indicated PEER's efficacy in decreasing emotional eating, with additional, secondary benefits including significant reductions in standardized BMI z-scores. Moreover, a 9-week DBT skills pilot study in school-aged youth provided evidence for reduced feelings of negative urgency, a trait that is associated with negative health-risk behaviors such as substance use and binge eating (Zapolski & Smith, 2017). At present, although research regarding the application of DBT to OW/OB youth is limited, the effectiveness of incorporating DBT skills in this context is promising.

CBT

There is a rich history of behavioral and cognitive behavioral techniques applied to the epidemic of childhood OW/OB (Boutelle et al., 2017; Epstein, Paluch, Kilanowski, & Raynor, 2004; Epstein et al. 2001; Israel, Stolmaker, & Andrian, 1985). Although this has been true for both individual and family-based interventions (Epstein, Valoski, Wing, & McCurley, 1994; Kalarchian et al., 2009), only one intervention for youth with OW/OB has explicit roots in CBT for EDs (Fairburn, 2008; 2013), while also incorporating health habits weight loss treatment (Saelens et al., 2002) and hunger and satiety awareness skills (Craighead, 2006). This Internet-facilitated intervention, Student Bodies 2-BED (SB2-BED; Jones et al., 2008), was evaluated in an RCT, in which both weight and ED symptoms (i.e., shape and weight concerns) were primary outcome measures. High school students, who endorsed frequent binge eating and were at or above the 85th percentile for age-adjusted BMI, were randomized to be in either SB2-BED or a wait list control (WLC) group. From baseline to 9-month follow-up, SB2-BED participants displayed significantly greater reductions in BMI and BMI z-score compared to those in the WLC condition. In addition, participants who completed the SB2-BED treatment experienced a significant decrease in weight and shape concerns from baseline to follow-up. This RCT demonstrates that a weight-management CBT intervention that includes components of CBT for EDs does not precipitate disordered eating in adolescents and, in fact, may decrease the development of full-threshold EDs.

The Body Project

The Body Project, an ED prevention program, utilizes dissonance-based techniques to reduce internalization of the thin ideal (Stice, Chase, Stormer, & Appel, 2001). This program is rooted in Festinger's (1957) cognitive dissonance theory, which posits that when individuals experience thoughts that do not align with their actions, they strive to reduce the psychological discomfort arising from this discrepancy by altering their beliefs. In the Body Project, participants critique and challenge the thin ideal of feminine beauty through a series of written, verbal, and behavioral activities, thereby evoking dissonance between actions and internalization of this attractiveness ideal. The Body Project has been shown to be successful in preventing EDs across age groups by targeting thin-ideal internalization and body dissatisfaction, two core ED risk factors (Stice, Rohde, Durant, Shaw, & Wade, 2013; Stice, Marti, Rohde, & Shaw, 2011; Stice, Rohde, Shaw, & Gau, 2011).

Beyond ED outcomes, some research on the Body Project has examined its effects on prevention of obesity and excess weight gain in children and adolescents. Findings showed a three-fold decrease in risk for obesity onset, approaching the effects of a healthy-weight intervention, at a 1-year follow-up for adolescent girls with baseline body image concerns (Stice, Shaw, Burton, & Wade, 2006). However, at a 3-year follow-up, only participants in the healthy weight intervention sustained a reduced risk for OW/OB (Stice, Marti, Spoor, Presnell, & Shaw, 2008).

Conclusion

Childhood obesity has been increasing exponentially, prompting clinical investigators to develop, adapt, and test a range of interventions aimed at prevention and early treatment. A number of evidence-based interventions, including family-based models, IPT, and DBT, have the potential to be applicable to OW/OB by targeting weight as a primary or secondary outcome. In the population of children affected by OW/OB, BED and AAN are two ED diagnoses requiring special attention. There is a dearth of RCTs supporting treatments for children and adolescents affected by BED and subthreshold BED, although LOC eating in youth has been better studied. Similarly, little is known regarding the efficacy of treatment targeting weight restoration and core ED pathology in youth with AAN, who often have a history of OW/OB. In summary, there are many gaps in our knowledge regarding evidence-based treatments for OW/OB with and without comorbid EDs; however, a number of promising interventions have been developed using principles and techniques from the ED literature and related fields of psychopathology. Efficacious interventions for OW/OB can have substantial clinical impact given the high population prevalence and importance of both physical and mental health correlates of this condition.

138 *Ashley F. Jennings et al.*

References

Agras, W. S., Walsh, B. T., Fairburn, C. G., Wilson, G. T., & Kraemer, H. C. (2000). A multicenter comparison of cognitive-behavioral therapy and interpersonal psychotherapy for bulimia nervosa. *Archives of General Psychiatry, 57*(5), 459–466. doi:10.1001/archpsyc.57.5.459.

American Psychiatric Association. (2013). *Diagnostic and statistical manual of mental disorders* (5th ed.). Arlington, VA: Author.

Ansell, E. B., Grilo, C. M., & White, M. A. (2011). Examining the interpersonal model of binge eating and loss of control over eating in women. *International Journal of Eating Disorders, 45*(1), 43–50. doi:10.1002/eat.20897.

Barlow, S. E., & Expert Committee (2007). Expert committee recommendations regarding the prevention, assessment, and treatment of child and adolescent overweight and obesity: Summary report. *Pediatrics, 120*(Suppl 4), S164–S192. doi:10.1542/peds.2007-2329c.

Berner, L. A., Shaw, J. A., Witt, A. A., & Lowe, M. R. (2013). The relation of weight suppression and body mass index to symptomatology and treatment response in anorexia nervosa. *Journal of Abnormal Psychology, 122*(3), 694–708. doi: 10.1037/a0033930.

Blewitt, C., Bergmeier, H., Macdonald, J. A., Olsson, C. A., & Skouteris, H. (2016). Associations between parent-child relationship quality and obesogenic risk in adolescence: A systematic review of recent literature. *Obesity Reviews, 17*(7), 612–622. doi:10.1111/obr.12413.

Boutelle, K. N., Braden, A., Knatz-Peck, S., Anderson, L. K., & Rhee, K. E. (2018). An open trial targeting emotional eating among adolescents with overweight or obesity. *Eating Disorders, 26*(1), 79–91. doi:10.1080/10640266.2018.1418252.

Boutelle, K., Cafri, G., & Crow, S. (2011). Parent-only treatment for childhood obesity: A randomized controlled trial. *Obesity, 19*(3), 574–580. doi:10.1038/oby.2010.238.

Boutelle, K., Rhee, K., Liang, J., Braden, A., Douglas, J., Strong, D., …, Crow, S. J. (2017). Effect of attendance of the child on body weight, energy intake, and physical activity in childhood obesity treatment: A randomized clinical trial. *JAMA Pediatrics, 171*(7), 622. doi:10.1001/jamapediatrics.2017.0651.

Byrne, M. E., LeMay-Russell, S., & Tanofsky-Kraff, M. (2019). Loss-of-control eating and obesity among children and adolescents. *Current Obesity Reports, 8*(1), 33–42. doi:10.1007/s13679-019-0327-1.

Cambuli, V. M., Musiu, M. C., Incani, M., Paderi, M., Serpe, R., Marras, V., …, Baroni, M. G. (2008). Assessment of adiponectin and leptin as biomarkers of positive metabolic outcomes after lifestyle intervention in overweight and obese children. *Journal of Clinical Endocrinology and Metabolism, 93*(8), 3051–3057. doi:10.1210/jc.2008-0476.

Chao, A. M., Wadden, T. A., Gorin, A. A., Shaw Tronieri, J., Pearl, R. L., Bakizada, Z. M., …, Berkowitz, R. I. (2017). Binge eating and weight loss outcomes in individuals with type 2 diabetes: 4-year results from the Look AHEAD study. *Obesity, 25*(11), 1830–1837. doi:10.1002/oby.21975.

Couch, S. C., Glanz, K., Zhou, C., Sallis, J. F., & Saelens, B. E. (2014). Home food environment in relation to child's diet quality and weight status. *Journal of the Academy of Nutrition and Dietetics, 114*(10), 1569–1579. doi:10.1016/j.jand.2014.05.015.

Couturier, J., Kimber, M., & Szatmari, P. (2013). Efficacy of family-based treatment for adolescents with eating disorders: A systematic review and meta-analysis. *International Journal of Eating Disorders, 46*, 3–11. doi:10.1002/eat.22042.

Craighead, L. (2006). *The appetite awareness workbook: How to listen to your body and overcome bingeing, overeating, and obsession with food*. Oakland, CA: Raincoast Books.

Dietz, L. J., Mufson, L., Irvine, H., & Brent, D. A. (2008). Family-based interpersonal psychotherapy for depressed preadolescents: An open-treatment trial. *Early Intervention in Psychiatry*, *2*(3), 154–161. doi: 10.1111/j.1751-7893.2008.00077.x.

Dimitropoulos, G., Kimber, M., Singh, M., Williams, E. P., Loeb, K. L., Hughes, E. K., …, Le Grange, D. (2019). Stay the course: Practitioner reflections on implementing family-based treatment with adolescents with atypical anorexia. *Journal of Eating Disorders*, *7*(10). doi:10.1186/s40337-019-0240-8.

Eddy, K. T., Tanofsky-Kraff, M., Thompson-Brenner, H., Herzog, D. B., Brown, T. A., & Ludwig, D. S. (2007). Eating disorder pathology among overweight treatment-seeking youth: Clinical correlates and cross-sectional risk modeling. *Behaviour Research and Therapy*, *45*(10), 2360–2371. doi:10.1016/j.brat.2007.03.017.

Elliott, C. A., Tanofsky-Kraff, M., Shomaker, L. B., Columbo, K. M., Wolkoff, L. E., Ranzenhofer, L. M., & Yanovski, J. A. (2010). An examination of the interpersonal model of loss of control eating in children and adolescents. *Behaviour Research and Therapy*, *48*(5), 424–428. doi:10.1016/j.brat.2009.12.012.

Epstein, L. H., Paluch, R. A., Kilanowski, C. K., & Raynor, H. A. (2004). The effect of reinforcement or stimulus control to reduce sedentary behavior in the treatment of pediatric obesity. *Health Psychology*, *23*(4), 371–380. doi:10.1037/0278-6133.23.4.371.

Epstein, L. H., Roemmich, J. N., & Raynor, H. A. (2001). Behavioral therapy in the treatment of pediatric obesity. *Pediatric Clinics of North America*, *48*(4), 983–993. doi:10.1016/S0031-3955(05)70352-7.

Epstein, L. H., Valoski, A., Wing, R. R., & McCurley, J. (1994). Ten-year outcomes of behavioral family-based treatment for childhood obesity. *Health Psychology*, *13*(5), 373–383. doi:10.1037/0278-6133.13.5.373.

Espel, H. M., Muratore, A. F., & Lowe, M. R. (2017). An investigation of two dimensions of impulsivity as predictors of loss-of-control eating severity and frequency. *Appetite*, *117*, 9–16. doi:10.1016/j.appet.2017.06.004.

Fairburn, C. G. (1991). Three psychological treatments for bulimia nervosa. *Archives of General Psychiatry*, *48*(5), 463–469. doi:10.1001/archpsyc.1991.01810290075014.

Fairburn, C. G. (2008). *Cognitive behavior therapy and eating disorders*. New York, NY: Guilford Press.

Fairburn, C. G. (2013). *Overcoming binge eating: The proven program to learn why you binge and how you can stop* (2nd ed.). New York, NY: Guilford Press.

Faith, M. S., Berkowitz, R. I., Stallings, V. A., Kerns, J., Storey, M., & Stunkard, A. J. (2004). Parental feeding attitudes and styles and child body mass index: Prospective analysis of a gene-environment interaction. *Pediatrics*, *114*(4), e429–E436. doi:10.1542/peds.2003-1075-L.

Festinger, L. (1957). *A theory of cognitive dissonance*. Stanford: Stanford University Press.

Flegal, K. M., Tabak, C. J., & Ogden, C. L. (2006). Overweight in children: Definitions and interpretation. *Health Education Research*, *21*(6), 755–760. doi:10.1093/her/cyl128.

Glasofer, D. R., Tanofsky-Kraff, M., Eddy, K. T., Yanovski, S. Z., Theim, K. R., Mirch, M. C., …, Yanovski, J. A. (2006). Binge eating in overweight treatment-seeking adolescents. *Journal of Pediatric Psychology*, *32*(1), 95–105. doi:10.1093/jpepsy/jsl012.

Golden, N. H., Katzman, D. K., Sawyer, S. M., Ornstein, R. M., Rome, E. S., Garber, A. K., …, Kreipe, R. E. (2015). Update on the medical management of eating

140   Ashley F. Jennings et al.

disorders in adolescents. *Journal of Adolescent Health, 56*(4), 370–375. doi:10.1016/j. jadohealth.2014.11.020.

Goldschmidt, A., Khoury, J., Jenkins, T., Bond, D., Thomas, J., Utzinger, L., ..., Mitchell, J. E. (2017). Adolescent loss-of-control eating and weight loss maintenance after bariatric surgery. *Pediatrics, 141*(1), e20171659. doi:10.1542/peds.2017-1659.

Goldschmidt, A. B., Lavender, J. M., Hipwell, A. E., Stepp, S. D., & Keenan, K. (2017). Emotion regulation and loss of control eating in community-based adolescents. *Journal of Abnormal Child Psychology, 45*(1), 183–191. doi:10.1007/s10802-016-0152-x.

Goldschmidt, A. B., Lavender, J. M., Hipwell, A. E., Stepp, S. D., & Keenan, K. (2018). Examining two prevailing models of loss of control eating among community-based girls. *Obesity, 26*(2), 420–425. doi:10.1002/oby.22101.

Goldschmidt, A. B., Wall, M. M., Loth, K. A., & Neumark-Sztainer, D. (2015). Risk factors for disordered eating in overweight adolescents and young adults. *Journal of Pediatric Psychology, 40*(10), 1048–1055. doi:10.1093/jpepsy/jsv053.

Gonçalves, S., Machado, B. C., Martins, C., Hoek, H. W., & Machado, P. P. P. (2016). Retrospective correlates for bulimia nervosa: A matched case-control study. *European Eating Disorders Review, 24*(3), 197–205. doi:10.1002/erv.2434.

Graziano, P. A., Calkins, S. D., & Keane, S. P. (2010). Toddler self-regulation skills predict risk for pediatric obesity. *International Journal of Obesity, 34*(4), 633. doi:10.1038/ijo.2009.288.

He, J., Cai, Z., & Fan, X. (2017). Prevalence of binge and loss of control eating among children and adolescents with overweight and obesity: An exploratory meta-analysis. *International Journal of Eating Disorders, 50*(2), 91–103. doi:10.1002/eat.22661.

Hilbert, A., & Brauhardt, A. (2014). Childhood loss of control eating over five-year follow-up. *International Journal of Eating Disorders, 47*(7), 758–761. doi:10.1002/eat.22312.

Israel, A. C., Stolmaker, L., & Andrian, C. A. (1985). The effects of training parents in general child management skills on a behavioral weight loss program for children. *Behavior Therapy, 16*(2), 169–180. doi:10.1016/S0005-7894(85)80043-5.

Jamilian, H. R., Malekirad, A. A., Farhadi, M., Habibi, M., & Zamani, N. (2014). Effectiveness of group dialectical behavior therapy (based on core distress tolerance and emotion regulation components) on expulsive anger and impulsive behaviors. *Global Journal of Health Science, 6*(7). doi:10.5539/gjhs.v6n7p116.

Janicke, D. M., Steele, R. G., Gayes, L. A., Lim, C. S., Clifford, L. M., Schneider, E. M., ..., Westen, S. (2014). Systematic review and meta-analysis of comprehensive behavioral family lifestyle interventions addressing pediatric obesity. *Journal of Pediatric Psychology, 39*(8), 809–825. doi:10.1093/jpepsy/jsu023.

Johnson, C., Henderson, M., Tripicchio, G., Rozin, P., Heo, M., Pietrobelli, A., ..., Faith, M. S. (2017). Observed parent-child feeding dynamics in relation to child body mass index and adiposity. *Pediatric Obesity, 13*(4), 222–231. doi:10.1111/ijpo. 12209.

Jones, M., Luce, K. H., Osborne, M. I., Taylor, K., Cunning, D., Doyle, A. C., & Taylor, C. B. (2008). Randomized, controlled trial of an internet-facilitated intervention for reducing binge eating and overweight in adolescents. *Pediatrics, 121*, 453–462. doi:10.1542/peds.2007-1173.

Kakinami, L., Barnett, T. A., Séguin, L., & Paradis, G. (2015). Parenting style and obesity risk children. *Preventive Medicine, 75*, 18–22. doi:10.1016/j.ypmed.2015.03.005.

Kalarchian, M., Levine, M., Arslanian, S., Ewing, L., Houck, P., Cheng, Y., ..., Marcus, M. D. (2009). Family-based treatment of severe pediatric obesity: Randomized, controlled trial. *Pediatrics, 124*(4), 1060–1068. doi:10.1542/peds.2008-3727.

Youth with Overweight/Obesity 141

Kass, A. E., Wilfley, D. E., Eddy, K. T., Boutelle, K. N., Zucker, N., Peterson, C. B., ..., Goldschmidt, A. B. (2017). Secretive eating among youth with overweight or obesity. *Appetite*, *114*, 275–281. doi:10.1016/j.appet.2017.03.042.

Kelly, N. R., Tanofsky-Kraff, M., Vannucci, A., Ranzenhofer, L. M., Altschul, A. M., Schvey, N. A., ..., Yanovski, S. Z. (2016). Emotion dysregulation and loss-of-control eating in children and adolescents. *Health Psychology*, *35*(10), 1110. doi: 10.1037/hea0000389.

Kessler, R. C., Berglund, P. A., Chiu, W. T., Deitz, A. C., Hudson, J. I., Shahly, V., ..., Xavier, M. (2013). The prevalence and correlates of binge eating disorder in the world health organization world mental health surveys. *Biological Psychiatry*, *73*(9), 904–914. doi:10.1016/j.biopsych.2012.11.020.

Klerman, G. L., Weissman, M. M., Rounsaville, B. J., & Chevron, E. S. (1984). *Interpersonal psychotherapy of depression*. New York, NY: Basic Books.

Kuczmarksi, R. J., Ogden, C. L., Guo, S. S., Grummer-Strawn, L. M., Flegal, K. M., Mei, Z., ..., Johnson, C. L. (2002). 2000 CDC growth charts for the United States: Methods and development. *Vital Health Statistics 11*(246), 1–190.

Le Grange, D., & Lock, J. (2007). *Treating adolescent bulimia: A family-based approach*. New York, NY: Guilford Press.

Linehan, M. M. (1993). *Cognitive behavioral therapy of borderline personality disorder*. New York, NY: Guilford.

Lock, J. & Le Grange, D. (2013). *Treatment manual for anorexia nervosa: A family-based approach* (2nd ed.). New York, NY: Guilford Press.

Loeb, K. L., Celio Doyle, A., Anderson, K., Parter, A., Sweeney, C., Hail, L., ..., Le Grange, D. (2015). *Family-based treatment for child and adolescent overweight and obesity: A transdevelopmental approach*. In K. L. Loeb, D. Le Grange, J. Lock, (Eds.), *Family therapy for adolescent eating and weight disorders: New applications* (pp. 177–229). New York Taylor & Francis.

Loeb, K. L., Le Grange, D., Celio Doyle, A., Crosby, R. D., Glunz, C., Laraque-Arena, D., ..., Gault, A. (2019). Adapting family-based treatment for pediatric obesity: A randomized controlled pilot trial. *European Eating Disorders Review*, *27*, 521–530.

McIntosh, V. V., Bulik, C. M., McKenzie, J. M., Luty, S. E., & Jordan, J. (2000). Interpersonal psychotherapy for anorexia nervosa. *International Journal of Eating Disorders*, *27*(2), 125–139. doi:10.1002/(sici)1098-108x(200003)27:2<125::aid-eat1>3.0.co;2-4.

Niemeier, B. S., Hektner, J. M., & Enger, K. B. (2012). Parent participation in weight-related health interventions for children and adolescents: A systematic review and meta-analysis. *Preventive Medicine*, *55*(1), 3–13. doi:10.1016/j.ypmed.2012.04.021.

Ogden, C. L., Carroll, M. D., Fryar, C. D., & Flegal, K. M. (2015). Prevalence of obesity among adults and youth: United States, 2011–2014. *NCHS Data Brief*, *219*, 1–8.

Ogden, C. L., Carroll, M. D., Kit, B. K., & Flegal, K. M. (2014). Prevalence of childhood and adult obesity in the United States, 2011–2012. *The Journal of the American Medical Association*, *311*(8), 806–814. doi:10.1001/jama.2014.732.

Ogden, C. L., Carroll, M. D., Lawman, H. G., Fryar, C. D., Kruszon-Moran, D., Kit, B. K., & Flegal, K. M. (2016). Trends in obesity prevalence among children and adolescents in the United States, 1988–1994 through 2013–2014. *The Journal of the American Medical Association*, *315*(21), 2292–2299. doi:10.1001/jama.2016.6361.

Ong, J. X., Ullah, S., Magarey, A., Miller, J., & Leslie, E. (2016). Relationship between the home environment and fruit and vegetable consumption in children aged 6–12 years: A systematic review. *Public Health Nutrition*, *20*, 464–480. doi:10.1017/s1368980016002883.

142 *Ashley F. Jennings et al.*

Pehlivanova, M., Wolf, D. H., Sotiras, A., Kaczkurkin, A. N., Moore, T. M., Ciric, R., ...,
Satterthwaite, T. D. (2018). Diminished cortical thickness is associated with impulsive
choice in adolescence. *The Journal of Neuroscience*, *38*(10), 2471–2481. doi:10.1523/
jneurosci.2200-17.2018.

Puhl, R. M., Latner, J. D., King, K. M., & Luedicke, J. (2014). Weight bias among
professionals treating eating disorders: Attitudes about treatment and perceived
patient outcomes. *International Journal of Eating Disorders*, *47*(1), 65–75. doi:10.1002/
eat.22186.

Ranzenhofer, L. M., Engel, S. G., Crosby, R. D., Anderson, M., Vannucci, A.,
Cohen, L. A., ..., Tanofsky-Kraff, M. (2014). Using ecological momentary assessment
to examine interpersonal and affective predictors of loss of control eating in adolescent
girls. *International Journal of Eating Disorders*, *47*(7), 748–757. doi:10.1002/eat.22333.

Rodgers, R., Paxton, S., Massey, R., Campbell, K., Wertheim, E., Skouteris, H., &
Gibbons, K. (2013). Maternal feeding practices predict weight gain and obesogenic
eating behaviors in young children: A prospective study. *International Journal of
Behavioral Nutrition and Physical Activity*, *10*(1), 24. doi:10.1186/1479-5868-10-24.

Roosen, M. A., Safer, D., Adler, S., Cebolla, A., & van Strien, T. (2012). Group
dialectical behavior therapy adapted for obese emotional eaters; a pilot study.
Nutricion Hospitalaria, *27*(4), 1141–1147. doi:10.3305/nh.2012.27.4.5843.

Saelens, B. E., Sallis, J. F., Wilfley, D. E., Patrick, K., Cella, J. A., & Buchta, R. (2002).
Behavioral weight control for overweight adolescents initiated in primary care.
Obesity Research, *10*, 22–32. doi:10.1038/oby.2002.4.

Safer, D., Robinson, A., & Jo, B. (2010). Outcome from a randomized controlled trial
of group therapy for BED: Comparing DBT adapted for binge eating to an active
comparison group therapy. *Behavior Therapy*, *41*(1), 106–120.

Safer, D. L., Telch, C. F., & Chen, E. Y. (2009). *Dialectical behavior therapy for binge eating
and bulimia*. New York, NY: Guilford Press.

Sawyer, S. M., Whitelaw, M., Le Grange, D., Yeu, M., & Hughes, E. K. (2016).
Physical and psychological morbidity in adolescents with atypical anorexia nervosa.
Pediatrics.137(4), e20154080. doi: 10.1542/peds.2015-4080.

Shank, L. M., Crosby, R. D., Grammer, A. C., Shomaker, L. B., Vannucci, A.,
Burke, N. L., ..., Tanofsky-Kraff, M. (2017). Examination of the interpersonal
model of loss of control eating in the laboratory. *Comprehensive Psychiatry*, *76*, 36–44.
doi:10.1016/j.comppsych.2017.03.015.

Shomaker, L. B., Tanofsky-Kraff, M., Elliott, C., Wolkoff, L. E., Columbo, K. M.,
Ranzenhofer, L. M., ..., Yanovski, J. A. (2009). Salience of loss of control for pediatric binge episodes: Does size really matter? *International Journal of Eating Disorders*,
43(8), 707–716. doi:10.1002/eat.20767.

Shomaker, L. B., Tanofsky-Kraff, M., Matherne, C. E., Mehari, R. D., Olsen, C. H.,
Marwitz, S. E., ..., Yanovski, J. A. (2015). A randomized, comparative pilot trial of
family-based interpersonal psychotherapy for reducing psychosocial symptoms,
disordered-eating, and excess weight gain in at-risk preadolescents with loss-of-
control-eating. *International Journal of Eating Disorders*, *50*(9), 1084–1094. doi:10.1002/
eat.22741.

Sonneville, K., Horton, N., Micali, N., Crosby, R., Swanson, S., Solmi, F., & Field, A.
(2013). Longitudinal associations between binge eating and overeating and adverse
outcomes among adolescents and young adults. *JAMA Pediatrics*, *167*(2), 149. doi:10.
1001/2013.jamapediatrics.12.

Speiser, P. W., Rudolf, M. C., Anhalt, H., Camacho-Hubner, C., Chiarelli, F., Eliakim, A., ..., Hochberg, Z. (2005). Childhood obesity. *The Journal of Clinical Endocrinology & Metabolism, 90*(3), 1871–1887. doi:10.1210/jc.2004-1389.

Stice, E., Cameron, R. P., Killen, J. D., Hayward, C., & Taylor, C. B. (1999). Naturalistic weight-reduction efforts prospectively predict growth in relative weight and onset of obesity among female adolescents. *Journal of Consulting and Clinical Psychology, 67*(6), 967–974. doi:10.1037/0022-006x.67.6.967.

Stice, E., Chase, A., Stormer, S., & Appel, A. (2001). A randomized trial of a dissonance-based eating disorder prevention program. *International Journal of Eating Disorders, 29*(3), 247–262. doi:10.1002/eat.1016.

Stice, E., Marti, C. N., Rohde, P., & Shaw, H. (2011). Testing mediators hypothesized to account for the effects of a dissonance-based eating disorder prevention program over longer term follow-up. *Journal of Consulting and Clinical Psychology, 79*(3), 398–405. doi:10.1037/a0023321.

Stice, E., Marti, C. N., Spoor, S., Presnell, K., & Shaw, H. (2008). Dissonance and healthy weight eating disorder prevention programs: Long-term effects from a randomized efficacy trial. *Journal of Consulting and Clinical Psychology, 76*(2), 329–340. doi:10.1037/0022-006x.76.2.329.

Stice, E., Presnell, K., & Spangler, D. (2002). Risk factors for binge eating onset in adolescent girls: A 2-year perspective investigation. *Health Psychology, 21*(2), 131–138. doi:10.1037/0278-6133.21.2.131.

Stice, E., Rohde, P., Durant, S., Shaw, H., & Wade, E. (2013). Effectiveness of peer-led dissonance-based eating disorder prevention groups: Results from two randomized pilot trials. *Behaviour Research and Therapy, 51*(4-5), 197–206. doi:10.1016/j.brat.2013.01.004.

Stice, E., Rohde, P., Shaw, H., & Gau, J. (2011). An effectiveness trial of a selected dissonance-based eating disorder prevention program for female high school students: Long-term effects. *Journal of Consulting and Clinical Psychology, 79*(4), 500–508. doi:10.1037/a0024351.

Stice, E., Shaw, H., Burton, E., & Wade, E. (2006). Dissonance and healthy weight eating disorder prevention programs: A randomized efficacy trial. *Journal of Consulting and Clinical Psychology, 74*(2), 263–275. doi:10.1037/0022-006x.74.2.263.

Stiles-Shields, C., Doyle, A. C., Le Grange, D., & Loeb, K. L. (2018). Family-based treatment for pediatric obesity: Case study of an adaptation for a non-psychiatric adolescent population. *Journal of Contemporary Psychotherapy, 49*(2), 111–118. 10.1007/s10879-018-9399-6.

Stiles-Shields, C., Hoste, R. R., Doyle, P. M., & Le Grange, D. (2012). A review of family-based treatment for adolescents with eating disorders. *Reviews on Recent Clinical Trials, 7*(2), 133–140.

Striegel-Moore, R. H., Fairburn, C. G., Wilfley, D. E., Pike, K. M., Dohm, F.-A., & Kraemer, H. C. (2005). Toward an understanding of risk factors for binge-eating disorder in black and white women: A community-based case-control study. *Psychological Medicine, 35*(6), 907–917. doi:10.1017/s0033291704003435.

Sung-Chan, P., Sung, Y. W., Zhao, X., & Brownson, R. C. (2013). Family-based models for childhood-obesity intervention: A systematic review of randomized controlled trials. *Obesity Reviews, 14*, 265–278. doi:10.1111/obr.12000.

Tanofsky-Kraff, M., Cohen, M. L., Yanovski, S. Z., Cox, C., Theim, K. R., Keil, M., ..., Yanovski, J. A. (2006). A prospective study of psychological predictors of body fat

144 *Ashley F. Jennings et al.*

gain among children at high risk for adult obesity. *Pediatrics, 117*(4), 1203–1209. doi:10.1542/peds.2005-1329.

Tanofsky-Kraff, M., Marcus, M. D., Yanovski, S. Z., & Yanovski, J. A. (2008). Loss of control eating disorder in children age 12 years and younger: Proposed research criteria. *Eating Behaviors, 9*(3), 360–365. doi:10.1016/j.eatbeh.2008.03.002.

Tanofsky-Kraff, M., Shomaker, L. B., Olsen, C., Roza, C. A., Wolkoff, L. E., Columbo, K. M., …, Yanovski, J. A. (2011). A prospective study of pediatric loss of control eating and psychological outcomes. *Journal of Abnormal Psychology, 120*(1), 108–118. doi:10.1037/a0021406.

Tanofsky-Kraff, M., Shomaker, L. B., Wilfley, D. E., Young, J. F., Sbrocco, T., Stephens, M., …, Yanovski, J. A. (2014). Targeted prevention of excess weight gain and eating disorders in high-risk adolescent girls: A randomized controlled trial. *American Journal of Clinical Nutrition, 100*(4), 1010–1018. doi:10.3945/ajcn.114.092536.

Tanofsky-Kraff, M., Shomaker, L. B., Wilfley, D. E., Young, J. F., Sbrocco, T., Stephens, M., …, Yanovski, J. A. (2017). Excess weight gain prevention in adolescents: Three-year outcome following a randomized controlled trial. *Journal of Consulting and Clinical Psychology, 85*(3), 218–227. doi:10.1037/ccp0000153.

Tanofsky-Kraff, M., Wilfley, D. E., Young, J. F., Mufson, L., Yanovski, S. Z., Glasofer, D. R., & Salaita, C. G. (2007). Preventing excessive weight gain in adolescents: Interpersonal psychotherapy for binge eating. *Obesity, 15*(6), 1345–1355. doi:10.1038/oby.2007.162.

Townshend, T. & Lake, A. (2017). Obesogenic environments: Current evidence of the built and food environments. *Perspectives in Public Health, 137*(1), 38–44. doi:10.1177/1757913916679860.

Webber, L., Cooke, L., Hill, C., & Wardle, J. (2010). Associations between children's appetitive traits and maternal feeding practices. *Journal of the American Dietetics Association, 110*(11), 1718–1722. doi:10.1016/j.jada.2010.08.007.

Wildes, J. E., Marcus, M. D., Kalarchian, M. A., Levine, M. D., Houck, P. R., & Cheng, Y. (2010). Self-reported binge eating in severe pediatric obesity: Impact on weight change in a randomized controlled trial of family-based treatment. *International Journal of Obesity, 34*(7), 1143–1148. doi:10.1038/ijo.2010.35.

Wilfley, D. E., Frank, M. A., Welch, R., Spurrell, E. B., & Rounsaville, B. J. (1998). Adapting interpersonal psychotherapy to a group format (IPT-G) for binge eating disorder: Toward a model for adapting empirically supported treatments. *Psychotherapy Research, 8*(4), 379–391. doi:10.1080/10503309812331332477.

Wilfley, D. E., Stein, R. I., Saelens, B. E., Mockus, D. S., Matt, G. E., Hayden-Wade, H. A., …, Epstein, L. H. (2007). Efficacy of maintenance treatment approaches for childhood overweight: A randomized controlled trial. *The Journal of the American Medical Association, 298*(14), 1661–1673. doi:10.1001/jama.298.14.1661.

Wilfley, D. E., Welch, R. R., Stein, R. I., Spurrell, E. B., Cohen, L. R., Saelens, B. E., …, Matt, G. E. (2002). A randomized comparison of group cognitive-behavioral therapy and group interpersonal psychotherapy for the treatment of overweight individuals with binge-eating disorder. *Archives of General Psychiatry, 59*(8), 713–721. doi:10.1001/archpsyc.59.8.713.

Wilson, G. T. (2011). Treatment of binge eating disorder. *The Psychiatric Clinics of North Aemerica, 34*(4), 773–783. doi:10.1016/j.psc.2011.08.011.

Young, J. F., Makover, H. B., Cohen, J. R., Mufson, L., Gallop, R. J., & Benas, J. S. (2012). Interpersonal psychotherapy-adolescent skills training: Anxiety outcomes and impact of comorbidity. *Journal of Clinical Child & Adolescent Psychology*, *41*(5), 640–653. doi:10.1080/15374416.2012.704843.

Young, J. F., Mufson, L., & Davies, M. (2006). Efficacy of interpersonal psychotherapy-adolescent skills training: An indicated preventive intervention for depression. *Journal of Child Psychology and Psychiatry*, *47*(12), 1254–1262. doi:10.1111/j.1469-7610.2006.01667.x.

Zapolski, T. C. & Smith, G. T. (2017). Pilot study: Implementing a brief DBT skills program in schools to reduce health risk behaviors among early adolescents. *The Journal of School Nursing*, *33*(3), 198–204. doi: 10.1177/1059840516673188.

7 Adapting Evidenced-Based Therapies for Avoidant/ Restrictive Food Intake Disorder

Kendra R. Becker, Lauren Breithaupt, Jenny H. Jo, Kamryn T. Eddy, and Jennifer J. Thomas

Brief History of the Development of the Avoidant/ Restrictive Food Intake Disorder (ARFID) Diagnosis

ARFID emerged as a new diagnosis in *Diagnostic and Statistical Manual of Mental Disorders*, 5th edition (*DSM-5*; APA, 2013) as an expansion and reformulation of the *DSM-IV* feeding disorder of infancy or early childhood. The *DSM-5* workgroup determined that a broader diagnosis was needed to improve clinical utility because research and clinical practice established that individuals present with feeding disturbances in the absence of low weight, that feeding difficulties can develop and persist beyond childhood, and that feeding disorders can co-occur with medical and psychological conditions (Bryant-Waugh, 2013; Thomas & Eddy, 2019). By allowing for a wider range of feeding difficulties to be recognized as clinically important feeding disturbances, *DSM-5* aimed to stimulate additional research and treatment development.

What is ARFID?

ARFID is characterized by a persistent pattern of eating that is limited in variety and/or volume of food and is associated with significant medical and/or psychosocial consequences (*DSM-5* Criterion A). As described in *DSM-5*, individuals with ARFID attribute their avoidant or restrictive eating to sensory sensitivity (e.g., aversions to certain tastes, textures, smells, or appearances of foods), lack of interest in eating or food (e.g., low appetite and/or lack of enjoyment of food), or fear of aversive consequences of eating (e.g., fear of choking, vomiting, abdominal pain, gastrointestinal (GI) distress/urgency, or allergic reactions). A novel hypothesis suggests that the three prototypic presentations are best understood within a three-dimensional framework which allows for the presentations to vary in severity and co-occur (Thomas et al., 2017). Early evidence suggests that more than half of patients with ARFID present with two or more of these prototypic presentations (Bryant-Waugh et al., 2019; Pulumo et al., 2016; Thomas & Eddy, 2019).

To qualify for a diagnosis of ARFID, feeding disturbances must be associated with significant medical and/or psychosocial impairment that

Adapting Evidenced-Based Therapies for ARFID 147

requires independent clinical attention. Negative consequences associated with ARFID presentations include one or more of the following: significant weight loss (or failure to achieve expected weight or height; *DSM-5* Criteria A1); a nutritional deficiency (*DSM-5* Criteria A2); dependence on energy-dense supplements, vitamin supplements, or enteral feeding (i.e., tube feeding; *DSM-5* Criteria A3); and/or psychosocial impairment (e.g., eating beforehand or packing separate meals when going to restaurants, eating alone because the variety and smell of other's food is intolerable; *DSM-5* Criteria A4). In addition, avoidant/restrictive eating cannot be attributed to other explanations such as a lack of resources, limited availability of food, or culturally sanctioned practices (*DSM-5* Criterion B) nor can they be motivated by weight or body shape concerns typical of classic eating disorders (*DSM-5* Criterion C). Furthermore, avoidant/restrictive eating behaviors cannot be fully accounted for by another medical or mental disorder (*DSM-5* Criterion D).

Box 7.1   Our Team's Operational Definitions for Criterion A of the ARFID Diagnosis in *DSM-5*

1   Criterion A1: Significant weight loss (or failure to achieve expected weight gain or faltering growth in children): We define low weight as a BMI ≤ 18.5 for adults aged 18 and older and a BMI percentile ≤ 10 for youth aged ≤ 17 years. Poor growth is evidenced by a height centile ≤ 10. We also classify an individual as meeting this criterion if a physician or other health care provider recommends significant weight gain (e.g., more than 10 pounds).

2   Criterion A2: Significant nutritional deficiency: For this criterion to be met, we rely on either a positive blood test for a nutritional deficiency or a nutritional deficiency diagnosis from a medical professional.

3   Criterion A3: Dependence on enteral feeding or oral nutritional supplements: We determine that this criterion is met if ≥ 50% of an individual's caloric needs are being met by either caloric supplements (e.g., Boost, Ensure, and Pediasure) or tube feeding or if a health care professional recommends a vitamin/multivitamin to supplement micronutrients.

4   Criterion A4: Psychosocial impairment: We determine psychosocial impairment to be present if a patient or their family report difficulty participating in age-appropriate activities (e.g., eating alone at school, unable to eat at the able with family, unable to attend holiday meals, avoiding social activities because of embarrassment around food options, and inability to travel).

148 *Kendra R. Becker et al.*

Challenges in Developing Treatment for ARFID

The ARFID diagnosis encompasses a heterogeneous patient group; thus, treatment must be flexible. Treatment strategies and targets may depend upon an individual's weight status, age, nutritional state, medical complications, and the complex nature of the possible presentation types (e.g., overlapping or independent motivations for avoidant/restrictive eating). In developing cognitive-behavioral therapy for ARFID (CBT-AR; Thomas & Eddy, 2019), our team carefully considered how these challenges may impact treatment goals.

ARFID Presents across the Weight Spectrum

The weight profiles of individuals with ARFID vary across the weight spectrum, from underweight to overweight, adding a special challenge in defining treatment plans and targets. Although avoidant/restrictive eating can lead to dangerously low weight or precipitous weight loss, individuals may also present as overweight or obese. It may also be uniquely difficult to determine appropriate weight ranges for those who have longstanding disruptions in eating behaviors and malnutrition (e.g., dating back to infancy or toddlerhood) such that premorbid functioning is difficult, if not impossible, to determine. Treatment must, therefore, accommodate individuals across the weight spectrum and be flexible to adapt to changes in weight gain goals. For example, if an adolescent starts to gain weight over the course of treatment, improved nutrition may allow for improvements in height as well, altering target weight range goals. In contrast, a weight target may need to be increased if a patient continues to exhibit delayed or disrupted pubertal development.

ARFID Presents in Children, Adolescents, and Adults

Feeding and eating disturbances are common in early childhood/infancy, with parents reporting at least one eating difficulty (e.g., eating a limited variety, stressful meals, and concern that child is not eating enough) occurring in roughly 25% of children (Chatoor, 2002; Micali et al., 2011). However, certain feeding patterns such as slow eating, picky eating, vomiting during mealtimes, and emotional undereating are associated with parental reports of poor child functioning and are associated with development of psychopathology (e.g., behavioral disorders, emotional disorders, somatic symptoms, and developmental disorders; Micali et al., 2011). These serious eating difficulties often do not resolve without intervention such that medical and psychosocial impairment may increase in severity and persist into adolescence and adulthood and are, therefore, encompassed by the ARFID diagnosis (Thomas & Eddy, 2019). Accordingly, successful ARFID treatment must be appropriate for different developmental periods by leveraging strengths of current child and adolescent therapies (e.g., mobilizing family support) without presenting materials (e.g., psychoeducation) or

Adapting Evidenced-Based Therapies for ARFID   149

strategies in a manner that is too rudimentary to be relevant/engaging for older adolescent or adult patients.

A Dimensional Understanding of ARFID Allows for Complex and Integrated Motivations for Avoidant/Restrictive Eating

As the three prototypic ARFID presentations can present individually or concurrently (Thomas et al., 2017), treatment needs will vary based on motivations for avoidant/restrictive eating such that some patients may need few interventions to address maintaining motivations, whereas others need more strategies to improve ARFID symptoms. For example, one individual may solely exhibit an aversion to food textures that are considered "mushy" or "wet" (e.g., fruits and noodles) and only accept crunchy and dry foods (e.g., pretzels, dry cereal, and chips), but be able to maintain a healthy weight on this diet. This patient's presentation would require only interventions to improve dietary variety. However, another individual may present for treatment after losing a significant amount of weight following the recent onset of a choking fear. The patient may also describe a long history of selective eating, typified by a sensory aversion to "slimy" foods including all fruits and vegetables, dating back to a very young age. Relevant interventions for this patient would include not only expansion of dietary range but also addressing eating fears and introducing weight regain strategies.

Cognitive Behavioral Therapy for ARFID (CBT-AR)

Development of CBT-AR

As ARFID is a newly defined diagnosis, no gold standard evidence-based treatment for ARFID yet exists. Our team is currently conducting pilot research on the efficacy of CBT-AR in children, adolescents, and adults (aged 10 and up) and exploring candidate neurobiological underpinnings that may underlie symptoms and improve with targeted treatment strategies. CBT-AR is modular in approach and designed to be flexibly adapted to apply to a broad range of patients across ages and with complex presentations of ARFID. However, CBT-AR is for patients who are able to comprehend the contents and aims of treatment as well as actively engage in sessions. Therefore, the treatment is for those patients who are at least 10 years of age. CBT-AR is a manualized treatment (Thomas & Eddy, 2019) delivered in four stages, spanning from 20 to 30 sessions in length, depending on whether weight gain is a treatment target. A total of 30 sessions are offered to provide additional time and interventions in support of weight gain/regain. CBT-AR can be delivered as a family-supported therapy or individual therapy and both versions follow the same basic principles and the same 20- to 30-session, four-stage format. Individual therapy is primarily designed for patients who are aged 16 years and older and who are not

150 *Kendra R. Becker et al.*

significantly underweight. Family-supported therapy is available to younger patients aged 10–15 years or for older adolescents who have low weight. As the treatment is modular, certain treatment strategies to address food selectivity, lack of interest in eating or food, and fears of eating can be implemented or not, depending on the patient's individual presentation.

CBT-AR borrows many of the basic principles and techniques from existing evidence-based treatments for pediatric feeding disorders, classic eating disorders (e.g., anorexia nervosa and bulimia nervosa), and anxiety disorders because ARFID shares similarities in clinical presentation with these disorders. However, because of the unique aspects of ARFID (e.g., clinical presentation of ARFID across ages, absence of weight/shape concerns, and disgust sensitivity), these techniques were not sufficient to fully resolve ARFID pathology, necessitating a novel approach. More specifically, interventions for pediatric feeding disorders typically target infants, toddlers, and young children and the applications utilized may not be developmentally appropriate for older children, adolescents, and adults with ARFID. Likewise, significant modifications to classic eating-disorder treatments were also needed to accommodate ARFID pathology because interventions for traditional eating disorders emphasize shape and weight concerns and body image disturbance. Thus, the treatment aims of these previous therapies did not sufficiently address the primary reasons for avoidant and restrictive eating in ARFID. There are also significant limitations in applying CBT for anxiety disorders to ARFID. Although individuals with some ARFID presentations, particularly sensory sensitivity and fear of aversive consequences, may endorse anxiety around trying new foods, it is unclear if the avoidance or restriction of food is wholly anxiety-based. Patients may avoid certain foods due to feelings of disgust or overall lack of appetite, in which case the anxiety techniques would not sufficiently address all symptoms. Furthermore, these anxiety-focused treatments also do not adequately address weight gain goals or nutritional deficiencies common in ARFID (Thomas & Eddy, 2019).

Deciding if CBT-AR is Appropriate

CBT-AR was specifically designed to be an adaptable outpatient treatment for ARFID, addressing many of the challenges in caring for ARFID patients. As previously mentioned, CBT-AR is most appropriate for patients aged 10 years and older, and if a developmental disorder is present, it should be of mild severity. This is because successful completion of CBT-AR depends on the patient comprehending and participating in interventions. Outpatient CBT-AR is appropriate only for patients who consume food orally and who do not rely on enteral feeding (e.g., tube feeding). Patients who do not meet these guidelines may require a different treatment approach or a higher level of care (e.g., inpatient or day hospitalization; Thomas & Eddy, 2019).

Determining Treatment Targets Prior to Beginning CBT-AR

We recommend that a licensed mental health clinician conduct a comprehensive psychiatric evaluation to assess the severity and presentation of ARFID symptoms and any comorbid psychopathology, as CBT-AR is only designed for individuals who meet criteria for ARFID. Importantly, we have not found that common co-occurring diagnoses (e.g., obsessive compulsive disorder, depression, generalized anxiety disorder, and attention deficit-hyperactivity disorder; Kambanis et al., 2020) prevent the successful completion of CBT-AR. However, determining that an additional ARFID diagnosis is appropriate and developing an accurate formulation of symptom maintenance depend on thorough assessment of psychological functioning. Currently, there are few measures that specifically evaluate ARFID pathology. On our team, we utilize the Pica, ARFID, and Rumination Disorder Interview (PARDI; Bryant-Waugh et al., 2019) for diagnostic assessment of ARFID symptoms. The PARDI includes subscales to evaluate the presence and severity of sensory sensitivity, lack of interest in eating or food, and fear of aversive consequences presentations to facilitate treatment planning (Bryant-Waugh et al., 2019). Other useful measures include the Eating Disorder Assessment for *DSM-5* (Sysko et al., 2015) and Structured Clinical Interview for *DSM-5* (First, Williams, Karg, & Spitzer, 2015) which are structured interviews and can be used to confer an ARFID diagnosis. Additionally, the Eating Disorders in Youth Questionnaire (Hilbert & van Dyck, 2016) and Nine Item ARFID screen (Zickgraf & Ellis, 2018) are available self-report measures that evaluate the severity of the specific psychopathology of ARFID.

Before beginning CBT-AR, it is critical to have a complete understanding of any medical complications. We recommend a consultation with a primary care physician or pediatrician in order to make several key treatment decisions: (1) if weight gain will be a goal of treatment based on current weight status and review of previous growth curves (height and weight); (2) if nutritional deficiencies are present and will need to be addressed; and (3) if other medical conditions fully explain the feeding disturbance, suggesting ARFID treatment is not recommended. This preliminary evaluation can also aid in determining medical stability for outpatient care; facilitate defining treatment goals such as setting a target weight; and determining if supplements are urgently needed even prior to introducing/reintroducing new foods (Thomas & Eddy, 2019).

Stage-Specific Interventions in CBT-AR

Stage 1

In the first stage of CBT-AR, the primary objective is early change in volume and/or variety. The therapist employs treatment strategies that encourage small early changes, which will support larger interventions later. Key elements include:

152 *Kendra R. Becker et al.*

(1) providing psychoeducation about ARFID and CBT-AR, (2) instituting in-session weighing, (3) establishing daily monitoring of dietary intake, (4) increasing weight (if needed), (5) increasing variability in eating routines, (6) creating a personalized formulation describing symptom maintenance in ARFID, and (7) establishing regular eating (Thomas & Eddy, 2019). These strategies are similar to those that are used in family-based therapy (FBT) for anorexia nervosa and bulimia nervosa (Grange & Lock, 2007; Lock & Le Grange, 2012) and CBT for eating disorders (Fairburn, 2008; Waller, Turner, Tatham, Mountford, & Wade, 2019). However, these core techniques have been adapted in CBT-AR to address the unique characteristics of ARFID. Utilization of different interventions and the order of interventions implemented depends on the patient's weight, nutritional status, the severity and presentations of avoidant/restrictive eating, and the format of therapy (family-supported or individual).

Psychoeducation

Psychoeducation is a core intervention in CBT-AR as it is for both FBT and CBT for classic eating disorders (Fairburn, 2008; Grange & Lock, 2007; Lock & Le Grange, 2012; Waller et al., 2019.). From the first session of CBT-AR, the therapist works to highlight that ARFID is a serious illness associated with a range of medical and psychosocial sequelae (Thomas & Eddy, 2019). A major focus of the psychoeducation materials in CBT-AR involves discussion of theorized biological contributions to ARFID symptoms. The therapist emphasizes how underlying biology (such as a heightened tendency toward anxiety, inappropriate brain and hormonal responses to food cues, and/or intense reactions to sensory experiences) engender food preferences or fears related to eating that may promote food avoidance and restriction. Although behaviors such as eating only preferred foods or restricting foods related to choking/vomiting/pain are understandable, the therapist assists the patient and/or family to understand that these eating patterns serve to maintain avoidant/restrictive eating behaviors (Thomas & Eddy, 2019).

Unlike more classic eating disorder symptoms, ARFID can onset in infancy or early toddlerhood, meaning that a patient's eating patterns may be long-standing without a clear picture of premorbid functioning (Thomas & Eddy, 2019). Thus, additional psychoeducation presented by the therapist during the first session of CBT-AR highlights reasonable expectations for families and patients (e.g., that treatment will not transform a patient into a gourmet or gourmand). However, achieving early changes in eating patterns is strongly emphasized, as in CBT and FBT, in order to achieve the best post-treatment outcomes (Thomas & Eddy, 2019).

In-Session Weighing

Weekly weighing is done in CBT-AR whether or not a patient needs to gain weight. For those patients who need to gain/regain weight, in-session weighing is used to set the tone for sessions such that the family and/or patient can evaluate if additional problem-solving is needed to increase intake to support weight gain/regain or if the patient is gaining as expected. Weekly weighing in CBT-AR for low-weight patients is, therefore, very similar to weighing in FBT. For patients without weight gain/regain goals, weekly weighing in CBT-AR is instead used as a marker of continued health during treatment (Thomas & Eddy, 2019). Importantly, in-session weighing does not serve as an exposure as it does in CBT or FBT for classic eating disorders, because individuals with ARFID are not restricting for weight/shape reasons and do not describe fears of out-of-control weight gain.

Self-/Parent-Monitoring

Daily dietary monitoring is a key intervention in CBT-AR as it is in CBT for traditional eating disorders (Fairburn, 2008; Thomas & Eddy, 2019; Waller et al., 2019). In family-supported CBT-AR, parents complete the dietary logs. Parents are asked to complete monitoring for younger patients and those who are low weight in order to actively engage the whole family in working to challenge ARFID. Assigning daily monitoring to parents conveys that younger and underweight patients need support to be successful in treatment and stresses that changes in the environment (e.g., removing accommodations and supervising all meals and snacks) as well as changes within the patient are needed for improvement in ARFID symptoms. Parents are asked to note which foods are eaten and when meals/snacks occur as well as emotions or thoughts that are described by the patient (Thomas & Eddy, 2019). During the individual format of CBT-AR, self-monitoring mirrors self-monitoring in CBT for other eating disorders (Fairburn, 2008; Thomas & Eddy, 2019; Waller et al., 2019).

Notably, CBT-AR requires the therapist to review monitoring records with an additional focus. Beyond checking for patient progress in eating regularly, therapists are also tasked with noting foods that the patient is eating that were not previously described as preferred foods, foods that occur in the logs infrequently but could be eaten more often to improve health status, and homework compliance. For example, later in treatment, reviewing records becomes vital in assessing if and when food tastings are occurring, if and when novel foods are being incorporated, hunger and fullness levels during the day, and emotions around food exposure (Thomas & Eddy, 2019).

Weight Gain/Regain

As with other eating disorders, weight gain/regain interventions for those with ARFID are generally most successful if they can be supported by family members (Lock & Le Grange, 2012). For all patients under 16 years old and for underweight patients who are living with their parents, family-supported CBT-AR is recommended. For underweight patients who are older than 16 and living independently (e.g., attending college), the individual format of

CBT-AR is recommended (Thomas & Eddy, 2019). Weight-gain/regain efforts begin at the first session of CBT-AR, and consumption of an additional 500 calories a day above and beyond what a patient is already eating is recommended to support a gain of approximately one to two pounds per week (Fairburn, 2008; Thomas & Eddy, 2019).

The foods avoided by individuals with ARFID are not necessarily high-calorie, high-fat, or high-sugar foods. Instead, individuals with ARFID are more likely to avoid low-calorie foods including vegetables, fruits, and proteins. This creates a key difference between weight gain/regain in ARFID compared to weight regain for classic eating disorders in that the goals of variety and volume are not one and the same, but rather represent two distinct goals. Thus, weight gain/regain and dietary variety in ARFID treatment often need to be addressed separately because eating feared low-calorie foods does not necessarily promote weight gain/regain (Thomas & Eddy, 2019). This distinction is particularly important for patients with multiple presentations of ARFID because goals to improve the patient's dietary range may diametrically conflict with a strict focus on early weight gain/regain. Parents and/or patients may want to focus on dietary variety for psychosocial reasons (e.g., making it easier to travel, eat meals away from the home, or prepare meals at home). However, weight gain/regain needs to be the primary goal for medical stability. To emphasize the importance of reaching a healthy weight range and provide motivation for a goal that the family and/or patient may be less motivated to pursue than expanding dietary variety, the therapist is direct about the consequences of malnutrition by providing a handout detailing the health risks of weight loss/persistent low-weight and introduces a main theme of CBT-AR: Volume before variety (Thomas & Eddy, 2019). This principle of volume before variety means that weight regain efforts in CBT-AR are achieved via increased intake of already preferred foods versus an introduction of new or reintroduced foods.

This distinction between weight gain/regain strategies in CBT-AR from FBT and CBT for traditional eating disorders are demonstrated most clearly during the in-session therapeutic meal. Similar to FBT, the family or patient brings a meal that is sufficient for weight gain (Lock & Le Grange, 2012). During the meal, the therapist helps the patient/family determine what is enough food for the patient to eat to support weight gain/regain and assists the parents in encouraging the patient to eat one more bite (Lock & Le Grange, 2012; Thomas & Eddy, 2019). However, unlike in FBT for anorexia nervosa or bulimia nervosa, the meal consists of the patient's preferred foods and family members are not encouraged to eat the same foods as the individual with ARIFD. This is because of the very limited range of foods that most patients with ARFID feel comfortable eating early in treatment. The therapist also may need to adopt a more direct style than is used in FBT. Parents of individuals with long-standing feeding difficulties may feel extremely disempowered regarding how to feed their child. In fact, many parents report receiving mixed messages from previous health care providers about the degree of caloric intake that is sufficient and the necessity (or not) of weight gain. This is unique from

Adapting Evidenced-Based Therapies for ARFID   155

cases of anorexia nervosa where there is a premorbid level of functioning where parents have confidence that their child was eating well, and providers are able to estimate more clearly appropriate growth curves (Thomas & Eddy, 2019).

As the same foods do not usually meet dietary volume and variety goals for ARFID patients, the therapist also asks the family/patient to bring a novel food to the in-session therapeutic meal. In addition to asking the individual with ARFID to eat one more bite (or more) than they felt ready to eat, the therapist also assists the family and/or patient to eat at least one (or more) bite of the novel food (Thomas & Eddy, 2019). The novel food can be a food that the patient used to eat consistently but has dropped or not eaten for three or more months, a variation on a preferred food (e.g., different brand or flavor), or even a completely new food that the patient feels ready to try. This additional challenge provides an opportunity for early change in variety despite the primary focus on volume at this stage. The expectation is that the patient will have at least one bite of the novel food (e.g., different flavor or brand of a preferred food) or food presentation (e.g., eating an apple with skin rather than peeled) providing an early example of how to include food tastings or incorporations during meals (Thomas & Eddy, 2019).

The final discussion point about the family meal in CBT-AR is that the intervention is also done in the individual format of treatment. Some adult patients may elect to include a significant other during the in-session meal for additional support. Others will complete the therapeutic meal alone with the therapist, in which case the therapist encourages and supports the patient directly in eating as well as coaching the patient in tasting the new food/novel food presentation (Thomas & Eddy, 2019).

Small Changes in Dietary Variety

For patients who are not underweight, CBT-AR maintains a focus on early changes to dietary intake. In place of increasing dietary volume, Stage 1 sessions focus on small changes to dietary routines such as reintroducing dropped foods, eating different brands or flavors of preferred foods, or breaking rigid routines around eating (e.g., having foods that are only eaten at lunch for dinner). This represents a stark difference from either FBT or CBT for eating disorders given that dropped foods in classical eating disorders are usually related to fears of weight gain and are targeted to test hypotheses about loss of control eating or weight gain (Fairburn, 2008; Grange & Lock, 2007; Lock & Le Grange, 2012; Waller et al., 2019).

Personalized Formulation

The family and/or the patient collaborates with the therapist to create a personalized formulation of ARFID symptoms in the second session of CBT-AR. The therapist highlights that biological vulnerabilities to sensory aspects of food, anxiety, and/or a lack of interest in eating underlie interactions with foods/eating that develop into problematic expectancies (Thomas & Eddy, 2019).

Similar to CBT for eating disorders, the formulation is used to identify dietary restriction in volume and/or variety as the primary culprit for maintaining the eating disturbance. In addition, as in CBT for classical eating disorders, the formulation is then used to highlight that the best target for therapeutic intervention is dietary restriction itself in order to correct malnutrition and cognitive distortions around food and/or eating (Fairburn, 2008; Thomas & Eddy, 2019).

Regular Eating

In CBT-AR, as in CBT for other eating disorders, after the patient or family has begun self-/parent-monitoring and understands via the personalized formulation how dietary restriction/avoidance maintains ARFID, the therapist introduces regular eating (Fairburn, 2008; Thomas & Eddy, 2019; Waller et al., 2019). Recommendations are exactly the same as those in CBT or FBT such that the therapist helps the patient/family move toward three meals and two snacks for non-underweight patients and three meals and three snacks for those who need to gain/regain (Fairburn, 2008; Thomas & Eddy, 2019). Importantly, regular eating is not framed, as it is in CBT, as a prevention method for binge eating (Fairburn, 2008). Instead, regular eating is introduced as the best approach to reset hormonal appetite cues for improved hunger and fullness awareness as well as a strategy for increasing opportunities for tastings and/or incorporations of novel foods (Thomas & Eddy, 2019).

Stage 2

The second stage of CBT-AR is similar to the second stage of CBT for eating disorders in that the therapist reviews the progress in treatment so far and begins planning for Stage 3, in which relevant maintaining mechanisms will be targeted (Fairburn, 2008). The key difference between CBT-AR and CBT for other eating disorders are the specific interventions used to assist the therapist, family, and/or patient in agreeing on which maintaining mechanisms to address in the next stage.

As in Stage 1, the CBT-AR therapist continues motivating the family and/or patient to reach their eating goals for recovery and does so by discussing potential consequences of an inadequate diet. The therapist introduces a chart describing common nutritional deficiencies to help the patient/family understand how failing to improve dietary variety may affect overall health and contribute to symptoms (e.g., fatigue, low mood, and weakened immune system). Using this chart, the therapist highlights foods rich in nutrients that are underrepresented in the patient's diet and asks the patient to identify which of these foods the patient might be willing to learn about (i.e., introduce in very small amounts at first) in the next stage. Thus, as in CBT for classic eating disorders, the therapist is capitalizing on a patient's desire to avoid certain symptoms to build motivation for thinking more flexibly about their eating habits (Fairburn, 2008; Thomas & Eddy, 2019; Waller et al., 2019).

Adapting Evidenced-Based Therapies for ARFID   157

A second strategy to build motivation in CBT-AR is the introduction of the United States Department of Agriculture's 2011 schematic of a balanced diet called the MyPlate schematic (to learn more visit www.chosemyplate.gov). The therapist uses this schematic to help the patient identify which of the five food groups (i.e., vegetables, fruits, protein, dairy and/or dairy substitutes, and grains) are well represented in their diet and which are not. Using the proportions exemplified in the MyPlate graphic as the ultimate goal, the therapist asks the patient to draw their typical intake from the five food groups as a pie chart with the size of each pie wedge representing how much of their diet is comprised of each food group. This intervention allows the therapist to set the treatment goal that the patient's typical plate at the end of treatment look closer to the MyPlate schematic via daily incorporations of foods from the under-represented groups (Thomas & Eddy, 2019).

The MyPlate intervention sets up the final intervention that is unique to CBT-AR in Stage 2: The Primary Food Group Building Blocks list. The Building Blocks worksheet is a comprehensive list of whole foods (e.g., cheese, tomatoes, and bread) that could be eaten individually or eventually used to build more complex foods (e.g., pizza, sandwiches, etc.). Although somewhat similar to the intervention described in CBT in which patients identify foods that they avoid at the grocery store due to concerns of gaining weight (Fairburn, 2008), the goal of selecting foods to learn about in CBT-AR is quite different as exposure to weight/shape fears is not targeted (Thomas & Eddy, 2019). Instead, the long list of foods, organized by the five food groups, is used to help the family and/or patient notice the variety possible in different food groups. For example, even if the patient has tried and disliked broccoli in the past, there are many other vegetables on the Building Blocks list that the patient may never have previously tried. The non-judgmental language and curious style of selecting possible foods to target in treatment is deliberate and removes the expectation that a patient must like or prefer every food they taste. Although the Building Blocks worksheet is introduced in Stage 2 of CBT-AR, it is used throughout Stage 3 as a way to track which foods have been tasted and incorporated. It is also used in Stage 4 to highlight changes in eating patterns achieved during treatment.

As in CBT (Fairburn, 2008), the CBT-AR therapist considers the progress in treatment so far around key Stage 1 goals (e.g., weight gain/regain, small changes in variety, self-monitoring, and regular eating) as well as data reviewed during the interventions in Stage 2, to decide which modules in Stage 3 should be addressed and in what order (Thomas & Eddy, 2019).

Box 7.2   Three Tips in Deciding Which Maintaining Mechanism to Target First

1   If a patient has a food or eating fear that has resulted in rapid weight loss, the first module in Stage 3 should likely be fear of aversive consequences. Often addressing a fear of choking/swallowing/

> vomiting/pain is necessary even before nutritional supplements can be taken by mouth or before a patient is able to eat enough preferred foods to gain/regain weight.
>
> 2   If a patient is at a low weight and still needs to gain more after Stages 1 and 2 (and is not limiting intake/foods because of a fear of aversive consequences), it is typically best to continue focusing on weight gain via the lack of interest module at the beginning of Stage 3. Not only will a patient learn additional skills for eating enough but will also be able to continue focusing on one primary goal (i.e., increasing volume) before trying to address a separate goal (e.g., expanding variety).
>
> 3   If a patient is not low weight, but has a clear nutritional deficiency, it is important for the patient to work with a medical professional to determine whether a dietary supplement is necessary. The patient should typically start Stage 3 with the sensory sensitivity module in order to promote food intake that will correct the deficiency.

Stage 3

The third stage of CBT-AR is the heart of the treatment. During Stage 3, patient-specific variations of exposures are used to address the maintaining mechanisms in order of the priority determined during the personalized formulation in Stage 1 and discussions in Stage 2. As such, Stage 3 is highly individualized, which also makes it the most variable part of treatment in terms of content and length. For example, for a patient at a healthy weight who presents with just one maintaining mechanism, Stage 3 may only last 14 sessions. However, a low-weight patient with more than one maintaining mechanism may need up to 22 sessions. Each maintaining mechanism is addressed sequentially, moving only to the next once the previously targeted mechanism has been, at minimum, partially resolved (Thomas & Eddy, 2019). Each maintaining mechanism is addressed by setting up exposures unique to the presentation. Below we highlight the adaptations to the core types of exposures used in CBT-AR Stage 3.

Food Exposures with Emphasis on Nonjudgmental Approach (Targeting Sensory Sensitivity)

Exposure is a highly effective way of increasing liking for novel foods in both children (Birch & Marlin, 1982) and adults (Methven, Langreney, & Prescott, 2012; Pliner, Pelchat, & Grabski, 1993). In CBT-AR, the therapist leads a patient through a concrete sensory exposure exercise, "The Five Steps," where the patient uses four of the five senses–sight, touch/texture, smell, taste–to approach a new food. The goal is to have the patient taste novel foods since there is no evidence that merely looking at novel food will increase preference for that food (Birch, McPhee, Shoba, Pirok, & Steinberg, 1987). Unlike food

Adapting Evidenced-Based Therapies for ARFID   159

exposures in CBT for classic eating disorders, anxiety is not the only emotion targeted by these food presentations as sensory exploration also facilitates degust tolerance (Thomas & Eddy, 2019).

Exposures during the sensory sensitivity module begin by having the patient/family bring in five foods identified during Stage 2 from the Building Blocks worksheet and leading the patient through the Five-Steps worksheet. The therapist asks the patient to explore the foods using nonjudgmental language, working toward having the patient taste the foods in session. After the exposure, the patient identifies which of the five foods brought to each session they are willing to continue tasting for homework. It is important to remember that at least one of the foods tasted in session should be tasted every day at home. Foods that are successfully tasted in session and at home are then targeted for incorporation into the patients diet.

Interoceptive Exposures and Pleasurable Eating (Targeting a Lack of Interest in Eating or Food)

Interoceptive exposures address internal body experiences, rather than external stimuli. Boswell, Anderson, and Anderson (2015) have recently described a series of interoceptive exposures for classic eating disorders that we have adapted for ARFID. Each exposure (e.g., chugging glasses of water) is designed to address the physical symptoms of bloating, nausea, or fullness that contribute to a lack of interest in eating or food. With practice, patients learn that these sensations are temporary, tolerable, and not associated with long-term negative consequences.

The therapist next supports a patient in enhancing the salience of hunger cues by instructing the patient/family to rate their levels of hunger/fullness on a scale of 1–7 using personalized anchors to increase awareness of hunger cues similar to Craighead's (2006) concept of appetite awareness. The patient/family is asked to rate their hunger/fullness as part of their homework on their self-/parent-monitoring records over the next week, aiming to record these physical sensations for at least two days.

At every session in this module, the patient also eats five of their preferred foods in a pleasurable eating exercise following the interoceptive exposures described above. This activity is done to help the patient attend to aspects of eating they enjoy while recalling or describing positive memories associated with their favorite foods. Pleasurable eating is used in this module to promote new learning of positive associations with food and eating.

Exposure to Fear Associated with Food and/or Eating (Targeting Fear of Aversive Consequences)

Patients with fears of eating (e.g., vomiting, choking, and abdominal pain) restrict their eating or eat a restricted range of foods to create a false feeling of safety, and, as a result, have limited opportunities to confirm or refute

160 *Kendra R. Becker et al.*

predictions that all eating situations or certain types of foods are dangerous. Together with the patient/family, the therapist works to create a fear and avoidance hierarchy containing foods or eating situations that the patient fears will elicit the feared feeding outcome (e.g., choking, nausea, allergic reaction, and pain). It is important to note that exposures during this module are completed with close consultation with a medical professional to develop exposures that address the patient's fear(s) *and* are safe for the patient to complete. For example, if a patient has a known food allergy but is eliminating all types of foods due to a fear of an allergic reaction, the therapist works with the patient's allergist to confirm which foods will be safe for the patient to consume.

Similar to CBT treatments for anxiety, the therapist assists the patient in first developing a Subjective Units of Distress (SUDS) scale to organize situations/foods from least to most frightening (Chorpita, Vitali, & Barlow, 1997; McNally, 1986; Nock, 2002). This scale should range from 0 to 100, with 0 representing no distress whatsoever and 100 representing the highest distress the patient can imagine. The therapist uses the patient's own words to describe distress and help create anchors of distress on the hierarchy. For younger adolescents and children, the therapist can present SUDS rating as a "fear thermometer" (as in Coping Cat; Kendall and Hedtke, 2006), ladder, or mountain to increase patient engagement and facilitate comprehension. For each step in the hierarchy, the therapist asks the patient (assisted by the family, if necessary) where this step falls on their SUDS scale. For example, if a patient had a fear of choking and is consuming only liquids and purees, the patient may first start by eating soft foods such as plain pasta or oatmeal. Higher SUDS-rated foods on the patient's generated hierarchy may include flaky foods such as crackers, stringy foods such as meats (e.g., pulled chicken) or certain vegetables (e.g., celery), or crunchy foods such as chips. The highest food on the hierarchy may be the very food itself that the patient choked on prior to the development of their fear. After each session, the patient continues to practice exposures at home and moves up their hierarchy toward the most feared outcome.

Stage 4

The final stage of CBT-AR includes discussions of progress made during treatment, strategies to maintain treatment gains, and relapse prevention as in all CBT treatments (Fairburn, 2008; Waller et al., 2019).

Stage 4 highlights the efforts by the patient/family in addressing ARFID symptoms. The therapist does this by using the Building Blocks worksheet to identify and count all the tasted foods and, of those foods, which foods have been incorporated. When discussing how success was possible, the therapist guides the patient/family in remembering exposures, regular eating, self-/parent-monitoring, and any tips that proved to be particularly helpful in moving foods from tasted to incorporated (e.g., using condiments or spices;

Adapting Evidenced-Based Therapies for ARFID 161

pairing a novel food with a preferred food; Thomas & Eddy, 2019). The therapist also highlights how much weight the patient has gained (if applicable) and which foods and changes to the eating schedule made weight gain/regain possible. Using these discussions of praise and reflection, the therapist reviews the original formulation to note how targeting food avoidance and restriction improved symptoms and, if present, where areas of continued work are possible to keep reducing the influence of ARFID on the patient's life.

A large part of Stage 4 is reviewing red flags that may signal the return of avoidant/restrictive eating in the future. Although some signs are also risky for relapse of traditional eating disorders including weight loss, reliance on safe foods, and avoidance of eating around others, some behaviors such as dropping new foods, no longer tasting new foods, and cutting out all foods from one food group are unique to ARFID. Similarly, some situations such as transitions to college may represent risk factors for both ARFID and traditional eating disorders but how these changes may increase risk for problematic eating behaviors differ and need to be discussed (e.g., college risks for ARFID are not related to increased focus on appearance but perhaps related to limited access to preferred foods in dining halls and changes in schedules making regular eating more effortful; Thomas & Eddy, 2019).

Importantly, and particularly for adolescent patients with ARFID, the family may have to maintain close vigilance around eating behaviors even after formal treatment to prevent backsliding. This is somewhat different from FBT for anorexia nervosa or bulimia nervosa in which a large part of the latter phases of treatment involves giving control back to an adolescent (Grange & Lock, 2007; Lock & Le Grange, 2012). For many cases of ARFID, parents may need to closely monitor food intake for a longer period of time to be sure that an adolescent with ARFID is continuing to eat regularly and ingest adequate calories/variety. Furthermore, parents will likely want to continue using The Five Steps and incorporation strategies to continue introducing new foods (perhaps ones that were not able to be addressed in treatment) so that there is continued flexibility around eating (Thomas & Eddy, 2019).

CBT-AR Case Examples

In order to demonstrate patient progress through Stages 1–4 of CBT-AR, we describe two cases below. Each patient agreed to have their anonymized case data included for educational purposes. The first case presentation describes an adult patient undergoing the individual format of CBT-AR and highlights weight re-gain for adult patients when family support is not available. The second case describes an adolescent undergoing the family-supported format of CBT-AR and highlights decision-making around the order of Stage 3 interventions as well as the successful implementation of CBT-AR interventions in the context of co-occurring psychopathology.

162 *Kendra R. Becker et al.*

Case Example 1: Individual CBT-AR with a 19-Year-Old Woman with Fear of Aversive Consequences and Low Weight

Jill was a 19-year-old White female referred to our outpatient eating disorder clinic after completing a partial hospitalization at a specialized eating-disorder treatment center following rapid weight loss. Jill reported that, after starting college, she began to experience marked GI symptoms including abdominal pain, bloating, and reflux. Subsequently, she began a self-determined elimination diet to systematically remove foods that she associated with pain. During this time, she saw many GI specialists and received a thorough GI workup (including a colonoscopy and esophagogastroduodenoscopy). Despite negative results, she continued to restrict her diet, moving from a healthy weight of 128 pounds , 65 inches (BMI = 21.3, healthy range) to 88 pounds (BMI = 14.4, underweight), with associated complications of hypotension, bradycardia, and amenorrhea. During treatment in a partial hospitalization program, she began reincorporating foods into her diet and weight was restored to 113 pounds (BMI = 18.8). At the time of her presentation to our clinic, she still needed to restore at least 10 pounds and was continuing to restrict volume and variety of foods for a fear of GI symptoms returning. She continued to engage in many safety behaviors that she felt prevented the GI distress such as cutting up foods into very small pieces and eating the exact same thing for each meal and snack. Jill denied shape/weight concerns and had no evidence of body image disturbance.

In Stage 1, the therapist worked with Jill to have her continue eating three meals and three snacks per day, comprised of preferred/safe high-energy foods. In order to continue to work on weight gain, Jill also added a typical snack food (e.g., banana, granola, or yogurt) to meals. These small changes helped her prepare for addressing her fears in Stage 3 by challenging her belief that rigidity in her diet prevented GI symptoms.

In Stage 2, after Jill had gained approximately 5 pounds, the therapist introduced her to the principles of avoidance exacerbating anxiety and the role gradual exposure plays to promote habituation and corrective learning. Jill identified foods she wanted to reincorporate using the Building Blocks worksheet. During Stage 2, all of the foods reintroduced were foods that Jill did not think would cause GI symptoms but were high in calories in order to support continued weight regain.

During Stage 3, Jill's weight continued to increase steadily, and the therapist began with the fear of aversive consequences module. Although Jill also reported low appetite, both Jill and her therapist believed that low appetite was secondary to the fears of GI symptoms. Jill was able to identify many safety behaviors that she perceived to lessen the GI symptoms. These safety behaviors were leading to social isolation and maintaining both her low weight and anxiety. For example, Jill would arrange her day to eat the majority of her meals and snacks at home in the event that she experienced GI symptoms. While eating at home, she would eat lying down, in bed,

Adapting Evidenced-Based Therapies for ARFID 163

watching movies on her computer to distract herself. In Stage 3, she created a hierarchy of new foods to incorporate back into her diet, starting first with energy-dense foods to continue advancing weight regain. She worked with the therapist to rank foods and eating situations using a 0–100 scale representing how scared Jill was that the foods and eating situations would cause GI symptoms. The exposures the therapist coached Jill to complete in treatment were first structured around eating feared foods and then progressed to eating feared foods in specific settings (i.e., at a restaurant) and during specific time periods (i.e., before she had to go to a class) that she previously avoided.

In order to continue to target Jill's feared outcomes and further support final weight regain, the therapist next introduced the lack of interest module and used interoceptive exposures (i.e., spinning in a chair to induce nausea and gulping glasses of water to induce fullness) to mimic GI distress. Jill was able to learn that, even if she felt some GI pain, it was temporary and she could eat anyway. She continued to gain weight steadily and the once challenging interoceptive exposures became much easier with repeated practice. The therapist then assisted Jill in focusing on the most feared situations on her hierarchy – eating around others in restaurants. For these exposures, the therapist assisted Jill in eating challenging foods while at restaurants.

By the end of Stage 4, Jill had reintroduced over 50 new foods, including some of her most feared foods (e.g., spicy foods) even in challenging settings (e.g., restaurants). Over the course of 23 CBT-AR sessions, she gained 12 pounds to reach 125 pounds, BMI = 20.7. She was eating all meals and snacks without any safety behaviors and was eating around friends at school and with her family at home. As a reward for her hard work, Jill planned a month-long European vacation with her sister, and she was excited (rather than afraid) to try new foods while there.

Case Example 2: Family-Supported CBT-AR with a 12-Year-Old Boy with Low Weight, Lack of Interest in Eating or Food, and Sensory Sensitivity

Diego was a 12-year-old Hispanic boy referred to our eating disorder specialty clinic by his pediatric gastroenterologist, who was concerned about his poor growth. At treatment presentation, Diego was 56 inches tall, weighed 61.6 pounds (BMI = 13.8, <1st percentile for sex and age), and had not begun puberty. He limited his food intake by both volume and variety and presented with lack of interest (eating very small portions) and sensory sensitivity (eating just a handful of dairy, grain, and protein foods). He had previously received diagnoses of high-functioning autism spectrum disorder (ASD) and attention-deficit/hyperactivity disorder (ADHD). Diego's family had immigrated to the United States from South America; his primary caregivers were his mother and maternal grandmother.

164 *Kendra R. Becker et al.*

In Stage 1, the therapist worked with Diego's mother and grandmother to feed him three meals and three snacks per day, comprising preferred, high-energy foods such as whole milk, pizza, chicken nuggets, hamburgers, ice cream, and supplement drinks (e.g., Boost). For the crucial first few weeks of treatment, Diego's mother stayed home from work (using the Family Medical Leave Act) and kept Diego home from school so she could closely supervise his meals and snacks. Once his mother returned to work, Diego's grandmother supervised his eating during the day. Throughout Stage 1, the therapist redirected Diego's mother and grandmother to focus on volume, rather than variety, as they were worried about his lack of fruit and vegetable intake.

In Stage 2, after Diego had gained approximately 10 pounds , the therapist worked with Diego to identify new foods to learn about in Stage 3, including fruits, vegetables, and traditional Latin American foods. His grandmother stopped attending sessions as his mother felt more confident in feeding Diego at home.

In Stage 3, the therapist began with the sensory sensitivity module given his mother's concerns about dietary variety. However, given that Diego's weight gain immediately stalled, the therapist suggested switching to the lack of interest module, to which Diego and his mother agreed. In the lack of interest module, Diego completed interoceptive exposures including spinning in a chair and gulping glasses of water (usually just one to two glasses as he had great difficulty tolerating fullness). After he had gained another five pounds , the therapist switched back to the sensory sensitivity module in which Diego tried a number of fruits, vegetables, and proteins. Diego also returned to school during Stage 3.

By the end of Stage 4, Diego had substantially increased his intake by both volume and variety. After completing 27 sessions of CBT-AR over the course of a year, he had grown 5.5 inches (to 61.5 inches), gained > 20 pounds (to 84.8 pounds), and incorporated nine novel foods including tangerines, yogurt, apple sauce, mozzarella sticks, chocolate muffins, and several types of fruit juice. Diego's mother reported that she did not have to push Diego to eat as much as she did at the beginning of treatment. Diego himself was pleased to have grown taller and begun pubertal development (i.e., facial hair and deeper voice). He still had further weight to gain, but his mother felt confident that she could continue to use CBT-AR strategies at home, and she and his therapist agreed that it would be most helpful for Diego clinically to refocus his continued psychiatric treatment on managing his ASD and ADHD.

Box 7.3 Five "Tips From the Trenches" in Treating Individuals with ARFID

1   Be prepared for allergic reactions: Individuals with sensory sensitivity presentations of ARFID may not be aware of previously undiagnosed food allergies because they have tasted few foods. A small minority of patients in our clinic were unaware of allergies and needed medical attention after a tasting session.

Therefore, we have received training in responding to mild allergic reactions and now have access to epinephrine autoinjector (EpiPens) in case of an unexpected allergic reaction. Notably, this has not occurred for patients with known food allergies who have disproportionate fears of having an allergic reaction (the fear of aversive consequences presentation), because we were already aware of the true risks before starting treatment with these patients and consulted with medical providers before beginning exposures.

2　Be prepared for patients to vomit during interoceptive exposures: Some patients with the lack of interest presentation have vomited after chugging water. Although we validate that no one enjoys vomiting, we also note that vomiting can be tolerated despite being unpleasant.

3　Stock up on food items that can be used for food tastings: Patients and/or their families sometimes forget to bring items for tasting sessions. We never want food tasting to be avoided in session if it is the planned activity for that session. Thus, at our clinic we keep several items available for tastings in case a patient attends a session without anything to practice. We make sure and let them know that we have these items, so that if they do forget food items, they are aware that they will practice with items available in the clinic.

4　Assess for weight and shape concerns during treatment: Although body image disturbance motivating restriction is a rule-out for a diagnosis of ARFID, some patients begin to express body image concerns during CBT-AR. This is most likely to happen, in our experience, when patients are gaining/regaining weight, particularly if they have never been at a healthy weight and see being low-weighted as a part of their identity or if they lost a substantial amount of weight rapidly prior to initiating treatment. We have found it helpful to routinely check in about these concerns while reviewing self-/parent-monitoring records. For some individuals, supplementing CBT-AR with psychoeducation about weight distribution with weight gain, appropriate mirror use, and body comparisons is sufficient for addressing these concerns. However, if additional weight/shape-motivated restrictive eating behaviors (e.g., refusing high-calorie foods) develop, we have also referred patients for FBT or CBT for traditional eating disorders.

5　Utilize reward systems: Patients with ARFID, especially younger individuals, may be less motivated to practice food tastings/ incorporations at home and/or feel unmotivated to increase their intake. As CBT-AR is a collaborative treatment, requiring engagement from both patients and their families, reward schedules can be very helpful in these circumstances. For example, a patient may receive an immediate $1 for every meal/snack eaten and an additional $2 for every day when *all* meals and snacks are eaten.

Future Research Directions

As no empirically-supported interventions for individuals with ARFID across the age and weight spectrum are yet available, treatment development and evaluation is vital for helping these patients. Published findings on ARFID treatments include case studies, case series, retrospective chart reviews, and treatment trials with only very young children. Although CBT-AR represents a new therapy and is in very early stages of outcome research, preliminary data on the efficacy of CBT-AR are promising. In a proof-of-concept study of CBT-AR, 20 children and adolescents with ARFID between the ages of 10 and 17 demonstrated significant decreases in PARDI scores, and the underweight subgroup gained significant weight (Thomas et al., 2020). Furthermore, 70% of the participants no longer met criteria for ARFID at the end of treatment (Thomas et al., 2020). Although encouraging, these data need support from large randomized-controlled trials in both children/adolescents and adults. Our team is currently exploring if changes in hypothesized underlying neurobiology (e.g., brain and hormonal functioning) correspond to treatment outcomes.

References

American Psychiatric Association. (2013). *Diagnostic and statistical manual of mental disorders (5th ed.)*. Arlington, VA: American Psychiatric Association Publishing.

Birch, L. L., & Marlin, D. W. (1982). I don't like it; I never tried it: Effects of exposure on two-year-old children's food preferences. *Appetite, 3*(4), 353–360. doi:10.1016/S0195-6663(82)80053-6.

Birch, L. L., McPhee, L., Shoba, B. C., Pirko, E., & Steinberg, L. (1987). What kind of exposure reduces children's food neophobia? *Appetite, 9*(3), 171–178. doi:10/1016/S0195-6663(87)80011-9.

Boswell, J. F., Anderson, L. M., & Anderson, D. A. (2015). Integration of interoceptive exposure in eating disorder treatment. *Clinical Psychology: Science and Practice, 22*(2), 194–210. doi:10.1111/cpsp.12103.

Bryant-Waugh, R. (2013). Avoidant restrictive food intake disorder: An illustrative case example. *International Journal of Eating Disorders, 46*(5), 420–423. doi:10.1002/eat.22093.

Bryant-Waugh, R., Micali, N., Cooke, L., Lawson, E. A., Eddy, K. T., & Thomas, J. J. (2019). Development of the Pica, ARFID, and Rumination Disorder Interview, a multi-informant, semi-structured interview of feeding disorders across the lifespan: A pilot study for ages 10–22. *International Journal of Eating Disorders, 52*(4), 378–387. doi:10.1002/eat.22958.

Chatoor, I. (2002). Feeding disorders in infants and toddlers: Diagnosis and treatment. *Child and Adolescent Psychiatric Clinics of North America, 11*(2), 163–183. doi:10.1016/S1056-4993(01)00002-5.

Chorpita, B. F., Vitali, A. E., & Barlow, D. H. (1997). Behavioral treatment of choking phobia in an adolescent: An experimental analysis. *Journal of Behavior Therapy and Experimental Psychiatry, 28*(4), 307–315. doi:10.1016/S0005-7916(97)00027-X.

Craighead, L. W. (2006). *The appetite awareness workbook: How to listen to your body and overcome bingeing, overeating & obsession with food*. Oakland, CA: New Harbinger Publications.

Adapting Evidenced-Based Therapies for ARFID 167

Eddy, K. T., Harshman, S. G., Becker, K. R., Bern, E., Bryant-Waugh, R., Hilbert, A., ... Thomas, J. J. (2019). Radcliffe ARFID Workgroup: Toward operationalization of research diagnostic criteria and directions for the field. *International Journal of Eating Disorders, 52*(4), 361–366. doi:10.1002/eat.23042.

Fairburn, C. G. (2008). *Cognitive behavior therapy and eating disorders.* New York, NY: Guilford Press.

First, M. B., Williams, J. B. W., Karg, R. S., & Spitzer, R. L. (2015). *Structured clinical interview for DSM-5- Research Version (SCID-5 for DSM-5, Research Version; SCID-5-RV).* Arlington, VA: American Psychiatric Association.

Hilbert, A., & van Dyck, Z. (2016). *Eating disorders in youth-questionnaire. English version.* University of Leipzig. http://nbn-resolving.de/urn:nbn:de:bsz:15-qucosa-197246.

Kambanis, P. E., Kuhnle, M., Wons, O. B., Jo, J., Keshishian, A. C., Hauser, K., ...Thomas, J. J. (2020). Prevalence and correlates of psychiatric comorbidities in children and adolescents with full and subthreshold avoidant/restrictive food intake disorder. *International Journal of Eating Disorders, 53*(2), 256–265.

Kendall, P. C., & Hedtke, K. (2006). *The coping cat workbook (2nd ed.).* Ardmore, PA: Workbook Publishing.

Le Grange, D. L., & Lock, J. (2007). *Treating bulimia in adolescents: A family-based approach.* New York, NY: Guildford Press.

Lock, J., & Le Grange, D. (2012). *Treatment manual for anorexia nervosa: A family-based approach (2nd ed.).* New York, NY: Guilford Press.

McNally, R. J. (1986). Behavioral treatment of a choking phobia. *Journal of Behavior Therapy and Experimental Psychiatry, 17*(3), 185–188. doi.:10.1016/0005-7916(86)90025-X.

Methven, L., Langreney, E., & Prescott, J. (2012). Changes in liking for a no added salt soup as a function of exposure. *Food Quality and Preference, 26*(2), 135–140. doi:10. 1016/j.foodqual.2012.04.012.

Micali, N., Simonoff, E., Elberling, H., Rask, C. U., Olsen, E. M., & Skovgaard, A. M. (2011). Eating patterns in a population-based sample of children aged 5 to 7 years: Association with psychopathology and parentally perceived impairment. *Journal of Developmental and Behavioral Pediatrics, 32*(8), 572–580. doi:10.1097/DBP. 0b013e31822bc7b7.

Nock, M. K. (2002). A multiple-baseline evaluation of the treatment of food phobia in a young boy. *Journal of Behavior Therapy and Experimental Psychiatry, 33*(3–4), 217–25. doi:10.1016/S0005-7916(02)00046-0.

Pliner, P., Pelchat, M., & Grabski, M. (1993). Reduction of neophobia in humans by exposure to novel foods. *Appetite, 20*(2), 111–123. doi:10.1006/appe.1993.1013.

Pulumo, R., Coniglio, K., Lawson, E. A., Micali, N., Hilderbrant, T., Asanza, E., ... Thomas, J. J. (2016, October). *DSM-5 Presentations of avoidant/restrictive food intake disorder: Are categories mutually exclusive or overlapping?* Poster session presented at the meeting of the Eating Disorders Research Society, New York, NY.

Sysko, R., Glasofer, D. R., Hildebrandt, T., Klimek, P., Mitchell, J. E., Berg, K. C., Peterson, C. B., Wonderlich, S. A., & Walsh, B. T. (2015). The eating disorder assessment for DSM-5 (EDA-5): Development and validation of a structured interview for feeding and eating disorders. *International Journal of Eating Disorders, 48*(5), 452–463. doi:10.1002/eat.22388.

Thomas, J. J., Becker, K. R., Kuhnle, M. C., Jo, J. H., Harshman, S. G., Wons, O., ... Eddy, K. T. (2020). Cognitive-behavioral therapy for avoidant/restrictive food intake disorder (CBT-AR): Feasibility, acceptability, and proof-of-concept for children and adolescents. *International Journal of Eating Disorders*. doi:10.1002/eat.23355.

Thomas, J. J., & Eddy, K. T. (2019). *Cognitive-behavioral therapy for avoidant/restrictive food intake disorder: Children, adolescents, & adults*. Cambridge, UK: Cambridge University Press.

Thomas, J. J., Lawson, E. A., Micali, N., Misra, M., Deckersbach, T., & Eddy, K. T. (2017). Avoidant/restrictive food intake disorder: A three-dimensional model of neurobiology with implications for etiology and treatment. *Current Psychiatry Reports*, *19*(8), 54. doi:10.1007/s11920-017-0795-5.

U.S. Department of Agriculture. ChoseMyPlate.gov Website. Washington, DC. https://www.choosemyplate.gov.

Waller, G., Turner, H. M., Tatham, M., Mountford, V. A., & Wade, T. D. (2019). *Brief cognitive behavioural therapy for non-underweight patients*. London, UK: Taylor and Francis Ltd.

Zickgraf, H. F., & Ellis, J. M. (2018). Initial validation of the nine item avoidant/restrictive food intake disorder screen (NIAS): A measure of three restrictive eating patterns. *Appetite*, *123*(1), 32–42. doi:10.1016/j.appet.2017.11.111.

8 Treating Eating-Related Problems in Non-Eating Disordered Populations

Rebecca Bernard, Jessie Menzel, and Kerri Boutelle

Introduction

Many eating-related issues are overlooked in health care as well as in mental health care. Eating behavior exists along a continuum, and can be considered non-disordered, disordered eating, or at the extreme end of the spectrum, meeting diagnostic criteria for an eating disorder. However, even at subthreshold levels, disordered eating has implications for physiological and psychological health. The presence of altered or abnormal eating in a patient should not be taken lightly. Disordered eating and eating disorders can result in severe medical complications, including an increased risk for mortality, and thus it is important to determine if the eating problem in the patient has had a physiological impact. Past research comparing patients with what was formally called eating disorder NOS (EDNOS) to those with full-syndrome anorexia nervosa (AN) or bulimia nervosa (BN) found that patients with EDNOS have higher mortality rates than the general population, and similar mortality rates as those with AN (Crow et al., 2009) in one study and BN (Fichter & Quadlfieg, 2016) in another. Thus, the presence of symptoms such as weight fluctuation, weight gain, restriction (reduced dietary intake), binge eating, and purging behavior should immediately signal a need for a more thorough medical and psychiatric assessment of a patient.

There are many medical and psychiatric conditions that may be associated with disordered eating. Certain medical conditions can lead to alterations in eating behavior, weight gain, weight loss, or change in appetite, including but not limited to inflammatory bowel disease (IBD), Chron's disease, celiac disease, functional gastrointestinal disorders, Prader–Willi syndrome, Marfan syndrome, food allergies, and diabetes mellitus. Additionally, many psychological illnesses may be associated with or result in some alteration of eating behavior, including depression, anxiety, sensory processing disorder, and autism spectrum disorder (ASD). In addition to severe medical complications, weight loss in and of itself has been associated with cognitive and personality changes such as increased rigidity, increased obsessionality and ritualistic behavior, increased anxiety, difficulty concentrating, flattened affect, and dysphoric mood (Keys, Brozek, Henschel, Mickelsen, & Taylor, 1950). Many of these changes resolve with restoration of a patient to a healthy weight, which suggests that certain interventions might be delayed until after resolution of weight loss to increase their efficacy, specifically certain pharmacological interventions (e.g., antidepressants; Marvanova & Gramith, 2018) and treatments for anxiety (e.g., exposure; Glover et al., 2012; Zeidan et al., 2011). Other eating disorder behaviors, such as purging/vomiting, misuse of laxatives or diuretics, and compulsive exercise should also be considered high risk or life-threatening behaviors depending on their frequency, intensity, and the weight status of the patient. These behaviors should be regarded in the same vein as suicidal behavior, substance-use, and self-injury both for their potential for causing harm to the patient as well as in their function for regulating emotions (Safer, Telch, & Chen, 2009). Overeating or binge eating, which can lead to weight gain and obesity, are not as acute as some of the above behaviors, however, should also not be ignored as they can also be associated with negative health sequelae in childhood and adulthood, including orthopedic and endocrine conditions, cardiovascular disease, cancer, and all-cause mortality (Daniels, 2006; Dietz, 1998; Dixon, 2010; Gunnell, Frankel, Nanchahal, Peters, & Davey Smith, 1998; Key et al., 2004; Reilly & Kelly, 2011; Sorof & Daniels, 2002) as well as psychiatric comorbidities (Rankin et al., 2016).

This chapter will cover assessment of disordered eating in non-eating disorder individuals, as well as conceptual and treatment options. In particular, this chapter will focus on co-occurring disordered eating in those with sensory issues, anxiety disorders, medical conditions that impact eating, and obesity.

Assessment of Disordered Eating

When treating a patient who presents with any kind of disordered eating, a thorough, multidisciplinary assessment is essential. Symptoms such as restriction, weight loss, weight gain, fluctuations in weight, bingeing, and purging warrant a thorough medical and psychiatric assessment. At a minimum, the goal of any assessment for disordered eating should be to ensure that the patient is free of medical and nutritional complications before proceeding with treatment. For children and adolescents, family members should be involved in the evaluation and assessment of eating problems. After assessing for medical stability and ruling out the presence of an acute eating disorder, the clinician may proceed with treatment to target the problematic eating behaviors. Continued monitoring of disordered eating and any associated medical complications should occur over the course of treatment.

In addition to being familiar with appropriate medical and psychiatric assessment of disordered eating, eating disorder therapists should be familiar with the assessment of other psychiatric conditions that may accompany disordered eating. As stated previously, many medical and psychiatric conditions may be accompanied by subthreshold symptoms of disordered eating. Many individuals with these conditions may present to an eating disorder therapist despite not having an eating disorder diagnosis because the problematic eating may be highly salient and concerning for patients, parents, and referring providers. Careful consideration and differential diagnosis of related medical and psychiatric disorders is essential to ensure that the eating disorder therapist is incorporating other necessary specialty providers in the assessment and treatment process. These providers or specialties may include (but are not limited to) gastroenterology (e.g., in the case functional gastrointestinal disorders), applied behavior analysis (e.g., in the case of ASD), occupational therapy/speech language pathology (e.g., in the case of sensory processing disorders), allergy/rheumatology (e.g., in a patient with food allergies), and endocrinology (e.g., in a patient with diabetes). The remainder of this chapter will focus on the discussion of several medical and psychiatric populations that commonly present with eating challenges and their associated treatment recommendations.

Selective Eating

Selective eating is defined as persistent refusal to eat specific foods or refusal to eat any type of food due to a negative response from certain food colors, textures or smells. Selective eating practically presents as consumption of a limited range of foods. Selective eating can be a symptom of AN, avoidant/restrictive food intake disorder (ARFID), or can be associated with sensory sensitivity. Differential diagnosis should include Diagnostic and Statistical Manual of Mental Disorders, 5th Edition (DSM-5) eating and feeding disorders, allergies or other organic issues (e.g., oral-motor dysfunction and medical conditions), and other psychiatric conditions (e.g., anxiety, mood disorders, attention-deficit/hyperactivity disorder, obsessive-compulsive disorder [OCD], etc.).

Sensory sensitivity is defined as a "style" of processing sensory input that is characterized by a lower neurological threshold for perceiving external stimuli (Dunn, 1997). The sensory properties of food are related to its palatability, and thus characteristics such as sight, taste, and texture influence approach and enjoyment of food (Hyde & Witherly, 1993). Individuals with sensory sensitivity experience sensory stimuli much more readily than others, or find it more overwhelming than others. Sensory sensitivity applies to taste, but also to tactile, auditory, olfactory, and visual sensations. Some research works suggest that sensory sensitivity in one domain may be correlated with heightened sensitivity in other domains, such as in the co-occurrence of tactile sensitivity and taste sensitivity (Nederkoorn, Jansen, & Havermans, 2015). Sensitivity to tastes and the textures of foods can result in an aversion and avoidance of foods with highly varied textures (e.g., pulpy fruits with seeds) and bitter tastes (e.g., vegetables; Coulthard & Blissett, 2009) but may also result in heightened preference for foods with highly palatable sensory properties (e.g., sweets; Naish & Harris, 2012). These strong preferences and aversions contribute to the development of food selectivity, or eating an

172   *Bernard, Menzel, and Boutelle*

inadequate variety of foods. The limited nature of the selective diet consequently places individuals at risk for nutritional deficiencies, poor growth, and psychosocial impairment (Zucker et al., 2015).

Sensory sensitivity and associated food selectivity most often present in younger, school-aged children. Indeed, appetites naturally become more selective in toddlerhood as children become more mobile and increase their exploration of the world around them (Cashdan, 1994). However, sensory sensitivity has been associated with selective eating across the lifespan. In an adult sample, the tendency to reject foods was associated with their sensory characteristics (Kauer, Pelchat, Rozin, & Zickgraf, 2015). Two special populations in which sensory issues and associated feeding difficulties are common include ASD and sensory processing (modulation) disorder.

ASD

Children with ASD are five times more likely to experience feeding problems compared to typically developing children (Sharp et al., 2013). These feeding difficulties most frequently take the form of selective eating. Although several factors likely contribute to selective eating problems in children with ASD (e.g., behavioral rigidity, parent–child interactions, and gastrointestinal symptoms; Sharp & Postorino, 2018), research suggests there is a link between sensory processing and selective eating in this group (Cermak, Curtin, & Bandini, 2010). The most frequently described sensory processing problem in children with ASD is tactile defensiveness, or an overresponsiveness to certain types of touch. Tactile defensiveness may contribute to oral defensiveness, or aversion to the texture/feel of food or activities in the mouth (e.g., toothbrushing). Indeed, several studies have specifically linked sensitivity to texture to food acceptance, with children with ASD self-selecting foods with more manageable textures (Ahearn, Castine, Nault, & Green, 2001; Twachtman-Reilly, Amaral, & Zebrowski, 2008). These preferred foods tend to be highly processed snacks and sweets, with corresponding rejection of fruits and vegetables (Martins, Young, & Robson, 2008; Schmitt, Heiss, & Campbell, 2008). Although most children with ASD are able to consume enough food to meet gross energy needs, they are at risk for deficits related to reduced dietary variety such as diet-related diseases (e.g., scurvy, rickets; [Sharp et al., 2013] and obesity [Croen et al., 2015]).

Sensory Processing Disorder

Sensory processing disorder (SPD) is a diagnosis that is not currently represented in the DSM-5 (American Psychiatric Association, 2013). SPD refers to difficulty integrating sensory information, resulting in odd responses to sensory stimuli and/or extreme distress. Jean Ayres (Ayres, 1972), an occupational therapist (OT), first described this condition and noted that individuals with SPD are overwhelmed or confused by sensory information

Non-Eating Disordered Populations   173

coming from not only the five traditional senses, but also proprioceptive (motor) and vestibular (balance) senses. In addition to its impact on food preference, individuals with SPD may also have difficulty eating due to their hypo- or hypersensitivity to sensory input. Examples of problems that may result from SPD include difficulty sitting still, playing with food, poor muscle tone (e.g., slumping), distractibility, and struggling with fine motor skills. There is a high degree of overlap between SPD and autism, with approximately 80% of children with ASD also endorsing sensory processing difficulties (Ben-Sasson et al., 2009).

Treatment of Selective Eating

Treatment of selective eating typically involves a multidisciplinary approach. Many individuals with sensory sensitivity and associated food selectivity may meet criteria for a feeding disorder or other eating disorder, such as ARFID (see Chapter 7). Thus, assessment of sensory sensitivity and food selectivity should include a physical evaluation for medical stability by a pediatrician. Dietitians or pediatricians may also play an important role in identifying major nutritional deficits and evaluating risk for diet-related diseases. OT or speech-language pathologists can provide comprehensive assessment of sensory deficits and recommend appropriate domains to target in treatment. These specialists should also assess for the presence of oral-motor dysfunction, which may contribute to the inability to tolerate/handle difficult textures during feeding.

Behavioral interventions are the only empirically supported treatment approaches for food selectivity related to sensory sensitivity (Sharp & Postorino, 2018). These interventions consist primarily of graduated exposure to the targeted texture/food with the goal of reducing the patient's aversive response to the associated sensory stimuli. Exposures are varied such that they range from easier to more challenging presentations of the sensory stimuli. For example, for individuals with aversion to specific textures, repeated exposures may consist of tasting foods with a smooth texture (e.g., purees) and progressing to more difficult textures over time (e.g., foods that are coarsely chopped). Exposures may also vary the volume of food presented, ranging from rice or pea-sized amount to full teaspoon bite sizes. Food chaining is a popularized method for progressing through tastes and textures, using preferred sensory aspects of food (e.g., flavor, shape, color, and texture) as a starting point for linking to new foods (Fraker, Fishbein, Cox, & Walbert, 2007). In these treatments, graduated exposure is often combined with contingency management procedures such as reinforcement for successful bite-acceptance and escape extinction to decrease refusal or disruptive behaviors.

Systematic research evaluating the efficacy of treatment for selective eating due to sensory sensitivity is sparse. The majority of treatment research in this area has been conducted in the context of pediatric feeding

174　*Bernard, Menzel, and Boutelle*

disorders in both ASD and medically compromised populations (Lukens & Silverman, 2014; Sharp, Jaquess, Morton, & Herzinger, 2010). Reviews of the treatment literature support the efficacy of behavioral interventions in the treatment of selective eating. However, the interventions in this area generally target a wide range of childhood feeding problems, not just food selectivity due to sensory sensitivity. Furthermore, many of the individuals included in these studies are preschool or school-aged. Data on interventions to target food selectivity due to sensory sensitivity in typically developing children, children who are not growth compromised, adolescents, and adults are lacking. These limitations make it difficult to generalize the effectiveness of these treatments to older ages and typically developing populations.

Food-Related Fear

It is well-documented that anxiety disorders and eating disorders are highly comorbid; an estimated 64% of individuals with an eating disorder have a lifetime history of an anxiety disorder (Swinbourne & Touyz, 2007). Body-focused anxiety (e.g., fear of weight gain) and food-related anxiety (e.g., foods associated with gaining weight) are common symptoms of eating disorders. However, several other fears may also impact eating and are likely to present in the context of other anxiety disorders (e.g., OCD and specific phobias). Examples of food-related fears include fear of poisoning, contamination, illness, allergic reaction, and spoilage and fears of vomiting, choking, or inability to swallow. Food-related fears may result in ritualistic eating (e.g., eating foods in a specific order), reassurance seeking, checking behaviors (e.g., expiration dates), and avoidance of specific food environments (e.g., restaurants and cafeterias). Fears may be specific to certain foods/food types or may generalize across eating.

The extent to which these food-related fears also result in reduced caloric intake in the context of anxiety disorders is not well known. One study examining individuals with specific fears of vomiting found that about a third of patients restricted their food intake leading to a body mass index (BMI) below 18.5 (underweight; Veale, Costa, Murphy, & Ellison, 2012). Significant disordered eating has also been documented in children diagnosed with pediatric acute-onset neuropsychiatric syndrome (Toufexis et al., 2015). Eating problems documented in this study were at times quite severe, with some cases associated with complete food refusal and greater than 10% of body weight lost. Contamination fears, choking fears, and vomiting fears were the most commonly reported anxieties. It should be noted that according to the DSM-5 (American Psychiatric Association, 2013), in cases where the eating disturbance is so pronounced that it constitutes the main focus of treatment, a diagnosis of ARFID or another eating disorder should be conferred (as opposed to a diagnosis of anxiety disorder or specific phobia).

Treatment of Food-Related Anxiety

Cognitive behavioral therapies are the treatment of choice for anxiety disorders in children and adults. Active treatment components typically include cognitive techniques (e.g., psychoeducation, cognitive restructuring, and expectancy modification) and behavioral techniques (e.g., exposure, behavioral experiments, and arousal-reduction strategies). Although both approaches are usually combined in treatment, exposure is considered an essential component of most anxiety treatments and the most effective treatment component for certain disorders (e.g., specific phobia; Olatunji, Cisler, & Deacon, 2010).

Exposure and response prevention is a specific treatment technique that involves "exposing" individuals to their fears in a controlled, safe environment without allowing for escape or avoidance from the fear. Exposure treatments are based on extinction theory, in which repeated presentations of a specific fear-eliciting object or situation (i.e., conditioned stimulus) in the absence of the aversive consequence with which it was previously paired (i.e., unconditioned stimulus) extinguishes conditioned fear responses, although modern conceptualizations focus on inhibition learning (Craske et al., 2008; Craske, Treanor, Conway, Zbozinek, & Vervliet, 2014). Recommendations regarding inhibition learning include the following: maximizing mismatches with expectancies (increasing discrepancy between expectancy and outcome), limiting distractions during exposures, cognitive interventions (heighten mismatches without providing a mental distraction that is used as a safety behavior), deepened extinction (e.g., use of two [or more] fear-provoking stimuli during exposure), elimination of safety behaviors, occasional reinforced extinction (sporadic pairing of an aversive outcome with the feared stimulus), cognitive enhancers (e.g., pharmacological intervention and brief bouts of exercise), affect labeling, positive mood induction, increased variability in exposures, spaced scheduling of exposure trials, shifting contexts across extinction training and subsequent renewal tests, the use of retrieval cues, and capitalization on reconsolidation (Weisman & Rodebaugh, 2018). Exposure is often combined with response prevention techniques (as in the case of OCD), which involves preventing individuals from engaging in safety behaviors which function to neutralize their fears (e.g., rituals and reassurance seeking). Exposures can be *in-vivo*, interoceptive, imaginal, or virtual. *In-vivo* exposures involve exposure to a specific cue (e.g., a dirty surface or expired food) in real life. Imaginal and virtual (reality) exposures are useful for exposure to a feared scenario or memory that would be unsafe or impossible to recreate in real life (e.g., a traumatic choking event). Interoceptive exposures involve induction of an uncomfortable or feared body sensation (e.g., difficulty breathing). Exposures can also be gradual or prolonged in nature. Over time, exposure to a feared stimulus theoretically leads to extinction of an individual's arousal in the face of their fear; eventually, the feared stimulus no longer triggers a feared response. No research has systematically evaluated the effectiveness of exposure-based treatments for food-related fears. A handful of single case

176   *Bernard, Menzel, and Boutelle*

studies document the use of exposure in the treatment of specific fears of vomiting (emetophobia; Maack, Deacon, & Zhao, 2013; Veale, 2009; Williams, Field, Riegel, & Paul, 2011) and choking (Ball & Otto, 1994; Chorpita, Vitali, & Barlow, 1997).

Disordered Eating Associated with Medical Diseases

There are many medical conditions that can influence eating behaviors. This section is not meant to be a comprehensive review but rather a discussion of some common medical conditions that can impact eating and later a general framework for treatment. It also is an important reminder for clinicians to assess a client's medical history so that medical issues that may impact psychological functioning are not overlooked.

Many medical conditions require significant dietary restrictions either lifelong (e.g., food allergies and celiac disease) or during periods of acute illness (e.g., Crohn's disease and ulcerative colitis). Other chronic medical conditions affect eating behaviors for a variety of reasons. These include the necessity of focus on food intake for disease management (e.g., diabetes and cystic fibrosis); concern about body image and being "different" from peers (common in many chronic medical conditions); and in some cases the medications used to treat the illness, which may have a known impact on appetite and food intake (e.g., chemotherapy and corticosteroids).

Food Allergies

In the United States, the prevalence of food allergies in children is estimated to be 3–6% (Sicherer, 2011). Common food allergies include milk, egg, soy, wheat, peanuts/tree nuts, and fish/shellfish (Branum & Lukacs, 2008). Some of these foods make up a large part of a developing child's diet and can greatly limit food options. The treatment for food allergies involves an elimination diet (i.e., eliminating these foods entirely) and finding alternative sources with similar nutrition. It is important to distinguish between a food allergy and food intolerance as perceived food allergies are common and can lead to unnecessarily restricted diets with severe consequence such as failure to thrive (Mehta, Groetch, & Wang, 2013). A food allergy is an immune response. The reaction to consuming a food that a child is allergic to is varied but can include mild symptoms like a tingling sensation in the mouth to more serious symptoms such as gastrointestinal (GI) distress, hives, vomiting, and in some cases, life-threatening anaphylaxis. For some children, the allergy resolves over time and for others it is a lifelong issue. Not surprisingly, these symptoms can lead to fear of new foods (Sicherer, Noone, & Muñoz-Furlong, 2001) and anxiety about eating (King, Knibb, & Hourihane, 2009), which places children at risk for avoiding foods and food refusal. Food intolerance does not involve the immune system and symptoms are less severe than a food allergy, most commonly involving GI symptoms. A suggested treatment approach to address disordered eating behaviors related to food allergies or intolerances is discussed below; however, an initial step is for the individual to undergo testing to determine if a food allergy is present if they have not already done so and subsequent consultation with the physician or immunologist regarding the results and food elimination recommendations.

GI Conditions

Certain GI conditions (e.g., IBD and gastroesophageal reflux disease) can present similarly as traditional eating disorders since the initial presentation may be nonspecific GI complaints such as weight loss/failure to gain, vomiting, or selective eating (Bern & O'Brien, 2013). For example, one of the symptoms of Crohn's disease is reduced appetite and weight loss due to changes in appetite and ability to digest and absorb food. Other symptoms include abdominal pain, diarrhea, bloody stools, and ulcers. The symptoms of Crohn's can lead to food preoccupation (e.g., avoiding foods that cause discomfort), fear of abdominal pain, dietary restriction, and even shape and weight concerns secondary to steroid medications (Quick, Byrd-Bredbenner, & Neumark-Sztainer, 2013). Management of IBD typically involves a prescribed dietary regimen (e.g., avoidance of foods that cause GI distress) and medications (e.g., corticosteroids), both of which affect eating behaviors. During an acute period of symptoms, required dietary restriction can be significant. The focus on diet is compounded by side effects of certain steroid medications including weight gain in part related to increased appetite (Aljebab, Choonara, & Conroy, 2017; Savas et al., 2017). It should be noted that many symptoms associated with GI conditions can be seen in patients with food allergies. For example, patients with eosinophilic gastrointestinal disorders such as eosinophilic esophagitis often have comorbid food allergies, making dietary recommendations even more challenging to follow.

Functional GI conditions (e.g., irritable bowel syndrome [IBS]) also involve GI symptoms that affect eating behavior. Symptoms vary but can include abdominal pain or cramping, bloating, gas, diarrhea or constipation, and mucus in the stool. Research has shown that functional GI symptoms are common in eating disorders (Abraham & Kellow, 2013; Boyd, Abraham, & Kellow, 2005) but also relatively common in the general population. In fact, IBS is estimated to affect 15–20% of children and adults and is the most common reason individuals seek treatment for GI symptoms (Quick et al., 2013). Avoiding foods that cause GI distress is often recommended and patients are cautioned to be wary of food allergies and intolerances, both of which place them at risk for eating-related issues.

Celiac disease, which presents as an inability to tolerate gluten, has some overlap with food allergies since the immune system is involved; however, resulting symptoms are primarily gastrointestinal. Research is limited; however, there is evidence to suggest changes in eating patterns for patients with celiac disease resulting in disordered eating behaviors and, in some cases,

178 Bernard, Menzel, and Boutelle

eating disorders (Quick et al., 2013). Treatment involves avoiding foods containing gluten such as foods made with wheat, barley, rye, and oats. Given the number of foods that contain these ingredients, it is not surprising that patients are at risk for disordered eating (Karwautz et al., 2008).

No matter what the cause, individuals with GI issues may be at risk for developing disordered eating habits that may require treatment. The result of the GI symptoms and, in some cases, the prescribed treatment can lead to general dietary restriction, elimination of specific foods or food groups (appropriate to condition or not) to avoid GI symptoms, and heightened fear of certain foods.

Other Chronic Illnesses Associated with Disordered Eating

There are many other chronic medical conditions that affect eating behaviors such as cancer, thyroid conditions, type I diabetes, and cystic fibrosis. Reviewing them all is beyond the scope of this chapter; however, it cannot be stressed enough that gaining a basic understanding of a patient's medical issues and how these can affect eating behavior is essential for treatment. For example, individuals with type 1 diabetes need to closely monitor food (carbohydrate) intake and administer insulin to properly digest food (Atkinson, Eisenbarth, & Michels, 2014). This vigilance about food, coupled with fluctuations in weight that can accompany type 1 diabetes, is a recipe for potential disordered eating and it is not uncommon for individuals to report withholding insulin in an effort to control weight at some point even if they do not develop BN, often referred to as diabulimia in this population (Quick et al., 2013). Individuals with cystic fibrosis also are at risk for disordered eating. Cystic fibrosis is an autosomal recessive disease involving elevated sweat chloride levels resulting in abnormal functioning of the lungs and pancreas. A common complication is low weight and malnutrition due to malabsorption of nutrients. A complex medical regimen is required which includes a high-calorie, high-fat diet and taking pancreatic enzymes to aid in proper digestion and absorption of food among many other treatment components (Rafeeq & Murad, 2017). Research has shown that the strict dietary regimen, which is quite different than the diets of healthy peers, and the focus on weight (usually to gain) and regular exercise (to improve pulmonary functioning) places patients at risk for disordered eating (Quick et al., 2013).

Treatment of Disordered Eating Secondary to Medical Issues

If a client has a medical condition, collaboration with the primary care physician and any medical specialists is essential for gaining a better understanding of the medical condition itself, the impact it may have on the client, and prescribed medications and side effects. If difficulty eating or overeating are related to the illness or its treatment, learning about the common issues with eating and the typical course for the illness/medical treatment can inform treatment. A key piece of information includes confirmation of the medical diagnosis and prescribed treatment since it is not uncommon for patients to have an incomplete or incorrect understanding of the diagnosis and treatment. With food allergies and celiac disease, confirmation of an allergy (or immune response to gluten in the case of celiac disease) versus food intolerance, often through laboratory testing, is important. Additionally, learning the prescribed dietary restrictions/changes helps to tease apart foods that must be avoided versus foods that may cause anxiety and/or physiological symptoms but are safe for the client to eat. Clinicians should keep in mind that even if changes in eating behaviors are not associated with the medical condition or treatment, the client still may experience psychological sequalae that can impact eating (e.g., symptoms of depression, anxiety, or medically related trauma). Continued collaboration with the client's medical provider(s) throughout psychological treatment is crucial for providing quality care.

Once the clinician has a good understanding of the physiological and psychological effects of the illness and any prescribed food restrictions, a treatment plan for disordered eating behaviors can be designed. There is a paucity of research examining interventions for disordered eating in medical populations. Studies are generally limited to case studies with a few exceptions of larger randomized control studies that can provide some guidance. For example, Be-In-CHARGE! is a behavioral and nutritional intervention designed for 4–12-year-old children with cystic fibrosis which incorporates child behavior management strategies such as differential attention and rewards to increase caloric intake and weight (Stark et al., 2009). Similarly, one group of researchers examined the use of motivational interviewing, goal setting, and problem-solving to increase healthy eating across meal settings in 8–16-year-old youths with type 1 diabetes, although this study did not target weight (Nansel et al., 2015). Fortunately, although research using psychological treatments to treat eating issues for a child with a specific medical condition may be lacking, clinicians can fall back on the more robust literature for evidence-based interventions for anxiety and eating disorders when providing treatment.

As mentioned above, an initial step is to collaborate with the medical team to determine if and how the medical illness or its treatment may affect eating behaviors. This collaboration should include any dietary recommendations or restrictions. This information is crucial for setting the stage for treatment. Early in treatment it is helpful to provide psychoeducation about the physiological and psychological effects of low weight and malnutrition and address any misconceptions the client and/or family members may have about the medical condition or its treatment. Individuals with chronic illnesses and parents of children with chronic illnesses may be hesitant or even highly resistant to making dietary changes if they believe these changes will result in physiological symptoms; thus, spending time reviewing and clarifying the medical team's recommendations until everyone is on the same page is a

180 *Bernard, Menzel, and Boutelle*

useful endeavor. Psychoeducation about the relationship between anxiety and physiological symptoms (e.g., headaches and GI distress) often is necessary to help clients understand how anxiety can cause or heighten physiological symptoms.

After setting the stage, ideally the family will be in agreement about prescribed dietary restrictions (or lack thereof). For patients who are underweight, clinicians can then utilize the weight restoration strategies identified in family-based treatment for AN (FBT for AN; Lock & Le Grange, 2012) while supporting the family in following any medically necessary food restrictions. A notable caveat is that treatment for patients with type I diabetes will likely need to have the dual focus of improving nutrition and adherence to the insulin regimen. Depending on the severity of low weight, starting with foods the client/parents are comfortable with is acceptable to achieve initial weight gain. For example, if the patient will only eat a few foods, initially increasing the portion sizes of these foods, possibly with the addition of supplements, can help with weight gain. Consistent with the FBT for AN approach, the therapist will support the parents in using their parenting knowledge and skills to increase their child's caloric intake and support weight gain. The family meal session of FBT for AN can be included to help assess family patterns and behaviors during meals and provide coaching to parents as needed on how to encourage appropriate food intake. If needed, behavior management techniques (e.g., contingency management, praise/reward, differential attention, etc.) and effective family communication skills can be taught. Basic relaxation strategies (e.g., diaphragmatic breathing) for the child also can be helpful.

After low weight has been addressed, treatment should be tailored to the specific presenting problem. Common treatment targets include anxiety about eating certain or new foods, stress management, body image issues, and self-esteem. Clinicians are encouraged to utilize techniques (e.g., exposure) from CBT-AR (see Chapter 7) and the interventions in this chapter for children with selective eating to address food related anxiety. Stress management techniques such as progressive muscle relaxation and guided imagery can be a heavier focus of treatment for IBS and there is evidence for using CBT, hypnotherapy, and acupuncture with children with IBS, although studies are relatively small (Sandhu & Paul, 2014). Patients who are experiencing poor self-esteem or body image will likely benefit from interventions to improve these domains (e.g., focusing on the function of body parts versus appearance, identifying parts of the body the client feels positively or neutral about, discussing and expanding areas of pride, etc.). Looking different than peers (e.g., smaller stature and changes in appearance due to side effects of medications) and being required to eat differently than peers coupled with not wanting to feel or be perceived as different from peers is a potential risk factor for a resurgence of symptoms if not addressed. Thus, for patients with chronic illnesses such as cystic fibrosis, IBD, and type 1 diabetes, it may be necessary to validate and then address concerns about feeling different from peers and improve overall coping with having a chronic medical condition (e.g.,

Non-Eating Disordered Populations 181

supportive therapy, cognitive restructuring, strengthening communication skills to help increase social support, etc.).

Treatment of Obesity

Obesity is another medical condition in which comorbid eating-related issues are often present. Approximately 35% of children and 70% of adults have overweight or obesity (Fryar, Carroll, & Ogden, 2016; Fryar, Carroll, & Ogden, 2018) which is associated with negative health sequelae in childhood and adulthood, including orthopedic and endocrine conditions, cardiovascular disease, cancer, and all-cause mortality (Daniels, 2006; Dietz, 1998; Dixon, 2010; Gunnell et al., 1998; Key et al., 2004; Oude Luttikhuis, Shrewsbury, O'Malley, Stolk, & Summerbell, 2009; Reilly & Kelly, 2011; Sorof & Daniels, 2002) as well as psychiatric comorbidities (Rankin et al., 2016), including depression (Halfon, Larson, & Slusser, 2013; Sutaria, Devakumr, Yasuda, Das, & Saxena, 2019), lower self-esteem (Blanco et al., 2020; Rankin et al., 2016), bullying and teasing (Rupp & McCoy, 2019), and weight bias (Puhl & Shuh, 2015). There is a common misperception that individuals with obesity merely need to eat less and exercise more; however, the causes and maintaining factors of obesity are numerous, complex, and not fully understood.

Many factors contribute to eating past nutritional needs, and ultimately obesity, including biological factors, environmental factors, and individual behavior. Genetics is an underappreciated factor that influences body weight and weight gain. Studies of the genetics of child and adult obesity suggest that genetics are responsible for 30–50% of the variance in body weight (Ahima et al., 1996; Berthoud, 2004, 2007; Drewnowski, 2004, 2010; Duffey & Popkin, 2013; Grill & Kaplan, 2002; Hill, Catenacci, & Wyatt, 2005; Kessler, 2009; Lowe, 2003; Lutter & Nestler, 2009; Nielsen & Popkin, 2003; Nogueiras et al., 2012; Popkin, Duffey, & Gordon-Larsen, 2005; Saper, Chou, & Elmquist, 2002; Schachter, 1968; Schwartz, Woods, Porte, Seeley, & Baskin, 2000; Small, 2009; Swanson, 2000; Swinburn et al., 2009; Thomas, Doshi, & Crosby, 2011). Unfortunately, today's environment is considered "obesogenic" (Brownell, 2004; Kessler, 2009; Lowe, 2003), in that it encourages excess energy intake and discourages energy expenditure (Berthoud, 2004). Calorically dense foods are easily available, highly variable, tasty, relatively inexpensive, and portable (Drewnowski, 2004, 2010; Duffey & Popkin, 2013; Nielsen & Popkin, 2003; Popkin et al., 2005). Excessive intake of highly palatable calorically dense foods is one of the most proximal causes of rising obesity rates during the past three decades (Hill et al., 2005; Swinburn et al., 2009).

Current research suggests that individuals are born with individual differences in appetitive traits, which are genetically determined early in life (Carnell & Wardle, 2008b; Llewellyn & Wardle, 2015; Schachter, 1971). These traits influence response to the current food environment, which is why some individuals gain weight in today's obesogenic environment and others

182 *Bernard, Menzel, and Boutelle*

do not. Appetitive traits, such as how quickly an individual feels full, is one of the mechanisms through which genetic predisposition leads to weight gain in an environment rich with food (Llewellyn, Trzaskowski, van Jaarsveld, Plomin, & Wardle, 2014).

The current model for the treatment of childhood obesity is a comprehensive family-based behavioral treatment (FBT for children with overweight or obesity), which combines nutrition and exercise education with behavior therapy techniques (Boutelle et al., 2017; Epstein, Roemmich, & Raynor, 2001; Wilfley et al., 2007). FBT for children with overweight or obesity was developed over 35 year ago and efficacy has been replicated over the years (Epstein, Paluch, Roemmich, & Beecher, 2007; Lloyd-Richardson et al., 2012; Young, Northern, Lister, Drummond, & O'Brien, 2007). FBT for children with overweight or obesity recommends the traffic-light diet, which categorizes foods into the three colors of the traffic light on the basis of energy density and focuses on reducing total energy intake. FBT for children with overweight or obesity also includes increasing physical activity and lifestyle activity, decreasing sedentary activity, stimulus control, problem-solving, planning for high-risk situations, and positive parenting skills (e.g., psychoeducation about basic behavioral principles and implementing a reward system). Self-monitoring of food intake is a key behavioral strategy focused on throughout treatment and goal-setting is used to shape healthy eating behaviors. Sessions focused on body acceptance, improving self-esteem, and strategies to manage teasing are often included. It is important to note that the goal of FBT for children with overweight or obesity is to help families engage in healthy lifestyle behaviors such as increasing consumption of vegetables and fruits, increasing physical activity, decreasing sedentary behavior, and developing strategies to manage the current food environment. Of note, FBT for children with overweight or obesity is not about aesthetics nor is it necessarily about significant weight loss, but rather the goal is to improve engagement in healthy lifestyle behaviors with resulting weight loss or even weight stabilization while the child continues to grow taller. Moreover, weight loss does not have to be significant to be beneficial. Studies with adults have shown that a reduction in weight by 5–10% is associated with decreased risk for disease (Blackburn, 1995; National Heart Lung & Blood Institute, 1998).

FBT for children with overweight or obesity is typically delivered in parent and child separate 1-hour groups, with 30 minutes of behavioral coaching with the child/parent dyad. Treatment is usually provided weekly for 6 months. Recently, research has focused on developing other models for the provision of the FBT for children with overweight or obesity. Parent-based therapy, which treats the parent without the child, has shown noninferiority to FBT for children with overweight or obesity, suggesting the outcomes are similar whether or not the child attends (Boutelle, Cafri, & Crow, 2011; Boutelle et al., 2017; Janicke et al., 2008). Other models have been tested to provide these treatment components in a less intensive program, such as a guided self-help program (Boutelle, Norman, Rock, Rhee, & Crow, 2013). Furthermore, these treatment components have been provided in primary care clinics (Quattrin et al., 2014). Alternative treatments for childhood overweight or obesity (e.g., family-based treatment for pediatric obesity; Loeb et al., 2019) are discussed in Chapter 6.

Behavioral treatments for obesity in adults first emerged in the late 1960's/ early 1970's and targeted modifying eating and exercise behaviors (Wing 2002). Over the years, the length of behavioral weight loss (BWL) treatments has increased and current interventions typically include weekly group or individual sessions offered across 6–12+ months. Similarly, the treatment components included have expanded and current BWL programs include dietary recommendations (e.g., education about nutrition, measuring portion sizes, and maintaining a balanced diet), guidelines for physical activity (e.g., increasing lifestyle activity and structured exercise, and decreasing sedentary behaviors), and behavioral skills. Behavior change skills include self-monitoring, goal setting, stimulus control, problem-solving, managing high-risk situations, meal planning, practicing slow eating, stress management, cognitive restructuring, improving social support, and lapse/relapse prevention (Brownell, 2000; Butryn, Webb, & Wadden, 2011; Diabetes Prevention Program [DPP] Research Group, 2002; Wadden & Butryn, 2003; Wadden & Foster, 2000). Like FBT for children with overweight or obesity, self-monitoring is a key intervention in BWL (Burke, Wang, & Sevick, 2011). Based on review of 89 behavior-based weight loss and maintenance programs, the U.S. Preventive Services Task Force (USPSTF; US Preventive Services Task Force et al., 2018) found that behavior-based interventions had greater weight loss at 12–18 months, less weight regain, and improved health outcomes (e.g., decreased risk of developing diabetes) when compared to control groups. Thus, the USPSTF recommended that individuals with a BMI $\geq$ 30 should be referred to intensive, multicomponent behavioral interventions and those with BMI $\geq$ 25–< 30 should be referred if they have medical complications. It should be noted that although BWL is considered the "gold standard" treatment for adults with overweight or obesity (Boutelle et al., 2019; Thomas, Bond, Raynor, Papandonatos, & Wing, 2019), not all adults achieve significant weight loss and/or are able to maintain weight loss.

Alternative Treatments for Overeating

A new emerging model for the treatment of obesity called regulation of cues (ROC) has been developed, which is based on the behavioral susceptibility theory of obesity (BST; Carnell, Benson, Pryor, & Driggin, 2013; Carnell & Wardle, 2008a; Llewellyn & Wardle, 2015). The BST states that individual characteristics in appetitive traits are genetically determined and influence how an individual interacts with the current food environment. The BST explains why some individuals gain weight and others are healthy weight in today's obesogenic environment. The BST focuses on the importance of

184 *Bernard, Menzel, and Boutelle*

eating onset (responsiveness to signals to start eating, i.e., food responsiveness) and eating offset (responsiveness to signals to stop eating, i.e., satiety responsiveness). This dual-susceptibility was first described in the 1960s by Stanley Schachter, whose Externality Theory hypothesized that individuals with overweight/obesity are more reactive to external cues to eat and less sensitive to internal satiety signals than their lean counterparts (Schachter, 1971; Schachter & Rodin, 1974). The ROC program uses psychoeducation and experiential learning approach to reduce responsiveness to food cues in the environment (to decrease eating onset when not physically hungry) and increasing sensitivity to satiety cues (for eating offset).

ROC integrates psychoeducation to improve the participant's awareness of the reasons why they overeat, and both lack of sensitivity to hunger and satiety cues and increased sensitivity to food cues are discussed. Physiological, neurobiological, and environmental models of overeating past nutritional needs are presented in lay language so that participants can understand their vulnerabilities in the current food environment. The ROC program provides psychoeducation by describing a "Tricky Hunger," defined as a way that the environment "tricks" the body into overeating beyond nutritional needs. Coping skills are taught to accompany each Tricky Hunger, and are presented to assist in mastery and tolerance of food cue responsivity. Coping skills include physiological skills (deep breathing, relaxation, and mindfulness), behavioral skills (delay and activity substitution), and distraction.

The ROC program teaches these concepts through experiential learning exercises with food. During the first half of treatment, participants are taught about hunger and satiety dysregulation. Participants learn to self-monitor their hunger, and are instructed to self-monitor hunger and satiety before, during and after each meal, as well as 10 and 20 minutes after eating for a minimum of two meals/snacks per day. Participants bring dinner to the clinic and groups start by eating dinner and monitoring their hunger with prompting from the interventionists. During the second half of treatment, participants learn to assess and rate their cravings (defined as urges to eat when not physically hungry). Participants also learn to self-monitor their cravings. They create a craving hierarchy (least to most highly craved foods), and they bring their highly craved foods to group and complete an exposure at each session. Exposures are conducted with three foods each session, and are only conducted when participants are not physically hungry. During the exposure, participants rate their cravings while looking at the food, holding the food, smelling the food, after taking two small bites of the food, and put the food down and rate their cravings at 30-second intervals with prompting from the interventionist. After 5 minutes, the participants dispose of the food without eating it and move onto the next food. After the final food exposure is complete and the food is thrown away, the exposure ends. In the final two treatment sessions, participants consume a meal and monitor their hunger at the beginning of the sessions and participate in exposure and monitor cravings at the end of the sessions.

Our pilot data suggest that influencing these appetitive behaviors offers a promising approach for weight-loss among adults who binge eat (Boutelle, Knatz, Carlson, Bergmann, & Peterson, 2017) as well as for children with overweight and obesity (Boutelle et al., 2014; Boutelle et al., 2011). Although the trials of this model are far from complete at this time, we believe that by targeting these proposed mechanisms of overeating, we can potentially develop more durable and long-lasting weight-loss for individuals with overweight and obesity.

Conclusions

Many medical and psychiatric conditions can have comorbid disordered eating. Although this disordered eating may be subthreshold for a formal DSM-5 eating disorder diagnosis, these symptoms can result in significant medical complications and warrant intervention. Multidisciplinary assessment is a clear first step to rule out eating and feeding disorders, assess for medical stability, and clarify any medical diagnoses/treatment that may affect eating. Established interventions for eating-related problems outside of traditional eating disorders are lacking. Treatment of problematic eating will need to be tailored to the specific eating issue. If low weight is a concern, this should be an initial treatment target. For certain eating issues treatments are more well researched (e.g., CBT interventions for food-related anxiety and FBT for children with overweight or obesity), whereas other eating issues (e.g., comorbid disordered eating in patients with chronic medical conditions) have limited literature on treatment and therapists will need to modify and/or combine existing treatments in order to effectively provide treatment.

References

Abraham, S., & Kellow, J. (2013). Do the digestive tract symptoms in eating disorder patients represent functional gastrointestinal disorders? *BMC Gastroenterology, 13*, 38. doi:10.1186/1471-230X-13-38.

Ahearn, W., Castine, T., Nault, K., & Green, G. (2001). An assessment of food acceptance in children with autism or pervasive developmental disorder-not otherwise specified. *Journal of Autism and Developmental Disorders, 31*(5), 505–511.

Ahima, R., Prabakaran, D., Mantrzoros, C., Qu, D., Lowell, B., Maratos-Flier, E., & Flier, J. (1996). Role of leptin in the neuroendocrine response to fasting. *Nature, 382*(6588), 250–252. doi:10.1038/382250a0.

Aljebab, F., Choonara, I., & Conroy, S. (2017). Systematic review of the toxicity of long-course oral corticosteroids in children. *PLoS One, 12*(1), e0170259. doi:10.1371/journal.pone.0170259.

American Psychiatric Association. (2013). *Diagnostic and statistical manual of mental disorders* (5th ed: DSM-5). Washington, D.C.: American Psychiatric Association.

Atkinson, M. A., Eisenbarth, G. S., & Michels, A. (2014). Type 1 diabetes. *Lancet, 383*(9911), 69–82. doi:10.1016/S0140-6736(13)60591-7.

186 *Bernard, Menzel, and Boutelle*

Ayres, A. (1972). *Sensory integration and learning disorders*. Los Angeles, CA. Western Psychological Services.

Ball, B., & Otto, M. (1994). Cognitive-behavioral treatment of choking phobia: 3 case studies. *Psychother & Psychosomatics, 62*(3–4), 207–211.

Ben-Sasson, A., Hen, L., Fluss, R., Cermak, S., Engel-Yeger, B., & Gal, E. (2009). A meta-analysis of sensory modulation symptoms in individuals with autism spectrum disorders. *Journal of Autism and Developmental Disorders, 39*(1), 1–11. doi:10.1007/s10803-008-0593-3.

Bern, E., & O'Brien, R. (2013). Is it an eating disorder, gastrointestinal disorder, or both? *Current Opinion in Pediatrics, 25*(4), 463–470. doi:10.1097/MOP.0b013e328362d1ad.

Berthoud, H. (2004). Neural control of appetite: Cross-talk between homeostatic and non-homeostatic systems. *Appetite, 43*(3), 315–317. doi:10.1016/j.appet.2004.04.009.

Berthoud, H. (2007). Interactions between the "cognitive" and "metabolic" brain in the control of food intake. *Physiology and Behavior, 91*(5), 486–498. doi:10.1016/j.physbeh.2006.12.016.

Blackburn, G. (1995). Effect of degree of weight loss on health benefits. *Obesity Research, 3*(Suppl 2), 211s–216s. doi:10.1002/j.1550-8528.1995.tb00466.x.

Blanco, M., Solano, S., Alcantara, A., Parks, M., Roman, F., & Sepulveda, A. (2020). Psychological well-being and weight-related teasing in childhood obesity: A case-control study. *Eating and Weight Disorders, 25*(3), 751–759. doi:10.1007/s40519-019-00683-y.

Boutelle, K., Cafri, G., & Crow, S. (2011). Parent-only treatment for childhood obesity: A randomized controlled trial. *Obesity (Silver Spring), 19*(3), 574–580. doi:10.1037/0278-6133.18.4.364.

Boutelle, K., Eichen, D., Peterson, C., Strong, D., Rock, C., & Marcus, B. (2019). Design of the PACIFIC study: A randomized controlled trial evaluating a novel treatment for adults with overweight and obesity. *Contemporary Clinical Trials, 84*, 105824. doi.org/10.1016/j.cct.2019.105824.

Boutelle, K., Knatz, S., Carlson, J., Bergmann, K., & Peterson, C. (2017). An open trial targeting food cue reactivity and satiety sensitivity in overweight and obese binge eaters. *Cognitive and Behavioral Practice, 24*(3), 363–373. doi:10.1016/j.cbpra.2016.08.003.

Boutelle, K., Norman, G., Rock, C., Rhee, K., & Crow, S. (2013). Guided self-help for the treatment of pediatric obesity. *Pediatrics, 131*(5), e1435–e1442. doi:10.1542/peds.2012-2204.

Boutelle, K., Rhee, K., Liang, J., Braden, A., Douglas, J., Strong, D., ..., Epstein, L. C., Sj. (2017). Effect of attendance of the child on body weight, energy intake, and physical activity in childhood obesity treatment: A randomized clinical trial. *JAMA Pediatrics, 171*(7), 622–628. doi:10.1001/jamapediatrics.2017.0651.

Boutelle, K., Zucker, N., Peterson, C., Rydell, S., Cafri, G., & Harnack, L. (2011). Two novel treatments to reduce overeating in overweight children: A randomized controlled trial. *Journal of Consulting and Clinical Psychology, 79*(6), 759–771. doi:10.1037/a0025713.

Boutelle, K., Zucker, N., Peterson, C., Rydell, S., Carlson, J., & Harnack, L. (2014). An intervention based on Schachter's externality theory for overweight children: The regulation of cues pilot. *Journal of Pediatric Psychology, 39*(4), 405–417. doi:10.1093/jpepsy/jst142.

Boyd, C., Abraham, S., & Kellow, J. (2005). Psychological features are important predictors of functional gastrointestinal disorders in patients with eating disorders. *Scandinavian Journal of Gastroenterology, 40*(8), 929–935.

Branum, A., & Lukacs, S. (2008). Food allergy among U.S. children: Trends in prevalence and hospitalizations. *NCHS Data Brief,* (10), 1–8.

Brownell, K. (2000). *The LEARN program for weight management.* Dallas, TX: American Health Publishing Company.

Brownell, K. (2004). Fast food and obesity in children. *Pediatrics, 113*(1 Pt 1), 132. doi:10.1542/peds.113.1.132.

Burke, L., Wang, J., & Sevick, M. (2011). Self-monitoring in weight loss: A systematic review of the literature. *Journal of the American Dietetic Association, 111*(1), 92–102. doi:10.1016/j.jada.2010.10.008.

Butryn, M. L., Webb, V., & Wadden, T. (2011). Behavioral treatment of obesity. *Psychiatric Clinics of North America, 34*(4), 841–859. doi: 10.1016/j.psc.2011.08.006.

Carnell, S., Benson, L., Pryor, K., & Driggin, E. (2013). Appetitive traits from infancy to adolescence: Using behavioral and neural measures to investigate obesity risk. *Physiology and Behavior, 121,* 79–88. doi:10.1016/j.physbeh.2013.02.015.

Carnell, S., & Wardle, J. (2008a). Appetite and adiposity in children: Evidence for a behavioral susceptibility theory of obesity. *American Journal of Clinical Nutrition, 88*(1), 22–29. doi:10.1093/ajcn/88.1.22.

Carnell, S., & Wardle, J. (2008b). Appetitive traits and child obesity: Measurement, origins and implications for intervention. *Proceedings of the Nutrition Society, 67*(4), 343–355. doi:10.1017/S0029665108008641.

Cashdan, E. (1994). A sensitive period for learning about food. *Human Nature, 5*(3), 279–291. doi:10.1007/BF02692155.

Cermak, S. A., Curtin, C., & Bandini, L. (2010). Food selectivity and sensory sensitivity in children with autism spectrum disorders. *Journal of the American Dietetic Association, 110*(2), 238–246. doi:10.1016/j.jada.2009.10.032.

Chorpita, B., Vitali, A., & Barlow, D. (1997). Behavioral treatment of choking phobia in an adolescent: An experimental analysis. *Journal of Behavior Therapy and Experimental Psychiatry, 28*(4), 307–315. doi:10.1016/S0005-7916(97)00027-X.

Coulthard, H., & Blissett, J. (2009). Fruit and vegetable consumption in children and their mothers. Moderating effects of child sensory sensitivity. *Appetite, 52*(2), 410–415. doi:10.1016/j.appet.2008.11.015.

Craske, M. G., KircanskI, K., Zelikowsky, M., Mystkowski, J., Chowdhury, N., & Baker, A. (2008). Optimizing inhibitory learning during exposure therapy. *Behaviour Research and Therapy, 46*(1), 5–27. doi:10.1016/j.brat.2007.10.003.

Craske, M. G., Treanor, M., Conway, C., Zbozinek, T., & Vervliet, B. (2014). Maximizing exposure therapy: An inhibitory learning approach. *Behaviour Research and Therapy, 58,* 10–23. doi:10.1016/j.brat.2014.04.006.

Croen, L., Zerbo, O., Qian, Y., Massolo, M., Rich, S., Sidney, S., & Krike, C. (2015). The health status of adults on the autism spectrum. *Autism, 19*(7), 814–823. doi:10.1177/1362361315577517.

Crow, S., Petersen, C., Swanson, S., Raymond, N., Specker, S., Eckert, E., & Mitchell, J. (2009). Increased mortality in bulimia nervosa and other eating disorders. *American Journal of Psychiatry, 166,* 1342–1346. doi:10.1176/appi.ajp.2009.09020247.

Daniels, S. (2006). The consequences of childhood overweight and obesity. *The Future of Children, 16*(1), 47–67.

188 *Bernard, Menzel, and Boutelle*

Diabetes Prevention Program (DPP) Research Group. (2002). The Diabetes Prevention Program (DPP): Description of lifestyle intervention. *Diabetes Care, 25*(12), 2165–2171.

Dietz, W. (1998). Health consequences of obesity in youth: Childhood predictors of adult disease. *Pediatrics, 101*(3 Pt 2), 518–525.

Dixon, J. (2010). The effect of obesity on health outcomes. *Molecular and Cellular Endocrinology, 316*(2), 104–108. doi:10.1016/j.mce.2009.07.008.

Drewnowski, A. (2004). Obesity and the food environment: Dietary energy density and diet costs. *American Journal of Preventive Medicine, 27*(Suppl 3), 154–162. doi:10.1016/j.amepre.2004.06.011.

Drewnowski, A. (2010). The cost of US foods as related to their nutritive value. *American Journal of Clinical Nutrition, 92*(5), 1181–1188. doi:10.3945/ajcn.2010.29300.

Duffey, K., & Popkin, B. (2013). Causes of increased energy intake among children in the U.S., 1977-2010. *American Journal of Preventive Medicine, 44*(2), e1–e8. doi:10.1016/j.amepre.2012.10.011.

Dunn, W. (1997). The impact of sensory processing abilities on the daily lives of young children and their families: A conceptual model. *Infant and Young Child, 9*, 23–35.

Epstein, L., Paluch, R., Roemmich, J., & Beecher, M. (2007). Family-based obesity treatment, then and now: Twenty-five years of pediatric obesity treatment. *Health Psychology, 26*(4), 381–391. doi:10.1037/0278-6133.26.4.381.

Epstein, L., Roemmich, J., & Raynor, H. (2001). Behavioral therapy in the treatment of pediatric obesity. *Pediatric Clinics of North America, 48*(4), 981–993. doi:10.1016/S0031-3955(05)70352-7.

Fichter, M., & Quadlfieg, N. (2016). Mortality in eating disorders - results of a large prospective clinical longitudinal study. *The International Journal of Eating Disorders, 49*(4), 391–401. doi:10.1002/eat.22501.

Fraker, C., Fishbein, M., Cox, S., & Walbert, L. (2007). *Food chaining: The proven 6-step guide to stop picky eating, solve feeding problems, and expand your child's diet.* Cambridge, MA: De Capo Press.

Fryar, C., Carroll, M., & Ogden, C. (2016). *Prevalence of overweight, obesity, and extreme obesity among adults aged 20 and over: United States, 1960–1962 through 2013–2014.* National Center for Health Statistics Health E-Stats.

Fryar, C., Carroll, M., & Ogden, C. (2018). *Prevalence of overweight, obesity, and severe obesity among children and adolescents aged 2–19 years: United States, 1963–1965 through 2015–2016.* National Center for Health Statistics Health E-Stats.

Glover, E., Jovanivic, T., Mercer, K., Kerley, K., Bradley, B., Ressler, K., & Norrholm, S. (2012). Estrogen levels are associated with extinction deficits in women with posttraumatic stress disorder. *Biological Psychiatry, 72*(1), 19–24. doi:10.1016/j.biopsych.2012.02.031.

Grill, H., & Kaplan, J. (2002). The neuroanatomical axis for control of energy balance. *Frontiers in Neuroendocrinology, 23*(1), 2–40. doi:10.1006/frne.2001.0224.

Gunnell, D., Frankel, S., Nanchahal, K., Peters, T., & Davey Smith, G. (1998). Childhood obesity and adult cardiovascular mortality: A 57-y follow-up study based on the Boyd Orr cohort. *American Journal of Clinical Nutrition, 67*(6), 1111–1118. doi:10.1093/ajcn/67.6.1111.

Halfon, N., Larson, K., & Slusser, W. (2013). Associations between obesity and co-morbid mental health, developmental, and physical health conditions in a nationally representative sample of US children aged 10 to 17. *Academic Pediatrics, 13*(1), 6–13. doi:10.1016/j.acap.2012.10.007.

Non-Eating Disordered Populations   189

Hill, J., Catenacci, V., & Wyatt, H. (2005). Obesity: Overview of an epidemic. *Psychiatric Clinics of North America, 28*(1), 1–23. doi:10.1016/j.psc.2004.09.010.

Hyde, R., & Witherly, S. (1993). Dynamic contrast: A sensory contribution to palatability. *Appetite, 21*(1), 1–16.

Janicke, D., Sallinen, B., Perri, M., Lutes, L., Huerta, M., Silverstein, J., & Brumback, B. (2008). Comparison of parent-only vs family-based interventions for overweight children in underserved rural settings: Outcomes from project STORY. *Archives of Pediatrics and Adolescent Medicine, 162*(12), 1119–1125. doi:10.1001/archpedi.162. 12.1119.

Karwautz, A., Wagner, G., Berger, G., Sinnreich, U., Grylli, V., & Huber, W. (2008). Eating pathology in adolescents with celiac disease. *Psychosomatics, 49*(5), 399–406. doi:10.1176/appi.psy.49.5.399.

Kauer, J., Pelchat, M., Rozin, P., & Zickgraf, H. (2015). Adult picky eating. Phenomenology, taste sensitivity, and psychological correlates. *Appetite, 90,* 219–228. doi:10.1016/j.appet.2015.03.001.

Kessler, D. (2009). *The end of overeating: Taking control of the insatiable American appetite.* New York, NY: Rodale.

Key, T., Schatzkin, A., Willett, W., Allen, N., Spencer, E., & Travis, R. (2004). Diet, nutrition and the prevention of cancer. *Public Health Nutrition, 7*(1A), 187–200. doi:10.1079/PHN2003588.

Keys, A., Brozek, J., Henschel, A., Mickelsen, O., & Taylor, H. (1950). *The biology of human starvation.* Minneapolis, MN: The University of Minnesota Press.

King, R., Knibb, R., & Hourihane, J. (2009). Impact of peanut allergy on quality of life, stress and anxiety in the family. *Allergy, 64*(3), 461–8. doi:10.1111/j.1398-9995. 2008.01843.x.

Llewellyn, C., Trzaskowski, M., van Jaarsveld, C., Plomin, R., & Wardle, J. (2014). Satiety mechanisms in genetic risk of obesity. *JAMA Pediatr, 168*(4), 338–344. doi:10. 1001/jamapediatrics.2013.4944.

Llewellyn, C., & Wardle, J. (2015). Behavioral susceptibility to obesity: Gene-environment interplay in the development of weight. *Physiology and Behavior, 152*(Pt B), 494–501. doi: 10.1016/j.physbeh.2015.07.006.

Lloyd-Richardson, E., Jelalian, E., Sato, A., Hart, C., Mehlenbeck, R., & Wing, R. (2012). Two-year follow-up of an adolescent behavioral weight control intervention. *Pediatrics, 130*(2), e281–e288. doi:10.1542/peds.2011-3283.

Lock, J., & Le Grange, D. (2012). *Treatment manual for anorexia nervosa: A family-based approach* (2nd ed.). New York, NY: Guilford Press.

Loeb, K., Le Grange D., Celio Doyle A., Glunz, C., Laraque-Arena, D., Hildebrandt, T., … Gault, A. (2019). Adapting family-based treatment for pediatric obesity: A randomized controlled pilot trial. *European Eating Disorders Review, 27,* 521–530. doi.org/10.1002/erv.2699.

Lowe, M. (2003). Self-regulation of energy intake in the prevention and treatment of obesity: Is it feasible? *Obesity Research, 11*(S10), 44S–59S. doi:10.1038/oby. 2003.223.

Lukens, C., & Silverman, A. (2014). Systematic review of psychological interventions for pediatric feeding problems. *Journal of Pediatric Psychology, 39,* 903–917. doi:10. 1093/jpepsy/jsu040.

Lutter, M., & Nestler, E. (2009). Homeostatic and hedonic signals interact in the regulation of food intake. *Journal of Nutrition, 139*(3), 629–832. doi:10.3945/jn.108.097618.

190 *Bernard, Menzel, and Boutelle*

Maack, D., Deacon, B., & Zhao, M. (2013). Exposure therapy for emetophobia: A case study with three-year follow-up. *Journal of Anxiety Disorders, 27*(5), 527–534. doi:10.1016/j.janxdis.2013.07.001.

Martins, Y., Young, R., & Robson, D. (2008). Feeding and eating behaviors in children with autism and typically developing children. *Journal of Autism and Developmental Disorders, 38*(10), 1878–1887. doi:10.1007/s10803-008-0583-5.

Marvanova, M., & Gramith, K. (2018). Role of antidepressants in the treatment of adults with anorexia nervosa. *Mental Health Clinician, 8*(3), 127–137. doi:10.9740/mhc.2018.05.127.

Mehta, H., Groetch, M., & Wang, J. (2013). Growth and nutritional concerns in children with food allergy. *Current Opinion in Allergy and Clinical Immunology, 13*(3), 275–279. doi:10.1097/ACI.0b013e328360949d.

Naish, K., & Harris, G. (2012). Food intake is influenced by sensory sensitivity. *PLoS One, 7*(8), e43622. doi:10.1371/journal.pone.0043622.

Nansel, T., Laffel, L., Haynie, D., Mehta, S., Lipsky, L. V., L. K. Butler, D., …, Liu, A. (2015). Improving dietary quality in youth with type 1 diabetes: Randomized clinical trial of a family-based behavioral intervention. *The International Journal of Behavioral Nutrition and Physical Activity, 12*, 58. doi:10.1186/s12966-015-0214-4.

National Heart Lung and Blood Institute. (1998). Clinical Guidelines on the Identification, Evaluation, and Treatment of Overweight and Obesity in Adults: the Evidence Report.

Nederkoorn, C., Jansen, A., & Havermans, R. (2015). Feel your food. The influence of tactile sensitivity on picky eating in children. *Appetite, 84*, 7–10. doi:10.1016/j.appet.2014.09.014.

Nielsen, S., & Popkin, B. (2003). Patterns and trends in food portion sizes, 1977-1998. *Journal of the American Medical Association, 289*(4), 450–453. doi:10.1001/jama.289.4.450.

Nogueiras, R., Romero-Pico, A., Vazquez, M., Novelle, M., Lopez, M., & Dieguez, C. (2012). The opioid system and food intake: Homeostatic and hedonic mechanisms. *Obesity Facts, 5*(2), 196–207. doi:10.1159/000338163.

Olatunji, B., Deacon, B. J., & Cisler, J. D. (2010). Efficacy of cognitive behavioral therapy for anxiety disorders: A review of meta-analytic findings. *Psychiatric Clinics of North America, 33*(3), 557–577. doi:10.1016/j.psc.2010.04.002.

Oude Luttikhuis, H., Shrewsbury, V., O'Malley, C., Stolk, R., & Summerbell, C. (2009). Interventions for treating obesity in children. Update in: Cochrane Database Syst Rev. 2019 Mar 07; 3: CD001872. *Cochrane Database of Systematic Reviews, 21*(1), CD001872. doi:10.1002/14651858.CD001872.pub2.

Popkin, B., Duffey, K., & Gordon-Larsen, P. (2005). Environmental influences on food choice, physical activity and energy balance. *Physiology and Behavior, 86*(5), 603–613. doi:10.1016/j.physbeh.2005.08.051.

Puhl, R., & Shuh, Y. (2015). Stigma and eating and weight disorders. *Current Psychiatry Reports, 17*(3), 552. doi:10.1007/s11920-015-0552-6.

Quattrin, T., Roemmich, J., Paluch, R., Yu, J., Epstein, L., & Ecker, M. (2014). Treatment outcomes of overweight children and parents in the medical home *Pediatrics, 134*(2), 290–297. doi:10.1542/peds.2013-4084.

Quick, V., Byrd-Bredbenner, C., & Neumark-Sztainer, D. (2013). Chronic illness and disordered eating: A discussion of the literature. *Advances in Nutrition, 4*(3), 277–286. doi:10.3945/an.112.003608.

Rafeeq, M., & Murad, H. (2017). Cystic fibrosis: Current therapeutic targets and future approaches. *Journal of Translational Medicine, 15*(1), 84. doi:10.1186/s12967-017-1193-9.

Rankin, J., Matthews, L., Cobley, S., Han, A., Sanders, R., Wiltshire, H., & Baker, J. (2016). Psychological consequences of childhood obesity: Psychiatric comorbidity and prevention. *Adolescent Health, Medicine and Therapeutics, 7,* 125–146. doi:10.2147/AHMT.S101631.

Reilly, J., & Kelly, J. (2011). Long-term impact of overweight and obesity in childhood and adolescence on morbidity and premature mortality in adulthood: Systematic review. *International Journal of Obesity, 35*(7), 891–898. doi:10.1038/ijo.2010.222.

Rupp, K., & McCoy, S. (2019). Bullying perpetration and victimization among adolescents with overweight and obesity in a nationally representative sample. *Childhood Obesity, 15*(5), 323–330. doi:10.1089/chi.2018.0233.

Safer, D., Telch, C., & Chen, E. (2009). *Dialectical behavior therapy for binge eating and bulimia.* New York, NY: The Guilford Press.

Sandhu, B., & Paul, S. (2014). Irritable bowel syndrome in children: Pathogenesis, diagnosis and evidence-based treatment. *World Journal of Gastroenterology, 20*(20), 6013–6023. doi:10.3748/wjg.v20.i20.6013.

Saper, C. B., Chou, T. C., & Elmquist, J. K. (2002). The need to feed: Homeostatic and hedonic control of eating. *Neuron, 36*(2), 199–211. doi:10.1016/S0896-6273(02)00969-8.

Savas, M., Wester, V., Staufenbiel, S., Koper, J., van den Akker, E., Visser, J., ... van Rossum, E. (2017). Systematic evaluation of corticosteroid use in obese and non-obese individuals: A multi-cohort study. *International Journal of Medical Sciences, 14*(7), 615–621. doi: 10.7150/ijms.19213.

Schachter, S. (1968). Obesity and eating. Internal and external cues differentially affect the eating behavior of obese and normal subjects. *Science, 161*(3843), 751–756.

Schachter, S. (1971). Some extraordinary facts about obese humans and rats. *American Psychologist, 26*(2), 129–144.

Schachter, S., & Rodin, J. (1974). *Obese humans and rats.* Hillsdale, NJ: Erlbaum.

Schmitt, L., Heiss, C., & Campbell, E. (2008). A comparison of nutrient intake and eating behaviors of boys with and without autism. *Topics in Clinical Nutrition, 23*(1), 23–31. doi:10.1097/1001.TIN.0000312077.0000345953.0000312076c.

Schwartz, M. W., Woods, S. C., Porte, D., Jr., Seeley, R. J., & Baskin, D. G. (2000). Central nervous system control of food intake. *Nature, 404*(6778), 661–671. doi:10.1038/35007534.

Sharp, W., Berry, R., McCracken, C., Nuhu, N., Marvel, E., Saulnier, C., ..., Jaquess, D. (2013). Feeding problems and nutrient intake in children with autism spectrum disorders: A meta-analysis and comprehensive review of the literature. *Journal of Autism and Developmental Disorders, 43*(9), 2159–2173. doi:10.1007/s10803-013-1771-5.

Sharp, W., Jaquess, D., Morton, J., & Herzinger, C. (2010). Pediatric feeding disorders: A quantitative synthesis of treatment outcomes. *Clinical Child and Family Psychology Review, 13*(4), 248–365. doi:10.1007/s10567-010-0079-7.

Sharp, W., & Postorino, V. (2018). Food selectivity in autism spectrum disorder. In L. A. Anderson, S. B. Murray, & W. H. Kaye (Eds.), *Clinical handbook of complex and atypical eating disorders.* New York, NY: Oxford University Press.

Sicherer, S. (2011). Epidemiology of food allergy. *Journal of Allergy and Clinical Immunology, 127*(3), 594–602. doi:10.1016/j.jaci.2010.11.044.

Sicherer, S., Noone, S., & Muñoz-Furlong, A. (2001). The impact of childhood food allergy on quality of life. *Annals of Allergy, Asthma & Immunology, 87*(6), 461–464. doi:10.1016/S1081-1206(10)62258-2.

Small, D. (2009). Individual differences in the neurophysiology of reward and the obesity epidemic. *International Journal of Obesity, 33*, Suppl 2: S44–S48. doi:10.1038/ijo.2009.71.

Sorof, J., & Daniels, S. (2002). Obesity hypertension in children: A problem of epidemic proportions. *Hypertension, 40*(4), 441–447. doi:10.1016/S1081-1206(10)62258-2.

Stark, L., Quittner, A., Powers, S., Opipari-Arrigan, L., Bean, J., Duggan, C., & Stallings, V. (2009). Randomized clinical trial of behavioral intervention and nutrition education to improve caloric intake and weight in children with cystic fibrosis. *Archives of Pediatrics and Adolescent Medicine, 163*(10), 915–921. doi:10.1001/archpediatrics.2009.165.

Sutaria, S., Devakumr, D., Yasuda, S., Das, S., & Saxena, S. (2019). Is obesity associated with depression in children? Systematic review and meta-analysis. *Archives of Disease in Childhood, 104*(1), 64–74. doi:10.1136/archdischild-2017-314608.

Swanson, L. (2000). Cerebral hemisphere regulation of motivated behavior. *Brain Research, 886*(1-2), 113–164. doi:10.1016/s0006-8993(00)02905-x.

Swinbourne, J., & Touyz, S. (2007). The co-morbidity of eating disorders and anxiety disorders: A review. *European Eating Disorders Review, 15*(14), 253–274. doi:10.1002/erv.784.

Swinburn, B., Sacks, G., Lo, S. K., Westerterp, K., Rush, E. C., Rosenbloom, M., ..., Ravusin, E. (2009). Estimating the changes in energy flux that characterize the rise in obesity prevalence. *American Journal of Clinical Nutrition, 89*(6), 1723–1728. doi:10.3945/ajcn.2008.27061.

Thomas, J., Bond, D., Raynor, H., Papandonatos, G., & Wing, R. (2019). Comparison of smartphone-based behavioral obesity treatment with Gold Standard Group Treatment and Control: A randomized trial. *Obesity (Silver Springs), 27*(4), 572–580. doi: 10.1002/oby.22410.

Thomas, J., Doshi, S., & Crosby, R. L. M. R. (2011). Ecological momentary assessment of obesogenic eating behavior: Combining person-specific and environmental predictors. *Obesity (Silver Springs), 9*(8), 1574–1579. doi:10.1038/oby.2010.335.

Toufexis, M., Hommer, R., Gerardi, D., Grant, P., Rothschild, L., D'Souza, P., ..., Murphy, T. (2015). Disordered eating and food restrictions in children with PANDAS/PANS. *Journal of Child and Adolescent Psychopharmacology, 25*(1), 48–56. doi:10.1089/cap.2014.0063.

Twachtman-Reilly, J., Amaral, S., & Zebrowski, P. (2008). Addressing feeding disorders in children on the autism spectrum in school-based settings: Physiological and behavioral issues. *Language, Speech, and Hearing Services in Schools, 39*(2), 261–272. doi:10.1044/0161-1461(2008/025).

US Preventive Services Task Force, Curry, S., Krist, A., Owens, D., Barry, M., Caughey, A., ..., Wong, J. (2018). Behavioral weight loss interventions to prevent obesity-related morbidity and mortality in adults. US Preventive Services Task Force recommendation statement. *Journal of the American Medical Association, 320*(11), 1163–1171. doi: 10.1001/jama.2018.13022.

Veale, D. (2009). Cognitive behaviour therapy for a specific phobia of vomiting. *The Cogn Behav Therapist, 2*, 272–288.

Veale, D., Costa, A., Murphy, P., & Ellison, N. (2012). Abnormal eating behaviour in people with a specific phobia of vomiting (emetophobia). *European Eating Disorders Review: The Journal of the Eating Disorders Association, 20*(5), 414–418. doi:10.1002/erv.1159.

Wadden, T., & Butryn, M. (2003). Behavioral treatment of obesity. *Endocrinology and Metabolism Clinics of North America, 32*(4), 981–1003.

Wadden, T., & Foster, G. (2000). Behavioral treatment of obesity. *Medical Clinics of North America, 84*(2), 441–461.

Weisman, J. S., & Rodebaugh, T. L. (2018). Exposure therapy augmentation: A review and extension of techniques informed by an inhibitory learning approach. *Clinical Psychology Review, 59*, 41–51. doi:10.1016/j.cpr.2017.10.010.

Wilfley, D., Tibbs, T., Van Buren, D., Reach, K., Walker, M., & Epstein, L. (2007). Lifestyle interventions in the treatment of childhood overweight: A meta-analytic review of randomized controlled trials. *Health Psychology, 26*(5), 521–532. doi:10.1037/0278-6133.26.5.521.

Williams, K., Field, D., Riegel, K., & Paul, C. (2011). Brief, intensive behavioral treatment of food refusal secondary to emetophobia. *Clinical Case Studies, 10*(4), 304–311. doi:10.1177/1534650111417144.

Wing, R. (2002). Behavioral weight control. In Wadden, T. A., & Stunkard, A. J. (Eds.), *Handbook of obesity treatment* (pp. 301–316). New York: The Guilford Press.

Young, K., Northern, J., Lister, K., Drummond, J., & O'Brien, W. (2007). A meta-analysis of family-behavioral weight-loss treatments for children. *Clinical Psychology Review, 27*(2), 240–249.

Zeidan, M., Igoe, S., Linnman, C., Vitalo, A., Levine, J., Klibanski, A., …, Milad, M. R. (2011). Estradiol modulates medial prefrontal cortex and amygdala activity during fear extinction in women and female rats. *Biological Psychiatry, 70*(10), 920–927. doi:10.1016/j.biopsych.2011.05.016.

Zucker, N., Copeland, W., Franz, L., Carpenter, K., Keeling, L., Angold, A., & Egger, H. (2015). Psychological and psychosocial impairment in preschoolers with selective eating. *Pediatrics, 136*(3), e582–e590. doi:10.1542/peds.2014-2386.

9 Eating Disorders and Disordered Eating in the Military Family

Alexandria Morettini, Natasha A. Schvey,
Dakota Gillmore, and Marian Tanofsky-Kraff

Introduction

The U.S. military currently counts just over 1.33 million active duty troops (Defense Manpower Data Center, 2018). Although military service members are trained to defend against threats to the nation, many also face internal threats, including personal and mental health challenges. One such challenge facing military personnel may be eating disorders and disordered eating attitudes and behaviors. A 2018 report by the Defense Health Agency described a 26% increase in eating disorder diagnoses among military personnel from 2013 to 2016 (Armed Forces Health Surveillance Branch, 2018). Evidence suggests that active duty service members may be at greater risk for eating disorders and associated psychopathology as compared to the general population (Antczak & Brininger, 2008). This may be because of a host of military-specific factors that jointly increase risk for disordered eating and inhibit help-seeking behaviors. The experiences of service members also impact military families. Preliminary findings suggest that the military family, comprising active duty personnel and their spouses and children, are at increased risk for psychological disturbances and associated comorbidities (Chandra, Martin, Hawkins, & Richardson, 2010; Jensen, Martin, & Watanabe, 1996; Nash & Litz, 2013; Paley, Lester, & Mogil, 2013; Peebles-Kleiger & Kleiger, 1994; Waasdorp, Caboot, Robinson, Abraham, & Adelman, 2007; Wadsworth, 2013).

Given the risks and demands faced by military personnel and their families, research and clinical practice must account for this population's unique needs. The purpose of this chapter, therefore, is to elucidate the specific risk factors for eating disorders facing the military family and offer considerations for treatment and prevention in this vulnerable population. We begin the chapter with a review of the estimated prevalence rates of eating disorders in the military family. Then, we discuss the unique demands facing the military family, with specific attention to how these demands may impact eating and weight. Next, we present a brief overview of the limited information on strategies for addressing disordered eating in the military family. Finally, we offer directions for future research to inform prevention and treatment strategies to best meet the unique needs of this population.

Eating Disorders in the Military Family 195

Prevalence of Disordered Eating in the Military Family

Prevalence among Military Service Members

Although data are sparse, it appears that the incidence of eating disorders among all service members rose significantly from 1998 to 2006 (Antczak & Brininger, 2008). More recently, diagnoses of eating disorders among military personnel increased by 26% from 2013 to 2016 (Armed Forces Health Surveillance Branch, 2018). Various reports suggest that rates of eating disorders in military personnel may be higher than in the civilian population (Peterson, Talcott, Kelleher, & Smith, 1995), with estimates ranging from 2% to 36% for the various disorders (Antczak & Brininger, 2008; McNulty, 1997a). By contrast, population-based studies of civilians report lifetime prevalence of anorexia nervosa (AN) of 0.6% (women 0.9%, men 0.3%), 1.0% for bulimia nervosa (BN; women 1.5%, men 0.5%), and 2.8% for binge-eating disorder (BED; women 3.5%, men 2.0%) (Hudson, Hiripi, Pope, & Kessler, 2007). Most of the eating disorder prevalence estimates of military personnel, however, are based on self-report surveys and medical records. Given that underreporting of medical and psychological symptoms is common in the military (Anestis, Mohn, Dorminey, & Green, 2019; Smith et al., 2016), these data may underestimate the scope and severity of the problem. Even with underreporting, self-report surveys among service members suggest high rates of eating disorders. In a sample of female service members from the Army, Air Force, and Navy ($N = 1,278$), 1% met criteria for AN, 8% for BN, and 63% for eating disorder not otherwise specified (EDNOS; which included BED until 2013) (American Psychiatric Association, 2013; Smith et al., 2012).

Similar to civilian samples, some data suggest that women appear to make up the majority of known eating disorder cases (Antczak & Brininger, 2008; Warner et al., 2007). One study identified 34% of active-duty Army women as at-risk for the development of an eating disorder, based on self-report questionnaires (Lauder, Williams, Campbell, Davis, & Sherman, 1999). When interviewed, 8% of the women met full criteria for an eating disorder, a rate that exceeds the prevalence of eating disorders observed in the general population (Hudson et al., 2007). Additional studies have found that 16% of female veterans report a lifetime eating disorder (Forman-Hoffman, Mengeling, Booth, Torner, & Sadler, 2012), and 30% of entry-level female Army service members report disordered eating (Warner et al., 2007). Although two studies have reported that female military members are at greater risk for eating disorders than their male counterparts (Antczak & Brininger, 2008; Warner et al., 2007), some data also indicate that males may be equally at risk. In civilian samples, males typically report fewer disordered eating *attitudes* than women; however, disordered eating *behaviors* have been shown to be comparable across sexes (Raevuori, Keski-Rahkonen, & Hoek, 2014). In the military, both sexes appear to experience high rates of eating disorders. Although the service-wide prevalence of disordered eating among males is unclear, surveys of both Navy men and women have found that across both sexes, approximately 50% of all personnel exhibited some form of broadly defined disordered eating behavior (McNulty, 1997a). One study reported that approximately 14% of male Navy service members endorsed binge eating, with 25% endorsing the behavior within the previous three months (McNulty, 1997b). In a sample of male Army personnel, rates of AN- and BN-related behaviors were endorsed at a rate ten times greater than the general population (Hudson et al., 2007). Importantly, the civilian data suggest that mortality risk from disordered eating may, in fact, be higher in men than women (Raevuori et al., 2014). Given the high proportion of male service members (Antczak & Brininger, 2008), eating disorders may be a significant threat to the readiness of the U.S. military.

As mentioned, the prevalence estimates for eating disorders in active duty military service members are likely an underestimation. Although many individuals, both civilian and military, choose not to seek treatment for their symptoms (Hart, Granillo, Jorm, & Paxton, 2011), the barriers to seeking treatment may be particularly pronounced in military members due to perceived stigmatization associated with an eating disorder diagnosis (Britt, Greene-Shortridge, & Castro, 2007) and potential consequences of being deemed unfit to serve. Many individuals who apply to enter the military are aware that acknowledgment of an eating disorder will lead to application rejection (Tanofsky-Kraff, Bulik, et al., 2013). This phenomenon may account for the underrepresentation of eating disorder diagnoses in medical records, explaining why individuals may be more willing to report eating disorder symptoms on surveys than during medical visits (perhaps due to greater perceived anonymity with survey questions; Keel, Crow, Davis, & Mitchell, 2002). Furthermore, service members, as well as health care providers, are aware that an eating disorder diagnosis may result in separation from service, further contributing to underreporting of disordered eating symptoms and potentially even a reluctance among health care providers to assess for problematic eating behaviors (Tanofsky-Kraff, Bulik, et al., 2013).

Binge Eating, Obesity, and Weight-Related Factors

The disordered eating behavior with the highest observed prevalence among military personnel is binge eating, a hallmark behavior of both BN and BED, and a strong contributor to the development and maintenance of obesity (American Psychiatric Association, 2013). In one sample of 489 Navy service members, 10% endorsed episodes of binge eating at least twice per week in the previous three months with an additional 30–40% endorsing binge-type behaviors and 11% reporting feeling "out of control" while eating (Carlton, Manos, & Van Slyke, 2005).

Several models have been used to explain binge eating pathology, each of which may be particularly salient among military personnel. For example, the well-defined restraint model identifies concerns over weight and shape as the primary contributor to a cycle of dietary restraint and binge eating behavior (Polivy & Herman, 1985). Although support for this theory is mixed (Harvey,

Rosselli, Wilson, DeBar, & Striegal-Moore, 2011; Stein et al., 2007; Stunkard & Allison, 2003), it is generally agreed that factors that increase emphasis on weight and shape may increase risk for eating disorders (Keel & Forney, 2013). Thus, military weight standards and fitness tests may contribute to eating disorder symptoms in the military by increasing the salience of weight and shape. A second model, affect regulation theory, describes binge eating as a coping mechanism used to reduce negative emotional states (Haedt-Matt & Keel, 2011). Weight and fitness standards, while increasing the emphasis on weight and shape, also contribute to anxiety and distress among military personnel (Carlton et al., 2005). Experiences of prolonged stress and associated negative affect are strongly linked with excess body weight and related metabolic dysfunction, further contributing to risk of eating disorders among this population (Chandola, Brunner, & Marmot, 2006). In effect, aspects of military service may contribute to a heightened risk for eating disorders through a cyclical pattern whereby an emphasis on weight and shape contributes to dietary restraint and psychological distress that, in turn, promote binge eating and weight gain.

Military Dependents

Considering the stressors facing military families and the links between psychological distress and disordered eating attitudes and behaviors (Goodman & Whitaker, 2002; Young-Hyman et al., 2006), military partners and children may be particularly vulnerable to unhealthy eating- and weight-related behaviors, such as using food to cope with the stressors of military life. However, very few studies have examined parental disordered eating and child eating behaviors in a military sample. One study, using a self-report questionnaire, found that 26% of military spouses were at risk for the development of an eating disorder, notably higher than the 7–9% identified by the same questionnaire in the general population (Waasdorp et al., 2007). Indeed, although additional studies are needed, disordered eating appears to be one of the most common psychiatric problems identified in this population (Waasdorp et al., 2007).

Limited data suggest that children of military personnel may be particularly vulnerable to the onset and maintenance of eating disturbances. One study found that among female adolescent military dependents, disordered eating behaviors and attitudes were reported by 21% of the sample (Waasdorp et al., 2007). In another study that compared female adolescent military dependents with overweight and obesity to their matched civilian counterparts, military dependents reported greater symptoms of disordered eating behaviors and attitudes, as well as depression (Schvey et al., 2015). Further, they reported significantly more binge-eating episodes per month, as compared to age- and sex-matched civilian peers. Recent data indicate that male adolescent military dependents may be as vulnerable to eating and weight-related pathology as their female counterparts. In fact, male and female adolescent military dependents reported comparable scores on global eating pathology, self-esteem, and social functioning

198 *Alexandria Morettini et al.*

(Quattlebaum et al., 2019). Therefore, it is plausible that both male and female adolescent military dependents may be at heightened risk for eating- and weight-related problems and associated psychosocial impairment.

Unique Demands Contributing to Disordered Eating in the Military Family

Military Service Requirements

Service members encounter many unique experiences and challenges that may adversely affect mental and physical health, including appearance standards, weight and fitness requirements, deployments, frequent relocations, and trauma exposure (Breland, Donalson, Nevedal, Dinh, & Maguen, 2017; McNulty, 2001; Mitchell, Porter, Boyko, & Field, 2016). Factors such as deployment, combat exposure and casualties, unit reassignments, and unexpected mobilization are all associated with higher levels of psychological distress (Maguen et al., 2011; Pflanz & Sonnek, 2002; Renshaw, Rodrigues, & Jones, 2009; Wells et al., 2010). Compounding these effects, current trends in the military have called for a reduction of personnel, thus resulting in greater individual responsibilities and longer, more frequent deployments (Karney, Crown, & Rand National Defense Research Institute, 2007). Long deployments and short dwell times between deployments are related to greater depression, anxiety, and acute stress (Mental Health Advisory Team VI, 2009), thus contributing to the high rates of mental health issues reported among Operation Iraqi Freedom veterans (Seal et al., 2009). Each of these factors is largely unique to military service members and places considerable strain on the physical and psychological health of service members and their families. Although several specific requirements of military service likely contribute to psychological distress and disordered eating, the impacts of weight and fitness standards, deployment, and trauma exposure have received the most attention in the literature to date, and provide some insight into the development and maintenance of disordered eating among this population.

Weight and Fitness Standards

To ensure physical readiness and maintain military appearance standards, the U.S. Department of Defense (DoD) has instituted strictly enforced fitness and weight standards across all branches of the military (Bray, Pemberton, & Hourani, 2009). The primary purpose of weight and fitness standards is to ensure that personnel are prepared for the physical demands of military service, based on the assumptions that proper body weight and physical fitness contribute to good health, physical and combat readiness, and a reduced likelihood of combat injury and mortality. Potential recruits must first meet weight and fitness standards prior to joining the service, and all service members must maintain weight and fitness retention standards throughout their term of service (Department of Defense, 2002; 2004). Those who fail to maintain an acceptable height–weight distribution or whose

Eating Disorders in the Military Family 199

appearance is not consistent with military appearance standards are subject to administrative action. Military appearance standards are set by each branch of service and describe grooming standards, ranks and insignias, and the proper wear of service-specific uniforms (Department of the Air Force, 2019; Department of the Army, 2017; Department of the Navy, 2019). For example, in Army Regulation 670-1: Wear and Appearance of Army Uniforms and Insignia, Soldiers are instructed on how to put forth a professional image and informed that "pride in appearance includes Soldiers' physical fitness and adherence to acceptable weight standards … ." Opportunities for positive personnel action, such as additional trainings and promotion, and the ability to deploy or re-enlist are regulated partly by the outcomes of fitness tests and adherence to body weight and appearance standards (Department of Defense, 2002; 2004). As a result, service members who repeatedly fail to maintain standards risk being unable to deploy or re-enlist, and may face early discharge from service (Department Defense, 2013; Haines & Neumark-Sztainer, 2006; McNulty, 1997b; 2001).

Factors that increase emphasis on weight and shape are known to increase risk for eating disorders in men and women (Keel & Forney, 2013). Therefore, it is plausible that military weight standards and fitness tests may contribute to eating disorder symptoms in the military by increasing the salience of weight and shape. Pressure to pass physical fitness testing, "make weight," and maintain one's military appearance may contribute to service members engaging in unhealthy weight control behaviors, including fasting, excessive exercise, self-induced vomiting, self-induced dehydration, and use of diet pills, laxatives, and diuretics (McNulty, 2001; Peterson et al., 1995). These behaviors may be characterized as symptomatic of situational eating disorders, defined as the symptoms of a full-syndrome eating disorder, but within the context of a particular time-frame or event (e.g., resulting from weigh-in and fitness test-related anxiety). A significant proportion of service members report anticipatory anxiety about fitness testing and have difficulty meeting weight and/or body fat standards (Armed Forces Health Surveillance Branch, 2011; Carlton et al., 2005). Indeed, in multiple studies, service members reported an increase in situational eating disorder-type behaviors (e.g., fasting and dehydration) immediately prior to fitness assessments (Lauder et al., 1999; McNulty, 1997b; 2001). Disordered eating behaviors are particularly concerning because they place individuals at risk for excessive weight gain and obesity (Stice, Cameron, Hayward, Taylor, & Killen, 1999; Tanofsky-Kraff & Yanovski, 2004), while promoting weight cycling, thereby potentially posing additional health risks (Brownell & Rodin, 1994).

Weight Stigma and Weight Bias Internalization

Weight stigmatization is defined as negative societal attitudes and prejudicial treatment due to one's high weight status (Puhl, Andreyeva, & Brownell, 2008; Puhl & Heuer, 2009; Seacat, Dougal, & Roy, 2016). Due to the pressure to meet weight and fitness standards, coupled with the military's cultural emphasis on leanness and fitness (Department of Defense, 2013;

Hodgdon & Naval Health Research Center, 1990; Tanofsky-Kraff, Sbrocco, et al., 2013), service members may be at considerable risk for both the experience and internalization of weight stigma as well as subsequent body dissatisfaction, compensatory behaviors, unhealthy weight control practices, and eating disorders (Antczak & Brininger, 2008; Forman-Hoffman et al., 2012; Lauder et al., 1999; McNulty, 1997b; 2001; Tanofsky-Kraff, Bulik, et al., 2013; Warner et al., 2007). Research among civilian samples demonstrates that individuals with overweight or obesity face frequent instances of weight stigma, though studies among military personnel are sparse (Brownell, Puhl, Schwartz, & Rudd, 2005; Puhl & Brownell, 2006; Puhl & Heuer, 2009; 2010). One study (Schvey et al., 2017) found that nearly half of service members with or at high-risk for obesity reported at least one instance of weight stigma in the military, including disciplinary action and name-calling. Importantly, the experience of weight stigma is associated with a host of harmful behaviors that collectively increase risk for eating disorders and obesity, including eating in secret, binge eating, and the use of compensatory behaviors, such as laxative misuse and purging (Ashmore, Friedman, Reichmann, & Musante, 2008; Schvey, Puhl, & Brownell, 2011; Sutin, Stephan, & Terracciano, 2015). Indeed, two recent studies of weight stigma in the U.S. military have documented associations of weight stigma with unhealthy weight control behaviors, depressive symptoms, and poor physical health (Schvey et al., 2017; Shank et al., 2019). Particularly relevant to the uniformed services, the experience of stigmatization and weight bias is also associated with lower motivation to exercise and the avoidance of physical activity altogether (Schvey, Roberto, & White, 2013; Vartanian & Novak, 2011; Vartanian & Shaprow, 2008).

In addition to facing weight stigma from others, individuals of all weight strata may also experience internalized weight bias, defined as the belief that negative weight-based stereotypes apply to oneself (e.g., "if only I had more willpower, I wouldn't be the weight that I am"). Research among civilians indicates that weight bias internalization is associated with eating pathology, such as binge eating and purging (Durso et al., 2012; Schvey et al., 2013), even among individuals without overweight/obesity (Schvey & White, 2015). Although in civilian populations, weight stigma is reported most frequently by those with an elevated body mass index (BMI; Carr & Friedman, 2005), it is plausible that in the military, wherein a lean body shape is highly valued and the determination of "military appearance" is subjective, individuals begin to experience weight stigma and weight bias internalization at lower BMIs. Given the occupational and social consequences of excess weight and failure to maintain proper military appearance (Armed Forces Health Surveillance Branch, 2011; Dall et al., 2007; Hodgdon & Naval Health Research Center, 1990; Sanderson, Clemes, & Biddle, 2011) service members of all weight strata may be vulnerable to both weight stigma and weight bias internalization, as well as their adverse effects on eating- and weight-related behaviors.

Trauma and Combat Exposure

Trauma is robustly associated with eating disorders among civilian populations (Brewerton, 2007). Given the high rates of trauma and adverse life events reported by members of the military family (Katon et al., 2015), it is critical to gain a better understanding of the association between trauma and eating pathology among service members. In one survey study of recent enlistees, being female, having overweight, having had previous psychiatric treatment, and reporting a history of verbal or sexual abuse in childhood or adolescence were all linked to disordered eating (Warner et al., 2007). In an examination of trauma among active duty service members in the Army, Navy, and Air Force, adverse life events, including trauma and interpersonally perpetrated experiences, were associated with disordered eating cognitions, attitudes, and behaviors (Bakalar et al., 2018). Although these findings mirror those in civilian samples, further exploration is warranted. Only two studies have investigated the influence of combat exposure on the development of eating disorders in women. One which utilized a broad-based survey reported that females who experienced deployment-related combat exposure were at especially high risk for eating disorders (Jacobson et al., 2009). The second study suggested that eating disorders were related to military sexual trauma but not to military combat exposure (Breland et al., 2018). As more women are entering the military and participating in combat positions not previously available to them, these data are of particular concern and highlight the need for more research on this emerging population (Cronk, 2016).

Deployment

There are limited data on the impact of deployment on eating disorders development and maintenance. Transitions between periods of deployment and homestays are biologically and psychologically complex. Many environmental factors change between deployment and homestead periods, including eating patterns and energy expenditure. Meals Ready-to-Eat contain ~1250–1500 kcal, are encouraged to be consumed in total, and are highly efficient energy-delivery systems to aid service members in combat. Care packages often contain high-fat/high-sugar foods and fast food establishments are ubiquitous on military bases and offer military discounts globally. Energy expenditure requirements typically increase during deployment and generally decrease after deployment; yet, eating behaviors may not change accordingly, placing service members at potential risk for eating disorders and/or weight cycling if these behaviors persist at home. Only one prospective study has examined the impact of deployment on disordered eating (Jacobson et al., 2009). Using data from the Millennium cohort, Jacobson et al. (2009) did not find a significant association between deployment and new-onset disordered eating behaviors. However, among deployed women, those exposed to combat were more likely to experience new-onset disordered eating (Jacobson et al., 2009). Additional studies are needed to further elucidate the impact of deployments on the emergence and maintenance of eating disorders.

Impacts on Military Dependents

Given that the experiences of service members are likely to affect all members of the military family, it is important to understand the effects of deployments and military-specific stressors on the health of the family as a whole. With longer, more frequent, and increasingly dangerous deployments in recent years (Karney et al., 2007), spouses and children of military personnel are subject to substantial stress during deployment. Low social support during a partner's deployment may exacerbate stress by placing increased burden on family members (e.g., financial, familial, and household responsibilities). Additionally, spousal and family stress (e.g., marital discord and financial strain) often extend past the period of deployment, considering the potential trauma (both physical and psychological) of returning spouses and subsequent re-acclimation to home life (Karney et al., 2007). Although literature on the impact of military-specific stressors on the eating behaviors of spouses and children is limited, high levels of psychological stress is consistently associated with excess weight and disordered eating (Goodman & Whitaker, 2002; Spoor, Bekker, Van Strien, & Van Heck, 2007; Young-Hyman et al., 2006). Although the exact mechanisms accounting for the risk of eating- and weight-related pathology in military spouses are unknown, it is plausible that military partners use food and unhealthy weight-control behaviors to cope with the stress of military life.

Children of military personnel are also exposed to stressors associated with their parents' military careers. In addition to parental deployment, military children often face a number of unique stressors, including parental absence during assignments and training, parental physical or psychological trauma or death, multiple geographic relocations, and maladaptive parental response to stress (Esposito-Smythers et al., 2011; Link & Palinkas, 2013; Paris, DeVoe, Ross, & Acker, 2010; Selected Populations Health et al., 2010). These unique demands contribute to high rates of psychological problems (Link & Palinkas, 2013) among this population, which may confer additional risk for eating disturbances. Additionally, parental modeling of extreme weight loss practices and situational eating disorders surrounding fitness tests may promote shape and weight concerns, dieting, and unhealthy weight-control behaviors among military children. Unlike healthful eating practices that involve eating in moderation and regular exercise, self-reported dieting – particularly efforts involving extreme restriction or purging behaviors – paradoxically predicts unhealthy weight gain (Stice et al., 1999), likely via promotion of overeating and binge eating (Field et al., 2012). Therefore, youth who adopt the extreme weight control behaviors of their parents may be at increased risk for disordered eating.

Furthermore, male children from military families represent a uniquely vulnerable, yet understudied, population. Male military personnel are subject to pressure to maintain a lean and muscular physique (Carlton et al., 2005; McNulty, 1997b), and boys may witness their fathers engaging in unhealthy weight control practices, extreme weight cycling surrounding fitness tests, or stress around diet and exercise. As males comprise approximately 85% of the U.S. military, sons of military personnel, who are more likely to join the military than their civilian peers (Kleykamp, 2006), are therefore at risk for modeling the behavior of their parents. Disordered eating and obesity within this population may therefore negatively impact the number of eligible volunteers for future military service. Notably, data from military families suggest that teen boys experience comparable levels of eating pathology as their female counterparts (Reed, Bell, & Edwards, 2011). Although additional studies are needed, existing data indicate that military boys and girls comprise a population that is particularly vulnerable to the development of disordered eating.

Veterans

An extensive body of literature suggests that military veterans may face high rates of eating- and weight-related psychopathology (Bartlett & Mitchell, 2015); thus, a thorough review is beyond the scope of this chapter. Though hospital-record-based research indicates fairly modest rates of eating disorders (e.g., 0.0007–2.8% among women and <0.001–0.3% among men; Curry et al., 2014; Striegel-Moore, Garvin, Dohm, & Rosenheck, 1999a; 1999b), survey data typically yield higher prevalence rates, likely due to underutilization of mental health services. Among female veterans, between 10.6% and 16% self-reported subthreshold or clinical levels of eating disorder symptoms (Arditte Hall, Bartlett, Iverson, & Mitchell, 2017b; Forman-Hoffman et al., 2012; Huston, Iverson, & Mitchell, 2018). Among male veterans, 4.1% met criteria for a probable eating disorder, whereas 24% reported binge eating, 11.7% reported fasting, 6.7% reported excessive exercise, and 3.3% reported laxatives, diuretics, and/or purging at least once per week (Arditte Hall, Bartlett, Iverson, & Mitchell, 2017a). Data consistently show that military veterans report high rates of binge eating; in one study of treatment-seeking veterans with overweight or obesity, the majority of the sample (77.6%) reported binge eating, whereas 6.1% reported high-frequency binge eating (defined as five or more binge episodes per week) (Masheb et al., 2015). In fact, male veterans may be more likely to report clinically significant binge eating than their female counterparts (Higgins et al., 2013). Of note, military-specific trauma and posttraumatic stress disorder (PTSD) are associated with eating disorder symptoms among both male and female veterans, thereby conferring additional risk on those with prior military service (Arditte Hall et al., 2017a; 2017b; Forman-Hoffman et al., 2012; Kimerling, Gima, Smith, Street, & Frayne, 2007). Further, one sample of female veterans identified binge eating, self-induced

204 *Alexandria Morettini et al.*

vomiting, and overexercise as three of the most frequently employed strategies for coping with combat exposure and military sexual trauma (Mattocks et al., 2012). In addition, high rates of overweight and obesity have been well documented among military veterans (Almond, Kahwati, Kinsinger, & Porterfield, 2008; Koepsell, Forsberg, & Littman, 2009; Nelson, 2006), which may place them at risk for unhealthy weight control practices and the onset of disordered eating.

Treatment of Disordered Eating in the Military

Treatment Strategies

Given the prevalence of eating disorders and unique risk factors facing military families, the development and implementation of accessible, effective, and culturally competent treatments is a priority. Complicating the challenge of finding culturally appropriate approaches for disordered eating in military families is that the majority of research on eating disorders in the military relies on retrospective data with veterans. Further, research has not shown whether the presentation and course of eating disorders in the active duty population differs from that of civilians or veterans, making tailored treatment recommendations difficult.

Currently, there are no national eating disorder treatment programs established specifically for service members or the military family. As a result, the quality and availability of eating disorder treatments may vary widely across geographic locations and military medical facilities. Given concerns about confidentiality and possible career implications, some service members may elect to receive treatment from civilian providers. Unfortunately, many civilian providers lack adequate military cultural competence and may fail to assess military-specific risk and protective factors, which may impede rapport and treatment effectiveness (Meyer & Wynn, 2018; Reger, Etherage, Reger, & Gahm, 2008). One potential solution to the lack of comprehensive eating disorder care within the Military Health System is the Patient-Centered Medical Home, which has been widely implemented. This is an interdisciplinary team-based patient-centered approach to health care, which may be particularly beneficial in promoting health among service members and dependents. Further, the practice of embedding behavioral health technicians within primary care settings may help to detect prodromal eating disturbances during routine medical visits and enables the early identification and treatment of eating disorders without requiring a separate visit to a behavioral health clinic.

Barriers to Care

Despite the prevalence of eating disorders in the military, relatively few service members seek mental health treatment. Particularly troubling is that these

Eating Disorders in the Military Family   205

members seek services at a low rate despite receiving no-cost health care services, which ostensibly should remove a significant barrier to treatment (Eaton et al., 2008; Hoge et al., 2004; Wilk, Hoge, Castro, Thomas, & Kim, 2010). Concerns unique to the military population compound the factors that already contribute to the underutilization of mental health services in the general population (Regier et al., 1993). Importantly, entry into service may be denied for those with a psychiatric diagnosis, and service members with eating disorders may find promotions and the ability to remain on active duty impacted. These policies serve as a barrier to care by disincentivizing the service member's acknowledgment of his or her disordered eating behavior and help-seeking behavior.

Other military-specific barriers include problems with logistical and command support, lack of time to participate in treatment (particularly given the multicomponent care often recommended for more severe eating disorder presentations), lack of proximal treatment options, and clinic schedules that are often incompatible with an individual's duty schedule (Eaton et al., 2008; Hoge et al., 2004; Kim, Thomas, Wilk, Castro, & Hoge, 2010). There are further occupational concerns among military service members (e.g., being separated from the military or unable to reenlist, being denied for promotion, or being unable to deploy), as well as a culture of stigmatizing mental health (e.g., being viewed as weak by one's peers and command and embarrassment or worry about who might find out about their participation in treatment), and beliefs about the utility of mental health care (e.g., an environment that emphasizes the importance of "toughing it out"). Internalized stigma, or "self-stigma," a significant barrier to mental health care, may also occur when the individual applies negative attributes about mental illness to themselves (Britt et al., 2007). Indeed, treatment-seeking behavior is lower in soldiers holding these self-stigmatizing views (Cooper, Corrigan, & Watson, 2003). Further, civilian data suggest that the stigma of having what is perceived as a "female" disorder may lead to greater shame among men with eating disorder symptoms, thereby reducing treatment-seeking behaviors (Griffiths, Mond, Murray, & Touyz, 2015). Given that males represent the majority of active duty service members, there may be a large proportion of personnel who resist treatment for disordered eating behaviors (Antczak & Brininger, 2008).

Challenges and Future Directions

The active duty military population is one that warrants further attention, given the dearth of systematic research on eating disorders in the military. However, there are significant challenges to conducting research in the military community that require consideration when developing research programs and delivering interventions. Frequent personnel moves and deployments can hamper data collection and complicate retention and the ability to conduct long-term follow-ups with participants. In addition, military personnel may not be eligible to receive compensation for their participation

206 *Alexandria Morettini et al.*

in research. More specifically, the 24 U.S. Code 30, Payment to Federal Employees and Military Personnel, mandates that:

> Payment to Federal Employees and Active Duty military personnel for participation in research while on duty is limited to blood donation and may not exceed $50 per blood draw. They may not receive any other payment or non-monetary compensation for participation unless they are off duty or on leave during the time they are participating in the protocol.

Thus, researchers may need to creatively incentivize participation in research aside from monetary compensation.

Though there are challenges, the Military Health System, a $50 billion federal organization that provides health care for over 9.3 million DoD beneficiaries (Gimbel, Pangaro, & Barbour, 2010) across the globe, also offers unique opportunities for research. The Military Health System oversees a primary care similar to civilian practices, including patient demographics, common diagnoses, and types of procedures (Jackson, Strong, Cheng, & Meyer, 1999). The Military Health System population is also highly diverse, enabling researchers to conduct adequately powered subgroup analyses in their research to elucidate differential risk based on race, ethnicity, income, or other relevant sociodemographic variables. Previous work with the Military Health System has provided a basis for strengthening the physician's training in evidence-based weight management approaches, in order to provide better treatment and prevention of obesity within the primary care setting (Terre, Hunter, Carlos Poston, Keith Haddock, & Stewart, 2007). Comprehensive health care and electronic medical records also enable the aggregation and analysis of large national datasets and many current and former military members live near bases, providing a robust population from which to recruit participants. In addition, given frequent relocations, deployments, and changes of duty station, researchers and clinicians may be able to extract biomedical data from the electronic medical record in lieu of in-person follow-up visits to enable large-scale longitudinal and prospective research.

Despite numerous studies testing interventions aimed at reducing and preventing eating disorders in veterans, we are unaware of research in active duty service members or their spouses. Our group is currently testing the effectiveness of interpersonal psychotherapy for preventing eating disorders and adult obesity in at-risk adolescent military dependent boys and girls due to high weight and loss-of-control eating and/or symptoms of anxiety (Spieker et al., 2015; Tanofsky-Kraff, 2012; Tanofsky-Kraff et al., 2009; 2017). In a pilot study, this approach was found to be feasible and acceptable in adolescent military dependent girls (Burke et al., 2016) and retrieval of long-term data through the Military Health System electronic database was effective. Further research piloting and testing evidence-based treatments in all members of the military family is warranted. Given the transience that characterizes military service and stigma associated with in-person counseling, telehealth methodology may also prove advantageous in treating service members and their family members (Jones, Etherage, Harmon, & Okiishi, 2012; Luxton, Mishkind, Crumpton, Ayers, & Mysliwiec, 2012). Research is needed to determine the feasibility and acceptability of eating disorder treatments delivered remotely among this population.

Conclusion

Despite evidence suggesting that prevalence rates of eating disorders among military service members and their families may be comparable to or higher than rates observed among civilians, there is a paucity of rigorous, nationally representative research within this population. Current estimates are largely based on medical records or questionnaires, both of which may be vulnerable to reporting bias. Given a number of military-specific risk factors, including weight and fitness standards, frequent relocations, combat-exposure and trauma, as well as culturally sanctioned negative attitudes toward obesity, military service members and their family members may be at considerable risk for the onset and maintenance of eating disorders. Further compounding this risk is the perception that mental health care will be ineffective, the concern that utilization of mental health care is a sign of weakness, or the fear that an eating disorder diagnosis may jeopardize one's career. As a result, military service members and their families may be highly vulnerable to eating disorders that are left untreated. Eating disorders within the military family represent a considerable threat to both public health and national security. Thus, rigorous nationally representative research is needed to elucidate prevalence rates and correlates of eating disorders in the military and culturally sensitive clinical research is needed to develop and implement effective treatment approaches that may be easily disseminated to service members and their families.

Disclaimer

The views presented here are those of the authors and are not to be construed as official or reflecting the views of the Uniformed Services University of the Health Sciences, the Department of Defense, or the U.S. Government.

References

Almond, N., Kahwati, L., Kinsinger, L., & Porterfield, D. (2008). The prevalence of overweight and obesity among US military veterans. *Military Medicine, 173*(6), 544–549.

American Psychiatric Association. (2013). *Diagnostic and statistical manual of mental disorders (5th ed.).* Washington, DC: American Psychiatric Publishing.

Anestis, M. D., Mohn, R. S., Dorminey, J. W., & Green, B. A. (2019). Detecting potential underreporting of suicide ideation among U.S. Military personnel. *Suicide and Life-Threatening Behavior, 49*(1), 210–220. doi:10.1111/sltb.12425.

Antczak, A. J., & Brininger, T. L. (2008). Diagnosed eating disorders in the U.S. military: A nine year review. *Eating Disorders, 16*(5), 363–377. doi:10.1080/10640260802370523.

Arditte Hall, K. A., Bartlett, B. A., Iverson, K. M., & Mitchell, K. S. (2017b). Eating disorder symptoms in female veterans: The role of childhood, adult, and military trauma exposure. *Psychological Trauma: Theory, Research, Practice, and Policy, 10*(3), 345–351.

Arditte Hall, K. A., Bartlett, B. A., Iverson, K. M., & Mitchell, K. S. (2017a). Military-related trauma is associated with eating disorder symptoms in male veterans. *International Journal of Eating Disorders, 50*(11), 1328–1331.

Armed Forces Health Surveillance Branch. (2011). Diagnoses of overweight/obesity, active component, U.S. Armed Forces 1998–2010. *Medical Surveillance Monthly Report, 18*, 7–11.

Armed Forces Health Surveillance Branch. (2018). Mental disorders and mental health problems, active component, U.S. Armed Forces, January 2000-December 2009. *MSMR, 25*(6), 18–25.

Ashmore, J. A., Friedman, K. E., Reichmann, S. K., & Musante, G. J. (2008). Weight-based stigmatization, psychological distress, & binge eating behavior among obese treatment-seeking adults. *Eating Behaviors, 9*(2), 203–209. doi:10.1016/j.eatbeh.2007.09.006.

Bakalar, J. L., Barmine, M., Druskin, L., Olsen, C. H., Quinlan, J., Sbrocco, T., & Tanofsky-Kraff, M. (2018). Childhood adverse life events, disordered eating, and body mass index in US military service members. *International Journal of Eating Disorders, 51*(5), 465–469.

Bartlett, B. A., & Mitchell, K. S. (2015). Eating disorders in military and veteran men and women: A systematic review. *International Journal of Eating Disorders, 48*(8), 1057–1069.

Bray, R. M., Pemberton, M. R., Hourani, L. L., Witt, M.,Rae Olmsted, K. L., Brown, J. M., Weimer, B. J., Lane, M. E., Marsden, M. E., Scheffler, S. A., Vandermaas-Peeler, R., Aspinwall, K. R., Anderson, E. M., Spagnola, K., Close, K.L., Gratton, J. L., Calvin, S. L., & Bradshaw, M. R. (2009). *2008 Department of Defense survey of health related behaviors among active duty military personnel*. Report prepared for TRICARE Management Activity, Office of the Assistant Secretary of Defense (Health Affairs) and U.S. Coast Guardunder Contract No. GS-10F-0097L.

Breland, J. Y., Donalson, R., Li, Y. M., Hebenstreit, C. L., Goldstein, L. A., & Maguen, S. (2018). Military sexual trauma is associated with eating disorders, while combat exposure is not. *Psychological Trauma: Theory, Research, Practice, and Policy, 10*(3), 276–281. doi:10.1037/tra0000276.

Breland, J. Y., Donalson, R., Nevedal, A., Dinh, J. V., & Maguen, S. (2017). Military experience can influence women's eating habits. *Appetite, 118*, 161–167. doi:10.1016/j.appet.2017.08.009.

Brewerton, T. D. (2007). Eating disorders, trauma, and comorbidity: Focus on PTSD. *Eating Disorders, 15*(4), 285–304.

Britt, T. W., Greene-Shortridge, T. M., & Castro, C. A. (2007). The stigma of mental health problems in the military. *Military Medicine, 172*(2), 157–161. doi:10.7205/MILMED.172.2.157.

Brownell, K., Puhl, R., Schwartz, M., & Rudd, L. (2005). *Weight bias: Nature, consequences, and remedies*. New York, NY: The Guilford Press.

Brownell, K. D., & Rodin, J. (1994). Medical, metabolic, and psychological effects of weight cycling. *Archives of Internal Medicine, 154*(12), 1325–1330. doi:10.1001/archinte.1994.00420120035004.

Burke, N. L., Schvey, N. A., Stojek, M., Ress, R., Barmine, M., Gorlick, J., ..., Tanofsky-Kraff, M. (2016). Feasibility of an adolescent eating disorder (ED) and obesity preventive intervention in a U.S. military treatment facility. Presented at the international conference on eating disorders, San Francisco, CA.

Carlton, J. R., Manos, G. H., & Van Slyke, J. A. (2005). Anxiety and abnormal eating behaviors associated with cyclical readiness testing in a naval hospital active duty population. *Military Medicine, 170*(8), 663–667.

Carr, D., & Friedman, M. A. (2005). Is obesity stigmatizing? Body weight, perceived discrimination, and psychological well-being in the United States. *Journal of Health and Social Behavior, 46*(3), 244–259. doi:10.1177/002214650504600303.

Chandola, T., Brunner, E., & Marmot, M. (2006). Chronic stress at work and the metabolic syndrome: Prospective study. *BMJ, 332*(7540), 521–524. doi:10.1136/bmj.38693.435301.80.

Chandra, A., Martin, L. T., Hawkins, S. A., & Richardson, A. (2010). The impact of parental deployment on child social and emotional functioning: Perspectives of school staff. *Journal of Adolescent Health, 46*(3), 218–223. doi:10.1016/j.jadohealth.2009.10.009.

Cooper, A. E., Corrigan, P. W., & Watson, A. C. (2003). Mental illness stigma and care seeking. *The Journal of Nervous and Mental Disease, 191*(5), 339–341. doi:10.1097/01.NMD.0000066157.47101.22.

Cronk, T. M. (2016). *Officials describe plans to integrate women into combat roles. DOD News*. https://www.defense.gov/Explore/News/Article/Article/648766/officials-describe-plans-to-integrate-women-into-combat-roles/.

Curry, J. F., Aubuchon-Endsley, N., Brancu, M., Runnals, J. J., Workgroup, R., Workgroup, V. M. A. M. R., & Fairbank, J. A. (2014). Lifetime major depression and comorbid disorders among current-era women veterans. *Journal of Affective Disorders, 152*, 434–440.

Dall, T. M., Zhang, Y., Chen, Y. J., Wagner, R. C. A., Hogan, P. F., Fagan, N. K., ... Tornberg, D. N. (2007). Cost associated with being overweight and with obesity, high alcohol consumption, and tobacco use within the military health system's TRICARE prime-enrolled population. *American Journal of Health Promotion, 22*(2), 120–139.

Defense Manpower Data Center (U.S.). (2018). *Military and Civilian Personnel by Service/Agency by State/Country*. Washington, DC.

Department of the Army. (2013). Army Regulation 600-9: The Army Body Composition Program. Washington, DC.

Department of Defense Physical Fitness and Body Fat Programs Procedures. (2002).

Department of Defense Physical Fitness and Body Fat Programs and Procedures. (2004).

Department of the Air Force. (2019). *Air Force Instruction 36-2903, Dress and Personal Appearance of Air Force Personnel*. Washington, DC.

Department of the Army. (2017). *Wear and Appearance of Army Uniforms and Insignia*. Washington, DC.

Department of the Navy. (2019). *NAVPERS 156651: United States Navy Uniform Regulations*. Washington, DC.

Durso, L. E., Latner, J. D., White, M. A., Masheb, R. M., Blomquist, K. K., Morgan, P. T., & Grilo, C. M. (2012). Internalized weight bias in obese patients with binge eating disorder: Associations with eating disturbances and psychological functioning. *International Journal of Eating Disorders, 45*(3), 423–427. doi:10.1002/eat.20933.

Eaton, K. M., Hoge, C. W., Messer, S. C., Whitt, A. A., Cabrera, O. A., McGurk, D., ..., Castro, C. A. (2008). Prevalence of mental health problems, treatment need, and barriers to care among primary care-seeking spouses of military service members involved in Iraq and Afghanistan deployments. *Military Medicine, 173*(11), 1051–1056. doi:10.7205/MILMED.173.11.1051.

Esposito-Smythers, C., Wolff, J., Lemmon, K. M., Bodzy, M., Swenson, R. R., & Spirito, A. (2011). Military youth and the deployment cycle: Emotional health consequences and recommendations for intervention. *Journal of Family Psychology, 25*(4), 497–507. doi:10.1037/a0024534.

Field, A. E., Sonneville, K. R., Micali, N., Crosby, R. D., Swanson, S. A., Laird, N. M., ..., Horton, N. J. (2012). Prospective association of common eating disorders and adverse outcomes. *Pediatrics, 130*(2), E289–E295. doi:10.1542/peds.2011-3663.

Forman-Hoffman, V. L., Mengeling, M., Booth, B. M., Torner, J., & Sadler, A. G. (2012). Eating disorders, post-traumatic stress, and sexual trauma in women veterans. *Military Medicine, 177*(10), 1161–1168.

Gimbel, R. W., Pangaro, L., & Barbour, G. (2010). America's "undiscovered" laboratory for health services research. *Medical Care, 48*(8), 751–756. doi:10.1097/MLR.0b013e3181e35be8.

Goodman, E., & Whitaker, R. C. (2002). A prospective study of the role of depression in the development and persistence of adolescent obesity. *Pediatrics, 110*(3), 497–504. doi:10.1542/peds.110.3.497.

Griffiths, S., Mond, J. M., Murray, S. B., & Touyz, S. (2015). The prevalence and adverse associations of stigmatization in people with eating disorders. *International Journal of Eating Disorders, 48*(6), 767–774. doi:10.1002/eat.22353.

Haedt-Matt, A. A., & Keel, P. K. (2011). Revisiting the affect regulation model of binge eating: A meta-analysis of studies using ecological momentary assessment. *Psychological Bulletin, 137*, 660–681.

Haines, J., & Neumark-Sztainer, D. (2006). Prevention of obesity and eating disorders: A consideration of shared risk factors. *Health Education Research, 21*(6), 770–782.

Hart, L. M., Granillo, T., Jorm, A. F., & Paxton, S. J. (2011). Unmet need for treatment in the eating disorders: A systematic review of eating disorder specific treatment seeking among community cases. *Clinical Psychology Review, 31*(5), 727–735. doi:10.1016/j.cpr.2011.03.004.

Harvey, K., Rosselli, F., Wilson, G. T., DeBar, L. L., & Striegal-Moore, R. H. (2011). Eating patterns in patients with spectrum binge eating disorder. *International Journal of Eating Disorders, 44*, 447–451.

Higgins, D. M., Dorflinger, L., MacGregor, K. L., Heapy, A. A., Goulet, J. L., & Ruser, C. (2013). Binge eating behavior among a national sample of overweight and obese veterans. *Obesity, 21*(5), 900–903.

Hodgdon, J. A., & Naval Health Research Center. (1990). Body composition in military services: Standards & methods.

Hoge, C. W., Castro, C. A., Messer, S. C., McGurk, D., Cotting, D. I., & Koffman, R. L. (2004). Combat duty in Iraq and Afghanistan, mental health problems, and barriers to care. *The New England Journal of Medicine, 351*(1), 13–22. doi:10.1056/NEJMoa040603.

Hudson J, Hiripi E., Pope H, Kessler R. (2007). The prevalence and correlates of eating disorders in the National Comorbidity Survey replication. *Biological Psychiatry, 61*(3), 348–358.

Huston, J., Iverson, K., & Mitchell, K. (2018). Associations between healthcare use and disordered eating among female veterans. *International Journal of Eating Disorders, 51*(8), 978–983.

Institute of Medicine (2010). *Returning home from Iraq and Afghanistan: Preliminary assessment of readjustment needs of veterans, service members, and their families.* Washington, DC: National Academies Press.

Jackson, J. L., Strong, J., Cheng, E. Y., & Meyer, G. (1999). Patients, diagnoses, and procedures in a military internal medicine clinic: Comparison with civilian practices. *Military Medicine, 164*(3), 194–197. doi:10.1093/milmed/164.3.194.

Jacobson, I. G., Smith, T. C., Smith, B., Keel, P. K., Amoroso, P. J., Wells, T. S., ... for the Millennium Cohort Study, T. (2009). Disordered eating and weight changes after deployment: Longitudinal assessment of a large U.S. Military cohort. *American Journal of Epidemiology, 169*(4), 415–427. doi:10.1093/aje/kwn366.

Jensen, P. S., Martin, D., & Watanabe, H. (1996). Children's response to parental separation during Operation Desert Storm. *Journal of the American Academy of Child and Adolescent Psychiatry, 35*(4), 433–441.

Jones, M. D., Etherage, J. R., Harmon, S. C., & Okiishi, J. C. (2012). Acceptability and cost-effectiveness of military telehealth mental health screening. *Psychological services, 9*(2), 132.

Karney, B. R., Crown, J. S., & Rand National Defense Research Institute. (2007). *Families under stress: An assessment of data, theory, and research on marriage and divorce in the military.*Santa Monica, CA: RAND Corporation.

Katon, J. G., Lehavot, K. P., Simpson, T. L.,Williams, E. C., Barnett, S. B., Grossbard, J. R., ..., Reiber, G. E. (2015). Adverse childhood experiences, military service, and adult health. *American Journal of Preventive Medicine, 49*(4), 573–582. doi:10.1016/j.amepre.2015.03.020.

Keel, P. K., Crow, S., Davis, T. L., & Mitchell, J. E. (2002). Assessment of eating disorders: Comparison of interview and questionnaire data from a long-term follow-up study of bulimia nervosa. *Journal of Psychosomatic Research, 53*(5), 1043–1047. doi:10.1016/S0022-3999(02)00491-9.

Keel, P. K., & Forney, K. J. (2013). Psychosocial risk factors for eating disorders. *International Journal of Eating Disorders, 65*, 433–439.

Kim, P. Y., Thomas, J. L., Wilk, J. E., Castro, C. A., & Hoge, C. W. (2010). Stigma, barriers to care, and use of mental health services among active duty and National Guard soldiers after combat. *Psychiatric Services, 61*(6), 582–588.

Kimerling, R., Gima, K., Smith, M. W., Street, A., & Frayne, S. (2007). The Veterans Health Administration and military sexual trauma. *American Journal of Public Health, 97*(12), 2160–2166.

Kleykamp, M. A. (2006). College, jobs, or the military? Enlistment during a time of war. *Social Science Quarterly, 87*(2), 272–290. doi:10.1111/j.1540-6237.2006.00380.x.

Koepsell, T. D., Forsberg, C. W., & Littman, A. J. (2009). Obesity, overweight, and weight control practices in US veterans. *Preventive Medicine, 48*(3), 267–271.

Lauder, T. D., Williams, M. V., Campbell, C. S., Davis, G. D., & Sherman, R. A. (1999). Abnormal eating behaviors in military women. *Medicine and Science in Sports and Exercise, 31*(9), 1265–1271.

Link, P. E., & Palinkas, L. A. (2013). Long-term trajectories and service needs for military families. *Clinical Child and Family Psychology Review, 16*(4), 376–393. doi:10.1007/s10567-013-0145-z.

Luxton, D. D., Mishkind, M. C., Crumpton, R. M., Ayers, T. D., & Mysliwiec, V. (2012). Usability and feasibility of smartphone video capabilities for telehealth care in the U.S. Military. *Telemedicine and e-Health, 18*(6), 409–412. doi:10.1089/tmj.2011.0219.

Maguen, S., Luxton, D. D., Skopp, N. A., Gahm, G. A., Reger, M. A., Metzler, T. J., & Marmar, C. R. (2011). Killing in combat, mental health symptoms, and suicidal ideation in Iraq war veterans. *Journal of Anxiety Disorders, 25*(4), 563–567. doi:10.1016/j.janxdis.2011.01.003.

Masheb, R. M., Lutes, L. D., Myra Kim, H., Holleman, R. G., Goodrich, D. E., Janney, C. A., ..., Damschroder, L. J. (2015). High-frequency binge eating predicts weight gain among veterans receiving behavioral weight loss treatments. *Obesity*, *23*(1), 54–61.

Mattocks, K. M., Haskell, S. G., Krebs, E. E., Justice, A. C., Yano, E. M., & Brandt, C. (2012). Women at war: Understanding how women veterans cope with combat and military sexual trauma. *Social Science and Medicine*, *74*(4), 537–545.

McNulty, P. A. F. (1997a). Prevalence and contributing factors of eating disorder behaviors in a population of female Navy nurses. *Military Medicine*, *162*(10), 703–706. doi:10.1093/milmed/162.10.703.

McNulty, P. A. F. (1997b). Prevalence and contributing factors of eating disorder behaviors in active duty Navy men. *Military Medicine*, *162*(11), 753–758. doi:10.1093/milmed/162.11.753.

McNulty, P. A. F. (2001). Prevalence and contributing factors of eating disorder behaviors in active duty service women in the Army, Navy, Air Force, and Marines. *Military Medicine*, *166*(1), 53–58. doi:10.1093/milmed/166.1.53.

Mental Health Advisory Team VI. (2009). *Operation Iraqi Freedom 07–09 report* Office of the Surgeon. Multinational Force-Iraq & Office of the Surgeon General (Army), Washington, DC. https://armymedicine.health.mil/Reports.

Meyer, E. G., & Wynn, G. H. (2018). The importance of US military cultural competence. In L. Weiss Roberts & C. H. Warner, *Military and Veteran Mental Health* (pp. 15–33). New York, NY: Springer.

Mitchell, K. S., Porter, B., Boyko, E. J., & Field, A. E. (2016). Longitudinal associations among posttraumatic stress disorder, disordered eating, and weight gain in military men and women. *American Journal of Epidemiology*, *184*(1), 33–47. doi:10.1093/aje/kwv291.

Nash, W. P., & Litz, B. T. (2013). Moral injury: A mechanism for war-related psychological trauma in military family members. *Clinical Child and Family Psychology Review*, *16*(4), 365–375. doi:10.1007/s10567-013-0146-y.

Nelson, K. M. (2006). The burden of obesity among a national probability sample of veterans. *Journal of General Internal Medicine*, *21*(9), 915–919.

Paley, B., Lester, P., & Mogil, C. (2013). Family systems and ecological perspectives on the impact of deployment on military families. *Clinical Child and Family Psychology Review*, *16*(3), 245–265. doi:10.1007/s10567-013-0138-y.

Paris, R., DeVoe, E. R., Ross, A. M., & Acker, M. L. (2010). When a parent goes to war: Effects of parental deployment on very young children and implications for intervention. *American Journal of Orthopsychiatry*, *80*(4), 610–618. doi:10.1111/j.1939-0025.2010.01066.x.

Peebles-Kleiger, M. J., & Kleiger, J. H. (1994). Re-integration stress for desert-storm families-wartime deployments and family trauma. *Journal of Traumatic Stress*, *7*(2), 173–194.

Peterson, A. L., Talcott, G. W., Kelleher, W. J., & Smith, S. D. (1995). Bulimic weight-loss behaviors in military versus civilian weight-management programs. *Military Medicine*, *160*(12), 616–620. doi:10.1093/milmed/160.12.616.

Pflanz, S., & Sonnek, S. (2002). Work stress in the military: Prevalence, causes, and relationship to emotional health. *Military Medicine*, *167*(11), 877–882. doi:10.1093/milmed/167.11.877.

Polivy, J., & Herman, C. P. (1985). Dieting and binging: A causal analysis. *American Psychologist*, *40*, 193–201.

Puhl, R., & Brownell, K. (2006). Confronting and coping with weight stigma: An investigation of overweight and obese adults. *Obesity*, *14*, 1802–1815.

Puhl, R., & Heuer, C. (2010). Obesity stigma: Important considerations for public health. *American Journal of Public Health*, *100*(6), 1019–1028. doi:10.2105/ajph.2009.159491.

Puhl, R. M., Andreyeva, T., & Brownell, K. D. (2008). Perceptions of weight discrimination: Prevalence and comparison to race and gender discrimination in America. *International Journal of Obesity*, *32*(6), 992–1000. doi:10.1038/ijo.2008.22.

Puhl, R. M., & Heuer, C. A. (2009). The stigma of obesity: A review and update. *Obesity*, *17*(5), 941–964. doi:10.1038/oby.2008.636.

Quattlebaum, M., Burke, N. L., Higgins Neyland, M. K., Leu, W., Schvey, N. A., Pine, A., ..., Tanofsky-Kraff, M. (2019). Sex differences in eating related behaviors and psychopathology among adolescent military dependents at risk for adult obesity and eating disorders. *Eating Behaviors*, *33*, 73–77. doi:10.1016/j.eatbeh.2019.04.001.

Raevuori, A., Keski-Rahkonen, A., & Hoek, H. W. (2014). A review of eating disorders in males. *Current Opinion in Psychiatry*, *27*(6), 426–430. doi:10.1097/YCO.0000000000000113.

Reed, S. C., Bell, J. F., & Edwards, T. C. (2011). Adolescent well-being in Washington State military families. *American Journal of Public Health*, *101*(9), 1676–1682. doi:10.2105/AJPH.2011.300165.

Reger, M. A., Etherage, J. R., Reger, G. M., & Gahm, G. A. (2008). Civilian psychologists in an Army culture: The ethical challenge of cultural competence. *Military Psychology*, *20*(1), 21–35.

Regier, D. A., Narrow, W. E., Rae, D. S., Manderscheid, R. W., Locke, B. Z., & Goodwin, F. K. (1993). The de facto US mental and addictive disorders service system: Epidemiologic catchment area prospective 1-year prevalence rates of disorders and services. *Archives of General Psychiatry*, *50*(2), 85–94. doi:10.1001/archpsyc.1993.01820140007001.

Renshaw, K. D., Rodrigues, C. S., & Jones, D. H. (2009). Combat exposure, psychological symptoms, and marital satisfaction in National Guard soldiers who served in Operation Iraqi Freedom from 2005 to 2006. *Anxiety, Stress & Coping*, *22*(1), 101–115. doi:10.1080/10615800802354000.

Sanderson, P. W., Clemes, S. A., & Biddle, S. J. H. (2011). The correlates and treatment of obesity in military populations: A systematic review. *Obesity Facts*, *4*(3), 229–237. doi:10.1159/000329450.

Schvey, N. A., Barmine, M., Bates, D., Oldham, K., Bakalar, J. L., Spieker, E., ..., Tanofsky-Kraff, M. (2017). Weight stigma among active duty US military personnel with overweight and obesity. *Stigma and Health*, *2*(4), 281.

Schvey, N. A., Puhl, R. M., & Brownell, K. D. (2011). The impact of weight stigma on caloric consumption. *Obesity*, *19*(10), 1957–1962.

Schvey, N. A., Roberto, C. A., & White, M. A. (2013). Clinical correlates of the Weight Bias Internalization Scale in overweight adults with binge and purge behaviours. *Advances in Eating Disorders*, *1*(3), 213–223. doi:10.1080/21662630.2013.794523.

Schvey, N. A., Sbrocco, T., Stephens, M., Bryant, E. J., Ress, R., Spieker, E. A., ..., Barmine, M. (2015). Comparison of overweight and obese military-dependent and civilian adolescent girls with loss-of-control eating. *International Journal of Eating Disorders*, *48*(6), 790–794.

Schvey, N. A., & White, M. A. (2015). The internalization of weight bias is associated with severe eating pathology among lean individuals. *Eating Behaviors*, *17*, 1–5. doi:10.1016/j.eatbeh.2014.11.001.

Seacat J. D., Dougal, S. C., & Roy D. (2016). A daily diary assessment of female weight stigmatization. *Journal of Health Psychology, 21*(2), 228–240.

Seal, K. H., Metzler, T. J., Gima, K. S., Bertenthal, D., Maguen, S., & Marmar, C. R. (2009). Trends and risk factors for mental health diagnoses among Iraq and Afghanistan veterans using Department of Veterans Affairs health care, 2002–2008. *American Journal of Public Health, 99*(9), 1651–1658. doi:10.2105/AJPH.2008.150284.

Shank, L. M., Schvey, N. A., Ekundayo, K., Schreiber-Gregory, D., Bates, D., Maurer, D., ..., Sbrocco, T. (2019). The relationship between weight stigma, weight bias internalization, and physical health in military personnel with or at high-risk of overweight/obesity. *Body Image, 28*, 25–33.

Smith, L., Westrick, R., Sauers, S., Cooper, A., Scofield, D., Claro, P., & Warr, B. (2016). Underreporting of musculoskeletal injuries in the U.S. Army: Findings from an infantry brigade combat team survey study. *Sports Health: A Multidisciplinary Approach, 8*(6), 507–513. doi:10.1177/1941738116670873.

Smith, T. J., Marriott, B. P., Dotson, L., Bathalon, G. P., Funderburk, L., White, A., ..., Young, A. J. (2012). Overweight and obesity in military personnel: Sociodemographic predictors. *Obesity, 20*(7), 1534–1538. doi:10.1038/oby.2012.25.

Spieker, E. A., Sbrocco, T., Theim, K. R., Maurer, D., Johnson, D., Bryant, E., ... Stephens, M. B. (2015). Preventing Obesity in the Military Community (POMC): The development of a clinical trials research network. *International Journal of Environmental Research and Public Health, 12*(2), 1174–1195.

Spoor, S. T. P., Bekker, M. H. J., Van Strien, T., & Van Heck, G. L. (2007). Relations between negative affect, coping, and emotional eating. *Appetite, 48*, 368–376.

Stein, R. I., Kenardy, J., Wiseman, C. V., Dounchis, J. Z., Arnow, B. A., & Wilfley, D. E. (2007). What's driving the binge in binge eating disorder?: A prospective examination of precursors and consequences. *International Journal of Eating Disorders, 40*, 195–203.

Stice, E., Cameron, R. P., Hayward, C., Taylor, C. B., & Killen, J. D. (1999). Naturalistic weight-reduction efforts prospectively predict growth in relative weight and onset of obesity among female adolescents. *Journal of Consulting and Clinical Psychology, 67*(6), 967–974. doi:10.1037/0022-006X.67.6.967.

Striegel-Moore, R. H., Garvin, V., Dohm, F. A., & Rosenheck, R. A. (1999a). Eating disorders in a national sample of hospitalized female and male veterans: Detection rates and psychiatric comorbidity. *International Journal of Eating Disorders, 25*(4), 405–414.

Striegel-Moore, R. H., Garvin, V., Dohm, F. A., & Rosenheck, R. A. (1999b). Psychiatric comorbidity of eating disorders in men: A national study of hospitalized veterans. *International Journal of Eating Disorders, 25*(4), 399–404.

Stunkard, A. J., & Allison, K. C. (2003). Binge eating disorder: Disorder or marker? *International Journal of Eating Disorders, 34*, 107–116.

Sutin, A. R., Stephan, Y., & Terracciano, A. (2015). Weight discrimination and risk of mortality. *Psychological Science, 26*(11), 1803–1811. doi:10.1177/0956797615601103.

Tanofsky-Kraff, M. (2012). Psychosocial preventive interventions for obesity and eating disorders in youths. *International Review of Psychiatry, 24*(3), 262–270.

Tanofsky-Kraff, M., Bulik, C. M., Marcus, M. D., Striegel, R. H., Wilfley, D. E., Wonderlich, S. A., & Hudson, J. I. (2013). Binge eating disorder: The next generation of research. *International Journal of Eating Disorders, 46*(3), 193–207. doi:10.1002/eat.22089.

Tanofsky-Kraff, M., Sbrocco, T., Theim, K. R., Cohen, L. A., Mackey, E. R., Stice, E., ..., Stephens, M. B. (2013). Obesity and the US military family. *Obesity, 21*(11), 2205–2220.

Tanofsky-Kraff, M., Shomaker, L. B., Wilfley, D. E., Young, J. F., Sbrocco, T., Stephens, M., ..., Olsen, C. H. (2017). Excess weight gain prevention in adolescents: Three-year outcome following a randomized controlled trial. *Journal of Consulting and Clinical Psychology, 85*(3), 218.

Tanofsky-Kraff, M., & Yanovski, S. Z. (2004). Eating disorder or disordered eating? Non-normative eating patterns in obese individuals. *Obesity Research, 12*(9), 1361–1366. doi:10.1038/oby.2004.171.

Tanofsky-Kraff, M., Yanovski, S. Z., Schvey, N. A., Olsen, C. H., Gustafson, J., & Yanovski, J. A. (2009). A prospective study of loss of control eating for body weight gain in children at high risk for adult obesity. *International Journal of Eating Disorders, 42*(1), 26–30.

Terre, L., Hunter, C., Carlos Poston, W. S., Keith Haddock, C., & Stewart, S. A. (2007). Treatment of obesity in the primary care setting: Are we there yet? *Eating Disorders, 15*(2), 135–143. doi:10.1080/10640260701190659.

Vartanian, L. R., & Novak, S. A. (2011). Internalized societal attitudes moderate the impact of weight stigma on avoidance of exercise. *Obesity, 19*(4), 757–762. doi:10.1038/oby.2010.234.

Vartanian, L. R., & Shaprow, J. G. (2008). Effects of weight stigma on exercise motivation and behavior: A preliminary investigation among college-aged females. *Journal of Health Psychology, 13*(1), 131–138. doi:10.1177/1359105307084318.

Waasdorp, C. E., Caboot, J. B., Robinson, C. A., Abraham, A. A., & Adelman, W. P. (2007). Screening military dependent adolescent females for disordered eating. *Military Medicine, 172*(9), 962–967. doi:10.7205/MILMED.172.9.962.

Wadsworth, S. M. (2013). Understanding and supporting the resilience of a new generation of combat-exposed military families and their children. *Clinical Child and Family Psychology Review, 16*(4), 415–420. doi:10.1007/s10567-013-0155-x.

Warner, C., Warner, C., Matuszak, T., Rachal, J., Flynn, J., & Grieger, T. A. (2007). Disordered eating in entry-level military personnel. *Military Medicine, 172*(2), 147–151. doi:10.7205/MILMED.172.2.147.

Wells, T. S., LeardMann, C. A., Fortuna, S. O., Smith, B., Smith, T. C., Ryan, M. A. K., ..., for the Millennium Cohort Study, T. (2010). A prospective study of depression following combat deployment in support of the wars in Iraq and Afghanistan. *American Journal of Public Health, 100*(1), 90–99. doi:10.2105/AJPH.2008.155432.

Wilk, J. E., Hoge, C. W., Castro, C. A., Thomas, J. L., & Kim, P. Y. (2010). Stigma, barriers to care, and use of mental health services among active duty and national guard soldiers after combat. *Psychiatric Services, 61*(6), 582–588. doi:10.1176/ps.2010.61.6.582.

Young-Hyman, D., Tanofsky-Kraff, M., Yanovski, S. Z., Keil, M., Cohen, M. L., Peyrot, M., & Yanovski, J. A. (2006). Psychological status and weight-related distress in overweight or at-risk-for-overweight children. *Obesity, 14*(12), 2249–2258. doi:10.1038/oby.2006.264.

10 Integrating Evidence-Based Treatments for Eating Disorder Patients with Comorbid PTSD and Trauma-Related Disorders

*Timothy D. Brewerton, Kathryn Trottier,
Julie Trim, Tricia Meyers, and Stephen Wonderlich*

Introduction

The association between trauma and resultant posttraumatic stress disorder (PTSD) and other trauma-related disorders in the predisposition, precipitation, and perpetuation of eating disorders (EDs) has been clearly established (Brewerton, 2015; 2018; Brewerton & Dennis, 2015). Compelling evidence from national representative samples, community and clinical samples, meta-analyses, and personal patient reports have demonstrated strong links between traumatic experiences and EDs, particularly those with binge-type features (Afifi et al., 2017; Brewerton, 2018; Brewerton, Alexander, & Schaefer, 2019; Brewerton, Cotton, & Kilpatrick, 2018; Brewerton & Dennis, 2015; Micali et al., 2017; Molendijk, Hoek, Brewerton, & Elzinga, 2017). In most but not all cases, the traumas were reported to have occurred prior to the onset of the ED. In the National Women's Study, the great majority of respondents with bulimia nervosa (BN) who reported rape were raped prior to the onset of binge eating (Dansky, Brewerton, O'Neil, & Kilpatrick, 1997). Furthermore, Tagay, Schlottbohm, Reyes-Rodriguez, Repic, and Senf (2014) also reported that most ED patients (67.7%) with PTSD reported that their first traumatic event occurred before the onset of their ED (Tagay et al., 2014). All PTSD-related symptom clusters, including intrusion, avoidance, hyperarousal, and dissociation, increased with the number of traumatic events.

It is not uncommon for ED-PTSD patients to have experienced multiple traumas and/or trauma types (Brewerton, 2018). Higher trauma "doses" have been linked to ED severity and comorbidities, including food addiction, substance use, and suicide (Afifi et al., 2017; Brewerton, 2007; 2017; Karr et al., 2013; Leonard, Steiger, & Kao, 2003; Molendijk et al., 2017; Schoemaker, Smit, Bijl, & Vollebergh, 2002). Trauma histories and PTSD have been reported to predict more complicated courses of illness, higher dropout rates, and worse outcomes following treatment (Brewerton, 2004; 2007; 2015; Carter, Bewell, Blackmore, & Woodside, 2006; Castellini et al., 2018; Fassino, Piero, Tomba, & Abbate-Daga, 2009; Ford & Kidd, 1998; Lonergan, 2014; Mahon, Bradley, Harvey, Winston, & Palmer, 2001; Vrabel, Hoffart, Ro, Martinsen, & Rosenvinge, 2010). Individuals with ED-PTSD may be more impulsive, prone to revictimization, and the subsequent perpetuation of PTSD (Brewerton et al., 2018).

Although there are several evidence-based treatments (EBTs) for both EDs and PTSD individually, there are few findings on integrated treatment approaches for this common comorbidity. Recent research suggests that ED clinicians view integrated treatment for individuals with ED and PTSD as a top priority, yet researchers have several concerns about administering such a treatment (Trottier, Monson, Wonderlich, MacDonald, & Olmsted, 2016). This is likely due, in part, to a paucity of research into integrated treatment approaches for individuals with these more complex presentations. Almost all controlled studies of the treatment of EDs have excluded individuals with significant comorbidity, and PTSD treatment studies have not systematically examined the course of treatment for an individual with an ED. The need for integrated treatment approaches for ED patients with trauma-related disorders has long been recognized.

This chapter will review the principles and treatment methods for individuals with ED-PTSD, and will provide the examples of treatment centers that are pioneering integrated care for their patients. The coordination or integration of EBTs such as cognitive behavioral therapy (CBT), cognitive processing therapy (CPT), prolonged exposure (PE), dialectical behavior therapy (DBT), family-based treatment (FBT), and trauma-focused CBT (TF-CBT) are recommended. To what extent, phasic, stepwise, or sequential treatment can be coordinated and utilized as opposed to more fully integrated treatment protocols will also be discussed. The principles of integrated treatment plans incorporating work on trauma and comorbid psychiatric disorders have been discussed previously (Brewerton, 2004; Trim, Galovski, Wagner, & Brewerton, 2017).

CBT for ED-PTSD: An Integration of Interventions from CBT-Enhanced and CPT

Background

Project Recover was initiated in 2013 by Trottier et al. at University Health Network (UHN) in Toronto in response to clinical observation of a bidirectional relationship between ED and trauma-related symptoms that appeared to maintain a significant proportion of patients' EDs. The aim of Project Recover has been to facilitate and enable full ED-PTSD recovery through an integration of EBTs for EDs and PTSD. The UHN Eating Disorder Program is a tertiary care center that provides inpatient and day hospital treatment to individuals with EDs where illness severity tends to be severe to extreme. This intensive phase of treatment is associated with large improvements in body mass index (BMI) and binge/purge frequencies, and behavioral remission rates have been on par with those seen in randomized clinical trials (RCTs) of CBT for EDs (Olmsted, McFarlane, Trottier, & Rockert, 2013). However, as is well known, relapse rates are high (Olmsted, MacDonald, McFarlane, Trottier, & Colton, 2015), and effective strategies to promote long-term recovery are needed.

Although trauma-related symptoms have not yet been empirically established as maintaining factors of EDs, a compelling rationale for developing and testing a protocol for treating ED-PTSD existed given the strength of documented associations between EDs and trauma-related variables, the fact that trauma exposure, and PTSD in particular, is associated with an array of psychiatric disorders, as well as clinician (Trottier, Monson, Wonderlich, & Olmsted, 2017) and patient perceptions (Thornley, Vorstenbosch, & Frewen, 2016) about the bidirectional and functional relationship between ED and trauma-related symptoms.

In response, Trottier and Monson (2014) developed Integrated CBT for ED-PTSD, an integrated individual CBT designed to be preceded by a period of nutritional stabilization and ED symptom interruption. Integrated CBT for ED-PTSD is an integration of the core interventions of CBT-enhanced (CBT-E; Fairburn et al., 2008) and CPT for PTSD (Resick, Monson, & Chard, 2014). CPT is an efficacious CBT for PTSD that is typically around 12 sessions (Watkins, Sprang, & Rothbaum, 2018). In CPT, the patient and therapist cognitively and emotionally process the traumatic event that happened as well as the impact that it has had on the individual. The focus is on identifying and modifying maladaptive beliefs or "stuck points" concerning why the traumatic event occurred as well as the implications of the trauma for the individual across the themes of safety, power/control, esteem, intimacy, and trust. The goal of treatment is to reconcile traumatic experiences with beliefs held by the individual about the world, themselves, and others, thereby helping patients to get "unstuck" in their recovery from the traumatic event and ameliorating the negative emotions and other symptoms of PTSD (Resick, Monson, et al., 2014).

Integrated CBT for ED-PTSD, which has been evaluated in empirical trials (Trottier et al., 2017), involves 16 individual therapy sessions over the course of 14 weeks. At the beginning of each session, both ED and PTSD practice/homework assignments are reviewed, along with the patient's self-monitoring records of their food intake and related events, thoughts, and feelings, in order to help set the session agenda. Each session covers the ED material and interventions first, followed by the PTSD material and interventions. Although the ED and PTSD work in each session is covered separately, within each part every opportunity is taken to explore and develop an understanding of how the ED and PTSD may be connected. For example, trauma-related symptoms are considered and included when developing an individualized formulation of ED maintenance. In addition, psychoeducation about how avoidance of trauma-related thoughts, feelings, and reminders by the use of ED behaviors can maintain PTSD is considered. Similarly, when the themes of safety, power/control, esteem, intimacy, and trust are introduced in the context of the PTSD treatment, the therapist and client together identify whether the trauma has led to disruptions in beliefs in each of these domains and consider how these negative beliefs may be related to their ED behaviors. For example, beliefs related to a lack of personal agency and the need to be in control are often related to food restriction and other behaviors aimed at controlling weight and/or shape. Further, once an intervention is introduced in the protocol, it may be used to address the symptoms of both the ED and PTSD, if appropriate. For example, the CBT-E problem-solving skill can be used to address any problems the individual may be facing, including those related to the trauma they experienced. Similarly, CPT worksheets designed to help patients challenge trauma-related stuck points can also be used to challenge ED-related beliefs that may be keeping the individual "stuck" in their ED.

Empirical Support

In one uncontrolled study, Integrated CBT for ED-PTSD was provided to ten individuals with co-occurring ED and PTSD following a course of intensive treatment (inpatient or partial hospital program [PHP] in the ED program at UHN; Trottier et al., 2017). There were statistically significant and large magnitude improvements in PTSD symptoms, depression, and anxiety over the course of the integrated individual therapy. Nearly 90% of the participants who were remitted from behavioral ED symptoms at the end of intensive treatment/start of integrated treatment maintained ED remission and also remitted from their PTSD over the course of integrated CBT for ED-PTSD. An initial RCT comparing integrated CBT for ED-PTSD with CBT for EDs alone is currently underway and in the final stages of data collection. The primary aim of this first RCT is to determine whether Integrated CBT for ED-PTSD is superior to CBT for EDs alone in addressing PTSD symptoms.

Two forms of CPT have been described in the literature. The original form of CPT included a written account (WA) of the index trauma (CPT-A). However, in a comparative study between CPT-A and CPT without the WA, the two forms were found not to be significantly different from each other (Resick, Suvak, & Wells, 2014; Resick et al., 2008). The only exception to this was in patients with prominent dissociative symptoms (Resick, Suvak, Johnides, Mitchell, & Iverson, 2012). Importantly, Resick et al. stated, "Written accounts may be needed to put a fragmented memory into a coherent story and context followed by cognitive therapy for any erroneous beliefs about their role in the event or implications about self or others" (Resick, Suvak, et al., 2014, p. 565). The creators of CPT hence recommend that patients be offered a choice of which form of CPT to pursue (Resick, Monson, & Chard, 2017). Given the association between ED and dissociation (Brewerton, Dansky, Kilpatrick, & O'Neil, 1999; Demitrack, Putnam, Brewerton, Brandt, & Gold, 1990; Moulton, Newman, Power, Swanson, & Day, 2015; Nagata, Kiriike, Kawarada, & Tanaka, 1999; Palmisano et al., 2018), CPT-A may be preferable for at least some individuals with ED-PTSD.

Application: Levels of Care

The current version of Integrated CBT for ED-PTSD was designed to be delivered on an outpatient basis following a period of nutritional stabilization and symptom interruption in intensive treatment. The protocol can readily be adapted for those who have not received a course of intensive ED treatment by adding in a number of sessions at the beginning of the individual therapy that focus on establishing a pattern of regular eating and interrupting binge eating and/or purging behaviors (i.e., CBT-E Stage 1 interventions).

CPT can also be initiated during more intensive levels of ED treatment. At UHN, CPT has been initiated at both inpatient and PHP levels of care. In these cases, CPT has been provided as an adjunct to intensive ED treatment according to the CPT manual with emphasis placed on considering how ED behaviors may be related to trauma-related beliefs and the tendency to avoid trauma-related thoughts, feelings, and situations. Monte Nido & Affiliates has also embarked on an integrated treatment approach utilizing CPT in higher levels of care, including residential, partial hospital, and intensive outpatient programs (Bunnell, Coffin, & Brewerton, 2018). Preliminary results of 80 patients in residential care indicate that ED-PTSD can be successfully treated concurrently at higher levels of care (Brewerton et al., 2019).

Vignette

Linda is a woman currently in her late 30s with a history of ED since adolescence. She first presented for the treatment of anorexia nervosa binge-eating/purging (AN-BP) type at UHN's ED program in her early 20s. Over the course of the 8 years between her first and last treatment, she received at least eight courses of intensive ED treatment including several from other treatment programs. Her AN-BP progressed from mild to extreme, her functioning declined severely, and she was told that she had reached "end state AN" by a physician in the year of her last admission. In her early admissions, she denied having ever experienced a trauma. However, in her later admissions, she disclosed that she was struggling with memories related to a sexual assault that had occurred in childhood. In part, this helped the treatment team to understand why she had always had great difficulty tolerating the contained environment of intensive treatment and accepting the need to eat according to the program's guidelines (e.g., requiring specific components in her meal). In her last treatment, she was admitted for inpatient treatment at a BMI of 13 with the goal of partial weight restoration. During her inpatient treatment, the treatment team worked collaboratively with her to maximize her autonomy and control over the ED treatment process, which enabled her to accept the refeeding and weight restoration process. After a period of initial nutritional stabilization, she was offered a course of CPT delivered twice weekly adjunct to her inpatient ED treatment. During CPT, she disclosed (for the first time in her life) the nature of two sexual assaults she had experienced and was able to resolve the self-blame she had experienced since childhood. Her need to be in control over her eating and her difficulty tolerating the controlled environment of intensive ED treatment and the limited choices regarding her food intake in treatment were closely tied to the nature of the traumas that she had experienced. She was able to accept the reality of what had happened to her, and the loss of control she had experienced during the traumas while rebuilding a realistic and adaptive sense of control over her current life. Linda was discharged from the hospital at a BMI of 16 and with her PTSD in full remission. She then received a brief course of outpatient CBT for AN to help her continue to restore her weight outside of the hospital environment. Linda chose to end her treatment at a BMI of 18 with the goal of continuing with normalized eating on her own. It has now been 4 years since her last treatment and she is fully recovered from her AN and PTSD. She was able to continue gaining weight on her own, and over time was able to return to working full time and develop hobbies. Her perception after 4 years of wellness is that her ED was maintained and worsened by her perceived need to avoid trauma-related memories, thoughts, and feelings, as well as the effects the sexual assaults had on her beliefs about trust, control, and safety. Her perception is that having received CPT during her ED treatment enabled her to recover from her ED. She believes that without it, she would have died due to complications of AN. She currently feels confident that she will continue to live a full life without the return of either her ED or PTSD.

Strengths and Weaknesses/Limitations

Integrated CBT for ED-PTSD is a blend of well-established, efficacious treatments for EDs and PTSD. Therapists who already have training in these therapies can readily implement the integrated protocol. That said, training therapists in evidence-based manualized treatments is resource-intensive and there are well-known barriers to successful dissemination and implementation, some of which may be compounded when multiple therapies are integrated. The fact that the protocol has been evaluated using research methods and that an RCT is underway to evaluate the treatment's efficacy are major strengths of the protocol. The treatment has not yet been implemented as a stand-alone outpatient individual therapy, so its feasibility and effectiveness in this context are unknown.

DBT–PE/DBT–CPT

Background and Research

Clinicians may shy away from offering trauma-focused treatment to their patients for several reasons (Brewerton et al., 2019; Trottier et al., 2016). These include uncertainty about how to best integrate trauma/PTSD treatment with ED treatment, concerns about patient readiness for trauma/

PTSD treatment, and fears about patient decompensation in the course of trauma work. Such concerns are not surprising in light of high rates of psychiatric comorbidity in the ED-PTSD population (Brewerton, 2007; Carter et al., 2006; Dansky et al., 1997). Research has demonstrated that ED-PTSD individuals have higher rate of substance use disorders and mood disorders (Dansky, Brewerton, & Kilpatrick, 2000), impulse control disorders (ICDs) (Fernandez-Aranda et al., 2008), and borderline personality disorder (BPD) (Brewerton, 2007; Hoerster et al., 2015; Wonderlich et al., 2007). It has been shown that these comorbidities impart greater ED psychopathology and may contribute to a more complicated course of treatment and recovery.

Stage-based treatments have emerged as a potential solution to the challenges of treating PTSD in patients with multiple comorbidities or high-risk behaviors. In stage-based treatment, following a complete assessment, the patient acquires skills and psychoeducation before starting trauma treatment. The rationale is that acquiring skills to regulate strong emotions and tolerate distress can prevent engagement in behaviors (e.g., ED behaviors, substance use, and self-harm) that are problematic and that may decrease the effectiveness of trauma treatment. Consequently, stage-based treatments often lead the therapist (and patient) to feel more confident about readiness to begin trauma treatment. Various stage-based treatments have been developed over the past few decades, including Skills Training in Affect and Interpersonal Regulation (STAIR) plus Exposure or Narrative Story Telling (Cloitre, Cohen, & Koenen, 2006; Cloitre, Petkova, Wang, & Lu Lassell, 2012; Cloitre et al., 2010) and DBT (Linehan, 1993). STAIR/Exposure is a weekly 16-session treatment: eight sessions for skills training and eight for exposure. The skills training interventions are adapted from DBT.

Although not a PTSD treatment, DBT (Linehan, 1993) is a stage-based treatment designed to help therapists prioritize treatment targets in emotionally dysregulated, multiproblem, and often high-risk patients. Expert DBT clinicians Harned (2014), Harned, Korslund, and Linehan (2014), and Harned, Korslund, Foa, and Linehan (2012) developed a comprehensive protocol for integrating trauma treatment with "full package" DBT (skill groups, individual sessions, and phone coaching and consultation for the therapists). PE was chosen as the PTSD treatment because exposure-based interventions are used frequently in DBT (Harned, Tkachuck, & Youngberg, 2013; Linehan, 1993). In the first stage of DBT PE, therapists focus on motivating patients to participate in PE, obtaining their commitment to refrain from self-harm and other problematic behaviors, and assisting them in creating a skills plan they can use following trauma exposures. Behaviorally specific readiness criteria are outlined, as are criteria for stopping and restarting trauma treatment if a higher target behavior occurs (e.g., self-harm and significant ED behaviors). Harned et al. (2013) suggested factors to take into account when deciding whether to "pause" PE, including the riskiness of the behavior, the degree to which the behavior interferes with the treatment, and the potential reinforcing and/or punishing effects of stopping PE. Typically, PE is temporarily stopped until the behavior is no longer occurring. When PE is on hold, sessions focus on addressing the higher target behaviors with standard DBT procedures (e.g., conducting a behavioral chain analysis on the behavior).

Research has demonstrated that DBT PE is not only effective in significantly reducing PTSD symptoms, but also leads to significant decreases in depression, dissociation, shame, trauma-related guilt cognitions, and anxiety (Harned et al., 2012; 2014). Harned et al. (2014) demonstrated in an RCT that, compared to women in the DBT only condition, women in the DBT PE condition were 2.4 times less likely to attempt suicide and 1.5 times less likely to self-injure during treatment.

Application: Levels of Care

The vast majority of research on DBT PE has been conducted in outpatient settings. With that said, there is no theoretical reason that DBT PE could not be applied in more intensive levels of care, as both DBT (Ben-Porath, Wisniewski, & Warren, 2009; Del Conte, Lenz, & Hollenbaugh, 2016; Lenz, Del Conte, Hollenbaugh, & Callendar, 2017) and PE (Beidel, Frueh, Neer, & Lejuez, 2017; Blount, Cigrang, Foa, Ford, & Peterson, 2014) have been integrated into IOP and PHP programs with effective results. In fact, delivering integrated PTSD treatment in an intensive setting appears to be an emerging trend. Recently, Meyers et al. (2017) described a 12-week DBT IOP (Intensive Outpatient Program) for non-ED veterans that included PE and found significant decreases in PTSD by the end of treatment. This is in line with recent research showing that "massed" PTSD treatment (i.e., treatment delivered more frequently in a shorter period) is an effective alternative to a traditional treatment course (Foa et al., 2018).

Another interesting question is whether components and principles of the DBT PE protocol (i.e., readiness criteria, review of higher treatment targets) could be applied to other PTSD treatments. The current PTSD literature indicates there is little to no difference in treatment outcome among the EBTs for PTSD. As noted previously, PE was chosen because exposure work is consistent with DBT, but there is no empirical data on whether DBT PE principles could be used with CPT or eye movement desensitization and reprocessing, for example.

Vignette

The following is an example of how DBT PE principles were applied in treating a patient in an ED PHP. Chloe was a 19-year-old Caucasian female who sought ED treatment at the request of her school. She reported a history of self-harm (hitting herself) starting at age 7, binge eating from ages 13 to 15, and since the age of 16, she had engaged in regular restriction, vomiting, and overexercise. Her BMI at admission was 17.4, and she was diagnosed with AN-BP. Chloe had prior ED treatment in which she restored weight, but she resumed behaviors and was back to a low weight a few months after discharge. At the onset of treatment, she reported a history of trauma that she began discussing for the first time 2 months prior. She disclosed that between the ages of 7 and 13, she was sexually, physically, and emotionally abused by her grandfather.

Although she was anxious about starting trauma treatment, Chloe was highly motivated to experience a decrease in PTSD symptoms (specifically, nightmares, hypervigilance, fear of men, and pervasive negative beliefs about herself and the world). Chloe and her therapist discussed where PTSD fell in her treatment hierarchy. Self-injurious behavior was the highest target, followed by restricting, purging, and overexercise. Chloe expressed a willingness to drastically reduce ED behaviors and stop self-harm immediately in order to work toward being ready for PTSD treatment. In the meantime, her therapist consulted with the treatment team about the DBT PE readiness criterion of "no life-threatening behaviors for at least 2 months." This was problematic because the average length of stay in treatment was 3 months (if 2 months were required, many patients in the program would not be able to start and complete trauma treatment). Her treatment team decided that because of the intensive treatment setting (i.e., PHP), 2 weeks of no self-harm seemed reasonable.

Chloe was presented with the option of PE or CPT, and she chose CPT. When all readiness criteria were met, she began weekly CPT with her therapist. She had no problems with CPT session attendance because she was already coming to the program every day as a patient of the ED PHP. Chloe's scores on the PTSD Checklist for DSM-5 (PCL-5; Weathers et al., 2013) increased by about 5–8 points during the first four sessions of CPT, suggesting a slight increase in PTSD symptoms. This increase was not considered problematic. Given that Chloe was no longer avoiding the trauma, she had more re-experiencing symptoms and more negative beliefs about herself and the world. In Session 5, her scores went down and continued to drop over time. She did not self-harm during the course of trauma treatment, and when she completed CPT, she declared that self-harming no longer "made sense" to her because she did not deserve to feel pain or be punished. Furthermore, her ED behaviors were almost nonexistent. She purged once through the course of CPT, she rarely restricted her food intake, and she was able to engage in healthy (moderate) exercise.

Strengths and Weaknesses/Limitations

Stage-based treatment may be an appealing approach to treating trauma in some ED-PTSD individuals. Teaching patients skills to regulate their emotions and tolerate distress may help reduce maladaptive behaviors during trauma treatment and therefore enhance treatment effectiveness. Additionally, it may provide reassurance to the therapist (and patient) about whether it is appropriate to start trauma treatment. This is beneficial in and of itself, and it also could give more reluctant therapists comfort or confidence in offering trauma treatment to their ED patients.

The DBT PE protocol is a particularly valuable stage-based treatment that may be well-suited to ED populations. Although no studies have been conducted on the DBT PE protocol in ED populations, there is little reason to believe it would not be effective. There have also been no studies on the use of DBT PE principles with other PTSD treatments. These are two areas of investigation that are much needed.

Integrating Trauma-Focused CBT and Family-Based Treatment for EDs

Background and Research

Psychological Trauma and ED Behaviors in Children and Adolescence

As has been highlighted earlier in this chapter, the empirical support for an association between experiences of trauma and ED behavior is strong and consistently reported (Molendijk et al., 2017). Furthermore, there is evidence that supports childhood trauma as a risk factor for ED behavior in younger individuals, ranging in age from 10 to 15 years old (Brewerton, 2002; 2007; Wonderlich et al., 2001). Consequently, it is likely that clinicians will encounter adolescent ED patients who have a significant trauma history resulting in a complex presentation of the ED, with features of PTSD. As trauma focused cognitive behavior therapy (TF-CBT) and family-based treatment (FBT) are the top treatment approaches for child and adolescent PTSD and ED, respectively, an integrated approach of these two treatments seems highly valuable. In this section, we will present integrated TF-CBT and FBT treatment and discuss considerations relevant for clinical practice.

Trauma-Focused Cognitive Behavior Therapy

TF-CBT is a family-focused treatment in which parents or caregivers participate with their traumatized child in a series of specific treatment components, which are delivered over several phases for a total of 12 sessions (Cohen, Mannarino, & Deblinger, 2006). The initial phase focuses on child and parent skill acquisition and stabilization. The middle phase of treatment focuses on the creation of a trauma narrative and processing of distressing or avoided memories and emotions with the child followed by conjoint sessions with the parents. The final phase focuses on integration and consolidation with an emphasis on reducing continued fears or avoidance through *in vivo* exposure as well as promotion of safety planning for the child.

FBT for AN and BN

One of the most effective treatments for adolescent EDs is FBT which was originally developed for the treatment of AN, and then later applied to adolescent BN (Lock and LeGrange, 2019). Traditional FBT is delivered in approximately 20 sessions that take place over the course of a year. FBT for AN is a behavioral treatment which targets family-based reactions to ED symptoms, such as food avoidance and weight loss. For example, in the treatment of AN, many of the ED behaviors are addressed through the inclusion of a family meal which can be conducted in an outpatient setting or possibly at the family home. During the meal, the therapist observes and coaches the parents in how to be consistent and successful in refeeding their child. As the child makes progress in terms of their caloric intake and weight gain, the treatment begins to broaden the target and promote a range of age appropriate activities while continuing to monitor eating behaviors for the adolescent. During this second phase, the child will take increasing amounts of control over their eating. Finally, in the last phase of the treatment, the family processes the impact of the AN on their lives and anticipates future struggles and conflicts that may involve eating or other problematic issues for the family.

Empirical Support

Currently, there is no empirical evidence regarding an integration of FBT and TF-CBT. However, each of these treatments has significant empirical support in terms of efficacy. For example, empirical support for FBT is robust, with RCTs completed in three different countries. Six of these studies focus on adolescents with AN and two on adolescents with BN. In AN, the remission rate for FBT averages approximately 38% and nearly three quarters of adolescents show significant improvements in weight and eating related psychopathology. For adolescents with BN, approximately 40% of the participants are abstinent from binge eating and purging for 1 month after treatment (Lock and LeGrange, 2019). Similarly, TF-CBT has been evaluated in 15 RCTs with a variety of different comparison conditions. These studies have included children from 3 to 18 years of age with a wide array of traumas experienced. In all of these studies, TF-CBT has been shown to be highly effective and superior to the comparison condition in terms of improving PTSD symptoms, as well as comorbid features such as depression, anxiety, and other behavioral problems (Cohen & Mannarino, 2015). In spite of the empirical support for each of these treatments, there is no protocol that integrates these treatments for traumatized, eating disordered youth, much less one that has been tested with rigorous empirical methods.

Levels of Care and Clinical Considerations in the Treatment of ED Adolescent with a Psychological Trauma History

TF-CBT and FBT are both typically delivered in an outpatient setting. Given there are no organized trials of an integrated approach, the most appropriate setting for such treatment is unknown. An integrated approach could feasibly be utilized in a higher level of care environment, particularly residential settings, if parents were able to be reliably included in sessions and a sufficient amount of time was available for the child and family to complete the treatment in the higher level of care. Otherwise, these treatments, alone or in combination, are likely to be effectively delivered in an outpatient setting.

Regardless of treatment setting, there is some reason to believe that clinicians may struggle with the integration of FBT and TF-CBT, particularly ED clinicians who are attempting to incorporate trauma-related treatment. In a recent review, McTavish et al. (2017) report that identifying child abuse is a significant challenge for professionals treating a variety of different forms of psychopathology, including EDs. They note that it may be difficult for practitioners to disentangle the symptoms of child abuse and associated PTSD from other forms of psychopathology that they are treating, which may in fact include EDs. Kimber et al. (2019) noted that the FBT manuals for AN and BN do not include any guidance on strategies for identifying or responding to child maltreatment when delivering FBT. In an effort to further understand this issue, the authors conducted an interview of FBT providers to clarify their experience with child maltreatment in the context of FBT. Interestingly, approximately two thirds of the respondents reported that they rarely see child abuse in the families with whom they work. Practitioners in the survey reported uncertainty about whether or not they would continue delivering FBT if trauma had been identified in their practice. They suggested that their decision whether or not to continue with FBT would depend on the nature and severity of the abuse and whether or not they perceived the abuse would interfere with the explicit ED treatment goals.

Although the study by Kimber et al. (2019) highlights some of the hesitations that ED clinicians have in addressing trauma in youth, we believe that such integration is logical and very possibly helpful for patients. We would offer the following thoughts to facilitate such clinically informed efforts for the traumatized ED youth: (1) It is important to consider whether one therapist will provide the comprehensive intervention or if separate ED experts and trauma experts will collaborate to provide concurrent, complementary interventions. As mentioned previously, there is no empirical evidence to guide this decision but for a variety of reasons, it would be most seamless to have one clinician involved as long as he or she has the appropriate training and consultation for both treatment modalities. In this case, the intervention would be sequential and follow the typical order of introduction of the TF-CBT PRACTICE components. PRACTICE is an acronym that denotes the typical therapeutic elements of TF-CBT, including psychoeducation and parenting skills, relaxation, affective expression and regulation, cognitive coping, trauma narrative development and processing, *in vivo* gradual exposure, conjoint parent–child sessions, and enhancing safety (Cohen et al., 2006). Weight restoration might be conceptualized as falling into the "enhancing safety component" of TF-CBT. (2) There are several similarities between these treatments that may facilitate integration. For example, both FBT and TF-CBT place a strong emphasis on the important role that caregivers can play in helping youth overcome symptoms, with parenting as a primary means of delivering the behavioral intervention early in the treatment. (3) Also, the two interventions include the promotion of early parental efficacy for caregivers and may facilitate their engagement in the treatment; this is a strength-based approach where the clinician is the expert in the treatment for ED or PTSD, but the caregiver is the expert for their child. (4) Both treatments address parental thoughts of shame/blame or other problematic cognitions, and a strong emphasis is placed on psychoeducation, alternative coping strategies and cognitive coping in both treatments. (5) Most notably, both interventions have a primary, ongoing emphasis on exposure to feared stimuli as an agent of change, and clinicians delivering either intervention should be experienced with this modality.

At the same time, there are some issues that need to be carefully considered when undertaking a comprehensive approach to TF-CBT and FBT for adolescent ED. For example, extra time may be needed for the screening and assessment of both PTSD and ED symptoms at intake with appropriate trauma informed feedback to follow. Also, it is important to note that TF-CBT is designed for nonoffending caregivers. For example, in the case of domestic violence, it would be imperative to evaluate whether or not the parent who displayed violence has initiated treatment to address this issue and is motived to change his or her patterns of behavior before involving them in either intervention. Knowledge of this past violent behavior should also be considered in terms of the appropriate balance of parental control and/or youth collaboration in the treatment plan to address ED behavior. Additional issues to consider include the possibility that the length of trauma-focused treatment will likely be extended due to the initial and sometimes ongoing need to focus on ED behaviors and/or weight restoration. A dietitian specifically trained to treat ED may help limit the total number of sessions with the mental health provider. Finally, time will also be required for case staffing and communication if two different therapists are providing separate but concurrent treatment of the ED and PTSD.

Vignette

Shawna was a 16-year-old female who was referred to a children's advocacy center for possible child abuse. Shawna had lived with her mother and stepfather and was attending her sophomore year of high school. She had a younger sister who was 11 years old. After evaluations by child protective services and the children's advocacy center, it was determined that Shawna had been neglected and physically and emotionally abused over the course of many years, primarily by her stepfather, but also her mother. She was placed with a foster family and over the next 6 months was noted to have lost a significant amount of weight, which prompted a referral to a local ED center. She was evaluated by a psychologist, dietician, and primary care provider and diagnosed with moderate AN with comorbid depression. She immediately began FBT with a psychologist and her foster parents were scheduled to attend all sessions.

At the feedback session, psychoeducation that included focused on ED and trauma symptoms was discussed. Shawna and her foster mother were provided with psychoeducation about the important role that caregivers can play in helping youth normalize eating and restore weight. Additionally, a trauma informed approach was used to discuss diagnostic impressions in order to promote an understanding of the "big picture" and how Shawna's experience of chronic abuse and neglect impacted her maladaptive attempts to cope with negative emotion through food restriction. Due to the safety concerns about her significant weight loss, initial sessions were focused on guiding foster parents on how they could monitor eating behaviors and incorporate energy dense foods. Given trust issues, this was done collaboratively, with Shawna meeting individually with the psychologist for a short period of time after the weigh in and at least one foster parent joining her for the remainder of the session. Shawna was initially reluctant to let her guard down and preferred to discuss her symptoms while alone with the psychologist. However, with gradual exposure to nutrition and strength-based discussions with her foster parents, she began to engage more openly and share her thoughts and feelings.

Over the course of 3 months of weekly family sessions, Shawna was able to restore most of her weight with improved eating patterns, although she continued to avoid eating a few foods that she felt were unhealthy and feared would lead to significant weight gain. At this point, the "big picture" was again discussed with a mutual agreement among all parties to continue to proceed with the remainder of the first phase of TF-CBT components. For Shawna, this included a weigh-in and brief discussion of goals to incorporate avoided foods, with the majority of the session focused on a specific CBT component. Shawna was seen individually during the first half of the session and a parallel process was used when meeting with foster parents individually during the second half of the appointment. Shawna was able to successfully create and share her trauma narrative with her foster parents, who responded supportively. Her desire to restrict food intake continued to decrease throughout the intervention, with Shawna taking on more independence for her eating behaviors. After approximately ten sessions, she "graduated" from TF-CBT. Due to the prospect of reunifying with her biological mother, she returned to therapy with her previous counselor for ongoing support and a specific intervention was developed to address the reunification process. The counselor maintained periodic contact with the TF-CBT team during the reunification.

Strengths and Limitations

FBT is an EBT for adolescents with AN and BN, and TF-CBT is an EBT for traumatized youth with posttraumatic stress symptoms. Clinicians delivering

FBT are likely to encounter adolescents with trauma-related symptoms, and currently FBT does not explicitly address how to manage such psychopathology. Consequently, clinicians may not have clear guidance about how to address trauma-related symptoms when providing FBT to patients. There is a need for clinical protocols that integrate FBT and TF-CBT for this population. Until such guidance is available, clinicians may need to use clinical judgement to modify FBT to address trauma-related symptoms in treatment. Fortunately, both treatments place a strong emphasis on family involvement and basic principles of gradual exposure to feared stimuli. Consequently, clinically meaningful integration seems possible and potentially quite useful.

Discussion

This chapter has presented an overview of potential integrated treatment strategies for patients with ED-PTSD, who are often severely traumatized, exhibit severe symptoms, have more comorbidities, and who are more likely to need higher levels of care due to treatment refractoriness (Brewerton, 2018; Brewerton et al., 2019; Chou, 2012; Molendijk et al., 2017). Some clinicians may make a presumptive diagnosis of complex PTSD (C-PTSD) in such patients. C-PTSD is a debatable diagnostic construct that encompasses more far-reaching and severe clinical characteristics in individuals with multiple traumas and/or trauma types usually occurring across childhood and adulthood. These characteristics typically include impairment of affect regulation, self-injurious behaviors (including ED behaviors), alcohol–drug abuse, amnesia/dissociation, somatization, alterations of self, distorted relations with others, and loss of sustaining beliefs (Courtois & Ford, 2009; Courtois, Ford, & Briere, 2015; Cloitre et al., 2011; Luxenberg, Spinazzola, & van der Kolk, 2001; Van der Kolk, 2002). One of the existing limitations in regards to diagnosing C-PTSD is the lack of a universally accepted measure of C-PTSD (Karatzias et al., 2016). However, it is expected to appear as a new diagnosis in ICD-11 (Ben-Ezra et al., 2018; Bottche et al., 2018; Brewin et al., 2017; Dokkedah, Oboke, Ovuga, & Elklit, 2015; Hyland et al., 2017; Sachser, Keller, & Goldbeck, 2017). It is notable in this discussion that EBTs used in the treatment of PTSD have also been reported to be beneficial for presumptive C-PTSD (Bongaerts, Van Minnen, & de Jongh, 2017; Hendriks et al., 2017; Resick, Nishith, & Griffin, 2003).

Although much remains to be learned in dealing with the complexities of ED-PTSD, experience with integrated treatments to date suggests that CPT or other EBTs for PTSD ideally be initiated once the individual has undergone a period of nutritional stabilization, established a more regular eating pattern, and experienced a significant reduction in any binge eating and/or purging symptoms (Brewerton, 2004; Trim et al., 2017). However, it should be noted that the majority of research on evidence-based PTSD treatments did not utilize a stage-based model, which are not necessarily required for effective PTSD treatment. De Johng et al. (2016) issued a statement paper arguing against the need for stage-based treatment. They cautioned that stage-based treatment may fragilize patients, and that it often delays PTSD treatment (sometimes resulting in the patient not receiving treatment). However, this has been challenged (Cloitre, 2016), and none of these authors have specifically addressed the ED-PTSD population. As noted by De Jongh et al. (2016), future research is needed to directly compare standard PTSD treatment with stage-based PTSD treatment. Nevertheless, the guidelines for C-PTSD that emphasize a stage-based treatment may be well suited to ED populations, especially those with dissociative symptoms (Brewerton, 2004; Cloitre et al., 2011; 2012; Herman, 1992; Trim et al., 2017). In addition, the International Society for Traumatic Stress Studies (ISTSS) guidelines state that there is some (albeit limited) data indicating that sequential, phase-based treatments can provide superior outcomes in those with C-PTSD (Cloitre, 2016). This begins with a thorough assessment, discussion of the adaptive links involved in ED-PTSD, establishment of safety and stability (including nutritional rehabilitation), and then proceeding to the trauma work proper when the patient is motivated and ready (Brewerton, 2004; Trim et al., 2017). The adoption of rational, individualized treatment plans that are tailored to the person's unique developmental and psychopathological features is essential for optimizing the successful treatment outcome of traumatized ED patients with comorbidity. Such an approach is in keeping with the evolution of personalized medicine, psychiatry, and psychology (Cloitre, 2015; Institute of Medicine, 2011; Ozomaro, Nemeroff, & Wahlestedt, 2013; Persons, 2008).

References

Afifi, T. O., Sareen, J., Fortier, J., Taillieu, T., Turner, S., Cheung, K., & Henriksen, C. A. (2017). Child maltreatment and eating disorders among men and women in adulthood: Results from a nationally representative United States sample. *The International Journal of Eating Disorders, 50*(11), 1281–1296. doi:10.1002/eat.22783.

Beidel, D. C., Frueh, B. C., Neer, S. M., & Lejuez, C. W. (2017). The efficacy of trauma management therapy: A controlled pilot investigation of a three-week intensive outpatient program for combat-related PTSD. *Journal of Anxiety Disorders, 50*, 23–32. doi:10.1016/j.janxdis.2017.05.001.

Ben-Ezra, M., Karatzias, T., Hyland, P., Brewin, C. R., Cloitre, M., Bisson, J. I., ..., Shevlin, M. (2018). Posttraumatic stress disorder (PTSD) and complex PTSD (CPTSD) as per ICD-11 proposals: A population study in Israel. *Depression and Anxiety, 35*(3)264–274 doi:10.1002/da.22723.

Ben-Porath, D. D., Wisniewski, L., & Warren, M. (2009). Differential treatment response for eating disordered patients with and without a comorbid borderline personality diagnosis using a dialectical behavior therapy (DBT)-informed approach. *Eating Disorders, 17*(3), 225–241. doi:10.1080/10640260902848576.

Blount, T. H., Cigrang, J. A., Foa, E. B., Ford, H. L., & Peterson, A. L. (2014). Intensive outpatient prolonged exposure for combat-related PTSD: A case study. *Cognitive and Behavioral Practice, 21*(1), 89–96. doi:10.1016/j.cbpra.2013.05.004.

Bongaerts, H., Van Minnen, A., & de Jongh, A. (2017). Intensive EMDR to treat patients with complex posttraumatic stress disorder: A case series. *Journal of EMDR Practice and Research, 11*(2), 84–95. doi:10.1891/1933-3196.11.2.84.

Bottche, M., Ehring, T., Kruger-Gottschalk, A., Rau, H., Schafer, I., Schellong, J., ..., Knaevelsrud, C. (2018). Testing the ICD-11 proposal for complex PTSD in trauma-exposed adults: Factor structure and symptom profiles. *European Journal of Psychotraumatology, 9*(1), 1512264. doi:10.1080/20008198.2018.1512264.

Brewerton, T. D. (2002). Bulimia in children and adolescents. *Child and Adolescent Psychiatry Clinics of North America, 11*(2), 237–256, viii.

Brewerton, T. D. (2004). Eating disorders, victimization, and comorbidity: Principles of treatment. In T. D. Brewerton (Ed.), *Clinical handbook of eating disorders: An integrated approach* (pp. 509–545). New York, NY: Marcel Decker.

Brewerton, T. D. (2007). Eating disorders, trauma, and comorbidity: Focus on PTSD. *Eating Disorders, 15*(4), 285–304. doi:10.1080/10640260701454311.

Brewerton, T. D. (2015). Stress, trauma, and adversity as risk factors in the development of eating disorders. In L. Smolak & M. Levine (Eds.), *Wiley handbook of eating disorders* (pp. 445–460). New York, NY: Guilford.

Brewerton, T. D. (2017). Food addiction as a proxy for eating disorder and obesity severity, trauma history, PTSD symptoms, and comorbidity. *Eating and Weight Disorders, 22*(2), 241–247. doi:10.1007/s40519-016-0355-8.

Brewerton, T. D. (2018). An overview of trauma-informed care and practice for eating disorders. *Journal of Aggression, Maltreatment & Trauma, 28*(4), 445–462. doi:10.1080/10926771.2018.1532940.

Brewerton, T. D., Alexander, J., & Schaefer, J. (2019). Trauma-informed care and practice for eating disorders: Personal and professional perspectives of lived experiences. *Eating and Weight Disorders, 24*(2), 329–338. doi:10.1007/s40519-018-0628-5.

Brewerton, T. D., Cotton, B. D., & Kilpatrick, D. G. (2018). Sensation seeking, binge-type eating disorders, victimization, and PTSD in the National Women's study. *Eating Behaviors, 30*, 120–124. doi:10.1016/j.eatbeh.2018.07.001.

Brewerton, T. D., Dansky, B. S., Kilpatrick, D. G., & O'Neil, P. M. (1999). Bulimia nervosa, PTSD, and forgetting: Results from the National Women's Study. In L. M. Williams & V. L. Banyard (Eds.), *Trauma and memory* (pp. 127–138). Durham: Sage.

Brewerton, T. D., & Dennis, A. B. (2015). Perpetuating factors in severe and enduring anorexia nervosa. In S. Touyz, P. Hay, D. Le Grange, & J. H. Lacey (Eds.), *Managing severe and enduring anorexia nervosa: A clinician's handbook*. New York, NY: Routledge.

Brewerton, T. D., McShane, M., Genet, J., Gavidia, I., Suro, G., Coffin, M., & Bunnell, D. (2019). *Assessment and treatment results using an integrated approach with cognitive processing therapy for eating disorders and PTSD in a residential treatment center*. Paper presented at the Eating Disorders Research Society, Chicago, IL.

Brewin, C. R., Cloitre, M., Hyland, P., Shevlin, M., Maercker, A., Bryant, R. A., ..., Reed, G. M. (2017). A review of current evidence regarding the ICD-11 proposals for diagnosing PTSD and complex PTSD. *Clinical Psychology Review, 58*. doi:1–1510.1016/j.cpr.2017.09.001.

Bunnell, D., Coffin, M. M., & Brewerton, T. D. (2018). *Decreasing avoidance: Integrating focused treatment for PTSD into treatment of eating disorders in higher levels of care*. Paper presented at the International Conference on Eating Disorders, Chicago, IL.

Carter, J. C., Bewell, C., Blackmore, E., & Woodside, D. B. (2006). The impact of childhood sexual abuse in anorexia nervosa. *Child Abuse and Neglect, 30*(3), 257–269. doi:10.1016/j.chiabu.2005.09.004.

Castellini, G., Lelli, L., Cassioli, E., Ciampi, E., Zamponi, F., Campone, B., ..., Ricca, V. (2018). Different outcomes, psychopathological features, and comorbidities in patients with eating disorders reporting childhood abuse: A 3-year follow-up study. *European Eating Disorders Review: The Journal of the Eating Disorders Association*, *26*(3), 217–229. doi:10.1002/erv.2586.

Chou, K. L. (2012). Childhood sexual abuse and psychiatric disorders in middle-aged and older adults: Evidence from the 2007 Adult Psychiatric Morbidity Survey. *Journal of Clinical Psychiatry*, *73*(11), e1365–e1371. doi:10.4088/JCP.12m07946.

Cloitre, M. (2015). The "one size fits all" approach to trauma treatment: Should we be satisfied? *European Journal of Psychotraumatology*, *6*, 27344. doi:10.3402/ejpt.v6.27344.

Cloitre, M. (2016). Commentary on De Jongh et al. (2016) critique of ISTSS complex PTSD guidelines: Finding the way forward. *Depression and Anxiety*, *33*(5), 355–366. doi:10.1002/da.22493.

Cloitre, M., Cohen, L. R., & Koenen, K. C. (2006). *Treating survivors of childhood abuse: Psychotherapy for the interrupted life*. New York, NY: Guilford Press.

Cloitre, M., Courtois, C. A., Charuvastra, A., Carapezza, R., Stolbach, B. C., & Green, B. L. (2011). Treatment of complex PTSD: Results of the ISTSS expert clinician survey on best practices. *Journal of Traumatic Stress*, *24*(6), 615–627. doi:10.1002/jts.20697.

Cloitre, M., Petkova, E., Wang, J., & Lu Lassell, F. (2012). An examination of the influence of a sequential treatment on the course and impact of dissociation among women with PTSD related to childhood abuse. *Depression and Anxiety*, *29*(8), 709–717. doi:10.1002/da.21920.

Cloitre, M., Stovall-McClough, K. C., Nooner, K., Zorbas, P., Cherry, S., Jackson, C. L., ..., Petkova, E. (2010). Treatment for PTSD related to childhood abuse: A randomized controlled trial. *American Journal of Psychiatry*, *167*(8), 915–924. doi:10.1176/appi.ajp.2010.09081247.

Cohen, J. A., & Mannarino, A. P. (2015). Trauma-focused cognitive behavior therapy for traumatized children and families. *Child and Adolescent Psychiatric Clinics of North America*, *24*(3), 557–570. doi:10.1016/j.chc.2015.02.005.

Cohen, J. A., Mannarino, A. P., & Deblinger, E. (2006). *Treating trauma and traumatic grief in children and adolescents*. New York, NY: Guilford Press.

Courtois, C. A., & Ford, J. D. (2009). *Treating complex traumatic stress disorders: An evidence-based guide*. New York. Guilford Press.

Courtois, C. A., Ford, J. D., & Briere, J. (2015). *Treatment of complex trauma: A sequenced, relationship-based approach*. New York. Guilford Publications.

Dansky, B. S., Brewerton, T. D., & Kilpatrick, D. G. (2000). Comorbidity of bulimia nervosa and alcohol use disorder: Results from the National Women's Study. *International Journal of Eating Disorders*, *27*, 180–190.

Dansky, B. S., Brewerton, T. D., O'Neil, P. M., & Kilpatrick, D. G. (1997). The National Womens Study: Relationship of victimization and posttraumatic stress disorder to bulimia nervosa. *International Journal of Eating Disorders*, *21*, 213–228.

De Jongh, A., Resick, P. A., Zoellner, L. A., van Minnen, A., Lee, C. W., Monson, C. M., ..., Bicanic, I. A. (2016). Critical analysis of the current treatment guidelines for complex PTSD in adults. *Depression and Anxiety*, *33*(5), 359–369. doi:10.1002/da.22469.

Del Conte, G., Lenz, A. S., & Hollenbaugh, K. M. (2016). A pilot evaluation of dialectical behavior therapy for adolescents within a partial hospitalization treatment milieu. *Journal of Child and Adolescent Counseling*, *2*(1), 16–32. doi:10.1080/23727810.2015.1134008.

Demitrack, M. A., Putnam, F. W., Brewerton, T. D., Brandt, H. A., & Gold, P. W. (1990). Relation of clinical variables to dissociative phenomena in eating disorders. *American Journal of Psychiatry, 147*(9), 1184–1188. doi:10.1176/ajp.147.9.1184.

Dokkedah, S., Oboke, H., Ovuga, E., & Elklit, A. (2015). ICD-11 trauma questionnaires for PTSD and complex PTSD: Validation among civilians and former abducted children in Northern Uganda. *Journal of Psychiatry, 18*(6). doi:10.4172/2378-5756.1000335.

Fairburn, C. G., Cooper, Z., Shafran, R., Bohn, K., Hawker, D. M., Murphy, R., & Straebler, S. (2008). Enhanced cognitive behavior therapy for eating disorders: The core protocol. In C. G. Fairburn (Ed.), *Cognitive behavior therapy and eating disorders* (pp. 47–193). New York, NY: Guilford Press.

Fassino, S., Piero, A., Tomba, E., & Abbate-Daga, G. (2009). Factors associated with dropout from treatment for eating disorders: A comprehensive literature review. *BMC Psychiatry, 9*, 67. doi:10.1186/1471-244X-9-67.

Fernandez-Aranda, F., Pinheiro, A. P., Thornton, L. M., Berrettini, W. H., Crow, S., Fichter, M. M., ..., Bulik, C. M. (2008). Impulse control disorders in women with eating disorders. *Psychiatry Research, 157*(1-3), 147–157. doi:10.1016/j.psychres.2007.02.011.

Foa, E. B., McLean, C. P., Zang, Y., Rosenfield, D., Yadin, E., Yarvis, J. S., ..., for the STRONG STAR Consortium (2018). Effect of prolonged exposure therapy delivered over 2 weeks vs 8 weeks vs present-centered therapy on PTSD symptom severity in military personnel: A randomized clinical trial. *Journal of the American Medical Association, 319*(4), 354–364. doi:10.1001/jama.2017.21242.

Ford, J. D., & Kidd, P. (1998). Early childhood trauma and disorders of extreme stress as predictors of treatment outcome with chronic posttraumatic stress disorder. *Journal of Traumatic Stress, 11*(4), 743–761. doi:10.1023/A:1024497400891.

Harned, M. S. (2014). The combined treatment of PTSD with borderline personality disorder. *Current Treatment Options in Psychiatry, 1*, 335–344.

Harned, M. S., Korslund, K. E., Foa, E. B., & Linehan, M. M. (2012). Treating PTSD in suicidal and self-injuring women with borderline personality disorder: Development and preliminary evaluation of a dialectical behavior therapy prolonged exposure protocol. *Behaviour Research and Therapy, 50*(6), 381–386. doi:10.1016/j.brat.2012.02.011.

Harned, M. S., Korslund, K. E., & Linehan, M. M. (2014). A pilot randomized controlled trial of dialectical behavior therapy with and without the dialectical behavior therapy prolonged exposure protocol for suicidal and self-injuring women with borderline personality disorder and PTSD. *Behaviour Research and Therapy, 55*, 7–17. doi:10.1016/j.brat.2014.01.008.

Harned, M. S., Tkachuck, M. A., & Youngberg, K. A. (2013). Treatment preference among suicidal and self-injuring women with borderline personality disorder and PTSD. *Journal of Clinical Psychology, 69*(7), 749–761. doi:10.1002/jclp.21943.

Hendriks, L., de Kleine, R. A., Heyvaert, M., Becker, E. S., Hendriks, G.-J., & van Minnen, A. (2017). Intensive prolonged exposure treatment for adolescent complex posttraumatic stress disorder: A single-trial design. *Journal of Child Psychology and Psychiatry, 58*(11), 1229-1238. doi:10.1111/jcpp.12756.

Herman, J. L. (1992). Complex PTSD: A syndrome in survivors of prolonged and repeated trauma. *Journal of Traumatic Stress, 5*(3), 377–391.

Hoerster, K. D., Jakupcak, M., Hanson, R., McFall, M., Reiber, G., Hall, K. S., & Nelson, K. M. (2015). PTSD and depression symptoms are associated with binge eating among US Iraq and Afghanistan veterans. *Eating Behaviors, 17*, 115–118.

Hyland, P., Shevlin, M., Brewin, C. R., Cloitre, M., Downes, A. J., Jumbe, S., ..., Roberts, N. P. (2017). Validation of post-traumatic stress disorder (PTSD) and complex PTSD using the International Trauma Questionnaire. *Acta Psychiatrica Scandinavica, 136*(3), 313–322. doi:10.1111/acps.12771.

Institute of Medicine. (2011). *Toward precision medicine: Building a knowledge network for biomedical research and a new taxonomy of disease*. Washington, DC: The National Academies Press.

Karatzias, T., Shevlin, M., Fyvie, C., Hyland, P., Efthymiadou, E., Wilson, D., ..., Cloitre, M. (2016). An initial psychometric assessment of an ICD-11 based measure of PTSD and complex PTSD (ICD-TQ): Evidence of construct validity. *Journal of Anxiety Disorders, 44,* 73–79. doi:10.1016/j.janxdis.2016.10.009.

Karr, T. M., Crosby, R. D., Cao, L., Engel, S. G., Mitchell, J. E., Simonich, H., & Wonderlich, S. A. (2013). Posttraumatic stress disorder as a moderator of the association between negative affect and bulimic symptoms: An ecological momentary assessment study. *Comprehensive Psychiatry, 54*(1), 61–69. doi:10.1016/j.comppsych.2012.05.011.

Kimber, M., McTavish, J. R., Couturier, J., Le Grange, D., Lock, J., & MacMillan, H. L. (2019). Identifying and responding to child maltreatment when delivering family-based treatment – A qualitative study. *International Journal of Eating Disorders*. doi:10.1002/eat.23036.

Lenz, A. S., Del Conte, G., Hollenbaugh, K. M., & Callendar, K. (2017). Emotional regulation and interpersonal effectiveness as mechanisms of change for treatment outcomes within a DBT program for adolescents. *Counseling Outcome Research and Evaluation, 7*(2), 73–85. doi:10.1177/2150137816642439.

Leonard, S., Steiger, H., & Kao, A. (2003). Childhood and adulthood abuse in bulimic and nonbulimic women: Prevalences and psychological correlates. *The International Journal of Eating Disorders, 33*(4), 397–405. doi:10.1002/eat.10176.

Linehan, M. M. (1993). *Cognitive-behavioral treatment of borderline personality disorder*. New York, NY: Guilford Press.

Lock, J., & Le Grange, D. (2019). Family-based treatment: Where are we and where should we be going to improve recovery in child and adolescent eating disorders. *International Journal of Eating Disorders, 52*(4), 481–487. doi:10.1002/eat.22980.

Lonergan, M. (2014). Cognitive behavioral therapy for PTSD: The role of complex PTSD on treatment outcome. *Journal of Aggression, Maltreatment & Trauma, 23,* 494–512. doi:10.1080/10926771.2014.904467.

Luxenberg, T., Spinazzola, J., & van der Kolk, B. A. (2001). Complex Trauma and Disorders of Extreme Stress (DESNOS) diagnosis. Part One: Assessment. *Directions in Psychiatry, 21*(25), 373–392.

Mahon, J., Bradley, S. N., Harvey, P. K., Winston, A. P., & Palmer, R. L. (2001). Childhood trauma has dose-effect relationship with dropping out from psychotherapeutic treatment for bulimia nervosa: A replication. *The International Journal of Eating Disorders, 30*(2), 138–148. doi:10.1002/eat.1066.

McTavish, J. R., Kimber, M., Devries, K., Colombini, M., MacGregor, J. C. D., Wathen, C. N., ..., MacMillan, H. L. (2017). Mandated reporters' experiences with reporting child maltreatment: A meta-synthesis of qualitative studies. *BMJ Open, 7*(10), e013942. doi:10.1136/bmjopen-2016-013942.

Meyers, L., Voller, E. K., McCallum, E. B., Thuras, P., Shallcross, S., Velasquez, T., & Meis, L. (2017). Treating veterans with PTSD and borderline personality symptoms in a 12-week intensive outpatient setting: Findings from a pilot program. *Journal of Traumatic Stress, 30*(2), 178–181. doi:10.1002/jts.22174.

Micali, N., Martini, M. G., Thomas, J. J., Eddy, K. T., Kothari, R., Russell, E., ..., Treasure, J. (2017). Lifetime and 12-month prevalence of eating disorders amongst women in mid-life: A population-based study of diagnoses and risk factors. *BMC Medicine, 15*(1), 12. doi:10.1186/s12916-016-0766-4.

Molendijk, M. L., Hoek, H. W., Brewerton, T. D., & Elzinga, B. M. (2017). Childhood maltreatment and eating disorder pathology: A systematic review and dose-response meta-analysis. *Psychological Medicine, 47*(8), 1402–1416. doi:10.1017/S0033291716003561.

Moulton, S. J., Newman, E., Power, K., Swanson, V., & Day, K. (2015). Childhood trauma and eating psychopathology: A mediating role for dissociation and emotion dysregulation? *Child Abuse and Neglect, 39*, 167–174. doi:10.1016/j.chiabu.2014.07.003.

Nagata, T., Kiriike, N., Kawarada, Y., & Tanaka, H. (1999). History of childhood sexual or physical abuse in Japanese patients with eating disorders: Relationship with dissociation and impulsive behaviours. *Psychological Medicine, 29*(4), 935–942.

Olmsted, M. P., MacDonald, D. E., McFarlane, T., Trottier, K., & Colton, P. (2015). Predictors of rapid relapse in bulimia nervosa. *The International Journal of Eating Disorders, 48*(3), 337–340. doi:10.1002/eat.22380.

Olmsted, M. P., McFarlane, T., Trottier, K., & Rockert, W. (2013). Efficacy and intensity of day hospital treatment for eating disorders. *Psychotherapy Research: Journal of the Society for Psychotherapy Research, 23*(3), 277–286. doi:10.1080/10503307.2012.721937.

Ozomaro, U., Nemeroff, C. B., & Wahlestedt, C. (2013). Personalized medicine and psychiatry: Dream or reality? *Psychiatryic Times, 30*(10), 1–3.

Palmisano, G. L., Innamorati, M., Susca, G., Traetta, D., Sarracino, D., & Vanderlinden, J. (2018). Childhood traumatic experiences and dissociative phenomena in eating disorders: Level and association with the severity of binge eating symptoms. *Journal of Trauma & Dissociation: The Official Journal of the International Society for the Study of Dissociation (ISSD), 19*(1), 88–107. doi:10.1080/15299732.2017.1304490.

Persons, J. B. (2008). *The case formulation approach to cognitive-behavior therapy*. New York, NY: Guilford Press.

Resick, P. A., Galovski, T. E., Uhlmansiek, M. O., Scher, C. D., Clum, G. A., & Young-Xu, Y. (2008). A randomized clinical trial to dismantle components of cognitive processing therapy for posttraumatic stress disorder in female victims of interpersonal violence. *Journal of Consulting and Clinical Psychology, 76*(2), 243–258. doi:10.1037/0022-006X.76.2.243.

Resick, P. A., Monson, C. M., & Chard, K. M. (2014). *Cognitive processing therapy: Veteran/military version: Therapist's manual*. Washington, DC: Department of Veterans Affairs.

Resick, P. A., Monson, C. M., & Chard, K. M. (2017). *Cognitive processing therapy for PTSD: A comprehensive manual*. New York, NY: The Guilford Press.

Resick, P. A., Nishith, P., & Griffin, M. G. (2003). How well does cognitive-behavioral therapy treat symptoms of complex PTSD? An examination of child sexual abuse survivors within a clinical trial. *CNS Spectrums, 8*(5), 340–355.

Resick, P. A., Suvak, M. K., Johnides, B. D., Mitchell, K. S., & Iverson, K. M. (2012). The impact of dissociation on PTSD treatment with cognitive processing therapy. *Depression and Anxiety, 29*(8), 718–730. doi:10.1002/da.21938.

Resick, P. A., Suvak, M. K., & Wells, S. Y. (2014). The impact of childhood abuse among women with assault-related PTSD receiving short-term cognitive-behavioral therapy. *Journal of Traumatic Stress, 27*(5), 558–567. doi:10.1002/jts.21951.

Sachser, C., Keller, F., & Goldbeck, L. (2017). Complex PTSD as proposed for ICD-11: Validation of a new disorder in children and adolescents and their response to trauma-focused cognitive behavioral therapy. *Journal of Child Psychology and Psychiatry and Allied Disciplines, 58*(2), 160–168. doi:10.1111/jcpp.12640.

Schoemaker, C., Smit, F., Bijl, R. V., & Vollebergh, W. A. (2002). Bulimia nervosa following psychological and multiple child abuse: Support for the self-medication hypothesis in a population-based cohort study. *The International Journal of Eating Disorders, 32*(4), 381–388. doi:10.1002/eat.10102.

Tagay, S., Schlottbohm, E., Reyes-Rodriguez, M. L., Repic, N., & Senf, W. (2014). Eating disorders, trauma, PTSD, and psychosocial resources. *Eating Disorders, 22*(1), 33–49. doi:10.1080/10640266.2014.857517.

Thornley, E., Vorstenbosch, V., & Frewen, P. (2016). Gender differences in perceived causal relations between trauma-related symptoms and eating disorders in online community and inpatient samples. *Traumatology, 22*(3), 222–232. doi:10.1037/trm0000071.

Trim, J. G., Galovski, T., Wagner, A., & Brewerton, T. D. (2017). Treating eating disorder - PTSD patients: A synthesis of the literature and new treatment directions. In L. K. Anderson, S. B. Murray, & W. H. Kaye (Eds.), *Clinical handbook of complex and atypical eating disorders* (pp. 40–59). New York, NY: Oxford University Press.

Trottier, K., & Monson, C. M. (2014). *Integrated cognitive behavioral therapy for co-occurring eating disorders and posttraumatic stress disorder*.

Trottier, K., Monson, C. M., Wonderlich, S. A., MacDonald, D. E., & Olmsted, M. P. (2016). Frontline clinicians' perspectives on and utilization of trauma-focused therapy with individuals with eating disorders. *Eating Disorders, 25*(1), 22–36. doi:10.1080/10640266.2016.1207456.

Trottier, K., Monson, C. M., Wonderlich, S. A., & Olmsted, M. P. (2017). Initial findings from project recover: Overcoming co-occurring eating disorders and posttraumatic stress disorder through integrated treatment. *Journal of Traumatic Stress, 30*(2), 173–177. doi:10.1002/jts.22176.

Van der Kolk, B. A. (2002). Assessment and treatment of complex PTSD. In R. Yehuda (Ed.), *Treating trauma survivors with PTSD* (pp. 127–156). Washington, DC: American Psychiatric Association Publishing.

Vrabel, K. R., Hoffart, A., Ro, O., Martinsen, E. W., & Rosenvinge, J. H. (2010). Co-occurrence of avoidant personality disorder and child sexual abuse predicts poor outcome in long-standing eating disorder. *Journal of Abnormal Psychology, 119*(3), 623–629. doi:10.1037/a0019857.

Watkins, L. E., Sprang, K. R., & Rothbaum, B. O. (2018). Treating PTSD: A review of evidence-based psychotherapy interventions. *Frontiers in Behavioral Neuroscience, 12*, 258. doi:10.3389/fnbeh.2018.00258.

Weathers, F. W., Blake, D. D., Schnurr, P. P., Kaloupek, D. G., Marx, B. P., & Keane, T. M. (2013). The Life Events Checklist for DSM-5 (LEC-5). Retrieved from www.ptsd.va.gov.

Wonderlich, S. A., Crosby, R. D., Mitchell, J. E., Thompson, K. M., Redlin, J., Demuth, G., ..., Haseltine, B. (2001). Eating disturbance and sexual trauma in childhood and adulthood. *The International Journal of Eating Disorders, 30*(4), 401–412.

Wonderlich, S. A., Rosenfeldt, S., Crosby, R. D., Mitchell, J. E., Engel, S. G., Smyth, J., & Miltenberger, R. (2007). The effects of childhood trauma on daily mood lability and comorbid psychopathology in bulimia nervosa. *Journal of Traumatic Stress, 20*(1), 77–87. doi:10.1002/jts.20184.

11 Treating Eating Disorders in Pregnancy and the Postpartum Period

Bronwyn Raykos and Hunna Watson

Introduction

Eating disorders primarily affect females of reproductive age. Clinicians are likely to encounter women who present for eating disorder treatment while pregnant, become pregnant during treatment, or attend treatment postpartum. We review peripartum-related (i.e., pregnancy and postpartum) guidance in evidence-based treatment manuals and share information from the clinical trenches in order to offer readers tools for patient engagement and clinical care.

Prevalence and Associated Risks

The prevalence of eating disorders in pregnant women is 2–5%: 0.1% for anorexia nervosa (AN), 0.2–0.7% for bulimia nervosa (BN), and 1.1–4.8% for binge eating disorder (BED) (dos Santos et al., 2017; Watson et al., 2013). Postpartum, the prevalence is 1% (Navarro et al., 2008). Having an eating disorder – either acute or lifetime – places women at risk of negative health outcomes. Unplanned pregnancies (Kimmel, Ferguson, Zerwas, Bulik, & Meltzer-Brody, 2016; Watson et al., 2014) and anxiety and depression during pregnancy and postpartum (dos Santos et al., 2017) are more common. Birth and obstetric complications, restricted or excessive fetal growth, and problems with child feeding and infant attachment are more likely (Watson, O'Brien, & Sadeh-Sharvit, 2018; Watson et al., 2014, 2017). Earlier breastfeeding cessation is more likely among women with eating disorders and, although the reasons are unknown, one etiology seems to be inadequate milk supply due to restrictive dieting postpartum (Kimmel et al., 2016).

Perinatal Course of Illness and Psychopathology

Pregnancy can influence illness course and features. For some women, the desire to promote fetal health during pregnancy abates eating disorders (Tierney, McGlone, & Furber, 2013). Pregnancy is a catalyst for remission or improvement in 29–78% (Kimmel et al., 2016). In pregnancy, behavioral symptoms such as purging and dietary restriction commonly decline, but cognitive symptoms stay elevated (Fogarty, Elmir, Hay, & Schmied, 2018; Mason, Cooper, & Turner, 2012;

Watson et al., 2014). Many women put their illness "on hold" when pregnant and resume the behaviors postpartum, as reminiscent of eating disorder inpatients who improve during hospitalization, but quickly deteriorate upon discharge (Mason et al., 2012). Symptom improvements in pregnancy may be short-lived in the postpartum, as fears of repercussion for the child in utero no longer abate disordered eating, weight and shape changes worsen body dissatisfaction, and the pull to return to comforting disordered eating behaviors can be overwhelming (Fogarty et al., 2018; Mason et al., 2012; Patel, Lee, Wheatcroft, Barnes, & Stein, 2005). Alternatively, some women experience diminished importance of the pursuit of weight/shape goals relative to the challenges and joys of motherhood.

For other pregnant women, weight and shape changes exacerbate the existing eating disorder or trigger a new eating disorder episode after a former recovery (Kimmel et al., 2016). Pregnancy-related eating issues – such as morning sickness, food aversions and cravings, food restrictions, hormone-regulated appetite changes, constipation and bloating, energy requirement guidelines, early fullness upon eating, heartburn, and acid reflux – can trigger disordered eating. These experiences may play into cognitive-behavioral mechanisms that maintain illness such as fear of weight gain, body dissatisfaction, perceived loss of control, restrictive eating, binge eating, and misinterpreting altered hunger and fullness sensations as weight gain.

Treatment for Pregnant and Postpartum Women

Recommendations

What are the current recommendations for treating eating disorders in pregnant and postpartum women? The simple answer is that empirically validated treatment manuals, research, and clinical practice guidelines lack guidance. A common practice is to administer evidence-based treatment as usual. We defer to clinical practice guidelines for fuller information on recommended treatments for eating disorders (Hilbert, Hoek, & Schmidt, 2017; National Institute for Health and Care Excellence, 2017). Cognitive-behavioral therapy (CBT) is the leading evidence-based treatment for adults with eating disorders (Hilbert et al., 2017; National Institute for Health and Care Excellence, 2017). There are two Food and Drug Administration (FDA)-approved medications for treating eating disorders – fluoxetine (Prozac) for BN and lisdexamfetamine (Vyvanse) for BED. Both are FDA Category C drugs for pregnant and breastfeeding women and are generally considered acceptable for use.

Cognitive-Behavioral Therapy

We focus on CBT, since it is currently the only recommended, evidence-based treatment applicable to all adult eating disorders. CBT is provided on an outpatient basis for 4–12 months (or in self-help form for less severe presentations; Fairburn, 2013). Inpatient settings can also provide CBT (Dalle Grave, Calugi,

Box 11.1 Evidence-Based Guidelines

- There is limited evidence-based guidance for treating eating disorders in pregnant and postpartum women.
- A common strategy is to follow evidence-based guidance for the general population.
- CBT is a recommended treatment for adult eating disorders.
- Two medications have been approved for treating eating disorders – an SSRI for BN and lisdexamfetamine for BED. These are FDA Category C drugs for pregnant and breastfeeding women, and are considered acceptable to use when benefits outweigh risks.

Conti, Doll, & Fairburn, 2013). CBT uses action-based, behavioral strategies to eliminate problematic eating, weight- and shape-related behaviors. Core strategies include developing a formulation, weekly weighing, daily self-monitoring of nutritional intake, eating disorder behaviors, and associated cognitions and affect, establishing regular meal patterns and normalizing the quantity and variety of nutritional intake, exposure and reduction of safety behaviors, addressing emotional triggers for disordered eating, challenging cognitions related to eating, weight, and shape and reducing overevaluation of weight, shape, and eating (Fairburn, 2008; Fairburn, Jones, Peveler, Hope, & O'connor, 1993; Fairburn et al., 1995; Waller & Raykos, 2019; Waller et al., 2007). The core pathology in the maintenance model widely accepted as underlying CBT is overevaluation of the importance of shape, weight, eating, and their control for evaluation of self-worth, which triggers vicious cycles of restricting and starvation, binge eating, and purging, and, in turn, greater focus on weight, shape, and eating (Byrne & McLean, 2002; Fairburn, Cooper, & Cooper, 1986; Fairburn, Cooper, & Shafran, 2003). The mechanisms of change in CBT are unclear due to a lack of dismantling studies. However, normalizing eating habits is important (Keys, Brožek, Henschel, Mickelsen, & Taylor, 1950; Waller, Evans, & Pugh, 2013). In the remainder of the chapter, we explore the augmentation of CBT for pregnant and postpartum women.

Augmentation of CBT for Peripartum Women

The content described in this section contains guidance on CBT augmentation and is tentative, since it is not supported by systematic evidence reviews or randomized controlled trials. No data exist on pregnant or postpartum populations (van Ravesteyn, Lambregtse-van den Berg, Hoogendijk, & Kamperman, 2017). Evidence-based CBT manuals (Fairburn, 2008; Waller, Turner, Tatham, Mountford, & Wade, 2019; Waller et al., 2007) scarcely touch on how therapeutic strategies might be adapted for women in peripartum. Yet clinicians working with patients require information and tools to apply. We augment guidance provided in CBT manuals with information from and for the "clinical trenches" based on the clinical practice of the author B.R. and her practice setting. The practice setting is a specialist, adult outpatient setting staffed by clinical psychologists where patients with a body mass index (BMI) ≥ 16 kg/m^2 receive evidence-based CBT (Fairburn, 2008; Waller et al., 2007; Waller et al., 2019). Several papers have evaluated CBT in the general population at this clinic (Byrne, Fursland, Allen, & Watson, 2011; Byrne et al., 2017). To enrich the reader's toolkit, we give a case example and clinical handouts, and cite scholarly literature to guide practice. We stress that we encourage adherence to CBT manuals as therapist drift from protocols leads to poorer patient outcomes in routine practice (Waller, 2009; Waller & Turner, 2016). Nevertheless, in clinical practice, we have found that there are certain important aspects of CBT where attention to pregnancy and postpartum issues might be a beneficial augmenting tool for a peripartum population. We detail these augmenting methods below for selected components of treatment.

Assessment

CBT Manual Guidance

There is limited guidance in CBT manuals – Waller et al. (2007) recommend assessing pregnancy-related events, including history of termination or miscarriage.

From the Clinical Trenches

There is a lack of validated instruments for peripartum women. Hence, the instruments used in non-pregnant populations are recommended, including the clinician-administered *Eating Disorder Examination* which yields Diagnostic and Statistical Manual of Mental Disorder (DSM)-based diagnoses, frequency of eating disorder behaviors, and ratings of symptom severity on Restraint, Eating Concern, Shape Concern, and Weight Concern subscales which sum to a Global score, and the self-report *Eating Disorder Examination-Questionnaire* which rates symptom severity over the previous 28 days (Cooper & Fairburn, 1987; Fairburn & Beglin, 1994; Fairburn & Beglin, 2008). The *Structured Clinical Interview for DSM* (SCID-IV) Eating Disorder module which is DSM-IV based is another option for diagnosis (First, Spitzer, Gibbon, Gibbon, & Williams, 1994). Research on DSM-5–based instruments is ongoing. The EDE has been updated to EDE-17.0D to generate DSM-5 diagnoses (freely available at https://www.credo-oxford.com/7.2.html) and there is supporting evidence for the *Eating Disorder Diagnostic Assessment for DSM-5* (Sysko et al., 2015). A clinician-administered interview for diagnosis of pica, avoidant/restrictive food intake disorder, and rumination disorder is under development (Bryant-Waugh et al., 2019).

> **Box 11.2 Assessment**
>
> - Consider using the *Eating Disorder Examination – Pregnancy Version* (EDE-PV) (Emery et al., 2017) to facilitate diagnosis and assessment.
> - Attend to whether cognitions and behaviors about eating, weight, and shape indicate pathology or pregnancy-related phenomena, and whether concerns are beyond the norm for pregnant and postpartum women.

We recommend a clinician-administered adaptation, the *Eating Disorder Examination – Pregnancy Version* (EDE-PV) (Emery, Grace, Kolko, & Levine, 2017). The core difference between the standard and pregnancy versions is that the symptom domains in the EDE-PV have probing to establish whether cognitions and behaviors are pathological or pregnancy-related. For example, dietary rules may be in effect because of pregnancy recommendations rather than eating disorder cognitions (i.e., gestational diabetes and avoidance of sweets). As other examples, some pregnant women avoid eating because eating triggers pregnancy nausea and some experience eating guilt related to the fetus's health and not for weight and shape.

If using traditional validated instruments such as the EDE, we recommend additional probing. Diagnosis is complicated by the overlap between normal pregnancy symptoms and eating disorder symptoms. A helpful practice is to assess symptoms before, during, and after pregnancy to understand the impact of peripartum on symptoms. Carefully consider whether body shape and weight concerns are out of proportion to normative responses to body weight and shape changes in pregnancy. Pregnancy (and postpartum) symptoms can look like eating disorder phenomena, for example, vomiting, eating/appetite changes, and drastic weight changes. Menstrual periods will be absent in pregnancy and in breastfeeding, so it is important to obtain history of menses prior to pregnancy. Patients commonly experience shame and guilt about their symptoms, and this may be exacerbated in peripartum women with concern for their fetus or newborn.

Sally was 13 weeks pregnant with her first baby when she attended her initial assessment. She was referred by her general practitioner who stated that Sally had become "extremely worried about her nutritional intake and weight although her weight gain (~3 kg/7 lb) was within the low normal expected range for pregnancy". During assessment, Sally was reluctant to discuss her eating disorder behaviors and became teary when asked about episodes of self-induced vomiting.

Therapist: Sally, I noticed that it is difficult for you to talk about some parts of the eating disorder like vomiting and I wonder whether you might be feeling uncomfortable when I ask you about this?

Sally:	I feel guilty. I know it is not good for the baby but I am finding it difficult to stop altogether.
Therapist:	Is stopping the vomiting something that you would most like to change in treatment?
Sally:	Yes, definitely. I want to stop vomiting and worrying about my weight all the time.
Therapist:	Well that sounds like it is one of the most important things for us to understand so that we can help you. How many times per week is that happening at the moment?... And when you do notice that happens? Has the vomiting changed since you found out you were pregnant?...

On completing the EDE interview, Sally met criteria for Other Specified Feeding or Eating Disorder. Although she had strict food rules, she was working hard to eat more regularly since she found out she was pregnant. Her BMI was 21, and she was vomiting three times per week – additional probing revealed that two episodes of vomiting were in response to pregnancy nausea and one episode was self-induced and compensatory (e.g., after breaking a dietary rule or overeating). In the past three months, Sally had engaged in objective binge eating on four occasions. Prior to pregnancy, Sally was restricting her intake to control her weight, often only eating two meals per day. She had been engaging in objective binge eating and compensatory self-induced vomiting three times per week. Sally had improved her eating behaviors significantly after learning that she was pregnant. The clinician noted that prior to pregnancy Sally met criteria for BN.

Establishing a Treating Team

CBT Manual Guidance

CBT manuals advise that women who are pregnant or breastfeeding may require more specialized interventions than CBT alone. Waller et al. (2007) suggested referral to a dietician due to the specific nutritional requirements of pregnancy and breastfeeding.

From the Clinical Trenches

The pregnant patient's obstetrician-gynecologist is ideally made aware of the patient's eating disorder status, since the potential increased risk of obstetric complications distinguishes a higher-risk pregnancy in need of closer monitoring. Inclusion of specialist team members for pregnant or postpartum women in addition to the CBT clinician differs markedly for each individual. We distinguish between patients who require a high level of specialist care, and those who require more limited specialist care.

1 Intensive specialist care: The National Institute for Health and Care Excellence guidelines (2017) advise considering more intensive care for pregnant women with current or remitted AN. Other indicators for

intensive specialist care peripartum include excessive vomiting, failure to meet expected goals of weight gain during pregnancy, or rapid weight loss postpartum. We recommend that a dietician is included as part of an intensive specialist care team and the patient is closely medically monitored. The CBT clinician should weigh the patient at each session and assess for signs of medical risk (e.g., dizziness, heart palpitations, and blood in vomit). Weekly updates to the dietician and medical team are required so that swift action can be taken in the event that the patient's health deteriorates or they are not responding to outpatient treatment. Current guidelines (e.g., Hay et al., 2014) advise that, for nonpregnant individuals, weight loss of 2 kg (4 lb) over 3 consecutive weeks of outpatient treatment is an indicator that urgent hospital admission is required. In pregnancy, the failure to gain weight may indicate need for hospital admission to ensure adequate nutrition for the patient and fetus. There are currently no medical guidelines on when to admit pregnant patients with eating disorders to hospital. Within local jurisdictions, some may exist[1]. If medical admission is required, outpatient CBT should be put on hold until the patient is medically stable and suitable for discharge back to the outpatient setting.

2   Limited specialist care: For all patients, liaising closely with obstetricians or other medical professionals (e.g., primary care practitioner) regarding the patient's medical risks and nutritional needs is important. However, for some peripartum women, only limited specialist input may be needed. A single session with a dietician may help normalize the nutritional requirements of pregnancy and/or breastfeeding, or seeing the dietician over a few sessions may help to ensure that the individual's nutrition is adequate for pregnancy and lactation. Seeking specialist input from a dietician can also be integrated as a means of gathering further evidence to test out beliefs related to eating and pregnancy.

After two sessions of CBT, Sally reported a pervasive belief that she was eating "too much for pregnancy," despite her obstetrician advising that her weight gain was "normal." She reported feeling highly anxious each time she ate, and restricting her intake in response to her anxiety. The CBT clinician asked Sally to generate some ideas about how she could test out whether or not her belief ("I am eating too much for pregnancy") was true. Sally decided to arrange an appointment with a dietician and to show the dietician 1 week of her self-monitoring. Sally predicted that the dietician would conclude that she was eating "at least 500 calories more than recommended in pregnancy." Sally rated the strength of her belief as 90%. Sally generated an alternative hypothesis that the dietician might conclude she was not eating enough and rated the strength of this belief as only 10%.

Sally returned to treatment the following week. The dietician had advised that Sally was undereating on most days and had provided a meal plan with suggestions of how she could increase her intake to meet the nutritional requirements of pregnancy. Sally expressed surprise and concluded that her original belief was not supported. The strength of this belief had reduced to 30%. She concluded that the alternative belief was supported, and although she was still not convinced this was true, she had increased her confidence in this belief to 60%. When reflecting

Box 11.3   Establishing a Treating Team

- Ideally, the obstetrician-gynecologist should be aware of the patient's eating disorder history, since the risk of obstetric and birth complications is increased.
- We recommend distinguishing whether the patient needs intensive or limited specialist care.
- Inclusion of a dietician in the treating team is a useful addition.

on what she had learned, Sally concluded, "Although I feel anxious about how much I am eating, there is no evidence that I am eating too much. Actually, I still need to eat more to meet the nutritional requirements of pregnancy." Sally planned to read over this conclusion when she was feeling anxious about eating, to sit with the anxiety until it passed, and to not adjust her eating based on her anxiety. The clinician asked if she needed to gather further information to test out this belief. Sally did not feel that she needed to return to see the dietician but was able to work with her CBT clinician to increase her intake in subsequent sessions.

Psychoeducation

CBT Manual Guidance

CBT manuals emphasize the importance of psychoeducation (Fairburn, 2008; Waller et al., 2007; Waller et al., 2019). Psychoeducation early in CBT focuses on the impact of starvation, practical information about nutritional intake (e.g., the advantages of regular eating, normalizing food intake, and nutritional needs), the ineffectiveness of extreme weight control methods (e.g., purging behaviors), and the physical and psychological consequences of disordered eating behaviors in the short and long term. Psychoeducation materials available in CBT manuals are applicable to all patients with eating disorders, including those who are pregnant or breastfeeding. The manuals do not specifically articulate how psychoeducation might be adapted for pregnant or postpartum women.

From the Clinical Trenches

We find that it is helpful to augment existing psychoeducation materials with materials that are specific to pregnancy and postpartum.

AMENORRHEA AND PREGNANCY

One of the physical health effects of eating disorders may be amenorrhea, or the loss of menstrual periods. Many patients assume that the presence of irregular

Box 11.4   Recommended Caloric Intake in Pregnancy and for Breastfeeding Women

- An additional 340–450 kcal per day is required in the second and third trimesters. Caloric intake will be higher in AN and underweight presentations to ensure adequate weight gain.
- Protein requirements are increased during pregnancy by an additional 21 g /0.7 oz per day (e.g., half a chicken breast or three serves of yoghurt).
- Getting a balance of macronutrients and taking recommended supplements (i.e., folate) is important.
- Breastfeeding at a healthy weight requires an additional 500 calories per day to support lactation. Age, BMI, activity level, and extent of breastfeeding affect individual estimates.

periods or amenorrhea means they are infertile and cannot conceive, leading to inadequate contraception use. Women with AN actually have a higher rate of unplanned pregnancies than women generally (Watson et al., 2014). Educating patients that pregnancy can occur even without menstrual periods, such as when ovulation occurs for the first time after a period of amenorrhea (when the first egg becomes fertilized), and that women who do not wish to conceive should use adequate contraception to reduce the risk of unplanned pregnancy, is important. Freely available handouts on "Eating Disorders and Pregnancy" and "Eating Disorders and Hormones" can be downloaded online (www.cci.health.wa.gov.au) and are also in Appendices A and B.

NUTRITIONAL INTAKE FOR PREGNANCY AND BREASTFEEDING

The clinician requires a basic knowledge of nutritional guidelines and recommended caloric intake for pregnant and breastfeeding women (Food Nutrition Board/Institute of Medicine, 2002). For those readers with interest – and useful for the dietician in the care team – a reading on nutritional care for women with eating disorders in pregnancy is here (Nickols-Richardson, 2018).

ACHIEVING A HEALTHY SET POINT WEIGHT

Reaching a genetically determined healthy set point weight range by normalizing eating is part of psychoeducation in CBT. Set point theory assists the clinician to set expectations for where a healthy weight range might be for the individual, based on their weight history, and to provide education about the need for 4 consecutive weeks of weighing before drawing conclusions about the trajectory of weight change or stability. The importance

Box 11.5 Recommended Weight Gain During Pregnancy

- BMI < 18.5 is 12.7–18 kg (28–40 lb)
- BMI 18.5-24.9 is 11.5–16 kg (25–35 lb)
- BMI 25-29.9 is 7–11.5 kg (15–25 lb)
- BMI over 30 is 5–9 kg (11–20 lb)

(Institute of Medicine (US) and National Research Council (US), 2009)

of providing psychoeducation on set point weight is not impacted by pregnancy. However, a notable difference is that many pregnant or breastfeeding women will not reach their set point weight within the time frame of CBT, which may range from 10 (Waller et al., 2019) to 40 sessions (Fairburn, 2008). Therefore, patients are likely to need to continue to work toward reaching their set point weight after treatment has ended. It may be tempting to continue treatment until set point weight is established; however, given the limited access to specialist eating disorder services and lack of evidence that longer dose improves CBT outcomes (Rose & Waller, 2017), we would not recommend this. Instead, reaching a healthy set point can be a focus of relapse prevention.

WEIGHT CHANGES IN PREGNANCY

The focus for pregnancy is on normalizing eating habits for pregnancy and accepting weight and shape changes rather than on reaching a healthy set point within the time constraints of CBT. Recommended weight gain during pregnancy depends on prepregnancy BMI. Expected weight gain should be informed by advice of the medical team involved in the patient's care and guidelines (Institute of Medicine (US) and National Research Council (US), 2009).

Understanding where and why weight is gained during pregnancy can help to challenge unhelpful cognitions. For instance, blood volume needs to increase to carry nutrients and oxygen to the baby and to protect the mother against excess blood loss during labor. Appendix A offers a psychoeducation handout for patients.

LAXATIVE SAFETY

Laxative misuse is common in patients. Stimulant laxatives (i.e., senna) are strongly advised against in pregnant and breastfeeding women. In the third trimester, they can stimulate uterine contractions, and they are partially absorbed by the gastrointestinal tract and can be excreted in breast milk.

Box 11.6 Psychoeducation

- Topics of suggested augmentations of psychoeducation materials:
  Adult women of reproductive age: Amenorrhoea and the probability of pregnancy.
  Peripartum women: Nutritional intake for pregnancy and breast-feeding, achieving a healthy set point weight, weight changes in pregnancy, and laxative safety.

Box 11.7 Formulation

- Case formulation is an important part of CBT. CBT manuals provide detailed guidance on formulations.
- Clinicians can link peripartum factors maintaining the eating problem into the formulation.

Case Formulation

CBT Manual Guidance

Case formulation is integral to CBT and is used to make sense of the patient's problem and to develop a treatment plan. Formulations are theoretically driven although individualized. Collaboratively making a visual diagram of factors that perpetuate the eating problem allows the patients to distance themselves from their eating disorder and to understand the relationship among symptoms. Formulation also allows the clinician to explain the rationale for CBT strategies (e.g., improving nutritional intake to reduce symptoms of starvation). CBT manuals explain how to construct a formulation, the theoretical underpinning, and contain examples of formulations (Fairburn, 2008; Waller et al., 2007).

From the Clinical Trenches

As formulations are always individualized, changes to the usual process of developing a case formulation are not necessary for peripartum. The "cognitions" to be addressed in CBT may be influenced by the peripartum phase, for example, weight gain and concern about "fatness" in pregnancy or feelings of loss of control after arrival of the newborn. The clinician should ensure that aspects of pregnancy or postpartum that maintain the eating problem are captured within the formulation, as can be seen in the example of Sally:

Therapist: Sally, what would you most like to change in treatment?
Sally: I am always so worried about my weight, I don't want to get fat.
Therapist: What do you worry about?
Sally: I am worried that I am eating too much for pregnancy and that I will gain too much weight. And I am also worried about not eating enough for my baby.
Therapist: When you worry about your eating and weight, what do you do?
Sally: I start to restrict what I am eating. I eat less than the dietician told me to eat and I avoid junk food. Also, my goal is to gain less weight than recommended for my BMI range. Later I might eat something I didn't want to eat or even binge. Then I make myself throw up and I feel guilty and worry about the baby even more.
Therapist: What happens to your worry about your eating and your weight when you eat something you didn't plan on eating or you binge?
Sally: I feel terrible, especially if I binge, and then I get even more worried about my weight. So, I try to have a healthier day the next day.
Therapist: Are there other times that you might try to restrict what you eat?
Sally: If I see the obstetrician and my weight has gone up then I freak out, I think I have gained too much weight and I want to restrict. I also freak out when I notice my clothes are getting tighter.

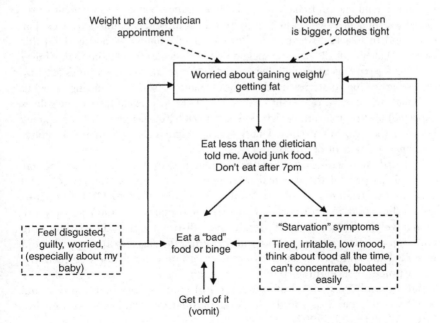

Figure 11.1 Sally's Clinical Formulation.

250 *Bronwyn Raykos and Hunna Watson*

Weekly Weighing

CBT Manual Guidance

Treatment manuals discuss weekly weighing only in the context of the general patient population, not specifically pregnant or postpartum women. We recommend following the guidance for weekly weighing. Obtaining a patient's predicted weight, weighing the patient at each session to determine actual weight, and plotting the weight on a chart that is shared and discussed openly is a non-negotiable component of CBT. Weighing is one aspect of monitoring medical risk in patients with eating disorders but is also a powerful behavioral experiment conducted with the patient each week that tests out their predictions about the impact of their eating (and changes to their eating) on their weight (Waller & Mountford, 2015; Waller et al., 2007). It is also an opportunity to provide psychoeducation about weight and weight fluctuations and other issues that maintain disordered eating or body dissatisfaction.

From the Clinical Trenches

Eating disorder cognitions related to weight are often very similar in pregnant and nonpregnant women (e.g., "my weight will increase uncontrollably if I eat regularly," "if I include an extra slice of bread I will gain 2 kg [4 lb]"). Clinicians are reminded that the actual pattern of weight change is not the key to addressing distorted cognitions. Rather, the central cognitive component of this intervention is about identifying and challenging the discrepancy between the patient's predicted weight (e.g., "I will gain 3 kg [6 lb] if I eat three meals and two snacks per day") and their actual weight (e.g., "the weight fluctuated by 500 g [1 lb] this week"). Waller et al. (2019) have suggested that clinicians should aim to maximize learning for patients by raising their anxiety prior to making predictions (e.g., by discussing eating patterns in depth immediately before predicting weight). Although the pattern of weight change will differ in pregnancy (weight gain is expected) and postpartum (weight loss is expected), challenging the discrepancy between the patient's predicted and actual weight change remains a central cognitive component of CBT.

A word of warning – pregnant women are often weighed at regular intervals as part of the medical management of their pregnancy (e.g., by general practitioners or obstetricians). This may lead to CBT clinicians concluding that it is unnecessary to weigh pregnant women as they are being weighed elsewhere. If weighing is distressing for the patient, the clinician may feel anxious about exacerbating the distress and opt to avoid this crucial component of treatment. Pregnancy does not diminish the importance of weighing patients at each session – the rationale for weighing and the process of weighing and charting predicted and actual weight is the same as for the general population (Waller & Mountford, 2015; Wallet et al., 2007).

> **Box 11.8 Weekly Weighing**
>
> - We recommend following CBT manual guidance on weekly weighing.
> - Four consecutive weeks of weighing are needed before drawing conclusions about the weight trajectory.
> - Weight gain is expected during pregnancy and weight loss is expected postpartum but the discrepancy between predicted and actual weight change remains a central cognitive target in CBT.

At 17 weeks gestation, Sally told her therapist that she had "suddenly popped out," (referring to her abdomen) and her anxiety about the number on the scale was high. She predicted that she had gained 3 kg (7 lb) "due to pregnancy" and she was 90% confident that her prediction was accurate. When weighed, Sally's weight was 1.5 kg (3 lb) higher than the previous week. The pattern of weights over the past 4 weeks indicated she had gained 0.5 kg (1 lb) per week on average. Sally was surprised and agreed that she was gaining weight within the expected range for pregnancy. She noted that the increase in her abdominal size and her tighter fitting clothing may be contributing to increased anxiety about weight gain. However, she remained anxious about weight gain ("what if I continue to eat regularly and gain 1.5 kg [3 lb] per week for the rest of the pregnancy?"). A further behavioral experiment was developed for the next 4 weeks such that Sally would continue to eat regularly and a sufficient quantity of food to see whether her predictions were accurate.

Self-Monitoring and Addressing Dietary Restriction and Dietary Restraint

CBT Manual Guidance

The manuals do not specifically address self-monitoring in the context of peripartum, yet the key principles hold. Existing manuals provide excellent guidance on using real-time self-monitoring to record the pattern and quality of nutritional intake and associated thoughts and feelings. Self-monitoring is a crucial component of CBT. Through self-monitoring, the therapist and patient can start to understand existing patterns that keep the eating disorder going and can work to increase the regularity, quantity, and variety of foods eaten to reduce eating disorder behaviors such as starvation and binge eating. Clinicians are referred to existing manuals for details on the rationale and approaches taken in CBT to address dietary restriction, dietary restraint, underweight, and other compensatory behaviors.

From the Clinical Trenches

Augmentations to CBT interventions may not be necessary for peripartum women. However, it is important to bear in mind that nutritional requirements

Box 11.9 Self-Monitoring and Addressing Dietary Restriction and Dietary Restraint

- The key principles within CBT manuals hold and can be readily applied to a postpartum population.
- Guilt and blame should not be imparted when the clinician is discussing restriction with pregnant and breastfeeding women.
- Women report being more motivated to reduce disordered eating behaviors when their baby is made 'more real' (e.g., researching fetus milestones and looking at ultrasounds).
- Breastfeeding might be an important goal for some women and can be used to help motivate good eating habits.

differ in pregnancy and postpartum (see psychoeducation). Because concern for the fetus is a strong motivator for reducing eating disorder symptoms in pregnancy, making the baby more "real" may accelerate improvements in eating habits. Qualitative research suggests that for some women, looking at ultrasound pictures and reading about fetal development encouraged them to change their behaviors during pregnancy (Mason et al., 2012; Tierney et al., 2013). Interventions should be delivered in a manner that does not exacerbate feelings of guilt or blame. Addressing restricting eating behaviors postpartum may help support breastfeeding as restricted intake might affect milk supply and contribute to the earlier discontinuation of breastfeeding seen in women with eating disorders (Watson et al., 2014). Although the evidence on discontinuation is mixed (Micali, Simonoff, & Treasure, 2009), breastfeeding might be an important goal for some women and can be used to motivate good eating habits. If a pregnant woman has made good changes to eating during pregnancy, it will be important to enquire about cognitions related to postpartum weight loss and nutrition and to address these using cognitive restructuring as part of relapse prevention. An example of how we augment existing CBT techniques for pregnancy is provided in Appendix C, in which Sally is asked to conduct a behavioral experiment to test out her fear that including bread at breakfast will exacerbate her pregnancy nausea.

Mood Intolerance and Emotional Triggers

CBT Manual Guidance

Existing manuals provide extensive clinical guidance on addressing eating disorder behaviors that are linked to events and moods, while not specifically addressing peripartum (Fairburn, 2008; Waller et al., 2007; Waller et al., 2019). Such strategies include psychoeducation about mood; self-monitoring of mood, associated

Box 11.10 Mood Intolerance and Emotional Triggers

- We have found that the content in CBT manuals is applicable to peripartum women and encourage readers to consult the manuals for detailed guidance.
- Unique contextual issues to consider include hormonal factors, peripartum anxiety and depression onset, and addressing perceptions of loss of control.

cognitions, and impact on eating disorder behaviors; urge surfing; mindful eating; developing alternative mood-modulatory strategies; binge analysis; proactive problem-solving; cognitive restructuring; and behavioral experiments to test out fears related to the patients' ability to tolerate negative feelings.

From the Clinical Trenches

Addressing mood intolerance and emotional triggers in treatment is much the same as for nonpregnant women. There are several factors one might consider when conceptualizing emotional triggers peripartum. Hormonal changes often temporarily contribute to greater instability in emotions. Postpartum anxiety and depression are more common in women who have eating disorders and screening is important (dos Santos et al., 2017). Peripartum women with eating disorders report, unsurprisingly, that this time of their lives carries a sense of loss of control, which triggers distress and attempts to reclaim control via eating disorder behaviors (Mason et al., 2012).

Overevaluation of Eating, Weight, and Shape

CBT Manual Guidance

The treatment content described in manuals is oriented toward a general population but can be readily applied to pregnant or postpartum women. A key strategy within CBT to address the overevaluation of eating, shape, and weight is the use of a self-evaluation pie chart (Fairburn, 2008; Waller et al., 2007). Patients are asked to identify aspects of their lives that influence how they judge themselves. The pie chart is used to indicate what proportion each aspect has in influencing how the patient feels about themselves and serves as a visual diagram of the degree to which overevaluation of weight, shape, and eating and their control may have become the most important aspect of self-evaluation. This allows the clinician to work with the patient using Socratic questioning to identify potential problems with this imbalance, and encourage a more balanced scheme for self-evaluation.

> **Box 11.11   Overevaluation of Eating, Weight, and Shape**
>
> - The treatment content in manuals is for a general population, but can be readily applied to pregnant or postpartum women.
> - The pie chart strategy is useful for working toward restoring balance to women's self-evaluation.
> - We suggest expanding the pie chart exercise to address the potential overevaluation of motherhood as part of relapse prevention or in the postpartum.

From the Clinical Trenches

Pregnancy and motherhood provide new avenues for self-evaluation. This can be protective as the importance of weight, shape, and eating may naturally diminish relative to the increased importance of motherhood. However, sometimes overevaluation of weight, shape, and eating may be replaced by similarly unhelpful overevaluation of motherhood, retaining an unbalanced pie chart. An unbalanced pie chart for self-evaluation will be problematic regardless of which aspect of life is driving the imbalance. We have found it helpful to expand this exercise so that patients also complete it in the context of considering motherhood. This may be completed during treatment as a relapse prevention strategy, or in the postpartum period.

Sally attended a routine follow-up appointment 10 weeks after the birth of her baby. She had been far less concerned about her weight, shape, and eating since completing treatment and was enjoying being a mother but she noticed that she was often self-critical about her role as a mother. When she was unable to pick her baby up within a few minutes of him crying, she became self-critical and concluded that she was "failing as a mom." She also compared herself negatively to other mothers, whom she perceived to be coping better than her ("they are always well groomed and they aren't having the same difficulties as me with breastfeeding," "some babies are sleeping through the night already and I am up four times"). She reported that she was so focussed on caring for her newborn that she often declined social invitations, had not exercised, and had not given herself permission to do things that she enjoyed (e.g., watching a TV show with her husband).

Therapist: Sally, when you were in treatment we talked about how shape, weight, and eating strongly influenced how you were evaluating yourself as a person. Do you remember we drew up a pie chart together?
Sally: Yes, I remember doing that.
Therapist: I wonder whether we might be able to draw up another pie chart for you that represents the things that are influencing how you feel about yourself now?
Sally: Well I guess being a good mom is probably the biggest thing that is influencing how I judge myself at the moment. I just don't want to do a bad job at that.

Therapist: What other things are influencing how you judge yourself at the moment? And what proportion of the pie chart would you give each of these aspects of your life?

Sally and the therapist draw up her pie chart.

☐ Being a good mom ☐ Friends ☐ Partner ☐ Weight/shape

Figure 11.2 Self-Evaluation Pie Chart.

Therapist: What do you notice about your pie chart?
Sally: I thought I was doing well because I haven't been worrying so much about my weight but it is still so unbalanced. I hadn't realized how much pressure I was putting on myself to be a good mom. I also haven't got many pieces in my pie chart at the moment, I have stopped doing a lot of the things that make me feel good about myself like seeing my friends. I went from being so focussed on my weight to focussing on being a good mom.
Therapist: So, what would help you feel like all your eggs aren't in the one basket now?
Sally: Well, I need to start doing some of the things that help me feel good about myself, like catching up with my friends. I saw a postnatal swimming class near my house and they have a crèche. That might be a good start.

Negative Body Image

CBT Manual Guidance

Existing manuals provide a range of techniques to address negative body image that can be applied readily to peripartum women. These include managing body checking, body avoidance, and comparison-making; discussing the functions of the body; mirror work (e.g., psychoeducation about perceptual distortions, mirror exposure); addressing misinterpretation of "feeling full" or "feeling fat" as weight gain, behavioral experiments and surveys to test out beliefs; and imagery rescripting.

From the Clinical Trenches

Existing strategies are appropriate for peripartum women; however, it can be helpful to augment these interventions by specifically focussing on pregnancy-related issues. Pregnant women who perceive weight changes as "getting fat" or "feeling fat" are likely to be more body dissatisfied, which is a trigger for eating disorder behaviors, than women who attribute weight gains to the necessary and appropriate physical demands of growing a baby (dos Santos et al., 2017). Psychoeducation and cognitive restructuring on the nature of these physical changes, recommended weight gain, and caloric intake requirements can be helpful for these patients (see psychoeducation).

Pregnancy and postpartum bring many potential triggers for negative body image and so ways of coping might need to be addressed. Others' comments about one's body, and clothes fitting tighter than prepregnancy, can be scary and difficult to tolerate. There are many unhelpful messages in the media, often by celebrities, promoting unrealistic and potentially dangerous postpartum weight loss. Setting realistic expectations about postpartum weight loss can help – that weight will normalize over time, without needing to deliberately restrict dietary intake. Unhealthy or quick-fix weight loss methods should be avoided, with a focus on allowing the body to return to its natural set point and ensuring adequate nutrition to sustain tasks such as breastfeeding. We encourage patients to abstain from dietary restriction for 12 months postpartum. Often an individual's weight/shape may differ after pregnancy and so a further goal may be on accepting such changes. Clinicians can address body image in the context of pregnancy and postpartum by normalizing body changes, proactive problem-solving to address body dissatisfaction triggers (e.g., comments from others and tight clothing) and conducting behavioral experiments and surveys that specifically address beliefs related to pregnancy body dissatisfaction. In line with existing CBT protocols, body image work should not commence until the patient has established appropriate nutritional intake and weight changes are appropriate for pregnancy. Working on body acceptance in patients who still require renourishment and weight regain is not appropriate.

Surveys

Surveys are a useful tool to address negative body image related to "mind-reading" predictions. Mind-reading predictions may be related to what other people consider to be important (e.g., "they will think I am fat rather than pregnant," "others will think I am a bad mother if I eat a high-calorie snack while pregnant"). Surveys can also address the patient's beliefs about the relationship between body weight/

Treatment in Pregnancy and Postpartum Period   257

> ## Box 11.12   Negative Body Image
>
> - The guidance in CBT manuals does not specifically address pregnancy and postpartum body image but is readily applicable.
> - Surveys are one of our favored methods for addressing negative body image and are underutilized. The goal of surveys is to explicitly challenge mind-reading predictions to break the cycle between unhelpful cognitions and disordered eating behaviors.
> - A helpful strategy for addressing negative body image in peripartum women is proactive problem-solving to address body dissatisfaction triggers (e.g., others' comments about pregnancy or postpartum weight, and tight clothing).
> - We discourage women from pursuing weight loss goals for 12 months postpartum so that the body can return to its natural set point and to ensure adequate nutrition to sustain tasks such as breastfeeding.

shape and other highly valued qualities (e.g., "people who lose weight quickly after pregnancy are successful, attractive, etc."). Surveys involve collecting objective data, using methods such as observing others, conducting a written survey, or interviewing others. Augmenting surveys for pregnancy may be helpful, although the process is the same as described in existing protocols.

Late in pregnancy, Sally reported feeling anxious about attending her friend's upcoming wedding. She told her therapist "I haven't worn a dress in so long. Everyone will think that I look like a whale and that I am unattractive." Sally and her clinician decided to test Sally's beliefs using a survey. The first step was to identify Sally's belief, to set up a survey to test out the belief, to generate specific mind-reading predictions, complete the survey, and to evaluate the outcome and revisit the original belief. Sally's completed survey is presented in Appendix D. It is important to work through all the steps for surveys to be effective.

Maintenance and Relapse Prevention

CBT Manual Guidance

CBT manuals emphasize the importance of discussing pregnancy as a potential trigger for a setback in the final stage of treatment when discussing maintenance and relapse prevention (Fairburn, 2008). This discussion is set in the context of considering events that may trigger an increase in shape- and weight-related concerns (e.g., weight loss due to illness, weight gain after being on vacation, or not returning to prepregnancy weight). Patients are also advised to continue weighing themselves at home when treatment ends, on a fortnightly to monthly basis so that they are not avoiding this task, and to identify any weight loss or weight gain if that were to occur.

258 *Bronwyn Raykos and Hunna Watson*

Box 11.13   Maintenance and Relapse Prevention

- Healthy set point may not be reached within the time constraints of CBT.
- Establish the expectation of regularly monitoring weight and working toward healthy set point postpartum.
- Provide psychoeducation on increased risk of depression and anxiety postpartum and encourage patients to seek help if these issues occur.
- Postpartum is a high-risk period for relapse of eating disorder behavior.
- Expanding the self-evaluation pie chart for motherhood can be a useful tool for relapse prevention.
- Provide a routine follow-up appointment postpartum to ensure that no new issues have emerged.

From the Clinical Trenches

Relapse prevention guidelines in CBT manuals are applicable to pregnancy and the postpartum period. For peripartum women who have not reached their set point weight range during treatment, it is particularly important to establish the expectation of regularly monitoring weight and working toward set point postpartum as part of relapse prevention. Providing women with psychoeducation that the postpartum period is associated with an increased risk of depression and anxiety in women with current or remitted eating disorders is also important. Changes in mood in the postpartum period may be a risk factor for a return to eating disorder symptoms and should not be ignored. At our clinic, we offer patients a routine follow-up appointment within 3 months postpartum to ensure that they are following their relapse prevention plan and that no new issues have emerged.

Considerations

There is no empirical evidence on whether general population recommendations for treatment apply equally well to peripartum women. Pregnant women are often excluded from psychotherapy intervention research. The assumption that effectiveness is equivalent may not hold true. For instance, CBT has lower effectiveness for major depression in the postpartum period (effect size: 0.36; confidence interval [CI]: 0.15–0.58) than in general (effect size: 0.51; CI: 0.36–0.68) and attrition is a higher concern in pregnancy and postpartum (Cuijpers, Brännmark, & van Straten, 2008). The clinical tools described are intended to align closely with existing CBT manuals and are not exhaustive as CBT interventions are described in detail in existing manuals. Customizing treatment delivery to peripartum may help to foster better outcomes and engagement. Such tailoring has been done for CBT for depression, anxiety, and insomnia (Green, Haber, Frey, & McCabe, 2015; Milgrom et al., 2015; Tomfohr-Madsen, Clayborne, Rouleau, & Campbell, 2017) but not in research on eating disorders.

Conclusions

Research on eating disorders in pregnancy and postpartum has focused mostly on adverse birth outcomes. There is very little research and guidance specific to treating pregnant and postpartum women. A common strategy is to follow evidence-based guidelines for the general population. Treatment guidelines recommend CBT for adults. Some research also supports the use of medication, especially in combination with psychotherapy. We strongly encourage clinicians to follow evidence-based treatment manuals. Nevertheless, existing manuals do not address issues relevant for peripartum women. We have suggested ways that CBT as usual may be augmented for pregnant and postpartum women based on treatment manuals, scholarly literature, and real-world practice. Providing care to pregnant and post-partum women offers the opportunity to promote the health and wellbeing of women and their babies during an important life transition. We hope this chapter helps clinicians in the clinical trenches who are treating women with eating disorders.

Note

1 In Western Australia, hospital admission guidelines for pregnant women with eating disorders have been developed. If you would like a copy, please email author B.R.

References

Bryant-Waugh, R., Micali, N., Cooke, L., Lawson, E. A., Eddy, K. T., & Thomas, J. J. (2019). Development of the Pica, ARFID, and Rumination Disorder Interview, a multi-informant, semi-structured interview of feeding disorders across the lifespan: A pilot study for ages 10–22. *International Journal of Eating Disorders, 52*, 378–387.

Byrne, S., Wade, T., Hay, P., Touyz, S., Fairburn, C., Treasure, J., ..., Fursland, A. (2017). A randomised controlled trial of three psychological treatments for anorexia nervosa. *Psychological Medicine, 47*(16), 2823–2833.

Byrne, S. M., Fursland, A., Allen, K. L., & Watson, H. (2011). The effectiveness of enhanced cognitive behavioural therapy for eating disorders: An open trial. *Behaviour Research and Therapy, 49*(4), 219–226.

Byrne, S. M., & McLean, N. J. (2002). The cognitive-behavioral model of bulimia nervosa: A direct evaluation. *International Journal of Eating Disorders, 31*(1), 17–31.

Cooper, Z., & Fairburn, C. (1987). The eating disorder examination: A semi-structured interview for the assessment of the specific psychopathology of eating disorders. *International Journal of Eating Disorders, 6*(1), 1–8.

Cuijpers, P., Brännmark, J. G., & van Straten, A. (2008). Psychological treatment of postpartum depression: A meta-analysis. *Journal of Clinical Psychology, 64*(1), 103–118.

Dalle Grave, R., Calugi, S., Conti, M., Doll, H., & Fairburn, C. G. (2013). Inpatient cognitive behaviour therapy for anorexia nervosa: A randomized controlled trial. *Psychotherapy and Psychosomatics, 82*(6), 390–398.

dos Santos, A. M., Benute, G. R. G., dos Santos, N. O., Nomura, R. M. Y., de Lucia, M. C. S., & Francisco, R. P. V. (2017). Presence of eating disorders and its relationship to anxiety and depression in pregnant women. *Midwifery, 51*, 12–15.

Emery, R. L., Grace, J. L., Kolko, R. P., & Levine, M. D. (2017). Adapting the Eating Disorder Examination for use during pregnancy: Preliminary results from a community sample of women with overweight and obesity. *International Journal of Eating Disorders, 5*(50), 597–601.

Fairburn, C. G. (2008). *Cognitive behavior therapy and eating disorders.* New York, NY: Guilford Press.

Fairburn, C. G. (2013). *Overcoming binge eating: The proven program to learn why you binge and how you can stop* (2nd ed.). New York, NY: Guilford Press.

Fairburn, C. G., & Beglin, S. (2008). Eating Disorder Examination Questionnaire (EDE-Q 6.0). In C. G. Fairburn (Ed.), *Cognitive behaviour therapy and eating disorders.* New York, NY: Guilford Press.

Fairburn, C. G., & Beglin, S. J. (1994). Assessment of eating disorders: Interview or self-report questionnaire? *International Journal of Eating Disorders, 16*(4), 363–370.

Fairburn, C. G., Cooper, Z., & Cooper, P. J. (1986). The clinical features and maintenance of bulimia nervosa. In K. D. Brownell & J. P. Foreyt (Eds.), *Handbook of eating disorders: Physiology, psychology and treatment of obesity, anorexia and bulimia* (pp. 389–404). New York, NY: Basic Books.

Fairburn, C. G., Cooper, Z., & Shafran, R. (2003). Cognitive behaviour therapy for eating disorders: A "transdiagnostic" theory and treatment. *Behaviour Research and Therapy, 41*(5), 509–528.

Fairburn, C. G., Jones, R., Peveler, R. C., Hope, R., & O'connor, M. (1993). Psychotherapy and bulimia nervosa: Longer-term effects of interpersonal psychotherapy, behavior therapy, and cognitive behavior therapy. *Archives of General Psychiatry, 50*(6), 419–428.

Fairburn, C. G., Norman, P. A., Welch, S. L., O'Connor, M. E., Doll, H. A., & Peveler, R. C. (1995). A prospective study of outcome in bulimia nervosa and the long-term effects of three psychological treatments. *Archives of General Psychiatry, 52*(4), 304–312.

First, M. B., Spitzer, R. L., Gibbon, R. L., Gibbon, M., & Williams, J. B. W. (1994). *Structured Clinical Interview for Axis I DSM–IV Disorders Patient Edition (SCID–I\p, Version 2.0).* New York, NY: Biometrics Research Department.

Fogarty, S., Elmir, R., Hay, P., & Schmied, V. (2018). The experience of women with an eating disorder in the perinatal period: A meta-ethnographic study. *BMC Pregnancy and Childbirth, 18*(1), 121.

Food Nutrition Board/Institute of Medicine. (2002). *Dietary Reference Intakes (DRI) and Recommended Dietary Allowances (RDA) for energy, carbohydrate, fiber, fats, fatty acids, cholesterol, proteins and amino acids.* Washington, DC: National Academy Press.

Green, S. M., Haber, E., Frey, B. N., & McCabe, R. E. (2015). Cognitive-behavioral group treatment for perinatal anxiety: A pilot study. *Archives of Women's Mental Health, 18*(4), 631–638.

Hay, P., Chinn, D., Forbes, D., Madden, S., Newton, R., Sugenor, L., ..., Ward, W. (2014). Royal Australian and New Zealand College of Psychiatrists clinical practice guidelines for the treatment of eating disorders. *Australian and New Zealand Journal of Psychiatry*, *48*(11), 977–1008.

Hilbert, A., Hoek, H. W., & Schmidt, R. (2017). Evidence-based clinical guidelines for eating disorders: International comparison. *Current Opinion in Psychiatry*, *30*(6), 423–437.

Institute of Medicine (US) and National Research Council (US). (2009). *Weight gain during pregnancy: Reexamining the guidelines*. Washington, DC: National Academies Press.

Keys, A., Brožek, J., Henschel, A., Mickelsen, O., & Taylor, H. L. (1950). *The biology of human starvation (2 volumes)*. Oxford, England: University of Minnesota Press.

Kimmel, M., Ferguson, E., Zerwas, S., Bulik, C., & Meltzer-Brody, S. (2016). Obstetric and gynecologic problems associated with eating disorders. *International Journal of Eating Disorders*, *49*(3), 260–275.

Mason, Z., Cooper, M., & Turner, H. (2012). The experience of pregnancy in women with a history of anorexia nervosa: An interpretive phenomenological analysis. *Journal of Behavioral Addictions*, *1*(2), 59–67.

Micali, N., Simonoff, E., & Treasure, J. (2009). Infant feeding and weight in the first year of life in babies of women with eating disorders. *Journal of Pediatrics*, *154*(1), 55–60. e51.

Milgrom, J., Holt, C., Holt, C. J., Ross, J., Ericksen, J., & Gemmill, A. W. (2015). Feasibility study and pilot randomised trial of an antenatal depression treatment with infant follow-up. *Archives of Women's Mental Health*, *18*(5), 717–730.

National Institute for Health and Care Excellence. (2017). *Eating disorders: Recognition and treatment*. London, UK: National Institute for Health and Care Excellence.

Navarro, P., García-Esteve, L., Ascaso, C., Aguado, J., Gelabert, E., & Martín-Santos, R. (2008). Non-psychotic psychiatric disorders after childbirth: Prevalence and co-morbidity in a community sample. *Journal of Affective Disorders*, *109*(1–2), 171–176.

Nickols-Richardson, S. M. (2018). Anorexia nervosa, bulimia nervosa, and binge-eating disorder during pregnancy. In C. J. Lammi-Keefe, S. C. Couch, & J. P. Kirwan (Eds.), *Handbook of nutrition and pregnancy* (2nd ed., pp. 247–71). Cham, Switzerland: Springer Nature.

Patel, P., Lee, J., Wheatcroft, R., Barnes, J., & Stein, A. (2005). Concerns about body shape and weight in the postpartum period and their relation to women's self-identification. *Journal of Reproductive and Infant Psychology*, *23*(4), 347–364.

Rose, C., & Waller, G. (2017). Cognitive–behavioral therapy for eating disorders in primary care settings: Does it work, and does a greater dose make it more effective? *International Journal of Eating Disorders*, *50*(12), 1350–1355.

Sysko, R., Glasofer, D. R., Hildebrandt, T., Klimek, P., Mitchell, J. E., Berg, K. C., ..., Walsh, B. T. (2015). The eating disorder assessment for DSM-5 (EDA-5): Development and validation of a structured interview for feeding and eating disorders. *International Journal of Eating Disorders*, *48*(5), 452–463.

Tierney, S., McGlone, C., & Furber, C. (2013). What can qualitative studies tell us about the experiences of women who are pregnant that have an eating disorder? *Midwifery*, *29*(5), 542–549.

Tomfohr-Madsen, L. M., Clayborne, Z. M., Rouleau, C. R., & Campbell, T. S. (2017). Sleeping for two: An open-pilot study of cognitive behavioral therapy for insomnia in pregnancy. *Behavioral Sleep Medicine*, *15*(5), 377–393.

van Ravesteyn, L. M., Lambregtse-van den Berg, M. P., Hoogendijk, W. J., & Kamperman, A. M. (2017). Interventions to treat mental disorders during pregnancy: A systematic review and multiple treatment meta-analysis. *PLoS One*, *12*(3), e0173397.

Waller, G. (2009). Evidence-based treatment and therapist drift. *Behaviour Research and Therapy*, *47*(2), 119–127.

Waller, G., Cordery, H., Corstorphine, E., Hinrichsen, H., Lawson, R., Mountford, V., & Russell, K. (2007). *Cognitive behavioral therapy for eating disorders: A comprehensive treatment guide*. Cambridge, UK: Cambridge University Press.

Waller, G., Evans, J., & Pugh, M. (2013). Food for thought: A pilot study of the pros and cons of changing eating patterns within cognitive-behavioural therapy for the eating disorders. *Behaviour Research and Therapy*, *51*(9), 519–525.

Waller, G., & Mountford, V. A. (2015). Weighing patients within cognitive-behavioural therapy for eating disorders: How, when and why. *Behaviour Research and Therapy*, *70*, 1–10.

Waller, G., & Raykos, B. (2019). Behavioral interventions in the treatment of eating disorders. *Psychiatric Clinics*, *42*(2), 181–191.

Waller, G., & Turner, H. (2016). Therapist drift redux: Why well-meaning clinicians fail to deliver evidence-based therapy, and how to get back on track. *Behaviour Research and Therapy*, *77*, 129–137.

Waller, G., Turner, H., Tatham, M., Mountford, V. A., & Wade, T. D. (2019). *Brief cognitive behavioural therapy for non-underweight patients: CBT-T for eating disorders*. London, UK: Routledge, Taylor & Francis Group.

Watson, H. J., O'Brien, A., & Sadeh-Sharvit, S. (2018). Children of parents with eating disorders. *Current Psychiatry Reports*, *20*(11), 101.

Watson, H. J., Torgersen, L., Zerwas, S., Reichborn-Kjennerud, T., Knoph, C., Stoltenberg, C., ..., Meltzer, H. (2014). Eating disorders, pregnancy, and the postpartum period: Findings from the Norwegian Mother and Child Cohort Study (MoBa). *Norsk Epidemiologi [Norwegian Journal of Epidemiology]*, *24*(1-2), 51–62.

Watson, H. J., Von Holle, A., Hamer, R. M., Berg, C. K., Torgersen, L., Magnus, P., ..., Bulik, C. M. (2013). Remission, continuation and incidence of eating disorders during early pregnancy: A validation study in a population-based birth cohort. *Psychological Medicine*, *43*(8), 1723–1734.

Watson, H. J., Zerwas, S., Torgersen, L., Gustavson, K., Diemer, E. W., Knudsen, G. P., ..., Bulik, C. M. (2017). Maternal eating disorders and perinatal outcomes: A three-generation study in the Norwegian Mother and Child Cohort Study. *Journal of Abnormal Psychology*, *126*(5), 552–564.

Appendix A

Eating Disorders & Pregnancy

For someone who has an eating disorder (or who has recently recovered) becoming pregnant can pose risks to both themselves and their baby. Pregnancy can also magnify issues the mother may struggle with, including those relating to food, eating, and body weight and shape.

Potential Risks to Mother and Baby

If a mother's nutrition is not sufficient during pregnancy, both mother and baby can be negatively affected. Mothers who are underweight or do not gain enough weight during pregnancy can experience malnutrition, low blood pressure, weakness, and fainting episodes Babies who do not receive adequate nutrition may not grow at the expected rate, and there is an increased risk of miscarriage, premature birth, low birth weight and long term developmental delays and problems.

Women who engage in purging behaviours may experience even poorer outcomes (such as dehydration, electrolyte imbalances and cardiac irregularities) because the mother's body is already allocating extra resources to the growing foetus.

Binge eating during pregnancy increases the risk of high blood pressure and gestational diabetes. This can affect the baby by causing rapid growth, high birth weight, and nutritional imbalances at birth.

Birth complications, difficult recovery, breastfeeding challenges and depression may also be more likely in mothers who have an eating disorder during pregnancy.

Changes in Nutritional Requirements

A mother's body needs extra energy and nutrients during the pregnancy and lactation period in order to maintain her wellbeing as well supporting the baby's healthy growth.
- In the first trimester folate, vitamins A and B6, and iron are particularly important for the development of the heart, brain and bones, as well as establishing the placenta and blood supply.
- In the second and third trimesters, extra energy and nutrients including protein, carbohydrates, and vitamins C and D are required to support development of the foetus' brain, nervous system, muscles and tissues, fat storage and facial features.
- Breastfeeding mothers will continue to need additional energy throughout nursing.

Strict food rules can interfere with adequate consumption of vital nutrients. A pregnant woman may need to overcome her fears about foods that contain these nutrients.

Weight Gain in Pregnancy

Weight gain (including fat storage) is a natural biological process during pregnancy. Some people can find the changes in the number on the scale distressing, so it is important to remember that weight gain is appropriate and necessary.

Factors that contribute to weight gain include:
    Your baby (~3-3.6kg)
    The placenta and amniotic fluid (~1.5kg)
    Uterine muscles (~1kg)
    Increased blood volume (~1.4-1.8kg)
    Fluid retention (~1-1.5kg)
    Breast tissue (~0.5-1kg)
    Fat storage for breastfeeding (~2.7-3.6kg)

At times the number on the scale can increase rapidly. This is due to normal growth fluctuations and hormonal changes. It's especially important to maintain adequate water intake to avoid dehydration and rebound swelling as the body seeks to secure nutritional resources.

Exposure to Triggers

Even people who have recently recovered from their eating disorder may be triggered when they are pregnant. This can be due to:
- Changes in body shape, in addition to increasing weight, which some people find difficult to accept.
- Other people (even strangers!) thinking that it's ok to comment on and touch a pregnant woman's body.
- Cravings and physical drives to eat more, which may trigger urges to overeat or binge.
- Morning sickness which may involve vomiting or food aversions similar to disordered eating behaviours.
- Having to limit exercise - pregnant women are recommended to do only a moderate amount of aerobic exercise, and some activities are not advised.

It is important that women who are pregnant (or hope to become pregnant) access support so they can prepare for any challenges they may face. Many women with eating disorders cope well with pregnancy, and even reduce or cease their eating disordered behaviours. However, it's still important to seek support as it's common for an increase in eating disordered thoughts and behaviours to occur after the baby is born. A healthcare professional with experience in eating disorders can offer assistance.

Developed in conjunction with Kate Fleming, Dietician
This document is for information purposes only. Please refer to the full disclaimer and copyright statement available at http://www.cci.health.wa.gov.au regarding the information from this website before making use of such information.
See website www.cci.health.wa.gov.au for more handouts and resources. Last updated 25/01/18.

Centre for Clinical Interventions
• Psychotherapy • Research • Training

Appendix B
Eating Disorders & Hormones

How Do Eating Disorders Affect Hormones?

Eating habits and weight play an important role in our hormone levels. Disordered eating, compensatory behaviours (e.g. excessive exercise), and weight (anorexia and obesity) can disrupt hormone production. Hormones that regulate metabolism, fertility, pregnancy, and bone health are particularly affected by disordered eating.

Fertility in Females and Males

When food is sparse the body reduces all processes that need large amounts of energy, such as pregnancy. Low levels of the hormones oestrogen, progesterone, and testosterone can result in a reduction of fertility or infertility in individuals with eating disorder.

In women, symptoms may include:
- Low libido (sexual desire);
- Absence of menstrual periods (*amenorrhoea*);
- Irregular menstrual periods

In men, symptoms may include:
- Low libido (sexual desire);
- Loss of early morning erections;
- Loss of nocturnal emissions ("wet dreams").

Hormonal changes associated with eating disorders are reversible. With time, adequate nutrition and maintaining a healthy body weight results in a return to normal sexual desire and normal physical functioning.

*NOTE: Even if you are experiencing signs of infertility, it is important to use contraception if you are sexually active. Ovulation and fertility may resume unexpectedly, making pregnancy possible.

Pregnancy

When pregnancy does occur, eating disorders can impact on reproductive hormones. Women who fall pregnant while they are underweight or obese are at higher risk of complications during pregnancy. Effects may include high blood pressure, gestational diabetes (especially in binge eating disorder), anaemia, and increased risk of miscarriage or complicated delivery. There can also be complications for the foetus, such as premature birth, low or high birth weight, feeding difficulties, and respiratory distress. Most pregnant women who have recovered from eating disorders have healthy pregnancies.

Bone Health & Osteoporosis

Eating disorders can have a significant impact on bone health. Osteoporosis causes bones to lose strength and become brittle and vulnerable to breaking easily. The main cause of osteoporosis is malnutrition and low weight. Many hormonal changes occur when a body has insufficient reserves of fat and muscles. These include changes to sex hormones (testosterone and oestrogen) as well as high levels of cortisol, low levels of IGF-1 and Leptin. Changes in these hormones can slow bone development and even cause bone loss. Although we cannot reverse damage to bone health, the only way to prevent further bone damage is by treating eating disorders early and involves reversing malnutrition and increasing weight to a healthy level. Previously it was believed that hormone replacements such as the oral contraceptive pill would assist bone health in individuals with eating disorders. However, possibly since a range of hormones is affected by malnutrition, research has found that hormone replacement is insufficient to protect bone density. The only effective treatment for osteoporosis in anorexia nervosa is weight re-gain.

Other Hormonal Effects

- Low levels of thyroid hormones may cause constipation and dry skin;
- Overeating/obesity can cause an increase in hormone levels that encourage the build up of body fat, making it even harder to lose weight;
- Low levels of stress hormones cause sleep problems, anxiety, depression, or panic (e.g. increased heart rate)
- Eating disorders may also impact on hormones involved in appetite, puberty and growth.

Seeking Help

If you have noticed any hormonal effects of your eating disorder, you should consult with a medical practitioner to get a medical assessment.

Appendix C Behavioral Experiment

Step 1: Identify the current belief. What am I afraid will happen?
If I eat two slices of bread as well as my fruit and yogurt for breakfast, my nausea will get worse and I will vomit

Step 2: Rate the strength of this belief. How much do I believe it will happen (0–100%)?
80%

Step 3: Identify the alternative belief. What else might happen?
I might be able to tolerate the extra food. My nausea could stay the same and I might not vomit.

Step 4: Rate the strength of this belief. How much do I believe it will happen (0–100%)?
15%

Step 5: Behavioral manipulation to test the two beliefs

Where, when and how will I test my prediction?
Eat two slices of bread as well as my fruit and yogurt for breakfast every day

Step 6: Agree to a timeframe (enough time to test whether either belief has support)
Time frame: *1 week*

Step 7: Evaluate the results

What actually happened?
At first I had to force myself to eat the bread and I felt quite full. After a few days I was used to it. My nausea didn't get worse. I also didn't feel so hungry by lunch time.

Which belief was supported by the evidence?
The alternative belief

Step 8: Revisit and re-rate the beliefs

What did I learn from this experiment? What do the results say about my original prediction? How am I going to use this information in the future?
It is good to know that if I eat more at breakfast I am not so hungry by lunch time and my nausea doesn't get worse. I am still afraid of gaining too much weight if I keep including two slices of bread each day. I can conduct another experiment to test out this fear.

How much do I believe my original belief (0–100%)? *30%*
How much do I believe the alternative belief (0–100%)? *60%*

Appendix D Survey

Step 1: Identify and rate my current beliefs about what other people think

Other people will think: *I am a whale and unattractive.* How much do I believe this (0–100%)? *95%*

Step 2: Set up survey questions that will allow the belief to be tested (e.g., photos)

I will ask my partner to take a photo of me in the dress I am planning to wear to the wedding and conduct a survey using the following questions:

1. What is the first thing you notice about this person's appearance? _____
2. On a scale from 0 to 10 please rate this person's overall body size:

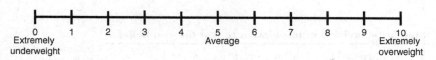

3. On a scale from 0 to 10 please rate how attractive this person is:

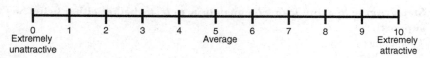

Step 3: Identify my predictions about how people will respond to the survey

Question 1 - Most people will notice that I am overweight
Question 2 - On average, people will rate my body weight as 9/10
Question 3 - On average, people will rate my attractiveness as 2/10

Step 4: Choose the appropriate people to ask *I will first conduct a survey at the clinic*

Step 5: Gather the data

Step 6: Compare the data with your predictions (in Step 3)

What actually happened? Were my predictions about how people would respond supported?

1. *Most people noticed that I was pregnant. I predicted they would comment on my weight;*
2. *Average body weight rating was 5/10. This was much lower than I predicted (9/10);*
3. *Average attractiveness rating was 8/10. This was much higher than I predicted (2/10)*

Step 7: Re-visit and re-rate the original belief (in Step 1)

What do the results say about the original belief? How am I going to use the information in the future? Is there anything else I need to do to test out this belief? *I overestimate my body size and underestimate my attractiveness. Calling myself a "whale" is unhelpful and keeps me feeling bad about my body. I can remind myself that I am nurturing a beautiful baby so of course my body has changed. The next step is to go to the wedding in the dress as an experiment.*

How much do I believe my original belief (0–100%)? *50%*

12 Tailoring Treatments to Middle-Aged and Older Adults

Lisa Smith Kilpela, Francesca Gomez, and Carolyn Becker

Introduction

Although a majority of the eating disorder (ED) literature focuses on adolescent and young adult females, the notion that ED pathology is a phenomenon limited to younger ages is false (Pike, Dunne, & Addai, 2013). Indeed, a growing body of research suggests that both EDs and ED risk factors (e.g., body dissatisfaction) are quite prevalent in middle-aged and older women (Gagne et al., 2012; Keel, Gravener, Joiner, & Haedt, 2010). Unfortunately, research also suggests that the majority of middle and late life individuals with EDs do not seek treatment for these symptoms (Mangweth-Matzek & Hoek, 2017). Moreover, for those who do make it into treatment, limited research exists to guide potentially necessary adaptations to treatments that were largely developed for younger populations.

The primary aim of this chapter is to provide clinicians with strategies to address the needs of middle-aged and older adult patients. Given the limited ED literature in this area that can be used to guide recommendations, we include general suggestions for tailoring evidence-based psychological interventions for older populations, and also rely on our own clinical experience. We start by summarizing evidence that EDs and their correlates exist in both middle-aged and older populations. We then briefly highlight some of the health risks associated with ED pathology that are particularly relevant in older populations. Next, we review the limited existing research on interventions designed to address ED pathology and key correlates in middle-aged and older adults. As life changes that are commonly experienced by middle-aged and older adults may trigger or exacerbate ED pathology, strategies to address such life changes are discussed. Aging is associated with numerous physical, medical, and cognitive changes that can impact the effectiveness of evidence-based psychological interventions, so we also consider recommendations from the literature for other problems (i.e., depression, anxiety, and insomnia) for advice on modifying ED interventions for older patients. The final section of this chapter outlines our experience with modifying a group-based dissonance intervention for middle-aged and older adults. Readers should note that because the existing literature on EDs in middle-aged and older men is virtually nonexistent, most of this chapter focuses on middle-aged and older women. We do not mean to imply that EDs are not a problem for men later in life; rather, we challenge the field to begin to address the lack of research focusing on middle-aged and older men (as well as middle-aged and older transgender individuals) so that in the future, chapters such as this one can also address these populations.

Prevalence and Correlates

Women

As noted above, research suggests that EDs are not uncommon among middle-aged and older women. For instance, Mangweth-Matzek et al. (2014) assessed ED symptoms and body image in women aged 40–60. In this community sample, 4.6% of women appeared to meet Diagnostic and Statistical Manual of Mental Disorders, 4th edition (DSM-IV) criteria for an ED and another 4.8% reported symptoms consistent with a subthreshold ED. Similarly, in an online sample of women aged 50 and above (N = 1,849), approximately 13% reported at least some current core ED symptoms; 7.8% of participants reported purging in the absence of binge eating in the last 5 years, and 3.5% endorsed currently binge eating at least once per week (Gagne et al., 2012).

With regards to older adult women, Thompson 2019 found that approximately 6% of women aged 65–90 (N = 97) met the clinical cutoff on the Eating Attitudes Test-26, whereas 12% endorsed objective binge episodes in the past month. In women aged 60–70 (Mangweth-Matzek et al., 2006), nearly 4% met full criteria for an ED; an additional 4.4% reported some ED symptoms (e.g., bingeing, purging, and fasting). Of the total sample, 56% used dietary restriction, 10% used fasting, and 6% used laxatives/diuretics for weight control.

One disadvantage of questionnaire-based studies is that they may overestimate the prevalence of ED symptoms. This is particularly the case with more ambiguous symptoms (e.g., binge eating) as compared to more concrete behaviors (e.g., self-induced vomiting; Fairburn & Beglin, 1994). One remedy is to utilize a two-stage detection strategy design, which combines questionnaire screening with follow-up interviewer-based assessment. Using this approach, Conceição, Gomes, Vaz, Pinto-Bastos, and Machado (2017) found that 3.25% of women aged 65–94 met DSM-5 criteria for an ED based on interview assessment. Overall, almost 6% of women reported binge eating. It is worth nothing that in middle-aged and older women, the distribution of ED diagnosis tends to be different than in younger women, with binge ED and other specified feeding and eating disorder (OSFED) being more prevalent, followed by bulimia nervosa. Rates of anorexia nervosa in later life are still not well understood (Mangweth-Matzek & Hoek, 2017).

Men

Unfortunately, very little research exists regarding the prevalence rates of EDs in men over the age of 40 (Reas & Stedal, 2015; Mitchell & Wolf, 2016; Mangweth-Matzek & Hoek, 2017). In one of the few studies to date,

Mangweth-Matzek, Kummer, and Pope (2016) assessed a community sample of 470 men aged 40–75; 6.8% of participants reported ED symptoms including binge eating only, binge eating and purging, or purging only. Among men who reported binging and purging, excessive exercise was the most frequently used compensatory behavior. In summary, evidence suggests that EDs affect men in midlife and beyond; however, more studies are needed to document the problem of eating disturbances in men.

Body Dissatisfaction and Other Correlates Among Women in Later-Life Stages

Body dissatisfaction is a well-established risk factor for ED pathology (Stice & Shaw, 2002). Multiple studies indicate that body dissatisfaction remains a problem for many women throughout mid- and late-life (Becker, Verzijl, Kilpela, Wilfred, & Stewart, 2017; Lewis & Cachelin, 2001; Pruis & Janowsky, 2010; Slevec & Tiggemann, 2011; Tiggeman, 2004). For instance, Bedford and Johnson (2006) compared body image attitudes between women aged 19–23 ($N = 49$) and older women aged 65–74 ($N = 51$). Despite the majority of women classifying themselves as being at the correct weight, approximately 78% of both younger and older women reported a negative body image. This is consistent with Gagne et al. (2012), who found that 70% of women aged 50+ reported dissatisfaction with current weight and shape; 71% also reported they were currently trying to lose weight. Similarly, among women aged 60–70, 60% endorsed body dissatisfaction (Mangeweth-Matzek et al., 2006). Finally, Jackson et al. (2014) found that 47% of middle-aged women reported body dissatisfaction; 73% reported being at least somewhat unsatisfied.

Other correlates of and risk factors for both ED pathology and body dissatisfaction have been identified in middle-aged and older women. For instance, in a literature review, Slevec & Tiggemann (2011) found that body mass index (BMI), sociocultural pressures, and internalization of the thin ideal, aging anxiety, sexual and physical abuse, and weight-related teasing were factors associated with ED pathology and body dissatisfaction in middle-aged women. Similarly, Carrard and Rothen (2020) found that in women aged 60–75, BMI, importance of appearance, and fear of age-related appearance changes were correlated with ED attitudes and behaviors. Finally, maladaptive perfectionism was significantly correlated with both ED attitudes and bulimic symptoms in women aged 65 and older (Thompson & Bardone-Cone, 2019).

Health Consequences of Disordered Eating in Older Adults

Unhealthy and disordered eating behaviors may incur substantial health risks (e.g., cardiovascular, metabolic, musculoskeletal, and gastrointestinal) as well as increased mortality at any age (Mehler, 2017a; 2017b); however, the potential for negative health consequences is often exacerbated in older adults. It is beyond the scope of this chapter to fully detail all the ways in which EDs can interact with the aging process, so this section highlights just a few key areas of concern by way of example. For instance, excessive caloric and nutrient restriction via strict fasting/dieting behaviors is particularly dangerous in older individuals, and increases risk for falls, fractures, and cognitive impairment (Marshall, Lengyel, & Utioh, 2012). Strict dieting and fasting behaviors also are associated with sarcopenia, osteoporosis, reduced immune function, and a series of cardiovascular and metabolic abnormalities (e.g., Marshall et al., 2012). Bulimic EDs have shared risk factors and high comorbidity with depression (Goldschmidt, Wall, Choo, Becker, & Neumark-Sztainer, 2016), which can potentiate or amplify existing medical morbidities and geriatric syndromes.

The health complications of ED pathology can reverberate further, causing interference with quality of life (Miller & Wolfe, 2008), ultimately undermining successful aging (Allaz, Bernstein, Vannes, Rouget, & Morabia, 1993). Clinicians working with older patients should make sure to get a detailed medical history and consult as needed with geriatric medical specialists. It is worth nothing that managing the interacting medical problems associated with EDs and aging (including the polypharmacy that is common in older adults) can be very stressful for clinicians, even medical providers with ED experience. Thus, we recommend setting a low threshold for engaging a medical provider with geriatric expertise.

Treatment of EDs in Middle-Aged and Older Adults: Current State of the Literature

To date, very limited research has addressed treatment for midlife and older adults with EDs and/or ED risk factors, such as body dissatisfaction. Moreover, to our knowledge, there are no data regarding long-term treatment effects, or recovery or remission rates, in middle-aged and older adults with EDs. In a systematic review of treatments for middle-aged women with EDs and body dissatisfaction, Lewis-Smith, Diedrichs, Rumsey, & Harcourt, (2016) identified 11 nonpharmacological interventions that targeted body image and/or disordered eating. Four of these comprised psychological/behavioral interventions (e.g., cognitive behavioral therapy [CBT] and mindfulness-based), whereas the remaining seven utilized a physical activity-based approach (e.g., yoga, Pilates, resistance training, dance, walking, and walking plus action planning). Seven of these interventions demonstrated positive effects immediately posttreatment on body image, but only two interventions significantly improved disordered eating. Furthermore, only three interventions demonstrated sustained improvements in body image at follow-up; two of these maintained effects on disordered eating. A critical caveat for even the effective programs, however, is that follow-up windows were fairly short (i.e., ranging from 2 weeks to 6 months). Of the effective interventions, two comprised CBT interventions and one utilized acceptance and commitment therapy (ACT). ACT is considered a third-wave behavioral intervention with a focus on mindfulness and a commitment to living according to one's values (Hayes, 2004).

With regards to older adults, these individuals are commonly excluded from both psychotherapy and pharmacotherapy clinical trials. Indeed, the majority of treatment research for EDs or body image typically cap age inclusion at either 60 or 65 years (Guerdjikova, O'melia, Mori, McCoy, & McElroy, 2012). Thus, no clinical guidelines exist for the treatment of EDs in older individuals; this is a major gap in the research literature. Although many theory-driven ED treatments have good empirical support, without major modifications, these treatments are unlikely to be appropriate for older individuals, who comprise a complex population with unique needs.

For instance, one of the first-line treatments for EDs is CBT (National Institute for Health and Care Excellence, 2017). Despite the benefit conferred by CBT in younger subjects, the efficacy of standard CBT for EDs in older populations is unknown. Furthermore, specific treatment strategies in CBT inadequately address psychosocial and biological experiences associated with aging. For example, one of the first targets in CBT for EDs is to regulate eating patterns using the guide of three meals and two snacks per day. Patients also are encouraged to maintain a food diary in which all intake is recorded in terms of time and context of consumption. For older women, transportation, physical, cognitive (including problems with literacy and memory), or financial limitations including food insecurity, as well as medical morbidities, and psychosocial stressors (e.g., caring for spouse/parent) can impede patients' ability to comply with treatment recommendations, which will, in turn, affect efficacy. Shame also may prevent older patient from explaining why they are unable to be adherent. Physical changes following menopause comprise additional stressors that can negatively impact treatment. Sleep disturbances, which are common in postmenopausal women, can increase risk for binge eating (Trace et al., 2012), yet CBT for EDs does not address sleep. In summary, research is critically needed to map out both the efficacy of existing treatments in older adults and to document the necessary adaptations needed to meet the needs of older adults.

Tailoring Treatment

Attending to the ED Stereotype

In the case of ED treatments for middle-aged and older adults, it is imperative to consider the stereotypes of EDs as disorders of youth. Although mental health diagnoses often come with self- and other-stigma, this phenomenon can be even more pronounced in middle-aged and older adults with EDs. Adults, later in life, may feel immense shame for having a "younger person's disorder" (Aziz, Rafferty, & Jurewicz, 2017) or perception that they should not care about their appearance, etc., at their age. Patients who feel this way may not adequately engage in treatment if shame and associated beliefs are not addressed.

Addressing Life Changes

Middle-aged and older women grapple with an array of aging-related life changes that (1) are commonly perceived as negative and unwanted, and (2) may contribute to the onset or maintenance of an ED. Despite the relative dearth of research on EDs in middle-aged and older women, researchers have long recognized that both fear of aging and age-related bodily changes appear to be associated with ED development in some women (Gupta, 1990; Lewis & Cachelin, 2001). As noted above, body dissatisfaction, which is a predictor of relapse in those who recover from an ED (Keel, Dorer, Franko, Jackson, and Herzog (2005), occurs across the lifespan (Peat, Peyeri, & Muehlenkamp, 2008) and may be impacted by the aging process. Middle-aged and older women contend with a wide range of body changes that move them away from Western appearance ideals, including, but not limited to changes in body composition (particularly during and after menopause), changes in metabolism and difficulty of losing or maintaining weight, and changes in muscle mass and skin tone/elasticity. Illness, such as cancer, may lead to other negative changes in the body including disfigurement resulting from surgery.

Changes in appearance that accompany aging also may meaningfully change how the world responds to women (e.g., when workers in a shop or restaurant ignore an older woman to attend to someone else) creating what is colloquially referred to as Invisible Woman Syndrome (https://thenewdaily.com.au/life/relationships/2016/07/30/invisible-woman-syndrome/). For women who have previously felt visible and recognized in their younger years, being passed over and ignored can represent a marked life change, which can increase grief and anxiety over losing a youthful appearance. It also may motivate increased desire to regain what has been lost. Although limited empirical research addresses the problem of invisibility in aging women, in a qualitative study of 44 women aged 50–70, Clark and Griffin (2008) found that women did report investing time to alter their appearance to combat aging-appearance-related invisibility.

Research is mixed as to the impact of aging on women's body image on a population-wide (i.e., nomothetic) level. Some research suggests that older women may decrease their investment in appearance as they age (see Peat et al., 2008 and Tiggemann, 2004 for review). Nonetheless, clinicians should remember that nomothetic research may fail to detect etiological factors that operate on an ideographic (i.e., individual) level, particularly when the existing research base is very limited, as is the case with the study of EDs in middle-aged and older women. As such, in the absence of sufficient data, it makes sense to use detailed functional assessment to determine the degree to which bodily changes appear to play a functional role in the development or maintenance of a specific middle-aged or older woman's ED.

Research with and clinical reports of middle-aged and older women also indicate that other types of life changes commonly associated with later stages of the lifespan appear to be associated with EDs and ED pathology (Lapid et al., 2010; Maine, Samuels, & Tantillo, 2015; McLean, Paxton, & Wertheim, 2010).

Examples of common later life changes include but are not limited to loss of a partner (via divorce or death), marital problems (e.g., marital dissatisfaction or remarriage of an ex-husband), medical illness, the need to simultaneously care for both children and aging parents (which can result in less time to care for oneself), children moving away (i.e., so-called empty nest), retirement, and the need to leave one's home secondary to a loss of functioning. Although some changes may be viewed as positive (e.g., time gained for self-care after children become independent), many changes are not. It is important to remember that negative life changes and EDs may have a reciprocal relationship. Negative life changes may exacerbate an existing ED, trigger relapse, or appear to play a causal role in the development of an ED that has just started. In turn, an ongoing ED may negatively impact interpersonal relationships and/or impair patients' ability to cope with stressors. As with body-related changes, careful functional analysis is warranted to assess whether there are functional relationships between life changes and ED symptomatology.

Unfortunately, as noted earlier, almost no research exists to guide recommendations as to how to modify existing evidence-based ED treatments for middle-aged and older women. Three commonsense strategies from existing evidence-based treatments, however, can be used to help middle-aged and older women cope with life changes when they appear to play a significant role in the ED clinical picture: interpersonal psychotherapy (IPT), problem-solving therapy, and acceptance-based strategies. Two of these strategies are already included in some evidence-based treatments (e.g., CBT-Enhanced [CBT-E]). Clinicians treating EDs in middle-aged and older women, however, may need to devote substantially more time to these strategies when life changes are a prominent component of the clinical picture. For this reason, we highlight them below.

Interpersonal Psychotherapy

IPT is an evidence-based treatment for EDs (Fairburn, 1997; Murphy, Straebler, Basden, Cooper, & Fairburn, 2012) that has largely been tested as a treatment for bulimia nervosa and binge ED, although one small trial with anorexia nervosa patients also exists. The rationale for IPT for EDs (IPT-ED) has typically been articulated with a focus on younger patients (Murphy et al., 2012); however, there are several good reasons to consider use with older women. First, IPT-ED is a modification of IPT for depression (Klerman, Weissman, Rounsaville, & Chevron, 1984; Weissman, Markowitz, & Klerman, 2017). Importantly, depression is a common co-occurring disorder with EDs in mid- and late-life women. For instance, Cumella and Kally (2008) found that 86% of older women presenting with a clinical ED severe enough for inpatient treatment met criteria for unipolar depression. Second, when life changes that have a strong interpersonal focus appear to play a role in triggering, maintaining, or exacerbating an ED, IPT-ED will both have significant face validity and offer an evidence-based approach for addressing the interpersonal problems. Core interpersonal domains directly addressed in IPT-ED include lack of intimacy and interpersonal deficits, interpersonal role disputes, role transitions, complicated grief, and life goals (Murphy et al., 2012). Although the evidence base of IPT-ED is small relative to the extensive evidence base for CBT and IPT-ED is discussed less frequently in the literature, there is reasonably robust support for this approach to treating EDs (see Murphy et al., 2012 for a review). Thus, IPT-ED can make a lot of sense for a patient like Charlene (see Box 12.1). Finally, although IPT and CBT are rather conceptually distinct, IPT actually serves as the Interpersonal Module for CBT-E (Fairburn, 2008).

Box 12.1   Case Illustration: Charlene

Charlene, a 72-year old woman, was referred for treatment of almost daily objective binge episodes. Charlene was distressed by both the binge eating behavior, which made her feel out of control, and the resulting weight gain. During assessment Charlene revealed that she had struggled with bulimia nervosa in college but had been symptom free until a year earlier when her beloved husband died after experiencing a cardiac arrest. Charlene reported she had had an active social life until then, but was increasingly isolated and lonely. For several months after the death of her husband, Charlene's friends invited her to various events, but she declined because she was "too depressed with grief." Over time, the invitations dried up and Charlene discovered that she had restarted binge eating, although she managed to refrain from resuming vomiting. As Charlene had been symptom free for almost 50 years until the loss of her husband and her social life, Charlene's therapist proposed they try IPT-ED as a first-line treatment. Charlene appreciated that IPT-ED had an evidence base for both EDs and depression as she felt she had struggled with her mood ever since the death of her husband. Charlene also agreed that interpersonal loss had triggered her relapse; thus, IPT-ED was intuitively appealing to Charlene as it seemed to "get to the heart of my problems."

Problem-Solving Therapy

Another strategy for addressing life changes is problem-solving therapy, which is typically viewed as falling under the broad CBT umbrella. As noted above, depression commonly co-occurs with EDs in older women, and problem-solving for depression is supported by a robust evidence base in older adults (Arean et al., 1993; Arean, Hegel, Vannoy, Fan, & Unuzter, 2008), including those with executive dysfunction (Arean et al., 2010). Problem-solving has also long been an optional component of CBT for EDs that is used to address eating behaviors that are impacted by outside events (e.g., life changes) and mood (Fairburn, 2008; Fairburn, Marcus, & Wilson, 1993). Additionally,

Box 12.2 Case Illustration: Dorothy

Dorothy, a 55-year old single mother of twins in high school, reported that the onset of her binge eating began after her mother was hospitalized for what was expected to be relatively routine surgery. Prior to the surgery, Dorothy's mother was not only high functioning, but she also helped Dorothy by cooking dinner for the family several nights per week and driving the girls to their sports practices. After the surgery, however, Dorothy's mother did not return to her baseline cognitive functioning. Dorothy suddenly found herself struggling to find affordable care for her mother, whereas she juggled the needs of both her job and her daughters without the support of her mother. Dorothy noted that, secondary to lack of time after her mother's surgery, she gave up key self-care behaviors (e.g., exercising several times per week) that helped her "stay even keeled and grounded." Dorothy reported that the binge eating seemed to have replaced her exercise and that it also worsened her postmenopausal weight gain, which, in turn, made her feel terrible about her body. Prior to seeking treatment, Dorothy had begun using laxatives as a method of purging. Dorothy's therapist used CBT to treat her ED, but allocated extra time to the use of problem-solving to help Dorothy with the problems that appeared to have triggered her ED. Problem-solving helped Dorothy to better cope with her problems and begin to allocate some time back to self-care.

problem-solving historically has been used to address a wide range of problems. Within problem-solving therapy, problems are construed as resulting from a person environment interaction that is rooted in either a real or perceived disparity between a person's ability to cope and the demands of the situation (Nezu, Nezu, & D'Zurilla, 2012).

As noted by Fairburn (2008), patients tend to like problem-solving and often find it highly effective. However, as also noted by Fairburn, quality training on problem-solving is critical to its effectiveness. Fairburn (2008, p. 136–9) outlines the steps of problem-solving in the context of EDs. Given that we are proposing greater use of problem-solving than might occur with younger patients, readers may want to gain some additional background in this treatment strategy. For those interested in more in-depth information about the conceptual background of problem-solving, Nezu et al. (2012) is a recommended source.

Acceptance Strategies

Acceptance strategies are a third option for addressing life changes in mid- and late-life women. Many acceptance-based interventions include the use of mindfulness, acceptance, and values-based strategies, and are considered third-wave CBT methods (Hayes, 2004). In acceptance-based theories of psychopathology, body image dissatisfaction (i.e., preoccupation with eating, weight, and/or shape) and eating disordered behaviors are conceptualized as serving an experiential avoidance function that helps patients escape from uncomfortable emotions or situations that are either perceived to be less controllable or more difficult (e.g., interpersonal conflict, loss, and grief).

Broadly speaking, acceptance-based strategies emphasize that acceptance of reality "as it is" serves as the foundation to change. Change, in this case, often means behaving in effective and values-consistent ways, versus spending time and energy fighting or avoiding reality. Avoidance of reality, in the case of body image disturbances, can look like avoidance of health behaviors (e.g., exercise) following weight gain during menopause. Alternatively, perseverating on body dissatisfaction, body checking, or eating behaviors may function to avoid empty nester syndrome or feelings of loneliness. In contrast, acceptance-based strategies take the approach that one can still engage in values-consistent behaviors even while experiencing discomfort. One of the prevailing acceptance-based approaches, ACT (Hayes, Strosahl, & Wilson, 1999), teaches patients to accept difficult personal experiences (e.g., thoughts, feelings, memories, and sensations), versus trying to push away or change them, and engage in values-consistent behaviors anyway (even with difficult experiences present).

As noted above, middle-aged and older adults experience aging-related changes in their body (e.g., loss of body function; changes in body appearance; medical conditions more common with aging; loss of reproductive ability for women; or cognitive decline) that are often very difficult to cope with and accept. Other psychosocial stressors associated with aging include role transitions in life (e.g., retirement, adult children moving away, etc.), loss of independence (e.g., assisted living, moving in with adult children, etc.), grief, and loss of social support. An acceptance-based approach teaches aging adults to accept these losses and associated difficult emotions (versus fighting or avoiding them) and to become more mindful of, and less influenced by, unhelpful thinking patterns. Notably, ACT strategies also emphasize an individual's values and a commitment to behave in ways that are consistent with their values (e.g., health-promoting behaviors such as exercise and healthy eating, calling family that has moved away, etc.) even in the context of difficult experiences, in order to enhance overall quality of life. As noted below, emphasizing values is recommended for tailoring interventions for older adults (Petkus & Wetherell, 2013).

Dialectical behavior therapy (DBT; Linehan, 1993; Linehan, 2013) offers additional strategies that fall under the realm of acceptance- or mindfulness-based therapies. From a DBT framework, disordered eating is conceptualized as an ineffective behavioral response to difficulties with emotion regulation, especially of negative emotions. Disordered eating behaviors then serve to alleviate, albeit temporarily, the discomfort of a negative emotion state. Notably, the affect regulation model of binge eating (Polivy & Herman, 1993) fits within

> **Box 12.3 Case Illustration: Sue**
>
> Sue, a 63-year-old married woman, initially presented to treatment for depressed mood. Upon evaluation, Sue reported significant body image disturbance that impacted her engagement in life activities and subsequent low mood. Sue stated that, prior to menopause, she was quite satisfied with her appearance and fully engaged in life. Following menopause, Sue became significantly distressed by her body shape changes – especially her stomach and arms – and began withdrawing from activities due to intense body shame. She was terrified that others would be "disgusted" by her body and would judge her at social gatherings or while exercising. She was worried that her husband now found her unattractive, so she stopped all intimacy with him in order to avoid the possibility of rejection by him. Every few months, Sue attempted extreme dieting, but "couldn't lose weight like I used to" and became more depressed. This frequently prompted night binge eating episodes, which accompanied postmenopausal sleep disturbances. Sue's therapist encouraged her to accept her difficult body image thoughts and discomfort while still engaging in values-consistent behaviors (e.g., physical activity and marital relationship), and to not act on urges to avoid situations where these difficult thoughts and feelings might arise, such as dining out with friends. Accepting difficult thoughts/fears while choosing to still engage in meaningful life activities helped alleviate Sue's body shame and depressed mood, and improved her overall health behaviors.

the DBT framework. In DBT, patients learn skills to improve emotion regulation abilities, to cope with difficult emotions without engaging in ineffective behaviors (e.g., bingeing or purging), and to reduce situations/contexts/events that can trigger negative emotions.

Although full-package DBT has demonstrated positive results in patients through midlife (e.g., DBT for binge ED M age = 50), clinicians also can integrate specific acceptance-based skills into other types of ED treatment of midlife and older adults for EDs or body dissatisfaction (i.e., a DBT-informed approach). Radical acceptance, which is the total and complete acceptance of the current situation with particular emphasis on things that cannot be changed via problem-solving, could be utilized as a strategy for accepting aging-related experiences such as body changes (function and appearance), losses and role transitions, development or management of chronic illness, interpersonal stressors (e.g., family caregiving roles, as noted above), etc. Radically accepting these aging-related experiences opens the doors for patients to engage in health behaviors consistent with their goals and values, even if they do not like these experiences. Additionally, mindfulness to current emotions and current thoughts can be

Middle-Aged and Older Adults 279

skills taught for "riding out" urges based on emotions or dysfunctional thinking without acting on them. For instance, helping patients resist urges to binge in the context of stress related to caring for an elderly parent. Finally, many of the distress tolerance skills taught in DBT with the goal of reducing acting on impulsive (and ineffective) urges may be relevant to incorporate when working with middle-aged or older adults with EDs. For guidance, clinicians can look to skills within the Core Mindfulness and Distress Tolerance modules to find acceptance-based strategies (Linehan, 2013).

Important Considerations When Working with Older Adults

By far, the bulk of the literature to date on psychotherapeutic interventions for older adults comprises treatments for geriatric depression, anxiety, and insomnia (Chand & Grossberg, 2013). Across studies, various recommendations exist for tailoring evidence-based interventions for older adults (e.g., CBT) to address a range of factors that can impede treatment effectiveness. Below, we have extrapolated those recommendations to address adaptations to treatments for EDs.

1 Cognitive status: An important consideration for treatment of older adults with EDs (or even serious body image concerns) is cognitive status. Specifically, increasing age is the most robust predictor of cognitive decline (Deary et al., 2009). Additionally, geriatric depression often presents similarly to biologically based neurocognitive impairment (e.g., memory problems, executive dysfunction, slowed processing speed, visuospatial deficits, impaired decision-making, and difficulties with problem-solving) and even failure to thrive. Given the association of EDs with symptoms of depression in adults across the lifespan, considerations regarding cognitive status are important when treating older adults with EDs. Recommended changes include:

   a   Memory and learning aids: One recommendation when conducting CBT with older adults is to increase the amount of written and visual aids, as well as multimodal presentation of information (Mackin & Arean, 2005; Stanley et al., 2003). This can include greater use of handouts, information sheets, note cards, visual graphs or colors for charting mood ratings, and enhanced use of external reminders (e.g., post-it notes and reminder calls from providers). Notably, including additional memory and learning aids for older adults appears to improve response rate (Chand & Grossberg, 2013). Reminder calls from clinicians also have improved compliance in studies of CBT for geriatric anxiety.

   b   Pacing of material: Processing speed slows with age. Use of structured material, more time to review information presented, external aids (e.g., taking notes), and less time pressure are associated with better uptake by older adults (Satre, Knight, & David, 2006). Slowing the pace of presenting material can help reduce time pressure; thus, preparing less material per therapy session and preparing to review/repeat information regularly can promote better uptake of information and, therefore, better response to treatment.

    c Emphasize behavioral strategies: For older adults with cognitive decline, prioritizing behavioral strategies over cognitive restructuring can be a more effective approach (i.e., increased emphasis on behavioral exposures, activity scheduling, behavioral rehearsal, and behavioral hierarchies). Furthermore, maladaptive thought patterns or core beliefs may have persisted for many years and, in some cases, even strengthened over a life course (Chand & Grossberg, 2013). Duration of dysfunctional thoughts and beliefs, paired with slowed processing and other potential cognitive decline, can slow and prolong the time needed for effective cognitive restructuring as compared to younger patients. This provides another reason for relying more heavily on behavioral strategies.

2 Increase psychoeducation and reduce jargon: There is a tendency among older cohorts to downplay psychological difficulties and to attribute psychological symptoms to physical ailments (Stanley et al., 2003). When working with older adults, it is important to dedicate substantial time and effort to patient education. It is also recommended that providers use lay language as opposed to psychological jargon (Stanley et al., 2003).

3 Understand the sociocultural context of older adults: There are various sociocultural considerations when working with older adults that can impact intervention-tailoring.

    a Living arrangements: It is important to inquire about living arrangements of older adults (e.g., living independently, assisted living, living with adult children/families, retirement communities, etc.). For patients not living independently, consultation with and possible involvement of care providers in treatment can be necessary (Satre et al., 2006). For older women living with partners or extended family, understanding pressures and expectations regarding food preparation and serving is important to assess. Older adults who have elderly parents cohabitating (especially if elderly parents have significant cognitive impairment, dementia, or Alzheimer's Disease) can have highly unpredictable schedules and caretaking expectations. Finally, refusal to eat may reflect unhappiness with living arrangements (e.g., nursing home) or passive suicide attempts (Aziz et al., 2017). Thus, understanding logistics around food preparation, planning, and inability to have consistent schedules is critical when implementing evidence-based treatment for EDs with older adults.

b   Education/literacy: Depending on factors such as year of birth, geographical location, and SES, older adults may have had vastly different exposure to schooling and, therefore, present with varying levels of literacy (Satre et al., 2006). Lower levels of literacy can impact a patient's ability to use food records or worksheets. Thus, it is important to assess and understand these factors, to approach this nonjudgmentally, and to tailor materials, home assignments, etc., as needed.

c   Financial considerations: As with other underserved populations, assessment and consideration of older adults' financial status (including health insurance) is important. Various factors can influence older adults' financial status, such as long-term disability, retirement, and family caregiving responsibilities. When discussing food planning, for instance, consider how financial status may impact feasibility of implementing food choice and preparation recommendations.

d   Social networks: With increasing age, individuals tend to have smaller social networks than younger individuals; however, older adults have greater emotional depth and investment in their relationships (Satre et al., 2006). Consideration of social support is important when tailoring treatment of EDs in older adults, especially in understanding factors that trigger or maintain ED behaviors (e.g., loneliness and loss of relationships).

e   Transportation: Older adults may have difficulties with transportation, secondary to inability to retain a driver's license, financial inability to own a vehicle, and physical decline that prevents use of public transportation independently. All of these can significantly affect older adults' access to treatment and contribute to higher rates of treatment dropout in this population (Stanley et al., 2003). Similar to other factors, transportation issues can also prevent older adults from following standard treatment recommendations in ED treatments (e.g., shopping for foods and regularly scheduled meals).

f   Disability and medical status: Although certainly not unique to older adults, increasing age is accompanied by more frequent physical disability, medical conditions, and acute medical conditions (e.g., illness or injury). Medical conditions more common in aging adults can directly impact eating behaviors. Loss of or damage to teeth and other dental problems, gastrointestinal and other digestive disorders, and cancer (treatments and illness) all can negatively impact eating behaviors. Even without substantial medical problems, older adults produce less saliva, which causes dry mouth and can make swallowing foods more difficult (e.g., Aziz et al., 2017). Slowed peristalsis, reduced bowel muscle tone, and sedentary lifestyle all contribute to slowed digestion, constipation, and the sensation of feeling full for longer in older adults. Of note, polypharmacy is extremely common among older adults, which can also impact digestion, appetite, and eating behaviors (e.g., Aziz et al., 2017).

For women, urinary incontinence is a frequent experience with aging, as well as associated medical conditions such as pelvic floor disorders, that can cause or exacerbate urinary incontinence. This can significantly impact older women's ability to engage in physical activity, complete activities out of the home, and can lead to seclusion behaviors. Each can elicit negative emotions that can prompt or exacerbate disordered eating urges and behaviors (Sanses, Kudish, & Guralnik, 2017).

g   Losses and transitions: As noted above, loss is a predominant and common theme among aging individuals. Older adults face multidimensional losses (e.g., loss of body function, loss of cognitive status, interpersonal loss and grief, and loss of independence). It is important to consider not only what are those losses, but also how losses and late life transitions can prompt maladaptive thoughts (e.g., thoughts of past mistakes, missed opportunities, and past conflicts or troubles) and emotions (regret, guilt, shame, or feelings of hopelessness, loss of self-worth, burdensomeness on family/friends; Chand & Grossberg, 2013; Satre et al., 2006). Such difficult thoughts and emotions can play a role in disordered eating onset or maintenance (Polivy & Herman, 1993).

h   Emphasis on religion/spirituality and values: For many older adults, thoughts on mortality and end-of-life issues are pronounced. Thus, it is recommended that psychotherapy for older adults can be enhanced by incorporating religion and spirituality (Mackin & Arean, 2005; Stanley et al., 2003; Stanley et al., 2011). Additionally, due to frequent losses and transitions experienced among older-aged individuals, integrating values-based strategies may be particularly effective for this population (Petkus & Wetherell, 2013). Incorporating an emphasis on values (which can include spiritual or religious values) is consistent with many acceptance-based and mindfulness-based interventions (e.g., ACT and DBT). With respect to values, older adults tend to be more invested in preserving their health, wellbeing, and body functionality for their children or grandchildren, which can serve as a key motivation for behavior change in this population (Aziz et al., 2017).

i   Group (versus individual) interventions: Although younger indi viduals can experience social isolation or difficulties maintaining interpersonal relationships, social isolation and loss of social support is a highly common experience of older adults (Satre et al., 2006; Stanley et al., 2003). Thus, group modalities may be especially useful. It is important to note, however, that ED clinicians should be mindful when working with mixed-age treatment groups. Specifically, older women may feel hesitant about participating in a treatment group with adolescents or young women. Furthermore, older women can take on more of a mothering/caretaking role for younger women in co-treatment settings and, in turn, focus less on their own recovery (Aziz et al., 2017).

j Caregiver considerations: Similar to family-based therapies employed in the treatment of childhood and adolescent EDs (Lock & Le Grange, 2005), older adults often have caregivers involved in their activities of daily living (ADLs) and instrumental ADLs that can be included in treatment planning. Depending on the patient's functional status, including caregivers in treatment modalities can be important in supporting the patient. For older adults with cognitive impairment, caregivers can be integral in the at-home implementation of treatment recommendations (e.g., timing of meals and monitoring of eating behaviors) and can serve as additional memory aids for the patient.

Case Example of Tailoring a CBT-Based Body Image Intervention for Adult Women: Development of the *Women's Body Initiative*

Recently, our team began the process of tailoring and pilot-testing a dissonance-based body image intervention for adult women. We first convened a focus group of women (over age 30) in the community and gathered feedback on logistical considerations (e.g., unanimous preference for four 1-hour sessions versus two 2-hour sessions), as well as preliminary content changes (e.g., greater focus on the aging body). Beginning with a series of beta tests using preparatory-to-pilot groups (i.e., no research data on outcomes), we systematically adapted the *Body Project* to adult women using both participant feedback and observations by the treatment developer (CBB), a trained co-facilitator, and a *Body Project* master trainer (LSK). On the basis of this process, we made the following modifications.

1   Content: First, we modified the appearance ideal discussion to explicitly elicit aging-related appearance content (e.g., no wrinkles, no dark/aging spots, nongray hair, no varicose veins, and taught skin on the legs and arms). Second, we added activities targeting: (1) age-related negative body-talk (i.e., old talk: Becker, Diedrichs, Jankowski, & Werchan, 2013); (2) advantages of aging; (3) advantages of accepting the aging process (versus fighting it tooth-and-nail); and (4) role-plays countering both perpetual youth and thinness.
2   Pacing: The *Body Project* manual provides estimated time allotments for each section within a session (e.g., costs associated with pursuing the thin-ideal: 20 minutes). However, once we began beta-testing the *Women's Body Initiative*, we found that the amount of time allotted to each activity was often insufficient. In contrast to college women and high school girls, adult women participating in these beta tests shared

more about their life story (e.g., personal examples and interpersonal relationships in the context of eating, weight, or appearance pressures). They also shared more about the emotional toll of longstanding body dissatisfaction (in some cases, histories of disordered eating, extreme weight cycling, etc.). Additionally, participants allocated more time for each participant to share her story, asked follow-up questions, provided validation, and/or shared their own stories in connection. Finally, participants used nonverbal behavior that demonstrated a desire to pause and think about questions before answering (e.g., furrowing brow and bringing a hand to the face in a classic "thinking pose" that conveyed the question was being seriously considered). All of these factors markedly reduced the amount of classic *Body Project* content that could be covered in a given period of time. Therefore, we modified the pacing in the manual to reflect additional time for reflection and these types of thoughtful, more in-depth personal discussions and personal history. It is worth noting that this was an iterative process that took place over several preparatory-to-pilot groups. After the first group, we allocated more time to activities, believing the new time allotments would be sufficient. However, in the next iteration, it was clear that even more time needed to be allocated. We share this to emphasize the marked difference in pacing with middle-aged and older women.

3   More home activities: To address content volume issues generated by slower pacing, we moved more material to homework. This, in turn, created more at-home written activities and reading material.

4   Loss as a common experience: Women very frequently discussed losses as contributing to body image dissatisfaction and/or dysregulated eating behaviors. Adult children moving away and feelings of loneliness, loss of body function (including metabolic function, aches and pains, changes in physical activity), loss of feeling attractive, and loss of societal acknowledgement (i.e., "invisibility syndrome") were all commonly described by participants as factors playing a role in body dissatisfaction. Indeed, body dissatisfaction takes on a multidimensional quality in older women that we see less often in younger women. More specifically, older women feel unhappy not only about the appearance of body changes with age (e.g., increased adipose tissue, wrinkled skin, etc.), but also how the body functions and feels.

5   Values and religion: Although we did not explicitly add religious- or values-based activities, participants brought up religion more often than we see with the traditional *Body Project*. For instance, religion came up in the letter to a younger woman encouraging her to let go of body image pressures, or as a reason to engage in self-love. Family was also a common value and motivation for improving body image (e.g., to set a good example for children and grandchildren).

6   Group Format: We maintained the small group format used in the traditional *Body Project*, which is consistent with recommendations for

tailoring interventions for older adults. Participants reported feeling supported by the group, sharing local resources (e.g., classes at local senior centers, free or low-cost services, and exercises important for aging, such as balance practice), and maintaining relationships with group members following completion of the program.

Summary and Conclusions

In this chapter, we provided a brief overview of the prevalence and correlates of EDs in middle-aged and older adults, as well as the limited existing research on ED and body image interventions for this population. As aging brings life experiences that can initiate or exacerbate EDs unique from younger individuals, we offered strategies for tailoring evidence-based psychological interventions for EDs in middle-aged and older populations. Given the limited literature on treating EDs in older populations, we incorporated recommendations from the literature for other psychopathology (e.g., geriatric depression) for advice on modifying ED interventions for older patients. Overall, although these strategies exist within formal treatment models, such strategies may involve more time or focus when life changes are a prominent component of the clinical picture. Thus, clinicians treating middle-aged and older adults should devote attention to evaluation and understanding of aging-related life experiences in the context of the EDs and body image disturbance.

References

Allaz, A. F., Bernstein, M., Rouget, P., Archinard, M., & Morabia, A. (1998). Body weight preoccupation in middle-age and ageing women: A general population survey. *International Journal of Eating Disorders, 23*(3), 287–294.

Allaz, A.F., Bernstein, M., Vannes, M.C., Rouget, P., & Morabia, A. (1993). Weight loss preoccupation in aging women: A review. *Journal of Nutrition and Healthy Aging, 3*(3), 177–181.

Arean, P., Hegel, M., Vannoy, S., Fan, M. Y., & Unuzter, J. (2008). Effectiveness of problem-solving therapy for older, primary care patients with depression: Results from the IMPACT project. *The Gerontologist, 48*(3), 311–323.

Arean, P. A., Perri, M. G., Nezu, A. M., Schein, R. L., Christopher, F., & Joseph, T. X. (1993). Comparative effectiveness of social problem-solving therapy and reminiscence therapy as treatments for depression in older adults. *Journal of Consulting and Clinical Psychology, 61*(6), 1003–1010.

Arean, P. A., Raue, P., Mackin, R. S., Kanellopoulos, D., McCulloch, C., & Alexopoulos, G. S. (2010). Problem-solving therapy and supportive therapy in older adults with major depression and executive dysfunction. *American Journal of Psychiatry, 167*(11), 1391–1398.

Aziz, V. M., Rafferty, D., & Jurewicz, I. (2017). Disordered eating in older people: Some causes and treatments. *BJPsych Advances, 23*(5), 331–337.

Becker, C. B., Diedrichs, P. C., Jankowski, G., & Werchan, C. (2013). I'm not just fat, I'm old: Has the study of body image overlooked "old talk"? *Journal of Eating Disorders, 1*(1), 6.

Becker, C. B., Verzijl, C. L., Kilpela, L. S., Wilfred, S. A., & Stewart, T. (2017). Body image in adult women: Associations with health behaviors, quality of life, and functional impairment. *Journal of health psychology, 24*(11), 1536–1547.

Bedford, J. L., & Johnson, C. S. (2006). Societal influences on body image dissatisfaction in younger and older women. *Journal of Women & Aging, 18*(1), 41–55.

Bock, J.-O., Luppa, M., Brettschneider, C., Riedel-Heller, S., Bickel, H., Fuchs, A., ..., Scherer M., (2014). Impact of depression on health care utilization and costs among multimorbid patients – Results from the MultiCare Cohort Study. *PLoS One 9*(3): e91973. https://doi.org/10.1371/journal.pone.0091973.

Carrard, I., & Rothen, S. (2020). Factors associated with disordered eating behaviors and attitudes in older women. *Eating and Weight Disorders, 25*, 567–575. https://doi.org/10.1007/s40519-019-00645-4.

Chand, S. P., & Grossberg, G. T. (2013). How to adapt cognitive-behavioral therapy for older adults. *Current Psychiatry, 12*(3), 10–15.

Clarke, L. H., & Griffin, M. (2008). Visible and invisible ageing: Beauty work as a response to ageism. *Ageing & Society, 28*(5), 653–674.

Conceição, E. M., Crosby, R., Mitchell, J. E., Engel, S. G., Wonderlich, S. A., Simonich, H. K., ..., Le Grange, D. (2013). Picking or nibbling: Frequency and associated clinical features in bulimia nervosa, anorexia nervosa, and binge eating disorder. *International Journal of Eating Disorders, 46*(8), 815–818.

Conceição, E. M., Gomes, F. V. S., Vaz, A. R., Pinto-Bastos, A., Machado, P. P. P. (2017). Prevalence of eating disorders and picking/nibbling in elderly women. *International Journal of Eating Disorders, 50*, 793–800. doi.org/10.1002/eat.22700.

Cornali, C., Franzoni, S., Frisoni, G. B., & Trabucchi, M. (2005). Anorexia as an independent predictor of mortality. *Journal of the American Geriatrics Society, 53*(2), 354–355. doi:10.2460/javma.241.10.1275.

Cumella, E. J., & Kally, Z. (2008). Profile of 50 women with midlife-onset eating disorders. *Eating Disorders, 16*(3), 193–203.

Currin, L., Schmidt, U., Treasure, J., & Jick, H. (2005). Time trends in eating disorder incidence. *The British Journal of Psychiatry, 186*(2), 132–135.

Deary, I. J., Corley, J., Gow, A. J., Harris, S. E., Houlihan, L. M., Marioni, R. E., ..., Starr, J. M. (2009). Age-associated cognitive decline. *British Medical Bulletin, 92*(1), 135–152.

Fairburn, C. G. (2008). *Cognitive behavior therapy and eating disorders*, New York, NY: Guilford Press.

Fairburn, C. G., & Beglin, S. J. (1994). Assessment of eating disorders: Interview or self-report questionnaire? *International Journal of Eating Disorders, 16*(4), 363–370.

Fairburn, C. G. (1997). Interpersonal psychotherapy for bulimia nervosa. In D. M. Garner & P. E. Garfinkel (Eds.), *Handbook of treatment for eating disorders* (pp. 278–294). New York: Guilford Press.

Fairburn, C. G., Marcus, M. D., & Wilson, G. T. (1993). Cognitive-behavioral therapy for binge eating and bulimia nervosa: A comprehensive treatment manual. In Wilson, G. T. and Fairburn, C. G. (Eds.) *Binge Eating: Nature, Assessment, and Treatment* (pp. 317–360). New York, NY: Guilford Press.

Fallaz, A. F., Bernstein, M., Van, M. N., Rouget, P., & Morabia, A. (1999). "Weight loss preoccupation in aging women": A review. *The Journal of Nutrition, Health & Aging, 3*(3), 177–181.

Gagne, D. A., Von Holle, A., Brownley, K. A., Runfola, C. D., Hofmeier, S., Branch, K. E., & Bulik, C. M. (2012). Eating disorder symptoms and weight and shape concerns in a large web-based convenience sample of women ages 50 and above: Results of the gender and body image (GABI) study. *International Journal of Eating Disorders*, *45*(7), 832–844.

Goldschmidt, A. B., Wall, M., Choo, T.-H. J., Becker, C., & Neumark-Sztainer, D. (2016). Shared risk factors for mood-, eating-, and weight-related health outcomes. *Health Psychology*, *35*(3), 245–. doi.org/10.1037/hea0000283.

Grilo, C. M., Crosby, R. D., Wilson, G. T., & Masheb, R. M. (2012). 12-month follow-up of fluoxetine and cognitive behavioral therapy for binge eating disorder. *Journal of Consulting and Clinical Psychology*, *80*(6), 1108–1113.

Grilo, C. M., Masheb, R. M., & Salant, S. L. (2005). Cognitive behavioral therapy guided self-help and orlistat for the treatment of binge eating disorder: A randomized, double-blind, placebo-controlled trial. *Biological Psychiatry*, *57*(10), 1193–1201.

Guerdjikova, A. I., O'melia, A. M., Mori, N., McCoy, J., & McElroy, S. L. (2012). Binge eating disorder in elderly individuals. *International Journal of Eating Disorders*, *45*(7), 905–908.

Gupta, M. A. (1990). Fear of aging: A precipitating factor in late onset anorexia nervosa. *International Journal of Eating Disorders*, *9*(2), 221–224.

Haines, J., & Neumark-Sztainer, D. (2006). Prevention of obesity and eating disorders: A consideration of shared risk factors. *Health Education Research*, *21*(6), 770–782, doi.org/10.1093/her/cyl094.

Hay, P. J., Mond, J., Buttner, P., Darby, A. (2008). Eating disorder behaviors are increasing: Findings from two sequential community surveys in South Australia. *PLoS One 3*(2): e1541. https://doi.org/10.1371/journal.pone.0001541.

Hayes, S. C. (2004). Acceptance and commitment therapy, relational frame theory, and the third wave of behavioral and cognitive therapies. *Behavior Therapy*, *35*(4), 639–665.

Hayes, S. C., Strosahl, K. D., & Wilson, K. G. (1999). *Acceptance and commitment therapy: An experiential approach to behavior change.* New York, NY: Guilford.

Iacovino, J. M., Gredysa, D. M., Altman, M., & Wilfley, D. E. (2012). Psychological treatments for binge eating disorder. *Current Psychiatry Reports*, *14*(4), 432–446.

Jackson, K. L., Janssen, I., Appelhans, B. M., Kazlauskaite, R., Karavolos, K., Dugan, S. A., ..., Kravitz, H. M. (2014). Body image satisfaction and depression in midlife women: The Study of Women's Health Across the Nation (SWAN). *Archives of Women's Mental Health*, *17*(3), 177–187.

Keel, P. K., Dorer, D. J., Franko, D. L., Jackson, S. C., & Herzog, D. B. (2005). Postremission predictors of relapse in women with eating disorders. *American Journal of Psychiatry*, *162*(12), 2263–2268.

Keel, P. K., Gravener, J. A., Joiner Jr, T. E., & Haedt, A. A. (2010). Twenty-year follow-up of bulimia nervosa and related eating disorders not otherwise specified. *International Journal of Eating Disorders*, *43*(6), 492–497.

Kessler, R. C., Berglund, P. A., Chiu, W. T., Deitz, A. C., Hudson, J. I., Shahly, V., ..., Xavier, M. (2013). The prevalence and correlates of binge eating disorder in the WHO World Mental Health Surveys. *Biological Psychiatry*, *73*(9), 904–914.

Klerman, G. L., Weissman, M. M., Rounsaville, B. J., & Chevron, E. S. (1984). *Interpersonal psychotherapy of depression.* Northvale, NJ: Jason Aronson.

Lapid, M. I., Prom, M. C., Burton, M. C., McAlpine, D. E., Sutor, B., & Rummans, T. A. (2010). Eating disorders in the elderly. *International Psychogeriatrics*, *22*(4), 523–536.

288 *Kilpela, Gomez, and Becker*

Lewis, D. M., & Cachelin, F. M. (2001). Body image, body dissatisfaction, and eating attitudes in midlife and elderly women. *Eating Disorders, 9*(1), 29–39.

Lewis-Smith, H., Diedrichs, P. C., Rumsey, N., & Harcourt, D. (2016). A systematic review of interventions on body image and disordered eating outcomes among women in midlife. *International Journal of Eating Disorders, 49*(1), 5–18.

Linehan, M. (1993). *Skills training manual for treating borderline personality disorder* (Vol. 29). New York: Guilford Press.

Linehan, M. M. (2013). *Dialectical behavior therapy.* Phoenix, AZ, USA: Milton H. Erickson Foundation.

Lock, J. & Le Grange, D. (2005). Family-based treatment of eating disorders. *International Journal of Eating Disorders, 37*(S1), S64–S67.

Mackin, R. S., & Arean, P. A. (2005). Evidence-based psychotherapeutic interventions for geriatric depression. *Psychiatric Clinics, 28*(4), 805–820.

Maine, M. D., Samuels, K. L., & Tantillo, M. (2015). Eating disorders in adult women: Biopsychosocial, developmental, and clinical considerations. *Advances in Eating Disorders: Theory, Research and Practice, 3*(2), 133–143.

Mangweth-Matzek, B., & Hoek, H. W. (2017). Epidemiology and treatment of eating disorders in men and women of middle and older age. *Current Opinion in Psychiatry, 30*(6), 446–451.

Mangweth-Matzek, B., Rupp, C. I., Hausmann, A., Assmayr, K., Mariacher, E., Kemmler, G., ..., Biebl, W. (2006). Never too old for eating disorders or body dissatisfaction: A community study of elderly women. *International Journal of Eating Disorders, 39*(7), 583–586.

Mangweth-Matzek, B., Hoek, H. W., Rupp, C. I., Lackner-Seifert, K., Frey, N., Whitworth, A. B., ..., Kinzl, J. (2014). Prevalence of eating disorders in middle-aged women. *International Journal of Eating Disorders, 47*(3), 320–324.

Mangweth-Matzek, B., Kummer, K. K., & Pope, H. G. (2016). Eating disorder symptoms in middle-aged and older men. *International Journal of Eating Disorders, 49*, 953–957.

Marshall, C., Lengyel, C. L., & Utioh, A. (2012). Body dissatisfaction among middle-aged and older women. *Canadian Journal of Dietetic Practice and Research, 73*(2), e241–e247.

Masheb, R. M., Dorflinger, L. M., Rolls, B. J., Mitchell, D. C., & Grilo, C. M. (2016). Binge abstinence is associated with reduced energy intake after treatment in patients with binge eating disorder and obesity. *Obesity, 24*(12), 2491–2496.

Masheb, R. M., Grilo, C. M., & Rolls, B. J. (2011). A randomized controlled trial for obesity and binge eating disorder: Low-energy-density dietary counseling and cognitive-behavioral therapy. *Behaviour Research and Therapy, 49*(12), 821–829.

McLean, S. A., Paxton, S. J., & Wertheim, E. H. (2010). Factors associated with body dissatisfaction and disordered eating in women in midlife. *International Journal of Eating Disorders, 43*(6), 527–536.

Mehler, P. S. (2017a). Medical complications of anorexia nervosa. *Eating disorders and obesity: A comprehensive handbook* (3rd ed., pp. 214–8). New York, NY: The Guilford Press.

Mehler, P. S. (2017b). Medical complications of bulimia nervosa. In *Eating disorders and obesity: A comprehensive handbook* (3rd ed., pp. 218–222). New York, NY: The Guilford Press.

Micali, N., Martini, M. G., Thomas, J. J., Eddy, K. T., Kothari, R., Russell, E., ..., Treasure, J. (2017). Lifetime and 12-month prevalence of eating disorders amongst women in mid-life: A population-based study of diagnoses and risk factors. *BMC Medicine, 15*(1), 12.

Midlarksy, E., Marotta, A. K., Pirutinsky, S., Morin, R. T., & McGowan, J. C. (2017). Psychological predictors of eating pathology in older adult women. *Journal of Women and Aging, 30*(2), 145–157. doi:10.1080/08952841.2017.1295665.

Miller, S. L., & Wolfe, R. R. (2008). The danger of weight loss in the elderly. *The Journal of Nutrition Health and Aging, 12*(7), 487–491.

Mitchell, J. E., & Crow, S. (2006). Medical complications of anorexia nervosa and bulimia nervosa. *Current Opinion in Psychiatry, 19*(4), 438–443.

Mitchell, K. S., & Wolf, E. J. (2016). PTSD, food addiction, and disordered eating in a sample of primarily older veterans: The mediating role of emotion regulation. *Psychiatry Research, 243*, 23–29.

Murphy, R., Straebler, S., Basden, S., Cooper, Z., & Fairburn, C. G. (2012). Interpersonal psychotherapy for eating disorders. *Clinical Psychology & Psychotherapy, 19*(2), 150–158.

Nezu, A. M., Nezu, C. M., & D'Zurilla, T. (2012). *Problem-solving therapy: A treatment manual.* New York, NY: Springer Publishing Company.

Paxton, S. J., McLean, S. A., Gollings, E. K., Faulkner, C., & Wertheim, E. H. (2007). Comparison of face-to-face and internet interventions for body image and eating problems in adult women: An RCT. *International Journal of Eating Disorders, 40*(8), 692–704.

Peat, C. M., Peyerl, N. L., & Muehlenkamp, J. J. (2008). Body image and eating disorders in older adults: A review. *The Journal of General Psychology, 135*(4), 343–358.

Persons, J. B. (2005). Empiricism, mechanism, and the practice of cognitive-behavior therapy. *Behavior Therapy, 36*(2), 107–118.

Persons, J. B. (2012). *The case formulation approach to cognitive-behavior therapy.* New York, NY: Guilford Press.

Petkus, A. J., & Wetherell, J. L. (2013). Acceptance and commitment therapy with older adults: Rationale and considerations. *Cognitive and Behavioral Practice, 20*(1), 47–56.

Pike, K. M., Dunne, P. E., & Addai, E. (2013). Expanding the boundaries: Reconfiguring the demographics of the "typical" eating disordered patient. *Current Psychiatry Reports, 15*(11), 411.

Polivy, J., & Herman, C. P. (1993). *Etiology of binge eating: Psychological mechanisms.*

Pruis, T. A., & Janowsky, J. S. (2010). Assessment of body image in younger and older women. *The Journal of General Psychology: Experimental, Psychological, and Comparative Psychology, 137*(3), 225–238.

Reas, D. L., & Stedal, K. (2015). Eating disorders in men aged midlife and beyond. *Maturitas, 81*(2), 248–255.

Sanses, T. V., Kudish, B., & Guralnik, J. M. (2017). The relationship between urinary incontinence, mobility limitations, and disability in older women. *Current Geriatrics Reports, 6*(2), 74–80.

Satre, D. D., Knight, B. G., & David, S. (2006). Cognitive-behavioral interventions with older adults: Integrating clinical and gerontological research. *Professional Psychology: Research and Practice, 37*(5), 489–498.

Saucier, M. G. (2004). Midlife and beyond: Issues for aging women. *Journal of Counseling & Development, 82*(4), 420–425.

Slevec, J. H., & Tiggemann, M. (2011). Predictors of body dissatisfaction and disordered eating in middle-aged women. *Clinical Psychology Review, 31*(4), 515–524.

Stanley, M. A., Beck, J. G., Novy, D. M., Averill, P. M., Swann, A. C., Diefenbach, G. J., & Hopko, D. R. (2003). Cognitive-behavioral treatment of late-life generalized anxiety disorder. *Journal of Consulting and Clinical Psychology, 71*(2), 309–319.

290 *Kilpela, Gomez, and Becker*

Stanley, M. A., Bush, A. L., Camp, M. E., Jameson, J. P., Phillips, L. L., Barber, C. R., ..., Cully, J. A. (2011). Older adults' preferences for religion/spirituality in treatment for anxiety and depression. *Aging & Mental Health, 15*(3), 334–343.

Stice, E., & Shaw, H. E. (2002). Role of body dissatisfaction in the onset and maintenance of eating pathology: A synthesis of research findings. *Journal of Psychosomatic Research, 53*(5), 985–993.

Tayback, M., Kumanyika, S., & Chee, E. (1990). Body weight as a risk factor in the elderly. *Archives of Internal Medicine, 150*(5), 1065–1072.

Thompson, K. A., & Bardone-Cone, A. M. (2019). Disordered eating behaviors and attitudes and their correlates among a community sample of older women. *Eating behaviors, 34*, 101301.

Tiggemann, M. (2004). Body image across the adult life span: Stability and change. *Body Image, 1*(1), 29–41.

Trace, S. E., Thornton, L. M., Runfola, C. D., Lichtenstein, P., Pedersen, N. L., & Bulik, C. M. (2012). Sleep problems are associated with binge eating in women. *International Journal of Eating Disorders, 45*(5), 695–703.

Tuffvesson, A. (2016, August 03). *Invisible woman syndrome: Do you have it?* Retrieved from https://thenewdaily.com.au/life/relationships/2016/07/30/invisible-woman-syndrome/.

Vander Wal, J. S. (2012). Night eating syndrome: A critical review of the literature. *Clinical Psychology Review, 32*, 49–59.

Weisenbach, S. L. & Kumar A. (2014). Current understanding of the neurobiology and longitudinal course of geriatric depression. *Current Psychiatry Reports, 16*:463.

Weissman, M., & Markowitz, J. (2007). *Clinician's quick guide to interpersonal psychotherapy.* New York, NY: Oxford University Press.

Weissman, M. M., Markowit, J. C., & Klerman, G. L. (2017). *The guide to interpersonal psychotherapy* (Updated and expanded edition). New York, NY: Oxford University Press.

Wilson, G. T., Grilo, C. M., & Vitousek, K. M. (2007). Psychological treatment of eating disorders. *American Psychologist, 62*(3), 199–216.

Part II

Applying Evidence-Based Treatments in Nontraditional Treatment Settings

13 Delivering Evidence-Based Treatments for Eating Disorders in the Home-Based Setting

Eva-Molly Petitto Dunbar, Christina C. Tortolani, Sandra M. Estrada, and Andrea Goldschmidt

Introduction

There are several interventions for eating disorders that have a strong evidence base. These include family-based treatment (FBT) for adolescents with anorexia nervosa (Lock & Le Grange, 2013); enhanced cognitive-behavioral therapy (CBT-E) for adolescents with bulimia nervosa (BN) and for adults across the diagnostic spectrum (Fairburn, 2008); and interpersonal psychotherapy (IPT) for adolescents and adults with binge eating-spectrum disorders (Wilson, Wilfley, Agras, & Bryson, 2010). Yet, despite research supporting their efficacy, implementation of these evidence-based treatments remains low outside of specialty research and private practice settings (Couturier & Kimber, 2015; Mussell et al., 2000). Many clients, particularly those of lower socioeconomic strata or from racial/ethnic minority backgrounds, may have difficulties accessing or engaging in treatment at these specialty practices due to transportation constraints, costs of treatment, language barriers, stigma associated with seeking treatment, and scheduling concerns (including family and work commitments that may make attendance by all family members challenging; Hart, Granillo, Jorm, & Paxton, 2011). Therefore, providing evidence-based treatments in settings other than traditional outpatient practices may improve access for clients who would otherwise receive no or suboptimal care. In particular, interventions delivered in the home offer an alternative to outpatient treatment that address many of the practical barriers that may limit client and family engagement (American Academy of Pediatrics, 2000; Cortes, 2004). In this chapter, we will describe the scientific premise and rationale for home-based behavioral treatment; review how home-based treatments have been utilized for other psychiatric disorders; discuss challenges and opportunities posed by the home-based treatment approach, particularly when applied to eating disorders; and present a clinical case in which a home-based model was applied to an evidence-based treatment for eating disorders. Although there are no published studies on home-based treatment for eating disorders, our group is currently testing FBT and CBT-E adapted for the home-based setting. Thus, most examples and case descriptions will be derived from these two treatment models. To conclude this chapter, we will discuss areas for future research with respect to home-based treatment, including exploration of other emerging treatments for eating disorders that may be amenable to delivery in the home.

Rationale for Home-Based Approaches

The theoretical premise for home-based treatment of maladaptive behavior derives, in part, from basic science research on learning and behavior change. This literature suggests that eliminating maladaptive behaviors (i.e., extinction) involves replacing these "old" behaviors with "new," inhibitory behaviors, a process which is sensitive to context (Bouton, 2014). That is, the context/setting in which learning of inhibitory behaviors occurs is itself a cue that becomes associated with the new behavior. Once the context is changed (and with it, contextual reminders to engage in the new behavior withdrawn), signals for the new behavior to occur are weakened (Podlesnik, Kelley, Jimenez-Gomez, & Bouton, 2017). Thus, intervention techniques designed to address eating disorder behaviors that are taught in a specific context/setting (e.g., outpatient therapy office) may not be adopted in other contexts/settings (e.g., dining room at home). These findings may explain the relatively high rates of relapse following treatment for eating disorders (McFarlane, Olmsted, & Trottier, 2008; Steinhausen, 2009), particularly those delivered in hospital-based settings which are highly structured and often fail to incorporate opportunities to generalize skills to external settings (i.e., treatment often takes place in locked units with few eating episodes occurring in external settings).

The primary goals of eating disorder treatment are to normalize eating behavior and to achieve weight restoration, where appropriate. This requires that meals and snacks occur multiple times a day, often across multiple settings (e.g., home, work, and school). According to behavior change theories, rates of eating disorder recovery should be maximized when treatment is delivered in as many naturalistic settings as possible, offering opportunities for adaptive behaviors (e.g., eating calorically appropriate meals and snacks without engaging in compensatory behaviors) to generalize to these multiple settings. Although it is not feasible for therapy to take place in every setting in which eating occurs, the home environment represents one setting in which numerous eating occasions may take place. Therefore, the home is a novel setting for delivering eating disorder treatment that may offer unique learning-related advantages to optimize treatment success.

As described later, home-based treatment can be costly, time-consuming, and resource intensive for clinicians, underscoring the importance of exercising caution in selecting treatments that are best suited for a home-based approach (Cortes, 2004). Indeed, although any type of treatment modality could potentially be adapted for delivery in the home-based setting, evidence-based treatments for eating disorders that include highly active components (e.g., behavioral exposures in CBT-E and supervised meals in FBT) may take particular advantage of the benefits offered by a home-based approach in terms of generalizability of learning. These treatments may ultimately prove to be more cost-effective when delivered in the home than interventions focused on providing support or validation, which offer no particular treatment-specific advantages when delivered in the home.

Overview of Home-Based Treatment

In recent years, there has been an increasing demand for home-based health care services, driven, in part, by a shift in demographics in the United States toward older age. As life expectancy has increased, so has the number of individuals managing multiple chronic health conditions and concomitant strains on functioning, including challenges with activities of daily living. Home-based health care was designed to help meet the needs of this segment of the population by helping individuals who wish to remain autonomous and self-sufficient for as long as possible receive quality health care at decreased cost (Landers et al., 2016).

In the medical field, a variety of home-based services may be provided, such as hospice care, nutrition education, medication management and education, physical rehabilitation, diagnostic testing (e.g., x-ray), nursing consultation, among others (Markle-Reid et al., 2006). Although home-based treatment may be common for the treatment of medical issues, in part because individuals with multiple health conditions that impact day-to-day functioning often have difficulties getting to a clinic, it has not been as well tested for psychiatric disorders. Yet, home-based treatment may offer similar accessibility benefits for individuals struggling with mental health issues (Maxfield & Segal, 2008).

Home-based mental health treatment is designed to offer intermediate care for those stepping down from inpatient or partial hospitalization, but not yet ready for outpatient psychotherapy, thus providing a short, intense "burst" of therapy to prepare clients for traditional weekly outpatient interventions. It may also be used as an alternative to requiring a higher level of care or for those who are unable (e.g., due to physical disability or emotional instability) or unwilling to seek therapeutic services outside of their homes (Edes et al., 2014). Home-based treatment is typically provided by community support organizations and child protective agencies, and involves the clinician providing services in the client's home. Because this model is resource intensive (e.g., involves travel time for clinicians in addition to actual face-to-face service time), third-party payers often adhere to strict guidelines regarding criteria required to qualify for home-based treatment (e.g., recipient's functioning must be impacted across multiple settings such as school, home, and community), and the frequency and duration of treatment (e.g., 3–5 hours of therapy per week for 6–10 weeks). Insurance coverage may also vary by state and insurance provider (e.g., commercial insurance versus government insurance providers). For example, in order to qualify for home-based services, clients insured under Medicare must be "homebound," i.e., unable to leave the home without taxing effort (Landers et al., 2016).

Families and clients who qualify for home-based mental health treatment are often more diverse in terms of socioeconomic status (SES) and race/ethnicity. In our experience working with one community mental health agency in Southern New England in the United States, clients are typically referred by the hospital or emergency room for step-down support and/or rapid stabilization. The clientele served is primarily insured by Medicaid, of a lower SES background (including many who are living in a single-caregiver home), has current or past involvement with a state agency, and may have recently immigrated with limited English-speaking abilities. In the context of these multiple presenting features, individuals served by the agency tend to be more psychosocially complex, including severe comorbidities (Cortes, 2004).

Training requirements for providing home-based treatment vary by agency. For example, some agencies require a minimum of a bachelor's degree, with group and individual supervision conducted by a licensed mental health provider. However, most agencies employ only master's-level clinicians. In contrast, the Veterans Health Administration's (VA) Home-Based Primary Care (HBPC) program, which offers home-based mental health services, requires providers to be doctoral level (e.g., psychologist or in some cases, a psychiatrist), as the population typically served often requires a range of complex psychological services (e.g., neuropsychological testing/interventions) that may exceed the training level of less-advanced clinicians (Karlin & Karel, 2013).

Home-Based Treatment for Other Health Conditions

Although home-based treatments for eating disorders have not been formally tested in rigorous empirical research studies, several prior studies have reported on the development and evaluation of home-based treatment for other health-related and psychiatric conditions. Home-based behavioral interventions have been found to be effective for mood disorders, anxiety disorders, and health-related conditions that often carry a mental health component, including diabetes, HIV/AIDS, and traumatic brain injury (Hicken & Plowhead, 2010). In addition, treating client's mental health issues in the home setting may reduce need for future psychiatric hospital admissions and emergency room visits by addressing emerging problems before they reach a crisis level.

There is a growing literature on the effectiveness and sustainability of community-based programs providing home-based mental health services (see Reifler & Bruce, 2014, for a review of ten "model" home-based programs for treating mental health concerns in homebound older adults), although studies tend to be feasibility studies and hence limited by small sizes. For example, Rowa et al. (2007) compared exposure with response prevention (ERP) in the office setting as compared to the home-based setting among 28 individuals with obsessive compulsive disorder (OCD). Both treatments evidenced similar rates of attrition, as well as equivalent levels of improvement in OCD symptoms and comorbid psychopathology over 3- and 6-month follow-up.

Thus, the authors concluded that home-based ERP may be useful for individuals who are unable to attend outpatient visits, those whose symptoms are less amenable to replication in an office environment, and those who find it challenging to try ERP on their own in their natural environments.

A 2010 systematic review by Ammerman et al. reported on home-based treatment of maternal depression. The authors describe studies in which they found that after 15 sessions of in-home cognitive behavior therapy (IH-CBT), a psychotherapy modeled after a cognitive-behavioral approach that is closely integrated with other ongoing home visitation services, mothers experienced significant decreases in depressive symptomatology. Furthermore, IH-CBT has been tested in a clinical trial (Ammerman et al., 2013) and has been incorporated into home visitation programs in ten states (Ammerman, Putnam, Teeters, & Van Ginkel, 2014). Ammerman, Putnam, Bosse, Teeters, and Van Ginkel (2010) also report on studies examining IPT delivered in the home setting by trained nurses for mothers with symptoms of depression. Results revealed a significant reduction in symptoms of depression after eight weekly sessions of IPT followed by an 8-week period during which clients could contact their clinician by phone. Taken together, CBT and IPT may be effectively incorporated into home visitation for postpartum depression.

Multisystemic therapy (MST) is a manualized evidenced-based family-based treatment (FBT) for youth with serious clinical problems, including substance use, criminal behavior, and conduct disorder. MST targets children and adolescents who are at risk of out-of-home placements (e.g., hospitalization, residential treatment, and incarceration), and is delivered in the client's natural setting, including the home, school, and community. It is typically delivered over a course of 4 months, where the clinician is available to be contacted by the family 24 hours a day. In MST, each case is seen by a team of three to four master's-level clinicians supervised by advanced trained MST doctoral or master's-level supervisors. Studies have demonstrated that MST is effective in improving family functioning, increasing school attendance, decreasing the client's psychiatric symptoms, reducing adolescent substance use, and decreasing long-term rates of rearrest (Sheidow & Woodford, 2003). In MST, the ecological conceptualization (taking into account the multiple contexts in which the child and family interact) of the cases is key to the treatment's success, which can be fully achieved as the treatment uses a home-based model of service delivery.

Another application of home-based treatment has been implemented within the VA, which began incorporating psychologists into their HBPC program in 2007. The HBPC approach utilizes a multidisciplinary continuity of care model in the home-based setting for veterans who have complicated health conditions that may not be appropriately managed in traditional clinic settings (Department of Veterans Affairs, 2019). The VA has identified home-based mental health treatment as improving access to mental health services, allowing for more efficient and accurate assessment and management in an underserved patient population. Although there are not currently any published data on the outcomes of this program, the VA describes potential

298　*Eva-Molly Petitto Dunbar et al.*

challenges and opportunities that psychologists may encounter in the home setting that may inform delivery of home-based services for other populations.

Although there is not yet an abundance of research on adapting psychosocial interventions for the home-based setting, the aforementioned examples suggest that this may be a promising avenue for improving access to mental health treatment while producing similar outcomes as traditional office-based approaches. Later we discuss considerations for adapting evidence-based eating disorder treatments to the home-based setting.

Home-Based Treatment Challenges and Opportunities

In addition to conferring specific benefits in terms of supporting new learning as described previously, providing psychotherapy for eating disorders in the home may provide several opportunities that would not otherwise be present in traditional therapy settings. For example, clinicians can canvas the home food environment to support appropriate food selection and meal preparation; gather information about the home which clients and families might not otherwise share; participate in family meals *in vivo* in the settings in which they typically occur; and observe behaviors and familial communication patterns that might not be evident in traditional treatment settings where clients may be less comfortable.

Opportunities

Access to Mental Health Services

In addition to improving access to treatment by addressing pragmatic barriers related to scheduling and travel, home-based treatment may improve the client's experience of mental health services in several ways. For example, clients may feel a greater sense of control in their own environment, which may, in turn, have a positive impact on the therapeutic alliance. Furthermore, the client may feel safe and comfortable in their home, which helps foster a positive environment for the therapeutic encounter. These experiences may lead to an increase in the acceptance of therapeutic interventions and decrease in the stigma associated with receiving mental health services in an office or agency that is open to the public (Hicken & Plowhead, 2010).

More Effective Treatment Planning

The clinician may observe behavior or communication patterns in the home that are not readily apparent in other settings (e.g., tendency to eat meals in front of the television, lack of dining room table or separated dining space), and which may either facilitate or impede behavior change. Understanding personal behavior patterns, family dynamics, and culture in a natural setting may aid in the treatment planning process (Reiter, 2000).

Improved Assessment

The home setting may provide the clinician with a more accurate picture of the client's daily routine, family functioning and food supply, including insight into the client's interactions with family members or roommates (e.g., involvement of client in meal preparation), information on the client's adherence to the treatment plan (e.g., checking the home for appropriate food choices and removing triggering environmental cues), and an opportunity to address safety concerns in the home (Hicken & Plowhead, 2010). In addition, the home setting offers clinicians an opportunity to witness treatment successes and challenges that the client may fail to report due to lack of awareness, self-report biases, and other sources of underreporting.

Support Outside of the Home

Because home-based treatment is not constrained to weekly, hour-long sessions, and always involves travel on the part of the provider, clinicians can be more creative in their use of therapy time. For example, clinicians can conduct restaurant exposures in locations that are frequented by the client, or assist with grocery shopping to provide psychoeducation and decrease burden on the client/family. In addition, the clinician can accompany the client to medical appointments, thus facilitating communication within a multidisciplinary team. Similarly, the clinician may attend school lunches and provide meal supervision in cases where the family is unable to do so and/or a qualified guidance counselor or school nurse is not available. During the process of reintroducing medically cleared physical activity, the clinician may accompany the client on a walk, which may provide a multitude of benefits, including helping the client process their thoughts and feelings about exercise in the moment (e.g., type of activity, boundaries set around the activity), ensuring that the client is walking at an appropriate pace and for an appropriate amount of time, and reminding the client to be more mindful while engaging in movement. Thus, providing home-based treatment may confer multiple advantages across other naturalistic settings as well.

In Vivo Interventions

The home-based setting can optimize the real-time practice of newly learned intervention skills by eliminating the need for clients to transport intervention materials to the office. For example, rather than relying on clients to remember to select a clothing item for a CBT-E behavioral exposure and bring it with them to the session, the clinician and client can collaboratively select an item directly from the client's closet. Similarly, in FBT, rather than directing the caregivers to bring a "family meal," which needs to be transportable and easily consumed in an office setting that may have limited food preparation facilities (e.g., microwave and utensils), the family meal(s) can occur with food the family already has in their home, in the setting where meals usually take place.

300   *Eva-Molly Petitto Dunbar et al.*

Challenges

Distractions

Distractions in the home setting are likely to be present to a much greater extent than in an office-based setting, and may interfere with the therapy process. Such distractions may include pets, electronics (e.g., televisions and telephones), visitors, or members of the household who are not involved in therapy (Maxfield, & Segal, 2008). These distractions may be managed through collaborative discussion about the importance of minimizing interruptions to therapy (to the extent possible) in order to facilitate a productive course of treatment and therapeutic relationship. Alternatively, the presence of distracting stimuli is a feature of everyday life that may interfere with the recovery process, and as such, may be useful to incorporate into therapy. For example, clinicians can assist clients in practicing problem-solving *in vivo* to minimize the impact of interruptions on compliance with the treatment plan (e.g., helping caretakers manage an adolescent leaving the dining room table to avoid eating, encouraging a client to stick with a difficult exposure which they might have ended prematurely without the clinician's support).

Role Confusion and Boundaries

The home environment has the potential to impact the nature of the therapeutic relationship (Knapp & Slattery, 2004). Given that treatment takes place in the client's home environment, the client may view the clinician as a visitor or guest rather than a health care provider, which may prompt him or her to focus on topics unrelated to treatment or ask the clinician for assistance with tasks unrelated to the treatment process. For example, in our work conducting home-based FBT, we have encountered ethical quandaries with families who were offered supportive services that initially were perceived as helpful, but later developed into concerns with appropriate boundaries (e.g., parents relying on clinician to supervise younger children during clinical interventions). In addition, clients may be more comfortable engaging in treatment interfering behaviors in the home setting relative to the office setting (e.g., locking themselves in the bedroom and refusing to take part in treatment). On the contrary, clinicians must delineate for themselves the extent to which they feel comfortable being an active participant in treatment versus a supportive coach (e.g., taking part in the family meal as a way to build rapport in the family's home). Taken together, the clinician must be clear in establishing the boundaries of the clinician–client relationship at the outset of treatment (e.g., clarifying the differences between clinician and visitor/guest).

Time Management

Home-based therapy sessions tend to be longer than the standard 50 minute office-based session, and include travel time to and from visits. Thus, there are

Eating Disorders in the Home-Based Setting   301

limitations on the number of clients that can feasibly be scheduled in 1 day and expectations for clinical productivity in the home-based setting must be modified (Mode of Therapy – Home Based Therapy, n.d.). Managed care requires the clinician to be flexible in adapting treatments to the home-based setting, as different insurance providers may have different requirements for the amount of time that the clinician spends providing treatment. For example, commercial insurance plans may require 6 hours of direct service per week, whereas state-funded plans may require 2 hours of in-home services per week. Thus, the clinician must adapt the treatment plan to fit the number of sessions covered by insurance while maintaining intervention fidelity and being careful not to introduce elements that may weaken the approach.

Safety

Clinicians may encounter safety issues in the home that would not be encountered or tolerated in the office environment (Lawson, 2005). These include the presence of dangerous pets, threats in the neighborhood, presence of firearms, relationships within the household that have the potential to escalate to violence, insect infestation, and unsanitary conditions, among others. It may not always be feasible for clinicians to take precautions to protect themselves from these issues (e.g., sitting by the door). Thus, the clinician must ensure proper safety precautions prior to home visits, including carrying a mobile communication device, alerting other clinicians (while being aware of Health Insurance Portability and Accountability Act concerns) as to where they are going and how long they are expected to be gone, and being familiarized with self-defense strategies.

Professional Competency / Complexity of Cases

Due to the intensity of treatment, including the complexity of clients' presenting concerns, travel time, and dose/duration of treatment, home-based treatment may present a higher than usual risk of burnout (which is already elevated in the treatment of clients with eating disorders) and significant turnover in staff. Therefore, receiving appropriate training and ongoing supervision and support is imperative (Lawson, 2005). Furthermore, as noted previously, families that qualify for home-based services often have a more severe and/or complicated presentation of illness and may have unique characteristics that make implementation of evidence-based treatments more challenging (e.g., involvement of child protective services). Therefore, careful consideration of the boundaries of competence and effects of the treatment on providers' own mental health is critical.

Confidentiality

Confidentiality may be impacted by the presence of friends, visitors, housemates, aides, etc. (Maxfield & Segal, 2008). In addition, there may be minimal private space in the client's home in which to engage in therapy sessions, which could impact disclosure of information during treatment. Thus, the clinician and client should discuss at the outset of treatment how to address issues that arise regarding confidentiality and privacy. For example, the clinician and client may decide to designate a part of the home for private sessions, which may require negotiation with other household members. Furthermore, the clinician and client should proactively discuss how to handle encounters with others during components of therapy that take place in the community (e.g., whether/how to introduce the clinician if the client sees an acquaintance during a restaurant exposure).

Case Presentation

Our group is currently testing the feasibility and effectiveness of home-based FBT for adolescents with restrictive eating disorders. FBT is currently the most efficacious outpatient behavioral intervention for adolescents with anorexia nervosa and related disorders, and may be an efficacious treatment for adolescents with BN as well. FBT is a highly structured behavioral approach in which caregivers are charged with the primary task of refeeding their ill child and normalizing his or her eating behaviors and weight status, with the ultimate goal of assisting the adolescent in achieving developmentally appropriate independence related to eating and other activities. To achieve this goal, treatment is typically delivered over 16 sessions (6–12 months of treatment) in three distinct phases whereupon caregivers' involvement is titrated down as the severity of the adolescent's eating disorder decreases.

In order for FBT to be adapted for the home-based setting, various elements of the treatment need to be modified or expanded. In traditional FBT, the second session consists of a family meal, which typically only occurs once during the course of treatment. The family meal provides an opportunity for the clinician to observe the family's current eating patterns and assist the caregiver with the task of refeeding the adolescent. In home-based FBT, the family meal may be conducted weekly or more, allowing for the goals of the meals to evolve with treatment. For example, initially the caregivers may be supporting the adolescent in completing one more bite than they had intended to complete, and this may then shift to 100% meal completion as treatment progresses. Additional sessions may involve a combination of family and individual sessions, and may include a focus on coping skills, meal supervision, parental support, or attending the client's medical appointments. Although individual treatment sessions with the adolescent are not included in standard FBT, they may be needed to supplement family sessions to meet third-party insurance requirements for home-based treatment frequency/intensity. The content of these sessions is selected to enhance, rather than contraindicate, the FBT approach, and to avoid introducing active components of other evidence-based treatments (e.g., meal planning, which might suggest that the adolescent rather than the parent is in control of food selection). Teaching adaptive coping, on the contrary, is purported to aid the client in tolerating FBT rather than undermining FBT interventions.

Eating Disorders in the Home-Based Setting 303

We present a case study that follows an adolescent and her family through a course of FBT that has been tailored to meet the unique constraints and opportunities of the home-based setting.

Case: Natalie

Presenting Problem and History

Natalie was a 16-year-old Latinx female from Colombia, living with her maternal grandmother, mother, and 6-year-old nephew. Natalie reported that her eating disorder developed 2 years ago, characterized by increasingly restricting her food intake, purging twice a week through vomiting, and water loading (five 0.5 L water bottles per day). She was attending a charter school that required a 1-hour commute and would restrict from 6 a.m. to 4 p.m. until she returned home. She also reported that her maternal grandmother's negative statements about the way she looked (e.g., "your thighs are so big," and "your butt is so low – you are like a duck") contributed to body image disturbance. Over the course of approximately 6 months, Natalie lost 9.10 kg. At this time, she was complaining of headaches, dizziness, fainting in school, and amenorrhea for the past 7 months. Her primary care provider sent her to a local children's hospital where she was admitted for 2 weeks and then discharged to an outpatient Spanish-speaking community mental health provider (who did not have any expertise in eating disorders). She was then referred for home-based FBT due to concerns surrounding her continued restrictive eating and an increase in symptoms of anxiety.

During the initial evaluation with the home-based therapist (who was a Spanish speaking, Latinx woman from Colombia), Natalie endorsed severe restrictive eating and excessive exercise. At the time of the intake, Natalie was at 93% of goal treatment weight (GTW). She also reported comorbid PTSD symptoms related to a previously undisclosed sexual assault and domestic violence in the family and symptoms of depression, including suicidal ideation, isolation, and sleep disturbances. Additionally, she reported intermittent self-injurious behaviors during times of high negative affect.

Natalie stated that she was raised by her mother and grandmother and had an adult sister who lived with them periodically. Natalie described high conflict between her mother and adult sister, which often resulted in physical altercations and police involvement. Her family history was notable for substance use and mood disorders, though her family's cultural values did not support open discussion of mental health diagnoses/treatment.

Treatment Summary

To adapt FBT for the home-based setting and to meet the needs of Natalie and her family, the clinician spent an average of 4 hours over 2–3 sessions per week delivering treatment, which included providing support in the home, school, and community. Sessions focused on weekly family meals, during which the clinician had the opportunity to observe and provide feedback on meal structure and caregivers' use of FBT-specific skills; and accompanying Natalie to her medical appointments to ensure appropriate collaboration between providers (adolescent medicine doctor within a local Eating Disorder Clinic). Natalie and her family engaged in FBT over the course of 21 weeks, which is longer than what is typically covered by third-party payers for home-based services. Figure 13.1 presents Natalie's weight trajectory throughout the treatment.

Over the course of treatment, Natalie completed Phase I and entered Phase II. The primary goals in Phase I were to provide psychoeducation to Natalie, her mother and grandmother, and school staff regarding eating disorders and their management; train all caregivers in meal supervision; and to return Natalie to her premorbid growth trajectory. As part of Phase II, once Natalie reached her GTW and conflict regarding eating was significantly decreased, independence over eating was gradually transferred back over to Natalie.

In order to accomplish these goals, and in line with standard FBT, the clinician first obtained a history of the illness; educated the family about the seriousness of the eating disorder; helped the family externalize the eating disorder as separate from Natalie; provided education and rationale for obtaining weekly exposed weights; observed the family's meals *in vivo*; provided support and empowerment to Natalie's caregivers in their efforts to refeed Natalie; communicated on a weekly basis with Natalie's outpatient medical providers; and facilitated food exposures in a wide variety of settings, including restaurants, food trucks, and cafes.

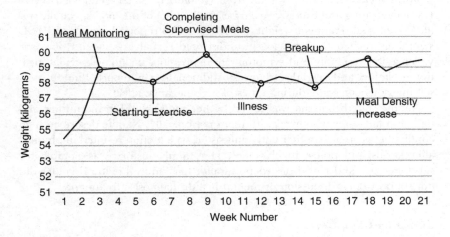

Figure 13.1 Natalie's Weight Gain Trajectory Throughout Home-Based FBT.

Specific adaptations for the home environment included weekly family meals, having the clinician attend medical appointments and supervise occasional meals when her mother and grandmother were unavailable, and conducting food exposures in the community.

Course of Treatment

Phase I

During the first 3 weeks of treatment (three sessions per week), Natalie's weight increased by 4.54 kg, which is a promising indicator of good treatment outcomes as demonstrated by research studies supporting early weight change as a marker of longer-term treatment response. During these first weeks in treatment, Natalie's grandmother and mother were appropriately mobilized in presenting and monitoring all of Natalie's meals (including preparing and packing her lunches, and communicating daily with the school nurse who was supervising snack and lunch). Food prepared represented calorically dense foods typical of Colombian culture (e.g., rice and beans, fried sweet plantains, and fried eggs). In addition, the clinician provided meal support at school twice a week and facilitated two family meals a week in the home. During this beginning phase, Natalie's grandmother provided the majority of meal support and supervision when her mother was working, but due to her continued criticism of Natalie (e.g., "why won't you just eat") and comments about Natalie's weight gain and shape, the clinician and mother decided that Natalie's grandmother should not provide meal supervision until she understood the consequence of her negative comments. Around Week 6, Natalie experienced a slight decrease in weight (~0.68 kg) corresponding to resumption of exercise, which had been approved by the medical outpatient provider. However, with the clinician's support and both Natalie and her mother's responsiveness to feedback, she gained 1.81 kg over the next 3 weeks (sessions 12–15). Natalie was completing 100% of her meals and snacks, and was being supervised at home by her clinician, mother, and grandmother; at school by the nurse; and in the community by her family and her clinician. The clinician then worked with Natalie's mother to present Natalie's feared foods (e.g., beef tacos with sour cream, fried steak, Burger King French Fries, and hamburgers) and they were able to successfully increase her variety of food choices to reflect pre-eating disorder eating.

Around Week 12, Natalie had a 1.81 kg weight loss due to illness, at which time her meals and snacks consisted primarily of foods that were low in energy density. Her weight continued to drop when her symptoms of anxiety and depression increased in the context of a relationship breakup and her adult sister moving back home. Her mother was not able to supervise meals due to the competing demand of helping her older daughter deal with an abusive relationship. However, by Week 18, Natalie had regained the 1.81 kg that she had lost and was again completing 100% of meals, which her mother was

306 *Eva-Molly Petitto Dunbar et al.*

continuing to present in the form of calorically dense food options (e.g., rice and beans, fried potatoes, and pasta with Alfredo sauce). During this time, Natalie's grandmother was able to provide more meal support without negative comments in the context of increased externalization of Natalie's eating disorder.

Phase II

Natalie entered Phase II around Week 18 when she achieved 100% of GTW, and demonstrated a consistent decrease in eating disorder symptoms and cognitions. Natalie was able to maintain her weight for the next several weeks and sessions decreased to twice a week. By session 21, her eating disorder symptoms and cognitions returned to within normal limits, she was completing meals on her own, and was successfully able to attend an overnight trip with her school. During the last session, Natalie shared her insights about eating disorder treatment: "Little things for you, mom, are big things for me," which Natalie's clinician and family recognized as significant in Natalie's family being able to openly discuss her eating disorder.

Phase III

Due to constraints around treatment length incurred by third-party payers, it is typical for individuals receiving home-based FBT treatment to complete Phase I, and enter into Phase II of treatment. However, if Natalie had progressed into Phase III of FBT while receiving home-based care, the goals would have been to review and problem-solve adolescent developmental issues, similar to standard outpatient FBT. Primary interventions in Phase III include educating the family on adolescent development and eating disorders, delineating and exploring adolescent themes, examining how caregivers are functioning together, and developing plans for relapse prevention. In the home setting, such interventions could be adapted by having the adolescent invite a friend to attend a therapy session so that the clinician can observe communication patterns and gain insight into the client's social functioning. In addition, the clinician can assess the family dynamics in the natural setting to help the family increase a sense of connection outside of the eating disorder. For example, subsequent to a family's report that the caregiver and adolescent are spending little quality time together, the clinician may observe that there is a television in the adolescent's room, which limits her time in "family" spaces. One intervention might be to suggest moving the television to another location to decrease the adolescent's sense of isolation, or to have the family engage in a group activity during the therapy session. Such interventions might not be appropriate or feasible in the office setting, as the family may lack awareness of the ways in which the physical layout of the home is interfering with family togetherness.

In summary, by the end of treatment, Natalie's mother and grandmother possessed the skills required to present appropriate meals, and Natalie's weight returned to its premorbid trajectory. Natalie completed Phase I of FBT and entered into Phase II by the end of home-based treatment, and was subsequently referred to outpatient therapy with a Spanish-speaking clinician for ongoing support around symptoms of anxiety and depression. She continued to follow up with the eating disorder outpatient medical team on a regular basis. This was a successful case despite the family's initial concerns about engaging in eating disorder treatment at a time when Natalie was experiencing heightened symptoms of anxiety and depression and beginning to disclose her trauma history to providers.

Home-Based FBT Successes and Challenges

In addition to challenges that would have been present in the context of FBT delivered in any setting (e.g., language barriers), conducting FBT with Natalie and her family presented several challenges specific to the home-based setting. One challenge included scheduling with Natalie's mother. Natalie's mother was a single parent and the sole financial provider for the family. Her work schedule varied and did not allow for frequent time-off requests. This might have presented more of a concern in an outpatient setting, where clinicians often schedule on the hour, and have fewer flexible hours (in particular, limited evening hours which often fill up quickly when working with school-aged clients). The home-based clinician needed to be flexible in accommodating the mother's work schedule, which sometimes meant late evening sessions.

At the start of treatment, Natalie and her family were primarily concerned with Natalie's symptoms of anxiety and depression. It was difficult for them to understand why treating the eating disorder was identified as a priority over treatment of comorbid psychopathology, which required a significant amount of psychoeducation from the clinician. The home-based setting enabled the clinician to highlight how Natalie's eating disorder was impacting the family and demonstrate why they needed to prioritize eating disorder treatment. For example, the clinician was able to show the family ways in which they had been accommodating Natalie's eating disorder, such as pointing out that they were demarcating specific foods in the home for Natalie only, as these were "safety" foods that the family had spent hours purchasing. Furthermore, the clinician pointed out the pictures of very slender models that Natalie had displayed around her room that may have been fueling Natalie's negative feelings about her body. These issues may not have been mentioned by the family in an office setting, whereas being in the home allowed Natalie's clinician to notice these eating disorder indicators and utilize them to drive home the importance of addressing AN as the primary diagnosis.

Finally, one of the main tenets of FBT is to empower parents/caregivers to manage the illness independently; however, the level of psychosocial stress that many clients in the home-based setting face (including Natalie's family) may contribute to the clinician struggling to balance empowering the caregivers to manage the illness, and disempowering them through intensive case

308   *Eva-Molly Petitto Dunbar et al.*

management. In Natalie's case, the clinician scheduled and attended medical appointments and provided transportation to ensure access to care, while at the same time communicating to the family that they had the tools to manage Natalie's care at home.

Despite these challenges, there were many opportunities presented by home-based FBT which may not have been possible in other settings. Successes to highlight in Natalie's case include the opportunity to train multiple generations of caregivers in the home in FBT despite the initial language barriers. For Natalie's family, treatment in the home setting allowed a level of comfort and safety to more easily express their emotions and genuinely engage in problem-solving around her eating. Other examples included navigating refeeding in the physical space of their apartment, where the clinician helped Natalie's grandmother to stay in the kitchen instead of going to her bedroom during meal supervision, and the clinician assessed food choices and preparation. For example, the clinician observed Natalie's grandmother making soups which are traditional in her culture but were not calorically dense enough, and was able to intervene in the moment by suggesting the grandmother add more oil and cream. The clinician was also able to target meal supervision at school by directly consulting with the school nurse in a face-to-face meeting, or helping Natalie's mother facilitate a meeting with the nurse, and developing a contingency plan to help Natalie reintegrate to social meals in the cafeteria when consistently eating 100% of her lunch. The family also moved from initial apprehension around a scale being brought into their home and engaging in exposed weighing, to being able to appropriately process and respond to weight data in sessions. Finally, the clinician was able to include natural supports outside of the family to help Natalie tolerate community-based meal exposures, including a friend who accompanied Natalie out to dinner with her and her family. On the contrary, in office-based FBT, a meal would not typically be conducted in the community, and a peer of the same age would likely not be included in treatment. Including a friend in treatment is consistent with the goals of Phase III, where eating may be social, and clinical attention is devoted to multiple domains of life rather than solely on food and weight, which is developmentally appropriate for an adolescent.

In the aforementioned case, consistent with an FBT approach, the caregivers are responsible for executing the core intervention strategies. Both learning and practicing these skills in the home may enhance generalizability and improve adherence and outcome. Here, the home-based setting has shown to be a promising alternative setting for delivering FBT treatment components.

Conclusions and Future Directions

Home-based treatment may be a powerful alternative approach to traditional clinic-based outpatient treatment that could overcome many barriers to treatment attendance and implementation. As such, adapting evidence-based treatments for the home setting has the potential to narrow treatment

Eating Disorders in the Home-Based Setting   309

disparities for clients with eating disorders who are underserved by current approaches. Despite its promise, however, there has been limited empirical testing of this home-based treatment as compared to traditional outpatient psychotherapy for psychiatric disorders in general, and no empirical testing in the eating disorder field. Therefore, future directions for research include rigorous empirical evaluation of the feasibility, acceptability, and effectiveness of delivering eating disorder interventions in the home-based setting. Our group is currently pilot testing outcomes of home-based FBT within a community-based behavioral health agency, and as such, much of this chapter has focused on adapting FBT for a home-based model. However, the development of research programs to adapt other treatments for eating disorders in the home setting and assess their effectiveness may also help increase the reach of eating disorder treatments. Examples of other treatments that have a strong evidence-base for eating disorders, or have shown promise in the treatment of eating disorders, that may be applied in the home include CBT-E, IPT, and dialectical behavior therapy (DBT). With this in mind, we provide several suggestions for possible adaptations.

CBT-E is a short-term, individual treatment focused on normalizing eating behaviors and modifying underlying attitudes and cognitions that contribute to the maintenance of eating disorder behaviors (e.g., overvaluation of shape and weight in one's self-evaluation; Fairburn, 2008). Another core strategy of CBT-E involves exposure to stimuli that are associated with the occurrence of eating disorder behaviors. The latter CBT-E technique could be particularly powerful when administered in the home setting. As one example, in the home-based setting, the clinician may collaborate with the client to select a challenging item of clothing from the client's closet for the client to wear in order to target the client's shape-related avoidance behaviors. The clinician may then help the client cope with subsequent distress by helping him or her engage in cognitive restructuring of thoughts that accompany such an exposure. In an office-based setting, the power of this type of exposure could be limited by the client having to remember to bring an item of clothing to the session, select a sufficiently challenging item, etc.

IPT is built on the foundation that through targeting interpersonal problems, psychological symptoms will resolve (Wilson et al., 2010). A key strategy involves taking an interpersonal inventory in which the clinician examines with the client the important people and interpersonal events in the client's life history and links them to the development of eating-related psychopathology. In the home setting, the clinician can directly observe current patterns of interpersonal functioning that may impact the maintenance of the eating disorder. These may include the ways that family members or partners interact either verbally or nonverbally, such as a partner placing their hand on the client's back while the client is experiencing distress during a meal. Observing the client's interpersonal functioning *in vivo* may help the client and therapist select an interpersonal problem area to focus on during treatment. For example, if role dispute is the selected interpersonal problem area, the client and their

310 *Eva-Molly Petitto Dunbar et al.*

partner may have had different conceptualizations about what is supportive during a difficult meal and the role that the partner has during the meal. Here the clinician can help the client identify and clarify differing expectations about the relationship. If grief is the selected problem area, the therapist may ask the client to select a picture of their deceased loved one and conduct an empty chair exercise with the client in the moment in order to assist the client in processing their feelings of grief. The clinician may also examine the client's home and assess what reminders the client has and what items they have kept from their loved one and assist the client in navigating what to do with them.

DBT is composed of four modules, which include mindfulness that focuses on acceptance and awareness of internal and external experiences as they arise in the moment; distress tolerance that promotes strategies to accept and tolerate difficult life events; emotion regulation that involves recognizing, labeling, and accepting emotions; and interpersonal effectiveness that helps develop effective communication (Linehan, 2014). In the home setting, the clinician may help the client practice the skills that the client has learned as part of the four DBT modules. For example, following a meal, in order to help the client manage difficult emotions and tolerate the refeeding process, the clinician may engage in a distress tolerance/mindfulness activity with the client. As part of an art project, the clinician may assist the client in creating a coping skills box, and then help the client find items throughout the home that are meaningful and engage the client's various senses (e.g., journal, stress ball, card from a loved one, etc.). The clinician may also invite other family members to participate in the activity. For example, a client's younger sibling may also create their own coping skills box, which may help strengthen their relationship and also help the client's sibling in coping with their own distressing emotions.

In summary, this chapter provides an initial framework for expanding eating disorder treatment to the home setting. We provide suggestions for addressing the complexities of home-based care and encourage continued research in this area in order to improve the reach and effectiveness of treatments for eating disorders. Attention to rigorous methods for implementing and evaluating these treatments will be important in advancing the field and, crucially, for improving long-term recovery for individuals with eating disorders.

References

American Academy of Pediatrics. (2000). Insurance coverage of mental health and substance abuse services for children and adolescents: A consensus statement. *Pediatrics, 106*(4), 860–862.

Ammerman, R. T., Putnam, F. W., Altaye, M., Stevens, J., Teeters, A. R., & Van Ginkel, J. B. (2013). A clinical trial of in-home CBT for depressed mothers in home visitation. *Behavior Therapy, 44*(3), 359–372.

Ammerman, R. T., Putnam, F. W., Bosse, N. R., Teeters, A. R., & Van Ginkel, J. B. (2010). Maternal depression in home visitation: A systematic review. *Aggression and Violent Behavior, 15*(3), 191–200.

Eating Disorders in the Home-Based Setting 311

Ammerman, R. T., Putnam, F. W., Teeters, A. R., & Van Ginkel, J. B. (2014). Moving beyond depression: A collaborative approach to treating depressed mothers in home visiting programs. *Zero to Three, 34*(5), 20–27.

Bouton, M. E. (2014). Why behavior change is difficult to sustain. *Preventive Medicine, 68,* 29–36.

Cortes, L. (2004). Home-based family therapy: A misunderstanding of the role and a new challenge for therapists. *The Family Journal, 12*(2), 184–188.

Couturier, J. L., & Kimber, M. S. (2015). Dissemination and implementation of manualized family-based treatment: A systematic review. *Eating Disorders, 23*(4), 281–290.

Department of Veterans Affairs. (2019). *Home based primary care.* Retrieved from https://www.va.gov/geriatrics/docs/Home_Based_Primary_Care.pdf.

Edes, T., Kinosian, B., Vuckovic, N. H., Olivia Nichols, L., Mary Becker, M., & Hossain, M. (2014). Better access, quality, and cost for clinically complex veterans with home-based primary care. *Journal of the American Geriatrics Society, 62*(10), 1954–1961.

Fairburn, C. G. (2008). *Cognitive behavior therapy and eating disorders.* New York, NY: Guilford Press.

Hart, L. M., Granillo, M. T., Jorm, A. F., & Paxton, S. J. (2011). Unmet need for treatment in the eating disorders: A systematic review of eating disorder specific treatment seeking among community cases. *Clinical Psychology Review, 31*(5), 727–735.

Hicken, B. L., & Plowhead, A. (2010). A model for home-based psychology from the Veterans Health Administration. *Professional Psychology: Research and Practice, 41*(4), 340–346.

Karlin, B. E., & Karel, M. J. (2013). National integration of mental health providers in VA home-based primary care: An innovative model for mental health care delivery with older adults. *The Gerontologist, 54*(5), 868–879.

Knapp, S., & Slattery, J. M. (2004). Professional boundaries in nontraditional settings. *Professional Psychology: Research and Practice, 35*(5), 553.

Landers, S., Madigan, E., Leff, B., Rosati, R., McCann, B. A., Hornbake, R., … Breese, E. (2016). The future of home health care: A strategic framework for optimizing value. *Home Health Care Management & Practice, 28*(4), 262–278.

Lawson, G. (2005). Special considerations for the supervision of home-based counselors. *The Family Journal, 13*(4), 437–444.

Linehan, M. (2014). *DBT Skills training manual.* New York, NY: Guilford Press.

Lock, J., & Le Grange, D. (2013). *Treatment manual for anorexia nervosa: A family-based approach* (2nd ed.). New York, NY: Guilford Press.

Markle-Reid, M., Browne, G., Weir, R., Gafni, A., Roberts, J., & Henderson, S. R. (2006). The effectiveness and efficiency of home-based nursing health promotion for older people: A review of the literature. *Medical Care Research and Review, 63*(5), 531–569.

Maxfield, M., & Segal, D. L. (2008). Psychotherapy in nontraditional settings: A case of in-home cognitive-behavioral therapy with a depressed older adult. *Clinical Case Studies, 7*(2), 154–166.

McFarlane, T., Olmsted, M. P., & Trottier, K. (2008). Timing and prediction of relapse in a transdiagnostic eating disorder sample. *International Journal of Eating Disorders, 41*(7), 587–593.

Mode of Therapy – Home Based Therapy. (n.d.). Retrieved from https://careersinpsychology.org/home-based-therapy/.

312   Eva-Molly Petitto Dunbar et al.

Mussell, M. P., Crosby, R. D., Crow, S. J., Knopke, A. J., Peterson, C. B., Wonderlich, S. A., & Mitchell, J. E. (2000). Utilization of empirically supported psychotherapy treatments for individuals with eating disorders: A survey of psychologists. *International Journal of Eating Disorders, 27*(2), 230–237.

Podlesnik, C. A., Kelley, M. E., Jimenez-Gomez, C., & Bouton, M. E. (2017). Renewed behavior produced by context change and its implications for treatment maintenance: A review. *Journal of Applied Behavior Analysis, 50*(3), 675–697.

Reifler, B. V., & Bruce, M. L. (2014). Home-based mental health services for older adults: A review of ten model programs. *The American Journal of Geriatric Psychiatry, 22*(3), 241–247.

Reiter, M. D. (2000). Utilizing the home environment in home-based family therapy. *Journal of Family Psychotherapy, 11*(3), 27–39.

Rowa, K., Antony, M. M., Summerfeldt, L. J., Purdon, C., Young, L., & Swinson, R. (2007). Office-based vs. home-based behavioral treatment for obsessive-compulsive disorder: A preliminary study. *Behaviour Research and Therapy, 45*(8), 1883–1892.

Sheidow, A. J., & Woodford, M. S. (2003). Multisystemic therapy: An empirically supported, home-based family therapy approach. *The Family Journal, 11*(3), 257–263.

Steinhausen, H. C. (2009). Outcome of eating disorders. *Child and Adolescent Psychiatric Clinics of North America, 18*(1), 225–242.

Wilson, G.T., Wilfley, D.E., Agras, W.S., Bryson, S.W. (2010). Psychological treatments of binge eating disorder. *Archives of General Psychiatry, 67*(1), 94–101.

14 Using Remote Methods to Deliver Evidence-Based Treatment for Eating Disorders

Claire Trainor, Sasha Gorrell, Kristen Anderson, and Daniel Le Grange

Introduction

Eating disorders (EDs) are serious psychiatric conditions with elevated costs of treatment, high mortality rates, and serious medical complications (Schaumberg et al., 2017). Due to the complexity of these illnesses, specialized, evidence-based treatment (EBT) is often required. EBTs, however, are not always available due to a limited number of adequately trained providers, particularly in rural environs or regions outside of those proximal to training sites (Murray & Le Grange, 2014). Further, due to high demand and extended wait lists (Bell & Newns, 2004), social stigma (Becker, Hadley Arrindell, Perloe, Fay, & Striegel-Moore, 2010), and high cost of treatment (Cachelin, Rebeck, Veisel, & Striegel-Moore, 2001), many of those who may otherwise be willing to seek treatment for EDs do not, leaving a significant number of individuals without access to specialty EBTs for their illness. Delivery access of EBTs for EDs can be enhanced with the use of remote methods, including telehealth; recent findings show promise for dissemination of cognitive behavioral therapy (CBT), enhanced cognitive behavioral therapy (CBT-E), and family-based treatment (FBT) for EDs. In the following discussion, current relevant evidence on remote treatment delivery methods for EBTs for ED is synthesized, and case vignettes demonstrating the use of these treatments is included at the end of each section. Clinical and theoretic implications are discussed along with critical directions for future research and practice.

Remote Delivery of EBT for EDs

Among adults, evidence supports the effectiveness of remote delivery methods (e.g., CBT via telehealth) for a wide range of mental health conditions including post-traumatic stress disorder (Germain, Marchand, Bouchard, Drouin, & Guay, 2009), obsessive-compulsive and related disorders, panic disorder, and depression (Griffiths, Blignault, & Yellowlees, 2006), with similar remission rates as when delivered face-to-face. For adolescents, there is evidence to support the use of videoconferencing for depression (Nelson, Barnard, & Cain, 2003), attention-deficit/hyperactive disorder (Myers et al., 2015), autism spectrum

314   *Claire Trainor et al.*

disorders (Little, Pope, Wallisch, & Dunn, 2018), and trauma-exposed youth (Stewart, Orengo-Aguayo, Cohen, Mannarino, & De Arellano, 2017). More recent work has extended the use of remote mental health treatment among both adults and adolescents with EDs.

Despite the severity of EDs and their long-term psychological and physical complications, there are remarkably few trained providers given the number of individuals who suffer from these disorders (Anderson, Byrne, Goodyear, Reichel, & Le Grange, 2015). A majority of these specialty ED treatment providers are located in urban areas located near clinical training sites, which increases the challenge for those living in remote areas to access necessary specialty treatment (Anderson et al., 2015; Murray & Le Grange, 2014). For adolescents in particular, there is a shortage of FBT-certified treatment providers, with an average of only one therapist available for every 2,000 adolescents with anorexia nervosa (AN) in the U.S.A. (Anderson et al., 2015). To help resolve this issue, and, in part, based upon the success of remote treatment options for other illnesses, research has begun to explore the use of computer or Internet-based interventions for EDs.

A majority of the studies examining the effectiveness of alternative treatment methods for ED have investigated CBT, CBT-E, and FBT. The range of methods has included e-mail, text messaging, and self-help programs in a CD-ROM format, as well as telemedicine and video conferencing. Much of this work has been implemented with adult patient populations diagnosed with bulimia nervosa (BN), binge eating disorder (BED), and other specified feeding and eating disorders (OSFED), particularly subthreshold BN or BED (Shingleton, Richards, & Thompson-Brenner, 2013). Considerably less research has examined remote delivery of treatments for AN, perhaps due to lower population base rates of the disorder, high treatment dropout rates, and lack of treatment acceptance (Schlegl, Bürger, Schmidt, Herbst, & Voderholzer, 2015). Anecdotally, some providers may be hesitant to provide remote treatment to individuals with AN due to increased medical risk, but more research is needed to understand the impact of medical severity on remote delivery methods for AN. Similarly, there is less evidence about the remote delivery of EBTs for adolescents with EDs as compared to that for adults (Anderson et al., 2015). While the evidence base is emerging, research to date indicates that telehealth interventions are promising for both adolescents and adults with EDs who may be unable or unwilling to seek in-person treatment. In the following, the current research evidence for remote treatment of CBT, CBT-E, and FBT is summarized; for each, an accompanying case vignette highlights clinical challenges that may arise with a remote treatment format.

Cognitive Behavioral Therapy

CBT is a short-term psychotherapy that has been used to treat transdiagnostic presentation of EDs (Agras, Fitzsimmons-Craft, & Wilfley, 2017; Murphy,

Straebler, Cooper, & Fairburn, 2010; Poulsen et al., 2014). Broadly speaking, CBT is aimed at disrupting the behaviors associated with EDs (e.g., purging) and identifying and challenging maladaptive, ED-related cognitions. Manualized CBT is designed to require approximately 6 months of treatment and is divided into four phases, each with a unique goal (Fairburn, 2008). Phase I focuses on engaging patients in treatment and establishing therapeutic alliance. Phase II is considered a transition period during which clinicians and patients evaluate how things have progressed since treatment began and engage in collaborative planning for the next phase. The majority of sessions occur in Phase III, which addresses the processes, thoughts, and beliefs maintaining the ED. The fourth and final phase focuses on sustaining progress that has been made, and relapse prevention. In the last four decades, CBT has emerged as the gold standard for adult BN and OSFED (Murphy et al., 2010), and provides more rapid symptom improvement than interpersonal psychotherapy for adults with BN (Agras et al., 2017). There is less evidence supporting the use of CBT for transdiagnostic EDs in children and adolescents (Le Grange & Loeb, 2014) and particularly for those with AN (Le Grange & Loeb, 2014).

Telemedicine

CBT demonstrates promising outcomes when delivered via remote treatment methods, mainly telemedicine and Internet interventions (Crow et al., 2009; Fernández-Aranda et al., 2009; Mitchell et al., 2008; Sánchez-Ortiz et al., 2011). In one study, adult women with BN or BED were randomized to receive 20 sessions of either face-to-face or telemedicine CBT (Crow et al., 2009). There were no differences in demographics or illness severity variables at baseline, and both groups performed similarly well in terms of outcomes. However, those in the telemedicine group had significantly lower average cost of treatment ($7,300.40) than those in the face-to-face condition ($9,324.68), largely due to reduced costs of transportation (Crow et al., 2009), indicating that telemedicine CBT may be a good alternative for adult BN patients who cannot access treatment in their local community.

Another Randomized Controlled Trial (RCT) explored differences in rates of abstinence from ED behaviors between face-to-face and telemedicine CBT (Mitchell et al., 2008). Adults with BN or EDNOS who reported binge eating and purging ($N = 128$) were randomized to receive 16 weeks of CBT for BN, delivered by trained therapists either in-person or via telemedicine. Binge eating and purging frequency were assessed at baseline, end-of-treatment, and at 3- and 12-month follow-up. Results did not indicate significant between-group differences in retention rates or baseline characteristics. At end-of-treatment, there were no significant between-group differences in abstinence rates. However, those in the face-to-face condition reported greater reductions in ED cognitions and depressive symptoms, though these differences were few in number (Mitchell et al., 2008).

Internet-Based Therapy

Other research has explored the effectiveness of CBT-informed treatment programs that do not involve meeting with a clinician, either face-to-face or via videoconferencing (Fernández-Aranda et al., 2009). Adult female patients with BN ($N = 62$) were assigned to either a waitlist condition or to receive a CBT-informed, Internet-based therapy (IBT) program (Fernández-Aranda et al., 2009). After initial evaluation, participants worked on their own for 4 months, and spoke with a coach once per week via a secured messaging module. Participants were also provided with psychoeducation and information about CBT concepts. All participants, regardless of condition, kept a food diary in which they recorded their binge eating and purging episodes. At end-of-treatment, individuals in the IBT group reported significant reductions in purging episodes compared to those on the waitlist. The IBT group also reported decreases in bulimic episodes, interpersonal distrust, maturity fears, and overall eating pathology (Fernández-Aranda et al., 2009). However, dropout rates in the IBT condition were high, particularly for those with higher baseline anxiety, lower reward-dependency, and higher baseline illness severity, indicating that this treatment may not be as effective for individuals with more severe ED symptoms or other personality traits (Fernández-Aranda et al., 2009). Further, this study did not collect follow-up data, so it is unclear whether treatment gains were maintained.

In college students with BN or EDNOS, Internet-based CBT may be effective in helping to improve ED symptoms and psychological health (Sanchez-Ortiz et al., 2010). In one study, undergraduates ($N = 76$) were randomized to receive either Internet-based CBT (iCBT) for 3 months or to a waitlist control group (Sánchez-Ortiz et al., 2011). iCBT is a brief, eight-session intervention including homework and self-assessment tools that is delivered online through downloaded modules (Williams, Aubin, Cottrell, & Harkin, 1998). In this protocol, each session took approximately 45 minutes, and each participant had a therapist who communicated via e-mail once every 1–2 weeks and responded to any other correspondence. Sessions were available for 24 weeks, but participants were encouraged to complete treatment within 8–12 weeks. Findings indicated that at 3 and 6 months post-treatment, those in the iCBT condition had significantly greater reductions in binge eating episodes, global eating pathology scores, affective symptoms, and quality of life as compared with waitlist controls (Sánchez-Ortiz et al., 2011).

Guided Self-Help

In addition to telemedicine or videoconferencing, some work has explored the use of CBT-based, guided self-help programs for adult BN, with promising findings (Ghaderi & Scott, 2003; Steele & Wade, 2008). While many of these programs used non-Internet-based forms of guided self-help (e.g., workbook or manual), other studies have examined technology-specific interventions.

In one self-management therapy study, adult women with BN or subthreshold BN (N = 141) completed a seven-module, CBT-informed program online (Carrard et al., 2006). The intervention lasted approximately 4 months, during which 25.2% of participants dropped out of treatment before termination. For the remainder of individuals, ED symptoms and general psychopathology improved after treatment, and 23% were completely symptom free at end-of-treatment. Those with improved baseline scores on general psychological health tended to have better outcomes than those with more severe psychopathology or worse scores for psychological health, indicating that this treatment option may not be as effective for those with more severe psychiatric symptoms (Carrard et al., 2011).

In another program, young adult females with BN or EDNOS (N = 38) participated in a CBT-informed, Internet-based, guided self-help program. This study used the same intervention described earlier, with seven modules delivered over approximately 6 months. Posttreatment, eating pathology scores decreased; the only subscales that did not change significantly were ineffectiveness, impulse regulation, and social insecurity (i.e., feelings of insecurity and tension in inter-personal relationships, and a preference to be alone over with others), indicating some improvement in psychological health after the intervention. Further, par-ticipants reported significant reductions in vomiting, dietary restraint, and weight phobia from pre- to post-treatment and at 2-month follow-up. Binge eating, however, did not decrease throughout treatment. Further, as binge eating and purging decreased, endorsement of exercise increased, indicating that individuals may have adopted a new mechanism for compensation during treatment (Nevonen, Mark, Levin, Lindström, & Paulson-Karlsson, 2006).

CBT-informed guided self-help has also demonstrated effectiveness in the treatment of BED (Carrard et al., 2011; Munsch et al., 2019; Shapiro et al., 2007). The first RCT to examine the use of Internet guided self-help for BED (N = 74 adult females) randomized half of the sample to receive a 6-month online program with a 6-month follow-up, with a corresponding wait-list condition. Those in the online intervention arm had access to a counselor via e-mail for questions and guidance. After 6 months, those receiving the intervention reported decreased binge eating behavior, decreased drive for thinness and body dissatisfaction, increased interoceptive awareness, and decreased overall ED symptoms; all of these changes were still present at 8-month follow-up (Carrard et al., 2011).

Additional research has compared group-format CBT, a CD-ROM administered CBT program, and a waitlist control group for adults with BED (Shapiro et al., 2007). In this study, adults with BED (N = 66) were randomized to receive one of the aforementioned conditions (n = 22 per group). The CBT CD-ROM intervention was based on the Cognitive Behavioral Manual for Healthy Weight Control (Bulik, 1997), and closely follows its guidelines. This program includes illustrations, photography, interactive activities, and video clips; it also features six characters with a history of overweight or obesity who act as models for the user. The

318 Claire Trainor et al.

intervention was designed to last 10 weeks, approximately the same amount of time as group-format CBT. At end-of-treatment, 13.3% and 12.5% of those in the CD-ROM condition reported abstinence from binge eating at post-treatment and follow-up, respectively; in the group treatment, these values were 7.7% and 22.2%, respectively. These differences were not significantly different. Overall, there were no differences in outcome between the active treatment conditions, and both groups did better than those in the waitlist condition. Further, those in the CD-ROM condition continued to use the program after treatment ended, indicating that its effects may be longer lasting, as participants continue to have access to the intervention (Shapiro et al., 2007).

CBT-informed guided self-help has also been explored as an alternative to FBT for adolescents with BN (Schmidt et al., 2007). In one study, adolescents ($N = 85$) with BN or EDNOS were randomized to receive either FBT or CBT guided self-care supported by a health professional. At the 6-month follow-up time point, those in the guided self-care group ($n = 44$) reported significantly greater decreases in binge eating and purging behavior than individuals in the FBT condition ($n = 41$). These differences, however, disappeared at 12-month follow-up. Further, the direct cost of treatment was significantly lower for those in the guided self-care condition than for those receiving FBT. CBT-based guided self-care for BN may also be a more acceptable treatment for adolescents, as it is more flexible and requires less family involvement, and may result in more rapid symptom reduction (Schmidt et al., 2007).

It is important, however, to note the lack of evidence for the remote delivery of CBT for individuals with AN and adolescents. In general, research on remote delivery for AN is lacking; this may be perhaps, in part, due to the ego-syntonic nature of the illness which may deter treatment-seeking, and increase dropout rates (Murphy et al., 2010; Schlegl et al., 2015). Further, the relative rarity of the disorder as well as medical complications that may necessitate a higher level of care may limit participation in research (Schlegl et al., 2015). Overall, evidence supports the use of CBT-based telehealth, IBT, and guided self-help for adults with BN and BED. In all of the aforementioned studies, remote treatment was effective in treating the disorder and resulted in significant improvements in behavioral and psychological symptoms.

The following clinical vignette demonstrates factors influencing why an individual may choose a remote treatment method, as well as some of the challenges that may arise using this treatment modality.

Clinical Vignette

Lucy is a 21-year-old college senior with a history of BN in high school for which she received FBT, and has been doing well since her treatment discharge. She lives with her two roommates in upstate New York; her family remains in Chicago, where she is from. However, due to school and social stressors, Lucy has noticed her urges to engage in binge eating behavior are becoming more frequent. She has also recently started purging again, although it has only been 1–2 times in the last 2 months. The only specialty ED provider near Lucy does not accept her insurance, and she cannot afford to pay out of pocket. While there is treatment available in New York City, Lucy does not feel like she can make the time commitment to travel there on a consistent basis, and feels something more flexible may be a better fit for her, given the varied nature of her academic schedule. She learned from a friend about a CBT-informed guided self-help program for BN or subthreshold BN and is on her first session in the program.

Throughout her time using the guided self-help program, Lucy notes a decrease in her urges to engage in binge eating and but has continued to purge. She has disclosed these episodes to her clinician via e-mail, who helped her to understand the circumstances that led to purging. She reports greater insight into why these urges have been arising and that they are particularly influenced by her upcoming graduation and recent break-up with her boyfriend of 3 years. Using this knowledge, Lucy is better able to understand the mechanisms that trigger her ED and to use adaptive coping skills when urges arise. Lucy has worked to implement regular eating and to stop skipping meals and snacks when her schedule is busy or overwhelming; early in treatment, she relied on cues from others eating to remind her that it is time for a meal or snack. Still, due to her busy schedule and low appetite, she frequently struggles to maintain regular eating, and still has urges to binge at least once a week.

Enhanced Cognitive Behavioral Therapy

CBT is currently the first-line treatment for adults with BN, although less effective in treating adults diagnosed with AN (Hay, 2013; Watson & Bulik, 2013). An enhanced form of CBT (CBT-E) was developed and manualized in an effort to improve transdiagnostic treatment outcomes (Fairburn, 2008). CBT-E is designed specifically for the treatment of EDs and provides enhanced, individualized treatment, even within a specific ED diagnosis (Cooper & Fairburn, 2011). CBT-E is primarily implemented as an outpatient treatment for adults with transdiagnostic EDs, and consists of 20 sessions over 20 weeks (less intense) or 40 sessions over 40 weeks (more intense). CBT-E is a four-phase treatment; the overall goals of the phases are the same as described earlier in CBT (Murphy et al., 2010). Through the use of ED-specific techniques, such as challenging maintaining mechanisms of the illness and changing ED behaviors, CBT-E has been shown to be effective in treating adults with BN (Wonderlich et al., 2014), adults with AN (Fairburn et al., 2013), and adolescents with AN (Dalle Grave, Calugi, Doll, & Fairburn, 2013).

Videoconference

Considerably less evidence exists regarding the implementation of CBT-E via remote practices. A small, single-case, multiple baseline study explored the efficacy of CBT-E via video-conference for adult females with BED or OSFED (Abrahamsson, Ahlund, Ahrin, & Alfonsson, 2018). In this study, five patients participated in the first phase of CBT-E via videoconferencing with a trained

320　*Claire Trainor et al.*

psychologist. The study design only examined changes after Phase I; participants were given the option to continue with treatment after this point in time, but no follow-up data were collected. Multiple baseline lengths were randomized to be between 14 and 35 days, after which participants began Phase I of CBT-E, as per the manual (Fairburn, 2008), with a trained psychologist via videoconference. This stage of treatment focuses on regular eating, which is associated with early symptom improvement (Zendegui, West, & Zandberg, 2014). The total study protocol lasted 55 days; depending on the baseline length, participants had between 20 and 41 days in treatment. During this time, patients met biweekly with a clinician; each received 7–11 total sessions, lasting between 20 and 46 minutes. While these individuals did not complete a full course of CBT-E, at the end of the first treatment phase, all five participants reported greater frequency of daily meals, and four participants reported significant decreases on measures of ED pathology. Individuals who reported depressed mood at baseline reported that mood improved after the intervention. Notably, participants reported good therapeutic alliance, and were satisfied with the mobile applications and videoconferencing platform used in this treatment (Abrahamsson et al., 2018).

Currently, researchers at the Centre for Research on Eating Disorders at Oxford (CREDO) are studying digital CBT-E treatment for adults with recurrent binge eating or BED (https://www.credo-oxford.com/5.1.html). This program is intended for individuals in the early stages of an ED and those who may not be able or willing to access face-to-face treatment. By providing treatment to those who would otherwise be unwilling or unable to attend face-to-face therapy, this treatment modality will be available to individuals who would otherwise not receive services.

In summary, existing evidence, while limited, provides guidance that CBT-E delivered via videoconferencing for BED is similarly effective to in-person CBT-E, and an online, guided self-help program for adults with BED is in current development. To date, no work has explored the use of a remote delivery format of CBT-E for BN or AN in adults or adolescents. The shortage of CBT research in adolescents may be further explained by the fact that most of the research in youth EDs has been conducted in trials that examine FBT, with considerably less investigation of CBT. The following clinical vignette provides an example of guided self-help for BED in an adult male and illustrates the challenges and successes of this treatment.

Clinical Vignette

Jackson is a 34-year-old male with a diagnosis of BED. He lives in Redding, California, with his fiancé and their two dogs. His mother left the family when he was young and his father is now deceased; he has two younger brothers, neither of whom lives nearby. He works as a lifeguard at the lake in the summer and performs odd jobs in the winter months. Jackson first began engaging in binge eating when he was 21 years old, following the death of his father. He received therapy for depression and post-traumatic stress disorder at that time, but has been unable to access care for his ED due to a shortage of specialized ED providers in his community. While he was able to keep his ED a secret from his fiancé for quite some time and was able to reduce the frequency of binge eating on his own, due to occupational stress and financial strain, his ED behaviors have escalated. His fiancé is aware of the ED symptoms, and has noticed significant changes in his mood; she has asked him to begin therapy. Jackson recently learned about an online CBT-E program for adults with BED, and hopes this will be helpful in reducing or eliminating his symptoms.

While the beginning of treatment is challenging for Jackson and he does not notice an immediate change in his ED cognitions or behavior, he continues with the program. Occasionally involving his fiancé for support around meals and as a model for appropriate eating patterns, Jackson begins to better understand what is maintaining his illness, including financial stress about his upcoming wedding and lingering trauma from his father's death. He also recognizes that his urges to engage in binge eating are stronger on days when he does not eat breakfast or lunch, so starts setting aside time the night before to prepare these meals. Jackson also starts to go on regular walks with his fiancé and their dogs, which helps him to feel more comfortable and confident in his body. He has learned to use coping skills such as distraction when he feels like he may engage in ED behavior, and will reach out to his fiancé for support in those moments.

Six months into treatment, Jackson has reduced his binge eating to once or twice a month, when he was previously binge eating daily. On the days he does engage in ED behaviors, he is able to understand what factors may have led him there and works to identify them earlier, in order to disrupt the behavior before it occurs. At this point, he decides to stop the program and practice the skills on his own, with the knowledge that he can start again whenever he may feel the need.

Family-Based Treatment

FBT, developed by Lock and Le Grange (2015), is a three-phase treatment for adolescents with AN. The first phase focuses on weight restoration and/or the disruption of binge eating and purging symptoms; in this phase, caregivers are responsible for refeeding, meal supervision, and weight gain. The second phase focuses on a return to independent eating; adolescents gradually start to choose their own meals and snacks, and begin to eat without adult supervision. The final phase focuses on typical adolescent issues and relapse prevention; clinicians work with families to determine what the child or adolescent needs to live a balanced, healthy life and the family begins to take steps toward those goals. FBT operates under the fundamental assumption that parents and caregivers are an essential part of treatment; as such, all family members are encouraged to attend sessions, which may pose significant challenges for families with two working parents, who have many other children, or who live far from treatment providers.

While the original treatment manual was developed for adolescent AN (Lock, Le Grange, Agras, & Dare, 2002), adaptations are available for BN (Le Grange & Lock, 2009), those under 12 (Lock, Le Grange, Forsberg, & Hewell, 2006), avoidant restrictive food intake disorder (Fitzpatrick, Forsberg, & Colborn, 2015), and transition-age youth (Dimitropoulos et al., 2015). Consistent research evidence

322 Claire Trainor et al.

demonstrates that FBT is an effective treatment for adolescent EDs, and yields higher remission rates than adolescent-focused therapy for AN (Lock et al., 2010), SPT for adolescents with BN (Le Grange, Crosby, Rathouz, & Leventhal, 2007), or CBT for adolescents with BN (Le Grange, Lock, Agras, Bryson, & Jo, 2015). FBT reduces the need for hospitalization (Madden et al., 2015) and is more cost-effective when compared to systemic family therapy (Agras et al., 2014).

Telehealth

While a majority of research in FBT has been focused on the use of this treatment as a face-to-face intervention for adolescent EDs, recent research has begun to investigate the use of a telemedicine format. One protocol for the remote delivery of FBT for adolescents with AN or atypical AN has been tested using a two-phase, iterative case series design (Anderson et al., 2015). Two waves of adolescents with AN or atypical AN and their families ($N = 10$, 5 per wave) received treatment from an FBT-certified clinician via video-conferencing. Similar to face-to-face FBT sessions, clinicians met first with the adolescents to briefly check in before bringing in the rest of the family; unlike standard FBT, in which the therapist weighs the adolescent, parents weighed their child before sessions and shared the weight with the therapist. Study patients continued to see a community-based medical provider during treatment to ensure safety for outpatient treatment, and these weights were also reported to the therapist. Duration of treatment was 6 months, over which participants received 20 FBT sessions. Scores on measures of ED pathology, depression, and self-esteem, as well as percent median BMI (%mBMI) were assessed at baseline, end-of-treatment, and 6-month follow-ups through a telehealth platform. Participants showed significant increases in %mBMI, and improved eating pathology, depression, and self-esteem at end-of-treatment and 6-month follow-up. These findings reveal that the delivery of FBT via telemedicine is feasible, with promising evidence of treatment outcomes that are similar to a face-to-face format (Anderson, Byrne, Crosby, & Le Grange, 2017).

Case report data also support the delivery of FBT via telehealth (Goldfield & Boachie, 2003). An adolescent female from rural Canada was admitted to a treatment program at a large, urban hospital, far from her home. While the patient's mother was able to attend family therapy at the hospital, her father and sister were unable to travel for weekly therapy sessions. After obtaining informed consent, the family participated in telehealth with the patient, mother, and therapist in one room, and the father and sister joining from their community via videoconference. At discharge, the patient had gained significant weight and was making progress toward psychological recovery. The family reported high levels of satisfaction and therapeutic alliance in this treatment, and reported they would participate in telehealth therapy again if necessary (Goldfield & Boachie, 2003). While, as a case example, this study is limited in its

Using Remote Methods   323

ability to support definitive claims, results are promising and indicate a need for further, adequately powered investigation.

Parent-Guided Self-Help

Similar to guided self-help for CBT, some research has examined the use of a parent-guided self-help program, specific to FBT for adolescent AN (Lock, Darcy, Fitzpatrick, Vierhile, & Sadeh-Sharvit, 2017). In one study, families of adolescents with AN (N = 19) were recruited to participate in a parental, guided self-help program, informed with key FBT principles (e.g., externalization of the illness and parental empowerment). Individuals were provided with codes to log onto a secure website, where they could access lecture materials, 25 short videos filmed by an FBT-certified clinician, reading assignments, and homework. There was also a guided portion of the program, which consisted of 12 sessions over 6 months, delivered by an FBT-trained provider; these sessions were similar to those that would occur in standard FBT. At the end-of-treatment, there were significant increases in %mBMI and decreased ED psychopathology. Parents in the intervention experienced significant increases in parental self-efficacy, a strong predictor of treatment outcome for adolescent AN (Byrne, Accurso, Arnow, Lock, & Grange, 2015). Overall, while this was a small sample, research indicates that the implementation of parent-guided self-help is feasible and acceptable, and may be an alternative for those who are unable to access care in person (Lock et al., 2017). In summary, for children and adolescents with AN, research, although limited, indicates that FBT telehealth has similar efficacy rates as face-to-face FBT. Additionally, the development of a guided self-help program for parents of children with EDs may allow additional support and be effective for those unable or unwilling to access in-person care. The following clinical vignette provides an example of telehealth for an adolescent female with AN, and potential challenges in treatment.

Clinical Vignette

Sarah is a 15-year-old female with a diagnosis of AN, restricting subtype. She lives with her mother, older sister, and younger brother approximately 3 hours outside of Denver, Colorado. Her parents divorced 3 years ago; her father lives nearby and sees the children two or three nights a week and on alternating weekends. She is an excellent student and has been running varsity cross-country since her freshman year in high school. In the last 4 months, Sarah has lost 14 pounds through restriction and compulsive exercise. Her primary medical doctor suggested that her parents find her a therapist and has recommended that she take a break from running due to risk for bradycardia and orthostasis. Due to their location, there are no FBT providers available for Sarah to see, and the only clinician in her town does not have training or experience with adolescent EDs. Her parents are incredibly concerned, but do not know how to support their daughter. Their primary medical doctor has connected them with a treatment provider in Denver who is FBT-certified and offers telehealth.

324 *Claire Trainor et al.*

Sarah, her parents, and her siblings begin weekly therapy sessions with the FBT-certified provider via telehealth. At the beginning of treatment, Sarah's parents take charge of her food and eating, including supervising her lunches at school, which Sarah complains about. Her parents express considerable concerns that they are not feeding her the right things and are unsure of how to help their daughter; their therapist helps to problem-solve and guides the parents in strategizing how to increase her nutrition. She progresses well through the first phase of treatment, gaining approximately 1–2 pounds per week.

After 4 months, Sarah is expressing interest in having autonomy over her food choices and believes she will be able to eat on her own at school. Her parents and therapist agree with her assessment, and she is allowed to pack her own lunch and eat with friends at school. The first 2 weeks that Sarah eats without supervision, she loses one pound; her parents and therapist give her on additional week to regain the weight or they will need to supervise her meals again. She is able to adequately increase her nutrition and gains two pounds between sessions, but Sarah reports that as she eats more food, her urges to exercise have been increasing. She denies any compulsive exercising or restricting, but her parents have noticed that, when she has autonomy over food choices, she rarely incorporates challenge or fear foods for herself.

Summary of Remote Delivery of EBTs

While literature on remote delivery of EBTs is still emerging, existing evidence summarily supports telehealth and Internet-based interventions for EDs. Research on technology-based CBT interventions includes telehealth, IBT, and guided self-help, particularly for adults with BN and BED, and, to a lesser extent, adolescents with BN. In all of these studies, remote treatment was effective at treating the ED and resulted in significant improvements in both behavioral and psychological symptoms. Further, existing evidence indicates that CBT-E delivered via videoconferencing for BED is similarly effective as in-person CBT-E, and additional research is exploring the delivery of this treatment through an online, guided self-help program for adults with BED. To date, no work has explored the use of a remote delivery form of CBT-E for BN or AN in adults or adolescents. For children and adolescents with AN, research, although limited, indicates that FBT telehealth has similar efficacy rates as face-to-face FBT. Additionally, the development of a guided FBT-based self-help program for parents of children with EDs may allow additional support and be effective for those unable or unwilling to access in-person care.

Challenges in Implementing Remote EBT for EDs

Alliance

One concern about the remote delivery of EBTs, particularly via videoconferencing or telehealth, is the potential negative impact on therapeutic alliance (Brenes, Ingram, & Danhauer, 2011). In adolescent samples with AN receiving outpatient FBT, alliance with the therapist predicts weight gain

(Pereira, Lock, & Oggins, 2006) and cognitive improvements post-treatment (Isserlin & Couturier, 2012). These findings also hold true for adolescents with AN treated in a partial hospitalization program using FBT adapted for higher levels of care (Rienecke, Richmond, & Lebow, 2016). Further, parent alliance is positively associated with weight gain and negatively associated with treatment dropout (Ellison et al., 2012; Isserlin & Couturier, 2012; Pereira et al., 2006). In adults with BN, better therapeutic alliance predicted greater reduction in bulimic behavior, regardless of treatment type (Accurso et al., 2015; Constantino, Arnow, Blasey, & Agras, 2005; Loeb et al., 2005). For adults with AN, alliance is predictive of better outcomes, including weight gain and cognitive improvements (Sly, Morgan, Mountford, & Lacey, 2013; Stiles-Shields et al., 2016).

Given the suggested importance of therapeutic alliance in ED treatment outcome, ensuring this relationship within technologically based treatments is essential. With patients not being physically present, it is possible that aspects of nonverbal communication (e.g., body language) may be more challenging to perceive via screen. Despite the increasing presence of technology in our lives, some patients may experience discomfort when talking on the phone or through video-chat, which may also impede alliance. Further, while patients are always able to leave during a session, the distance granted by telehealth may make departing a screen session easier than walking away from an in-person provider. Notably, while many of the aforementioned studies did not examine therapeutic alliance during remote treatment, the few that did report no differences in alliance between face-to-face and telehealth treatment (Anderson et al., 2017; Goldfield & Boachie, 2003). Moving forward, providers using technology for treatment should be aware of possible challenges in the cultivation of alliance in an effort to increase acceptability of these delivery methods.

Implementation

While preliminary evidence supports the remote dissemination of EBTs for EDs, there are acknowledged challenges associated with its implementation, particularly in regards to the scalability of both guided and unguided self-help programs. For the former, some sort of supervision or guidance is still necessary and, as such, providers would need to be trained in how to support individuals throughout these interventions (Cooper & Bailey-Straebler, 2015). Guided self-help programs, which often adhere to the CBT treatment model, have similar efficacy as face-to-face treatment for a variety of psychiatric conditions (Bashshur, Shannon, Bashshur, & Yellowlees, 2016); as such, determining the most cost- and time-effective way to train clinicians would be beneficial. Unguided self-help programs are easier to scale, as they require no additional training of providers; however, evidence suggests that unguided self-help programs are not as effective as guided self-help (Cooper & Bailey-Straebler, 2015; Fairburn & Patel, 2017), and may not demonstrate symptom

326 *Claire Trainor et al.*

improvement for adults with BED, when tested in active control conditions (Grilo, White, Gueorguieva, Barnes, & Masheb, 2013). Further, dropout rates in unguided programs tend to be higher than in a clinical setting (Fairburn & Patel, 2017). If these remote treatments were to be widely disseminated, steps would need to be taken to design programs that minimize attrition.

For those who do fully participate in remote therapy formats, it is possible that programs, which rely heavily on Internet usage or mobile apps, will be more effective for younger individuals who feel comfortable and competent using technology. For individuals raised with access to mobile device communication, treatment provided through these mechanisms may feel familiar and comfortable, especially compared to meeting face-to-face with a therapist. Alternatively, it is possible that these programs may be challenging for those not as technologically savvy, creating an additional barrier to care. Further, little research has examined whether the form of the treatment matters for the illness. For example, individuals with EDs whose brains are malnourished may find it difficult to focus on remote delivery format programs that require reading or focusing for extended periods of time. More research, including studies that are adequately powered to allow for moderation analyses, are needed to determine for whom remote treatment may be most effective.

There are also questions about the cost of telehealth and IBT as compared to standard formats that require evaluation before remote interventions can be widely implemented. One study found that telehealth CBT for BN was significantly less costly than face-to-face treatment (Crow et al., 2009); however, this study is the only of its kind. Other literature examining insurance claims for mental health and substance use services delivered via telehealth reveals decreasing trends for average reimbursements from 2009 to 2013 (Wilson, Rampa, Trout, & Stimpson, 2017). Further, reimbursements for non-telehealth formats tended to be nearly twice as much as those for telehealth, and reimbursement rates were lower for telehealth than face-to-face services for 9 out of the top 10 telehealth services (Wilson et al., 2017). Determining the optimal way to bill telehealth sessions to insurance may help to reduce the burden of cost associated with this form of treatment. It is important to note that these costs are only associated with services that require a clinician, such as IBT and telehealth; as such, unguided self-help would not be impacted by insurance and therefore potentially more cost-effective for patients.

Future Directions

While preliminary research supports the effectiveness of remote delivery of EBTs for EDs, future work is needed to both test the treatment formats themselves, as well as to determine for whom remote delivery may be most effective. For example, some work indicates that remote treatments may not be as effective for those with greater baseline severity or certain personality traits (Carrard et al., 2011; Fernández-Aranda et al., 2009) but little else is known about the impact of baseline moderators on overall remote treatment outcomes.

Larger, controlled studies are necessary, particularly for the remote delivery of CBT-E and FBT. Many of the CBT for BN studies were controlled, but only compared the telehealth or self-help intervention with a waitlist group. The only existing telehealth study for FBT did not compare directly to face-to-face treatment, although remission rates were similar to what is found in other studies (Anderson et al., 2015). While some work has been initiated to investigate the process of training providers, CBT-E does not currently have any published evidence on remote telehealth; the only existing literature is in guided self-help. Future research should compare telehealth or videoconferencing directly to face-to-face treatment, possibly in RCTs with adequate power to detect differences. For CBT-E, research should begin by exploring efficacy of videoconferencing and then broaden the scope to a larger, controlled study. These studies would also provide the opportunity to test for moderators and mediators influencing outcomes. Future work should also strive to include historically underserved or marginalized populations, including those from low-income backgrounds, ethnic minorities, and individuals who live in rural areas.

One of the greatest challenges in accessing care is the shortage of specialized providers and as such, future research may explore web-based training and supervision for EBTs, as was proposed for FBT (Lock & Le Grange, 2018). This would allow more providers to access training with lower costs and a more flexible time commitment, and increase the number of individuals trained in the use of EBTs for EDs. CREDO also provides web-centered training in CBT-E and behavioral activation for EDs (https://www.credo-oxford.com), which is a helpful resource for those who are unable to attend in-person training. Research is needed to understand the best mechanisms by which to identify and train clinicians in the community, particular in environs where few or no providers have experience with EDs and thus may be unwilling or unable to provide treatment to these individuals and families. Additionally, there is the possibility for qualitative research in this area, focusing on clinician testimonials and beliefs to help improve future trainings.

Regarding guided self-help, more research is needed to understand exactly how much guidance is necessary. Guided self-help is more effective in decreasing ED pathology and behaviors than unguided self-help (Cooper & Bailey-Straebler, 2015; Fairburn & Patel, 2017), but less is known about how frequently providers must meet with patients before meaningful advantages in symptom relief will become apparent. In the aforementioned guided self-help treatments, most participants received a weekly contact with a clinician, either through e-mail or messaging boards, similar to the frequency of meetings with an in-person clinician. It is possible, however, that less frequent meetings may be similarly effective, and future research is needed to determine where this threshold may lie.

Not only are EDs tremendously challenging for the individual with the disorder, but caregivers of those with AN or BN experience substantial caregiver burden and strain (Graap et al., 2008; Treasure et al., 2001). As such, interventions that support caregivers also benefit their loved ones. There is possibility for the integration of technology into caregiver support, as well as treatment for ill individuals. Currently, researchers' are exploring the efficacy of a web-based intervention for carers of individuals with AN using We Can, a web-based intervention to support caretakers (Spencer et al., 2019). Participants in this study receive either clinician messaging support, moderated carer chatroom support, or an online forum for 12 weeks. Primary outcome variables are caregiver depression and anxiety, and secondary outcome variables include quality of life, alcohol and drug use, caregiver behavior, and acceptability of the program (Spencer et al., 2019). Results from this trial will hopefully help the field better understand web-based interventions for carers of those with EDs, which, while they do not directly treat the individual, may be helpful in strengthening their support networks, thereby further facilitating their recovery.

Technology also has tremendous potential for ED prevention. Internet-based interventions for college women with body image concerns are similarly effective to group interventions, and more effective than educational videos or brochures aimed at reducing ED risk factors (e.g., body image dissatisfaction and symptoms associated with weight gain) (Stice, Durant, Rohde, & Shaw, 2014; Stice, Rohde, Durant, & Shaw, 2012). An 8-week online CBT program (Student Bodies; Taylor et al., 2006) has also demonstrated decreased weight and shape concerns for college women, and these changes continued for 2 years of follow-up. Further evidence indicates that text messaging interventions are useful in maintaining gains made while in an inpatient treatment setting for adults with BN or EDNOS (Bauer, Okon, Meermann, & Kordy, 2012). Future research may consider how to adapt these prevention interventions for children and adolescents at risk for EDs, or to target other vulnerable populations such as pregnant women, athletes, LGBTQ+ individuals, and those in the military.

Summary and Conclusions

In sum, preliminary evidence supports the remote delivery of EBTs for EDs. The majority of research has examined the use of CBT for adults with BN and BED, CBT-E for BED, and FBT for adolescents with AN or atypical AN. These treatments, however, are not without challenges, and more work is needed to more fully appreciate the clinical impact and scalabilities of care. Future research should consider the training of clinicians in EBTs for remote dissemination, larger, controlled studies comparing the same treatment delivered via technology versus face-to-face, and the use of technology in prevention for those at high risk of developing an ED.

References

Abrahamsson, N., Ahlund, L., Ahrin, E., & Alfonsson, S. (2018). Video-based CBT-E improves eating patterns in obese patients with eating disorder: A single case multiple baseline study. *Journal of Behavior Therapy and Experimental Psychiatry, 61*, 104–112. https://doi.org/10.1016/J.JBTEP.2018.06.010.

Using Remote Methods 329

Accurso, E. C., Fitzsimmons-Craft, E. E., Ciao, A., Cao, L., Crosby, R. D., Smith, T. L., ... Peterson, C. B. (2015). Therapeutic alliance in a randomized clinical trial for bulimia nervosa. *Journal of Consulting and Clinical Psychology, 83*(3), 637–642. https://doi.org/10.1037/ccp0000021.

Agras, W. S., Fitzsimmons-Craft, E. E., & Wilfley, D. E. (2017). Evolution of cognitive-behavioral therapy for eating disorders. *Behaviour Research and Therapy, 88*, 26–36. https://doi.org/10.1016/J.BRAT.2016.09.004.

Agras, W. S., Lock, J., Brandt, H., Bryson, S. W., Dodge, E., Halmi, K. A., ... Woodside, B. (2014). Comparison of 2 family therapies for adolescent anorexia nervosa: A randomized parallel trial. *JAMA Psychiatry, 71*(11), 1279. https://doi.org/10.1001/jamapsychiatry.2014.1025.

Anderson, K. E., Byrne, C. E., Crosby, R. D., & Le Grange, D. (2017). Utilizing Telehealth to deliver family-based treatment for adolescent anorexia nervosa. *International Journal of Eating Disorders, 50*(10), 1235–1238. https://doi.org/10.1002/eat.22759.

Anderson, K. E., Byrne, C., Goodyear, A., Reichel, R., & Le Grange, D. (2015). Telemedicine of family-based treatment for adolescent anorexia nervosa: A protocol of a treatment development study. *Journal of Eating Disorders, 3*, 25. https://doi.org/10.1186/s40337-015-0063-1.

Bashshur, R. L., Shannon, G. W., Bashshur, N., & Yellowlees, P. M. (2016). The empirical evidence for telemedicine interventions for mental disorders. *Telemedicine Journal and E-Health: The Official Journal of the American Telemedicine Association, 22*(2), 87–113. https://doi.org/10.1089/tmj.2015.0206.

Bauer, S., Okon, E., Meermann, R., & Kordy, H. (2012). Technology-enhanced maintenance of treatment gains in eating disorders: Efficacy of an intervention delivered via text messaging. *Journal of Consulting and Clinical Psychology, 80*(4), 700–706. https://doi.org/10.1037/a0028030.

Becker, A. E., Hadley Arrindell, A., Perloe, A., Fay, K., & Striegel-Moore, R. H. (2010). A qualitative study of perceived social barriers to care for eating disorders: Perspectives from ethnically diverse health care consumers. *International Journal of Eating Disorders, 43*(7), 633–647. https://doi.org/10.1002/eat.20755.

Bell, L., & Newns, K. (2004). What factors influence failure to engage in a supervised self-help programme for bulimia nervosa and binge eating disorder? *European Eating Disorders Review, 12*(3), 178–183. https://doi.org/10.1002/erv.554.

Brenes, G. A., Ingram, C. W., & Danhauer, S. C. (2011). Benefits and challenges of conducting psychotherapy by telephone. *Professional Psychology: Research and Practice, 42*(6), 543–549. https://doi.org/10.1037/a0026135.

Bulik, C. M. (1997). *Cognitive-behavioral modules for successful weight control.* Eating Disorders Clinic, MCV Hospitals at Virginia Commonwealth University.

Byrne, C. E., Accurso, E. C., Arnow, K. D., Lock, J., & Grange, D. Le. (2015). An exploratory examination of patient and parental self-efficacy as predictors of weight gain in adolescents with anorexia nervosa. *The International Journal of Eating Disorders, 48*(7), 883. https://doi.org/10.1002/EAT.22376.

Cachelin, F. M., Rebeck, R., Veisel, C., & Striegel-Moore, R. H. (2001). Barriers to treatment for eating disorders among ethnically diverse women. *The International Journal of Eating Disorders, 30*(3), 269–278. Retrieved from http://www.ncbi.nlm.nih.gov/pubmed/11746286.

Carrard, I., Crépin, C., Rouget, P., Lam, T., Golay, A., & Van der Linden, M. (2011). Randomised controlled trial of a guided self-help treatment on the Internet for binge

330 *Claire Trainor et al.*

eating disorder. *Behaviour Research and Therapy, 49*(8), 482–491. https://doi.org/10. 1016/j.brat.2011.05.004.

Carrard, I., Rouget, P., Fernández-Aranda, F., Volkart, A.-C., Damoiseau, M., & Lam, T. (2006). Evaluation and deployment of evidence based patient self-management support program for bulimia nervosa. *International Journal of Medical Informatics, 75*, 101–109. https://doi.org/10.1016/j.ijmedinf.2005.07.031.

Constantino, M. J., Arnow, B. A., Blasey, C., & Agras, W. S. (2005). The association between patient characteristics and the therapeutic alliance in cognitive-behavioral and interpersonal therapy for bulimia nervosa. *Journal of Consulting and Clinical Psychology, 73*(2), 203–211. Retrieved from https://psycnet.apa.org/doiLanding? doi=10.1037%2F0022-006X.73.2.203.

Cooper, Z., & Bailey-Straebler, S. (2015). Disseminating evidence-based psychological treatments for eating disorders. *Current Psychiatry Reports, 17*(3), 551. https://doi.org/ 10.1007/s11920-015-0551-7.

Cooper, Z., & Fairburn, C. G. (2011). The evolution of "enhanced" cognitive behavioral therapy for eating disorders: Learning from treatment nonresponse. *Cognitive and Behavioral Practice, 18*(3), 394–402. https://doi.org/10.1016/j.cbpra.2010.07.007.

Crow, S. J., Mitchell, J. E., Crosby, R. D., Swanson, S. A., Wonderlich, S., & Lancanster, K. (2009). The cost effectiveness of cognitive behavioral therapy for bulimia nervosa delivered via telemedicine versus face-to-face. *Behaviour Research and Therapy, 47*(6), 451–453. https://doi.org/10.1016/J.BRAT.2009.02.006.

Dalle Grave, R., Calugi, S., Doll, H. A., & Fairburn, C. G. (2013). Enhanced cognitive behaviour therapy for adolescents with anorexia nervosa: An alternative to family therapy? *Behaviour Research and Therapy, 51*(1), R9–R12. https://doi.org/10.1016/ j.brat.2012.09.008.

Dimitropoulos, G., Freeman, V. E., Allemang, B., Couturier, J., McVey, G., Lock, J., & Le Grange, D. (2015). Family-based treatment with transition age youth with anorexia nervosa: A qualitative summary of application in clinical practice. *Journal of Eating Disorders, 3*(1), 1. https://doi.org/10.1186/s40337-015-0037-3.

Ellison, R., Rhodes, P., Madden, S., Miskovic, J., Wallis, A., Baillie, A., … Touyz, S. (2012). Do the components of manualized family-based treatment for anorexia nervosa predict weight gain? *International Journal of Eating Disorders, 45*(4), 609–614. https://doi.org/10.1002/eat.22000.

Fairburn, C. (2008). *Cognitive behavior therapy and eating disorders.* Chichester, England: Guilford Press.

Fairburn, C. G., Cooper, Z., Doll, H. A., O'Connor, M. E., Palmer, R. L., & Dalle Grave, R. (2013). Enhanced cognitive behaviour therapy for adults with anorexia nervosa: A UK–Italy study. *Behaviour Research and Therapy, 51*(1), R2–R8. https://doi.org/10.1016/J.BRAT.2012.09.010.

Fairburn, C. G., & Patel, V. (2017). The impact of digital technology on psychological treatments and their dissemination. *Behaviour Research and Therapy, 88*, 19–25. https://doi.org/10.1016/j.brat.2016.08.012.

Fernández-Aranda, F., Núñez, A., Martínez, C., Krug, I., Cappozzo, M., Carrard, I., … Lam, T. (2009). Internet-based cognitive-behavioral therapy for bulimia nervosa: A controlled study. *Cyberpsychology & Behavior, 12*(1), 37–41. https://doi.org/10.1089/ cpb.2008.0123.

Fitzpatrick, K. K., Forsberg, S., & Colborn, D. (2015). Family-based therapy for avoidant restrictive food intake disorder: Families facing food neophobias. In K. L.

Loeb, D. Le Grange, & J. Lock (Eds.), *Family Therapy for Adolescent Eating and Weight Disorders: New Applications* (1st ed., pp. 256–276). New York: Routledge.

Germain, V., Marchand, A., Bouchard, S., Drouin, M. S., & Guay, S. (2009). Effectiveness of cognitive behavioural therapy administered by videoconference for posttraumatic stress disorder. *Cognitive Behaviour Therapy*, *38*(1), 42–53, https://doi.org/10.1080/16506070802473494.

Ghaderi, A., & Scott, B. (2003). Pure and guided self-help for full and sub-threshold bulimia nervosa and binge eating disorder. *British Journal of Clinical Psychology*, *42*(3), 257–269. https://doi.org/10.1348/01446650360703375.

Goldfield, G. S., & Boachie, A. (2003). Delivery of family therapy in the treatment of anorexia nervosa using Telehealth. *Telemedicine Journal and e-Health* (Vol. 9). Retrieved from www.liebertpub.com.

Graap, H., Bleich, S., Herbst, F., Trostmann, Y., Wancata, J., & de Zwaan, M. (2008). The needs of carers of patients with anorexia and bulimia nervosa. *European Eating Disorders Review*, *16*(1), 21–29. https://doi.org/10.1002/erv.804.

Griffiths, L., Blignault, I., & Yellowlees, P. (2006). Telemedicine as a means of delivering cognitive-behavioural therapy to rural and remote mental health clients. *Journal of Telemedicine and Telecare*, *12*(3), 136–140. https://doi.org/10.1258/135763306776738567.

Grilo, C. M., White, M. A., Gueorguieva, R., Barnes, R. D., & Masheb, R. M. (2013). Self-help for binge eating disorder in primary care: A randomized controlled trial with ethnically and racially diverse obese patients. *Behaviour Research and Therapy*, *51*(12), 855–861. https://doi.org/10.1016/j.brat.2013.10.002.

Hay, P. (2013). A systematic review of evidence for psychological treatments in eating disorders: 2005–2012. *The International Journal of Eating Disorders*, *46*(5), 462–469. https://doi.org/10.1002/eat.22103.

Isserlin, L., & Couturier, J. (2012). Therapeutic alliance and family-based treatment for adolescents with anorexia nervosa. *Psychotherapy*, *49*(1), 46–51. https://doi.org/10.1037/a0023905.

Le Grange, D., Crosby, R. D., Rathouz, P. J., & Leventhal, B. L. (2007). A randomized controlled comparison of family-based treatment and supportive psychotherapy for adolescent bulimia nervosa. *Archives of General Psychiatry*, *64*(9), 1049. https://doi.org/10.1001/archpsyc.64.9.1049.

Le Grange, D., & Lock, J. (2009). *Treating bulimia in adolescents: A family-based approach* (1st ed.). New York, NY: Guilford Press.

Le Grange, D., Lock, J., Agras, W. S., Bryson, S. W., & Jo, B. (2015). Randomized clinical trial of family-based treatment and cognitive-behavioral therapy for adolescent bulimia nervosa. *Journal of the American Academy of Child & Adolescent Psychiatry*, *54*(11), 886–94.e2. https://doi.org/10.1016/j.jaac.2015.08.008.

Le Grange, D., & Loeb, K. L. (2014). Family-based treatment for adolescent eating disorders: A transdiagnostic approach. In J. Ehrenreich-May & B. Chu (Eds.), *Transdiagnostic mechanisms and treatment for youth psychopathology* (pp. 363–385). New York, NY: Guilford Press.

Little, L. M., Pope, E., Wallisch, A., & Dunn, W. (2018). Occupation-based coaching by means of telehealth for families of young children with autism spectrum disorder. *American Journal of Occupational Therapy*, *72*(2), 1–7. https://doi.org/10.5014/ajot.2018.024786.

Lock, J., Darcy, A., Fitzpatrick, K. K., Vierhile, M., & Sadeh-Sharvit, S. (2017). Parental guided self-help family based treatment for adolescents with anorexia

332 *Claire Trainor et al.*

nervosa: A feasibility study. *International Journal of Eating Disorders, 50*(9), 1104–1108. https://doi.org/10.1002/eat.22733.

Lock, J., & Le Grange, D. (2015). *Treatment manual for anorexia nervosa: A family-based approach (2nd ed.).* New York, NY: The Guilford Press.

Lock, J., & Le Grange, D. (2018). Family-based treatment: Where are we and where should we be going to improve recovery in child and adolescent eating disorders. *International Journal of Eating Disorders, 52*(4), 481–487. https://doi.org/10.1002/eat.22980.

Lock, J., Le Grange, D., Agras, W. S., & Dare, C. (2002). *Treatment manual for anorexia nervosa: A family-based approach (1st ed.).* New York. NY: Guilford Press.

Lock, J., Le Grange, D., Agras, W. S., Moye, A., Bryson, S. W., & Jo, B. (2010). Randomized clinical trial comparing family-based treatment with adolescent-focused individual therapy for adolescents with anorexia nervosa. *Archives of General Psychiatry, 67*(10), 1025–1032. https://doi.org/10.1001/archgenpsychiatry.2010.128.

Lock, J., Le Grange, D., Forsberg, S., & Hewell, K. (2006). Is family therapy useful for treating children with anorexia nervosa? Results of a case series. *Journal of American Academy of Child and Adolescent Psychiatry, 45*(11), 1323–1328. https://doi.org/10.1097/01.chi.0000233208.43427.4c.

Loeb, K. L., Wilson, G. T., Labouvie, E., Pratt, E. M., Hayaki, J., Walsh, T. B., … Fairburn, C. G. (2005). Therapeutic alliance and treatment adherence in two interventions for bulimia nervosa: A study of process and outcome. *Journal of Consulting and Clinical Psychology, 737*(6), 1097–1106. Retrieved from https://psycnet.apa.org/doiLanding?doi=10.1037%2F0022-006X.73.6.1097.

Madden, S., Miskovic-Wheatley, J., Wallis, A., Kohn, M., Lock, J., Le Grange, D., … Touyz, S. (2015). A randomized controlled trial of in-patient treatment for anorexia nervosa in medically unstable adolescents. *Psychological Medicine, 45*(2), 415–427. https://doi.org/10.1017/S0033291714001573.

Mitchell, J. E., Crosby, R. D., Wonderlich, S. A., Crow, S., Lancaster, K., Simonich, H., … Cook Myers, T. (2008). A randomized trial comparing the efficacy of cognitive–behavioral therapy for bulimia nervosa delivered via telemedicine versus face-to-face. *Behaviour Research and Therapy, 46*(5), 581–592. https://doi.org/10.1016/J.BRAT.2008.02.004.

Munsch, S., Wyssen, A., Vanhulst, P., Lalanne, D., Steinemann, S. T., & Tuch, A. (2019). Binge-eating disorder treatment goes online - feasibility, usability, and treatment outcome of an Internet-based treatment for binge-eating disorder: Study protocol for a three-arm randomized controlled trial including an immediate treatment, a waitlist, and a placebo control group. *Trials, 20*(1), 128. https://doi.org/10.1186/s13063-019-3192-z.

Murphy, R., Straebler, S., Cooper, Z., & Fairburn, C. G. (2010). Cognitive behavioral therapy for eating disorders. *The Psychiatric Clinics of North America, 33*(3), 611–627. https://doi.org/10.1016/j.psc.2010.04.004

Murray, S. B., & Le Grange, D. (2014). Family therapy for adolescent eating disorders: An update. *Current Psychiatry Reports, 16*(5), 447. https://doi.org/10.1007/s11920-014-0447-y.

Myers, K., Vander Stoep, A., Zhou, C., McCarty, C. A., Katon, W., & Stoep, V. (2015). Effectiveness of a Telehealth service delivery model for treating attention-deficit/hyperactivity disorder: A community-based randomized controlled trial. *54*(4), 263–274. https://doi.org/10.1016/j.jaac.2015.01.009.

Nelson, E.-L., Barnard, M., & Cain, S. (2003). Treating childhood depression over videoconferencing. *Telemedicine Journal and e-Health, 9*(1), 49–55. https://doi.org/10.1089/153056203763317648.

Nevonen, L., Mark, M., Levin, B., Lindström, M., & Paulson-Karlsson, G. (2006). Evaluation of a new Internet-based self-help guide for patients with bulimic symptoms in Sweden. *Nordic Journal of Psychiatry, 60*(6), 463–468. https://doi.org/10.1080/08039480601021993.

Pereira, T., Lock, J., & Oggins, J. (2006). Role of therapeutic alliance in family therapy for adolescent anorexia nervosa. *International Journal of Eating Disorders, 39*(8), 677–684. https://doi.org/10.1002/eat.20303.

Poulsen, S., Lunn, S., Daniel, S. I. F., Folke, S., Mathiesen, B. B., Katznelson, H., & Fairburn, C. G. (2014). A randomized controlled trial of psychoanalytic psychotherapy or cognitive-behavioral therapy for bulimia nervosa. *American Journal of Psychiatry, 171*(1), 109–116. https://doi.org/10.1176/appi.ajp.2013.12121511.

Rienecke, R. D., Richmond, R., & Lebow, J. (2016). Therapeutic alliance, expressed emotion, and treatment outcome for anorexia nervosa in a family-based partial hospitalization program. *Eating Behaviors, 22*, 124–128. https://doi.org/10.1016/J.EATBEH.2016.06.017.

Sánchez-Ortiz, V. C., Munro, C., Stahl, D., House, J., Startup, H., Treasure, J., … Schmidt, U. (2011). A randomized controlled trial of internet-based cognitive-behavioural therapy for bulimia nervosa or related disorders in a student population. *Psychological Medicine, 41*(2), 407–417. https://doi.org/10.1017/S0033291710000711.

Schaumberg, K., Welch, E., Breithaupt, L., Hübel, C., Baker, J. H., Munn-Chernoff, M. A., … Bulik, C. M. (2017). The science behind the academy for eating disorders' nine truths about eating disorders. *European Eating Disorders Review: The Journal of the Eating Disorders Association, 25*(6), 432–450. https://doi.org/10.1002/erv.2553.

Schlegl, S., Bürger, C., Schmidt, L., Herbst, N., & Voderholzer, U. (2015). The potential of technology-based psychological interventions for anorexia and bulimia nervosa: A systematic review and recommendations for future research. *Journal of Medical Internet Research, 17*(3), e85. https://doi.org/10.2196/jmir.3554.

Schmidt, U., Lee, S., Beecham, J., Perkins, S., Treasure, J., Yi, I., … Eisler, I. (2007). A randomized controlled trial of family therapy and cognitive behavior therapy guided self-care for adolescents with bulimia nervosa and related disorders. *American Journal of Psychiatry, 164*(4), 591–598. https://doi.org/10.1176/ajp.2007.164.4.591.

Shapiro, J. R., Reba-Harrelson, L., Dymek-Valentine, M., Woolson, S. L., Hamer, R. M., & Bulik, C. M. (2007). Feasibility and acceptability of CD-ROM-based cognitive-behavioural treatment for binge-eating disorder. *European Eating Disorders Review, 15*(3), 175–184. https://doi.org/10.1002/erv.787.

Shingleton, R. M., Richards, L. K., & Thompson-Brenner, H. (2013). Using technology within the treatment of eating disorders: A clinical practice review. *Psychotherapy, 50*(4), 576–582. https://doi.org/10.1037/a0031815.

Sly, R., Morgan, J. F., Mountford, V. A., & Lacey, J. H. (2013). Predicting premature termination of hospitalised treatment for anorexia nervosa: The roles of therapeutic alliance, motivation, and behaviour change. *Eating Behaviors, 14*(2), 119–123. https://doi.org/10.1016/j.eatbeh.2013.01.007.

Spencer, L., Schmidt-Hantke, J., Allen, K., Gordon, G., Potterton, R., Musiat, P., … Schmidt, U. (2019). *A web-based intervention for carers of individuals with anorexia nervosa (We Can): Trial protocol of a randomised controlled trial investigating the effectiveness of*

334 *Claire Trainor et al.*

different levels of support. Internet Interventions, 16, 76–85 https://doi.org/10.1016/j. invent.2018.02.005.

Steele, A. L., & Wade, T. D. (2008). A randomised trial investigating guided self-help to reduce perfectionism and its impact on bulimia nervosa: A pilot study. *Behaviour Research and Therapy, 46*(12), 1316–1323. https://doi.org/10.1016/j.brat.2008. 09.006.

Stewart, R. W., Orengo-Aguayo, R. E., Cohen, J. A., Mannarino, A. P., & De Arellano, M. A. (2017). A pilot study of trauma-focused cognitive-behavioral therapy delivered via Telehealth technology. *Child maltreatment, 22*(4), 324–333. https://doi.org/10.1177/1077559517725403.

Stice, E., Durant, S., Rohde, P., & Shaw, H. (2014). Effects of a prototype Internet dissonance-based eating disorder prevention program at 1- and 2-year follow-up. *Health Psychology: Official Journal of the Division of Health Psychology, American Psychological Association, 33*(12), 1558–1567. https://doi.org/10.1037/hea0000090.

Stice, E., Rohde, P., Durant, S., & Shaw, H. (2012). A preliminary trial of a prototype internet dissonance-based eating disorder prevention program for young women with body image concerns. *Journal of Consulting and Clinical Psychology, 80*(5), 907–916. https://doi.org/10.1037/a0028016.

Stiles-Shields, C., Bamford, B. H., Touyz, S., Le Grange, D., Hay, P., & Lacey, H. (2016). Predictors of therapeutic alliance in two treatments for adults with severe and enduring anorexia nervosa. *Journal of Eating Disorders, 4,* 13. https://doi.org/10.1186/s40337-016-0102-6.

Taylor, C. B., Bryson, S., Luce, K. H., Cunning, D., Doyle, A. C., Abascal, L. B., ... Wilfley, D. E. (2006). Prevention of eating disorders in at-risk college-age women. *Archives of General Psychiatry, 63*(8), 881. https://doi.org/10.1001/archpsyc.63.8.881.

Treasure, J., Murphy, T., Szmukler, T., Todd, G., Gavan, K., & Joyce, J. (2001). The experience of caregiving for severe mental illness: A comparison between anorexia nervosa and psychosis. *Social Psychiatry and Psychiatric Epidemiology, 36*(7), 343–347. https://doi.org/10.1007/s001270170039.

Watson, H. J., & Bulik, C. M. (2013). Update on the treatment of anorexia nervosa: Review of clinical trials, practice guidelines and emerging interventions. *Psychological Medicine, 43*(12), 2477–2500. https://doi.org/10.1017/S0033291712002620.

Williams, C., Aubin, S., Cottrell, D., & Harkin, P. J. R. (1998). *Overcoming bulimia: A self-help package.* Leeds, UK: University of Leeds Press.

Wilson, F. A., Rampa, S., Trout, K. E., & Stimpson, J. P. (2017). Telehealth delivery of mental health services: An analysis of private insurance claims data in the United States. *Psychiatric Services, 68,* 1303–1306. https://doi.org/10.1176/appi.ps. 201700017.

Wonderlich, S. A., Peterson, C. B., Crosby, R. D., Smith, T. L., Klein, M. H., Mitchell, J. E., & Crow, S. J. (2014). A randomized controlled comparison of integrative cognitive-affective therapy (ICAT) and enhanced cognitive-behavioral therapy (CBT-E) for bulimia nervosa. *Psychological Medicine, 44*(03), 543–553. https://doi.org/10.1017/S0033291713001098.

Zendegui, E. A., West, J. A., & Zandberg, L. J. (2014). Binge eating frequency and regular eating adherence: The role of eating pattern in cognitive behavioral guided self-help. *Eating behaviors, 15*(2), 241–243. https://doi.org/10.1016/J.EATBEH. 2014.03.002.

15 Using FBT and Adjunctive Family Interventions in a Partial Hospitalization Program for Adolescents with Eating Disorders

Terra L. Towne, Stephanie K. Peck, and Roxanne E. Rockwell

Introduction

The role of family involvement in adolescent eating disorders treatment has significantly evolved since the early application of treatments that intentionally excluded parents and prescribed adolescent autonomy around food (Harper, 1983). The development of family therapy for adolescent anorexia nervosa at the Maudsley Hospital in London in the late 1970s marked a pivotal paradigm shift toward viewing families as an important resource in the recovery of adolescents (Dare & Eisler, 1997). This specific family-focused treatment approach serves as the theoretical foundation for many present-day eating disorder treatments, including family-based treatment (FBT) for adolescent anorexia nervosa (Lock & Le Grange, 2012) and adolescent bulimia nervosa (Le Grange & Lock, 2007). Indeed, involving parents in their child's treatment has consistently yielded improvements in psychological and medical morbidities (Eisler et al., 1997; Eisler, Simic, Russell, & Dare, 2007; Lock, Couturier, & Agras, 2006) and is deemed an acceptable approach by both parents and adolescents (Le Grange, Crosby, Rathouz, & Levethal, 2007). FBT has proven efficacious in the treatment of adolescent anorexia nervosa (Lock et al., 2010) and bulimia nervosa (Le Grange et al., 2007; Le Grange, Lock, Agras, Bryson, & Jo, 2015) and is considered the first-line treatment for these disorders in adolescents (Lock & Le Grange, 2019; Reinecke, 2017). However, despite the bulk of evidence supporting family involvement, many treatment centers delivering higher levels of care, such as residential and partial hospitalization programs, do not involve families at the levels recommended in FBT. One barrier involves adapting treatments that were primarily designed for and tested on medically stable outpatients to more intensive treatment settings (e.g., inpatient, partial-hospitalization, and intensive outpatient programs; Murray et al., 2015). Such adaptations pose the unique challenge of both structuring treatment in ways that promote FBT principles in a broader treatment context where adolescents receive some aspects of treatment without families present and providing additional tools to

336 *Towne, Peck, and Rockwell*

families for whom outpatient FBT was insufficient or not indicated. This chapter will discuss the implementation of FBT and adjunctive family interventions at the University of California, San Diego Eating Disorders Center's adolescent partial hospitalization program (UCSD PHP) in the United States.

Partial Hospitalization Program Background

General Overview

The UCSD PHP is a 6 day per week program that patients attend for either 10 hours or 6 hours per day depending on the level of care needed. The treatment program is based on a blended orientation of FBT (Lock & Le Grange, 2012) and dialectical behavior therapy (DBT; Linehan, 2015). FBT serves as the theoretical foundation for PHP family programming and the primary treatment modality utilized in family therapy, whereas DBT guides adolescent-specific programming and is one of the primary treatment modalities used in individual therapy. Each PHP treatment day is comprised of group therapy and structured meals and snacks, and 3 days of the week involve intensive family programming. Adolescents receive weekly family and individual therapy, and each adolescent is assigned a dietitian and psychiatric provider. Dietitians are typically consultants to the family therapist and meet with parents as needed to provide dietary consultation. Adolescents may meet with their dietitian depending on their stage of treatment. This practice may stray from core FBT principles in some cases, whereas, in others, it is used to assist adolescents who are regaining independence around food in Phase II of FBT. Adolescents are seen weekly by their psychiatric provider, who consults with parents to provide medication recommendations and updates. All patients are medically monitored throughout treatment.

Adolescent and Family Programming Overview

Adolescent-specific programming, which comprises the bulk of the treatment week, involves various therapy groups in addition to structured meals and snacks that are eaten with other patients and supervised by program staff. The majority of adolescent therapy groups are focused on specific aspects of DBT (e.g., mindfulness and applied DBT). Other core groups include cognitive-behavioral therapy (Beck, 2011), cognitive remediation therapy (Tchanturia, Davies, Reeder, & Wykes, 2010), anxiety management, challenging perfectionism, self-compassion, nutrition, and behavioral activation (Lejuez, Hopko, Acierno, Daughters, & Pogoto, 2011). Parents attend 2 half days of family programming per week and a full day of family programming every Saturday. Over half of family programming is spent with their children during which families partake in multifamily meals, activities, groups, and DBT skills training. Parents spend the remainder of family programming in parent-only groups including psychoeducation,

FBT and Family Interventions for Adolescents

nutrition, process, and Parent Management Training (PMT; Kazdin, 1997). See Figure 15.1 for a complete program schedule.

Individual Therapy

Adolescents receive weekly individual therapy sessions while enrolled in PHP. The primary goals of individual therapy are twofold. First and foremost, the individual therapist aims to connect with the patient and serve as their advocate and support throughout their PHP treatment course, similar to the role of siblings in outpatient FBT. Second, the therapist aims to facilitate the patient's awareness, management, and appropriate expression of emotions through the use of skills. This involves reviewing patient diary cards (i.e., a self-report tracking tool used to measure daily emotions, urges, ineffective behaviors, and skill use), and conducting behavior chain analysis to identify why an ineffective behavior occurred and when and how the patient could have intervened. Consistent with full model DBT, individual therapists provide patients with their personal cell phone numbers, which patients can text or call for skills coaching outside of program hours. In addition to helping adolescents refrain from ineffective behaviors (e.g., self-harm and food restriction) by engaging in skills, or skills coaching, the adolescent PHP often

MONDAY	TUESDAY	WEDNESDAY	THURSDAY	FRIDAY	SATURDAY (PARENTS / PATIENTS)
BREAKFAST	BREAKFAST	BREAKFAST	BREAKFAST	BREAKFAST	MULTIFAMILY BREAKFAST
DAILY CHECK-IN	DAILY CHECK-IN	DAILY CHECK-IN	DAILY CHECK-IN	DAILY CHECK-IN	
DBT INTERPERSONAL EFFECTIVENESS	COGNITIVE-BEHAVIORAL THERAPY / BREAK THE CYCLE	EXPRESSIVE ARTS / SPORT PARTICIPANT	NUTRITION	RADICALLY OPEN DBT / DBT EMOTION REGULATION	TEEN PROCESS
Bathroom Break / AM SNACK	Bathroom Break / AM SNACK	Bathroom Break / AM SNACK	Bathroom Break / AM SNACK	Bathroom Break / AM SNACK	PARENT PSYCHOEDUCATION / AM SNACK
SCHOOL	SCHOOL	SCHOOL	SCHOOL	SCHOOL	CONTRIBUTE
Bathroom Break	Bathroom Break	Bathroom Break	Bathroom Break	Bathroom Break	
LUNCH & PRIVILEGES/ WALK	LUNCH & PRIVILEGES/ WALK	LUNCH & PRIVILEGES/ WALK	LUNCH & PRIVILEGES/ WALK	LUNCH & PRIVILEGES/ WALK	MULTIFAMILY LUNCH
PROCESS / SPORT PARTICIPANT	PROCESS	PROCESS	PROCESS / BODY IMAGE	PROCESS	FAMILY-BASED ACTIVITY & CHECKOUT
COMMUNITY MEETING & LEVEL SHEETS	BREATH RE-TRAINING	SKILLS IN ACTION / COOKING CLASS	LEVEL 1 YOGA / LEVEL 2 YOGA	PROBLEM SOLVING	
Bathroom Break / PM SNACK	Bathroom Break / PM SNACK	Bathroom Break / PM SNACK	Bathroom Break / PM SNACK	Bathroom Break / PM SNACK	
PRIVILEGES	GROUP HOMEWORK	PRIVILEGES	GROUP HOMEWORK	MEDIA AWARENESS	
MINDFULNESS			PARENT MANAGEMENT TRAINING	CLEAN UP	
SELF-COMPASSION	MULTIFAMILY DBT SKILLS TRAINING	DBT DISTRESS TOLERANCE	ANXIETY MANAGEMENT / PARENT NUTRITION	Bathroom Break / PRIVILEGES	
Bathroom Break	Bathroom Break	Bathroom Break	Bathroom Break	Bathroom Break	
DINNER/ PRIVILEGES	MULTIFAMILY DINNER WITH COACHING	DINNER/ PRIVILEGES	MULTIFAMILY DINNER WITH COACHING	DINNER/ PRIVILEGES	
REWARD/BEHAVIOR CHAIN ANALYSIS	PARENT PSYCHOEDUCATION / CHALLENGING PERFECTIONISM	COGNITIVE REMEDIATION THERAPY	MULTIFAMILY ACTIVITY	LIVING LIFE OUTSIDE YOUR DISORDER	

Figure 15.1 UCSD Adolescent Partial Hospitalization Program Schedule.

338 *Towne, Peck, and Rockwell*

simultaneously serves the purpose of providing support and validation in highly distressing situations in which family relations are tense due to parents asserting control over their child's recovery. The intensity of DBT work in the PHP can promote recovery, even in the absence of motivation, as adolescents learn skills to accept reality (e.g., parents will never stop fighting the eating disorder), cope with uncomfortable emotions (e.g., shame after mealtime), and improve communication with their parents to better meet their needs (e.g., asking for a reward in exchange for meeting a recovery goal).

Family-Supported Treatment Components

Overview

Family- and parent-focused interventions at the UCSD PHP are incorporated in both family groups and weekly family therapy sessions. Such interventions are based upon FBT and multifamily therapy for anorexia nervosa (MFT-AN; Lock & Le Grange, 2012; Simic & Eisler, 2012; Simic & Eisler, 2016), temperament-based treatment (TBT-S; Hill, Knatz Peck, Wierenga, & Kaye, 2016; Kaye et al., 2014; Knatz, Wierenga, Murray, Hill, & Kaye, 2015), and various behavioral strategies for both parents and patients (Kazdin, 1997; Knatz Peck, 2016; Linehan, 2015). Consistent with the key tenets of FBT, each family- and parent-focused intervention functions to educate and empower parents, build parental self-efficacy, help parents view the eating disorder as separate from the child, and reduce familial blame surrounding the development of the eating disorder. Moreover, family programming aims to expand upon FBT tenets to provide families with a scientific understanding of eating disorders, more tools and "how to's" for facilitating behavior change among adolescents, and opportunities for increased connection and learning within individual families and among families in treatment. Involving parents in intensive treatment from the outset allows for maximal learning to take place and massed practice shaping eating behavior over an extended period of time, theoretically resulting in early treatment response and the skillset to sustain recovery progress beyond PHP.

Family-Based Treatment

A core component of treatment is weekly family therapy, in which FBT is the most commonly employed treatment modality. FBT is a manualized family therapy that centrally leverages parental resources toward combatting the eating disorder. Parents are considered the experts on their children and tasked with the responsibility of helping them recover, whereas family therapists serve as consultants throughout this treatment process. Two key tenets of FBT that are emphasized in the PHP involve aligning parents with one another, and empowering and mobilizing them to restore their child to a healthy weight, normalize their eating, and reduce their eating disorder behaviors. Although it is not possible to employ FBT adherent to the outpatient model in the context of a PHP, the latter was designed to initially provide respite for family members while they are receiving intensive psychoeducation and tools and then gradually taper off the time spent in program. The majority of families presenting for treatment at the PHP have gone through other treatment unsuccessfully, and the goal here is to reduce their sense of disempowerment, perhaps exacerbated by perceived past failures, and provide parents with opportunities within the program to build self-efficacy. Family sessions closely resemble outpatient FBT but are adapted in several ways in an effort to underscore FBT tenets while both considering the limitations and maximizing the benefits of the intensive treatment setting.

Parent Mobilization

An FBT intervention utilized in the initial family session involves presenting parents with information on the mortality rate, medical risks, and time-sensitive prognosis of eating disorders. This is often referred to as "orchestrating an intense scene," in which family therapists mobilize parents to take action by rendering their anxiety about the effects of eating disorders greater than their reticence about fighting their child's illness. Although this is an important intervention for providing treatment rationale and fostering parental buy-in, Murray et al. (2015) caution against its use when there are few opportunities for parents to build mastery in challenging the eating disorder, such as in intensive treatment settings with limited parental involvement. Indeed, elevated anxiety in the absence of these opportunities may exacerbate feelings of helplessness or overreliance on the treatment team or program.

The success of facilitating this therapeutic bind for families enrolled in the UCSD PHP is dependent on how it is adapted given the clinical context. Families often present to a PHP following inpatient hospitalization or having previously received outpatient FBT. Such families may already be aware of both the seriousness of eating disorders and the rationale for parental involvement. Rather than reiterating this information, mobilization can be facilitated by presenting data most relevant to the patient's current stage of treatment. As noted by Murray et al. (2015), parents of patients who admit to the PHP immediately following inpatient hospitalization could be informed of the high premature treatment drop-out rates in PHP settings and high relapse rates following hospital-driven weight restoration (Girz, LaFrance Robinson, Foroughe, Jasper, & Boachie, 2013). The ultimate goal of this adaptation is to raise parental anxiety about the serious risks associated with their child's stage of treatment to enhance their motivation for and vigilance toward treatment attendance and adherence. Additionally, parents may already be highly anxious, and as a result, derive little to no benefit from further elevation of their anxiety. At worst, further elevating anxiety could exacerbate feelings of hopelessness and guilt and impair their ability to act in this context. This is occasionally the case for families who are readmitted to the UCSD PHP or

340   Towne, Peck, and Rockwell

are admitted in the middle of or following an unsuccessful course of outpatient FBT. Parents may feel defeated and question the utility of parent involvement for their family or their personal ability to effect change. Although these concerns should be examined to ensure treatment appropriateness, parents may benefit from the family therapist instilling hope and normalizing the often nonlinear nature of eating disorder recovery. Specifically, family therapists can provide assurance that FBT can fail because of the severity of the illness and that continued parental involvement during the PHP will help them learn and practice new skills, receive feedback and support from professionals, and ultimately result in a more sustainable transition home.

Parent Empowerment

Family therapists can enhance parent empowerment throughout the child's treatment by emphasizing parental contributions to their child's recovery steps. Consistent with FBT's prioritization of parent-driven weight restoration for patients who are underweight, therapists at the UCSD PHP often present weight graphs to parents in a way that compares weight progress made in program with weight progress made over the weekend, during which adolescents spend the majority of time with their families. Evidence of weekend weight gain can assure parents they are capable of ensuring meal compliance without therapeutic assistance, serving their child enough food, appropriately balancing their child's activity level and intake, and potentially reducing compensatory eating disorder behaviors. Family therapists can also bring attention to parent successes observed during multifamily meals, such as insisting on 100% meal completion or successfully implementing a new meal coaching strategy. Similarly, family therapists may inform parents of a positive change in their child that occurred during program (e.g., increased group participation or provided recovery-minded advice to a peer), which was likely influenced by a parent decision or change (e.g., using a validation strategy or awarding an extra walk after a challenge meal). These techniques are particularly important in shaping parents' perception of an objective recovery success, as parents often note confusion about evaluating progress in recovery and may perceive their child's distress as a parental failure or shortcoming. Sharing markers that predict long-term recovery (e.g., restoring 2.5 kg by the 4th week of treatment) with parents is often beneficial, both as an objective marker of success and as a motivational tool. When progress is not being made in any of the aforementioned areas, family therapists can continue to empower parents (if clinically appropriate) by creating opportunities during FBT sessions for parents to set achievable goals for getting on track and problem-solve accomplishing these goals.

Family Therapist as Consultant

Although FBT tasks parents with the responsibility of normalizing their child's eating and deriving their own ideas and strategies for how to accomplish this

FBT and Family Interventions for Adolescents   341

feat, the family therapist can simultaneously encourage parents to utilize the increased support offered by the PHP setting. FBT sessions can be spent brainstorming or deriving strategies that promote the child's recovery. Although the family therapist should facilitate parents coming up with their own ideas, parents who struggle to do so can be encouraged to reach out to other families for suggestions or advice. Many families create recovery rules or contracts that apply to their child's eating, communication, or eating disorder behaviors both during and outside of program. The family therapist can work with the parents to ensure the program is upholding these same expectations and reporting back when expectations are not met. For example, if parents set a rule that the child must complete a food exposure every day of the week, the family therapist can report back to the family whether or not the exposure was successfully completed in program. Furthermore, the family therapist can facilitate communication among staff to ensure parents' requests are accommodated (e.g., dietary staff selecting a group "surprise snack" based on the exposure food or plating the exposure food for the adolescent at varying meals/snacks throughout the week). Utilizing the support offered by the PHP can ensure consistency in recovery expectations across settings, theoretically increasing the likelihood that the adolescent's ability to follow these expectations will generalize to the home environment. Therapists supporting parent-derived rules and expectations also reiterates to the adolescent that their parents, as opposed to program therapists, are in charge and know what is best for their recovery. Although this may be upsetting to the adolescent, it often helps build trust in their parents' knowledge and abilities. The additional support offered by the PHP does not replace parents' responsibility for creating recovery rules for their child or upholding preestablished contingencies for following or breaking rules (e.g., presenting the exposure food for night snack when it is not successfully consumed in program).

Multifamily Meals

The UCSD program is structured such that parents have ample opportunities to build self-efficacy around mealtimes and influence their child's eating behavior, which have been implicated as robust predictors of positive treatment outcome (Ellison et al., 2012). An important component of family programming is multifamily meals. During multifamily meals, parents plate food from a buffet (depending on the phase of treatment, this involves plating in the absence of their child or providing oversight and feedback while their child plates him or herself), and the whole family eats together, often at the same table as other families in treatment. Plating meals in program allows parents to practice serving quantities of food that meet their child's nutritional needs, present a united front with their partner, and manage distress, both their own and that of their child, upon presenting an appropriately-sized, balanced meal. Consistent with FBT tenets, parents are held responsible for helping their child complete the meal, whereas program therapists observe from a distance and provide meal-coaching consultation directly to parents as needed. This allows parents, as opposed to program therapists, to problem-solve their child's noncompliance and practice implementing meal-coaching strategies (e.g., facilitating distractions and prompting additional bites) in a supportive environment. An example of meal-coaching consultation is provided in Figure 15.2. Moreover, multifamily meals provide family therapists with invaluable *in vivo* observations that often serve as a microcosm of mealtimes outside of program. Family therapists can use these observations as tangible examples during FBT sessions to provide affirmation for success or help parents address a problem. Multifamily meals are used as an alternative or in addition to the traditional family meal that takes place in the second FBT session, as the greater proximal distance from program therapists while eating in the meal room may have greater ecological validity.

Temperament-Based Treatment

TBT-S (Hill et al., 2016; Kaye et al., 2014; Knatz et al., 2015) is a multifamily, neurobiologically based approach developed and implemented at the UCSD Eating Disorders Center and Center for Balanced Living in Columbus, OH. US. Although FBT mobilizes parents to take responsibility for refeeding their child and/or normalizing their eating, parents often struggle to understand eating disorder symptomatology and feel ill-equipped to navigate barriers to

---

Mother: walks to side of room to consult with therapist while other therapists in the room supervise her daughter

Mother: (appearing frustrated) She says she's done. I don't know what to do.

Therapist: How much has she eaten?

Mother: About a quarter. And she hasn't touched the roll.

Therapist: Okay. What have you tried so far?

Mother: Well she actually started on her own but stopped after 5 bites. We started playing Uno, and I was prompting her to eat before every turn. But it's not working anymore; she's adamant.

Therapist: It sounds like you were really effective in getting her going, and now you need to do something else. You know your daughter best. What do you think would be compelling to her?

Mother: I don't know. She chooses the eating disorder over everything. Except maybe school.

Therapist: How could you use school to get her to start eating again?

Mother: We've never taken away school before. I don't know. She does have a lot of homework, and it's been hard to get it all done being here 10 hours a day. Could I tell her she can't do her homework tonight unless she finishes dinner?

Therapist: That's a great idea!

Figure 15.2 Meal-Coaching Consultation Example During Multifamily Meal.

FBT and Family Interventions for Adolescents 343

accomplishing these goals. A hallmark of TBT-S that works to address this issue is the focus on the neurobiologically influenced temperament and personality traits (e.g., heightened anxiety) that predispose individuals to the development of eating disorders (Kaye et al., 2014; Kaye, 2008). Contrary to treatments viewing these traits as targets to be altered, TBT-S utilizes a strengths-based approach to help families understand and capitalize on their child's unique and adaptive temperament profile to meet recovery goals (Knatz et al., 2015). To do so, families learn about the etiological mechanisms of eating disorders, undergo experiential activities demonstrating how these traits are experienced (both cognitively and neurologically) by their child, and derive strategies and coping mechanisms to "work with" their child's traits and compensate for alterations in brain circuitry that perpetuate maladaptive behaviors. This approach has demonstrated acceptability, feasibility, and preliminary effectiveness in two open treatment trials (Marzola et al., 2015; Wierenga et al., 2018).

Components of TBT-S are woven throughout family programming in the adolescent PHP. One such component involves providing families with interactive lectures presented by neuroscientists with expertise in eating disorders. Lectures are intended to reduce guilt and blame surrounding the development of eating disorders by dispelling common misconceptions about their etiology and providing compelling, empirical evidence that they are powerful, biologically based illnesses. To do so, experts present brain imaging data, many of which were collected at the UCSD Eating Disorders Center, that implicate differences in reward and punishment sensitivity, interoceptive awareness, anxiety, and cognitive flexibility among individuals with eating disorders. These data illustrate how together these alterations can manifest as severe anticipatory anxiety about eating, fear of negative consequences resulting from eating, and altered hunger and satiety, providing a rational explanation for seemingly illogical eating disorder behaviors. Information provided in lectures facilitates treatment buy-in by both establishing the scientific credibility of the treatment program and providing a science-based rationale for parental involvement in treatment.

The UCSD PHP has implemented several experiential exercises from TBT-S into their multifamily groups. Experiential group exercises are highly interactive demonstrations that effectively bring to life the imaging findings presented during expert lectures. The purpose of experiential exercises is to enhance parental empathy, increase understanding of eating disorder symptoms and behaviors (many of which adolescents may struggle to understand or articulate themselves), and brainstorm and practice strategies for navigating this altered circuitry. For example, one experiential exercise created by Dr. Laura Hill of the Center for Balanced Living involves creating and acting out a "gauntlet" of the thoughts, feelings, body sensations, and urges that a patient experiences surrounding mealtimes (e.g., anticipatory worry while waiting for parents to serve dinner; Hill et al., 2016). To represent alterations in the insula that influence hunger and satiety, parents walk blindfolded through the gauntlet while

344 Towne, Peck, and Rockwell

navigating both external barriers and eating disorder voices that occur prior to, during, and following every meal. Families are given the opportunity to brainstorm and implement techniques for successfully navigating the gauntlet (e.g., distractions to shift their attention, verbal or physical guidance from another person, and structuring barriers in a way they can be anticipated), which have broader implications for useful recovery strategies (e.g., ensuring meals and snacks are at the same time every day). This exercise allows parents to experience a powerful snapshot of the anxiety and inhibition around food experienced by individuals with eating disorders and begin conversations with their child about how best to provide support around mealtimes to ensure recovery goals are met. In addition to building empathy, it highlights the improbability of even the most motivated adolescents to fully recover on their own and stresses the necessity of some form of parental guidance.

Parent Management Training

Although parents are charged with the enormous responsibility of restoring their child's health, they may feel unprepared to manage the resistance, emotional dysregulation, and behavioral outbursts that often accompany the changes necessary for recovery. This perceived unpreparedness may be exacerbated in families who had few opportunities to set rules or discipline their child prior to the onset of the eating disorder, which parents often attribute to their child's good behavior, agreeableness, and tendency to comply with rules. Although reminding parents of these emotional and behavioral discrepancies may assist them in separating the illness from their child, parents also need tangible strategies to influence their child's behavior.

PMT is a 13-session parent-focused, behavioral intervention that first demonstrated efficacy for the treatment of children with oppositional and antisocial behaviors (Kazdin, 1997). While enrolled in the PHP, parents receive weekly group PMT. The goal of PMT is to increase the child's adaptive functioning and facilitate effective parent–child interactions by helping parents understand their role in maintaining behavior and teaching them to appropriately shape behavior through the use of operant conditioning (Kazdin, 2005). To do so, parents learn about behavioral principles, provide real-life examples for the group to discuss, and role play behavioral strategies (e.g., attending to desired behavior and giving effective directions) with fellow parents before practicing them for homework.

Although definitive dismantling studies in PMT are lacking (Kazdin, 2005), one potential mechanism of change is parents' increased use of positive reinforcement, particularly the reinforcement of positive opposites, and the child's associated learning that occurs as a result. Punishment strategies are taught as part of PMT but are typically deemphasized in comparison to reinforcement, as there is weak evidence of their long-term effectiveness for decreasing target behaviors (Patterson, Reid, & Dishion, 1992). Although this model makes conceptual sense for patients with bulimia nervosa, who are generally highly sensitive to reward (Orberndorfer et al., 2013) and may behave impulsively despite negative consequences (Harrison, O'Brien, Lopez, & Treasure, 2010), it may benefit from adaptation for patients with anorexia nervosa, who tend to anticipate and avoid negative consequences (Bischoff-Grethe et al., 2018) and are generally insensitive to reward but highly sensitive to punishment (Harrison, Sternheim, O'Hara, Oldershaw, & Schmidt, 2016; Wierenga et al., 2014). This is often illuminated in conversations with parents of children with anorexia, who describe difficulties with reinforcing behaviors such as meal completion when their child does not want verbal praise nor tangible rewards for this behavior. Although punishment itself does not facilitate new learning, it may enhance motivation, and, in turn, desired behavior change, among patients who are sensitive to punishment. In the absence of data to guide decisions about the application of PMT to an eating disorders population, PMT may be adapted to the individual needs of the families, and parents can be encouraged to simultaneously reinforce desirable behaviors and consider their child's temperament when learning to shape behavior.

Behavioral Contracting

Behavioral contracts are powerful recovery tools that provide families with a comprehensive treatment roadmap (Knatz Peck, 2016). The creation of such a roadmap is accomplished by defining rules and expectations surrounding eating disorder recovery markers and creating associated behavioral contingencies for each. The combination of outlining each recovery expectation in writing and providing a tool for which associated contingencies will be upheld may render the behavioral contract more useful than less specific recovery plans. Furthermore, although implementation of a well-developed behavioral contract can be anxiety-provoking and undesirable for adolescents, it may play to the strengths of several neurobiologically influenced temperament and personality traits common to individuals with eating disorders (Knatz Peck, 2016). Specifically, high achievement orientation, cognitive rigidity, and perfectionistic tendencies may enhance the adolescent's motivation to comply with expectations, whereas uncertainty intolerance and harm avoidance may be assuaged by the transparency and predictability of the contract. The development of a tangible written document may also help parents promote recovery by mitigating their own anxiety and facilitating consistency in both their expectations and implementation of contingencies.

While in treatment, family therapists frequently assist families with the development of behavioral contracts, which can be implemented with a primary goal of promoting recovery throughout PHP treatment, staying recovered upon discharge, achieving a life worth living goal (e.g., discharging from treatment or returning to sports), or avoiding an undesirable consequence (e.g., hospitalization or delaying college). When developing a behavioral contract, parents are encouraged to brainstorm and clearly define behaviors that are incompatible with recovery (e.g., restricting) and any other clinically relevant behaviors (e.g., isolation after meals) they wish to include in the contract. One important aspect of the contract is the creation of concrete rule sets for each identified behavior that emphasize adaptive, alternative behaviors as opposed to "dead man's goals" (i.e., behaviors that can be accomplished by a dead person). For example, setting the recovery rule that an adolescent must spend time with their family or engage in distractions in the living room for 45 minutes after meals has much greater utility than a rule stating that purging is not allowed.

The primary goal of setting behavioral contingencies is to motivate adolescents to behave in ways that align with recovery expectations by making recovery less undesirable than the natural and parent-enforced consequences of having an eating disorder. The effective use of contingencies is partially dependent on the adolescent's perception of the rewards and consequences. As such, it can be helpful to enlist adolescents' input to create strong behavioral contingencies. Adolescents can also request commitments of their parents (e.g., not discussing the next meal while eating or spending time together without mentioning the disorder) to be included in the contract. Parent commitments are included in behavioral contracts to validate adolescents' requests during a challenging process in which they have little control and help parents help their children meet recovery expectations.

Multifamily Therapy

Multifamily therapy groups are an integral component of family programming in the adolescent PHP, as they provide valuable opportunities to relate to and learn from others, and consolidate understanding and mastery of therapeutic material. Two types of evidence-informed multifamily groups provided at the PHP include an adaptation of MFT-AN (Simic & Eisler, 2012; Simic & Eisler, 2015) that is inclusive of all eating disorders and a DBT skills group (Linehan, 2015).

MFT-AN is a systemic family therapy that was derived from its well-established single-family format, family therapy for AN (Eisler, Simic, Blessitt, & Dodge, 2016), and demonstrated greater comparative efficacy despite vast similarities in treatments (Eisler, Simic, Blessitt, Dodge, & team, 2016), suggesting a unique benefit of interfamily interactions. Multifamily groups typically begin with a small group discussion or activity, many of which are recycled or adapted from MFT-AN. One MFT-AN technique involves the creation of "adoptive families" in which patients are paired with small groups of parents and siblings to whom they are not related (Simic & Eisler, 2012; Simic & Eisler, 2015). Adoptive families can be utilized to facilitate open communication around important topics that are often emotionally charged when discussed among parents and their children. For example, one multifamily activity involves tasking patients with compiling a list of effective and ineffective mealtime strategies to share and discuss with their adoptive family. This activity provides parents with a space to ask candid questions and receive both helpful general suggestions (e.g., no commenting on appearance or discussing calories) and opinions on nuanced topics such as how parents can simultaneously validate and disagree with their child (e.g., when patients express sadness and frustration about being "too fat") or how parents can recognize their child's hard work without "upsetting the eating disorder." Following activities or small group discussions, families come together in a large process group to reflect on what they heard, allowing parents to learn from their child through the voice of another parent. Consistent with the overarching principles of MFT-AN, the interactive group format aims to facilitate self-reflection and learning, reductions in guilt and blame, hope for recovery, and connection and support among group members.

In line with a growing body of evidence supporting the use of DBT for the treatment of eating disorders (Ben-Porath, Wisniewski, & Warren, 2010; Brown et al., 2018) and early DBT skills acquisition as a predictor of decreased symptomatology in adults at PHP discharge (Brown et al., 2019), families attend a multifamily DBT skills group on a weekly basis. All DBT groups begin with a mindfulness activity used to refocus the group on the present moment followed by reviewing the applied homework and teaching a new skill to the group. Families are equipped with mindfulness, distress tolerance, emotion regulation, and interpersonal effectiveness skills that can be applied to both recovery (e.g., when a friend restricts in program, when eating disorder urges are high) and everyday life (e.g., getting invited to a birthday party or asking to push back curfew) situations. The primary goal of DBT skills training is to equip patients and parents with the appropriate tools to effectively recognize, express, and cope with intense uncomfortable emotions. Although the DBT skills group is a manualized treatment, acronyms and examples are adapted as appropriate to better meet the needs of an adolescent eating disorders population. For example, the "I" in the Temperature, Intense Exercise, Paced Breathing, Paired Muscle Relaxation skill, which stands for "intense exercise" in traditional DBT, is reframed as "intense sensations." This adaptation is used to promote new, less destructive methods of managing crisis urges (e.g., ripping paper and listening to loud music) and discourage reliance on negative affect motivated exercise, which is associated with eating disorder behaviors (De Young & Anderson, 2010).

In addition to bolstering their own coping and communication skills, parent involvement in multifamily DBT presents many opportunities to influence their child's behavior and build self-efficacy in return. Parents may be able to effect increased skill use in their child by modeling appropriate homework completion and engagement in the group or reinforcing their child for engaging in skills on their own. Further, having learned the skills themselves, parents can more easily identify when their child could benefit from skills and attempt to facilitate their child's use of a specific skill (e.g., facilitating the use of distraction during meals by playing a funny cat video). The opportunities for therapeutic family interactions beyond PHP highlight the many advantages of multifamily groups that would not be possible if treatment were delivered in a solely individual format.

Summary

The UCSD PHP adapts FBT for a PHP treatment setting, fostering FBT principles through both family therapy and adjunctive family- and parent-focused interventions. Parents are centrally and intensively involved in PHP family programming to increase their knowledge of eating disorders, become better equipped with recovery tools, and practice and gain confidence in challenging their child's eating disorder, allowing for a smoother transition home and eliminating their child's need to readjust to parental involvement upon discharge. This eclectic treatment approach was tested among a transdiagnostic adolescent eating disorder sample who received treatment at the UCSD PHP (Reilly et al., in press). The sample reported eating disorder symptoms comparable to those of residential and other PHP samples; 27.1% of adolescents were referred from an inpatient eating disorders unit, 58.1% were diagnosed with a psychiatric comorbidity, and the average duration of illness was 2.17 years (SD = 1.84). When full remission is stringently defined (i.e., weight above 95% of estimated body mass index, eating disorder psychopathology within one standard deviation of a nonclinical community sample, as per the Eating Disorder Examination Questionnaire (Fairburn & Beglin, 2008), and abstinence from binging and purging for the prior 28 days), 40.3% of adolescents achieved full remission at 12-month follow-up, and 59.7% achieved partial or full remission (Reilly et al., in press). These outcomes are similar to those reported by Bryson and colleagues (2018) in the only other adolescent PHP outcome study including follow-up data past discharge. Importantly, significant mean improvements in the areas of weight, eating disorder psychopathology, and binging and purging from pre to posttreatment were maintained at follow-up periods (Reilly et al., 2018), suggesting progress made in PHP is sustainable at home over time. Given the dearth of effectiveness research on adolescent PHP outcomes and poor long-term retention rates for these open trials, more naturalistic studies are needed to better qualify outcome data from the UCSD PHP. Upon improving retention rates, moderators and mediators can be explored to determine for whom treatment works and the specific program components accounting for treatment outcome, respectively. This will be particularly important in tailoring the treatment approach and testing theoretical assumptions of FBT as they relate to a PHP setting.

References

Beck, J. S. (2011). *Cognitive behavior therapy: Basics and beyond.* New York, NY: The Guilford Press.

Ben-Porath, D. D., Wisniewski, L., & Warren, M., (2010). Outcomes of a day treatment program for eating disorders using clinical and statistical significance. *Journal of Contemporary Psychotherapy, 40*(2), 115–123. doi: 10.1007/s10879-009-9125-5.

Bischoff-Grethe, A., Wierenga, C. E., Berner, L. A., Simmons, A. N., Bailer, U., Paulus, M. P., & Kaye, W. H. (2018). Neural hypersensitivity to pleasant touch in women remitted from anorexia nervosa. *Translational Psychiatry, 8*(1), 1–13. doi: 10.1038/s41398-018-0218-3.

FBT and Family Interventions for Adolescents   349

Brown, T. A., Cusack, A., Anderson, L. K., Trim, J., Nakamura, T., Trunko, M. E., & Kaye, W. H. (2018). Efficacy of a partial hospital programme for adults with eating disorders. *European Eating Disorders Review*, *26*(3), 241–252. doi: 10.1002/erv.2589.

Brown, T. A., Cusack, A., Anderson, L. K., Reilly, E. E., Berner, L. A., Wierenga, C. E., ... Kaye, W. H. (2019). Early versus later improvements in Dialectical behavior therapy skills use and treatment outcome in eating disorders. *Cognitive Therapy and Research*, *43*(4), 759–768. doi: 10.1007/s19698-019-10006-1.

Bryson, A. E., Scipioni, A. M., Essayli, J. H., Mahoney, J. R., & Ornstein, R. M. (2018). Outcomes of low-weight patients with avoidant/restrictive food intake disorder and anorexia nervosa at long-term follow-up after treatment in a partial hospitalization program for eating disorders. *International Journal of Eating Disorders*, *51*(5), 470–474. doi: 10.1002/eat.22853.

Dare, C. & Eisler, I. (1997). Family therapy for anorexia nervosa. In D. M. Garner & P. E. Garfinkel (Eds.). *Handbook of treatment for eating disorders* (pp. 307–24). New York, NY: The Guilford Press.

De Young, K. P. & Anderson, D. A. (2010). Prevalence and correlates of exercise motivated by negative affect. *International Journal of Eating Disorders*, *43*(1), 50–58. doi: 10.1002/eat.20656.

Eisler, I., Dare, C., Russell, G. F. M., Szmukler, G. I., Le Grange, D., & Dodge, E. (1997). Family and individual therapy in anorexia nervosa: A five-year follow-up. *Archives of General Psychiatry*, *54*(11), 1025–1030. doi: 10.1001/archpsyc.1997.01830230063008.

Eisler, I., Simic, M., Russell, G., & Dare, C. (2007). A randomized controlled treatment trial of two forms of family therapy in adolescent anorexia nervosa: A five-year follow-up. *Journal of Child Psychology & Psychiatry*, *48*(6), 552–556. doi: 10.1111/j.1469-7610.2007.01726.x.

Eisler, I., Simic, M., Blessitt, E., Dodge, L., & team (2016). *Maudsley service manual for child and adolescent eating disorders. Child and adolescent eating disorders service, South London and Maudsley NHS Foundation Trust.* https://www.national.slam.nhs.uk/wp-content/uploads/2011/11/Maudsley-Service-Manual-for-Child-and-Adolescent-Eating-Disorders-July-2016.pdf.

Eisler, I., Simic, M., Hodsoll, J., Asen, E., Berelowitz, M., Connan, F., ... Landau, S. (2016). A pragmatic randomized multi-centre trial of multifamily and single family therapy for adolescent anorexia nervosa. *BMC Psychiatry*, *16*(1), 422–437. doi: 10.1186/s12888-016-1129-6.

Ellison, R., Rhodes, P., Madden, S., Miskovic, J., Wallis, A., Baillie, A., ... Touyz. S. (2012). Do the components of manualized family-based treatment for anorexia nervosa predict weight gain? *International Journal of Eating Disorders*, *45*(4), 609–614. doi: 10.1002/eat.22000.

Fairburn, C. G. & Beglin, S. J. (2008). Eating disorder examination questionnaire (6.0). In Fairburn C. G. (Ed.) *Cognitive behavior therapy and eating disorders*. New York, NY: The Guilford Press.

Girz, L., LaFrance Robinson, A., Foroughe, M., Jasper, K., & Boachie, A. (2013). Adapting family-based therapy to a day hospital programme for adolescents with eating disorders: Preliminary outcomes and trajectories of change. *Journal of Family Therapy*, *35*, 102–120. doi: 10.1111/j.1467-6427.2012.00618.x.

Harper, M. (1983). Varieties of parenting failures in anorexia nervosa: Protection and parentectomy, revisited. *Journal of the American Academy of Child Psychiatry*, *22*(2), 134–139. doi: 10.1016/S0002-7138(09)62326-8.

350 Towne, Peck, and Rockwell

Harrison, A., O'Brien, N., Lopez, C., & Treasure, J. (2010). Sensitivity to reward and punishment in eating disorders. *Psychiatry Research, 177*(1–2), 1–11.

Harrison, A., Sternheim, L., O'Hara, C., Oldershaw, C., & Schmidt, U. (2016). Do reward and punishment sensitivity change after treatment for anorexia nervosa? *Personality and Individual Differences, 96*, 40–46. doi: 10.1016/j.paid.2016.02.051.

Hill, L., Knatz Peck, S., Wierenga, C. E., & Kaye, W. H. (2016). Applying neurobiology to the treatment of adults with anorexia nervosa. *Journal of Eating Disorders, 4*(31), 1–13. doi: 10.1186/s40337-016-0119-x.

Kaye, W. H. (2008). Neurobiology of anorexia and bulimia nervosa. *Physiology Behavior, 94*(1), 121–135.

Kaye, W. H., Wierenga, C. E., Knatz, S., Liang, J., Boutelle, K., Hill, L., & Eisler, I. (2014). Temperament-based treatment for anorexia nervosa. *European Eating Disorders Review, 23*(1), 12–18. doi: 10.1002/erv.2330.

Kazdin, A. E. (1997). Parent management and training: Evidence, outcomes, and issues. *Journal of the American Academy of Child & Adolescent Psychiatry, 36*(10), 1349–1356.

Kazdin, A. E. (2005). *Parent management training: Treatment for oppositional, aggressive, and antisocial behavior in children and adolescents.* New York, NY: Oxford University Press.

Knatz Peck, S. (2016). *Behavioral contracts for eating disorders: A tool to enhance motivation and elicit change.* In S. B. Murray, L. K. Karwoski, & L. Cohn (Eds.), *Innovations in family therapy for eating disorders: Novel treatment developments, patient insights, and the role of carers* (pp. 286–295). New York, NY: Routledge Taylor & Francis Group.

Knatz, S., Wierenga, C. E., Murray, S. B., Hill, L., & Kaye, W. H. (2015). Neurobiologically informed treatment for adults with anorexia nervosa: A novel approach to a chronic disorder. *Dialogues of Clinical Neuroscience, 17*(2), 229–236.

Le Grange, D., Crosby, R., Rathouz, P., Leventhal, B. (2007). A randomized controlled comparison of family-based treatment and supportive psychotherapy for adolescent bulimia nervosa. *Archives of General Psychiatry, 64*(9), 1049–1056. doi: 10.1001/archpsyc.64.9.1049.

Le Grange, D., & Lock, J. (2007). *Treating bulimia in adolescents: A family-based approach .* New York, NY: The Guilford Press.

Le Grange, D., Lock, J., Agras, W. S., Bryson, S. W., & Jo, B. (2015). Randomized clinical trial of family-based treatment and cognitive-behavioral therapy for adolescent bulimia nervosa. *Journal of the American Academy of Child & Adolescent Psychiatry, 54*(11), 886–894. doi: 10.1016/j.jaac.2015.08.008.

Lejuez, C. W., Hopko, D. R., Acierno, R., Daughers, S. B., & Pagoto, S. L. (2011). Ten year revision of the brief behavioral activation treatment for depression: Revised treatment manual. *Behavior Modification, 35*(2), 111–161. doi: 10.1177/0145445510390929.

Linehan, M. M. (2015). *DBT skills training manual (2nd ed.).* New York, NY: The Guilford Press.

Lock, J. & Le Grange, D. (2019). Family-based treatment: Where are we and where should we be going to improve recovery in child and adolescent eating disorders? *International Journal of Eating Disorders, 52*(4), 481–487. doi: 10.1002/eat.22980.

Lock, J., Couturier, J., & Agras, W. S. (2006). Comparison of long term outcomes in adolescents with anorexia nervosa treated with family therapy. *American Journal of Child & Adolescent Psychiatry, 45*(6), 666–672. doi: 10.1097/01.chi.0000215152.61400.ca.

Lock, J. & Le Grange, G. (2012). *Treatment manual for anorexia nervosa: A family-based approach (2nd ed.).* New York, NY: The Guilford Press.

FBT and Family Interventions for Adolescents 351

Lock, J., Le Grange, D., Agras, W. S., Moye, A., Bryson, S. W., & Jo, B. (2010). Randomized clinical trial comparing family-based treatment with adolescent-focused individual therapy for adolescents with anorexia nervosa. *Archives of General Psychiatry, 67*(10), 1025–1032. doi: 10.1001/archgenpsychiatry.2010.128.

Marzola, E., Knatz, S., Murray, S. B., Rockwell, R., Boutelle, K., Eisler, I., & Kaye, W. H. (2015). Short-term intensive family therapy for adolescent eating disorders: 30-month outcome. *European Eating Disorders Review, 23*(3), 208–210. doi: 10.1002/erv.2353.

Murray, S. B., Anderson, L. K., Rockwell, R., Griffiths, S., Le Grange, D., & Kaye, W. H. (2015). Adapting family-based treatment for adolescent anorexia across higher levels of patient care. *Eating Disorders: The Journal of Treatment & Prevention, 23*(4), 302–314. doi: 10.1080/10640266.2015.1042317.

Orberndorfer, T. A., Frank, G. F., Simmons, A. N., Wagner, A., McCurdy, D., Fudge, J. L., ... Kaye, W. H. (2013). Altered insula response to sweet taste processing after recovery from anorexia and bulimia nervosa. *Journal of American Psychiatry, 170*(10), 1143–1151. doi: 10.1176/appi.ajp.2013.11111745.

Patterson, G. R., Reid, J. B., & Dishion, T. J. (1992). *Antisocial boys*. Eugene, OR: Castalia.

Reinecke, R. D. (2017). Family-based treatment of eating disorders in adolescents: Current insights. *Adolescent Health, Medicine and Therapeutics, 8*, 69–79. doi: 10.2147/AHMT.S115775.

Simic, M., & Eisler, I. (2012). Family and multifamily therapy. In J. Fox & K. Goss (Eds.), *Eating and its disorders*. Oxford, UK: Willey-Blackwell.

Simic, M. & Eisler, I. (2015). Multi family therapy. In K. Loeb, D. Le Grange, & J. Lock (Eds.), *Family therapy for adolescent eating and weight disorders: New applications*. (pp. 110–138) New York, NY: Routledge.

Tchanturia, K., Davies, H., Reeder, C., & Wykes, T. (2010). *Cognitive remediation therapy for anorexia nervosa*. Retrieved from https://www.national.slam.nhs.uk/wp-content/uploads/2014/04/Cognitive-remediation-therapy-for-Anorexia-Nervosa-Kate-Tchantura.pdf.

van Langenberg, T., Duncan, R. E., Allen, J. S., Sawyer, S. M., Le Grange, D., & Hughes, E. K. (2018). "They don't really get heard": A qualitative study of sibling involvement across two forms of family-based treatment for adolescent anorexia nervosa. *Eating Disorders, 26*(4), 373–387. doi: 10.1080/10640266.2018.1453632.

Wierenga, C. E., Bischoff Grethe, A., Melrose, A. J., Irvine, Z., Torres, L., Bailer, U. F., Simmons, ... Kaye, W. H. (2014). Hunger does not motivate reward in women remitted from anorexia nervosa. *Biological Psychiatry, 77*(7), 642–652. doi: 10.1016/j.biopsych.2014.09.024.

Wierenga, C. E., Hill, L., Knatz Peck, S., McCray, J., Greathouse, L., Peterson, D., Scott, A., Eisler, I., & Kaye, W. H. (2018). The acceptability, feasibility, and possible benefits of a neurobiologically-informed 5-day multifamily treatment for adults with anorexia nervosa. *International Journal of Eating Disorders, 51*(8), 863–869. doi: 10.1002/eat.22876.

16 Ensuring Continuity of Family-Based Care across Levels of Treatment

Renee D. Rienecke and Elizabeth Wallis

Introduction

Family-based treatment (FBT) has emerged as the first line of treatment for adolescents with anorexia nervosa (AN). FBT is an outpatient approach that is designed to circumvent the ego-syntonic nature of AN by temporarily putting parents in charge of their child's weight restoration and return to physical health (Lock & Le Grange, 2013). This is accomplished by parents making all eating-related decisions for their child, much as a treatment team would do on an inpatient unit. Once patients have gained weight, are eating more willingly, and their thinking is less influenced by the eating disorder, responsibility over eating is gradually returned to them. Treatment ends with an assessment of the adolescent's current developmental status and remaining developmental challenges, with a focus on ways to navigate these challenges without returning to eating disordered behavior.

Although FBT is an outpatient treatment that cannot be replicated in higher levels of care, the efficacy of FBT (Lock et al., 2010) and its ability to be disseminated (Couturier, Isserlin, & Lock, 2010) have led to efforts to incorporate the principles of FBT into intensive outpatient settings (Marzola et al., 2015), partial hospitalization/day hospital programs (Easton et al., 2017; Girz, Robinson, Foroughe, Jasper, & Boachie, 2013; Henderson et al., 2014; Hoste, 2015; Martin-Wagar, Holmes, & Bhatnagar, 2018; Ornstein, Lane-Loney, & Hollenbeak, 2012), and inpatient units (Halvorsen, Reas, Nilsen, & Rø, 2018). Factors such as length of stay, distance to the treatment setting, and program philosophy have traditionally limited the extent to which families are involved in residential programs, although some programs do include families to a limited degree. Although the evidence base is fairly small, results suggest that FBT principles can successfully be incorporated into higher levels of care, given that programs adhere to the core FBT tenets. These include parental empowerment, taking an agnostic view of the illness, taking a non-authoritarian therapeutic stance in the treatment, externalization of the illness, and a pragmatic focus on symptom reduction. This chapter will explore ways in which treatment programs offering higher levels of care can stay true to these tenets, thus enabling continuity of care across treatment levels.

Parental Empowerment

Empowering parents to take charge of the recovery process is at the heart of FBT, which views parents as their child's best resource and the primary agents of change in treatment. Parents choose all meals and snacks for their child in the first phase of treatment, monitor all eating, and sometimes manage significant resistance to weight gain. The therapist conveys confidence in the parents' ability to take on this often formidable task, encouraging parents to break free from unhelpful patterns and accommodating behaviors that may have allowed the eating disorder to continue unchallenged.

Although parental empowerment is a critical FBT tenet, it may also be the most difficult to incorporate into higher levels of care. In some ways, the very concept of a higher level of care is in direct contradiction to the notion of parental empowerment. How does a treatment provider convey confidence in a parent's ability to bring about recovery, while simultaneously removing the patient from their parents for treatment? Programs wishing to avoid parental disempowerment must consider ways to address this from the beginning of the treatment process. Given that the majority of a patient's recovery is likely to take place on an outpatient basis at home with his or her parents, including parents from the start is a worthwhile endeavor, and one that makes sense from a practical perspective. One way to accomplish this is to consider the overall message that the treatment program is sending to families.

In many programs offering higher levels of care, parents deliver their child to the care of the treatment team and their involvement in treatment is minimal until the child returns home. In addition to possibly conveying the message that parents are not equipped to manage their child's recovery, it may also send the message that parental involvement is not important. Programs wishing to avoid sending this message may specifically tell families that the program is not a place to drop off their child to be "fixed" by the treatment team, and that their involvement is critical to their child's success (Hoste, 2015). Parents should then be involved throughout the treatment, to whatever extent is allowed by the treatment setting parameters. There are many ways to do this, some of which are outlined below.

When deciding how to include parents in a family-based program, it is useful to keep in mind the parental role in outpatient manualized FBT, and then involve parents in a way that most closely approximates that role. Requiring parental involvement at meals should be considered an important component of family-based programs offering higher levels of care. For example, the partial hospitalization program (PHP) described by Hoste (2015), which offered programming 5 days a week for 6 hours a day, required at least one parent to be present for breakfast every day. Practical barriers, such as missing work, were addressed in part by an early breakfast time, allowing parents to be with their child for breakfast and then be finished by 8:00 am, with the option of staying for snack and/or lunch if their schedules allowed. To achieve parental empowerment in a higher level of care, however, parental presence alone is not sufficient. Several day programs (Henderson et al., 2014; Hoste, 2015; Martin-Wagar et al., 2018) put parents partially or entirely in charge of choosing meals for their child while in the program, giving them the same responsibilities they would have in outpatient FBT, and preparing parents for the larger role they will take on once their child steps down to a lower level of care.

This level of parental involvement has a significant impact on the role of team members during meal support. When parents are present, team members should be there to support and coach parents through difficult meals, but should not take over the refeeding process for them. This can be quite tempting to do, especially when a parent is obviously struggling with a meal or directly asking for help. In outpatient FBT, parents are in charge of every step of the refeeding process, from deciding what is going to be made for a meal, to grocery shopping, to preparing the meal, to serving it and ensuring that it is eaten. Consider what a different experience it must be to come to a treatment program, have the food prepared for you, and have a team around you in the event that anything goes wrong. One might argue that it serves as necessary support for struggling parents, but it also runs the risk of sending the message, however inadvertently, that parents cannot handle the eating disorder on their own, thus leading to parental disempowerment. Team members must be trained to possibly sit with some discomfort if parents, for example, specifically ask a team member to take over a difficult meal. Team members may need to coach parents to continue to work with the child rather than turning it over to the "professionals." The team must convey confidence in the parents' ability to manage the eating disorder with the proper guidance and support.

An additional way to empower parents in levels of care such as PHP or intensive outpatient programs (IOP) may include instilling confidence in parents' ability to choose meals and snacks by focusing on total calories needed rather than providing them with a meal plan to follow. The emphasis in FBT is on overall caloric guidelines. Parents are not given a meal plan, in part because this may send the message to parents that they do not, in fact, know how to feed their child, and instead need a professional to tell them what to do and how to do it. Meal plans are also not provided because some patients have a tendency to adhere rigidly to the plan and become fixated on following it exactly, rather than eating in a flexible and spontaneous manner. In residential programs this may be more difficult, as patients are often on very specific meal plans based on an exchange system, in which foods are grouped together to have a similar number of calories and nutrients so that they can then be exchanged with other food items on the same list. However, when a patient is nearing discharge it may be helpful to consider including parents in meal planning and transitioning from an exchange system, which may be necessary in a residential setting, to a system in which parents are able to confidently make eating-related decisions to continue the recovery process without needing to follow a meal plan. It may also be helpful to focus less in residential settings on a child mastering the exchange system and eating on a rigid meal plan, but rather on professionals helping to ensure the child meets his or her nutritional needs and incorporating some flexibility of meals and snacks early on to empower parents to take over when the child steps down to a lower level of care.

When a child is in an inpatient setting, the medical complications of their eating disorder may dictate many aspects of care, which must be advised by the medical team. The medical team should be responsible for laboratory monitoring, additional testing, and monitoring for risk of refeeding syndrome. This may also mean that the medical team, with a dietitian, prescribes a safe calorie goal early in hospitalization. Team members should then put parents in charge whenever possible once they have been introduced to FBT and its tenets. This requires clinicians to provide parents with a first session or overview of FBT while hospitalized (if they are hospitalized at the time of diagnosis or if the family has not yet participated in FBT). Points that are emphasized in the first session include psychoeducation about the medical and psychological complications that are associated with eating disorders and an emphasis on externalization of the illness, explaining to parents that the child is not purposely being difficult when she refuses to eat, but that her behavior and thoughts are being driven by the eating disorder. The ego-syntonic nature of anorexia is discussed and presented as a rationale for parental participation in the refeeding process: the eating disorder will not allow the patient to make healthy choices about her eating, so for the time being, parents must step in and make these decisions for her.

There are few studies examining parents' experiences of FBT in an inpatient setting. A recent study reported favorable outcomes in relation to weight restoration, disordered thinking, and clinical impairment after a family-based inpatient admission for AN (Halvorsen et al., 2018). In this study, parents stayed with their children during the first phase of hospitalization and were trained in FBT principles adapted for an inpatient setting. All meals were eaten in a family dining area, and frequent family meetings and treatment team meetings reinforced FBT principles and ensured adequate medical monitoring and weight gain. Patient outcomes at the end of hospitalization and long-term were encouraging, though the average length of hospitalization was 20.6 weeks. Though this length of hospitalization is much longer than an acute inpatient stay in the United States, it is worth considering ways in which findings from this study may be used to inform the development of best practice principles around shorter term inpatient stays to empower parents to the degree needed to continue to help their child in a less restrictive setting.

In addition, inpatient settings are often medical units with providers who may not be familiar with eating disorder care, or that are not staffed to provide the one-on-one support that may be needed early in treatment. Although patients may need more strictly prescribed calories and macronutrients to monitor for refeeding syndrome and other complications while on an inpatient unit, parents could still be involved in choosing the actual food and timing of meals, thus reinforcing parental empowerment and the concept

356 *Renee D. Rienecke and Elizabeth Wallis*

that nutritional restoration must be the most important goal for the child during the initial stages of treatment and recovery. In the same way that an inpatient registered dietitian (RD) might plan with the child and medical team, a parent could be incorporated into meal planning and receive additional coaching and education from an RD early in the child's recovery. Parents could also be involved in the discussion of privileges and activities outside of meals while in the hospital, to the extent that it is medically safe.

Physicians in acute settings report challenges in caring for patients and families with eating disorders. Specifically, physicians report uncertainty as to how to involve parents and patients in treatment decisions, particularly if the patient is not aligned with the treatment decision (as is often the case in eating disorder treatment; Davidson, Branham, Dasey, & Reidlinger, 2019). Physicians also reported the need for increased training, support, and education around eating disorder conceptualization to improve their confidence and their ability to better engage patients and families.

Family-centered care (FCC) is an approach to health care that is seen as a partnership between parents and professionals, and has been incorporated into multiple health care systems. It is based on the principles of information sharing, respecting and honoring differences, partnership and collaboration, negotiation, and care in the context of family and community (Kuo et al., 2012). Examples of FCC may be as straightforward as treating parents and families with respect, to allowing parents to be in the room with their child during medical procedures. Among parents of children with cancer, FCC has been shown to improve parental self-efficacy, leading to enhanced psychological well-being (Salvador, Crespo, & Barros, 2019). The principles of FCC may further inform ways to incorporate families into inpatient treatment for eating disorders (Silber, Lyster-Mensh, & DuVal, 2011) and may provide a more familiar framework for physicians in inpatient care settings to conceptualize eating disorder treatment. Considering this model, along with improved education and training around eating disorder symptoms and cognitions, may better allow inpatient physicians to empower parents to help their child recover while still attending to the patient's medical needs.

With the above discussion in mind, let us consider the case of CM, a 13-year-old female with AN, restricting type. Because of the rapidity and significance of her weight loss, she required hospital admission for medical stabilization at her first appointment with the eating disorder outpatient team. Additionally, the family had researched FBT and the evidence-base and was aligned with this treatment approach and sought care specifically with this in mind. While inpatient, CM had significant resistance to meal support and would become very anxious and agitated before and after meals, sometimes attempting to lock herself in her hospital room, or hide in the hospital playroom before meals. CM's anxiety was unsettling to the inpatient staff who did not have significant eating disorder experience, and they often expressed feeling overwhelmed by the agitation, frequently seeking medications from the physician team to assist in managing CM, and struggling to engage in productive meal support.

Ensuring Continuity of Family-Based Care 357

Although CM was ultimately discharged to begin FBT after she was medically stable, the family expressed much more apprehension about their ability to manage her weight restoration at home, citing specifically the inpatient staffs' discomfort. CM also attempted to help with the meal and snack selection, as had been the case while she was in the hospital. CM and her family required significant support from the outpatient team to feel sufficiently empowered to engage in FBT and help their daughter recover.

As discussed previously, a number of changes while CM was inpatient might have better prepared the family to implement FBT at home, such as removing CM from decisions about meals and snacks, training the staff in adequate meal support, and helping the staff to better employ behavioral techniques to manage anxiety and agitation. Additionally, staff training may have helped them to feel less overwhelmed by the anxiety and agitation, which they inadvertently projected to the family, who then doubted their own ability to feed their daughter at home.

Taking an Agnostic View of the Eating Disorder

Viewing eating disorders from an agnostic perspective involves taking a non-blaming stance in regard to etiology. That is, parents are not blamed for causing the eating disorder, and adolescents are not blamed for developing it. The focus of treatment is not on attempting to uncover the possible underlying cause of the eating disorder, but rather on a rapid return to physical and mental health.

Creating a philosophy of agnosticism in a treatment program should perhaps begin with psychoeducation for its team members. Outdated notions about the causes of eating disorders and the role of the family in the onset and maintenance of eating disorders are unfortunately still quite common, both among the lay public (Ebneter & Latner, 2013; Le Grange, Lock, Loeb, & Nicholls, 2010; Roehrig & McLean, 2010) and among treatment providers (Dryer, Tyson, & Kiernan, 2013; Jones, Saeidi, & Morgan, 2013). The development and implementation of an onboarding process that includes psychoeducation on eating disorders and on FBT may be a helpful first step in ensuring that team members are conceptualizing issues of etiology accurately, and that they are in agreement in regard to their understanding of and approach to treating eating disorders. Murray, Griffiths, and Le Grange (2014) found that team members' collegial alliance was related to treatment outcome for patients in FBT, highlighting the importance of unity among team members, which may be enhanced when each member has gone through the same training prior to joining the team.

An example of this is the training provided in the program described by Hoste (2015). When joining the program, all team members, including those not providing any clinical services, participate in an extensive FBT training, and are provided with general didactics on eating disorders. This is in part to ensure that the team members are "speaking the same language," much as parents are asked to provide a united front against the eating disorder in FBT

358　*Renee D. Rienecke and Elizabeth Wallis*

(Lock & Le Grange, 2013). When possible, this level of training would be desirable for all new additions to a treatment team. In practice, this may not always be feasible, particularly in inpatient settings or settings with high turnover rates. In these cases, a more basic form of training, or alternate form of training such as video training, may need to be required, with the goal of eliminating outdated beliefs about the etiology of eating disorders and ensuring that the team believes in, and models for families, an agnostic view of the cause of eating disorders.

At higher levels of care, particularly inpatient settings in which children with eating disorders are cared for along with children with other medical and psychiatric illnesses, staff education as to this principle is imperative. In a typical inpatient children's hospital, staff are required to be facile with the treatment of many childhood illnesses and may not see inpatients with eating disorders or even general mental health concerns with the frequency needed to reach an adequate level of confidence and competence. With multiple staff caring for patients in this type of setting, without adequate education and support, parents may hear different messages from different providers, which can disrupt treatment and contribute to parents' confusion about the treatment process.

In addition, although the comorbid presence of both medical and psychiatric illnesses is increasingly common (Bardach et al., 2014; Doupnik et al., 2017), hospital staff may align as capable of treating one or the other. Even with the presence of psychiatric consultation services, there is significant unmet patient need (Bierenbaum, Katsikas, Furr, & Carter, 2013). Recent studies show high rates of mental health symptoms in children hospitalized with medical concerns (as defined by known mental health diagnosis, positive mental health screen, or receipt of mental health services in the 12 months prior to hospitalization), furthering the need for education and support for an integrated care of medical and psychological needs of children in inpatient settings (Doupnik et al., 2017).

In addition to training team members, educating families is critical to ensuring that they also maintain an agnostic perspective. Depending on the structure of the treatment setting, this may be done through weekly family therapy meetings (e.g., Girz et al., 2013; Henderson et al., 2014; Hoste, 2015; Martin-Wagar et al., 2018; Ornstein et al., 2012), multifamily groups (e.g., Girz et al., 2013; Hoste, 2015; Martin-Wagar et al., 2018), and/or requiring all families to participate in an "introduction to FBT" prior to joining a residential program or PHP. For example, one PHP (Hoste, 2015) requires all families to participate in the first two sessions of manualized FBT prior to joining the PHP. This provides an opportunity for families to learn about their role in treatment and for therapists to provide psychoeducation about the disorder before families join the therapeutic milieu. Thus, patients and parents start treatment knowing what is expected of them and being familiar with the treatment philosophy of the program, including the agnostic view of the illness. An introductory FBT session may also be possible to incorporate into an inpatient setting prior to involving parents in meal planning and treatment decision making, particularly if families will be stepping down to outpatient FBT.

Non-Authoritarian Therapeutic Stance

Taking a non-authoritarian stance toward treatment means that the FBT therapist does not dictate treatment decisions, but rather encourages families to come up with their own solutions. The therapist is seen as an expert on eating disorders and on the treatment approach, but parents are seen as the experts on their child and their family. The FBT therapist is active in treatment, but believes that the solutions generated by parents will be more effective and more suitable for their family than anything that the therapist could prescribe.

Adopting this stance in treatment can be challenging, particularly when parents are directly asking for a specific plan to bring about weight restoration for their son or daughter. However, this may be somewhat easier to navigate when the family is seen once a week in outpatient FBT and by necessity is forced to figure out many things on their own, as opposed to when the family is seen daily or almost daily in programs offering higher levels of care. Again, appropriate training of the treatment team is critical. Team members must not approach treatment thinking they know best, that there is one correct way to do FBT, or that there is a "one-size-fits-all" approach, and they may need to resist the urge to come to the family's "rescue" and take over the process for them. It is useful to keep in mind that as treatment providers, we are seeing a small part of each family's daily life, with limited knowledge of likes, dislikes, routines, habits, and ethnic, cultural, and religious backgrounds – all things that can impact eating behavior. Families know themselves best, and with appropriate support, most succeed in identifying ways to manage the recovery process without being given a specific blueprint for how to achieve it.

Taking a non-authoritarian therapeutic stance may be the most challenging FBT principle for physicians working in higher levels of care to adopt, particularly in inpatient settings. Those responsible for monitoring and managing medical symptoms, severity and complications are used to practicing in a hierarchical setting, with some collaboration with patients and families when appropriate (Crowe, Clarke, & Brugha, 2017). Although parents cannot be made responsible for the medical management of their child, in order to support FBT principles, there should be a non-authoritarian balance with parents in a decision-making role concerning food, meals, and weight restoration, while adhering to necessary medical monitoring. A model of shared-decision making (SDM) may be suitable to adopt in this scenario, in which parents and physicians work together, sharing the best available evidence when faced with the task of making a decision, and supporting parents to consider their options in order to reach an informed and collaborative plan (Elwyn et al., 2012). SDM is a familiar model for many medical professionals and supports a non-authoritarian approach in which families and physicians collaborate, and both parties agree with the guiding clinical principles. In the case of eating disorders, when patients may have significant ambivalence about recovery and difficulty separating eating disorder thoughts from healthy cognitions, parents can very much partner in SDM to support FBT practices. SDM principles as applied to FBT may include supporting parental authority as an expert on their child and discussion of treatment options. Medical providers and inpatient teams less familiar with FBT should also be educated on the successes of parental-driven weight restoration and be encouraged to think of it as a tool in improving care for hospitalized patients with eating disorders (Gusella, Campbell, & Lalji, 2017).

Consider the case of GR, a 15-year-old male with AN, binge/purge type. GR was engaged in outpatient FBT and was approximately 88% of his expected body weight (EBW) when he was hospitalized after an unrelated leg injury requiring orthopedic surgery. His surgical recovery required a several day hospital stay, and his inpatient team had little familiarity with eating disorders or FBT. Because the family had been successfully weight-restoring their son for several months, they were able to confidently discuss with the surgical team how to manage nutrition while hospitalized. The surgical team then consulted with the patient's primary eating disorder team, who helped to support the family and the surgical team in this collaboration, even adjusting surgery times to limit the length of time that GR would need to fast in preparation for surgery and anesthesia. The surgical attending was also able to reinforce good nutrition needed for GR's injury recovery, supporting the family in their role, and providing positive reinforcement to GR as he met these goals. As a result of this collaboration, GR continued to gain weight while hospitalized and following surgery.

Externalization of the Illness

Externalization of the illness involves treating the patient and the eating disorder as two very separate entities, and emphasizing to parents that their child does not resist eating because he or she is obstinate or wants attention, but because the child is in the grip of a powerful disorder that is impacting thoughts, behaviors, and emotions, particularly when it comes to issues of food, eating, weight, and shape. Families will often name the eating disorder, sometimes "Ed," to further highlight the differences between their healthy child and the illness. Externalization is crucial for parents, as parents who truly understand this concept seem to be less critical of their ill child, and parental criticism has been shown in numerous studies to be related to poor treatment outcome (e.g., Allan, Le Grange, Sawyer, McLean, & Hughes, 2018; Rienecke, Accurso, Lock, & Le Grange, 2016).

Similar to adopting an agnostic view of the illness, successfully externalizing the illness is facilitated by education of both the team and the families. This may be done during the onboarding process for team members, and during therapeutic interventions with families, whether this is in family therapy sessions, multifamily groups, or "introduction to FBT" sessions (Hoste, 2015). Families have said that it is extremely helpful to have all team members refer to the eating disorder as "the disorder," rather than attributing unwanted behavior to their child. This also helps to create a non-blaming atmosphere in the

Ensuring Continuity of Family-Based Care 361

clinic and can ease the guilt patients often feel about the resistance that the disorder can display in response to meals. In settings such as inpatient units, where patients with a variety of illnesses are cared for, team members should be reminded regularly to use non-blaming language and to think carefully about offering a consistent and united message to parents. If possible, multi-disciplinary rounds should include FBT clinicians (or other experts) to reinforce the language and approach with patients even while they are hospitalized.

Pragmatic Focus on Symptom Reduction

A focus on symptom reduction involves encouraging families to pour their energy and attention into the weight restoration process, and putting other issues – for example, concerns about social isolation or increased irritability – on hold until later in treatment. This is in part because these symptoms are often secondary to malnutrition (Kalm & Semba, 2005) and will resolve themselves with the resolution of low weight. This is also in part because discussion of these other issues takes the focus off the hard work of the behavioral change necessary to bring about weight restoration.

In the context of residential programs or PHPs, a primary focus on symptom reduction may be achievable in some ways but more difficult in others. Higher levels of care have the potential to emphasize weight restoration and establish regular patterns of eating above all else, given that the patient has several, if not all, meals at the treatment center. However, programs wishing to stay true to the core tenets of FBT must carefully consider the ways in which they manage food refusal. If a patient is reluctant to finish his or her meal, then ideally a staff member or parent would stay with the patient until the food is eaten, as might happen at home in outpatient FBT. In reality, limited staff or parent availability or limited parental involvement, as well as the need to follow the program schedule, will at times result in partial completion of meals. If the patient is then allowed to join in another activity, such as a group therapy session, following the meal, it may send the message that food is not the top priority and group therapy sessions are equally, if not more, valuable. Given the limited research evidence to support the use of group interventions for adolescents with eating disorders (Downey, 2014), it may be premature to send this message.

Group therapy also has the potential to reduce the focus on eating disorder symptom reduction in other ways. Many groups offered in treatment programs are not directly related to disordered eating. Although they may be helpful in a general sense, prioritizing participation in group therapy sessions over meal completion may send a message that is incompatible with this core tenet of FBT. Although it is certainly not possible, or desirable, to eliminate group therapy from higher levels of care, it is worthwhile to be cognizant of the prioritization of, and emphasis on, different components of the therapy program, and to focus on group therapies that have empirical support for their use with patients with eating disorders, such as dialectical behavior therapy

(Peterson, Van Diest, Mara, & Matthews, 2019) or cognitive remediation therapy (Pretorius et al., 2012).

Treatment programs may want to consider full meal completion as a necessary part of the treatment day and adjust staff or parent responsibilities accordingly. In one program, parents of patients who were particularly struggling during meals were sometimes asked to be present at all meals and snacks, rather than just the required breakfast (Hoste, 2015). Although this is a significant demand on the parent's time, outpatient FBT can be just as demanding, if not more so. Some parents must take leave from work during the initial weeks of treatment in order to ensure that they have adequate time to prepare and monitor all meals. However, when parents are taught the basics of FBT and understand the treatment philosophy, they are often willing to do whatever is necessary to help their child recover. Parents are told that the intervention has to be more powerful than the disorder, and that eating disorders are quite powerful. Partial meal completion in higher levels of care may also disempower parents when the child transitions to outpatient treatment, as parents may get the message that professionals could not ensure meal completion, so parents may wonder how they will be able to do so at home.

With this in mind, it is important to consider secondary gain in certain situations. For example, if a patient does not finish a meal and is then not allowed to go to group therapy, patients may purposely not eat to avoid attending groups. This will be important to ascertain with the help of the treatment team and the patient's parents. Sending the message that nutrition is paramount in the initial stages of treatment for an eating disorder is important, while attempting to individualize the process and take into consideration ways in which resistance may manifest itself in the treatment setting.

A related consideration in many programs offering higher levels of care is the use of nutritional supplements if meals are not completed. Although this may be necessary in an inpatient unit where acute medical complications need to be addressed as quickly as possible, it may be less desirable in PHPs or even residential programs. From an FBT perspective, offering a nutritional supplement to a patient who is unable to finish a meal is seen as negotiating with the eating disorder. Rather than giving in to the eating disorder's demands, it may be preferable to have the expectation that 100% of meals and snacks are completed, as is the expectation in outpatient FBT. At times, this means sitting with a patient for as long as is necessary for him or her to finish the meal. Again, given limited staff availability, this may not be possible in a residential setting, but it may be more feasible in a PHP where parents may be able to step in for team members. Another option is described by Hoste (2015), in which food that is not finished during the treatment day is sent home with families at the end of the day. The expectation is that parents will ensure that the food, or its caloric equivalent, is consumed at home, thereby driving home the message that not eating is not an option, and that the food may be consumed at the PHP or at home, but it must be consumed. Parents are helped to understand the inherent limitations of the PHP setting and the inability for staff to always stay with a

Ensuring Continuity of Family-Based Care 363

struggling patient past the allotted meal time, in order to avoid sending the message that the PHP team was unable to encourage the child to eat so parents must finish the task. The extent to which parents follow through on this plan varies from family to family, but an important consideration is the underlying message of this approach – that the food must be eaten – and its ability to be implemented across multiple levels of care, staying consistent with the overall goals of FBT. In support of this approach, the program demonstrated significant improvements in expected body weight from baseline to the end of treatment in the PHP (Hoste, 2015), and at 3-month follow-up (Rienecke & Richmond, 2018), in addition to improvements in eating disorder psychopathology.

Additional Considerations

When planning the incorporation of FBT principles into higher levels of care, it is also useful to consider the extent to which individual therapy is used in treatment. In outpatient FBT, the therapist meets at the beginning of each session with the adolescent alone for 5–10 minutes, but the majority of the session is usually spent with the whole family together. This is in part because parents are the primary agents of change in the recovery process, so the treatment necessarily should focus on ensuring that parents get the support, guidance, and information they need to be successful. This is also in part because adolescents with AN often have limited cognitive capacity to successfully engage in individual therapy, and are often highly ambivalent about the prospect of recovery. In fact, parent-focused treatment, which is similar to FBT but the therapist only meets with the parents while a nurse meets briefly with the adolescent, is just as effective as FBT (Le Grange et al., 2016). However, many higher levels of care include individual therapy in their programs, sometimes multiple times per week. To what extent this therapy is evidence-based, or even useful, is unclear. Partial and residential programs may want to consider whether time is better spent on family rather than individual sessions. The family-based nature of the PHP/IOP described in Hoste (2015) prioritized meetings with parents over individual meetings with patients, which were not automatically offered as part of the program. Meetings with parents may be particularly important as a patient is preparing for discharge, when parents will soon be largely responsible for their child's continued progress through the recovery process. Additionally, parents transitioning to outpatient FBT from a PHP/IOP incorporating individual therapy may be confused as to why the focus on individual therapy has shifted, or why something that was previously emphasized in treatment as important has been reduced or eliminated. If they feel as though a change in approach is negative, they may be less likely to adhere to FBT principles or even continue to participate in treatment. Individual therapy might best be incorporated as needed once weight restoration is achieved to address any residual concerns or comorbid psychiatric illnesses, rather than during weight restoration when it may be of limited benefit.

364 *Renee D. Rienecke and Elizabeth Wallis*

Conclusions

Incorporating FBT principles across higher levels of care is a challenge for treatment programs, but efforts to achieve this have resulted in promising outcomes (Girz et al., 2013; Halvorsen et al., 2018; Henderson et al., 2014; Hoste, 2015; Martin-Wagar et al., 2018; Marzola et al., 2015; Ornstein et al., 2012; Rienecke & Richmond, 2018). Although whether these programs are more effective than non-FBT-based programs is a question that remains to be answered empirically, parental involvement in the treatment of adolescents with eating disorders is recommended (NICE, 2017) and it is worth considering ways to include parents across levels of treatment to ensure continuity of care. Using the main principles of FBT as a guide, programs can consider ways to stay true to the tenets of FBT and involve parents to the greatest extent possible given the structure of the particular program. Even in inpatient settings, which offer the most restrictive and perhaps most rigid treatment, there are ways to involve parents in the treatment process, ensuring that those who are often the most invested in a patient's recovery are able to contribute in meaningful ways.

References

Allan, E., Le Grange, D., Sawyer, S. M., McLean, L. A., & Hughes, E. K. (2018). Parental expressed emotion during two forms of family-based treatment for adolescent anorexia nervosa. *European Eating Disorders Review, 26*, 46–52.

Bardach, N. S., Coker, T. R., Zima, B. T., Murphy, J. M., Knapp, P., Richardson, L. P., ..., Mangione-Smith, R. (2014). Common and costly hospitalizations for pediatric mental health disorders. *Pediatrics, 133*, 602–609.

Bierenbaum, M. L., Katsikas, S., Furr, A., & Carter, B. D. (2013). Factors associated with non-reimbursable activity on an inpatient pediatric consultation-liaison service. *Journal of Clinical Psychology in Medical Settings, 20*, 464–472.

Couturier, J., Isserlin, L., & Lock, J. (2010). Family-based treatment for adolescents with anorexia nervosa: A dissemination study. *Eating Disorders: The Journal of Treatment & Prevention, 18*, 199–209.

Crowe, S., Clarke, N., & Brugha, R. (2017). 'You do not cross them': Hierarchy and emotion in doctors' narratives of power relations in specialist training. *Social Science & Medicine, 186*, 70–77.

Davidson, A. R., Braham, S., Dasey, L., & Reidlinger, D. P. (2019). Physicians' perspectives on the treatment of patients with eating disorders in the acute setting. *Journal of Eating Disorders, 7*, DOI: 10.1186/s40337-018-0231-1.

Doupnik, S. K., Henry, M. K., Bae, H., Litman, J., Turner, S., Scharko, A. M., & Feudtner, C. (2017). Mental health conditions and symptoms in pediatric hospitalizations: A single-center point prevalence study. *Academic Pediatrics, 17*, 184–190.

Downey, J. (2014). Group therapy for adolescents living with an eating disorder: A scoping review. *SAGE Open, 4*, 1–11, DOI: 10.1177/2158244014550618.

Dryer, R., Tyson, G. A., & Kiernan, M. J. (2013). Bulimia nervosa: Professional and lay people's beliefs about the causes. *Australian Psychologist, 48*, 338–344.

Easton, E., Manwaring, J., Salada, G., Hartman, G., Bermudez, O., & Johnson, C. (2017). Family in Residence Program: A family empowerment model for higher

Ensuring Continuity of Family-Based Care 365

levels of care. In S. B. Murray, L. K. Anderson, & L. Cohn (Eds.), *Innovations in family therapy for eating disorders* (pp. 161–175). New York, NY: Routledge.

Ebneter, D. S., & Latner, J. D. (2013). Stigmatizing attitudes differ across mental health disorders: A comparison of stigma across eating disorders, obesity, and major depressive disorder. *Journal of Nervous and Mental Disease, 201*, 281–285.

Elwyn, G., Frosch, D., Thomson, R., Joseph-Williams, N., Lloyd, A., Kinnersley, P., ..., Barry, M. (2012). Shared decision making: A model for clinical practice. *Journal of General Internal Medicine, 27*, 1361–1367.

Girz, L., Robinson, A. L., Foroughe, M., Jasper, K., & Boachie, A. (2013). Adapting family-based therapy to a day hospital programme for adolescents with eating disorders: Preliminary outcomes and trajectories of change. *Journal of Family Therapy, 35*, 102–120.

Gusella, J. L., Campbell, A. G., & Lalji, K. (2017). A shift to placing parents in charge: Does it improve weight gain in youth with anorexia? *Paediatrics & Child Health, 22*, 269–272.

Halvorsen, I., Reas, D. L., Nilsen, J-V., & Rø, Ø. (2018). Naturalistic outcome of family-based inpatient treatment for adolescents with anorexia nervosa. *European Eating Disorders Review, 26*, 141–145.

Henderson, K., Buchholz, A., Obeid, N., Mossiere, A., Maras, D., Norris, M., ... Spettigue, W. (2014). A family-based eating disorder day treatment program for youth: Examining the clinical and statistical significance of short-term treatment outcomes. *Eating Disorders: The Journal of Treatment & Prevention, 22*, 1–18.

Hoste, R. R. (2015). Incorporating family-based therapy principles into a partial hospitalization programme for adolescents with anorexia nervosa: Challenges and considerations. *Journal of Family Therapy, 37*, 41–60.

Jones, W. R., Saeidi, S., & Morgan, J. F. (2013). Knowledge and attitudes of psychiatrists towards eating disorders. *European Eating Disorders Review, 21*, 84–88.

Kalm, L. M., & Semba, R. D. (2005). They starved so that others be better fed: Remembering Ancel Keys and the Minnesota Experiment. *The Journal of Nutrition, 135*, 1347–1352.

Kuo, D. Z., Houtrow, A. J., Arango, P., Kuhlthau, K. A., Simmons, J. M., & Neff, J. M. (2012). Family-centered care: Current applications and future directions in pediatric health care. *Maternal and Child Health Journal, 16*, 297–305.

Le Grange, D., Hughes E. K., Court, A., Yeo, M., Crosby, R. D., & Sawyer, S. (2016). Randomized clinical trial of parent-focused treatment and family-based treatment for adolescent anorexia nervosa. *Journal of the American Academy of Child & Adolescent Psychiatry, 55*, 683–692.

Le Grange, D., Lock, J., Loeb, K., & Nicholls, D. (2010). Academy for Eating Disorders Position Paper: The role of the family in eating disorders. *International Journal of Eating Disorders, 43*, 1–5.

Lock, J., & Le Grange, D. (2013). *Treatment manual for anorexia nervosa: A family-based approach* (2nd ed.). New York: Guilford Press.

Lock, J., Le Grange, D., Agras, W. S., Moye, A., Bryson, S. W., & Jo, B. (2010). Randomized clinical trial comparing family-based treatment with adolescent-focused individual therapy for adolescents with anorexia nervosa. *Archives of General Psychiatry, 67*, 1025–1032.

Martin-Wagar, C. A., Holmes, S., & Bhatnagar, K. A. C. (2018). Predictors of weight restoration in a day-treatment program that supports family-based treatment for adolescents with anorexia nervosa. *Eating Disorders: The Journal of Treatment & Prevention, 27*, 400–417. DOI: 10.1080/10640266.2018.1528085.

Marzola, E., Knatz, S., Murray, S. B., Rockwell, R., Boutelle, K., Eisler, I., & Kaye, W. H. (2015). Short-term intensive family therapy for adolescent eating disorders: 30-month outcome. *European Eating Disorders Review, 23*, 210–218.

Murray, S. B., Griffiths, S., & Le Grange, D. (2014). The role of collegial alliance in family-based treatment of adolescent anorexia nervosa: A pilot study. *International Journal of Eating Disorders, 47*, 418–421.

National Institute for Health and Care Excellence (2017). Eating disorders: Recognition and treatment. National Institute for Health and Care Excellence. NICE guideline (NG69).

Ornstein, R., Lane-Loney, S., & Hollenbeak, C. (2012). Clinical outcomes of a novel, family-centered partial hospitalization program for young patients with eating disorders. *Eating and Weight Disorders, 17*, e170–e177.

Peterson, C. M., Van Diest, A. M. K., Mara, C. A., & Matthews, A. (2019). Dialectical behavioral therapy skills group as an adjunct to family-based therapy in adolescents with restrictive eating disorders. *Eating Disorder: The Journal of Treatment & Prevention, 28*, 67–79. DOI: 10.1080/10640266.2019.1568101.

Pretorius, N., Dimmer, M., Power, E., Eisler, I., Simic, M., & Tchanturia, K. (2012). Evaluation of a cognitive remediation therapy group for adolescents with anorexia nervosa: Pilot study. *European Eating Disorders Review, 20*, 321–325.

Rienecke, R. D., Accurso, E. C., Lock, J., & Le Grange, D. (2016). Expressed emotion, family functioning, and treatment outcome for adolescents with anorexia nervosa. *European Eating Disorders Review, 24*, 43–51.

Rienecke, R. D., & Richmond, R. L. (2018). Three-month follow-up in a family-based partial hospitalization program. *Eating Disorders: The Journal of Treatment & Prevention, 26*, 278–289.

Roehrig, J. P., & McLean, C. P. (2010). A comparison of stigma toward eating disorders versus depression. *International Journal of Eating Disorders, 43*, 671–4.

Salvador, Á., Crespo, C., & Barros, L. (2019). The benefits of family-centered care for parental self-efficacy and psychological well-being in parents of children with cancer. *Journal of Child and Family Studies, 28*, 1926–1936. DOI: 10.1007/s10826-019-01418-4.

Silber, T. J., Lyster-Mensh, L. C., & DuVal, J. (2011). Anorexia nervosa: Patient and family-centered care. *Pediatric Nursing, 37*, 331–333.

17 Primary Care-Based Treatment for Eating Disorders

Richard Chung and Devdutta Sangvai

A Diverse Array of Clinical Vignettes in Primary Care

An 8-year-old girl with cerebral palsy, neurodevelopmental disability, gastrostomy tube dependence, and malnutrition
An 11-year-old boy with autism, weight loss, and picky eating
A 12-year-old girl with body image concerns and questions about dieting
A 15-year-old boy with obesity, binge episodes, and secretive eating
A 17-year-old girl with female athlete triad
A 22-year-old man with chemotherapy-associated depression and restrictive eating
A 27-year-old woman with anorexia nervosa in remission
A 42-year-old woman with severe chronic anorexia nervosa and malnutrition

Introduction

Eating disorders care in specialized treatment centers offers intensive multidisciplinary care for severely impacted individuals. Although these venues are essential in the treatment course of many individuals, the landscape for combatting eating disorders more generally is far more expansive. Whether a preteen manifesting a diathesis for disordered eating behaviors or an older adult living with recalcitrant anorexia nervosa who has been unable to engage in more intensive treatments, primary care is a key nexus that draws together the wide range of eating disorder experiences into a versatile treatment context that can play a key role throughout the course of many complex eating disorders. To fully understand the potential of primary care in facilitating evidence-based treatment of eating disorders, it is essential to first understand the essence of primary care, current evolutions in primary care, and anticipated future realities.

The Importance of Primary Care: A Key Nexus of Treatment for a Wide Range of Patients and Experiences

Primary care has long been the true foundation of healthcare practice and therefore an appropriate centerpiece for early recognition, proactive management, and longitudinal family- and patient-centered care of eating disorders. Effective primary care is founded on deep longitudinal relationships and trust building that undergirds a whole-person perspective that is crucial for managing chronic illnesses over time. Although some primary care clinicians may offer more specialized condition-specific or age-specific services, at core, primary care is generalized and whole-person oriented, including behavioral and mental health services. As such, it is well-positioned to recognize the underpinnings and implications of disordered eating within the broader context of the rest of a person's life. In this regard, primary care has notable advantages as compared to specialty settings to not only address eating disorders but also to create a long-term holistic scaffolding for ongoing care and recovery across a variety of domains. The challenge in a nonspecialty setting is to draw in adequate specialized knowledge and skills to allow for the core strengths of primary care to emerge and synergize with those elements (Homan, Sim, Crowley, Lebow, & Kransdorf, 2019).

Although specialty eating disorders treatment venues are not widely or equitably available, primary care clinics are key fixtures across communities of all sorts. As such, equipping primary care clinicians to recognize and actively manage eating disorders in these settings is crucial to allow for sufficient access to needed services and the avoidance or mitigation of disparities in eating disorders care and outcomes. Although there is substantial ongoing need for training and support (Currin, Waller, & Schmidt, 2009; Thaler et al., 2018), there is also great opportunity to leverage the reach of primary care to offer care for patients who otherwise might go unrecognized and unsupported.

A key challenge in integrating consistent high-quality eating disorders treatment into primary care is the variegated nature of primary care contexts. These variations derive from the breadth of contexts and patients served by these venues and the variable and disproportionate resourcing available. Some clinics are child-focused, others adult-focused, and still others offer services across the lifespan. Some venues serve as fully fledged primary care medical homes, which provide patient-centered, comprehensive, and well-coordinated services addressing the full breadth of health needs. Others may not have sufficient resourcing and may simply provide preventive services without genuine wraparound capabilities. These distinctions modulate the breadth and quality of eating disorder services that might be available in specific primary care settings in terms of surveillance for, diagnosis and assessment of, and management of disordered eating.

There is also wide variation in terms of behavioral health service integration. In many regions and settings, mental health services remain exclusively

Primary Care-Based Treatment 369

consultative and pristinely siloed from primary care, whereas in other contexts, colocated integrated services are available. Clearly from the vantage point of eating disorders treatment, this domain is crucial in understanding how a psychologically rooted disorder can be feasibly addressed in a primary care setting. Accessing appropriate psychological treatment options in a feasible and sustainable way is crucial, whether in the medical home or otherwise. Further, other supports such as dietetics consultation are variable and typically lacking in many settings.

The resourcing and capabilities of specific primary care settings are also related to the broader context of options for consultative support, either at an outpatient level or at higher levels of care. What is available based on the region, patient and payer characteristics, and other variables will often determine how a primary care clinician approaches eating disorders management. This includes wide variation throughout the hierarchy of services including hospitalization for medical stabilization. These variations will constrain or broaden what clinicians may feel comfortable in pursuing. Some may do more in a low-resource context out of necessity, whereas others may do less for fear of entering into suffering that cannot be reasonably addressed. Others may need to limit their own interest in caring for patients with eating disorders based on availability of other clinicians to provide call coverage and other backup.

Evidence-Based Eating Disorder Treatment in Primary Care Settings: Key Functions and Necessary Adaptations

In considering eating disorders treatment in primary care settings, a key question is what the core nidus of specialty eating disorder treatment is that truly could be universalized and what the modular aspects are that might be specific to certain resource settings. A fundamental goal broadly is to provide guidance and support for clinicians in any settings to prevent, recognize, assess, and begin management of an eating disorder. This basic and essential function is often the key difference between long-smoldering difficulty and increasingly difficult subsequent intervention, and proactive intervention on nascent eating difficulties. Providing for a basic foundation of expertise and practice across the far reach of primary care will push back against the disparity that plagues this domain of care. However, beyond establishing foundational practice elements, another goal is to recognize the variability inherent in primary care settings and leverage resources appropriately to offer even greater treatment capacity when possible.

General Care Considerations

Primary care teams are a constellation of varied health professionals playing different roles in preventing and managing health problems among diverse populations of patients. Given the nature of eating disorders, a more diverse team and greater integration are likely to be beneficial. The contributions of the primary medical clinician, nurses, mental health clinicians, dietitians, care coordinators, schedulers, and staff assistants all affect the complex and longitudinal demands of complex eating disorders care. The degree of integration of different disciplines will determine the function of each team member and the flow of care. The type of venue, whether pediatric, adult-centered, or otherwise will also critically define the scope and dynamics of care.

A key issue in a nonspecialized setting is providing for sufficient training and clinical experiences for different members of the care team. Specifically, given the complexity of disordered eating, this training requires rich exploration of the psychological underpinnings of eating disorders by clinicians who are typically not primarily trained in behavioral health services. This challenge may affect not only knowledge and clinical skills but also personal investment, confidence, and comfort in care for these patients. This may represent a true cultural shift within a clinical team or practice setting and require focused efforts over an extended period of time to build up adequate treatment capacity within a team (Sim et al., 2010).

Key functions of primary care-based treatment include proactive, developmentally appropriate anticipatory guidance, education, and prevention; assessment of physical growth and development during childhood and adolescence; recognition of anthropometric changes over time; screening and early recognition of risk and morbidity; proactive management of subclinical disordered eating; initial assessment and management of progressive concern; management of physical symptoms that emerge as a consequence of disordered eating; longitudinal care and support; surveillance of medical treatment and recovery markers; oversight of transitions of care; aftercare and relapse prevention; and management of the interface between healthcare settings and home- and community-based realities (Lenton-Brym, Rodrigues, Johnson, Couturier, & Toulany, 2019). All of these tasks can be accomplished by a primary care clinician with sufficient training, experience, and ancillary supports. Key themes that undergird successful primary care management include fluidity of communication and access, patient engagement and activation, continuity of care, care coordination, interprofessional collaboration, quality measurement, and closed-loop referral management and coordination.

Although specialty settings are typically keenly focused on the eating disorder at hand, primary care clinicians and teams have the benefit of having a broader mandate and perspective, which may, in some cases, facilitate eating disorder-specific care. By providing services that range the full gamut of health needs, clinicians may cultivate a degree of trust and a broader relational context that may be helpful when difficult conversations related to disordered eating are needed. Primary care settings can also partner effectively with specialty consultants to offer a broader whole-person perspective and buttress a patient's engagement in specialty services over time by providing a trusted foothold and facilitator.

Screening

Primary care settings have the advantage of having a reach that far exceeds specialty settings. As such, primary prevention and screening are domains in which primary care can truly change the landscape of eating disorders management by facilitating earlier intervention and care. Indeed, screening and early recognition of a range of health difficulties is a central function of primary care in general. Aside from community-based screening, primary care visits are typically the first opportunity for difficulties to be elucidated and explored. Although validated screening measures such as the screen for disordered eating (SDE), the eating disorders screen for primary care (EDS-PC), and the SCOFF screener are available (Maguen et al., 2018), broad-based screening is uncommon largely due to an insufficient evidence based to warrant universal screening in clinical settings already tasked with the time demands of screening for everything from depression, to cervical cancer, to high blood pressure (Yarnall & Pollack, 2003).

Further, although eating disorders represent a substantial burden of suffering and cost, they are comparatively uncommon next to other major morbidities in each relevant age group, including obesity. As such, when clinicians often find themselves promoting weight loss efforts in the face of overweight and obesity, a patient with binge eating disorder or even a restrictive eating disorder may not be readily recognized. It is not uncommon for the only examination of eating and body concerns to be a brief review of growth charts among children or a review of general anthropometrics over time among adults. Improving our capacity to screen in a structured and evidence-based way and to support clinicians in recognizing earlier and more subtle manifestations of disordered eating beyond progressed physical deterioration and overt compromise is crucial.

Diagnosis

Beyond screening and elucidating nascent difficulties, formulating specific diagnostic impressions and initial treatment plans is also within the purview of primary care clinicians. Many eating disorders are shrouded in secrecy and are not actively volunteered by those who are suffering. As such, recognizing constellations of signs and symptoms and having a backdrop of understanding and experience to draw connections accordingly is essential. Initial treatment plans might include laboratory and other diagnostic and assessment steps, dietary recommendations, physical activity guidance, home-based behavioral management strategies, and guidance regarding engagement with school, work, social media (Sindani & Shensa, 2016), or other day-to-day activities.

Ongoing Management

Primary care teams are tasked with addressing every health need, whether eating disorder related or not. A key challenge is balancing a keen awareness of the pernicious nature of eating disorder morbidities and the broad range of health manifestations they bring, with the reality that all patients may also encounter other common and less-common morbidities completely distinct from the eating disorder. It is often tempting to attribute most new symptoms or concerns to disordered eating, but a balanced and comprehensive approach is always necessary.

The waxing and waning course of many eating disorders also necessitates long-term continuity of care and constant vigilance for worsening. Primary care settings can offer a versatile setting for ongoing monitoring for difficulties and changes. Further, primary care settings can maintain close personal connection and support through the management of other health needs even when the eating disorder may be quiescent. This continuous connection can be crucial in consolidating progress, and avoiding backsliding into difficulty.

Behavioral Health

Most primary care settings lean heavily toward assessment and management of physical health conditions. The ability of primary care clinicians and settings to genuinely address psychological and behavioral concerns is far less certain and consistent, and tends to be focused on mood disorders such as depression and anxiety, and less on eating disorders. There are ongoing efforts to truly integrate behavioral health services, not only geographically into colocated settings, but also into the clinical approach and decision-making of individual clinicians through advancement in initial continuing education offerings. This will necessarily be an ongoing process and current-state approaches may continue to be deeply rooted generationally. However, settings with colocated mental health teams and/or close integration with outside partners can provide a flexible and comprehensive approach to care. Psychotherapeutic modalities may even be provided in medical home settings by colocated clinicians with expertise and experience (Rose & Waller, 2017). Both individual and family based modalities can feasibly be provided, and even preferentially so, if appropriate clinicians are colocated. Telehealth provides another established avenue to deliver services to patients with anorexia nervosa (Goldfield & Boachie, 2003) and bulimia nervosa (Bakke & Mitchell, 2001).

Nutrition

Dietetic support can also be useful in the context of the medical home to ensure that specific recommendations are supported by the primary care team and accountability galvanized through each point of contact. Further, a deeper recognition of social drivers that may facilitate or hinder nutritional improvement is critical and often more richly provided by medical home teams with holistic perspectives and access to community-based supports that might be drawn into treatment planning.

Pharmacotherapy

Although there are limited pharmacologic options for the treatment of eating disorders per se (Medication Choices), pharmacotherapy may be managed in primary care. Many clinicians, particularly among adolescent and adult-focused settings are increasingly comfortable in addressing common psychological morbidities such as comorbid anxiety and mood disorders in primary care without the direct involvement of psychiatric consultants. Given the substantial comorbidity involved in disordered eating, this contribution can be meaningful.

Community and Home

Another aspect that modulates expectations for evidence-based treatment in primary care is the fluidity of boundaries as to what constitutes a medical home or even more broadly, a medical neighborhood. Many true medical homes may avidly incorporate community partners and home-based treatment options in the neighborhood of services for a particular patient. This broader perspective may continue to extend the collective view as to what can be accomplished in primary care as opposed to more specialized settings, especially as payment and resource landscapes evolve to increase value across the spectrum of care.

The Future of Primary Care-Based Eating Disorders Treatment: How to Improve and How We Can Get There

Finally, in thinking about the future of primary care-based eating disorders treatment, it is crucial to recognize the monumental shifts afoot in the broader landscape of healthcare transformation in the United States. Although many of these changes are particular to the United States, similar pressures are likely omnipresent, regardless of setting. In particular, the U.S. healthcare system is actively evolving in terms of payment models in the context of value-based pressures. There are broad changes as well in terms of standards of care with respect to behavioral health integration and primary care management of psychological morbidities. There are also shifts in terms of how patients and families engage with healthcare teams leveraging technologies such as telehealth, widely varying sources of health information and perspectives through the Internet and social media, and the broad forces of consumerism.

The prodigious changes in the payment landscape in the United States. driven by a broad-based focus on value among all involved parties will create pressure to innovate the care of eating disorders and likely intensify interest in creating genuine footholds for treatment in nonhospital settings such as community-based medical homes, other community-based care settings, and home-based and telehealth contexts. There is great opportunity to innovate care toward value and mitigate what often can be extremely expensive treatment options among those most several affected. Indeed, the total cost of care for management of an illness that typically does not involve costly procedures but rather behavioral interventions is a key target for improving efficiencies and gaining value. The extension of the medical home not upward into more intensive medicalized care venues, but outward into community- and home-based care options holds great promise for not only constraining costs, but also providing better experiences for patients and families.

Leveraging the full potential of primary care settings in the management of eating disorders will require ongoing advocacy to strengthen education and training of healthcare professionals in managing these disorders, to continue to grow the treatment resources available to different communities and patients with differential resources, and to continue to mitigate the disparity and stigma that affects most behavioral health domains. These efforts will require an intersectoral approach that draws together the perspectives and influence of healthcare professionals, patients and families, and communities for the benefit of those who suffer from these conditions. Concomitantly, payment reform and parity for mental health will need to advance to increase access for patients.

All of these changes and trends may support the creation of true advanced medical homes for eating disorders that draw together the key elements of evidence-based treatment and integrate community, home, and technological supports. Indeed, improvements in primary care settings may be the crucial ingredient in reimagining eating disorders care going forward. Continuous improvement and innovation at the point of care in the face of the varied and complex nature of eating disorders demands a full-spectrum approach involving a wide range of key players. As such, there are innumerable opportunities to reimagine the eating disorders management. Primary care will always remain a key player.

References

Bakke, B., & Mitchell, J. (2001). Administering cognitive-behavioral therapy for bulimia nervosa via telemedicine in rural settings. *The International Journal of Eating Disorders, 30*, 454–7.

Currin, L., Waller, G., & Schmidt, U. (2009). Primary care physicians' knowledge of and attitudes toward the eating disorders: Do they affect clinical actions? *The International Journal of Eating Disorders, 42*(5), 453–8.

Goldfield, G. S., & Boachie, A. (2003). Delivery of family therapy in the treatment of anorexia nervosa using telehealth. *Telemedicine and e-Health, 9*, 111–4.

Homan, K. J., Sim, L. A., Crowley, S. L., Lebow, J. R., & Kransdorf, L. N. (2019). Medical assessment and triage of pediatric patients with anorexia nervosa in primary care. *Journal of Developmental and Behavioral Pediatrics, 40*(2), 92–98.

Lenton-Brym, T., Rodrigues, A., Johnson, N., Couturier, J., & Toulany, A. (2019). A scoping review of the role of primary care providers and primary care-based interventions in the treatment of pediatric eating disorders. *Eating Disorders, 21*, 1–20.

Maguen, S., Hebenstreit, C., Li, Y., Dinh, J. V., Donalson, R., Dalton, S., ... Masheb, R. (2018). Screen for disordered eating: Improving the accuracy of eating disorder screening in primary care. *General Hospital Psychiatry, 50*, 20–25.

Medication Choices to assist in the treatment of eating disorders. mirror-mirror.org/eating-disorder-medication.htm. Accessed May 19, 2019.

Rose, C., & Waller, G. (2017). Cognitive-behavioral therapy for eating disorders in primary care settings: Does it work, and does a greater dose make it more effective? *The International Journal of Eating Disorders, 50*(12), 1350–5.

Sim, L. A., McAlpine, D. E., Grothe, K. B., Himes, S. M., Cockerill, R. G., & Clark, M. M. (2010). Identification and treatment of eating disorders in the primary care setting. *Mayo Clinic Proceedings, 85*(8), 746–51.

Sindani, J. E., & Shensa, A. (2016). The association between social media use and eating concerns among U.S. young adults. *Journal of the Academy of Nutrition and Dietetics, 116*, 1465–72.

Thaler, L., Freiwald, S., Paquin Hodge, C., Fletcher, E., Cottier, D., Kahan, E., ... Steiger, H. A. (2018). Tertiary-care/primary-care partnership aimed at improving care for people with eating disorders. *Community Mental Health Journal, 54*(8), 1154–61.

Yarnall, K. S. H., & Pollack, K. I. (2003). Primary care: Is there enough time for prevention? *American Journal of Public Health, 93*, 635–41.

18 eHealth Interventions for Eating Disorders

Johanna Sander, Sally Bilić, and Steffi Bauer

Introduction

Over the past two decades, modern technology, particularly the Internet, has emerged as a resource offering an enormous potential for health care. eHealth, i.e., services focusing on the provision of health information and on improving health outcomes using the Internet and related technologies (e.g., e-mail, instant messaging, computer, and smartphone applications), have been integrated into the prevention and treatment of various health conditions, and have also been increasingly applied in the field of eating disorders (EDs). One reason for this development is the hope that eHealth may help to address major challenges of conventional health care, i.e., the limited reach of most available prevention programs and the so-called "treatment gap." This phenomenon describes the fact that by far not all individuals affected by EDs have access to evidence-based care (Hart, Granillo, Jorm, & Paxton, 2011; Kazdin, Fitzsimmons-Craft, & Wilfley, 2017; Patel et al., 2010). It is caused partly by the characteristics of our service systems, such as treatment costs, long waiting times, or a lack of health care professionals specialized in EDs which lead to a limited availability of appropriate treatment (e.g., in rural areas). Barriers to help-seeking on the side of the individual include the feelings of shame and stigmatization, limited mental health literacy, a lack of insight into the severity of the illness, and ambivalence to change (Ali et al., 2017).

It is assumed that technology-enhanced interventions offer advantages over conventional face-to-face (f2f) interventions in various respects. They are easily accessible and may be used anonymously and independently of time and place. Thus, they promise to reach currently underserved populations that may not have access to expert care or may be reluctant to seek help from their local health care providers. Furthermore, technology allows providers to flexibly adapt content and intensity of an intervention to the needs of individual users and also to latest scientific evidence. In addition, eHealth interventions are assumed to be more resource-friendly and cost-effective than conventional health care while potentially having a larger reach.

Over the past 20 years, a number of eHealth interventions for the prevention, early intervention, self-help, and treatment of EDs have been developed and evaluated. In this chapter, we introduce two main areas of application, i.e., stand-alone programs that are not integrated into conventional f2f interventions, and approaches that combine eHealth and conventional care. Following a summary of the state of science concerning empirically supported eHealth interventions in the field of EDs, implications for clinical practice and future research priorities are discussed.

Stand-Alone Interventions

Prevention and Early Intervention

One of the first and most studied Internet-based ED prevention programs is *Student Bodies* (*SB*), an 8-week structured online intervention targeting body dissatisfaction and excessive weight concerns based on the principles of cognitive-behavioral therapy (CBT). The efficacy of *SB* has been studied in more than ten clinical trials in different target groups mostly in the United States and Germany. In a randomized controlled trial (RCT) with 480 college-age women at risk for an ED, *SB* significantly reduced weight and shape concerns for up to 2 years. In a subgroup of women with elevated body mass index (BMI) and compensatory behaviors, the ED onset rate was significantly lower in the *SB* intervention relative to the control group (Taylor et al., 2006). In another trial, the effects of *SB* were studied in women with high weight and shape concerns, and subthreshold ED symptoms (e.g., bingeing, compensatory behaviors, and restrictive eating). Compared to a waitlist control group, *SB* improved ED-related attitudes, reduced subjective and objective binges and purging episodes, and led to higher abstinence rates from disordered eating at 6-month follow-up (Jacobi, Volker, Trockel, & Taylor, 2012). Findings of another study suggested that a guided discussion group improves the efficacy of *SB* in reducing weight and shape concerns in a sample of high-risk women, thus having an added value for the intervention while being cost-effectively deliverable (Kass et al., 2014). In a recent RCT including a very high ED-risk sample with comorbid depression, the subgroup with the highest shape concerns had a significantly lower ED onset rate than the control group (Taylor et al., 2016). Recently, *SB* was integrated into the *Healthy Body Image Program* which includes an online screening tool and several tailored online interventions for individuals across the ED risk spectrum. About 2,500 students were screened for ED risk factors as part of the first state-wide implementation of the *Healthy Body Image Program* in public universities in Missouri, which equals a participation rate of approximately 2.5% of the undergraduates at the participating universities. Depending on their risk/symptom status, participants were allocated to a universal prevention program, a selective prevention program, a guided self-help intervention, or in-person care. Uptake of the interventions ranged from 44% to 51% with higher ED risk being associated with a higher enrollment rate (Fitzsimmons-Craft et al., 2018). Research evaluating the costs of the interventions compared to standard care demonstrated that a stepped care approach integrating online prevention, online guided self-help, and conventional psychotherapy for those who do not benefit from online help is associated with modest cost savings compared to conventional care (Kass, Balantekin, & Fitzsimmons-Craft, 2017).

Another evidence-based prevention program that has been primarily evaluated in the f2f setting is the *Body Project* (*BP*). The *BP* is a prevention program for women at risk for EDs that focuses on maladaptive social comparison, self-objectification, and body dissatisfaction while employing cognitive dissonance-based techniques (Stice, Chase, Stormer, & Appel, 2001). The *BP* aims to elicit cognitive dissonances between behaviors (e.g., dieting) and attitudes (e.g., costs of pursuing the thin ideal) to achieve behavioral change. The *BP* has been evaluated in numerous research projects in terms of efficacy (i.e., risk factor reduction and prevention of illness onset), effectiveness, and dissemination (Becker & Stice, 2017). More recently, an online version of the *BP*, i.e., the *eBody Project*, was developed. Stice, Durant, Rohde, and Shaw (2014) analyzed post-intervention effects of a prototype of this Internet-based version of the *BP*. Results indicated similar effects for the *eBody Project* as compared to the original *BP*. However, effects decreased more rapidly for the *eBody Project* (Stice et al., 2014; Stice, Rohde, Durant, & Shaw, 2012). In a more recent study, the *eBody Project* was inferior to the clinician- and peer-led group-based versions of the *BP* in reducing risk factors, such as thin-ideal internalization, body dissatisfaction, and negative affect (Stice, Rohde, Shaw, & Gau, 2017). Still, all interventions were more effective than an educational video control condition. Another online intervention based on cognitive dissonance theory was studied by Chithambo and Huey (2017). They conducted an RCT comparing this intervention and another preventive intervention based on CBT and a control condition. Both interventions were superior relative to the control group in reducing body dissatisfaction, thin-ideal internalization, and depression. The CBT-based intervention was associated with greater reductions in ED pathology. Moderation analyses revealed that both interventions were more effective for individuals from ethnic minorities (i.e., Asian, Latino, Black, multiethnic, and others) than for Whites (Chithambo & Huey, 2017).

Media Smart-Targeted is a technology-enhanced adaption of a school-based program (*Media Smart*) and consists of nine interactive modules. The program targets weight concerns and its cognitive components (e.g., media internalization). *Media Smart* has been successfully evaluated in terms of reduction of ED risk factors and onset of clinically relevant weight and shape concerns (Wilksch & Wade, 2009; Wilksch et al., 2015). In a recent RCT with 575 women, the online version of this program, *Media Smart-Targeted*, was compared to *Student Bodies* and a control condition (i.e., an e-mail on how to improve body image). The results showed relatively low uptake of both interventions and no difference in terms of effectiveness between the three groups when intention-to-treat analyses were conducted. Completer analyses indicated that the outcome in the *Media Smart-Targeted* condition was superior to the control group and the *Student Bodies* condition (Wilksch et al., 2018).

ProYouth is a European Internet-based program combining prevention and early intervention. It aims to raise awareness around ED, to provide psychoeducation

eHealth Interventions for Eating Disorders   379

and online support, and to detect problematic ED-related attitudes and behaviors early. An online screening and supportive monitoring tool allows providers and users to tailor the intensity of support to individuals' risk profiles and to track relevant symptoms and behaviors over time. Participants can also use an online forum for peer-to-peer support and chats to seek advice from psychological experts. In case participants are in need of more intense support, the program aims at facilitating access to f2f treatment (Bauer et al., 2013). In contrast to most other eHealth interventions, *ProYouth* follows a flexible and individualized approach with respect to frequency, duration, and intensity of support. Findings confirmed the expected patterns of use on an interindividual and intraindividual level, i.e., participants with more severe ED symptoms used the program more and participants used the program more intensively during times of increased symptom severity. This suggests that an individualized approach may optimize resource allocation (Kindermann, Moessner, Ozer, & Bauer, 2017). In addition, there is preliminary evidence that *ProYouth* may enhance help-seeking behaviors (Kindermann, Ali, Minarik, Moessner, & Bauer, 2016), and may serve as a stepping stone to regular health care (Moessner, Minarik, Ozer, & Bauer, 2016a). However, it was also found that the participants who were at risk for an ED but did not report severe impairment hardly used the program. Therefore, enhanced versions of *ProYouth* including a dissonance-based and a CBT-based module are currently studied in terms of their efficacy and cost-effectiveness in an at-risk sample (Bauer et al., 2019b).

Box 18.1   Summary

Overall, systematic reviews and meta-analyses indicate that participation in ED prevention programs may improve individuals' ED-related attitudes, and reduce ED-related risk-factors, symptoms, and rates of illness onset (Le, Barendregt, Hay, & Mihalopoulos, 2017; Watson et al., 2016). To some extent, this seems to be the case for stand-alone Internet-based prevention programs as well (Beintner, Jacobi, & Taylor, 2012; Melioli et al., 2016; Wade & Wilksch, 2018), where approaches based on cognitive dissonance, media literacy, and CBT have been found to be promising examples. However, there is still a need for more high-quality efficacy trials and research into the long-term effectiveness and cost-effectiveness of such eHealth prevention programs.

Self-Help and Treatment Interventions

Technology-based self-help offers either unguided or guided access to information and materials related to EDs and ways to overcome them. Unguided technology-enhanced self-help is basically a more or less interactive but automated equivalent to traditional self-help books where users work through materials on their own. Guidance may be provided by professionals, peers, or recovered individuals via various forms of technology, e.g., phone, text messages, e-mail, moderated discussion forums, online chat, or video conferencing. Frequency and intensity of support vary largely between different interventions.

In the field of EDs, the majority of online self-help and treatment approaches are based on CBT principles. Most available interventions address individuals affected by full- or subthreshold bulimia nervosa or binge eating disorder. Various programs have been evaluated in the treatment of bulimia nervosa. For example, Sanchez-Ortiz et al. (2011) compared a multimedia CBT program (*Overcoming Bulimia Online*) to a waitlist control condition in a sample of students. Over eight sessions, participants had access to exercises, self-assessment tools, and support from CBT therapists via e-mail once every 1–2 weeks. After 3 months of participation, the intervention group showed significantly larger improvements regarding ED symptoms, binge eating episodes, affective symptoms, and quality of life. Intervention effects were maintained and further improved at follow-up.

Instead of using a waitlist control group, Wagner et al. (2013) compared a CBT-based Internet-delivered guided self-help intervention for patients with bulimia nervosa (*SALUT-BN*) to a conventional bibliotherapeutic approach based on a self-help book. The online intervention included weekly e-mail contact with a trained psychologist over a period of 4–7 months. The program content was structured consecutively, and psychologists were able to review patients' progress online. The bibliotherapeutic intervention was based on CBT as well and included 15 chapters with similar content. The results showed that binge eating, vomiting, and dieting were significantly reduced in both groups with largest improvements occurring during the first 4 months of intervention. However, no superiority of the online intervention over bibliotherapy was found.

Highly relevant for research and clinical practice is obviously the direct comparison between an online intervention and evidence-based f2f psychotherapy. Therefore, Bulik et al. (2012) conducted an RCT comparing an Internet-based version of CBT for bulimia nervosa delivered via an online chat group versus conventional group-based f2f CBT. At the end of the treatment, the online intervention was inferior to the f2f intervention in improving abstinence from bingeing and purging behaviors, and in reducing the frequency of these behaviors. However, group differences were no longer salient at 12-month follow-up (Zerwas et al., 2017). A cost-effectiveness analysis confirmed the online intervention to be a comparably cost-effective treatment as conventional f2f CBT, while coming along with possible advantages in their reach and accessibility, especially in regard to individuals with an unmet need for treatment (Watson et al., 2018).

In the field of binge eating disorder, an online program was developed on the basis of the self-help book "Overcoming Binge Eating" (Fairburn, 1995). The online program (*SALUT-BED*) consists of 11 modules with lessons and exercises based on CBT, and a self-monitoring diary with automated feedback. It also includes weekly e-mail guidance by a psychologist. In comparison to a waitlist control condition, the intervention group showed significantly larger improvements in binge eating behavior, drive for thinness, body dissatisfaction, and interoceptive awareness at the end of treatment as well as at follow-up (Carrard et al., 2011).

Promising results were also found for another guided Internet-based intervention for binge eating disorder. The program consists of 11 structured writing exercises mainly focusing on body image, problem solving, and relapse prevention. It also includes regular feedback by a therapist via e-mail. Participants further have access to CBT-based psychoeducational information provided via a webpage, an online diary on daily eating or activities, and week plans to implement daily structure. Compared to the waitlist control condition, participants in the online program reported significantly fewer objective binge eating episodes at the end of intervention, as well as significant reductions in dietary restraint, and weight and shape concerns from pre- to post-assessment, all of which were maintained at follow-up (Wagner et al., 2016).

The aforementioned *SALUT-BED* program was also studied in an large RCT in terms of its efficacy in comparison to conventional outpatient CBT for full-syndrome or subthreshold binge eating disorder (de Zwaan et al., 2017). The results showed that both groups improved, but did not differ in general psychopathology, BMI, and quality of life. However, findings demonstrated superiority of f2f CBT over online-guided self-help with respect to key BED binge eating disorder symptoms, i.e., the online intervention was more successful in reducing the number of objective binge eating days at the end of treatment and at 6-month follow-up, as well as in reducing ED psychopathology at 6-month follow-up. At 1.5-year follow-up, these group differences disappeared. The authors assume that Internet-based guided self-help interventions might act with a slower trajectory of improvement than f2f treatment. A cost-effectiveness analysis of the online intervention compared to CBT revealed no significant differences in costs, with only a tendency for CBT being more effective but also more costly (Koenig et al., 2018).

Another RCT compared an Internet-based self-help intervention for individuals with self-reported ED symptoms (*Featback*) to a waitlist control condition (Aardoom et al., 2016). Participants were assigned to one of three *Featback* conditions with either (1) no personal support, (2) low (i.e., once a week) therapeutic support, or (3) high (i.e., three times a week) therapeutic support. Participants in all conditions had access to the basic *Featback* program offering psychoeducation, and a fully automated supportive self-monitoring and feedback system. After 8 weeks of participation, all *Featback* groups were superior to the waitlist control condition in reducing bulimic psychopathology, depression, anxiety, and preservative thinking. More intense contact with a therapist had no added value regarding effectiveness and satisfaction, but those with digital therapist support reported significantly higher satisfaction with the intervention.

Box 18.2 Summary

In summary, research indicates that Internet-based stand-alone interventions for self-help and treatment are superior to no intervention. However, current online interventions do not seem to be more effective than conventional self-help (Wagner et al., 2013), and at least in the short term are less effective than f2f psychotherapy for bulimia nervosa and binge eating disorder (de Zwaan et al., 2017; Zerwas et al., 2017). Therefore, conventional psychotherapy should remain the treatment of choice for these disorders. However, eHealth may be a viable alternative for populations who would otherwise stay without professional support because conventional treatment is not available or accessible for them. Future studies should give special consideration to the benefits of technology-based interventions in terms of reducing barriers to treatment, enhancing help-seeking behavior, and facilitating access to conventional evidence-based treatment.

Combination of eHealth and Conventional Treatment

eHealth may be combined with conventional f2f treatment in two different ways. One option is to combine both formats in a sequential way ("stepped care"), i.e., an eHealth intervention of lower intensity and lower cost precedes or follows conventional f2f care. For example, current treatment guidelines for bulimia nervosa and binge eating disorder in the U.K. recommend participation in a self-help program as the first step within a multilevel stepped care treatment approach (National Institute for Health & Care Excellence, 2017). The original idea underlying stepped care is that the treatment starts with an intervention of the lowest intensity and costs that may be beneficial to the patient. Individuals who do not benefit from this first level are moved to a more intense form of treatment. Thus, the treatment becomes more individualized and efficient because the type and intensity of intervention are adapted based on the patients' specific needs. However, there are also approaches where all participants would undergo the same steps of care, e.g., by participating in a program to prepare them for treatment ("step up") or to prevent relapse after treatment termination ("step down").

The second option to combine eHealth and conventional care is to integrate both formats, i.e., eHealth interventions or eHealth modules are offered in parallel to conventional care ("blended treatment"). For example, online or mobile programs may be used to monitor patients' progress continuously over the course of therapy, to send reminders or motivational messages to maintain engagement in therapy or to offer additional support beyond that available in f2f sessions. Also, patients may be encouraged to work through psychoeducational materials or to complete certain tasks or homework electronically in-between f2f treatment sessions.

Stepped Care

Preparation for Treatment

A lack of specialized health care providers leads to long waiting times for many individuals affected by EDs. eHealth may be used to bridge waiting periods in order to prevent symptom deterioration and to prepare patients for their subsequent treatment. To date, such interventions for EDs are scarce but research from other mental health fields shows that their implementation might be beneficial for individuals with EDs as well (Kenter, Cuijpers, Beekman, & van Straten, 2016; Kok, van Straten, Beekman, & Cuijpers, 2014; Zimmer et al., 2015). In the field of EDs, an RCT investigating the efficacy of an 8-week Internet-based self-help program (*everyBODY Plus*) for individuals with bulimia nervosa, binge eating disorder, or other specified feeding or EDs awaiting f2f outpatient treatment is currently being conducted in Germany and the U.K. Compared to the control group, *EveryBODY Plus* is assumed to be associated with a more rapid reduction of core ED symptoms and higher rates of abstinence from ED behaviors (Vollert et al., 2019).

Another challenge in ED treatment is sufferers' high ambivalence to change and their reluctance to enter treatment when it is recommended to them. The *MotivATE* program consisting of four web-based modules of 15–20 minutes each was developed in the U.K. to increase motivation to change and attendance at specialist ED services (Denison-Day, Muir, Newell, & Appleton, 2019; Muir et al., 2017). Findings showed that access to the *MotivATE* intervention did not significantly affect service uptake. However, secondary analysis of data on program utilization revealed that only one-third of the intervention group actually registered to the program, and that among those who did register attendance to the specialized service was significantly higher. However, findings do not allow for conclusions on whether *MotivATE* actually improved motivation and ambivalence to change, or if individuals that were more motivated showed higher engagement within the study.

Aftercare

Patients with EDs are at high risk of relapse following treatment termination. eHealth interventions may be used to maintain the gains patients achieved during treatment by supporting them in the challenging transition phase after discharge. Therefore, Fichter et al. (2012) conducted an RCT examining the effects of a CBT-based relapse prevention program for patients with anorexia nervosa. The

384   *Johanna Sander, Sally Bilić, and Steffi Bauer*

program ran for nine months after participants' discharge from inpatient specialized ED treatment, and the intervention was compared to treatment as usual. Results showed that the 40% of intervention participants who completed all modules gained significantly more weight than the control group patients. Findings indicate the intervention may be beneficial if participants' adherence to the program can be maintained.

Several technology-enhanced aftercare interventions have been developed and evaluated for individuals with bulimia nervosa. In a first study, the efficacy of a supportive monitoring system based on mobile phones and text messaging was investigated. The 4-month intervention allows participants to report on key bulimic symptoms on a weekly basis and to receive tailored feedback depending on symptom level and changes over time. The feedback messages also serve as a reminder of CBT-based strategies learned during inpatient treatment. An RCT confirmed the intervention to be efficacious in terms of increasing abstinence rates from bulimic behaviors at 8-month follow-up and in terms of reducing relapse rates (Bauer, Okon, Meermann, & Kordy, 2012). A similar monitoring system was part of an Internet-based aftercare intervention (*EDINA*) following outpatient treatment in Hungary. In addition to the supportive monitoring, patients had access to online psychoeducation, a discussion board, and therapist-guided chat sessions. In an RCT, the intervention was shown to be feasible and well accepted. However, differences in ED-related impairment at the end of the 4-month intervention, which was in favor of the intervention group, did not reach statistical significance (Gulec et al., 2014).

In another study, a CBT-oriented aftercare program for patients with bulimia nervosa (*IN@*) was developed. It consists of 11 sessions to be completed within 9 months. Additionally, the intervention includes an online discussion group, feedback, and support provided by a moderator through e-mail and chat. Results of an RCT could not show the efficacy of the intervention, i.e., abstinence rates from binge eating did not differ significantly between the intervention and control group. Similarly, no group differences were found for the frequency of binge eating episodes, compensatory behaviors, and meeting of diagnostic criteria for any ED (Beintner & Jacobi, 2019; Jacobi et al., 2017).

Blended Treatment

Blended treatment, i.e., the integration of eHealth into f2f treatment, offers various possibilities of application such as the implementation of continuous monitoring procedures. For example, text messages for daily self-monitoring of binge eating and purging episodes were incorporated into CBT for bulimia nervosa. Participants received daily automated feedback according to their self-reported symptoms while undergoing CBT-based group treatment over a period of 12 weeks. Treatment acceptability and compliance with the self-monitoring tool were high, suggesting text messaging to be beneficial in improving adherence and engagement in CBT for EDs. However, due to the pilot nature of this research, no conclusions could be drawn on potential effects on treatment efficacy (Shapiro et al., 2010).

More recently, smartphone applications have been introduced to monitor symptom development over time and/or to provide support to individuals affected by EDs (e.g., Anastasiadou, Folkvord, & Lupianez-Villanueva, 2018; Fairburn & Rothwell, 2015; Juarascio, Manasse, Goldstein, Forman, & Butryn, 2015; Tregarthen, Lock, & Darcy, 2015). Some of these programs may also be integrated into conventional care for EDs, but it is currently unknown what the best way to do so is. Hildebrandt et al. (2017) investigated the efficacy of a self-monitoring smartphone application (*Noom Monitor*) that was provided as an add-on to CBT-based therapist-guided self-help for patients with bulimia and binge eating disorder. For intervention group participants, therapists had access to a summary of participants' data. The results showed greater (but small-sized) reductions in binge eating and purging in the intervention group compared to the self-help program alone, indicating the added value of the *Noom Monitor*. However, due to the small sample size, results have to be considered preliminary.

In an ongoing trial, researchers investigate the potential of another smartphone app (*Jourvie*) as an add-on to a weight management intervention for adolescents with anorexia nervosa who are waiting for the start of outpatient psychotherapy (Kolar, Hammerle, Jenetzky, & Huss, 2017). Even though it makes intuitive sense to integrate such mobile interventions into conventional health care for various reasons (e.g., availability, ease of use, self-monitoring, and opportunity to interact with a clinician), it has to be noted that the evidence base is still weak, and that there is a clear need for adequately powered RCTs to investigate the efficacy of such tools. In addition, challenges and potential negative effects of integrating mobile interventions into regular care need to be investigated, on the side of both patients and clinicians using the app. For example, qualitative research in a Danish sample of ED patients and clinicians who utilized the widely used app *Recovery Record* while patients underwent specialized ED treatment showed that part of the patient sample experienced the app as obstructive (Lindgreen, Lomborg, & Clausen, 2018), and part of the therapist sample was concerned about potential harmful effects on the therapeutic bond and about the additional workload on the side of professionals using the app (Lindgreen, Clausen, & Lomborg, 2018).

The concept of blended treatment has also been applied to the setting of family-based treatment which is considered the treatment of choice for adolescents with anorexia nervosa (Lock et al., 2010). As EDs present a burden not only for the affected person but also for their parents, Binford Hopf et al. developed a therapist-guided chat intervention to support parents in parallel to the participation of their families in f2f family-based treatment. Findings of a pilot study provided preliminary support for the potential of this eHealth intervention as adjunct to f2f treatment (Binford Hopf, Le Grange, Moessner, & Bauer, 2013).

Another form of blended care concerns the integration of conventional treatment and virtual reality (VR). VR is a computer technology that creates virtual physical environments in which the user's presence is simulated. In the field of ED treatment, it allows, e.g., to expose users to different types and amounts of food or to changes in body shape. Recent reviews show that VR-based interventions have indeed been used most often to virtually work on patients' body image and to expose them to various virtual food stimuli (Clus, Larsen, Lemey, & Berrouiguet, 2018), and that they have the potential to significantly enhance conventional care for EDs (Riva, 2017). Promising findings have been reported particularly for the use of VR in the context of cue exposure therapy which aims at changes of underlying behavioral patterns through exposition to craving eliciting stimuli (De Carvalho, Dias, Duchesne, Nardi, & Appolinario, 2017). As findings of studies on repeated sessions of exposure to virtual food demonstrated reduced negative emotional response, VR may be beneficial in progressively reducing food-related anxiety, which is considered a specific anticipatory reaction associated with binge eating episodes in individuals with bulimia nervosa (Clus et al., 2018; Pla-Sanjuanelo et al., 2017). Similar to other technology-enhanced interventions, open questions relate to potential risks and disadvantages of integrating VR into care for EDs.

Box 18.3 Summary

In summary, a variety of technology-enhanced interventions have been introduced to the ED field with the idea of complementing conventional care. Periods before the beginning of treatment and after its termination offer opportunities for providers to use eHealth interventions to extend their reach and provide additional support to affected individuals. Initial, but still limited empirical support currently exists on the efficacy of such sequential interventions for treatment preparation and aftercare. The same is true for blended treatment. Overall, more research is needed to identify which interventions work for specific patient populations in which settings and under which circumstances.

Implications for Research and Practice

Implications for Clinical Practice

Without a doubt, technology-enhanced interventions will play an increasing role in the delivery of preventive and therapeutic mental health services in the future. Technology plays such a big role in patients' and therapists' daily lives and in their communication routines that its integration into health care has become an obvious next step. Even though further research is needed, the available evidence indicates that eHealth interventions are promising tools and offer new opportunities for the prevention, self-help, and treatment of EDs. However, it is also clear that eHealth interventions are not suitable and beneficial for all individuals at risk of or affected by EDs, and that not all potential participants are interested in using this type of intervention. A lack of adherence and high dropout rates has been found particularly for stand-alone interventions, but almost nothing is known about the specific factors that contribute to this phenomenon nor on characteristics of individuals who terminate interventions prematurely. Similarly, it is currently unclear which populations benefit most from which type of intervention, so that target groups currently need to be defined by expert opinion and based on available reports and publications of what worked for which population.

While making the decision to offer technology-enhanced services as a clinician or provider, a number of aspects need to be taken into consideration from the outset. One of the most important aspects is obviously whether an intervention is offered as only means of support (i.e., stand-alone) or as adjunct to another intervention that involves personal f2f contact between client and provider. Furthermore, professionals need to determine the type of care and exact interventions they want to offer, the extent to which they want to integrate eHealth into their clinical work (full-time versus part-time), and they need to define exact procedures for usage of the intervention both for patients and themselves. It is important for the client–therapist communication, the therapeutic relationship, and also for clinicians' workload that there are clear rules for frequency and intensity of the technology-based interaction (e.g., how many contacts during which time period, how quickly does a clinician respond to clients' messages, and availability/office hours of the clinician). Therapists who work with Internet-based interventions have reported concerns about the loss of nonverbal information (e.g., in chat or e-mail contact) and the need to put more effort into establishing a robust therapeutic relationship (Anastasiadou et al., 2018). Also, clinicians need to pay attention to practical issues (e.g., technical requirements for utilization of certain eHealth interventions, which hardware/software is needed, and technical support) as well as to legal and ethical issues related to privacy, confidentiality, insurance, and data security. Finally, it is of utmost importance that emergency and safety procedures are clearly defined, for example, which measures take place if a participant in an online intervention reports suicidal thoughts or other life-threatening conditions such as severe underweight or medical complications in anorexia nervosa.

Independent of the specific eHealth interventions described in this chapter, it appears that one major advantage of the use of technology in mental health care is the possibility to implement online screening and monitoring procedures, i.e., to invite participants to complete questionnaires on ED-related risk factors, attitudes and behaviors at regular intervals. Such tools are used for various reasons: First, they allow clinicians and providers to track individuals' ED-related impairment over time which is relevant in almost all areas of health care. For example, in the field of prevention, continuous monitoring may help to identify illness onset which allows to initiate timely treatment which is assumed to improve chances for recovery. Similarly, in the field of aftercare, monitoring systems allow detection of relapses as soon as they occur and may thus help to prevent another full episode of the illness. In the context of stepped care, monitoring is essential to determine when a specific intervention is no longer sufficient and a participant should receive more intense interventions. A second advantage of screening and monitoring systems is that they allow to provide feedback to clients on their individual risk profile or symptom level. As with other forms of mental illness, EDs are characterized by poor mental health literacy, i.e., a lack of knowledge about the illness and treatment options. Therefore, providing feedback to participants may help them to gain more insight into their ED-related impairment and inform them about appropriate next steps (e.g., f2f consultation with an ED professional). Supportive monitoring and feedback may also serve as an efficacious minimum eHealth intervention itself as could be shown in the field of relapse prevention (Bauer et al., 2012) and self-help (Aardoom et al., 2016).

Nowadays, more and more smartphone applications are available for mental health in general and also for EDs. They may serve as useful tools to implement monitoring systems due to the portability and permanent availability of the device. However, only few of the currently available apps offer the possibility for users to share their monitoring entries with clinical experts and/or to interact with a clinician. Furthermore, most apps have not been subject to any kind of evaluation or research and there is currently no full-size RCT indicating the efficacy of any app (Anastasiadou et al., 2018). Overall, the validity of the content of apps for EDs as well as the potential benefits and risks related to their use are largely unknown (Fairburn & Rothwell, 2015). At the same time, it should be noted that individuals affected by EDs are interested in using apps and many do so independent of whether they are currently in treatment or not. Download numbers of the most prominent app in the ED field (*Recovery Record*; Tregarthen et al., 2015) illustrate the potential reach of such programs. They also point to the need for clinicians to ask clients who present for treatment about their usage of and experience with ED-related apps and discuss if and how they should be used in parallel to treatment.

Future Research Priorities

Research in the field of technology-enhanced care is challenging due to the fast speed of technological development and the relatively slow speed of evaluation research. However, it is of utmost importance that a solid evidence base is established before an intervention is implemented in clinical settings. A number of review papers and meta-analyses have confirmed that eHealth interventions may reduce risk factors and symptoms related to EDs (Aardoom, Dingemans, Spinhoven, & Van Furth, 2013; Bauer & Moessner, 2013; Loucas et al., 2014; Melioli et al., 2016). However, they have also concluded that there is a limited number of high-quality RCTs and that evidence in many areas should be considered preliminary. This is particularly true for the field of mobile interventions that use, e.g., smartphone applications to provide support (Anastasiadou et al., 2018). Therefore, the most important priority for future research remains the evaluation of interventions in terms of their efficacy and cost-effectiveness, but also with respect to potential side effects or harm that may be associated with their use. In such trials, researchers should carefully decide upon the control group(s) to which they compare a given eHealth intervention. This decision is related to the specific target group(s) for which the intervention has been developed. For example, if an eHealth intervention should be offered to patients as an alternative to an evidence-based f2f intervention, it is necessary to demonstrate that it is equally efficacious or not substantially inferior to this existing f2f intervention. However, if an intervention is supposed to support individuals who normally have no access to expert f2f treatment (e.g., in underserved regions or countries) or who are not willing to utilize such treatment, it might well be worth to test its efficacy in comparison to treatment as usual or a no-intervention control group.

In general, it is essential for research in this field that new interventions are conceptualized and evaluated based on the conditions of specific populations and health care systems. For example, although some barriers to treatment (e.g., shame and stigmatization) may be universal, individuals from low-income countries or countries with poor health care and insurance coverage face different challenges with respect to care compared to those who have free access to expert treatment. Thus, different eHealth solutions may be needed for these different populations: Those with access to expert care may benefit most from online interventions that encourage them to seek f2f treatment, that support them during waiting times for or in parallel to f2f treatment, or that help them navigate their way through the health care system. In contrast, stand-alone online interventions may be most suitable for individuals where no high-quality f2f care is available. In case of a lack of treatment providers, such interventions may be offered unguided, i.e., as pure self-help. They may thus be delivered to large groups of users without prior training of professionals.

Related to this, there is a need for more research into the reach and dissemination of eHealth interventions (Bauer & Moessner, 2013; Lipson et al., 2017; Nacke et al., 2019). Although the potential reach of such programs is obviously huge due to the permanent availability of the Internet, their actual reach still needs to be investigated in more detail. So far, most studies include relatively small samples and it is unclear to which extent underserved populations may be reached by eHealth interventions. It has been shown to be challenging to convince young people to sign up for and utilize technology-enhanced ED prevention programs (Fitzsimmons-Craft et al., 2018; Moessner, Minarik, Ozer, & Bauer, 2016b). Also, it has been found that different access paths via which participants reach an Internet-based intervention and specific recruitment strategies (e.g., via high schools versus online/social media) result in user groups with different characteristics (sociodemographic and ED-related impairment) and different duration and intensity of program use (Bauer et al., 2019a), but it is largely unknown what the most promising ways are to recruit individuals for participation in eHealth interventions. These aspects as well as the costs of intervention delivery and the cost-effectiveness of dissemination strategies are important to study when we aim for the sustained implementation of eHealth interventions into routine health care (Minarik, Moessner, Özer, & Bauer, 2013; Moessner et al., 2016b).

Conclusion

eHealth interventions offer many opportunities for the prevention, self-help, and treatment of EDs. As stand-alone interventions, they promise to reduce the treatment gap by providing support to individuals who do not have access to evidence-based care. However, it is currently unknown what the best way is to disseminate eHealth interventions to large underserved populations and how to encourage them to use such interventions. Future research needs to determine the public health impact of eHealth for EDs by studying not only the efficacy, effectiveness, and cost-effectiveness of such interventions but also dissemination strategies and their reach.

As adjunct to conventional f2f care, eHealth offers innovative ways for treatment providers to extend their reach, e.g., by conducting treatment preparation or aftercare via technology-enhanced interventions. Also, eHealth tools may be integrated into conventional care ("blended treatment"). The use of online screening and monitoring programs allows for tracking patients' ED-related impairment over time and adjusting treatment accordingly. Thus, eHealth may contribute to more flexible and individualized delivery of evidence-based interventions which may ultimately result in an optimization of care for EDs. However, research in this field is still in the early stages and a number of important questions need to be addressed before eHealth may fully unfold its potential.

References

Aardoom, J. J., Dingemans, A. E., Spinhoven, P., & Van Furth, E. F. (2013). Treating eating disorders over the Internet: A systematic review and future research directions. *The International Journal of Eating Disorders*, *46*(6), 539–52. doi:10.1002/eat.22135.

Aardoom, J. J., Dingemans, A. E., Spinhoven, P., van Ginkel, J. R., de Rooij, M., & van Furth, E. F. (2016). Web-based fully automated self-help with different levels of therapist support for individuals with eating disorder symptoms: A randomized controlled trial. *Journal of Medical Internet Research*, *18*(6), e159. doi:10.2196/jmir.5709.

Ali, K., Farrer, L., Fassnacht, D. B., Gulliver, A., Bauer, S., & Griffiths, K. M. (2017). Perceived barriers and facilitators towards help-seeking for eating disorders: A systematic review. *The International Journal of Eating Disorders*, *50*(1), 9–21. doi:10.1002/eat.22598.

Anastasiadou, D., Folkvord, F., & Lupianez-Villanueva, F. (2018). A systematic review of mHealth interventions for the support of eating disorders. *European Eating Disorders*

Review: *The Journal of the Eating Disorders Association, 26*(5), 394–416. doi:10.1002/erv.2609.
Bauer, S., Bilic, S., Özer, F., & Moessner, M. (2019a). Dissemination of an Internet-based program for the prevention and early intervention in eating disorders: Relationship between access paths, user characteristics, and program utilization. *Zeitschrift für Kinder- und Jugendpsychiatrie und Psychotherapie, 48,* 25–32. doi:10.1024/1422-4917/a000662.
Bauer, S., Bilic, S., Reetz, C., Ozer, F., Becker, K., Eschenbeck, H., ..., ProHEAD Consortium (2019b). Efficacy and cost-effectiveness of Internet-based selective eating disorder prevention: Study protocol for a randomized controlled trial within the ProHEAD Consortium. *Trials, 20*(1), 91. doi:10.1186/s13063-018-3161-y.
Bauer, S., & Moessner, M. (2013). Harnessing the power of technology for the treatment and prevention of eating disorders. *The International Journal of Eating Disorders, 46*(5), 508–15. doi:10.1002/eat.22109.
Bauer, S., Okon, E., Meermann, R., & Kordy, H. (2012). Technology-enhanced maintenance of treatment gains in eating disorders: Efficacy of an intervention delivered via text messaging. *Journal of Consulting and Clinical Psychology, 80*(4), 700–6. doi:10.1037/a0028030.
Bauer, S., Papezova, H., Chereches, R., Caselli, G., McLoughlin, O., Szumska, I., ..., Moessner, M. (2013). Advances in the prevention and early intervention of eating disorders: The potential of Internet-delivered approaches. *Mental Health & Prevention, 1*(1), 26–32. doi:10.1016/j.mhp.2013.10.003.
Becker, C. B., & Stice, E. (2017). From efficacy to effectiveness to broad implementation: Evolution of the Body Project. *Journal of Consulting and Clinical Psychology, 85,* 767–82.
Beintner, I., & Jacobi, C. (2019). Internet-based aftercare for women with bulimia nervosa following inpatient treatment: The role of adherence. *Internet Interventions, 15,* 67–75. doi:10.1016/j.invent.2018.11.004.
Beintner, I., Jacobi, C., & Taylor, C. B. (2012). Effects of an Internet-based prevention programme for eating disorders in the USA and Germany – A meta-analytic review. *European Eating Disorders Review: The Journal of the Eating Disorders Association, 20*(1), 1–8. doi:10.1002/erv.1130.
Binford Hopf, R. B., Le Grange, D., Moessner, M., & Bauer, S. (2013). Internet-based chat support groups for parents in family-based treatment for adolescent eating disorders: A pilot study. *European Eating Disorders Review: The Journal of the Eating Disorders Association, 21*(3), 215–23. doi:10.1002/erv.2196.
Bulik, C. M., Marcus, M. D., Zerwas, S., Levine, M. D., Hofmeier, S., Trace, S. E., ..., Kordy, H. (2012). CBT4BN versus CBTF2F: Comparison of online versus face-to-face treatment for bulimia nervosa. *Contemporary Clinical Trials, 33*(5), 1056–64. doi:10.1016/j.cct.2012.05.008.
Carrard, I., Crepin, C., Rouget, P., Lam, T., Golay, A., & Van der Linden, M. (2011). Randomised controlled trial of a guided self-help treatment on the Internet for binge eating disorder. *Behaviour Research and Therapy, 49*(8), 482–91. doi:10.1016/j.brat.2011.05.004.
Chithambo, T. P., & Huey, S. J., Jr. (2017). Internet-delivered eating disorder prevention: A randomized controlled trial of dissonance-based and cognitive-behavioral interventions. *The International Journal of Eating Disorders, 50*(10), 1142–51. doi:10.1002/eat.22762.
Clus, D., Larsen, M. E., Lemey, C., & Berrouiguet, S. (2018). The use of virtual reality in patients with eating disorders: Systematic review. *Journal of Medical Internet Research, 20*(4), e157. doi:10.2196/jmir.7898.

De Carvalho, M. R., Dias, T. R. S., Duchesne, M., Nardi, A. E., & Appolinario, J. C. (2017). Virtual reality as a promising strategy in the assessment and treatment of bulimia nervosa and binge eating disorder: A systematic review. *Behavioral Sciences (Basel)*, *7*(3), 43–63. doi:10.3390/bs7030043.

de Zwaan, M., Herpertz, S., Zipfel, S., Svaldi, J., Friederich, H. C., Schmidt, F., ..., Hilbert, A. (2017). Effect of Internet-based guided self-help vs individual face-to-face treatment on full or subsyndromal binge eating disorder in overweight or obese patients: The INTERBED randomized clinical trial. *JAMA Psychiatry*, *74*(10), 987–95. doi:10.1001/jamapsychiatry.2017.2150.

Denison-Day, J., Muir, S., Newell, C., & Appleton, K. M. (2019). A web-based intervention (MotivATE) to increase attendance at an eating disorder service assessment appointment: Zelen randomized controlled trial. *Journal of Medical Internet Research*, *21*(2), e11874. doi:10.2196/11874.

Fairburn, C. G. (1995). *Overcoming binge eating*. New York, NY: Guilford Press.

Fairburn, C. G., & Rothwell, E. R. (2015). Apps and eating disorders: A systematic clinical appraisal. *International Journal of Eating Disorders*, *48*(7), 1038–46.

Fairburn, C. G., & Wilson, G. T. (2013). The dissemination and implementation of psychological treatments: Problems and solutions. *The International Journal of Eating Disorders*, *46*(5), 516–21. doi:10.1002/eat.22110.

Fichter, M. M., Quadflieg, N., Crosby, R. D., & Koch, S. (2017). Long-term outcome of anorexia nervosa: Results from a large clinical longitudinal study. *The International Journal of Eating Disorders*, *50*(9), 1018–30. doi:10.1002/eat.22736.

Fichter, M. M., Quadflieg, N., Nisslmuller, K., Lindner, S., Osen, B., Huber, T., & Wunsch-Leiteritz, W. (2012). Does Internet-based prevention reduce the risk of relapse for anorexia nervosa? *Behaviour Research and Therapy*, *50*(3), 180–90. doi:10.1016/j.brat.2011.12.003.

Fitzsimmons-Craft, E. E., Firebaugh, M.-L., Graham, A. K., Eichen, D. M., Monterubio, G. E., Balantekin, K. N., ..., Wilfley, D. E. (2018). State-wide university implementation of an online platform for eating disorders screening and intervention. *Psychological Services*, *16*(2), 239-249. doi:10.1037/ser0000264.

Gulec, H., Moessner, M., Túry, F., Fiedler, P., Mezei, A., & Bauer, S. (2014). A randomized controlled trial of an Internet-based posttreatment care for patients with eating disorders. *Telemedicine and e-Health*, *20*(10), 916–22.

Hart, L. M., Granillo, M. T., Jorm, A. F., & Paxton, S. J. (2011). Unmet need for treatment in the eating disorders: A systematic review of eating disorder specific treatment seeking among community cases. *Clinical Psychology Review*, *31*(5), 727–35. doi:10.1016/j.cpr.2011.03.004.

Hildebrandt, T., Michaelides, A., Mackinnon, D., Greif, R., DeBar, L., & Sysko, R. (2017). Randomized controlled trial comparing smartphone assisted versus traditional guided self-help for adults with binge eating. *The International Journal of Eating Disorders*, *50*(11), 1313–22. doi:10.1002/eat.22781.

Jacobi, C., Beintner, I., Fittig, E., Trockel, M., Braks, K., Schade-Brittinger, C., & Dempfle, A. (2017). Web-based aftercare for women with bulimia nervosa following inpatient treatment: Randomized controlled efficacy trial. *Journal of Medical Internet Research*, *19*(9), e321. doi:10.2196/jmir.7668.

Jacobi, C., Volker, U., Trockel, M. T., & Taylor, C. B. (2012). Effects of an Internet-based intervention for subthreshold eating disorders: A randomized controlled trial. *Behaviour Research and Therapy*, *50*(2), 93–99. doi:10.1016/j.brat.2011.09.013.

Juarascio, A. S., Manasse, S. M., Goldstein, S. P., Forman, E. M., & Butryn, M. L. (2015). Review of smartphone applications for the treatment of eating disorders. *European Eating Disorders Review: The Journal of the Eating Disorders Association, 23*(1), 1–11. doi:10.1002/erv.2327.

Kass, A. E., Balantekin, K. N., & Fitzsimmons-Craft, E. E. (2017). *The economic case for digital interventions for eating disorders among United States college students. 50*(3), 250–8. doi:10.1002/eat.22680.

Kass, A. E., Trockel, M., Safer, D. L., Sinton, M. M., Cunning, D., Rizk, M. T., ..., Taylor, C. B. (2014). Internet-based preventive intervention for reducing eating disorder risk: A randomized controlled trial comparing guided with unguided self-help. *Behaviour Research and Therapy, 63*, 90–98. doi:10.1016/j.brat.2014.09.010.

Kazdin, A. E., Fitzsimmons-Craft, E. E., & Wilfley, D. E. (2017). Addressing critical gaps in the treatment of eating disorders. *The International Journal of Eating Disorders, 50*(3), 170–89. doi:10.1002/eat.22670.

Kenter, R. M., Cuijpers, P., Beekman, A., & van Straten, A. (2016). Effectiveness of a Web-Based Guided Self-help Intervention for Outpatients with a Depressive Disorder: Short-term Results from a Randomized Controlled Trial. *Journal of Medical Internet Research, 18*(3), e80. doi:10.2196/jmir.4861.

Kindermann, S., Ali, K., Minarik, C., Moessner, M., & Bauer, S. (2016). Enhancing help-seeking behavior in individuals with eating disorder symptoms via Internet: A case report. *Mental Health & Prevention, 4*(2), 69–74. doi:10.1016/j.mhp.2016.04.002.

Kindermann, S., Moessner, M., Ozer, F., & Bauer, S. (2017). Associations between eating disorder related symptoms and participants' utilization of an individualized Internet-based prevention and early intervention program. *The International Journal of Eating Disorders, 50*(10), 1215–21. doi:10.1002/eat.22774.

Kok, R. N., van Straten, A., Beekman, A. T., & Cuijpers, P. (2014). Short-term effectiveness of web-based guided self-help for phobic outpatients: Randomized controlled trial. *Journal of Medical Internet Research, 16*(9), e226. doi:10.2196/jmir.3429.

Kolar, D. R., Hammerle, F., Jenetzky, E., & Huss, M. (2017). Smartphone-enhanced low-threshold intervention for adolescents with anorexia nervosa (SELTIAN) waiting for outpatient psychotherapy: Study protocol of a randomised controlled trial. *BMJ Open, 7*(10), e018049.

Koenig, H. H., Bleibler, F., Friederich, H. C., Herpertz, S., Lam, T., Mayr, A., ..., Egger, N. (2018). Economic evaluation of cognitive behavioral therapy and Internet-based guided self-help for binge-eating disorder. *The International Journal of Eating Disorders, 51*(2), 155–64. doi:10.1002/eat.22822.

Le, L. K., Barendregt, J. J., Hay, P., & Mihalopoulos, C. (2017). Prevention of eating disorders: A systematic review and meta-analysis. *Clinical Psychology Review, 53*, 46–58. doi:10.1016/j.cpr.2017.02.001.

Lindgreen, P., Clausen, L., & Lomborg, K. (2018). Clinicians' perspective on an app for patient self-monitoring in eating disorder treatment. *Int J Eat Dis, 51*(4), 314–21.

Lindgreen, P., Lomborg, K., & Clausen, L. (2018). Patient experiences using a self-monitoring app in eating disorder treatment: Qualitative study. *JMIR mHealth and uHealth, 6*(6), e10253. Lindgreen, P.,

Lipson, S. K., Jones, J. M., Taylor, C. B., Wilfley, D. E., Eichen, D. M., Fitzsimmons-Craft, E. E., & Eisenberg, D. (2017). Understanding and promoting treatment-seeking for eating disorders and body image concerns on college campuses through online screening, prevention and intervention. *Eating Behaviors, 25*, 68–73. doi:10.1016/j.eatbeh.2016.03.020.

Lock, J., Le Grange, D., Agras, W. S., Moye, A., Bryson, S. W., & Jo, B. (2010). Randomized clinical trial comparing family-based treatment with adolescent-focused individual therapy for adolescents with anorexia nervosa. *Archives of General Psychiatry, 67*(10), 1025–32. doi:10.1001/archgenpsychiatry.2010.128.

Loucas, C. E., Fairburn, C. G., Whittington, C., Pennant, M. E., Stockton, S., & Kendall, T. (2014). E-therapy in the treatment and prevention of eating disorders: A systematic review and meta-analysis. *Behaviour Research and Therapy, 63*, 122–31. doi:10.1016/j.brat.2014.09.011.

Melioli, T., Bauer, S., Franko, D. L., Moessner, M., Ozer, F., Chabrol, H., & Rodgers, R. F. (2016). Reducing eating disorder symptoms and risk factors using the Internet: A meta-analytic review. *The International Journal of Eating Disorders, 49*(1), 19–31. doi:10.1002/eat.22477.

Minarik, C., Moessner, M., Özer, F., & Bauer, S. (2013). Implementierung und dissemination eines Internet basierten programms zur prävention und frühen intervention bei essstörungen. *Psychiatrische Praxis, 40*, 332–8.

Moessner, M., Minarik, C., Ozer, F., & Bauer, S. (2016a). Can an Internet-based program for the prevention and early intervention in eating disorders facilitate access to conventional professional healthcare? *Journal of Mental Health, 25*(5), 441–7. doi:10.3109/09638237.2016.1139064.

Moessner, M., Minarik, C., Ozer, F., & Bauer, S. (2016b). Effectiveness and cost-effectiveness of school-based dissemination strategies of an Internet-based program for the prevention and early intervention in eating disorders: A randomized trial. *Prevention Science, 17*(3), 306–13.

Muir, S., Newell, C., Griffiths, J., Walker, K., Hooper, H., Thomas, S., …, Appleton, K. M. (2017). MotivATE: A pretreatment web-based program to improve attendance at UK outpatient services among adults with eating disorders. *JMIR Research Protocols, 6*(7), e146. doi:10.2196/resprot.7440.

Nacke, B., Beintner, I., Gorlich, D., Vollert, B., Schmidt-Hantke, J., Hutter, K., …, Jacobi, C. (2019). everyBody-Tailored online health promotion and eating disorder prevention for women: Study protocol of a dissemination trial. *Internet Interventions, 16*, 20–25. doi:10.1016/j.invent.2018.02.008.

National Institute for Health and Care Excellence. (2017). *Eating disorders: Recognition and treatment.* London: National Institute for Health and Care Excellence.

Patel, V., Maj, M., Flisher, A. J., De Silva, M. J., Koschorke, M., Prince, M., & WPA Zonal and Member Society Representatives. (2010). Reducing the treatment gap for mental disorders: A WPA survey. *World Psychiatry: Official Journal of the World Psychiatric Association, 9*(3), 169–76. doi:10.1002/j.2051-5545.2010.tb00305.x.

Pla-Sanjuanelo, J., Ferrer-Garcia, M., Vilalta-Abella, F., Riva, G., Dakanalis, A., Ribas-Sabate, J., … Gutierrez-Maldonado, J. (2017). Testing virtual reality-based cue-exposure software: Which cue-elicited responses best discriminate between patients with eating disorders and healthy controls? *Eating and Weight Disorders, 24*(4), 757–765. doi:10.1007/s40519-017-0419-4.

Riva, G. (2017). Letter to the editor: Virtual reality in the treatment of eating and weight disorders. *Psychological Medicine, 47*(14), 2567–8. doi:10.1017/S0033291717001441.

Sanchez-Ortiz, V. C., Munro, C., Stahl, D., House, J., Startup, H., Treasure, J., …, Schmidt, U. (2011). A randomized controlled trial of Internet-based cognitive-behavioural therapy for bulimia nervosa or related disorders in a student population. *Psychological Medicine, 41*(2), 407–17. doi:10.1017/S0033291710000711.

Shapiro, J. R., Bauer, S., Andrews, E., Pisetsky, E., Bulik-Sullivan, B., Hamer, R. M., & Bulik, C. M. (2010). Mobile therapy: Use of text-messaging in the treatment of bulimia nervosa. *The International Journal of Eating Disorders*, *43*(6), 513–9. doi:10.1002/eat.20744.

Stice, E., Chase, A., Stormer, S., & Appel, A. (2001). A randomized trial of a dissonance-based eating disorder prevention program. *The International Journal of Eating Disorders*, *29*(3), 247–62. doi:10.1002/eat.1016.

Stice, E., Durant, S., Rohde, P., & Shaw, H. (2014). Effects of a prototype Internet dissonance-based eating disorder prevention program at 1- and 2-year follow-up. *Health Psychology*, *33*(12), 1558–67. doi:10.1037/hea0000090.

Stice, E., Rohde, P., Durant, S., & Shaw, H. (2012). A preliminary trial of a prototype Internet dissonance-based eating disorder prevention program for young women with body image concerns. *Journal of Consulting and Clinical Psychology*, *80*(5), 907–16. doi:10.1037/a0028016.

Stice, E., Rohde, P., Shaw, H., & Gau, J. M. (2017). Clinician-led, peer-led, and Internet-delivered dissonance-based eating disorder prevention programs: Acute effectiveness of these delivery modalities. *Journal of Consulting and Clinical Psychology*, *85*(9), 883–95. doi:10.1037/ccp0000211.

Taylor, C. B., Bryson, S., Luce, K. H., Cunning, D., Doyle, A. C., Abascal, L. B., …, Wilfley, D. E. (2006). Prevention of eating disorders in at-risk college-age women. *Archives of General Psychiatry*, *63*(8), 881–8. doi:10.1001/archpsyc.63.8.881.

Taylor, C. B., Kass, A. E., Trockel, M., Cunning, D., Weisman, H., Bailey, J., …, Wilfley, D. E. (2016). Reducing eating disorder onset in a very high risk sample with significant comorbid depression: A randomized controlled trial. *Journal of Consulting and Clinical Psychology*, *84*(5), 402–14. doi:10.1037/ccp0000077.

Tregarthen, J. P., Lock, J., & Darcy, A. M. (2015). Development of a smartphone application for eating disorder self-monitoring. *The International Journal of Eating Disorders*, *48*(7), 972–82. doi:10.1002/eat.22386.

Vollert, B., Beintner, I., Musiat, P., Gordon, G., Gorlich, D., Nacke, B., …, Jacobi, C. (2019). Using Internet-based self-help to bridge waiting time for face-to-face outpatient treatment for Bulimia Nervosa, Binge Eating Disorder and related disorders: Study protocol of a randomized controlled trial. *Internet Interv*, *16*, 26–34. doi:10.1016/j.invent.2018.02.010.

Wade, T. D., & Wilksch, S. M. (2018). Internet eating disorder prevention. *Current Opinion in Psychiatry*, *31*(6), 456–61. doi:10.1097/YCO.0000000000000450.

Wagner, B., Nagl, M., Dolemeyer, R., Klinitzke, G., Steinig, J., Hilbert, A., & Kersting, A. (2016). Randomized controlled trial of an Internet-based cognitive-behavioral treatment program for binge-eating disorder. [Randomisierte kontrollierte Prüfung eines Internet-basierten kognitiv-vehaltenstherapeutischen Behandlungsprogramms der Binge Eating-Störung]. *Behavior Therapy*, *47*(4), 500–14. doi:10.1016/j.beth.2016.01.006.

Wagner, G., Penelo, E., Wanner, C., Gwinner, P., Trofaier, M. L., Imgart, H., …, Karwautz, A. F. (2013). Internet-delivered cognitive-behavioural therapy v. conventional guided self-help for bulimia nervosa: Long-term evaluation of a randomised controlled trial. *British Journal of Psychiatry*, *202*, 135–41. doi:10.1192/bjp.bp.111.098582.

Watson, H. J., Joyce, T., French, E., Willan, V., Kane, R. T., Tanner-Smith, E. E., …, Egan, S. J. (2016). Prevention of eating disorders: A systematic review of randomized, controlled trials. *The International Journal of Eating Disorders*, *49*(9), 833–62. doi:10.1002/eat.22577.

396 *Johanna Sander, Sally Bilić, and Steffi Bauer*

Watson, H. J., McLagan, N., Zerwas, S. C., Crosby, R. D., Levine, M. D., Runfola, C. D., ..., Crow, S. J. (2018). Cost-effectiveness of Internet-based cognitive-behavioral treatment for bulimia nervosa: Results of a randomized controlled trial. *Journal of Clinical Psychiatry*, *79*(1), 16m11314. doi:10.4088/JCP.16m11314.

Wilksch, S. M., O'Shea, A., Taylor, C. B., Wilfley, D., Jacobi, C., & Wade, T. D. (2018). Online prevention of disordered eating in at-risk young-adult women: A two-country pragmatic randomized controlled trial. *Psychological Medicine*, *48*(12), 2034–44. doi:10.1017/S0033291717003567.

Wilksch, S. M., Paxton, S. J., Byrne, S. M., Austin, S. B., McLean, S. A., Thompson, K. M., ..., Wade, T. D. (2015). Prevention across the spectrum: A randomized controlled trial of three programs to reduce risk factors for both eating disorders and obesity. *Psychological Medicine*, *45*(9), 1811–23.

Wilksch, S. M., & Wade, T. D. (2009). Reduction of shape and weight concern in young adolescents: A 30-month controlled evaluation of a media literacy program. *Journal of the American Academy of Child and Adolescent Psychiatry*, *48*(6), 652–61.

Zerwas, S. C., Watson, H. J., Hofmeier, S. M., Levine, M. D., Hamer, R. M., Crosby, R. D., ..., Bulik, C. M. (2017). CBT4BN: A randomized controlled trial of online chat and face-to-face group therapy for bulimia nervosa. *Psychotherapy and Psychosomatics*, *86*(1), 47–53. doi:10.1159/000449025.

Zimmer, B., Moessner, M., Wolf, M., Minarik, C., Kindermann, S. & Bauer, S. (2015). Effectiveness of an Internet-based preparation for psychosomatic treatment: Results of a controlled observational study. *Journal of Psychosomatic Research*, *79*(5), 399–403.

Afterword: Novel Research, Training, and Supervision Opportunities for Evidence-Based Treatment Adaptations

Carol B. Peterson, Emily M. Pisetsky, and Lisa M. Anderson

Introduction

Significant advances in treatment outcome research have facilitated remission and recovery for many individuals who have struggled with eating disorders (EDs). Unfortunately, in spite of such advances, EDs continue to cause significant health, psychological, and interpersonal issues; financial burden; as well as mortality (Crow et al., 2009; Klump, Bulik, Kaye, Treasure, & Tyson, 2009). In addition, a majority of individuals with EDs do not have access to treatment (Innes, Clough, & Casey, 2017). Recent advances in the field of EDs include a broadening of diagnostic criteria in the *DSM-5* (Call, Walsh, & Attia, 2013), facilitating the potential increase of treatment resource availability and the expansion of evidence-based treatments beyond narrow diagnostic categories. Indeed, evidence-based treatments for EDs have been increasingly implemented in more heterogeneous ED populations. For example, more recent ED treatment outcome studies have increasingly included participants meeting broadly defined diagnostic criteria (e.g., Strandskov et al., 2017; Thompson-Brenner et al., 2016; Wonderlich et al., 2014), in contrast to earlier randomized controlled trials that were limited to participants meeting strict criteria for anorexia nervosa (AN) or bulimia nervosa (BN). The development of enhanced cognitive behavioral therapy (CBT-E), a transdiagnostic ED treatment (Fairburn, 2008), is especially notable for its emphasis on individualized formulations that encompass a full range of ED symptoms and behaviors. Another advancement in psychopathology research, including EDs, is the increasing focus on dimensional nosology and measurement (Kelly, Clarke, Cryan, & Dinan, 2018; Luo, Donnellan, Burt, & Klump, 2016). Expanding the dimensional conceptualization and measurement of EDs has facilitated the recognition that individuals who do not meet all of the diagnostic criteria for AN, BN, or binge eating disorder (BED) nonetheless experience co-occurring psychopathology, health problems, and impairment at comparable levels to those with formal AN, BN, and BED diagnoses (Agras, Crow, Mitchell, Halmi, & Bryson, 2009). These findings, along with data from empirical classification studies (Wonderlich, Joiner, Keel, Williamson, & Crosby, 2007), the high prevalence of diagnostically "subthreshold" EDs in clinical settings (Fairburn & Bohn, 2005), and the desire to reduce the number of individuals with clinically significant EDs assigned to the "Not Otherwise Specified" category of *DSM-IV* (Call et al., 2013), have contributed to changes in *DSM-5* and conceptualization of ED psychopathology more broadly as well as increased access to treatment for more individuals with EDs.

The recent broadening of ED diagnostic criteria occurs in a context, however, in which the accessibility of evidence-based ED treatments is limited and many, if not the majority, of individuals with EDs do not receive adequate treatment (Fairburn & Patel, 2014). Health disparities in accessing ED treatment are particularly pronounced (Becker, Franko, Speck, & Herzog, 2003; Cachelin & Striegel-Moore, 2006). The reasons for this inaccessibility are multifaceted and complex, involving problems with financial resources, dissemination, training, and the research/practice "gap" (Kazdin, Fitzsimmons-Craft, & Wilfley, 2017). As highlighted in the previous chapters, however, another source of inaccessibility is the limited scope of applications of ED evidence-based treatments. Traditionally, evidence-based treatment development involves the writing and pilot testing of a treatment manual, the development of adherence measures and therapist training procedures, the determination of treatment outcome measures, and the investigation of the treatment in a randomized controlled trial (RCT). This process is highly rigorous with an emphasis on strict definitions, reliability, and reproducibility. Although these high standards are intentionally rigid in the context of science, they have resulted in limited applications of evidence-based treatments. This tendency is reinforced by grant and peer-review procedures which, by definition, emphasize scientific rigor. In the process of establishing efficacy in RCTs and effectiveness in clinical settings, evidence-based treatment investigations have often restricted the heterogeneity of samples as well as the flexibility of interventions and assessments in the interest of scientific rigor. The emphasis on scientific rigor in evidence-based ED treatments may have contributed to the relatively slow process of broadening the applications and adaptations of these interventions.

In contrast to other psychiatric disorders such as depression and anxiety, ED treatment outcome is a "younger" field with the early RCTs not published until the late 1970s and early 1980s. As a result, our evidence-based treatments have developed a robust body of supporting research only relatively recently (Hollon & Wilson, 2014; Kass, Kolko, & Wilfley, 2013). Given the increasingly strong empirical support for these existing treatments, broadening their content and scope is both appropriate and impactful. These adaptations also reflect the growing awareness of the heterogeneity of ED presentations and populations impacted by EDs. For these reasons, the timing is optimal for this volume and its emphasis on the critical importance of adapting evidence-based ED treatments to novel populations and settings. As illustrated in the previous chapters, these adaptations will broaden the accessibility of our treatments, address ED heterogeneity, and advance the implementation of our evidence-based treatments. In addition, these adaptations may increase both the efficacy and effectiveness of ED evidence-based treatment, a necessity given the rates of treatment nonresponse and relapse among individuals with EDs. (Kass et al., 2013; Linardon & Wade, 2018; Linardon, 2018).

Although enthusiasm for these adaptations should not be tempered, the importance of scientific rigor remains critical. Additional considerations that have been highlighted in previous chapters are essential in the context of ED treatment research, training, and supervision, including cultural humility, ethics, and the challenges of emerging technologies. The following sections highlight considerations for clinicians and researchers as well as those with lived experiences in the context of these treatment adaptations including research, training, and supervision.

Research

The importance of conducting research on adaptations of evidence-based treatments cannot be overemphasized. Comprehensive information regarding treatment protocols, manuals, training procedures, and outcome data is critical to examine these adaptations rigorously, to disseminate information in the scientific and clinical communities, and to facilitate global implementation of these adaptations. These data will also facilitate the iterative process of refining and strengthening these adaptations. The following sections address specific considerations in this type of research (see Box A.1).

Assessment

A foundation of all treatment outcome research, assessment includes questionnaires, clinical interviews, and observational data that are used to determine eligibility of participants, characterize clinical samples, and measure treatment outcome. The adaptation of evidence-based treatments to novel populations requires a thorough determination of the appropriateness of established interviews

---

Box A.1   Research Considerations for Adaptations of Evidence-Based Treatment Investigations

- Optimal assessment measures
- Appropriateness of treatment outcome definitions
- Ethics of consent and confidentiality
- Cultural adaptations
- Treatment predictors, moderators, and mediators
- Therapist fidelity, competency, and adherence
- Treatment acceptability and retention
- Cost-efficacy and stepped care designs

400 *Peterson, Pisetsky, and Anderson*

and questionnaires for use in research with these specific populations. For example, the reliability and validity of established assessment instruments may not replicate in cross-cultural samples (Franko et al., 2004). In addition, the items in widely used ED assessment measures may not adequately assess variables relevant to specific populations and may be experienced by participants as confusing, irrelevant, insensitive, or even offensive, particularly content related to body image (Hildebrandt, Walker, Alfano, Delinsky, & Bannon, 2010; Mitchison & Mond, 2015). For these reasons, the content of assessment instruments must be scrutinized, edited, and, ideally, pilot tested to ensure acceptability across populations. As evidence-based treatments are adapted for broader populations, these cultural adaptations will inform our treatment outcome measures (Hinton & Patel, 2017). Investigating the psychometrics of established as well as novel assessment measures by examining internal consistency, inter-rater reliability, test–retest reliability, and validity in psychometric and treatment studies will serve the dual purpose of providing support of these assessment measures in novel populations and broadening the scope of these instruments' reliability and validity.

Adapting assessment measures to unique settings can also require innovation, including the use of technology-based measurements in telehealth and e-health delivery. The use of state-of-the-art research techniques including ecological momentary assessment (EMA) in which participants are signaled to respond to handheld technology (typically mobile phones) in "real time" can also enhance the ecological validity and accuracy of treatment outcome measurement (Engel et al., 2016). Portable technology-based assessment administration can also be used in nontraditional clinical settings including home-based care. Certain technology-based assessments (e.g., text or email links to self-report questionnaires) have the additional benefit of being more easily administered during treatment follow-up than in-person assessments. However, off-site technology-based assessment administration, while both convenient and scalable, may reduce the reliability and accuracy of self-report data. In selecting assessment measures, investigators must balance the potential advantages of technology-based assessment, including the potential of increased self-disclosure (Keel, Crow, Davis, & Mitchell, 2002), with the risks of incomplete or inaccurate data.

Treatment Outcome Definitions

Adapting evidence-based treatments to novel populations and settings requires a re-examination of treatment outcome definitions. In novel samples, traditional *DSM-5* criteria-based assessment measures may be too narrow to capture the range and complexity of relevant constructs for good treatment outcome. Broadening treatment outcome conceptualization may include variables related to care providers, medical outcomes (e.g., among pregnant samples and for bariatric surgery patients), developmental milestones in youth samples, observation of food intake among individuals with ARFID, specific comorbidity (e.g., trauma), group cohesion, and family-based functioning. Adapting existing measures and developing novel assessments for these

Afterword 401

variables may require additional psychometric support, as described previously, but can provide valuable resources for ongoing outcome assessment of these treatment adaptations across settings.

In the context of treatment adaptation, prioritizing measures of treatment acceptability including self-report and rates of retention as well as therapeutic alliance, participant motivation, and intervention adherence will be particularly useful in establishing feasibility and facilitating treatment refinements. Given the iterative and ongoing nature of treatment adaptation, qualitative data in which participants can describe their evaluations of their treatment experiences in confidential survey-based measures as well as interview assessments can also provide valuable data for further adaptations of treatment manuals and procedures. Follow-up assessments after the end of treatment are particularly informative with respect to longer-term treatment efficacy and effectiveness.

Ethics

The involvement of caregivers in ED treatment has advanced ED treatment outcome considerably. As adaptations of evidence-based treatments – which include partners, supportive others, and caregivers – continue, research investigations will need to continue to focus on ethical considerations including confidentiality, consent, and assent procedures in the context of treatment and data collection. Because consent procedures, including determining the capacity to provide consent, can be particularly challenging when conducted electronically, establishing specialized consent procedures for telehealth, e-health, and m-health is an especially important priority. Issues of confidentiality and consent in research can also be complicated in group treatments when participants are asked to evaluate their treatment experiences including group coherence. Careful consideration of research consent, in particular, and ethics, in general, are essential in these types of adaptation studies.

Other Research Considerations

As noted previously, the increasing emphasis on dimensional measures of psychopathology and treatment outcome has continued to advance the ED field and can help guide measurement selection in adaptation studies (Kelly et al., 2018; Luo et al., 2016). Dimensional assessment can also facilitate research of hypothesized ED maintenance mechanisms that can be targeted to increase treatment efficacy. Frequent administration of measures throughout treatment to assess hypothesized mechanistic variables can be used in mediation analyses to identify specific changes in variables that are associated with treatment outcome (Kraemer, Wilson, Fairburn, & Agras, 2002). For example, if an adapted treatment targets family-based variables, these constructs can be measured throughout treatment to determine if changes impact outcome. When feasible, incorporating neurobiological and neurocognitive measures, including fMRI, into treatment outcome measurement can provide informative data about ED maintenance mechanisms (Wildes & Marcus, 2015). However, the feasibility of incorporating this type of assessment is limited in community-based settings outside of medical centers and is often cost prohibitive in many community-based research studies.

Identifying treatment moderators and predictors is potentially valuable in determining whether certain participant characteristics are associated with better or poorer outcome (Kraemer et al., 2002). A comprehensive baseline assessment to examine hypothesized moderators may include symptom severity, personality factors, interpersonal variables, demographic measures, and/or co-occurring psychopathology. Moderator and mediator examinations can also potentially contribute to the development of personalized psychotherapy (Cuijpers, Ebert, Acarturk, Andersson, & Cristea, 2016). Research investigations of treatment adaptations to novel populations and settings can include context-specific moderator assessments like food insecurity, adverse childhood experiences, family income, and education that may be related to specific populations and settings.

Emerging evidence-based treatment outcome investigations can examine factors that have been studied in traditional treatment outcome research including rapid response, treatment attrition, sudden gains, and relapse. In addition to the innovative applications of evidence-based treatment described in previous chapters, future research can continue to investigate treatment delivery methods. Further examinations of cost-efficacy, self-help approaches, and stepped care designs will also continue to advance the field, particularly treatment implementation, as well as improve access to care. Treatment delivery by nonspecialists, as well as technology-based administration, may be particularly impactful in dissemination and accessibility (Fairburn & Patel, 2014; Kazdin et al., 2017).

Finally, treatment outcome research, particularly in novel settings, needs to balance comprehensive assessment and standardization of treatment procedures with the potential burden on participants and staff (Peterson, 2010). Because increasing assessment and research burden can lead to declining data quality, investigators establishing research protocols should strive for the optimal balance between scientific rigor and acceptability among participants and staff.

Training

Cultural Adaptations

The importance of cultural representation among health care providers, including therapists, is critically important. As described by Kazdin and colleagues (2017), "a mismatch of race/ethnicity and culture between prospective client and therapist at minimum adds another obstacle for receiving services" whereas "...forming an alliance, being able to communicate in one's primary language, and having a shared view of psychological problems can all depend on having a match between therapist and patient in relation to race/ethnicity and culture (p. 174)." These considerations are particularly important when selecting therapists and interventionists for adaptations of evidence-based ED treatment. Given

Afterword 403

the crucial importance of the assessment interview in engaging the patient or research participant and the necessity of alliance for the gathering of accurate clinical data (Peterson, 2005), representation of race or ethnicity and culture among clinical interviewers is potentially as crucial as it is for therapists. Cultural representation is especially critical in the selection of assessment and therapist supervisors in the context of training as well as ongoing interpretation of clinical data, particularly in cultural adaptations of evidence-based treatment.

Training Assessment Interviewers

Clinical interviewers need expertise in the measure being administered as well as the ED psychopathology that is being assessed. Strong interpersonal skills and a capacity to develop rapport is as important in administering clinical assessment interviews as it is in providing treatment (Peterson, 2005). A strong alliance between a clinical interviewer and a patient or research participant not only improves the quality of data obtained during the interview but can also increase engagement in subsequent treatment.

Traditional assessment training procedures typically involve a didactic review of the clinical interview, role playing, and observation as well as audio or video review with supervision and feedback. Inter-rater reliability is extremely important to prevent clinical raters from "drift." Regular meetings with clinical interviewers in which the supervisor reviews questions and case examples are also extremely helpful in increasing reliability and building assessment skills. In evidence-based treatment adaptation research, clinical interviewers may require specialized training to work with novel populations and to administer assessment interviews in nontreatment settings. Practice clinical interviews can increase assessor confidence and improve technique.

Training Therapists

Traditional didactic workshops combined with treatment manual readings increase knowledge but do not consistently result in changes in treatment techniques (Herschell, Kolko, Baumann, & Davis, 2010); therefore, therapist training in the context of adaptations of evidence-based treatment in both clinical and research settings should ideally use state-of-the-art approaches including train-the-trainer models, competency-based learning, and interactive technology-based learning modules (Kazdin et al., 2017). Train-the-trainer approaches involve training one member of the staff who then trains other on-site staff. This approach emphasizes active learning, modeling, supportive interactions, and the development of mastery (Beidas & Kendall, 2010). Based on recent findings indicating that therapist self-efficacy may increase treatment fidelity (Brown & Perry, 2018), train-the-trainer and similar approaches may be especially beneficial to treatment fidelity by increasing therapists' sense of mastery in their skills and techniques. Successful train-the-trainer approaches that have been used in eating disorders (e.g.,

404   *Peterson, Pisetsky, and Anderson*

Zandberg & Wilson, 2013) can be adapted to other samples and settings in evidence-based treatment adaptations.

Adaptations of evidence-based treatments using technology-based administration including telehealth and e-health may find technology-based learning modules and competency-based education approaches especially well-suited for therapist training. These approaches typically facilitate learning using a web-based interactive curriculum that enables therapists to learn at their own pace. As a result, this type of training is both cost-effective and scalable (Fairburn & Cooper, 2011; Fairburn & Patel, 2014). Online technology-based training is also advantageous in providing a standardized learning experience across sites and locations in multisite programs and research.

Traditional approaches to therapist training and monitoring are also potentially useful in adaptation research. The use of "checklists" (paper or electronic) to help therapists' ensure that specific content is covered in therapy sessions can increase treatment fidelity. This approach is especially helpful for therapists who were trained in the traditional form of an evidence-based treatment and are implementing an adapted format. Regular (e.g., weekly and monthly) group or individual supervision sessions in which study therapists review cases, discuss recordings of therapy sessions, and receive feedback from the therapy supervisor are also useful for increasing therapists' skills, preventing drift, and improving treatment fidelity and adherence.

Treatment implementation programs and treatment outcome studies examining therapist competency, fidelity, and adherence in adapted treatments can use or revise existing measures for use in novel populations and settings (e.g., Forsberg et al., 2015). In traditional treatment outcome studies, these measures are typically based on ratings of audio or visual recordings of therapy sessions, although innovative approaches that are less time-intensive and costly, including a review of session handouts, are being examined (Wiltsey Stirman et al., 2018). Given inconsistent findings in the correlation between treatment fidelity and treatment outcome, recognizing and understanding the complexity of this relationship remains a priority when examining these variables (Farmer, Mitchell, Parker-Guilbert, & Galovski, 2017; Tschuschke et al., 2015).

Supervision

Although supervision in clinical settings as well as in implementation and treatment outcome research typically emphasizes therapist training, supervision of clinical assessment interviewing is also a priority. Supervision is used in most training approaches including train-the-trainer models. Best practices in supervision typically include audio or video review of therapy sessions along with verbal and/or written feedback provided to the trainee. As described earlier, supervision is traditionally administered in face-to-face dyadic or group meetings but can also be delivered via teleconference or videoconference. Recent advances in technology-based supervision (e.g., Rousmaniere & Frederickson, 2013; Rousmaniere, 2014) may be especially useful for training and monitoring clinicians in different locations as well as in multisite e-health programs.

Providing supervision in the context of adapted evidence-based treatment requires specialized skills and knowledge. In monitoring adapted evidence-based treatments among novel populations, supervisors may need to have expertise in cultural adaptations, developmental considerations, family- and carer-based interactions, and technology-based treatment administration in addition to advanced expertise in their knowledge about eating disorders and evidence-based treatment. Effective supervision also requires an understanding of the potential challenges for clinicians in conducting evidence-based treatments as well as strategies that can be used to help clinicians address these challenges (Waller, 2016; Waller et al., 2013).

Conclusions

Empirical testing of adaptations of evidence-based ED treatments to novel populations and nontraditional settings necessitates thoughtful considerations of research methods including measurement and definitions of treatment outcome in order to optimally extend established procedures. Similarly, high-quality training and supervision of treatment therapists and research assessors in the context of these adaptations requires an integration of validated procedures and techniques with innovative approaches. State-of-the-art training and supervision approaches including train-the-trainer models and technology-based interactive curriculum can be used in evidence-based treatment adaptions. Data collection using well-suited assessment measures of baseline characteristics and thoughtfully defined treatment outcomes, as well as potential moderators and mediators, can be used to refine treatment adaptations and establish efficacy and effectiveness of adapted evidence-based treatments.

References

Agras, W. S., Crow, S., Mitchell, J. E., Halmi, K. A., & Bryson, S. (2009). A 4-year prospective study of eating disorder NOS compared with full eating disorder syndromes. *International Journal of Eating Disorders, 42*, 565–570.

Becker, A. E., Franko, D. L., Speck, A., & Herzog, D. B. (2003). Ethnicity and differential access to care for eating disorder symptoms. *International Journal of Eating Disorders, 33*, 205–212.

Beidas, R. S., & Kendall, P. C. (2010). Training therapists in evidence-based practice: A critical review of studies from a systems-contextual perspective. *Clinical Psychology: Science and Practice, 17*, 1–30.

Brown, C. E., & Perry, K. N. (2018). Cognitive behavioural therapy for eating disorders: How do clinician characteristics impact on treatment fidelity? *Journal of Eating Disorders, 6*, 19.

Cachelin, F. M., & Striegel-Moore, R. H. (2006). Help seeking and barriers to treatment in a community sample of Mexican American and European American women with eating disorders. *International Journal of Eating Disorders, 39*, 154–161.

Call, C., Walsh, B. T., & Attia, E. (2013). From DSM-IV to DSM-5: Changes to eating disorder diagnoses. *Current Opinion in Psychiatry, 26*, 532–536.

Crow, S. J., Peterson, C. B., Swanson, S. A., Raymond, N. C., Specker, S., Eckert, E. D., & Mitchell, J. E. (2009). Increased mortality in bulimia nervosa and other eating disorders. *American Journal of Psychiatry, 166*, 1342–1346.

Cuijpers, P., Ebert, D. D., Acarturk, C., Andersson, G., & Cristea, I. A. (2016). Personalized psychotherapy for adult depression: A meta-analytic review. *Behavior Therapy, 47*, 966–980.

Engel, S. G., Crosby, R. D., Thomas, G., Bond, D., Lavender, J. M., Mason, T., …, Wonderlich, S. A. (2016). Ecological momentary assessment in eating disorder and obesity research: A review of the recent literature. *Current Psychiatry Reports, 18*, 37.

Fairburn, C. G., *Cognitive-behavioral therapy and eating disorders.* 2008. New York, NY: Guilford Press.

Fairburn, C. G., & Bohn, K. (2005). Eating disorder NOS (EDNOS): An example of the troublesome "not otherwise specified" (NOS) category in DSM-IV. *Behaviour Research and Therapy, 43*, 691–701.

Fairburn, C. G., & Cooper, Z. (2011). Therapist competence, therapy quality, and therapist training. *Behaviour Research and Therapy, 49*, 373–378.

Fairburn, C. G., & Patel, V. (2014). The global dissemination of psychological treatments: A road map for research and practice. *American Journal of Psychiatry, 171*, 495–498.

Farmer, C. C., Mitchell, K. S., Parker-Guilbert, K., & Galovski, T. E. (2017). Fidelity to the cognitive processing therapy protocol: Evaluation of critical elements. *Behavior Therapy, 48*, 195–206.

Forsberg, S., Fitzpatrick, K. K., Darcy, A., Aspen, V., Accurso, E. C., Bryson, S. W., …, Lock, J. (2015). Development and evaluation of a treatment fidelity instrument for family-based treatment of adolescent anorexia nervosa. *International Journal of Eating Disorders, 48*, 91–99.

Franko, D. L., Striegel-Moore, R. H., Barton, B. A., Schumann, B. C., Garner, D. M., Daniels, S. R., …, Crawford, P. B. (2004). Measuring eating concerns in black and white adolescent girls. *International Journal of Eating Disorders, 35*, 179–189.

Herschell, A. D., Kolko, D. J., Baumann, B. L., & Davis, A. C. (2010). The role of therapist training in the implementation of psychosocial treatments: A review and critique with recommendations. *Clinical Psychology Review, 30*, 448–466.

Hildebrandt, T., Walker, D. C., Alfano, L., Delinsky, S., & Bannon, K. (2010). Development and validation of a male specific body checking questionnaire. *International Journal of Eating Disorders, 43*, 77–87.

Hinton, D. E., & Patel, A. (2017). Cultural adaptations of cognitive behavioral therapy. *Psychiatric Clinics, 40*, 701–714.

Hollon, S. D., & Wilson, G. T. (2014). Psychoanalysis or cognitive–behavioral therapy for bulimia nervosa: The specificity of psychological treatments. *American Journal of Psychiatry, 171*, 13–16.

Innes, N. T., Clough, B. A., & Casey, L. M. (2017). Assessing treatment barriers in eating disorders: A systematic review. *Eating disorders, 25*, 1–21.

Kass, A. E., Kolko, R. P., & Wilfley, D. E. (2013). Psychological treatments for eating disorders. *Current Opinion in Psychiatry, 26*, 549–555.

Kazdin, A. E., Fitzsimmons-Craft, E. E., & Wilfley, D. E. (2017). Addressing critical gaps in the treatment of eating disorders. *International Journal of Eating Disorders, 50*, 170–189.

Afterword 407

Keel, P. K., Crow, S., Davis, T. L., & Mitchell, J. E. (2002). Assessment of eating disorders: Comparison of interview and questionnaire data from a long-term follow-up study of bulimia nervosa. *Journal of Psychosomatic Research, 53*, 1043–1047.

Kelly, J. R., Clarke, G., Cryan, J. F., & Dinan, T. G. (2018). Dimensional thinking in psychiatry in the era of the Research Domain Criteria (RDoC). *Irish Journal of Psychological Medicine, 35*, 89–94.

Klump, K. L., Bulik, C. M., Kaye, W. H., Treasure, J., & Tyson, E. (2009). Academy for eating disorders position paper: Eating disorders are serious mental illnesses. *International Journal of Eating Disorders, 42*, 97–103.

Kraemer, H. C., Wilson, G. T., Fairburn, C. G., & Agras, W. S. (2002). Mediators and moderators of treatment effects in randomized clinical trials. *Archives of General Psychiatry, 59*, 877–883.

Linardon, J. (2018). Rates of abstinence following psychological or behavioral treatments for binge-eating disorder: A meta-analysis. *International Journal of Eating Disorders, 51*, 785–797.

Linardon, J. & Wade, T. D. (2018). How many individuals achieve symptoms abstinence following psychological treatments for bulimia nervosa? A meta-analytic review. *International Journal of Eating Disorders, 51*, 287–294.

Luo, X., Donnellan, M. B., Burt, S. A., & Klump, K. L. (2016). The dimensional nature of eating pathology: Evidence from a direct comparison of categorical, dimensional, and hybrid models. *Journal of Abnormal Psychology, 125*, 715–726.

Mitchison, D., & Mond, J. (2015). Epidemiology of eating disorders, eating disordered behaviour, and body image disturbance in males: A narrative review. *Journal of Eating Disorders, 3*, 20.

Peterson, C. B. (2005). Conducting the diagnostic interview. In J. E. Mitchell & C. B. Peterson (eds), *Assessment of eating disorders* (pp. 32–58). New York, NY: Guilford.

Peterson, C. B. (2010). Assessment of eating disorder treatment efficacy. In C. M. Grilo and J. E. Mitchell (eds), *The treatment of eating disorders: A clinical handbook* (pp. 524–534). New York, NY: Guilford.

Rousmaniere, T. G. (2014). Technology-assisted supervision and training. In C. E. Watkins, Jr. Milne, D. (Eds.), *International handbook of clinical supervision* (pp. 204–237). Oxford, UK: Wiley.

Rousmaniere, T. G., & Frederickson, J. (2013). Internet-based one-way-mirror supervision for advanced psychotherapy training. *The Clinical Supervisor, 32*, 40–55.

Strandskov, S. W., Ghaderi, A., Andersson, H., Parmskog, N., Hjort, E., Wärn, A. S., …, Andersson, G. (2017). Effects of tailored and ACT-Influenced Internet-based CBT for eating disorders and the relation between knowledge acquisition and outcome: A randomized controlled trial. *Behavior Therapy, 48*, 624–637.

Thompson-Brenner, H., Shingleton, R. M., Thompson, D. R., Satir, D. A., Richards, L. K., Pratt, E. M., & Barlow, D. H. (2016). Focused vs. Broad enhanced cognitive behavioral therapy for bulimia nervosa with comorbid borderline personality: A randomized controlled trial. *International Journal of Eating Disorders, 49*, 36–49.

Tschuschke, V., Crameri, A., Koehler, M., Berglar, J., Muth, K., Staczan, P., …, Koemeda-Lutz, M. (2015). The role of therapists' treatment adherence, professional experience, therapeutic alliance, and clients' severity of psychological problems: Prediction of treatment outcome in eight different psychotherapy approaches. Preliminary results of a naturalistic study. *Psychotherapy Research, 25*, 420–434.

Waller, G. (2016). Treatment protocols for eating disorders: Clinicians' attitudes, concerns, adherence and difficulties delivering evidence-based psychological interventions. *Current Psychiatry Reports, 18*, 36.

Waller, G., Mountford, V. A., Tatham, M., Turner, H., Gabriel, C., & Webber, R. (2013). Attitudes towards psychotherapy manuals among clinicians treating eating disorders. *Behaviour Research and Therapy, 51*, 840–844.

Wildes, J. E., & Marcus, M. D. (2015). Application of the Research Domain Criteria (RDoC) framework to eating disorders: Emerging concepts and research. *Current Psychiatry Reports, 17*, 30.

Wiltsey Stirman, S. W., Marques, L., Creed, T. A., Gutner, C. A., DeRubeis, R., Barnett, P. G., …, Jo, B. (2018). Leveraging routine clinical materials and mobile technology to assess CBT fidelity: The Innovative Methods to Assess Psychotherapy Practices (imAPP) study. *Implementation Science, 13*, 69.

Wonderlich, S. A., Joiner Jr., T. E., Keel, P. K., Williamson, D. A., & Crosby, R. D. (2007). Eating disorder diagnoses: Empirical approaches to classification. *American Psychologist, 62*, 167–180.

Wonderlich, S. A., Peterson, C. B., Crosby, R. D., Smith, T. L., Klein, M. H., Mitchell, J. E., & Crow, S. J. (2014). A randomized controlled comparison of integrative cognitive-affective therapy (ICAT) and enhanced cognitive-behavioral therapy (CBT-E) for bulimia nervosa. *Psychological Medicine, 44*, 543–553.

Zandberg, L. J., & Wilson, G. T. (2013). Train-the-trainer: Implementation of cognitive behavioural guided self-help for recurrent binge eating in a naturalistic setting. *European Eating Disorders Review, 21*, 230–237.

Index

Boldfaced page numbers refer to tables; page numbers in italics refer to figures.

AAN in youth with OW/OB 130–1, **131**
AAT (Appetite Awareness Training) 9
acceptance and commitment therapy (ACT) 110
acceptance strategies 276–9
adolescents: alternative caregivers and support persons 76–9; FBT and adjunctive family interventions in partial hospitalization program 335–48
adults, treating: alternative caregivers and support persons 81–6, **90**, 92–3; middle-aged and older adults *see* middle-aged and older adults, treating
aftercare 383–4
agnostic view of eating disorders 357–8
alternative caregivers and support persons in eating disorder treatment 74–94; career skills workshops and self-help 91–2; overview 74–5, 93–4; treating adolescents 76–9; treating adults 81–6, **90**, 92–3; treating transitional-age youth 79–81; UCAN and UNITE 86–91
American Psychological Association: guidelines on diversity 3
anorexia nervosa: sex differences in prevalence rates and presentations 33–4
Appetite Awareness Training (AAT) 9
avoidant/restrictive food intake disorder (ARFID) 146–66, 171, 173; CBT-AR case examples 161–5; challenges in developing treatment 148–9; cognitive behavioral therapy for ARFID (CBT-AR) 149–51; future research directions 166; overview 146–7, 166; stage-specific interventions in CBT-AR 151–61

bariatric surgery, eating disorder treatment before and after 103–23; binge eating disorder/LOC eating 105–7; graze eating 105–7; night eating syndrome (NES) and sleep-related eating disorder (SRED) 106, 108; overview 103–5, 122–3; postsurgical disordered eating 106–8; postsurgical treatment 114–22, **117**–**18**; presurgical disordered eating 105–6; presurgical treatment 108–14, **110**; prevalence of EDs before and after bariatric surgery 105–8; subthreshold disorders 106, 108
behavioral contracting 345–6
behavioral health: primary–care-based treatment for eating disorders 372
Be-In-CHARGE 179
binge eating disorder (BED): bariatric surgery and 105–7; sex differences in prevalence rates and presentations 35; in youth with OW/OB 129–30
blended treatment: eHealth interventions 384–6
body dissatisfaction and other correlates among women in later-life stages 270
Body Project (BP) 9, 137, 378
bulimia nervosa: sex differences in prevalence rates and presentations 34–5

410   *Index*

career skills workshops and self-help: alternative caregivers and support persons in eating disorder treatment 91–2

case formulation 248–9

CBT-E (enhanced cognitive behavioral therapy) *see* enhanced cognitive behavioral therapy (CBT-E)

children: of military personnel 202–3

cognitive behavioral therapy (CBT): for ARFID (CBT-AR) 149–51, 161–65; body image intervention 283–5; ED-PTSD 217–21; post-bariatric surgery intervention 115–17, **117–18**; pre-bariatric surgery intervention **110**, 110–11; pregnancy and the postpartum period, treating ED in 239–58; remote methods to deliver evidence-based treatment 314–18; youth with OW/OB 136

community and home: primary–care-based treatment for eating disorders 373

confidentiality 302–3

cultural adaptations of evidence-based treatments for eating disorders 3–22, 402–3; culturally tailored treatment studies 12–15; interpreters, use of 19–20; level of acculturation and acculturative stress 18–19; literature review 5–18; overview 3–5, **6**–7, *8*, 20–2, *21*; prevalence studies 5–9; racially and ethnically diverse individuals 15–18; treatment studies 9–15, **10–11**

dialectical behavior therapy (DBT): LGBTQIA+ individuals 62; trauma-focused treatment 221–5; youth with OW/OB 135–6

DSM-5 Cross-Cultural Issues Subgroup 4

Eating Disorder Diagnostic Assessment for DSM-5 241

Eating Disorder Examination (ED) 241–2

Eating Disorder Examination–Pregnancy Version (EDE-PV) 242

Eating Disorder Examination Questionnaire (EDE-Q) 39–40

eating disorder NOS (EDNOS) 169

eating disorders (EDs): home-based *see* home-based setting for ED; LGBTQIA+ individuals

see LGBTQIA+ individuals with eating disorders; middle-aged and older adults *see* middle-aged and older adults, treating; military families *see* military families, eating disorders and disordered eating in; in non-eating disordered populations *see* non-eating disordered populations, eating-related problems in; patients with comorbid PTSD and trauma-related disorders 216–31; overview 216–17, 230–1; pregnancy and the postpartum period *see* pregnancy and the postpartum period, treating ED in; prevalence before and after bariatric surgery 105–8; primary–care-based treatment *see* primary–care-based treatment for eating disorders; remote methods to deliver care *see* remote methods to deliver evidence-based treatment; sex differences in prevalence rates and presentations of EDs 33–5

eating disorders screen for primary care (EDS-PC) 371

eBody Project 378

ECHOMANTRA 84

ED (Eating Disorder Examination) 241–2

EDE-PV (Eating Disorder Examination–Pregnancy Version) 242

EDE-Q (Eating Disorder Examination Questionnaire) 39–40

EDNOS (eating disorder not otherwise specified) 169

EDS-PC (eating disorders screen for primary care) 371

eHealth interventions 376–90; blended treatment 384–6; combination of eHealth and conventional treatment 382–6; feature research priorities 388–90; implications for research and practice 386–90; overview 376–7, 390; self-help and treatment interventions 379–82; stand-alone interventions 377–9; stepped care 383–4

e-mail 314

enhanced cognitive behavioral therapy (CBT-E): alternate caregivers 89, **90**, 91; home-based setting 293, 294, 309; LGBTQIA+ individuals 62; remote methods to deliver evidence-based treatment 319–20

ethics 401

externalization of the illness 360–1

Index 411

family-based care, ensuring continuity of 352–64; externalization of the illness 360–1; non-authoritarian therapeutic stance 359–60; overview 352, 364; parental empowerment 353–7; pragmatic focus on symptom reduction 361–3; taking an agnostic view of the eating disorder 357–8

family-based treatment (FBT): for AN (FBT-AN) 76–8; LGBTQIA+ individuals 62; for pediatric obesity (FBT-PO) 135; remote methods to deliver evidence-based treatment 321–4; for transition age youth (FBT-TAY) 80–1; for youth with OW/OB 134–5

family-based treatment (FBT) and adjunctive family interventions in partial hospitalization program for adolescents 335–48; behavioral contracting 345–6; family-supported treatment components 338–41; individual therapy 337–8; multifamily meals 341–2, *342*; multifamily therapy 346–7; overview 335–7, *337*, 348; parent management training 344–5; temperament-based treatment 342–3

food allergies 176–7

food-related fear 174–6

gender dysphoria 57

gender identity: should not be confused or conflated with sexual orientation 53

gender minority and sexual minority populations: prevalence of eating disorders among 58–61

general couple therapy 88

GI conditions: non-eating disordered populations 177–8

graze eating: treatment before and after bariatric surgery 105–7

guided self-help 316–17

health consequences of disordered eating 270–1

home-based setting for ED treatment 293–310; case presentation 302–8; challenges 300–2; future directions 308–10; opportunities 298–9; other health conditions 296–8; overview 293–6, 308–10; rationale for home-based approaches 294–5

hospitalization for adolescents *see* family-based treatment (FBT) and adjunctive

family interventions in partial hospitalization program for adolescents

individual therapy 337–8

integrated CBT for ED-PTSD 217–19

internet-based therapy 315–16

interpersonal psychotherapy (IPT): middle-aged and older adults 274–5; youth with OW/OB 132–4

interpreters, use of 19–20

Jourvie (smart-phone app) 385

Latinas, comprehensive ED intervention approach for *21*

level of acculturation and acculturative stress 18–19; cultural adaptations and 18–19

LGBTQIA+ individuals with eating disorders 50–68; epidemiology and engagement 51–61; gathering information on sexual orientation and gender 51–5; overview 50–1, 68; prevalence of eating disorders among sexual minority and gender minority populations 58–61; theoretical frameworks for understanding disparities in eating disorder risk 55–8; treatment 61–8, *67*

life changes, addressing 273–4

LOC (loss-of-control) eating 129–30; bariatric surgery and 105–7

majority–minority nation 3

Maudsley eating disorder collaborative care skills workshops 91

Maudsley Model of Treatment for Adults with Anorexia Nervosa (MANTRA) 84–5

Media Smart-Targeted 378

medical diseases, disordered eating associated with 176–81

men, middle-aged and older: prevalence of eating disorders in 269–70

men, modifying treatments to recognize the pursuit of muscularity and related eating psychopathology 31–45; anorexia nervosa 33–4; binge eating disorder 35; bulimia nervosa 34–5; future research directions 42–4; gold standard assessments 39–41; medical complications of EDs in males 32–3; muscle dysmorphia 41–2;

412 *Index*

muscular-oriented disordered eating 35–9; overview 31–2, 44–5; sex differences in prevalence rates and presentations of EDs 33–5

middle-aged and older adults, treating 268–85; acceptance strategies 276–9; addressing life changes 273–4; attending to the ED stereotype 272; body dissatisfaction and other correlates among women in later-life stages 270; CBT-based body image intervention 283–5; current state of the literature 271–2; health consequences of disordered eating 270–1; important considerations 279–83; interpersonal psychotherapy 274–5; overview 268–9, 285; prevalence and correlates 269–70; problem-solving therapy 275–6; tailoring treatment 272–83

military families, eating disorders and disordered eating in 194–207; challenges and future directions 205–7; disclaimer 207; overview 194, 207; prevalence 195–8; treatment 204–5; unique demands contributing to disordered eating 198–204

MOET (Muscularity Oriented Eating Test) 40

mood intolerance and emotional triggers 252–3

multifamily meals 341–2, *342*

multifamily therapy 346–7

Multisystemic therapy (MST) 297

muscle dysmorphia (MD): pursuit of muscularity and related eating psychopathology among men 41–2

muscle growth 37–8

muscle leanness 38

Muscularity Oriented Eating Test (MOET) 40

National Women's Study 216

New Maudsley Method 91

night eating syndrome (NES): treatment before and after bariatric surgery 106, 108

non-authoritarian therapeutic stance 359–60

non-eating disordered populations, eating-related problems in 169–85; alternative treatments for overeating 183–5; ASD 172; assessment 170–1; disordered eating associated with

medical diseases 176–81; food allergies 176–7; food-related fear 174–6; GI conditions 177–8; obesity 181–3; overview 169–70, 185; selective eating 171–4; sensory processing disorder (SPD) 172–3

novel research, training, and supervision opportunities for evidence-based treatment adaptations 397–405; overview 397–9, 405; research 399–402; supervision 404–5; training 402–4

nutrition: primary–care-based treatment for eating disorders 372

obesity *see* overweight/obesity

older adults *see* middle-aged and older adults, treating

ongoing management: primary–care-based treatment for eating disorders 371–2

Overcoming Binge Eating 14

Overcoming Bulimia Online 380

overeating, alternative treatments for 183–5

overweight/obesity 128; comorbid with ED 128; within ED 128; FBT for children with 182–3; non-eating disordered populations 181–3; youth with *see* youth with overweight/obesity, evidence-based treatments for

parental empowerment 353–7

parent-guided self-help 323

parent management training 344–5

partial hospitalization program for adolescents *see* family-based treatment (FBT) and adjunctive family interventions in partial hospitalization program for adolescents

partner-assisted interventions 87

pharmacotherapy 373

postpartum period *see* pregnancy and the postpartum period, treating ED in

postsurgical disordered eating: bariatric surgery and 106–8

pregnancy and the postpartum period, treating ED in 238–59, 263–7; augmentation of CBT for peripartum women 240–59; CBT treatment 239–58; hormones and eating disorders 264; overview 238, 258–9, 263–4; perinatal course of illness and

Index 413

psychopathology 238–9; prevalence and associated risks 238; recommended caloric intake in pregnancy and for breastfeeding women 246; recommended weight gain during pregnancy 247; treatment 239–58

presurgical disordered eating: bariatric surgery and 105–6

primary–care-based treatment for eating disorders 367–74; behavioral health 372; community and home 373; diagnosis 371; future improvements 373–4; general care considerations 369–70; importance of primary care 368–9; key functions and necessary adaptations 369–73; nutrition 372; ongoing management 371–2; overview 367, 373–4; pharmacotherapy 373; screening 371

problem-solving therapy 275–6

Project Recover 217

ProYouth 378–9

psychoeducation 245, 248

PTSD and trauma-related disorders, ED patients with 216–31; CBT for ED-PTSD 217–21; DBT–PE/DBT–CPT 221–5; integrating trauma-focused CBT and family-based treatment for EDs 225–30; overview 216–17, 230–1

QTPOC (queer trans people of color) 60

racially and ethnically diverse individuals 15–8

Recovery Record (app) 385

regulation of cues (ROC) 183–4

remote methods to deliver evidence-based treatment 313–28; challenges 324–6; clinical vignettes 318–21, 323–4; cognitive behavioral therapy 314–18; enhanced cognitive behavioral therapy 319–20; family-based treatment 321–4; future directions 326–8; overview 313, 324, 326–30; parent-guided self-help 323; telehealth 322–3; videoconference 319–20

research: novel research, training, and supervision opportunities for evidence-based treatment adaptations 399–402

ROC (regulation of cues) 183–4

SALUT-BED (internet-based self-help intervention for binge-eating disorder patients) 380–1

SALUT-BN (internet-based self-help intervention for bulimia patients) 380

SCOFF screener 371

screen for disordered eating (SDE) 371

SDM (shared-decision making) 359–60

selective eating 171–4

self-help: and eHealth treatment interventions 379–82; programs in CD-ROM format 314

sensory processing disorder (SPD) 172–3

sexual minority and gender minority populations: prevalence of eating disorders among 58–61

sexual orientation: should not be confused or conflated with gender identity 53

sexual orientation and gender, gathering information on 51–5

shared-decision making (SDM) 359–60

sleep-related eating disorder (SRED) 106, 108

stand-alone eHealth interventions 377–9

stepped care: eHealth interventions 383–4

Student Bodies 2 BED (SB2-BED) 136

Student Bodies (SB) 377–8

subthreshold disorders: bariatric surgery and 106, 108

supervision: novel research, training, and supervision opportunities for evidence-based treatment adaptations 404–5

telehealth 322–3

telemedicine 315–16

temperament-based treatment 342–3

text messaging 314

training: novel research, training, and supervision opportunities for evidence-based treatment adaptations 402–4

transitional-age youth (TAY), treating: alternative caregivers and support persons in eating disorder treatment 79–81

trauma-focused CBT and family-based treatment for EDs 225–30

treatment studies 9–15, **10–11**; of cultural adaptations 9–15, **10–11**

Uniting Couples in the Treatment of Anorexia Nervosa (UCAN) 85–8

Uniting couples In the Treatment of Eating disorders (UNITE) 86–8

414   *Index*

veterans 203–4
videoconferencing 319–20

weekly weighing 250
women, middle-aged and older *see* middle-aged and older adults, treating

youth with overweight/obesity, evidence-based treatments for 128–37; AAN in youth with OW/OB 130–1, **131**; adapting ED interventions to prevent or treat OW/OB in youth 132–7, *133*; BED in youth with OW/OB 129–30; the Body Project 137; CBT 136; DBT 135–6; family-based therapy for adolescent EDs 134–5; IPT 132–4; overview 128, 137; weight and EDs 128–9